●●● Concepts, Applications, and Skill Development for Success in Today's Workplace! ●●●

Using a three-pronged approach of concepts, applications, and skill development, Lussier's *Management Fundamentals* gives students a solid foundation of management concepts and skills that they can immediately put to use in the workplace. Proven skill-building exercises, behavioral models, self-assessments, and group exercises throughout the text help students realize their managerial potential. This text is written with the learning needs of today's students in mind: "learning by doing—how to manage!"

●●● Praise for Management Fundamentals ●●●

"In this ever-changing world in which we live, we need a text like this one to keep us on top of our game. This text is progressive, relevant, and provides so many opportunities to apply the principles. I just love the text!"

Amy Wojciechowski, West Shore Community College

"Dr. Lussier provides the academic community with another outstanding form of scholarship. The material is fresh, current, and presented in a fashion that students understand and can relate [to]."

Joseph Adamo, Cazenovia College

"Lussier excels at introducing students to the complexities inherent in management and organizations in a way that remains accessible, informative, and compelling."

Eric S. Ecklund, Saint Francis University

"Lussier provides a textbook that applies to the 'real world' of business. It is suitable for planning interactive lessons and assessment of learning."

Melanie Jacks Hillburn, Lone Star College

Active Learning Approach:

The three-pronged approach provides students with multiple ways to apply content. Lussier:

- Provides clear and complete understanding of core management **concepts** and functions as well as current trends and new challenges facing managers today

- Emphasizes active learning by providing students with a wide range of **applications** and examples

- Focuses on student **skill development,** helping students hone skills they can use in their daily lives and on the job

IDEAS ON MANAGEMENT at Volkswagen Group

Volkswagen means "people's car." The German MNC Volkswagen Group is one of the world's leading automobile manufacturers and the largest carmaker in Europe. The Group comprises 12 brands from seven European countries: Volkswagen Passenger Cars, Audi, SEAT, ŠKODA, Bentley, Bugatti, Lamborghini, Porsche, Ducati, Volkswagen Commercial Vehicles, Scania, and MAN. Each brand has its own character and operates as an independent subsidiary. In Western Europe, almost one in four new cars (24.4 percent) is made by the Volkswagen Group. Volkswagen activities may focus on the automobile, but the Volkswagen Group is far more than just a carmaker, as a wide variety of mobility-related services round out its portfolio.

Volkswagen Group has a goal of becoming the world's largest automaker. To that end, it continues to be innovative. Group Research has its headquarters in Wolfsburg and researches for all Group brands. International trend scouting and technology scouting form part of its strategic orientation, and it also operates from research bases in the U.S., Japanese, and Chinese markets.

Uniting a wide variety of brands and companies with all their individual characteristics and focuses under one umbrella is a great challenge, especially as the Volkswagen Group is committed to maintaining their individual identities. But this is the only way all the brands and companies can make their own contributions to the common value stream and form cornerstones of the Group.

1. Where is Volkswagen Group on the mechanistic and organic continuum?
2. What are the important organizational principles guiding Volkswagen in achieving its goal of becoming the world's largest automaker?
3. Is Volkswagen more centralized or decentralized?
4. What is Volkswagen Group's organizational design?
5. What prioritization issues does Volkswagen face?

You'll find answers to these questions throughout the chapter. To learn more about the Volkswagen Group, visit its website at www.volkswagenag.com.

Sources: Information for the case was taken from Volkswagen's website at http://www.volkswagenag.com, accessed June 26, 2013.

7 Organizing and Delegating Work

• • • Learning Outcomes

After studying this chapter, you should be able to:

7-1. Explain the difference between mechanistic and organic organizations and the environments in which they are more effective.

7-2. Discuss the difference between formal and informal authority and centralized and decentralized authority.

7-3. List and briefly explain the four levels of authority.

7-4. Explain what an organization chart is and list the four aspects of a firm that it shows.

7-5. Discuss the difference between internal and external departmentalization.

7-6. Explain the difference between job simplification and job expansion.

7-7. Explain how to set priorities by answering three priority questions and determining whether activities have high, medium, or low priority.

7-8. List the four steps in the delegation process.

7-9. Define the key terms found in the chapter margins and listed following the Chapter Summary.

• • • Chapter Outline

Organizational Considerations and Principles
  Organizational Considerations
  Principles of Organization
Authority
  Formal and Informal Authority and Scope and Levels of Authority
  Centralized and Decentralized Authority
  Line and Staff Authority
Organizational Design
  Organization Chart
  Departmentalization

Multiple Departmentalization
Reengineering Contemporary Organizational Designs
Job Design
  Job Simplification
  Job Expansion
  Work Teams
  The Job Characteristics Model
Organizing Yourself and Delegating
  Setting Priorities
  Delegating

- ***New* Chapter 3: Managing in a Global Diverse Environment** has been added to this edition, providing new coverage on the global environment, cultural considerations, and managing a diverse workforce.

- ***New*** **and expanded coverage** of timely topics such as social entrepreneurship, workplace diversity, creativity, innovation, technology, social loafing, team leadership, and international assignments.

- ***New* cases** on Sheryl Sandberg, Target, Google, Apple, LEGO, Blackberry, Costco, and Richard Branson.

• • • CASE: BLACKBERRY TRIES TO NAVIGATE A TURNAROUND STRATEGY

Remember when BlackBerry was so popular that it was just about the only cell phone that people bought? Well, with the soaring popularity of Apple iPhones and Samsung smartphones with Android operating systems, BlackBerry is quickly losing market share.

In 2003, BlackBerry introduced the first of what the company feels was the beginning of the modern smartphone. This was a device that not only functioned as a telephone but also allowed for the sending and receiving of email and text messages as well as web browsing. One of the main focuses of the early BlackBerry was to allow for mobile email. Clearly people who were on the go needed a way to access their email without having to find a computer—and BlackBerry was an early entrant into the marketplace. (BlackBerry, "A Short History of the Blackberry," http://www.bbcnw.com/a-short-history-of-the-blackberry.php.)

• • • CASE: RICHARD BRANSON (VIRGIN AIRLINES) ON MANAGING A GROWING ENTREPRENEURIAL BUSINESS

Sir Richard Branson is the slightly eccentric founder of United Kingdom-based Virgin Group, which consists of more than 400 companies around the world, including the airlines Virgin Atlantic and Virgin America, wireless company Virgin Mobile, and international health club Virgin Active. (Richard Branson, "Richard Branson on the Secret to Virgin's Sustained Success," *Entrepreneur,* http://www.entrepreneur.com/article/228382#ixzz2fXCblfIp.)

Richard Branson is well known as a guru of entrepreneurship. You could call him a change agent in his own company since he is always inspiring everyone who works for him to look for industries they can enter and provide the spark for a discontinuous change on the way business is done in that industry.

Enhanced Applications & Skill Development:

Revised and updated pedagogical features in every chapter enrich the reading experience and encourage students to connect chapter material to their everyday lives.

4-1 SELF ASSESSMENT

Decision-Making Styles

Individuals differ in the way they approach decisions. To determine whether your decision-making style is reflexive, reflective, or consistent, evaluate each of the following eight statements using the scale below. Place a number between 1 (indicating "This behavior is common for me") and 5 (indicating "This behavior is not common for me") on the line preceding each statement.

This behavior is common for me.   This behavior is not common for me.

1	2	3	4	5

1. ____ Overall, I make decisions quickly.
2. ____ When making decisions, I go with my first thought or hunch.
3. ____ When making decisions, I don't bother to recheck my work.
4. ____ When making decisions, I gather little or no information.
5. ____ When making decisions, I consider very few alternative options.
6. ____ When making decisions, I usually decide well before any deadline.
7. ____ When making decisions, I don't ask others for advice.
8. ____ After making decisions, I don't look for other alternatives or wish I had waited longer.

____ Total score

Self Assessments help students gain personal knowledge of management functions in the real world.

"This is a good way for students to test their skills and knowledge of application."

Michael Provitera, Barry University

4-1 JOIN THE DISCUSSION ETHICS & SOCIAL RESPONSIBILITY

Avoiding Taxes

Many large corporations have an objective to pass less taxes and are using corporate tax loopholes to avoid paying taxes. **Walmart** and **Apple** are such companies. Apple CEO Tim Cook was quoted in the press as defending Apple tax avoiding practices saving $44 billion in offshore income from 2009-2012, and it also has three Irish subsidiaries that claim to have no residence anywhere for tax purposes. Some companies have moved headquarters out of the United States to countries with lower tax rates to save money.

It is not known just how many corporations are engaging in these kinds of activities. What is known, though, is that as these corporations continue taking advantage of corporate tax loopholes, the more taxes ordinary families and small businesses pay.

1. Although it is legal, is it ethical for Apple, Walmart, and other corporations to take advantage of tax loopholes to save money?
2. If you became CEO of one of these corporations, would you continue to take advantage of the tax loopholes? Why or why not?
3. What is the government's role and responsibility regarding tax loopholes?

Join the Discussion boxes provide opportunities for classroom discussion around ethical dilemmas.

"It gets students accustomed to thinking ethically."

Michael Provitera, Barry University

4-1 APPLYING THE CONCEPT

Steps in Decision Making

Identify the step in the decision-making model represented by each statement.

step 1
step 2
step 3
step 4
step 5
step 6

____ 1. "Andrea, is the machine still jamming, or has it stopped?"
____ 2. "I don't understand what we are trying to accomplish."
____ 3. "What symptoms have you observed to indicate that a problem even exists?"
____ 4. "Probability theory should be used to help us in this situation."
____ 5. "We will use the brainstorming technique to solve the problem."

Applying the Concept features ask students to determine the most appropriate concept to be used in a specific short example.

"Love the **Applying the Concept** boxes. I use them on slides in my class to test their knowledge and thinking."

Frank Armstrong, Ferris State University

Work Application Questions challenge students to apply concepts to their own work experience, helping bridge the gap between theory and real-world practice.

WORK
APPLICATION 7-5

Describe the type of authority (centralized or decentralized) used in an organization you work for or have worked for.

Models and Exhibits illustrate key management processes and concepts, providing students with visual tools they can use on the job.

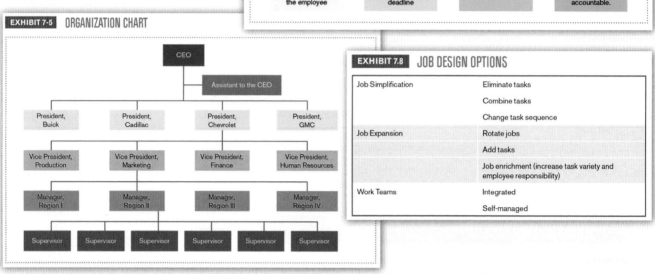

MODEL 7-1 THE DELEGATION PROCESS

Step 1 Explain the need for delegating and the reasons for selecting the employee → **Step 2** Set objectives that define responsibility, level of authority, and deadline → **Step 3** Develop a plan → **Step 4** Establish control checkpoints and hold employees accountable.

EXHIBIT 7-5 ORGANIZATION CHART

CEO — Assistant to the CEO
President, Buick | President, Cadillac | President, Chevrolet | President, GMC
Vice President, Production | Vice President, Marketing | Vice President, Finance | Vice President, Human Resources
Manager, Region I | Manager, Region II | Manager, Region III | Manager, Region IV
Supervisor | Supervisor | Supervisor | Supervisor | Supervisor | Supervisor

EXHIBIT 7.8 JOB DESIGN OPTIONS

Job Simplification	Eliminate tasks
	Combine tasks
	Change task sequence
Job Expansion	Rotate jobs
	Add tasks
	Job enrichment (increase task variety and employee responsibility)
Work Teams	Integrated
	Self-managed

• • • SKILL BUILDER 4-1: MAKING A DECISION USING THE DECISION-MAKING MODEL

Select a problem or opportunity that you now face. Remember, a problem exists when objectives are not being met—when there is a difference between what is happening and what you want to happen. The problem or opportunity may be from any facet of your life—work, college, sports, a relationship, a purchase to be made in the near future, where to go on a date, and so on. Use the decision-making model outline that follows to solve your problem or take advantage of the opportunity.

Objective

To improve your ability to make decisions.

Skills

The primary skills developed through this exercise are:
Management skill—decision making (conceptual, diagnostic, analytical, critical thinking, and quantitative reasoning)
AACSB competency—analytic skills
Management function—primarily planning (but decisions are made when organizing, leading, and controlling)

Step 1. Classify and Define the Problem or Opportunity

Decision structure. Do you need to make a programmed or a nonprogrammed decision?

Decision condition. Are you facing a condition of uncertainty, of risk, or of certainty?

Decision-making type. Is a rational or bounded rational decision appropriate? (Continue to follow all steps in the decision-making model even if a bounded rational decision is appropriate.)

Select the appropriate level of participation. Should the decision be made by an individual or a group? (If a group decision is appropriate, use a group for the following steps in the model. But remember to maximize the advantages and minimize the disadvantages of group decision making.)

Define the problem. List the symptoms and causes of the problem (or opportunity); then write a clear statement of it.

Step 2. Set Objectives and Criteria

Write down what is to be accomplished by the decision and the standards that any alternative must meet to be selected as the decision that will accomplish the objective. (Specify "must" and "want" criteria if appropriate for the decision.)

Objective: Criteria: (must) and (want)

Step 3. Generate Creative and Innovative Alternatives

• • • SKILL BUILDER 4-2: WHAT INFORMATION DO YOU NEED?

Using the Vroom Model

You read about the Vroom participative decision-making model in this chapter. Using the appropriate version of the model (time-driven or development-driven), determine which leadership style to use for each situation below.

Note that this skill builder is based on leadership and can be used with Chapter 12.

Objective

To determine the appropriate leadership style.

Skills

The primary skills developed through this exercise are:

1. *Management skill*—decision making (conceptual, diagnostic, analytical, critical thinking, and quantitative reasoning)

2. *AACSB competency*—analytic skills

3. *Management function*—primarily planning (but decisions are made when organizing, leading, and controlling)

Situation 1

You are the manager of the production department for a company that manufactures a mass-produced product. You have two production machines in your department with 10 people working on each. You have an important order that needs to be shipped first thing tomorrow. Your boss has made it very clear that you must meet this deadline. It's 2:00 P.M., and you are right on schedule to meet the order deadline. At 2:15, an employee tells you that one of the machines is smoking a little and making a noise. If you keep running the machine, it may make it until the end of the day and you will deliver the important shipment on time. If you shut down the machine, the manufacturer will not be able to check it until tomorrow and you will miss the deadline. You call your boss, but there is no answer; there is no telling how long it will take for the boss to get back to you if you leave a message. There are no higher-level managers to consult, and no one with

more knowledge of the machine than you. Which leadership style should you use?

Step 1. Which version of the model should you use? (_____ time-driven _____ development-driven)

Step 2. How did you answer the model's questions? Did you skip any questions?

Step 3. Which leadership style is the most appropriate?

_ Decide _ Consult individuals _ Consult group _ Facilitate _ Delegate

Situation 2

You are the leader of your church, with 125 families (200 members). You have a doctor of religious studies degree with just two years' experience as the head of a church; you have not taken any business courses. The church has one paid secretary, three part-time program directors for religious instruction, music, and social activities, plus many volunteers. The paid staff members serve on your advisory board with 10 other church members who are primarily business leaders in the community. You develop a yearly budget, which is approved by the advisory board. The church's source of income is weekly member donations. The advisory board doesn't want the church to operate in the red, and the church has very modest surplus funds. Your volunteer accountant, who is a board member, asks to meet with you. During the meeting,

Skill Builder Exercises help students develop skills that can be used in their personal and professional lives. AACSB competencies are included to enhance student analytic skills.

"I do find these skill developments effective and compelling, with the **Skill Builders** as the best part. They are great tools for student involvement and knowledge."

Joseph Adamo, Cazenovia College

"I LOVE the student skill-development section where students can assess their skills and see where they are strong and where they need to improve. Those surveys are priceless as far as I am concerned."

Frank Armstrong, Ferris State University

IDEAS ON MANAGEMENT at Volkswagen Group

Volkswagen means "people's car." The German MNC Volkswagen Group is one of the world's leading automobile manufacturers and the largest carmaker in Europe. The Group comprises 12 brands from seven European countries: Volkswagen Passenger Cars, Audi, SEAT, ŠKODA, Bentley, Bugatti, Lamborghini, Porsche, Ducati, Volkswagen Commercial Vehicles, Scania, and MAN. Each brand has its own character and operates as an independent subsidiary. In Western Europe, almost one in four new cars (24.4 percent) is made by the Volkswagen Group. Volkswagen activities may focus on the automobile, but the Volkswagen Group is far more than just a carmaker, as a wide variety of mobility-related services round out its portfolio.

Volkswagen Group has a goal of becoming the world's largest automaker. To that end, it continues to be innovative. Group Research has its headquarters in Wolfsburg and researches for all Group brands. International trend scouting and technology scouting form part of its strategic orientation, and it also operates from research bases in the U.S., Japanese, and Chinese markets.

Uniting a wide variety of brands and companies with all their individual characteristics and focuses under one umbrella is a great challenge, especially as the Volkswagen Group is committed to maintaining their individual identities. But this is the only way all the brands and companies can make their own contributions to the common value stream and form cornerstones of the Group.

1. Where is Volkswagen Group on the mechanistic and organic continuum?
2. What are the important organizational principles guiding Volkswagen in achieving its goal of becoming the world's largest automaker?
3. Is Volkswagen more centralized or decentralized?
4. What is Volkswagen Group's organizational design?
5. What prioritization issues does Volkswagen face?

You'll find answers to these questions throughout the chapter. To learn more about the Volkswagen Group, visit its website at www.volkswagenag.com.

Sources: Information for the case was taken from Volkswagen's website at http://www.volkswagenag.com, accessed June 26, 2013.

Ideas on Management Opening Cases

"I really like this. How current companies are doing business is extremely important to student learning."

Thomas D. Foreback, University of Cincinnati

4.5 Describe when to use rational versus bounded rational decision making and group versus individual decision making.

Use rational decision making with a group when faced with a nonprogrammed decision with high risk or uncertainty. Use bounded rational decision making and make an individual decision when faced with a programmed decision with low risk or certainty. However, this is a general guide; there may be exceptions to the rule.

4.6 State the difference between an objective and "must" and "want" criteria.

An objective is the end result you want to achieve when making the decision. "Must" criteria are the requirements that an alternative must meet to be selected. "Want" criteria are desirable but are not necessary for an alternative to be selected.

4.7 State the difference between creativity and innovation.

Creativity is a way of thinking that generates new ideas. Innovation is the implementation of new ideas for products and processes.

4.8 List and explain the three stages in the creative process.

The three stages are (1) preparation—developing familiarity with the problem; (2) incubation and illumination—taking a break from the problem and perhaps getting an idea for the solution; and (3) evaluation—making sure the idea will work.

4.9 Describe the differences among quantitative techniques, the Kepner-Tregoe method, and cost-benefit analysis for analyzing and selecting an alternative.

Quantitative techniques and the Kepner-Tregoe method are management science approaches; cost-benefit analysis is not. Quantitative methods use math to objectively select the alternative with the highest value. The Kepner-Tregoe method uses math, with some subjectivity in selecting and weighting criteria, to select the alternative with the highest value. Cost-benefit analysis is primarily based on subjective analysis; it can use some math, but alternatives do not have a final number value to compare.

KEY TERMS

brainstorming
consensus mapping
creative process
creativity
criteria
decision making

decision-making conditions
decision-making model
devil's advocate approach
innovation
nominal grouping
nonprogrammed decisions

participative decision-making model
problem
problem solving
programmed decisions
synectics

KEY TERM REVIEW

Complete each of the following statements using one of this chapter's key terms.

1. A _____ exists whenever objectives are not being met.
2. _____ is the process of taking corrective action to meet objectives.
3. _____ is the process of selecting a course of action that will solve a problem.
4. The steps of _____ include (1) classifying and defining the problem or opportunity, (2) setting objectives and criteria, (3) generating creative and innovative alternatives, (4) analyzing alternatives and selecting the most feasible, (5) planning and implementing the decision, and (6) controlling the decision.
5. For _____, which are recurring or routine, the decision maker should use decision rules or organizational policies and procedures.
6. For _____, which are significant, nonrecurring, and nonroutine, the decision maker should use the decision-making model.
7. The three _____ are certainty, risk, and uncertainty.
8. _____ are the standards that an alternative must meet to be selected as the decision that will accomplish the objective.
9. _____ is a way of thinking that generates new ideas.
10. _____ is the implementation of a new idea.
11. The three stages in the _____ are (1) preparation, (2) incubation and illumination, and (3) evaluation.
12. With the _____, group members focus on defending a proposed solution to a problem while others try to come up with criticisms of why the solution will not work.

13. _____ is the process of suggesting many possible alternatives without evaluation.
14. _____ is the process of generating novel alternatives through role playing and fantasizing.
15. _____ is the process of generating and evaluating alternatives using a structured voting method.
16. _____ is the process of developing group agreement on a solution to a problem.
17. The _____ is a time-driven or development-driven decision tree that assists a users in selecting one of five leadership styles to use in a given situation to maximize a decision.

REVIEW QUESTIONS

1. What is the relationship among the management functions, problem solving, and decision making?
2. Why is it necessary to determine the decision structure and decision-making conditions?
3. What is the current trend concerning the use of groups to solve problems and make decisions?
4. Is a decrease in sales and/or profits a symptom or a cause of a problem?
5. Would a maximum price of $1,000 to spend on a stereo be an objective or a criterion?
6. Is there really a difference between creativity and innovation?
7. What is the major difference between nominal grouping and consensus mapping?
8. Why are generating and analyzing alternatives separate steps in the decision-making model?
9. What quantitative techniques are commonly used to compare alternatives?
10. When is the cost-benefit analysis commonly used?
11. For what is Vroom's participative decision-making model primarily used?

COMMUNICATION SKILLS

The following critical-thinking questions can be used for class discussion and/or as written assignments to develop communication skills. Be sure to give complete explanations for all questions.

1. Are problem solving and decision making really all that important? How do you rate your decision-making ability?
2. Which potential advantage and disadvantage of group problem solving and decision making do you think arises most frequently?
3. Are creativity and innovation really important to all types of businesses? Is it important to evaluate a creative idea before it becomes an innovation?
4. What is the role of intuition in decision making? Should managers use more objective or subjective intuition techniques when making decisions?
5. Have you ever used any of the techniques for analyzing and selecting an alternative? If so, which one(s)?
6. Should managers be ethical in their decision making? If so, how should ethics be used in decision making?
7. Have you or someone you know experienced escalation of commitment? If so, explain.
8. Do men and women make decisions differently?
9. Have you ever made a decision with information that was not timely, of good quality, complete, and/or relevant? If so, was the decision a good one? Why or why not?

CASE: THE COCA-COLA COMPANY

Coca-Cola was created by Dr. John Stith Pemberton, a pharmacist in Atlanta, Georgia. It went on sale in a drug store for five cents a glass as a soda fountain drink on May 8, 1886. Today, The Coca-Cola Company is the largest beverage company in the world. It has grown to become the world's most recognized brand, with more than 3,500 products sold in 200 countries. Coca-Cola is ranked in the top 60 Fortune 500 Companies, top 210 Fortune Global 500 Companies, top 5 of the Fortune World's Most Admired Companies, and its CEO Muahtar Kent is ranked in the Fortune top 10 Businessperson of the Year.

Coke was one of the first U.S. companies to go international. The company began building its global network in the 1920s. One of the first countries the company expanded to was China, opening its first bottling plants in Tianjin and Shanghai in 1927. In recent years, it has spent more than 2 billion expanding operations in China. In the late 2000s, The Coca-Cola Company was looking for new ways to expand in China. Coca-Cola announced a bid for Huiyuan, one of China's top local brands and the country's largest maker of 100 percent fruit juice. The deal would have been the largest for The Coca-Cola Company

---

End-of-chapter Pedagogy and Cases allow students to test their understanding of key concepts.

"Probably the most comprehensive coverage of a case study that I have ever read."

Michael Provitera, Barry University

Open Online Resources:

SAGE provides comprehensive and free online resources at www.sagepub.com/Lussier6e designed to support and enhance both instructors' and students' experiences.

Instructors benefit from access to the password-protected **Instructor Teaching Site**, which includes

- Test bank in Word and Respondus
- PowerPoint lecture slides
- Author-created instructor's manual that includes annotated lecture outlines with answers to all in-text questions
- Web resources
- Ideas for classroom activities
- Select SAGE journal articles with critical-thinking questions
- Sample syllabi
- Exhibits and models from the text
- Common course cartridges for course management systems
- Video links with discussion questions

Students increase their understanding of management concepts through the free, open-access **Student Study Site**, which includes

- Mobile-friendly eflashcards
- Mobile-friendly self-quizzes
- Web resources
- Study questions
- Chapter outlines
- Select SAGE journal articles for each topic and chapter with critical-thinking questions
- Video links with discussion questions

Management Fundamentals
Concepts, Applications, & Skill Development

Sixth Edition

To my wife, Marie, and our six children:
Jesse, Justin, Danielle, Nicole, Brian, and Renee

Management Fundamentals
Concepts, Applications, & Skill Development

Sixth Edition

Robert N. Lussier
Springfield College

Los Angeles | London | New Delhi
Singapore | Washington DC

Los Angeles | London | New Delhi
Singapore | Washington DC

FOR INFORMATION:

SAGE Publications, Inc.
2455 Teller Road
Thousand Oaks, California 91320
E-mail: order@sagepub.com

SAGE Publications Ltd.
1 Oliver's Yard
55 City Road
London EC1Y 1SP
United Kingdom

SAGE Publications India Pvt. Ltd.
B 1/I 1 Mohan Cooperative Industrial Area
Mathura Road, New Delhi 110 044
India

SAGE Publications Asia-Pacific Pte. Ltd.
3 Church Street
#10-04 Samsung Hub
Singapore 049483

Acquisitions Editor: Patricia Quinlin
Associate Editor: Maggie Stanley
Editorial Assistant: Dori Zweig
Project Editor: Veronica Stapleton Hooper
Copy Editor: Kim Husband
Typesetter: C&M Digitals (P) Ltd.
Proofreader: Wendy Jo Dymond
Indexers: Sheila Bodell and Julie Grayson
Interior Designer Gail Buschman
Cover Designer: Gail Buschman
Marketing Manager: Liz Thornton

Printed in the United States of America

A catalog record of this book is available from the Library of Congress.

ISBN 978-1-4833-5226-8

This book is printed on acid-free paper.

15 16 17 18 19 10 9 8 7 6 5 4 3 2 1

··· Brief Contents

··· Detailed Contents

PART I · THE GLOBAL MANAGEMENT ENVIRONMENT

Chapter 3. Managing Diversity in a Global Environment   60

PART II · PLANNING

Chapter 4. Creative Problem Solving and Decision Making   92

PART III · ORGANIZING

Chapter 8.   Managing Team Work   214

Chapter 9.   Human Resources Management   248

Chapter 13. Communication and Information Technology 382

PART 5 · CONTROLLING

Chapter 14. Managing Control Systems, Finances, and People 416

Chapter 15. Operations, Quality, and Productivity 446

···Preface

In his book *Power Tools,* John Nirenberg asks, "Why are so many well-intended students learning so much and yet able to apply so little in their personal and professional lives?" The world of management has changed and so should how it is taught. Increasing numbers of students want more than just an understanding of the concepts of management. They also want skills they can use in their everyday lives at work. It's not enough to learn about management; they want to learn how to *be* managers. This is why I wrote this book.

If you have been in education for some years, you know that the learning style of today's students is different than it was 20 or even 10 years ago. This can be attributed in part to lowering academic standards at all levels. If you look at the textbooks over time, they keep getting smaller as authors cut out material. When writing this sixth edition, I decided to set a higher standard. I've actually added more material while making the text more concise and added more than 1,300 new references so that 95 percent of the references in this edition are new. Compare the contents to any major competitor and you will find that the real difference is that I offer superior application and skill-development options.

I personally developed the total package to have the following competitive advantages:

- A unique **"how-to-manage"** approach
- Eight types of high-quality **application materials** using the concepts to develop critical-thinking skills
- Five types of high-quality **skill-builder exercises** to develop management skills that can be utilized in students' professional and personal lives
- A **flexible** package—with all these features, instructors can design the course by selecting the features that meet their needs
- A **lower price** to students than major competitors

DESIGNED TO MEET A VARIETY OF LEARNING STYLES

Today's traditional students are being called "Digital Millennials" or "NetGens." Today's students need to be engaged, as the old primary lecture method is no longer effective. My text is very flexible and can be used with the traditional lecture method. But it also offers a wide range of engaging activities to select from that best meet the professor and student goals and preferred teaching/learning styles. Many of the specific learning preferences of NetGens have been addressed in the book's overall approach, organization, and distinctive features.

- **Active Learning.** A design for active learning is addressed with a wide variety of activities and skill-building tools. The text includes six types of **applications** and four types of **skill-building** activities to help students develop actual skills that can be used immediately in their own lives.
- **Practical Approach.** Students are provided with **immediate feedback** and ongoing **self-assessment** opportunities found in the Work Applications, Applying the Concepts, and Self-Assessments. Organizational tools such as **checklists**, summaries, and **"how-to"** instructions are integrated throughout. Reviewers consistently state that Lussier books have the highest quality and quantity of practical applications and pedagogical tools.

- **Accessible Content.** Text material presents management concepts followed by application material so that students can break up the reading while applying the concepts and getting feedback. The boxed items are not just passively reading an example; they engage the student to come up with an answer. Students especially like self-assessments within the chapters. Content is **chunked** into easily digested segments to help students process new ideas and concepts.

- **Online Resources.** The text is accompanied by a password-protected **instructor website** and an open-access **student website** (see the following for more details). Also, while all the elements in the text are designed to be used by individuals, they can also be used in groups settings, making *Management Fundaments* an ideal text for ***online courses.***

INTEGRATED THREE-PRONGED APPROACH

Based on my experience teaching management courses for more than 25 years, I created course materials that develop students into managers. As the title of this book implies, it involves a balanced, three-pronged approach to the curriculum:

1. A clear understanding of management **concepts**
2. The **application** of management concepts for critical thinking in the real world
3. The development of management **skills**

I wrote this text and its supporting ancillary package to support these three distinct but integrated parts. This text follows a management-functions approach covering all the traditional concepts and current topics. The applications develop students' critical-thinking skills as they require them to apply specific concepts to their own work experience (part time, summer, or full time), to short situations, and to cases. In addition, this text meets the challenge of the AACSB call for skills development. Since I wrote almost every exercise and application in the package, the material is completely integrated to create a seamless experience in the classroom or online.

Because these three key elements of concepts, applications, and skills are integrated throughout the chapters, you won't find them in broad general sections. However, they are identified clearly and are delineated in some detail for your reference in this preface. Recognizing the diverse needs of students and faculty, they can be used flexibly to fit any classroom. Instructors can create their course by using only features that fit with their objectives.

My goal is to make both students and instructors successful in and out of the classroom by providing learning features that not only teach about management but also help students become managers.

CONCEPTS

This text covers all key management topics and concepts. It is comprehensive in scope, as shown by the detailed learning outcomes at the front of each chapter. Each outcome is reinforced and identified throughout the chapter. Key terms are highlighted in **green** to emphasize the vocabulary of management for students.

Current Management Issues

Because this text takes an integrated approach to the subject of management, it is not cluttered with extraneous boxes. Instead, current topics as described by the

AACSB, such as sustainability, globalization, diversity, quality, productivity, and participative management and teams, are covered throughout the chapters.

End-of-Chapter Material Reinforcement of Concepts

Each chapter ends with a **Chapter Summary** that reinforces every Learning Outcome. A **Key Term Review** section enables the readers to quiz themselves on the definitions, making it an active glossary. In addition, each chapter includes an average of 13 **Review Questions** to support and reinforce the key concepts that appear in the chapters.

APPLICATIONS

Powerful learning takes place when theory is put within the context of the real world. Using this text, students are challenged to apply the concepts they learn to actual business situations, especially as they have experienced them personally. Students must think critically as they apply specific concepts to their own work experience, short situations, and cases.

Ideas on Management Opening Cases

At the beginning of each chapter, information about an actual manager and organization is presented. The case is followed by four to eight questions to get students involved. Throughout the chapter, the answers to the questions are given to illustrate how the organization actually uses the text concepts to create opportunities and solve problems through decision making. The students get a real-world example illustrated extensively throughout the chapter, beginning with the opening pages.

Real-World Examples

Company examples illustrate how businesses use the text concepts. There are hundreds of examples altogether, with an average of eight per chapter. Text concepts come alive as students see how actual organizations use them to succeed. Companies featured include **Microsoft**, the **New York Yankees, eBay, Yahoo!, Google, MTV, Blockbuster, Intel, Walmart, Dell Computer**, and **Apple**, among many others. The organization names are highlighted throughout the text in bold font.

Work Applications

Open-ended questions called Work Applications require students to explain how the text concepts apply to their own work experience; more than 160 of these are strategically placed throughout the text. Student experience can be present, past, summer, full-time or part-time employment, or volunteer work. The questions help students bridge the gap between theory and their real world.

Applying the Concept

Every chapter contains a series of three to six Applying the Concept boxes that require the student to determine the management concept being illustrated in a specific short example. There are 15 to 25 objective questions per chapter for development of student critical-thinking skills.

Join the Discussion: Ethics and Social Responsibility Dilemmas

There are 40 ethical dilemma boxed items, with at least two to three included per chapter. Many of the dilemmas include information from companies such as

Gap, Land's End, Monsanto, Arthur Andersen, Global Crossing, SAP, and **JetBlue Airways**. Each dilemma has two to four questions for class discussion.

End-of-Chapter Cases

Following the review and communication questions, students are presented with a case on an actual manager or organization. The student learns how the manager or organization applies the management concepts from that chapter. **Case questions** require the student to apply management practices and concepts to the actual organization. Chapters 2 through 15 also include **cumulative case questions** that relate case material to concepts from prior chapters. Thus, students continually review and integrate concepts from previous chapters.

SKILL DEVELOPMENT

The difference between learning about management and learning to be a manager is the acquisition of skills. This text focuses on skill development so students can use what they learn on the job. The skill material is integrated throughout the text, but instructors can choose how to incorporate the material into their classroom or online experience—individually or as groups, inside the class or as outside group projects.

Students can actually develop a skill that can be used on the job. The features listed in the following paragraphs include true skill building, such as step-by-step models, and skill-builder exercises. Other features support skill building, such as self-assessments and group exercises.

Step-by-Step Models

The book contains approximately 25 detailed sets of how-to steps for handling day-to-day management functions. They are integrated into the context of the chapter or skill-building exercise being taught. For example, models teach students how to set objectives and priorities, how to handle a complaint, and how to discipline an employee. This feature directly teaches students how to be managers.

Skill Builders

Chapters contain an average of three Skill Builders, all of which have been class tested to be the best found in any text on the market. Full support of more than 40 activities can be found in the Instructor's Manual, including detailed information, timing, answers, and so on. All exercises and their uses are optional in the classroom. There are three primary types of exercises:

1. Individual Focus: Around half are those in which participants are required to make individual decisions prior to or during class. These answers can be shared in class for discussion, or the instructor may elect to go over recommended answers.
2. Group Focus: Around a quarter are those in which participants discuss the material presented and may select group answers.
3. Role-Play Focus: Around a quarter are those in which participants are presented with a model and given the opportunity to use the model, usually in groups of three.

Self-Assessments

Scattered throughout the text are more than 20 Self-Assessments, with at least one per chapter. Students complete these assessments to gain personal knowledge.

All information for completing and scoring the assessments is contained within the text. Self-knowledge leads students to an understanding of how they can and will operate as managers in the real world. Many of the assessments are tied to exercises within the book, thus enhancing the impact of the activities.

Communication Skills

There are approximately 150 critical-thinking questions (an average of 10 per chapter) that can be used for class discussion and/or written assignments to develop communication skills.

NEW TO THE SIXTH EDITION

I am really excited about this new sixth edition. I have totally updated and reorganized parts of it.

- The book is now full color, includes photos, and is significantly less expensive than the previous edition. Around 95 percent of the references are new to this edition, with an average of more than 80 references per chapter.

- There is a new chapter—Chapter 3: Managing Diversity in a Global Environment.

- Some of the chapters have been reorganized and some of the topics moved. Chapter 1's topic, entrepreneurship, has been moved to Chapter 6 (Managing Change, Innovation, and Entrepreneurship), and its appendix on the history of management is now within the chapter. The global and diversity parts of Chapter 2 have been moved into the new Chapter 3 with increased coverage. Managing Teams is now Chapter 8, moved up from Chapter 12. The sequence of the leadership chapters 10 through 13 has been changed.

- New topics include the transition to management, being a team leader, social entrepreneurship, the Foreign Corrupt Practices Act, international assignments, creativity, innovation killers, intuition in decision making, incremental and discontinuous change, mechanistic versus organic organization, social loafing, human resource information system (HRIS), changing organizational behavior (OB) foundations, Manager Acquired Needs Profile, visionary leaders, workplace deviance,

- Virtually every opening case has been updated or replaced and shortened a bit. There are 10 new end-of-chapter cases (75 percent) and the others are updated or changed. The objective questions have been eliminated, but the cumulative case questions remain.

- The Test Bank continues to measure application and skill development, and the AACSB competencies tested are also identified.

Chapter 1. Management and Its History

- New integrated material on the history of management has been incorporated in the chapter. The material on entrepreneurship has been moved to Chapter 6.

- Three new Exhibits for resources, management functions, and management skills

- New focus on knowledge in the section on information resources

- New introduction to the skills section revised AACSB competencies

- New sections discussing the transition to management (managing people) and being a team leader.

Chapter 2. The Environment: Culture, Ethics, and Social Responsibility

- The first section on the internal environment has been reorganized to begin with the mission combined with management and culture, followed by resources combined with structure, and ending with the systems process.

- Revised Join the Discussion: Auto Fuel Efficiency has been changed to focus on increases in miles per gallon.

- Revised sections "Does It Pay to Be Ethical?" and "Does It Pay to Be Socially Responsible?" have been rewritten with all new references and now include a discussion of social entrepreneurship.

- New discussion on the Foreign Corrupt Practices Act in the Managing Ethics section

- Revised section on sustainability has been moved into the social responsibility section.

- The material on global management has been moved to a new Chapter 3.

- New end-of-chapter case on LEGO and sustainable environmental decisions

- Ninety-eight percent of the references are new to this edition.

Chapter 3. Managing Diversity in a Global Diverse Environment

- New chapter addresses the opportunities and challenges of managing a diverse workforce and managing in a global society.

- New material on *global new venture/global start-up* and *subsidiaries* in the section on classifying businesses in the global village

- New and expanded coverage of trade agreements and foreign trade

- New and expanded coverage on taking a business global includes new examples as well as advantages and disadvantages of each of the methods described.

- New discussion on think globally, act locally in the section on practices of global companies.

- New and expanded coverage of diversity includes discussion of age, sex, race, ability, and other aspects.

- New self-assessment for diversity. The Self-Assessment now includes attitudes toward minorities as well as women's advancement.

- New discussion policies and practices in the managing of diversity

- New sections on Hofstede national cultural diversity and international assignments

- New end-of-chapter case on Sheryl Sandberg's *Lean In*

- New Skill Builder 3–1 exercise focusing on the global environment, diversity, and global management practices

- Ninety-nine percent of the references are new to this edition.

Chapter 4. Creative Problem Solving and Decision Making

- Updated Ideas on Management case and end-of-chapter case

- Reorganized and streamlined coverage. The first major section has been reorganized. The first two sections have been combined as Problem Solving and Decision-Making Interrelationships, and the Decision Making in the Global Village section has been moved up, putting the Decision-Making Model section last.

- New subsection on creativity and innovation killers in the reorganized section on generate creative and innovative alternatives

- New section titled "Intuition" to discuss its role in decision making
- Revised section on Vroom's participative decision-making model is now reorganized and condensed.
- Ninety-four percent of the references are new to this edition.

Chapter 5. Strategic and Operational Planning

- Revised Ideas on Management case features a new focus on CEO Schultz and new questions.
- Reorganized and streamlined coverage
- Expanded coverage of vision in the mission section
- Streamlined coverage of analyzing the environment and industry and competitive situation
- New corporate objective examples
- Streamlined coverage of the portfolio analysis
- The Entrepreneurial Strategy Matrix has been removed.
- Material from Appendix B has been moved into the chapter. Material on time management has been integrated into the operational planning section, and most of it has been rewritten.
- New subsection discussing multitasking has been integrated into the operational planning section.
- New end-of-chapter case on BlackBerry
- The Time Management Skill Builder is now within the chapter as a third activity.
- Ninety-six percent of the references are new to this chapter.

Chapter 6. Managing Change, Innovation, and Entrepreneurship

- Chapter 6 remains as Chapter 6. However, the title has been changed to reflect that the diversity section has been moved to Chapter 3 and that the section on entrepreneurship has been moved here from Chapter 1, reorganized, and mostly rewritten.
- New focus on change, innovation, and entrepreneurship. Material on diversity has been moved to Chapter 3.
- Now includes reorganized, rewritten, and expanded material on entrepreneurship from Chapter 1
- Revised section on forms of change includes new discussion of incremental and discontinuous change
- New section on managing innovation during incremental and discontinuous change
- Condensed coverage of organizational development
- New end-of-chapter case on Richard Branson (Virgin Airlines) on managing a growing entrepreneurial business
- Ninety-eight percent of the references are new to this chapter.

Chapter 7. Organizing and Delegating Work

- Chapter 7 was Chapter 5 in the previous edition.
- New coverage of the need to consider mechanistic versus organic organization and the environment, strategy, size, and technology in the section on organization considerations

- The section on principles of organization now states differences between the use of the principles in mechanistic and organic organizations.
- Reorganized section on authority has been reorganized and includes a discussion contrasting mechanistic and organic organizations.
- The subsection New Approaches to Departmentalization has been changed to Reengineering Contemporary Organizational Designs to add a discussion of reengineering.
- New end-of-chapter case on Costco
- Ninety-six percent of the references are new to this edition.

Chapter 8. Managing Team Work

- Chapter 8 was Chapter 12 in the fifth edition. The chapter title has changed to Managing Teams. The chapter has been moved up so that students get an earlier understanding of teamwork as it flows from Chapter 7's discussion on the increased use of team structures.
- New introduction to teams discussing the relationship between team structure and the need for teamwork skills as both a group member and manager
- New emphasis on how groups enforce norms
- The major section the Stages of Group Development and Styles of Leadership has been changed to Stages of Group Development and Management Styles to better place the focus on managing teams as stated in the chapter title.
- New subsection on team rewards and recognition. Social loafing has also been added.
- New end-of-chapter case on teamwork at Target
- Ninety-nine percent of the references are new to this chapter.

Chapter 9. Human Resources Management

- Chapters 9 was Chapter 7 in the fifth edition, with the same chapter title. The introduction to the human resource management process has been rewritten with all new references.
- New subsection on harassment and sexual harassment
- New discussion of why candidates should be informed that they didn't get the job and what to say to them
- Human resource information system (HRIS) has also been introduced with application forms. The difference between mechanistic and organic organization evaluations is explained.
- The Retaining Employees and Loss of Employees sections have been combined, titled Retaining and Terminating Employees, and the introduction has been rewritten with new references.
- New case on Google's Human Resource Management

Chapter 10. Organizational Behavior: Power, Politics, Conflict, and Stress

- Chapter 10 was Chapter 8 in the fifth edition, with the same chapter title.
- Revised or reorganized with the first four major sections having been combined under one title, Organizational Behavior (OB) Foundations
- The section on the Big Five personality traits has been rewritten with more descriptive traits listed for each dimension.

- New section on changing OB foundations explains how we can change our own personality, perception, and attitudes and how managers can change employee OB foundations.
- Revised and streamlined coverage on stress
- Ninety-five percent of the references are new to this chapter.

Chapter 11. Motivating for High Performance

- Chapter 11 was Chapter 11 in the fifth edition, with the same chapter title. The first section title is the same, but its subsection titles have been changed and the introduction has been rewritten.
- The subsection Acquired Needs Theory has been reorganized and condensed, and it now includes the Manager Acquired Needs Profile.
- The Employee Rewards and Recognition section title has been changed to Motivating Employees with Rewards and Recognition. The two subsections on reward and recognition programs have been combined and completely rewritten.
- While retaining the classical motivation theory references, new ones are added for a total of 79 percent new references to this edition.

Chapter 12. Leading With Influence

- Chapter 12 was Chapter 9 in the fifth edition, with the same chapter title.
- Reorganized to better follow the historic progression of leadership theories. New discussion on an overview of the leadership theories and a new Exhibit 12–1 listing the four leadership classes and their leadership theories.
- New section on contemporary leadership theories has been revised, adding visionary leaders.
- Significantly revised coverage of charismatic and transformational leaders
- While retaining the classical leadership theory references, new ones are added for a total of 80 percent new references to this edition.
- New case on Apple's leadership transition from Steve Jobs to Tim Cook

Chapter 13. Communication and Information Technology

- Chapter 13 was Chapter 10 with the same title in the fifth edition.
- Rewritten introduction to the first section
- Reorganized, revised, and streamlined coverage of information technology
- New Join the Discussion: Ethics & Social Responsibility 13–1 the Grapevine
- The chapter has been updated, and 93 percent of the references are new to this edition.

Chapter 14. Managing Control Systems, Finances, and People

- Chapter 14 was Chapter 13 in the fifth edition, with the chapter title changed to Managing Control Systems, Finances, and People.
- The subsection Functional Area/Department Control Systems has been consolidated.
- Streamlined coverage of establishing control systems and control frequency and methods
- The Human Controls section title has been changed to Managing People.

- New coverage of workplace deviance in section on discipline
- The chapter has been updated, and 95 percent of the references are new to this chapter.

Chapter 15. Operations, Quality, and Productivity

- Chapter 15 was Chapter 14 with the same title in the fifth edition.
- Revised coverage of time-based competition and operations now includes a short discussion on the transition from manufacturing to services and how technology and 3-D printing are transforming operations and will bring back some jobs to the United States.
- Streamlined coverage of resources and technology management has been shortened by deleting the discussion on ways of managing manufacturing technology and ways of managing service technology.
- The subsection on facilities layout has been rewritten with new examples to better distinguish among the four layouts.
- The two subsections on facility location and capacity planning have been combined and shortened.
- The subsection titled Productivity Measures for the Functional Areas has been deleted, including Exhibit 14–11 Financial Area Ratios and its accompanying Applying the Concept.
- The chapter has been updated, and 95 percent of the references are new to this edition.

ANCILLARY SUPPORT FOR THE INSTRUCTOR

Just as businesses must be integrated across functions and departments for success, text and ancillary material must also be integrated to create the optimum student learning experience. Many of our key supplements have been described to you as part of the support for our three-pronged approach to the management curriculum. The following paragraphs describe all elements of the text package, which are designed to create a successful classroom environment. Password-protected Instructor Teaching Site at **www.sagepub.com/lussier6e** includes the following resources:

- **Author-Created Instructor's Manual.** The instructor's manual, written by the author, Robert N. Lussier, Springfield College, was designed to ensure that every faculty member would receive complete, integrated support for teaching. The manual contains the following for each chapter of the book: a detailed outline for lecture enhancement, Work Application student sample answers, Review Questions and Communication Skills answers, Applying the Concept answers, cases, instructions on use of videos, and skill-builder ideas (including setup and timing). The instructor's manual also includes ideas on how to use the special features of the text in the classroom, with emphasis on creating an interactive learning environment. Skill Builders in the text have reinforcement and assessment questions in the corresponding Test Bank chapter, a unique feature of the Lussier text package. The Instructor's Manual contains detailed answers for all of the skills features in the text, including timing, information, answers, logistics for instructor use, and follow-up questions for student debriefing. The manual also explains how to test on skill building.

- **A Microsoft® Word® test bank**, is available, written by the author, Robert N. Lussier, Springfield College, and Charles J. Mambula I, Langston University. The test bank is structured around the book's three-pronged approach, testing students' understanding of management concepts, applications, and skills. Containing multiple choice, true/false, and essay questions for each chapter, the test bank provides you with a diverse range of pre-written options as well as the opportunity for editing any question and/or inserting your own personalized questions to effectively assess students' progress and understanding.

- **A Respondus electronic test bank** is available and can be used on PCs. written by the author, Robert N. Lussier, Springfield College, and Charles J. Mambula I, Langston University, the test bank is structured around the book's three-pronged approach, testing students' understanding of management concepts, applications, and skills. Containing multiple choice, true/false, and essay questions for each chapter, the test bank provides you with a diverse range of pre-written options as well as the opportunity for editing any question and/or inserting your own personalized questions to effectively assess students' progress and understanding.

- Editable, chapter-specific **Microsoft® PowerPoint® slides** offer you complete flexibility in easily creating a multimedia presentation for your course. The slides highlight essential content, features, and artwork from the book. Created by Andreas Bechrakis, Miami Dade College.

- **Class activities** provide lively and stimulating exercises to be used in or out of the classroom for groups or individuals.

- Links to engaging **video resources** with discussion questions and web resources provide you and your students with media resources to further explore key concepts.

- Access to full-text **SAGE journal articles** have been carefully selected for each chapter. Discussion questions for each article guide students' reading.

- Sample syllabi for semester and quarter courses provide suggested models for use when creating the syllabi for your courses.

- In-text **exhibits and models** are provided online to use in teaching aids such as PowerPoints, handouts, and lecture notes.

ANCILLARY SUPPORT FOR THE STUDENTS

Open-access Student Study Site at **www.sagepub.com/lussier6e** includes the following resources:

- **Mobile-friendly eFlashcards** reinforce understanding of key terms and concepts that have been outlined in the chapters

- **Mobile-friendly web quizzes** allow for independent assessment of progress made in learning course material

- Links to engaging **video resources** with discussion questions and web resources provide you and your students with media resources to further explore key concepts

- Access to full-text **SAGE journal articles** which have been carefully selected for each chapter; discussion questions for each article help guide your reading

···Acknowledgments

The authorship of a publishing project of this magnitude is only one aspect of a complex process. Many hardworking individuals gave great effort to create this text and package. I wish to express my special gratitude to the fine people at SAGE Publications. Specifically, I would like to thank my acquisitions editor Patricia Quinlin, associate editor Maggie Stanley, marketing manager Liz Thornton, production editor Veronica Stapleton Hooper, and designer Gail Buschman.

I would like to acknowledge that David Kimball of the Elms College wrote eight new end-of-chapter cases.

In addition, the reviewers of the project provided me with great ideas and inspiration for writing. The reviewers overwhelmingly confirmed the basic philosophical premise behind the book—teaching students how to be managers—and I am very grateful for their valuable input:

Joseph Adamo, Cazenovia College

Frank Armstrong, Ferris State University

Jeffrey C. Bauer, University of Cincinnati, Clermont College

Charlotte Davis, Concord University.

Eric S. Ecklund, Saint Francis University

Thomas D. Foreback, University of Cincinnati, Clermont College

Pope Gondwe. University of Namibia and Polytechnic of Namibia

Melanie Jacks Hillburn, Lone Star College—North Harris

Janet Kuser Komarnicki, Fisher College

Edward G. Lewis, University of Denver

Kimberly LaComba, Saint Mary-of-the-Woods College

Sharon Lobel, Seattle University

Charles Jabani Mambula, Langston University

Dr. John Michaels, California University of Pennsylvania

Diane Minger, Cedar Valley College

Fereshteh Mofidi, Peralta College/Merritt College

Dr. Clara Munson, Albertus Magnus College

Jane Murtaugh, College of DuPage

Robert D. Nale, Coastal Carolina University

Laura L. Paglis, University of Evansville

Alex Pomnichowski, Ferris State University

Michael Provitera, Barry University

Kenneth Rasheed, Chattahoochee Technical College

Herbert Sherman, Long Island University

Neil Trotta, Fisher College

Amy Wojciechowski, West Shore Community College

Patricia Wyatt, Bossier Parish Community College

I hope everyone who uses this text enjoys teaching from these materials as much as I do.

Contact Me With Feedback

I wrote this book for you. Let me know what you think of it. More specifically, how can it be improved? I will respond to your feedback. If I use your suggestion for improvement, your name and college will be listed in the acknowledgments section of the next edition.

Robert N. Lussier
Springfield College

rlussier@springfieldcollege.edu

... About the Author

Robert N. Lussier is a professor of management at Springfield College and has taught management for more than 25 years. He has developed some innovative and widely copied methods for applying concepts and developing skills that can be used in one's personal and professional life.

Dr. Lussier is a prolific writer, with more than 400 publications to his credit. His articles have been published in the *Academy of Entrepreneurship Journal, Business Horizons, Entrepreneurship Theory and Practice, Family Business Review, Journal of Business Strategies, Journal of Management Education, Journal of Small Business Management, Journal of Small Business Strategy, SAM Advanced Management Journal,* and several others. He also has a Human Resource Management textbook with (John Hendon) published by SAGE.

When not writing, he consults to a wide array of commercial and nonprofit organizations. In fact, some of the material in the book was developed for such clients as Baystate Medical Center, Coca-Cola, Friendly Ice Cream, Institute of Financial Education, Mead, Monsanto, Smith & Wesson, the Social Security Administration, the Visiting Nurses Association, and YMCAs.

Dr. Lussier holds a bachelor of science in business administration from Salem State College, two master's degrees in business and education from Suffolk University, and a doctorate in management from the University of New Haven.

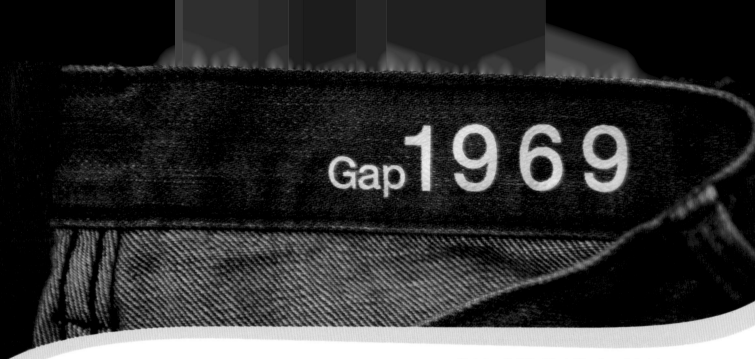

Gap 1969

Photo from David Paul Morris/Bloomberg via Getty Images.

1 Management and Its History

• • • Learning Outcomes

After studying this chapter, you should be able to:

1-1. Describe a manager's responsibility. PAGE 2

1-2. List and explain the three management skills. PAGE 6

1-3. List and explain the four management functions. PAGE 7

1-4. Identify the three management role categories. PAGE 9

1-5. List the hierarchy of management levels. PAGE 11

1-6. Describe the three different types of managers. PAGE 13

1-7. Describe the differences among management levels in terms of skills needed and functions performed. PAGE 14

1-8. State the major similarities and differences between the classical and behavioral theorists. PAGE 16

1-9. Describe how systems theorists and contingency theorists differ from classical and behavioral theorists. PAGE 19

IDEAS ON MANAGEMENT at Gap Inc.

Back in 1969, Doris and Don Fisher opened the first Gap store because Don couldn't find a pair of jeans that fit. The Fishers grew their company thoughtfully and transformed retailing. Customers responded. Today, **Gap Inc.** is one of the world's largest specialty retailers, offering clothing, accessories, and personal care products for men, women, children, and babies under the Gap, Banana Republic, Old Navy, Piperlime, and Athleta brand names. Gap brand includes Gap, GapKids, babyGap, and GapBody. The company also operates Gap Outlet and Banana Republic Factory Outlet stores. Gap Inc. has around 3,400 stores worldwide. In 2012, it moved up to be ranked number 179 on the *Fortune* 500 list with $15.7 billion in revenues and profits of $1.1 billion. In the specialty apparel retail industry, it was ranked second to TJX.

1. What resources does Gap Inc. use to sell its merchandise? PAGE 4
2. What management functions are performed at Gap stores? PAGE 7
3. What levels and types of managers have careers at Gap Inc.? PAGE 9

You'll find answers to these questions about management at **Gap** throughout the chapter, and you will also learn about Gap manager Bonnie Castonguary and her experiences in managing several stores for this casual-look retailer. To learn more about the Gap, visit its website at www.gapinc.com.

Source: Information for the case was taken from Gap's website at http://www.gapinc.com, accessed April 10, 2013; Largest U.S. corporations—*Fortune* 500, *Fortune* (May 20, 2013), 1–20.

WHY STUDY MANAGEMENT?

It's natural at this point to be thinking, "What can I get from this book?" or "What's in it for me?" These common questions are seldom asked or answered directly. The short answer is that the better you can work with people—and this is what most of this book is about—the more successful you will be in both your personal and your professional

• • • Chapter Outline

lives.[1] If you are a manager, or want to be a manager someday, you need good management skills to be successful.[2] Even if you are not interested in being a manager, you still need management skills to succeed in today's workplace.[3] The old workplace, in which managers simply told employees what to do, is gone. Today, employees want to be involved in management,[4] and organizations expect employees to work in teams and share in decision making and other management tasks.[5]

The study of management also applies directly to your personal life. You communicate with and interact with people every day; you make personal plans and decisions, set goals, prioritize what you will do, and get others to do things for you. Are you ever in conflict with family and friends, and do you ever feel stressed? This book can help you develop management skills that you can apply in all of those areas. In this chapter, you will learn what management is all about, and we begin the discussion of how you can develop your management skills.

LO 1-1

Describe a manager's responsibility.

WHAT IS A MANAGER'S RESPONSIBILITY?

This interview with Bonnie Castonguary, a store manager for **Gap** Inc., provides an overview of the manager's job and responsibility.

Q: What was your progression to your present job as store manager?

A: I started as a store manager in training. I replaced a woman on maternity leave as acting store manager, and then I had my first store. After a while, I was promoted to larger stores with more sales volume. A few years later, I was promoted to manager of [a] Gap outlet store. . . . My next career advancement is to general manager . . . I would still be in one store, but I would assist the district manager by overseeing other stores in my district.

Q: Briefly describe your job.

A: **Gap** Inc.'s two-page "Position Overview Store Management" form, which also contains a detailed summary for each level of management, presents this general summary: "The Store Management team manages the sales, operations, and personnel functions of the store to ensure maximum profitability and compliance with company procedures. The Team includes Assistant Managers, Associate Managers, the Store Manager, and/or the General Manager." [See Exhibit 1-1 for Castonguary's description of a typical Monday.]

Q: What do you like best about being a manager?

A: You don't have time to get bored on the job because you are always doing something different.

Q: What do you like least about being a manager?

A: Dealing with difficult performance problems of employees and customers, and always being on call. When I'm not at work, I'm still on call when there are problems at the store. This could mean going to the store at 2:00 A.M. to shut off the alarm.

Q: What advice would you give to college graduates without any full-time work experience who are interested in a management career after graduation?

A: You need to be dedicated and hardworking. You must take great pride in your work. You have to be willing to take on a lot of responsibility. Remember, your employees are always looking to you to set the example; when you make a mistake (which you will do), it affects your staff. You have to be a self-starter. As a store manager you have to motivate employees, but your boss is not around much to motivate you.

EXHIBIT 1-1   A DAY IN THE LIFE OF A MANAGER

8:00 A.M.

- Enter the store and walk the sales floor to ensure a proper closing took place the night before.
- Project the payroll cost for the week as a percentage of my forecasted sales, and call it in.
- Perform opening procedures on the controller (computer that records sales transactions and inventory count for all cash registers in the store).

8:30 A.M.

- Walk the sales floor with staff and assign projects for them to create new displays for merchandise during the day (create a "to do" list for employees and myself).

9:00 A.M.

- Before the store opens, call voice mail and check email for messages left by other store managers or my boss, the district manager.
- Make business telephone calls for the day.

9:30 A.M.

- Assign sales associates to store zones.
- Put money in computer cash register drawers.

10:00 A.M.

- Open the store.
- Make sure sales associates are in their zones on the floor for proper floor coverage.
- Make sure everyone who enters the store is greeted and has his or her needs determined.
- Provide floor coverage. (Help out as needed—greet customers, assist customers with sales, stock shelves, assist at the changing room, etc.)

12:00 P.M.

- Do business analysis for previous month from operating statement and gross margin reports.

12:30 P.M.

- Provide floor coverage as needed for staggered employee breaks.

1:30–2:30 P.M. MY BREAK, THEN:

- Prepare customer request transfers (merchandise our store has but other stores do not have) to be delivered. Enter transfers into computer and get merchandise.

3:00 P.M.

- Leave for district meeting.

3:15 P.M.

- Drop off transfers and pick up another store manager; continue on to district meeting.

4:00 P.M.

- Meeting is conducted by district manager with the seven general and store managers.
- Meeting begins with discussion of the following topics:
  - Previous week's sales, previous week's payroll, payroll projections for next month (cost as a percentage of sales), cleanliness, and standards of the stores.
  - New information items, mail, general discussion, questions, etc.
- Meeting ends with a walk-through of the store at which the meeting is held. During a walk-through, the host store manager discusses new display ideas that the other store managers may want to use. In addition, the other store managers give the host manager ideas for improving the store visually. In other words, this is a time to share ideas that will help all team members in the Gap district.

6:00 P.M.

- Call my store to see how sales are going for the day, then leave for home.

WORK
APPLICATION 1-1

Describe the specific resources used by a present or past boss. Give the manager's job title and department.

Organizational Resources

A **manager** is *responsible for achieving organizational objectives through efficient and effective utilization of resources.* Efficient means doing things right so as to maximize the utilization of resources. Effective means doing the right thing in order to attain an objective; a manager's effectiveness reflects the degree to which he or she achieves objectives.[6] The **manager's resources** are *human, financial, physical, and informational.* Bundling your resources efficiently and effectively can give you an advantage over your competitors.[7] The resources are listed in Exhibit 1-2.

EXHIBIT 1-2   MANAGEMENT RESOURCES
Management Resources
Human
Financial
Physical
Informational

Human Resources. Human resources are people. Managers are responsible for getting the job done through employees.[8] People are the manager's most valuable resource;[9] treat them well and they will be more productive.[10] Throughout this book, we focus on how managers work with employees to accomplish organizational objectives.

Financial Resources. It takes money to make money, and without proper finances, you don't have a business.[11] Most managers have a budget stating how much it should cost to operate their department/store for a set time. In other words, a budget defines the financial resources available.

Physical Resources. Getting the job done requires effective and efficient use of physical resources through control mechanisms.[12] Managers are responsible for keeping equipment in working condition and for making sure that necessary materials and supplies are available. Deadlines might be missed and present sales and future business lost if physical resources are not available and used and maintained properly.[13]

Informational Resources. You can't manage an organization without communicating information on how to transform resources into performance.[14] Information should be based on knowledge,[15] so managers need to disseminate knowledge,[16] and employees need to share their knowledge.[17]

Resources and Performance. Managers have a profound impact on the performance of their organizations.[18] So how you manage the four resources affects organizational performance.[19] The level of organizational **performance** *is based on how effectively and efficiently managers utilize resources to achieve objectives.* Managers are responsible for and evaluated on how well they meet organizational strategies and objectives through utilization of resources.[20] Selecting the right resources—being effective—and using them efficiently results in high levels of performance.[21]

Gap (Case Question 1) has around 136,000 people (human resources), sales of more than $15 billion a year (financial), $7.5 billion in (physical) assets including 3,400 stores with fixtures to display its merchandise, and a complex computer system (information) to coordinate business globally. Starting with one small store with limited resources, the company grew to the point of Gap's performance being high with more than $1.1 billion in profits.

manager The individual responsible for achieving organizational objectives through efficient and effective utilization of resources.

manager's resources Human, financial, physical, and informational resources.

performance Means of evaluating how effectively and efficiently managers utilize resources to achieve objectives.

WHAT DOES IT TAKE TO BE A SUCCESSFUL MANAGER?

Now that you have an idea of what management is, let's focus on some of the qualities, skills, and competencies necessary to be a successful manager.

Management Qualities

Over the years, numerous researchers have attempted to answer the question, "What does it take to be a successful manager?" In a *Wall Street Journal* Gallup survey, 782 top executives in 282 large corporations were asked, "What are the most important traits for success as a supervisor?"[22] Before you read what these executives replied, complete the Self-Assessment on management traits to find out if you have these qualities. It is said that to "know thyself" is the foundation of leadership development,[23] and self-awareness is critical for success,[24] so you will have the opportunity to complete self-assessments in every chapter.

The executives in the Gallup survey identified integrity, industriousness, and the ability to get along with people as the three most important traits for successful managers. Other necessary traits included business knowledge, intelligence, leadership ability, education, sound judgment, ability to communicate, flexibility, and ability to plan and set objectives.

1-1 SELF ASSESSMENT

Management Traits

The following 15 questions relate to some of the qualities needed to be a successful manager. Rate yourself on each item by indicating with a number (1–4) how well each statement describes you.

1. The statement does not describe me at all.
2. The statement somewhat describes me.
3. The statement describes me most of the time.
4. The statement describes me very accurately

_____ 1. I enjoy working with people. I prefer to work with others rather than working alone.
_____ 2. I can motivate others. I can get people to do things they may not want to do.
_____ 3. I am well liked. People enjoy working with me.
_____ 4. I am cooperative. I strive to help the team do well rather than to be the star.
_____ 5. I am a leader. I enjoy teaching, coaching, and instructing people.
_____ 6. I want to be successful. I do things to the best of my ability to be successful.
_____ 7. I am a self-starter. I get things done without having to be told to do them.
_____ 8. I am a problem solver. If things aren't going the way I want them to, I take corrective action to meet my objectives.
_____ 9. I am self-reliant. I don't need the help of others.
_____ 10. I am hardworking. I enjoy working and getting the job done.
_____ 11. I am trustworthy. If I say I will do something by a set time, I do it.
_____ 12. I am loyal. I do not do or say things to intentionally hurt my friends, relatives, or coworkers.
_____ 13. I can take criticism. If people tell me negative things about myself, I give them serious thought and change when appropriate.
_____ 14. I am honest. I do not lie, steal, or cheat.
_____ 15. I am fair. I treat people equally. I don't take advantage of others.
_____ TOTAL SCORE (add numbers on lines 1–15; the range of possible scores is 15–60)

In general, the higher your score, the better your chances of being a successful manager. You can work on improving your integrity (items 11–15), industriousness (items 6–10), and ability to get along with people (items 1–5) both in this course and in your personal life. As a start, review the traits listed here. Which ones are your strongest and your weakest? Think about how you can improve in the weaker areas—or, even better, write out a plan.

LO 1-2

List and explain the three management skills.

WORK APPLICATION 1-2

Identify a specific manager, preferably one who is or was your boss, and explain what makes him or her successful or unsuccessful. Give examples.

Management Skills

Skills involve the ability to perform some type of activity or task.[25] **Management skills** *include (1) technical, (2) interpersonal, and (3) decision-making skills.* All employees today need good management skills.[26] Because management skills are so important, the focus of this book is on skill building. If you work at it, you can develop your management skills through this course.

Technical Skills. **Technical skills** *involve the ability to use methods and techniques to perform a task.* Technical skills are also called business skills, and they are the easiest of the three management skills to develop.[27] When managers are working on budgets, for example, they may need computer skills in order to use spreadsheet software such as **Microsoft** Excel®. Most employees are promoted to their first management position primarily because of their technical skills. Technical skills vary widely from job to job; therefore, this course does not focus on developing these skills.

EXHIBIT 1-3   **MANAGEMENT SKILLS**

Management Skills
Decision-Making Skills
Interpersonal Skills
Technical Skills

Interpersonal Skills. **Interpersonal skills** involve *the ability to understand, communicate, and work well with individuals and groups through developing effective relationships.* Interpersonal skills are sometimes also referred to as human or people skills, as well as soft skills. The resources you need to get the job done are made available through relationships, both inside (employees) and outside (customers, suppliers, others) the firm.[28] You need to develop your interpersonal skills to be effective.[29] Sir Richard Branson, of **Virgin Group**, says, "You definitely need to be good with people to help bring out the best in people."[30] Businesses seek employees with good interpersonal skills.[31] Unfortunately, college grads have been criticized as lacking the skills necessary to effectively manage people.[32] You can develop your interpersonal skills, and they are based on several other skills that you will learn throughout the book, including ethical, diversity, power, political, negotiation, conflict, networking, communication, motivation, and teamwork skills.

Decision-Making Skills. Clearly, the decisions you have made over your lifetime have affected you today. Leadership decisions determine the success or failure of organizations,[33] so organizations are training their people to improve their decision-making skills.[34] **Decision-making skills** *are based on the ability to conceptualize situations and select alternatives to solve problems and take advantage of opportunities.* Decision-making skills are based on several other skills you will learn throughout the book, including conceptual; diagnostic, analytical, critical-thinking, quantitative reasoning, and time-management skills.

To summarize, technical skills are primarily concerned with things, interpersonal skills are primarily concerned with people, and decisional skills are primarily concerned with ideas and concepts.[35] Review the management skills in Exhibit 1-3; then complete Applying the Concept 1.

AACSB Competencies

In addition to qualities and skills, the AACSB (Association to Advance Collegiate Schools of Business) has established standards for accreditation of business schools. The standards do not require any specific courses in the curriculum. Normally, the

management skills The skills needed to be an effective manager, including technical, interpersonal, and decision-making skills.

technical skills The ability to use methods and techniques to perform a task.

interpersonal skills The ability to understand, communicate, and work well with individuals and groups through developing effective relationships.

decision-making skills The ability to conceptualize situations and select alternatives to solve problems and take advantage of opportunities.

1-1 APPLYING THE CONCEPT

Management Skills

Identify each activity as being one of the following types of management skills:

A. technical
B. interpersonal
C. decision making

_____ 1. The manager is giving an employee a sincere "thank you" for finishing the job ahead of schedule.

_____ 2. The manager is scheduling employee work hours for next week.

_____ 3. The manager is writing an email.

_____ 4. The manager is running a machine for an employee who is out sick.

_____ 5. The manager is trying to figure out why the department is behind schedule.

---

degree program includes learning experiences in such general-knowledge and skill areas as communication abilities, ethical understanding and reasoning abilities, analytic skills, use of information technology, dynamics of the global economy, multicultural and diversity understanding, and reflective thinking skills.[36]

Supervisory Ability

Professor Edwin Ghiselli conducted a study to determine the traits that contribute to success as a manager.[37] Ghiselli identified six traits as important, although not all are necessary for success. These six traits, in reverse order of importance, include initiative, self-assurance, decisiveness, intelligence, need for occupational achievement, and supervisory ability. The number one trait, supervisory ability, includes skills in planning, organizing, leading, and controlling. These four areas of supervisory ability are more commonly referred to as the _management functions_, which you will learn about in the next section.

This book includes Skill Builders at the end of each chapter to foster the development of your management qualities, skills, competencies, and supervisory ability. Each exercise identifies the area of development.

WHAT DO MANAGERS DO?

Having discussed what a manager is responsible for and what it takes to be a successful manager, our next question is, "What do managers do?" In this section, you will learn about the four functions performed by managers and the three roles that all managers play.

Management Functions

The four **management functions** (**Case Question 2**) include _planning, organizing, leading, and controlling._ Managers perform the management functions through using organizational resources to achieve organizational objectives through others, usually in teams.[38] All of the Skill Builder exercises identify the management function skill being developed through the activity. Exhibit 1-4 lists the four functions of management.

Planning—Based on Objectives. Planning is typically the starting point in the management process, and you should begin with a clear objective.[39] **Planning** is the process of setting objectives and determining in advance exactly how the objectives

WORK
APPLICATION 1-3

Select a manager, preferably one who is or was your boss, and state the specific management skills he or she uses on the job.

LO 1-3

List and explain the four management functions.

management functions Planning, organizing, leading, and controlling.

planning The process of setting objectives and determining in advance exactly how the objectives will be met.

EXHIBIT 1-4 MANAGEMENT FUNCTIONS

Management Functions
Planning
Organizing
Leading
Controlling

will be met. The objective is the end result, and the plan specifies exactly what needs to happen to accomplish your objective.[40] So before we do things, we should have an objective stating the end result and a plan for how to complete it. You should realize how important it is to set and pursue your objectives[41] and that the other three functions also focus on achieving your objectives. You will learn how to write effective objectives and plans in Part II: Planning, Chapters 4 through 6.

Organizing. Performance is based on how managers organize their resources.[42] *Organizing is the process of delegating and coordinating tasks and allocating resources to achieve objectives.* An important part of coordinating human resources is to assign people to various jobs and tasks. An important part of organizing, sometimes listed as a separate function, is staffing. *Staffing* is the process of selecting, training, and evaluating employees. You will learn how to organize in Part III: Organizing, Chapters 7 through 9.

Leading. The ability to lead is an important skill for everyone, especially for managers.[43] **Leading** *is the process of influencing employees to work toward achieving objectives.* Managers must communicate the objectives to employees and motivate them to achieve those objectives. You will learn how to lead in Part IV: Leading, Chapters 10 through 13.

Controlling. Objectives will not be met without consistent follow-through.[44] **Controlling** *is the process of monitoring progress and taking corrective action when needed to ensure that objectives are achieved.* An important part of controlling is monitoring and measuring progress toward the achievement of objectives and taking corrective action when necessary.[45] Although it will happen, don't view missing a deadline or an objective as OK; get back on track—no excuses.[46] You will learn how to control in Part V: Controlling, Chapters 14 through 15.

Growing **Gap Inc.** took lots of planning. Bonnie Castonguary has to plan displays and schedule employees. The entire company has an organizational structure based on territory. Castonguary has full responsibility for selecting, training, and evaluating her store's employees. Great success comes from effectively leading employees by motivating them. Controlling is also important at Gap. Castonguary is consistently taking corrective action with inventory to make sure her store has the right products available in the right quantities and the prices to satisfy customers.

Nonmanagement Functions. All managers perform the four functions of management as they get work done through employees. However, many managers perform nonmanagement, or employee, functions as well. For example, at the **Gap**, Bonnie Castonguary spent from 10:00 to 12:00 and 12:30 to 1:30 primarily waiting on customers, which is a nonmanagement function. Many managers are called working managers because they perform both management and employee functions.

The Transition to Management—Managing People. Going from being an employee to being a manager is not an easy transition.[47] New managers tend to view themselves as the boss, telling others what to do, making decisions, and getting things done, but with time they realize their job is to manage people. They also don't

WORK APPLICATION 1-4

Identify a specific manager, preferably one who is or was your boss, and give examples of how that person performs each of the four management functions.

organizing The process of delegating and coordinating tasks and allocating resources to achieve objectives.

leading The process of influencing employees to work toward achieving objectives.

controlling The process of monitoring progress and taking corrective action when needed to ensure that objectives are achieved.

1-2 APPLYING THE CONCEPT

Management Functions

Indicate which type of function the manager is performing in each situation:

A. planning
B. organizing
C. leading
D. controlling
E. nonmanagement

_____ 6. The manager is encouraging an employee to get an important order ready today.

_____ 7. The manager is conducting a job interview to fill the position of a retiring employee.

_____ 8. The production manager is making copies in the office.

_____ 9. The manager is determining how many units were produced during the first half of the shift.

_____ 10. The manager is teaching the waiter how to use the computer ordering system.

realize just how hard the job really is and how much more work managers do than employees who constantly interrupt them, putting demands on their time. Because most new managers are used to doing nonmanagement functions, which they tend to enjoy, they often do the work for employees when their actual job is to train them to do their job, help them improve their performance, and solve problems to make their jobs easier and less frustrating. As a manager, you will likely need to perform nonmanagement functions, but be sure to focus on planning, organizing, leading, and controlling to get the job done through people.

Management Roles

Managers have a set of distinct roles (**Case Question 3**).[48] A *role* is a set of expectations of how one will behave in a given situation. Henry Mintzberg identified ten roles that managers embody as they accomplish management functions. Studies have supported Mintzberg's management role theory. Mintzberg grouped these roles into three **management role categories:**[49] *interpersonal, informational, and decisional roles.*

LO 1-4

Identify the three management role categories.

Interpersonal Roles. Interpersonal roles include figurehead, leader, and liaison. When managers play interpersonal roles, they use their human and communication skills as they perform management functions. Managers play the *figurehead* role when they represent the organization or department in ceremonial and symbolic activities. The manager of the **Gap** store at which Bonnie Castonguary attended the district meeting played the figurehead role when she greeted visitors and gave them a tour of the store. Managers play the *leader*

EXHIBIT 1-5 MANAGEMENT ROLES

Management Roles
Interpersonal—figurehead, leader, liaison
Informational—monitor, disseminator, spokesperson
Decisional—entrepreneur, disturbance handler, resource allocator, negotiator

role when they motivate, train, communicate with, and influence others. Throughout the day, Castonguary performed the leader role as she directed employees to maintain floor coverage. Managers play the *liaison* role when they interact with people outside of their unit to gain information and favors. Castonguary was a liaison at the district meeting, which included the store walk-through.

management role categories The categories of roles—interpersonal, informational, and decisional—managers play as they accomplish management functions.

Informational Roles. Informational roles include monitor, disseminator, and spokesperson. When managers play informational roles, they use their human and communication skills. Managers play the *monitor* role when they read and talk to others to receive information. Bonnie Castonguary was continually monitoring the store to ensure full floor coverage. Managers play the *disseminator* role when they send information to others. Castonguary played the disseminator role when she was at the district meeting. Managers play the spokesperson role when they provide information to people outside the organization. Castonguary played the *spokesperson* role when she made business calls in the morning and gave the interview to the author of this book.

Decisional Roles. Decisional roles include entrepreneur, disturbance handler, resource allocator, and negotiator. When managers play decisional roles, they use their conceptual and decision-making management skills. Managers play the *entrepreneur* role when they innovate and initiate improvements. Bonnie Castonguary played this role when she had the staff set up new displays to help improve store sales. Managers play the *disturbance-handler* role when they take corrective action during disputes or crisis situations. Castonguary had to deal with a customer who was not satisfied when an employee would not give a cash refund for merchandise returned. Managers play the *resource-allocator* role when they schedule, request authorization, and perform budgeting and programming activities, as when Castonguary allocated sales associates to zones on the floor. Managers perform the *negotiator* role when they represent their department or organization during nonroutine transactions to gain agreement and commitment. Castonguary played the negotiator role when she made business calls to outside contractors.

WORK
APPLICATION 1-5

Identify a specific manager, preferably one who is or was your boss, and give examples of how that person performs roles in each of the three management role categories. Be sure to identify at least one of the three or four roles in each category.

1-3   APPLYING THE CONCEPT

Management Roles

Identify each of the managerial activities as part of one of the three role categories:

   A.   interpersonal role
   B.   informational role
   C.   decisional role

_____ 11. The manager reads *The Wall Street Journal* while having coffee first thing in the morning.

_____ 12. The manager shows an employee how to fill out a form.

_____ 13. The manager discusses how much it will cost for a new machine.

_____ 14. The sales manager resolves a complaint with a customer.

_____ 15. The manager develops a new meal for the restaurant.

The Systems Relationship Among the Management Skills, Functions, and Roles

The management skills are interrelated. For example, a first-line supervisor's technical skills will affect his or her interpersonal and decision-making skills and vice versa. A manager's skills also affect the implementation of the management functions and roles.[50]

The management functions are not steps in a linear process. Managers do not usually plan, then organize, then lead, and then control. The functions are distinct yet interrelated. Managers often perform them simultaneously. In addition, each function depends on the others. For example, if you start with a poor plan, the objective will not be met even if things are well organized, led, and controlled. Or, if you start with a great plan but are poorly organized or lead poorly, the objective may not be met. Plans without controls are rarely implemented effectively. Remember that the management functions are based on setting objectives (planning) and achieving them (through organizing, leading, and controlling).

How well a manager plays the various management roles is also affected by his or her management skills. The ten management roles are also integrated with the management functions. Certain management roles are played when performing the different management functions.

Exhibit 1-6 illustrates the interrelationship of management skills, functions, and roles.

EXHIBIT 1-6   MANAGEMENT SKILLS, FUNCTIONS, AND ROLES

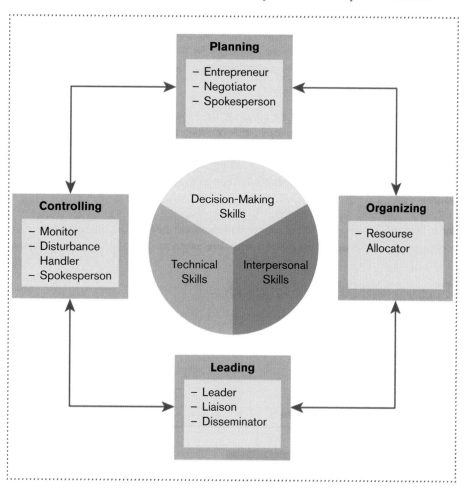

DIFFERENCES AMONG MANAGERS

There are many differences in levels of management, types of managers, management skills needed, management functions performed, roles played, and the functions of managers in large businesses versus small businesses and for-profit versus not-for-profit businesses.

The Three Levels of Management

Managers differ in the level of management, and there are also nonpermanent managers called team leaders, as well as nonmanager operative employees. There

LO 1-5

List the hierarchy of management levels.

are also different types of managers by level of management. Let's cover these concepts in this sequence.

The three **levels of management** *are top managers, middle managers, and first-line managers.* The three levels relate to each other as described here. See Exhibit 1-7 for an illustration of the three levels of management and operative employees.

Top Managers. Top managers—people in executive positions—have titles such as chief executive officer (CEO), president, or vice president. Most organizations have relatively few top management positions. Top managers are responsible for managing an entire organization or major parts of it. They develop and define the organization's purpose, objectives, and strategies and often get the credit or blame for the performance of their firms.[51] They report to other executives or boards of directors and supervise the activities of middle managers.

Middle Managers. People in middle-management positions have titles such as sales manager, branch manager, or department head. Middle managers are responsible for implementing top management's strategy by developing short-term operating plans. They generally report to executives and supervise the work of first-line managers.

First-Line Managers. Examples of titles of first-line managers are team or crew leader, supervisor, head nurse, and office manager. These managers are responsible for implementing middle managers' operational plans. They generally report to middle managers. Unlike those at the other two levels of management, first-line managers do not supervise other managers; they supervise operative employees.

levels of management Top managers, middle managers, and first-line managers.

Team Leader. This is a newer management position needed in organizations that focus on a team-based structure.[52] They are often called a project or program

EXHIBIT 1-7   MANAGEMENT LEVELS AND FUNCTIONAL AREAS

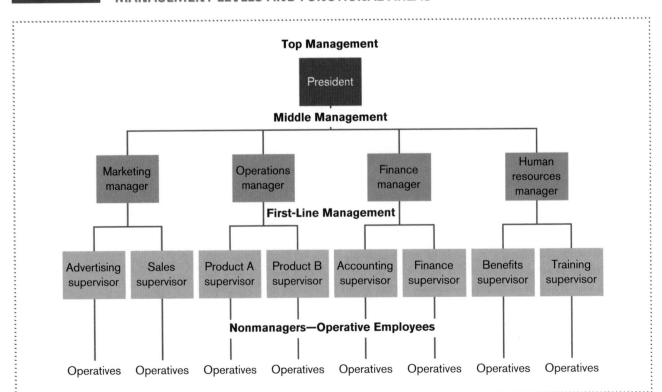

Executive Compensation

Eight CEOs, led by J.C. Penny, made more than 1,000 times their average workers' salary. Oracle's CEO made an estimated $189,000 per hour. Some say top executives are being overpaid. Fortune 500 CEOs all make millions.

However, not everyone agrees. In capitalist countries, talented CEOs, like in pro sports, are entitled to fetch their price. Top executives should be paid multimillion-dollar compensation packages; after all, if it weren't for effective CEOs, companies would not be making the millions of dollars of profits they make each year. CEOs deserve a piece of the pie they help create.

1. Do executives deserve to make 300 times more than the average worker?

2. Is it ethical for managers to take large pay increases when laying off employees?
3. Is it ethical for managers to get pay raises when their companies lose money?
4. Are companies being socially responsible when paying executives premium compensation?

Sources: Information taken from the AFL-CIO's website at http://www.aflcio.org/corporatewatch/paywatch/pay/index.cfm, accessed April 15, 2013; R. Lowenstein, "Is Any CEO Worth $189,000 per Hour?" *BusinessWeek* (February 20–26, 2012), 8–9; R. Fisman and T. Sullivan, "In Defense of the CEO," *Wall Street Journal* (January 12–13, 2013), C1–C2; E. D. Smith and P. Kuntz, "Some CEOs Are More Equal than Others," *BusinessWeek* (May 6–12, 2013), 70–73.

---

leader or task force or committee leader. The team leader facilitates team activities to achieve a goal rather than telling people what to do.

Higher-level managers may also be team leaders who supervise a small group of people to achieve a goal. Nonmanagement operative employees may also be team leaders who manage a team until the goal is completed. The team leader is not usually a permanent management position and thus is not a level in the hierarchy of management. You will learn more about teams and how to lead them in Chapter 8.

Nonmanagement Operative Employees. Operative employees are the workers in an organization who do not hold management positions. They commonly report to first-line managers and possibly to team leaders. They make the products, wait on customers, perform repairs, and so on.

Types of Managers by Level. The three **types of managers** are general managers, functional managers, and project managers. Top-level and some middle managers are general managers because they supervise the activities of several departments that perform different activities. Middle and first-line managers are often functional managers who supervise the completion of related tasks. Project managers are often team leaders.

The four most common business functional areas include marketing, operations/production, finance/accounting, and human resources/personnel management, as shown in Exhibit 1-7. A *marketing* manager is responsible for selling and advertising products and services. A *production* manager is responsible for making a product, such as a **Ford** Mustang, whereas an operations manager is responsible for providing a service, such as a loan by **Bank of America**. (However, both product and service organizations now use the broader term *operations*.) An *accounting* manager is responsible for keeping records of sales and expenses (accounts receivable and payable) and determining profitability, whereas a financial manager is responsible for obtaining the necessary funds and investments. The term *finance* is commonly used to mean both accounting and financial activities. A human resources manager (known in the past as a *personnel manager*) is responsible for forecasting future employee needs and recruiting, selecting, evaluating, and compensating employees.

WORK APPLICATION 1-6

Identify the levels of management in a specific organization by level and title. Be sure to give the organization's name.

LO 1-6

Describe the three different types of managers.

WORK APPLICATION 1-7

Identify which type of boss you have now or have had previously. If that person is or was a functional manager, be sure to specify the functional tasks of the department.

types of managers General managers, functional managers, and project managers.

1-4   APPLYING THE CONCEPT

Differences Among Management Levels

Identify the level of management in the following five instances:

    A. top
    B. middle
    C. first-line

____ 16. Managers who are supervised directly by executives.

____ 17. Managers who have a greater need for technical skills.

____ 18. Managers who spend more time planning and organizing.

____ 19. Managers who oversee the performance of operative employees.

____ 20. Managers who develop short-term operating plans.

A *project manager* coordinates employees and other resources across several functional departments to accomplish a specific goal or task, such as developing and producing a new breakfast cereal for **Kellogg's** or a new aircraft at **Boeing**.

LO 1-7

Describe the differences among management levels in terms of skills needed and functions performed.

Differences in Management Skills and Functions

Differences in Management Skills. All managers need technical, interpersonal, and decision-making skills. However, the relative importance of these types of skills varies with the level of management. At all three levels of management, the need for interpersonal skills remains fairly constant. However, top-level managers have a greater need for decision-making skills, whereas first-line managers have a greater need for technical skills. Middle managers tend to need all three skills, but the mix required differs somewhat from organization to organization.

Differences in Management Functions. All managers perform the four management functions: planning, organizing, leading, and controlling. However, the time spent on each function varies with the level of management. First-line managers spend more time leading and controlling, middle-level managers spend equal time on all four functions, and top managers spend more time planning and organizing.

Exhibit 1-8 summarizes the primary skills needed and functions performed at each of the three management levels.

EXHIBIT 1-8   SKILLS NEEDED AND FUNCTIONS PERFORMED AT DIFFERENT MANAGEMENT LEVELS

Management Level	Primary Management Skills Needed	Primary Management Functions Performed
Top	Decision-Making and Interpersonal Skills	Planning and Organizing
Middle	Balance of all Three	Balance of all Four
First-Line	Technical and Interpersonal Skills	Leading and Controlling

Differences in Size and Profits

Large-Business versus Small-Business Managers. Research suggests that entrepreneurs behave differently than managers in large companies.[53] There are few people who are both good entrepreneurs and good managers.[54] Bonnie Castonguary works for a large organization—**Gap** Inc. Her independent store resembles a small business, but it has the support of a large organization. Exhibit 1-9 lists some of the differences between large and small businesses. However, these are general statements; many large and small businesses share certain characteristics. Most large businesses, including **Apple**, started as small businesses and grew.

Managers of For-Profit versus Not-For-Profit Organizations. Is the manager's job the same in for-profit and not-for-profit organizations? Although some noteworthy differences exist, the answer is basically yes. All managers need management skills, perform management functions, and play management roles regardless of the organization type. Bonnie Castonguary works for a for-profit business. Employees of the **United Way of America, American Red Cross,** and **Girl Scouts of the United States of America** work for the public (not-for-profit) sector.

In the past, it was common to classify both non-governmental and governmental organizations together into one group called not-for-profits. However, the current trend is to distinguish not-for-profit organizations into non-governmental organizations (NGOs) and governmental organizations. **Doctors Without Borders** is an example of an NGO, operating independently of political aid or policies, while the **Federal Emergency Management Agency (FEMA)** is an example of a governmental organization, supported and funded by the government.

Exhibit 1-10 lists some of the differences between for-profit and not-for-profit organizations.

Steve Jobs cofounded Apple with Steve Wozniak in his parents' garage with no employees and grew the company to become one of the largest corporations in the world. Photo from Time & Life Pictures/Getty Images.

EXHIBIT 1-9 DIFFERENCES BETWEEN LARGE AND SMALL BUSINESSES

Functions and Roles	Large Business	Small Business
Planning	Commonly have formal written objectives and plans with a global business focus.	Commonly have informal objectives and plans that are not written with a global focus.
Organizing	Tend to have formal organization structures with clear policies and procedures, with three levels of management. Jobs tend to be specialized.	Tend to have informal structures without clear policies and procedures, with fewer than three levels of management. Jobs tend to be more general.
Leading	Managers tend to be more participative, giving employees more say in how they do their work and allowing them to make more decisions.	Entrepreneurs tend to be more autocratic and want things done their way, often wanting to make the decisions.
Controlling	Tend to have more sophisticated computerized control systems.	Tend to use less sophisticated control systems and to rely more on direct observation.
Important management roles	Resource allocator.	Entrepreneur and spokesperson.

EXHIBIT 1-10 DIFFERENCES AMONG FOR-PROFIT AND NOT-FOR-PROFIT ORGANIZATIONS

Function	For-Profit	Not-for-Profit	
		Non-Governmental Organizations	Governmental Organizations
Ownership and Profits	The primary universal measure of performance is bottom-line profit. Owners are entitled to take profits out of the firm.	Organizations are mission driven; like all businesses, profits are the objective. However, any excess revenue remains in the organization. There are no individual owners.	Organizations are mission driven; however, unlike non-governmental organizations, profits are not the goal. Ownership is an entity of a function of government.
Revenues	Raised primarily through sales.	Raised through donations, grants, memberships, and investments, as well as sales	Raised through taxes, fees, and sales.
Staffing	Primarily all paid employees.	Both volunteer workers and paid employees.	Primarily all paid employees, with some entities relying on volunteers.

Source: Dr. Kathryn Carlson Heler, Professor at Springfield College, 2010. Used with permission.

LO 1-8

State the major similarities and differences between the classical and behavioral theorists.

A BRIEF HISTORY OF MANAGEMENT

There are two primary reasons you should be concerned about the history of management: to better understand current developments and to avoid repeating mistakes. Early literature on management was written by management practitioners who described their experiences and attempted to extrapolate basic principles. More recent literature comes from researchers. There are different classifications of management approaches, or schools of management thought. In this appendix you will learn about five management theories: the classical, behavioral, management science, systems, and contingency theories.

Classical Theory

The **classical theorists** *focus on the job and management functions to determine the best way to manage in all organizations.* In the early 1900s, managers began an organized approach to increasing performance by focusing on the efficiency of managing jobs. This focus later changed to a concern for managing departments and organizations. Scientific management stressed job efficiency through the development of technical skills, while administrative theory stressed rules and the structure of the organization.

Scientific Management. Frederick Winslow Taylor (1856–1915), an engineer known as the Father of Scientific Management, focused on analyzing jobs and redesigning them so that they could be accomplished more efficiently. As he searched for the best way to maximize performance, he developed "scientific management" principles, including the following:

1. Develop a procedure for each element of a worker's job.
2. Promote job specialization.
3. Select, train, and develop workers scientifically.
4. Plan and schedule work.
5. Establish standard methods and times for each task.
6. Use wage incentives such as piece rates and bonuses.[55]

classical theorists Researchers who focus on the job and management functions to determine the best way to manage in all organizations.

Frank Gilbreth (1868–1924) and his wife Lillian Gilbreth (1878–1972) used time-and-motion studies to develop more efficient work procedures. Their work was popularized in a book titled *Cheaper by the Dozen* (and later two movies and a television comedy of the same name), which described their application of scientific management practices to their family of 12 children. When Frank died, the children ranged in age from 2 to 19 years old. Lillian continued her work as a consultant but changed the focus of her work to become a pioneer in industrial psychology. Lillian became a professor of management at Purdue University and is commonly referred to as the First Lady of Management.

Another person who made important contributions to scientific management was Henry Gantt (1861–1919). He developed a method for scheduling work over time that is still widely used today. You will learn how to develop a Gantt chart in Chapter 15.

Administrative Theory. Henri Fayol (1841–1925) was a French engineer who is sometimes referred to as the Father of Modern Management. Fayol was a pioneer in the study of the principles and functions of management. He made a clear distinction between operating and managerial activities. Fayol identified five major functions of management: planning, coordinating, organizing, controlling, and commanding. In addition to his five management functions, Fayol also developed 14 principles that are still used today.[56] Most principles-of-management textbooks are organized on the basis of the functions of management.

Two other contributors to administrative management are Max Weber (1864–1920) and Chester Barnard (1886–1961). Max Weber was a German sociologist who developed the *bureaucracy concept*. The aim of his concept of bureaucracy was to develop a set of rules and procedures to ensure that all employees were treated fairly. Chester Barnard studied authority and power distributions in organizations. He raised awareness of the informal organization—cliques and naturally occurring social groupings within formal organizations.

Mary Parker Follett (1868–1933) stressed the importance of people rather than engineering techniques. Follett contributed to administrative theory by emphasizing the need for worker participation, conflict resolution, and shared goals. The trend today is toward increasingly higher levels of employee participation. Barnard's and Follett's contributions led to the development of behavioral theory.

People are the most important resource that organizations have. Mary Parker Follett's work, which focused on interactions between management and employees, still influences organizations today. Photo from Monkeybusinessimages/iStockphoto.

Many companies still use classical management techniques successfully today. **McDonald's** system of fast-food service is one good example of a company that uses these techniques. Managers at **Monsanto** also use classical techniques, such as time-and-motion studies and organization principles that you will learn about in Chapter 7. Large organizations that are downsizing to cut costs by laying off employees and becoming more efficient are using a classical management approach.

Behavioral Theory

The **behavioral theorists** *focus on people to determine the best way to manage in all organizations.* In the 1920s, management writers began to question the classical approach to management and changed their focus from the job itself to the

behavioral theorists Researchers who focus on people to determine the best way to manage in all organizations.

people who perform the job. Like the classicists, behaviorists were looking for the best way to manage in all organizations. However, the behavioral approach to management stressed the need for human skills rather than technical skills.

Elton Mayo (1880–1949) pioneered the *human relations* movement. Mayo headed a group of Harvard researchers in conducting the Hawthorne studies, a landmark series of studies of human behavior in **Western Electric**'s Hawthorne plant (Cicero, Illinois) from 1927 to 1932. Like Taylor, Mayo wanted to increase performance; however, he viewed determining the best work environment as the means to this end. Mayo's research suggested that a manager's treatment of people had an important impact on their performance. In other words, treating people well and meeting their needs frequently results in increased performance. The *Hawthorne effect* refers to the phenomenon that just studying people affects their performance.[57]

Abraham Maslow (1908–1970) developed the *hierarchy of needs* theory.[58] Maslow is one of the earliest researchers to study motivation, and motivation is still a major area of research. You will learn more about Maslow's hierarchy of needs and other motivation theories in Chapter 11.

Douglas McGregor (1906–1964) developed *Theory X* and *Theory Y*. McGregor contrasted the two theories, based on the assumptions that managers make about workers. Theory X managers assume that people dislike work and that only if managers plan, organize, and closely direct and control their work will workers perform at high levels. Theory Y managers assume that people like to work and do not need close supervision. McGregor did not give specific details on how to manage; he suggested a reorientation in managerial thinking.[59]

Behaviorists believed that happy employees would be productive. However, later research suggested that a happy worker is not necessarily a productive worker. As you can see, the classical and behavioral theories are very different, yet both kinds of theorists claim that their approach is the best way to manage in all organizations.

The behavioral approach to management is still evolving and being used in organizations. The current term for studying people at work is the *behavioral science approach*, which draws from economics, psychology, sociology, and other disciplines. Most of the material in the chapters in Parts III and IV is based on behavioral science research. Managers all over the globe use behavioral sciences in dealing with people.

Management Science

The **management science theorists** *focus on the use of mathematics to aid in problem solving and decision making.* During World War II, a research program began to investigate the applicability of quantitative methods to military and logistics problems. After the war, business managers began to use management science (math). Some of the mathematical models are used in the areas of finance, management information systems (MIS), and operations management. The use of computers has led to an increase in the use of quantitative methods by managers all over the globe. Because management science stresses decision-making skills and technical skills, it is more closely aligned with classical management theory than with behavioral theory. You will learn more about management science in the chapters in Parts II and V. Management science is not commonly used in organizing and leading.

management science theorists Researchers who focus on the use of mathematics to aid in problem solving and decision making.

Integrative Perspective

The integrative perspective has three components: systems theory, sociotechnical theory, and contingency theory.

Systems Theory. The systems theorists *focus on viewing the organization as a whole and as the interrelationship of its parts.* In the 1950s, management theorists attempted to integrate the classical, behavioral, and management science theories into a holistic view of the management process. Systems theorists began by assuming that an organization is a system that transforms inputs (resources) into outputs (products and/or services).

LO 1-9

Describe how systems theorists and contingency theorists differ from classical and behavioral theorists.

According to Russell Ackoff, the commonly used classical approach to problem solving is a reductionist process. Managers tend to break an organization into its basic parts (departments), understand the behavior and properties of the parts, and add the understanding of the parts together to understand the whole. They focus on making independent departments operate as efficiently as possible. According to systems theorists, the reductionist approach cannot yield an understanding of the organization, only knowledge of how it works. Because the parts of a system are interdependent, even if each part is independently made to perform as efficiently as possible, the organization as a whole may not perform as effectively as possible. For example, all-star athletic teams are made up of exceptional players. But because such players have not played together as a team before, the all-star team may not be able to beat an average team in the league.[60]

Systems theory stresses the need for conceptual skills in order to understand how an organization's subsystems (departments) interrelate and contribute to the organization as a whole. For example, the actions of the marketing, operations, and financial departments (subsystems) affect each other; if the quality of the product goes down, sales may decrease, causing a decrease in finances. Before managers in one department make a decision, they should consider the interrelated effects it will have on the other departments. The organization is a system (departments), just as the management process is a system (planning, organizing, leading, and controlling), with subsystems (parts of departments) that affect each other. So, in other words, when you have a problem to solve, do not break it into pieces; focus on the whole.

According to Harold Koontz, Daniel Katz, Robert Kahn, and others, the systems approach recognizes that an organization is an open system because it interacts with and is affected by the external environment.[61] For example, government laws affect what an organization can and cannot do, the economy affects the organization's sales, and so on. You will learn more about open systems and the organizational environment in Chapter 2.

Over the years, systems theory lost some of its popularity. However, today one of the major trends is toward total quality management (TQM), which takes a systems approach to management. You will learn more about TQM in Chapters 2 and 15.

Sociotechnical Theory. The sociotechnical theorists *focus on integrating people and technology.* Sociotechnical theory was formulated during the 1950s and 1960s by Eric Trist, Ken Bamforth, Fred Emery, and others.[62] They realized, as today's managers do, that a manager must integrate both people and technology. To focus on one to the exclusion of the other leads to lower levels of performance. Much of current behavioral science work is in agreement with sociotechnical theory.

systems theorists Researchers who focus on viewing the organization as a whole and as the interrelationship of its parts.

sociotechnical theorists Researchers who focus on integrating people and technology.

Contingency Theory. The contingency theorists *focus on determining the best management approach for a given situation.* In the 1960s and 1970s, management researchers wanted to determine how the environment and technology affected the organization. Tom Burns and George Stalker conducted a study to determine how the environment affects a firm's organization and management systems. They identified two different types of environments: stable (where there is little change) and innovative (great changes). The researchers also identified two types

contingency theorists Researchers who focus on determining the best management approach for a given situation.

of management systems: mechanistic (similar to bureaucratic classical theory) and organic (nonbureaucratic, similar to behavioral theory). They concluded that in a stable environment, the mechanistic approach works well, whereas in an innovative environment, the organic approach works well.[63]

Joan Woodward conducted a study to determine how technology (the means of producing products) affects organizational structure. She found that organizational structure did change with the type of technology. Woodward concluded that the mechanistic or classical approach worked well with mass-production technology (such as that of an automobile assembly line), whereas the organic or behavioral approach worked well with small-batch (custom-made) products and long-run process technology (such as that for refining crude oil).

These contingency theories may be historic, but they still influence present-day organizational structures. We will revise them in Chapter 7, Organizing and Delegating Work.

Comparing Theories

Exhibit 1-11 reviews the theories covered in this appendix. Throughout this book, you will learn to take an integrative perspective using systems and contingency theories, combined with some management science, to ensure that you maximize development of your management skills. For example, Skill Builder 4 at the end of this chapter uses a contingency approach.

EXHIBIT 1-11 COMPARING THEORIES

Classical	Behavioral	Management Science	Systems Theory	Sociotechnical Theory	Contingency Theory
Attempts to develop the best way to manage in all organizations by focusing on the jobs and structure of the firm.	Attempts to develop a single best way to manage in all organizations by focusing on people and making them productive.	Recommends using math (computers) to aid in problem solving and decision making.	Manages by focusing on the organization as a whole and the interrelationship of its departments rather than on individual parts.	Recommends focusing on the integration of people and technology.	Recommends using the theory or the combination of theories that meets the given situation.

Managing the Old versus New Workplace

In the old workplace, managers used an autocratic leadership style with a local domestic view, jobs were specialized and routinely performed by individuals, employees were homogeneous, and change was slow. In the new workplace, managers use a more participative leadership style with a global view, jobs are more flexible and performed by teams, employees are diverse, and change is rapid.[64]

Knowledge Management. Today's leaders focus on learning and knowledge management,[65] because the acquisition of knowledge and the ability to learn are important to organizational success.[66] Knowledge workers process information rather than physical goods.[67] **Knowledge management** *involves everyone in an organization in sharing knowledge and applying it to continuously improve products and processes. Learning* is the process whereby knowledge is created through the transformation of experience.[68] Knowledge sharing provides opportunities for mutual learning.[69] *Learning*

knowledge management Involving everyone in an organization in sharing knowledge and applying it continuously to improve products and processes.

organizations have everyone engaged in identifying and solving problems, enabling change, and continuous improvement. They share three characteristics: a team-based structure, participative management, and the sharing of information through knowledge management.[70]

Evidence-Based Management (EBM). Knowledge management is all about learning new things and applying the knowledge in order to improve. It goes hand in hand with *evidence-based management* (EBM), which is the systematic use of the best available evidence to improve management practice.[71] Throughout this book, you will learn about management and how to apply the knowledge to develop management skills based on EBM that you can use in your personal and professional lives.

In today's global business world, knowledge management is especially important as although people working for the same company may be scattered across the world, they still need to share their knowledge and best practices so that the entire organization can continually improve. Photo from Ridofranz/iStockphoto.

OBJECTIVES OF THE BOOK

This book takes a "how-to" approach to management, as research has shown that knowledge is more likely to be implemented when it is acquired from learning by doing rather than from learning by reading, listening, or thinking.[72] As indicated by its subtitle, "Concepts, Applications, and Skill Development," this book uses a three-pronged approach, with these objectives:

- To teach you the important concepts of management
- To develop your ability to apply the management concepts through critical thinking
- To develop your management skills in your personal and professional lives

The book offers some unique features to further each of these three objectives, as summarized in Exhibit 1-12.

Management Concepts

Throughout this book, you will learn management concepts and see how they relate to organizational success, as well as to the difficulties and challenges managers face. Your knowledge of management concepts is vital to your success as a manager. This book offers the six features listed in Exhibit 1-12 to help you learn management concepts.

Application of Management Concepts

Understanding theory and concepts is essential before moving to the next level: applying the concepts,[73] which requires critical thinking.[74] One of the criticisms of management education is the focus on teaching theory without the application to practice, called the knowing-doing gap and practice gap.[75] As shown in Exhibit 1-12, this book offers seven features to help you develop the critical-thinking skills you will need to apply the concepts.

Development of Management Skills

The third and highest-level objective is to develop the management skills that you can use in your personal and professional lives as both a leader and a follower.[76]

EXHIBIT 1-12   FEATURES OF THIS BOOK'S THREE-PRONGED APPROACH AND TABLE OF CONTENTS

		Table of Contents
Features That Present Important Concepts	• Text discussions of management research • Step-by-step behavior models • Learning Outcomes • Chapter summaries and glossaries • Key Term Review • Review questions	I. THE GLOBAL MANAGEMENT ENVIRONMENT 1. Management and Its History 2. The Environment: Culture, Ethics, and Social Responsibility 3. Managing Diversity in a Global Environment
Features That Help You Apply What You Learn	• Ideas on Management cases • Organizational examples • Work Applications • Applying the Concept • Cases • Videos • Ethics and Social Responsibility	II. PLANNING 4. Creative Problem Solving and Decision Making 5. Strategic and Operational Planning 6. Managing Change Innovation and Entrepreneurship III. ORGANIZING 7. Organizing and Delegating Work 8. Managing Team Work 9. Human Resources Management Appendix: Career Management and Networking
Features That Foster Skill Development	• Self-Assessments • Communication Skills • Behavior Modeling training • Skill Builder exercises	IV. LEADING 10. Organizational Behavior: Power, Politics, Conflict, and Stress 11. Motivating for High Performance 12. Leading With Influence V. CONTROLLING 13. Communication and Information Technology 14. Managing Control Systems, Finances, and People 15. Operations, Quality, and Productivity

You can develop your management skills.[77] This book offers four features to help you do so.

Practice. As with just about everything in life, you cannot become skilled by simply reading about or trying something once. Developing management skills takes persistence and practice,[78] which is not something everyone wants to do.[79] The great **Green Bay Packers** football coach Vince Lombardi said that leaders are made by effort and hard work. If you want to develop your management skills, you must not only learn the concepts in this book but also practice with the applications and skill-building exercises.[80] But most important, to be successful, you need to practice using your skills in your personal and professional lives to gain experience.[81]

Flexibility. This book has so many features that it is unlikely that all of them can be covered in class during a one-semester course. Your instructor will select the features that best meet the course objectives and the amount of time available, but you may want to cover some or all of the other features on your own or with the assistance of others.

Organization of the Book

This book is organized into five parts, with Part I covering the introductory information and Parts II through V covering the four functions of management discussed in this chapter. Part II, which covers planning, includes three chapters. Part III on organizing has three chapters and an appendix. Part IV covers leading and includes four chapters. Finally, Part V, which covers controlling, contains two chapters. See Exhibit 1-12 for the table of contents.

• • • CHAPTER SUMMARY

1-1. Describe a manager's responsibility.

A manager is responsible for achieving organizational objectives through efficient and effective use of resources. *Efficient* means doing things right, and *effective* means doing the right thing. The manager's resources include human, financial, physical, and informational resources.

1-2. List and explain the three management skills.

The three management skills are technical, interpersonal, and decision-making skills. Technical skills involve the ability to use methods and techniques to perform a task. Interpersonal skills involve the ability to understand, communicate, and work well with individuals and groups through developing effective relationships. Decision-making skills are based on the ability to conceptualize situations and select alternatives to solve problems and take advantage of opportunities.

1-3. List and explain the four management functions.

The four management functions are planning, organizing, leading, and controlling. Planning is the process of setting objectives and determining in advance exactly how the objectives will be met. Organizing is the process of delegating and coordinating tasks and allocating resources to achieve objectives. Leading is the process of influencing employees to work toward achieving objectives. Controlling is the process of establishing and implementing mechanisms to ensure that the organization achieves its objectives.

1-4. Identify the three management role categories.

Managers play the interpersonal role when they act as figurehead, leader, or liaison. Managers play the informational role when they act as monitor, disseminator, or spokesperson. Managers play the decisional role when they act as entrepreneur, disturbance handler, resource allocator, or negotiator.

1-5. List the hierarchy of management levels.

The three hierarchy levels are top managers (e.g., operations executive), middle managers (e.g., marketing manager), and first-line managers (e.g., accounting supervisor).

1-6. Describe the three different types of managers.

A general manager supervises the activities of several departments or units that perform different activities. Functional managers supervise related activities such as marketing, operations, finance, and human resources management. A project manager coordinates employees and other resources across several functional departments to accomplish a specific task.

1-7. Describe the differences among management levels in terms of skills needed and functions performed.

Top managers have a greater need for decision-making skills than do first-line managers. Middle managers have a need for all three skills. First-line managers have a greater need for technical skills than do top managers.

1-8. State the major similarities and differences between the classical and behavioral theorists.

Both classical and behavioral theorists wanted to find the best way to manage in all organizations. However, the classicists focused on the job and management functions, whereas the behaviorists focused on people.

1.9. Describe how systems theorists and contingency theorists differ from classical and behavioral theorists.

The classical and behavioral and the systems theorists differ in the way they conceptualize the organization and its problems. The classical and behavioral theorists use a reductionist approach by breaking the organization into its component parts to understand the whole (sum of parts = whole). Systems theorists look at the organization as a whole and the interrelationship of its parts to understand the whole (whole = interrelationship of parts).

The classical and behavioral theorists seek the best management approach in all organizations. The contingency theorists propose that there is no best approach for all organizations; they seek to determine which management approach will work best in a given situation.

• • • KEY TERMS

• • • KEY TERM REVIEW

Complete each of the following statements using one of this chapter's key terms:

1. A _____ is responsible for achieving organizational objectives through efficient and effective utilization of resources.

2. The _____ include human, financial, physical, and informational.

3. The level of organizational _____ is based on how effectively and efficiently managers utilize resources to achieve objectives.

4. _____ include technical, interpersonal, and decision-making skills.

5. _____ involve the ability to use methods and techniques to perform a task.

6. _____ involve the ability to understand, communicate, and work well with individuals and groups through developing effective relationships.

7. _____ are based on the ability to conceptualize situations and select alternatives to solve problems and take advantage of opportunities.

8. The four _____ include planning, organizing, leading, and controlling.

9. _____ is the process of setting objectives and determining in advance exactly how the objectives will be met.

10. _____ is the process of delegating and coordinating tasks and allocating resources to achieve objectives.

11. _____ is the process of influencing employees to work toward achieving objectives.

12. _____ is the process of monitoring progress and taking corrective action when needed to ensure that objectives are achieved.

13. The _____ include interpersonal, informational, and decisional.

14. There are three _____: top managers, middle managers, and first-line managers.

15. There are three _____: general, functional, and project.

16. The _____ focus on the job and management functions to determine the best way to manage in all organizations.

17. The _____ focus on people to determine the best way to manage in all organizations.

18. The _____ focus on the use of mathematics to aid in problem solving and decision making.

19. The _____ focus on viewing the organization as a whole and as the interrelationship of its parts.

20. The _____ focus on integrating people and technology.

21. The _____ focus on determining the best management approach for a given situation.

22. _____ involves everyone in an organization in sharing knowledge and applying it to continuously improve products and processes.

• • • REVIEW QUESTIONS

1. What are a manager's resources?
2. What are the three management skills?
3. What are the four functions of management?
4. What are the three management role categories?
5. What are the three levels of management?
6. What are the three types of managers?
7. What are the objectives of this book?

• • • COMMUNICATION SKILLS

The following critical-thinking questions can be used for class discussion and/or as written assignments to develop communication skills. Be sure to give complete explanations for all questions.

1. Are you interested in being a manager?

2. Why is it important to take this course in management?

3. Is it more important for managers to be efficient or effective? Can you improve both at the same time?

4. Is management ability universal? In other words, can a good manager in one environment (e.g., computers) also be effective in another (e.g., banking)?

5. Some people say the hard skills (technical, finance, quantitative analysis) are more important for

managers than soft skills (interpersonal), and some say the opposite is true. What is your view?

6.   Is your college professor a manager? Why or why not?

7.   When a good employee is promoted to management, which management level is the promotion usually

to, and how do the management skills and functions change with the job promotion?

8.   When an employee is promoted to manager, do most organizations provide some type of training? Should they? Why or why not?

• • • CASE: MICROSOFT AND THE BILL & MELINDA GATES FOUNDATION

In 1975, Bill Gates and Paul Allen founded Microsoft, based on their vision of using a new technology to change the way business was done and to benefit and transform society. In their view, the future was in computer software, not hardware. At the time, IBM saw its business as primarily selling mainframe computers; the company's mission later expanded to include the sale of PC hardware. Bill Gates convinced IBM to use Microsoft software to operate its PCs. Although IBM eventually realized the value of developing its own PC operating systems and software, the company did not have much success.

Even when IBM acquired Lotus Development Corporation in 1995 in an effort to add software (Lotus Notes, Lotus 1–2-3, Ami Pro) to its product line, the company was too late to catch up with Microsoft. And over the years, with competition from IBM clones, IBM continued to lose PC market share to competitors; eventually, the company's share of the PC market dropped below 5 percent. IBM's PC division was bought by Chinese company Lenovo on May 1, 2005.

Over the past 35 years, Microsoft has been a technology leader in transforming the way people work, play, and communicate. Microsoft Windows and other Microsoft operating systems and office software have dominated the market and continue to do so. Microsoft's mission and values are "to help people and businesses throughout the world realize their full potential." Microsoft has eight business divisions: (1) Interactive Entertainment Business (gaming, music, and video across multiple screens, including Xbox 360), (2) Microsoft Business Solutions (consulting), (3) Microsoft Office Division (Office and other software), (4) Online Services Division (Bing and MSN), (5) Server and Tools Division (infrastructure software, developer tools, and cloud platform), (6) Skype (Skype and Lync), (7) Windows & Windows Live Division (all Windows businesses), (8) Windows Phone Division (new line taking Microsoft more mobile).

Under Gates's leadership, Microsoft Corporation flourished, consistently landing in *Fortune*'s 100 Best Companies to Work For and the *Fortune* 500. Gates has also been recognized for his exceptional leadership, landing at number one on the *Forbes* 400 list several times and on the *Forbes* list of the World's Richest People. He

was also recognized by *Time* magazine in its *Time* 100 list as one of the 100 people who most influenced the 21st century, as well as one of the 100 most influential people.

Gates's role at Microsoft for most of its history was primarily a management and executive role. He was known as a demanding and verbally combative boss, consistently encouraging creativity and recognizing employee achievements. He demanded that his colleagues be well informed, logical, vocal, and thick-skinned. Gates also met regularly with Microsoft's senior managers and program managers. During these meetings, Gates often interrupted presentations and proposals with such comments as "That's the stupidest thing I've ever heard!" The target of his outburst would then have to defend the proposal in detail until, hopefully, Gates was fully convinced.

Effective July 2008, Gates transitioned out of his day-to-day CEO role at Microsoft. Steve Ballmer is the current CEO. Gates continues to serves as chairman of the board and an advisor on key development projects. Gates now spends more of his time with the Bill & Melinda Gates Foundation he and his wife started to give most of their wealth away to help others.

The Bill & Melinda Gates Foundation works to help all people lead healthy, productive lives. In developing countries, it focuses on improving people's health and giving them the chance to lift themselves out of hunger and extreme poverty. In the United States, it seeks to ensure that all people—especially those with the fewest resources—have access to the opportunities they need to succeed in school and life.

Guided by the belief that every life has equal value, the Foundation is led by CEO Jeff Raikes and co-chair William H. Gates Sr., under the direction of Bill and Melinda Gates and Warren Buffett. The Gateses and Buffett are also active fund-raisers, working to get more wealthy people to give to the Foundation, which currently has assets valued at more than $38.3 billion. The Foundation gave away more than $27.6 billion to people in more than 100 countries and all 50 states through its three Grantmaking areas: (1) Global Development Program, (2) Global Health Program, and (3)United States Program.

Case Questions

1. Which resources play important roles in the success of Microsoft?

2. Give examples of some of the tasks Bill Gates performed while CEO of Microsoft in each of the four management functions.

3. Give examples of some of the tasks Bill Gates performed while CEO of Microsoft in each of the three management roles.

4. Do you think you would like to work for someone like Bill Gates? Explain your answer.

5. Are Bill Gates and Microsoft ethical and socially responsible?

6. Are Bill Gates and the Bill and Melinda Gates Foundation ethical and socially responsible?

Sources: Information for this case was taken from the Microsoft website at http://www.microsoft.com and the Bill & Melinda Gates Foundation, http://www.gatesfoundation.org, accessed May 1, 2013.

• • • SKILL BUILDER 1-1: GETTING TO KNOW YOU

Objectives

1. To get acquainted with some of your classmates

2. To gain a better understanding of what the course covers

3. To get to know more about your instructor

Skills

The primary skills developed through this exercise are:

1. Management skill—interpersonal

2. AACSB competency—communication

3. Management function—leading

4. Break into groups of five or six, preferably with people you do not know. Have each member tell his or her name and two or three significant things about himself or herself. Then ask each other questions to get to know each other better.

5. Can everyone in the group address every other person by name? If not, have each member repeat his or her name. Then each person in the group should repeat the names of all the group members until each person knows everyone's first name.

Discussion

What can you do to improve your ability to remember people's names?

1. Elect a spokesperson for your group. Look over the following categories and decide on some specific questions you would like your spokesperson to ask the instructor from one or more of the categories. The spokesperson will not identify who asked the questions. You do not have to have questions for each area.

- Course expectations. What do you expect to cover or hope to learn from this course?

- Doubts or concerns. Is there anything about the course that you don't understand?

- Questions about the instructor. List questions to ask the instructor in order to get to know him or her better.

2. Each spokesperson asks the instructor one question at a time until all questions have been answered. Spokespeople should skip questions already asked by other groups.

Apply It

What did I learn from this experience? How will I use this knowledge in the future?

• • • SKILL BUILDER 1-2: COMPARING MANAGEMENT SKILLS

Objective

To better understand the importance of good management skills and functions.

Skills

The primary skills developed through this exercise are:

1. Management skill—decision making

2. AACSB competency—analytic

3. Management function—planning

Compare Your Supervisors' Management Skills

Recall the best supervisor or boss you ever worked for and the worst one you ever worked for. Compare these two people by writing brief notes in the following chart about each person's management skills and ability to perform the four management functions.

Management Skills and Functions		
Best Supervisor or Boss		Worst Supervisor or Boss
	Technical	
	Interpersonal	
	Decision Making	
	Planning	
	Organizing	
	Leading	
	Controlling	

Apply It

What did I learn from this exercise? How will I use this knowledge in the future?

Based on your own experiences with a good boss and a poor one, what do you believe are the key differences between good and poor managers?

• • • SKILL BUILDER 1-3: CAREERS

Objective

To think about your career.

Skills

The primary skills developed through this exercise are:

1. Management skill—decision making
2. AACSB competency—reflective thinking
3. Management function—planning

Discussion Questions

1. When you graduate, do you want to work in a for-profit or not-for-profit organization as an employee, manager, or entrepreneur?

2. Regarding a career plan, do you believe your answer will change with time? If yes, how?

Apply It

What did I learn from this exercise? How will I use this knowledge in the future?

• • • SKILL BUILDER 1-4: MANAGEMENT STYLES

Note that this Skill Builder is based on leadership and can also be used with Chapter 12.

Objectives

1. To learn your preferred management style
2. To learn how to match a situation to an appropriate management style

Skills

The primary skills developed through this exercise are:

1. Management skill—decision making
2. AACSB competency—analytic
3. Management function—leading

Self-Assessment of Your Preferred Management Style

Following are 12 situations. Select the one alternative that most closely describes what you would do in each

situation. Don't be concerned with trying to pick the right answer; select the alternative you would really use. Circle a, b, c, or d. (Ignore the C _____ preceding each situation and the S _____ following each answer choice; these will be explained later.)

C _____ 1. Your rookie crew seems to be developing well. Their need for direction and close supervision is diminishing. What do you do?

   a. Stop directing and overseeing performance unless there is a problem. S _____

   b. Spend time getting to know them personally, but make sure they maintain performance levels. S _____

   c. Make sure things keep going well; continue to direct and oversee closely. S _____

   d. Begin to discuss new tasks of interest to them. S _____

C _____ 2. You assigned Jill a task, specifying exactly how you wanted it done. Jill deliberately ignored your directions and did it her way. The job will not meet the customer's standards. This is not the first problem you've had with Jill. What do you decide to do?

    a.   Listen to Jill's side, but be sure the job gets done right. S _____

    b.   Tell Jill to do it again the right way and closely supervise the job. S _____

    c.   Tell her the customer will not accept the job and let Jill handle it her way. S _____

    d.   Discuss the problem and solutions to it. S _____

C _____ 3. Your employees work well together and are a real team; the department is the top performer in the organization. Because of traffic problems, the president has approved staggered hours for departments. As a result, you can change your department's hours. Several of your workers are in favor of changing. What action do you take?

    a.   Allow the group to decide the hours. S _____

    b.   Decide on new hours, explain why you chose them, and invite questions. S _____

    c.   Conduct a meeting to get the group members' ideas. Select new hours together, with your approval. S _____

    d.   Send out a memo stating the hours you want. S _____

C _____ 4. You hired Rahim, a new employee. He is not performing at the level expected after a month's training. Rahim is trying, but he seems to be a slow learner. What do you decide to do?

    a.   Clearly explain what needs to be done and oversee his work. Discuss why the procedures are important; support and encourage him. S _____

    b.   Tell Rahim that his training is over and it's time to pull his own weight. S _____

    c.   Review task procedures and supervise his work closely. S _____

    d.   Inform Rahim that his training is over and that he should feel free to come to you if he has any problems. S _____

C _____ 5. Padma has had an excellent performance record for the last five years. Recently you have noticed a drop in the quality and quantity of her work. She has a family problem. What do you do?

    a.   Tell her to get back on track and closely supervise her. S _____

    b.   Discuss the problem with Padma. Help her realize that her personal problem is affecting her work. Discuss ways to improve the situation. Be supportive and encourage her. S _____

    c.   Tell Padma you're aware of her productivity slip and that you're sure she'll work it out soon. S _____

    d.   Discuss the problem and solution with Padma and supervise her closely. S _____

C _____ 6. Your organization does not allow smoking in certain areas. You just walked by a restricted area and saw Joan smoking. She has been with the organization for ten years and is a very productive worker. Joan has never been caught smoking before. What action do you take?

    a.   Ask her to put the cigarette out; then leave. S _____

    b.   Discuss why she is smoking and what she intends to do about it. S _____

    c.   Give her a lecture about not smoking and check up on her in the future. S _____

    d.   Tell her to put the cigarette out, watch her do it, and tell her you will check on her in the future. S _____

C _____ 7. Your employees usually work well together with little direction. Recently a conflict between Sue and Tom has caused problems. What action do you take?

    a.   Call Sue and Tom together and make them realize how this conflict is affecting the department. Discuss how to resolve it and how you will check to make sure the problem is solved. S _____

    b.   Let the group resolve the conflict. S _____

    c.   Have Sue and Tom sit down and discuss their conflict and how to resolve it. Support their efforts to implement a solution. S _____

    d.   Tell Sue and Tom how to resolve their conflict and closely supervise them. S _____

C _____ 8. Hector usually does his share of the work with some encouragement and direction. However, he has migraine headaches occasionally and doesn't pull his weight when this happens. The others resent doing Hector's work. What do you decide to do?

    a.   Discuss his problem and help him come up with ideas for maintaining his work; be supportive. S _____

    b.   Tell Jim to do his share of the work and closely watch his output. S _____

    c.   Inform Hector that he is creating a hardship for the others and should resolve the problem by himself. S _____

d. Be supportive but set minimum performance levels and ensure compliance. S _____

C _____ 9. Barbara, your most experienced and productive worker, came to you with a detailed idea that could increase your department's productivity at a very low cost. She can do her present job and this new assignment. You think it's an excellent idea. What do you do?

a. Set some goals together. Encourage and support her efforts. S _____

b. Set up goals for Barbara. Be sure she agrees with them and sees you as being supportive of her efforts. S _____

c. Tell Barbara to keep you informed and to come to you if she needs any help. S _____

d. Have Barbara check in with you frequently so that you can direct and supervise her activities. S _____

C _____10. Your boss asked you for a special report. Franco, a very capable worker who usually needs no direction or support, has all the necessary skills to do the job. However, Franco is reluctant because he has never done a report. What do you do?

a. Tell Franco he has to do it. Give him direction and supervise him closely. S _____

b. Describe the project to Franco and let him do it his own way. S _____

c. Describe the benefits to Franco. Get his ideas on how to do it and check his progress. S _____

d. Discuss possible ways of doing the job. Be supportive; encourage Franco. S _____

C _____11. Jean is the top producer in your department. However, her monthly reports are constantly late and contain errors. You are puzzled because she does everything else with no direction or support. What do you decide to do?

a. Go over past reports, explaining exactly what is expected of her. Schedule a meeting so that you can review the next report with her. S _____

b. Discuss the problem with Jean and ask her what can be done about it; be supportive. S _____

c. Explain the importance of the report. Ask her what the problem is. Tell her that you expect the next report to be on time and error free. S _____

d. Remind Jean to get the next report in on time without errors. S _____

C _____12. Your workers are very effective and like to participate in decision making. A consultant was hired to develop a new method for your department using the latest technology in the field. What do you do?

a. Explain the consultant's method and let the group decide how to implement it. S _____

b. Teach the workers the new method and supervise them closely as they use it. S _____

c. Explain to the workers the new method and the reasons it is important. Teach them the method and make sure the procedure is followed. Answer questions. S _____

d. Explain the new method and get the group's input on ways to improve and implement it. S _____

To determine your preferred management style, circle the letter you selected for each situation.

	Autocratic	Consultative	Participative	Empowering
1.	c	b	d	a
2.	b	a	d	c
3.	d	b	c	a
4.	c	a	d	b
5.	a	d	b	c
6.	d	c	b	a
7.	d	a	c	b
8.	b	d	a	c
9.	d	b	a	c
10.	a	c	d	b
11.	a	c	b	d
12.	b	c	d	a
Totals				

Now add up the number of circled items per column. The column with the most items circled suggests your preferred management style. Is this the style you tend to use most often?

Your management style flexibility is reflected in the distribution of your answers. The more evenly distributed the numbers, the more flexible your style. A total of 1 or 0 for any column may indicate a reluctance to use that style.

Learn More about Management Styles

According to contingency theorists, there is no best management style for all situations. Instead, effective managers adapt their styles to individual capabilities or group situations. Following is a discussion of how to use the Situational Management model 1–1; refer to it as you read about it.

••• MODEL 1-1 SITUATIONAL MANAGEMENT

Step 1. Determine the capability level of employees on a continuum from C1 to C4; follow the arrow left to right.

Step 2. Match the management style (S1A, S2C, S3P, S4E) with the employee capability level; follow the arrow down from the capability-level box to the management-style box.

CAPABILITY LEVEL (C)

Employee Ability and Motivation to Perform the Task

(C1) Low Low Ability or Low Motivation →	(C2) Moderate Low Ability/ High Motivation →	(C3) High High Ability/ Lower Motivation →	(C4) Outstanding High Ability/ High Motivation
Employees are unable to perform the task without supervision or lack motivation (unwillingness to perform.	Employees have moderate ability and are motivated to do the task with supervision.	Employees have the ability to do the task but need some motivation (they are reluctant or need confidence buildup).	Employees have the ability and motivation to perform the task without direction or support.

MANAGEMENT STYLE (S)

Directive and Supportive Behavior Manager Needs to Give Employee to Perform the Task

(S1A) Autocratic High Directive/ Low Supportive	(S2C) Consultative High Directive/ High Supportive	(S3P) Participative Low Directive/ High Supportive	(S3E) Empowerment Low Directive/ Low Supportive
Manager tells employees what to do and how to do it and closely oversees performance. Manager makes decisions without any employee input.	Manager sells employees on doing the task and oversees performance. Manager typically gets input from individual employees when making decisions.	Manager develops motivation by developing confidence. Manager typically has a group meeting to get employee input into decisions.	Manager assigns tasks and lets the employees do it on their own. Manager lets the employee or group make decision.

1. Manager–Employee Interactions. Managers' interactions with employees can be classified into two distinct categories: directive and supportive.

- *Directive behavior.* The manager focuses on directing and controlling behavior to ensure that tasks get done and closely oversees performance.

- *Supportive behavior.* The manager focuses on encouraging and motivating behavior without telling employees what to do. The manager explains things and listens to employees' views, helping employees make their own decisions by building up confidence and self-esteem.

As a manager, you can focus on directing (getting the task done), supporting (developing relationships), or both.

2. Employee Capability. There are two distinct aspects of employee capability.

- *Ability.* Do employees have the knowledge, experience, education, skills, and training to do a particular task without direction?

- *Motivation.* Do the employees have the confidence to do the task? Do they want to do the task? Are they committed to performing the task? Will they perform the task without encouragement and support?

Employee capability may be measured on a continuum from low to outstanding. As a manager, you assess each employee's capability level and motivation:

- *Low.* The employees can't do the task without detailed directions and close supervision. Employees in this category are either unable or unwilling to do the task.

- *Moderate.* The employees have moderate ability and need specific direction and support to get the task done properly. The employees may be highly motivated but still need direction.

- *High.* The employees have high ability but may lack the confidence to do the job. What they need most is support and encouragement to motivate them to get the task done.

- *Outstanding.* The employees are capable of doing the task without direction or support.

Most people perform a variety of tasks on the job. It is important to realize that employee capability may vary depending on the specific task. For example, a bank teller may handle routine transactions with great ease but falter when opening new or special accounts. Employees tend to start working with low capability, needing close direction. As their ability to do the job increases, their managers can begin to be supportive and probably cease close supervision. As a manager, you must gradually develop your employees from low to outstanding levels over time.

3. Four Management Styles. The four situational management styles are autocratic, consultative, participative, and empowering.

- An *autocratic style* is highly directive and less concerned with building relationships. The autocratic style is appropriate when interacting with low-capability employees. When interacting with such employees, give very detailed instructions describing exactly what the task is and when, where, and how to perform it. Closely oversee performance and give some support. The majority of time with the employees is spent giving directions. Make decisions without input from the employees.

- A *consultative style* involves highly directive and highly supportive behavior and is appropriate when interacting with moderately capable employees. Give specific instructions and oversee performance at all major stages of a task. At the same time, support the employees by explaining why the task should be performed as requested and answering their questions. Work on relationships as you explain the benefits of completing the task your way. Give fairly equal amounts of time to directing and supporting employees. When making decisions, you may consult employees, but retain the final say. Once you make the decision, which can incorporate employees' ideas, direct and oversee employees' performance.

- A *participative style* is characterized by less directive but still highly supportive behavior and is appropriate when interacting with employees with high capability. When interacting with such employees, spend a small amount of time giving general directions and a great deal of time giving encouragement. Spend limited time overseeing performance, letting employees do the task their way while focusing on the end result. Support the employees by encouraging them and building up their self-confidence. If a task needs to be done, don't tell them how to do it; ask them how they will accomplish it. Make decisions together or allow employees to make decisions subject to your limitations and approval.

- An *empowering style* requires providing very little direction or support for employees and is appropriate when interacting with outstanding employees. You should let them know what needs to be done and answer their questions, but it is not necessary to oversee their performance. Such employees are highly motivated and need little, if any, support. Allow them to make their own decisions, subject to your approval. Other terms for empowerment are *laissez-faire* and *hands off.* A manager who uses this style lets employees alone to do their own thing.

Apply Management Styles

Return to the portion of the exercise in which you assessed your preferred management style. Identify the employee capability level for each item; indicate the capability level by placing a number from 1 to 4 on the line marked "C" before each item. (1 indicates low capability; 2, moderate capability; 3, high capability; and 4, outstanding capability.) Next, indicate the management style represented in each answer choice by placing the letter A (Autocratic), C (Consultative), P (Participative), or E (Empowering) on the line marked "S" following each answer choice. Will your preferred management style result in the optimum performance of the task?

Let's see how you did by looking back at the first situation.

C _____ 1. Your rookie crew seems to be developing well. Their need for direction and close supervision is diminishing. What do you do?

    a.   Stop directing and overseeing performance unless there is a problem. S _____

    b.   Spend time getting to know them personally, but make sure they maintain performance levels. S _____

    c.   Make sure things keep going well; continue to direct and oversee closely. S _____

    d.   Begin to discuss new tasks of interest to them. S _____

- As a rookie crew, the employees' capability started at a low level, but they have now developed to the moderate level. If you put the number 2 on the C line, you were correct.

- Alternative a is E, the empowering style, involving low direction and support. Alternative b is C, the consultative style, involving both high direction and high support. Alternative c is A, the autocratic style, involving high direction but low support. Alternative d is P, the participative style, involving low direction and high support (in discussing employee interests).

- If you selected b as the management style that best matches the situation, you were correct. However, in the business world, there is seldom only one way to handle a situation successfully. Therefore, in this exercise, you are given points based on how successful your behavior would be in each situation. In situation 1, b is the most successful alternative because it involves developing the employees gradually; answer b is worth 3 points. Alternative c is the next-best alternative, followed by d. It is better to keep things the way they are now than to try to rush employee development, which would probably cause problems. So c is a 2-point answer, and d gets 1 point. Alternative a is the least effective because you are going from one extreme of supervision to the other. This is a 0-point answer because the odds are great that this approach will cause problems that will diminish your management success.

The better you match your management style to employees' capabilities, the greater are your chances of being a successful manager.

Apply It

What did I learn from this skill-building experience? How will I use this knowledge in the future?

Your instructor may ask you to do Skill Builder 5 in class in a group. If so, the instructor will provide you with any necessary information or additional instructions.

• • • STUDENT STUDY SITE

Visit the Student Study Site at **www.sagepub.com/lussier6e** to access to these additional study tools:

- Mobile-compatible self-assessment quizzes
- Mobile-compatible key term flashcards
- Video Links
- SAGE Journal Articles
- Web Links

Gap1969

2

The Environment
Culture, Ethics, and Social Responsibility

• • • **Learning Outcomes**

After studying this chapter, you should be able to:

2-1. Explain the five internal environmental factors.
PAGE 36

2-2. List and explain the need for the two primary principles of total quality management (TQM).
PAGE 38

2-3. Describe the three levels of organizational culture and their relationship to each other. PAGE 40

2-4. Describe how the nine external environmental factors—customers, competitors, suppliers, labor

force, shareholders, society, technology, the economy, and governments—can affect the internal business environment. PAGE 42

2-5. Compare the three levels of moral development.
PAGE 48

2-6. Explain the stakeholders' approach to ethics. PAGE 50

IDEAS ON MANAGEMENT at Amazon.com

E-commerce pioneer Jeff Bezos launched **Amazon.com** as an online bookstore in July 1995. The company expanded to sell a wide variety of products and then to produce consumer electronics such as the Amazon Kindle e-book reader and the Kindle Fire tablet computer, and it is a major provider of cloud computing services. It is also going after the video market with the Kindle TV Set-Top Box. The focus continues to be on customer service. Amazon.com continues to be an e-commerce global leader as a *Fortune* 500 company, ranked in the top 50 with sales exceeding $61 billion. However, it has acquired a collection of unrelated businesses, including buying the troubled old-media *Washington Post* newspaper in 2013.

Jeff Bezos changed the way people buy books and then the way we read them with e-book readers and tablets. Bezos wasn't the first to develop an e-reader—others had flopped—but Amazon made the Kindle easy to use and popularized it, leading to tablets like the iPad. Amazon has transformed itself and the whole digital media business. Amazon is reinventing media, racing against Apple and Google to build the most comprehensive array of devices and services. *Fortune* named Bezos the best CEO in 2012, and he has an estimated net worth of $21 billion.

1. Who is Amazon.com's top manager, and what is the company's mission, major resource, systems process, and structure? PAGE 39
2. What type of culture does Amazon.com have? PAGE 42
3. How does the external environment affect Amazon.com? PAGE 44
4. What types of things does Amazon.com do to be ethical, socially responsible, and sustainable? PAGE 54

You'll find answers to these questions throughout the chapter. To learn more about Amazon, visit its website at www.amazon.com.

Sources: Information for this case was taken from the Amazon.com website at http://www.amazon.com, accessed May 5, 2013; Stone and Kucera (2012); Stone (2012).

• • • Chapter Outline

The Internal Environment
  Mission, Management, and Culture
  Resources and Structure
  Systems Process
Organizational Culture
  Organizational Culture Artifacts, Levels, and Strength
  Managing, Changing, and Merging Cultures
  Learning Organizations
The External Environment
  External Environmental Factors
  Dynamic Environments and Interactive Management

Business Ethics
  Does Ethical Behavior Pay?
  How Personality Traits and Attitudes, Moral Development, and the Situation Affect Ethical Behavior
  How People Justify Unethical Behavior
  Simple Guides to Ethical Behavior
  Managing Ethics
Social Responsibility and Sustainability
  Social Responsibility to Stakeholders
  Does It Pay to Be Socially Responsible?
  Sustainability

LO 2-1

Explain the five internal environmental factors.

WORK APPLICATION 2-1

For each work application in this chapter, use a different organization, or several different ones, for your examples.

State the mission of an organization, preferably an organization you work for or have worked for.

EXHIBIT 2-1   Internal Environmental Means and Ends

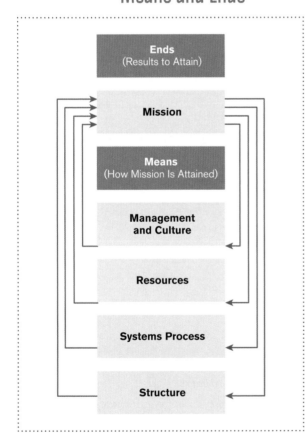

internal environment Factors that affect an organization's performance from within its boundaries.

mission An organization's purpose or reason for being.

stakeholders People whose interests are affected by organizational behavior.

THE INTERNAL ENVIRONMENT

Organizations are created to produce products and/or services for customers, and they need to establish their boundaries in the environment. The organization's **internal environment** *includes the factors that affect its performance from within its boundaries.* They are called internal factors because they are within the organization's control, as opposed to external factors, which are outside the organization's control. The five internal environmental factors that we'll talk about in this section are presented in Exhibit 2-1.

Mission, Management, and Culture

Here we discuss the first two parts of the internal environment.

Mission. The organization's **mission** *is its purpose or reason for being.* It provides an organization's identity by answering the questions, "Who are we as an organization?" and "What industries do we compete in?"[1]

Here are some example mission statements:

- **Toyota's** mission is to attract and attain customers with high-valued products and services and the most satisfying ownership experience.[2]
- **Walmart's** mission is to help people save money so they can live better.[3]
- The mission of **Springfield College** is to educate students in spirit, mind, and body for leadership in service to humanity by building upon its foundation of Humanics and academic excellence.[4]

The mission should be relevant to all stakeholders,[5] especially employees.[6] **Stakeholders** *are people whose interests are affected by organizational behavior.* Among a company's stakeholders are employees, shareholders, customers, suppliers, and the government. More about these stakeholders appears throughout this chapter.

Management and culture. Managers are responsible for the organization's performance.[7] Clearly, **FedEx**—to take one highly visible example of a successful firm—would not be the success it is today without its founder and CEO, **Frederick W. Smith**.

An **organizational culture** *consists of the values, beliefs, and assumptions about appropriate behavior that members of an organization share.* Think of the culture as the organization's personality. Good cultures don't happen by accident.[8] Managers, with employees, make the culture part of the environment so everyone knows what they should be doing at work and how to do it.

Because culture is such an important part of management, we will discuss it in more detail after we have discussed the other four internal environmental factors.

Resources and Structure

Resources. As stated in Chapter 1, organizational resources include human, financial, physical, and informational. Human resources are responsible for achieving the organization's mission and objectives.[9] **FedEx** has thousands of employees delivering millions of packages daily worldwide. Physical resources at FedEx include aircraft and ground vehicles. Financial resources are necessary to purchase and maintain the physical resources and to pay employees. Informational resources include the FedEx computer system. As a manager, you will be responsible for using these four types of resources to achieve your organization's mission.[10]

Structure. *Structure* refers to the way in which an organization groups its resources to accomplish its mission. As discussed in Chapter 1, an organization is a system structured into departments such as finance, marketing, production, human resources, and so on. Each of these departments affects the organization as a whole, and each department is affected by the other departments. All of an organization's resources must be structured effectively to achieve its mission. As a manager, you will be responsible for part of the organization's structure. You will learn more about organizational structure in Chapters 7 through 9.

Systems Process

Organizations structure resources to transform inputs into outputs.[11] The **systems process** *is the technology used to transform inputs into outputs.* The systems process has four components:

1. *Inputs.* Inputs are an organization's resources (human, financial, physical, and informational) that are transformed into products or services. At **FedEx**, the primary input is the millions of packages to be delivered worldwide daily.

2. *Transformation.* Transformation is the conversion of inputs into outputs. At FedEx, the packages (input) go to the hub (transformation), where they are sorted for delivery.

3. *Outputs.* Outputs are the products or services offered to customers. At FedEx, the packages are delivered to customers; the service of package delivery is FedEx's output.

4. *Feedback.* Feedback provides a means of control to ensure that the inputs and transformation process are producing the desired results.[12] FedEx uses computers to gain feedback by tracking packages to help ensure that they are delivered on time.

WORK
APPLICATION 2-2

Illustrate the systems process for an organization you work for or have worked for.

EXHIBIT 2-2 THE SYSTEM PROCESS

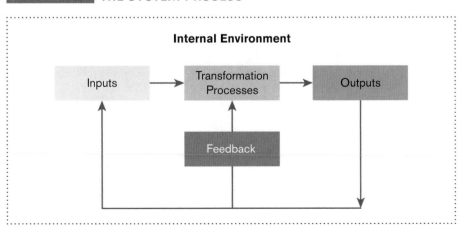

organizational culture The values, beliefs, and assumptions about appropriate behavior that members of an organization share.

systems process The method used to transform inputs into outputs.

WORK
APPLICATION 2-3

Identify the quality and value of a product you purchased recently.

LO 2-2

List and explain the need for the two primary principles of total quality management (TQM).

Managers with a systems perspective view the organization as a process rather than as separate departments. The focus is on the interrelationship of all of these functions as the inputs are converted into outputs.[13] See Exhibit 2-2 for an illustration of the systems process.

Quality is an important internal factor within the systems process. Customers determine **quality** by comparing a product's actual functioning to their requirements to determine value. **Customer value** is the perceived benefit of a product, used by customers to determine whether to buy the product. Customers don't simply buy a product itself. They buy the benefit they expect to derive from that product. Value is what motivates us to buy products.

Total quality management (TQM) is the commonly used term for stressing quality within an organization. **Total quality management (TQM)** *is the process*

quality A measure of value determined by comparing a product's actual functioning to requirements.

customer value The perceived benefit of a product, used by customers to determine whether or not to buy the product.

total quality management (TQM) The process that involves everyone in an organization focusing on the customer to continually improve product value.

EXHIBIT 2-3 COMPONENTS OF THE INTERNAL ENVIRONMENT

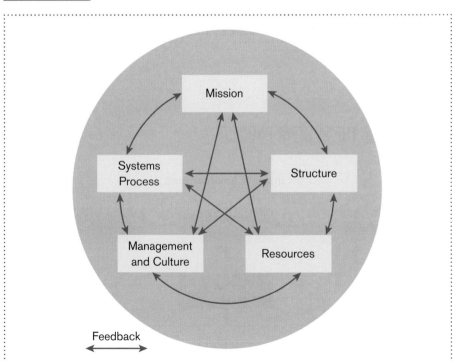

2-1 APPLYING THE CONCEPT

The Internal Environment

Identify the internal environmental factor underlying each statement.

A. management and culture
B. mission
C. resources
D. systems process
E. structure

_____ 1. "We deliver pizza and buffalo wings."

_____ 2. "We are planning to split the accounting clerks into an accounts receivable and accounts payable staff."

_____ 3. "We focus on the customer experience for repeat business."

_____ 4. "We take these chemicals and make them into a liquid, which then goes into these molds. When it's hard, we have outdoor chairs."

_____ 5. "Management does not trust us. All the major decisions around here are made by top-level managers."

that involves everyone in an organization focusing on the customer to continually improve product value. The two primary principles of TQM are (1) focusing on delivering customer value and (2) continually improving the system and its processes. The Japanese term for continuous improvement is *kaizen.* You will learn more about quality and TQM in Chapter 15. See Exhibit 2-3 for a review of the components of the internal environment.

Amazon.com's (Case Question 1) top manager is still its founder Jeff Bezos, who is the company's president, CEO, and chairman of the board. Amazon .com's mission is to be the Earth's most customer-centric company, where customers can find and discover anything they might want to buy online. Amazon .com endeavors to offer its customers the lowest possible prices. Its primary resources are the Internet and its computer system. Its primary systems process inputs are customer product orders that are filled and shipped to the customer, resulting in an output of sales that have created customer value. Amazon .com's primary structure is having a U.S. headquarters and subsidiaries in other countries.

ORGANIZATIONAL CULTURE

An organization's culture is manifested in the core values and principles that leaders preach and practice and in its employees' attitudes and behavior.[14] Fostering the right organizational culture is one of the most important responsibilities of a chief executive.[15] Examples of aspects of organizational culture include the casual dress and long workdays of **Microsoft**; the rigid work rules and conservative dress code at the **Bank of America**; the emphasis at **Southwest Airlines** on fun and excitement, which founder Herb Kelleher explains in an orientation video set to rap music; and **FedEx's** people-service-profit philosophy and its goal to ensure time-certain delivery. Recruiters seek employees who fit their culture.

In this section, we discuss how employees learn organizational culture, the three levels of culture, strong and weak cultures, managing and changing cultures, and organizational learning.

Organizational Culture Artifacts, Levels, and Strengths

Learning the Organizational Culture through Artifacts. Organizational culture is primarily learned through observing people and events in the organization.

Southwest Airlines prides itself on being a fun place to work while getting the job done. Having a fun-loving attitude is part of its organizational culture. Photo from Zack Wittman/Mlive.com/Landov.

Simply, you watch and listen to people and learn the culture of what you should and shouldn't do. More complex, there are five artifacts of organizational culture, which are important ways that employees learn about it:[16]

1. *Heroes,* such as founders **Tom Watson** of **IBM**, **Sam Walton** of **Walmart**, **Herb Kelleher** of **Southwest Airlines**, and others who have made outstanding contributions to their organizations.

2. *Stories,* often about founders and others who have made extraordinary efforts, such as Sam Walton visiting every **Walmart** store yearly, or someone driving through a blizzard to deliver a package for **UPS**. Public statements and speeches can also be considered stories.

3. *Slogans,* such as **McDonald's** Q, S, C, V (or quality, service, cleanliness, and value).

4. *Symbols,* such as plaques, pins, jackets, or a **Mary Kay Cosmetics** pink Cadillac. Symbols convey meaning.

5. *Ceremonies,* such as awards dinners for top achievers at **GE**.

LO 2-3

Describe the three levels of organizational culture and their relationship to each other.

Three Levels of Culture. The three **levels of culture** *are behavior, values and beliefs, and assumptions.* Exhibit 2-4 illustrates the three levels of culture.

1. **Behavior**—Behavior includes the observable things that people do and say or the actions employees take. Heroes, stories, slogans, symbols, and ceremonies are all part of behavior-level culture.

2. **Values and Beliefs**—Values represent the way people believe they ought to behave. Values and beliefs guide decision making and shape the behavior that results in level 1 culture. Although organizations use heroes, stories,

EXHIBIT 2-4   THREE LEVELS OF ORGANIZATIONAL CULTURE

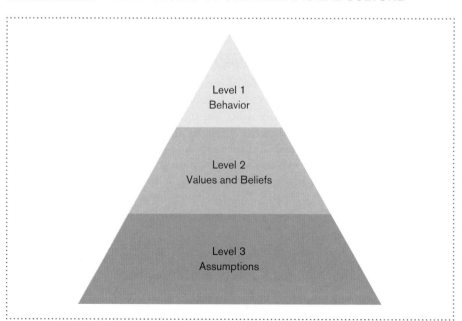

levels of culture Behavior, values and beliefs, and assumptions.

symbols, and ceremonies to convey the important values and beliefs, the slogan is critical to level 2 culture. A *slogan* expresses key values.

3. **Assumptions**—Assumptions are values and beliefs that are so deeply ingrained that they are considered unquestionably true and taken for granted.[17] Because assumptions are shared, they are rarely discussed. They serve as an "automatic pilot" to guide behavior. Assumptions are often the most stable and enduring part of culture and are difficult to change.

Strong and Weak Cultures. Organizational cultural strength is characterized by a continuum from strong to weak. Organizations with strong cultures have employees who subconsciously know the shared assumptions; consciously know the values and beliefs; agree with the shared assumptions, values, and beliefs; and behave as expected. Organizations with many employees who do not behave as expected have weak cultures. In a strong culture, the group peer pressures nonconformists to behave as expected.[18]

The primary benefits of a strong culture include easier communication and cooperation. Employees exhibit unity of direction, and consensus is easier to reach. The primary disadvantage is the threat of becoming stagnant.

WORK APPLICATION 2-4

Identify the cultural heroes, stories, symbols, slogans, and ceremonies for an organization you are/were a member of.

WORK APPLICATION 2-5

Describe the organizational culture at all three levels for a firm you work for or have worked for. Does the organization have a strong or a weak culture?

2-2 APPLYING THE CONCEPT

Strong and Weak Cultures

Identify whether each statement reflects an organization with a strong or weak culture.

A. strong culture
B. weak culture

____ 6. "Walking around this department during my job interview, I realized I'd have to wear a jacket and tie every day."

____ 7. "I'm a little tired of hearing about how our company founders conducted business. We all know the stories, so why do people keep telling them?"

____ 8. "I've never attended a meeting with people who all seem to act the same. I guess I can just be me rather than trying to act in a manner acceptable to others."

____ 9. "It's hard to say what is really important because management says quality is important, but they force us to work at too fast a pace and they know we send out defective products just to meet orders."

____ 10. "I started to tell this ethnic joke and the other employees all gave me a dirty look."

Managing, Changing, and Merging Cultures

Good cultures don't happen by accident; they are developed.[19] **Symbolic leaders** *articulate a vision for an organization and reinforce the culture through slogans, symbols, and ceremonies.* They may also tell stories and draw people's attention to heroes. Larry Page of **Google** and Jeff Bezos of **Amazon.com** are often cited as examples of great symbolic leaders.[20] Symbolic leaders manage, change, and merge cultures.

Organizational culture can be managed by drawing attention to heroes and using stories, symbols, slogans, and ceremonies. If any of these five artifacts of a strong culture are missing or weak, top management can work to strengthen the culture. However, strengthening an organizational culture is not a program with a starting and ending date; it is an ongoing process.[21]

Organizational cultures often need to be changed to ensure organizational success. However, changing cultures is not easy. Alan Mulally changed **Ford**'s organizational culture after the company was close to bankrupt. **BP** brought in new CEO Bob Dudley to help change its organizational culture after the disastrous 2010 oil spill in the Gulf of Mexico.

symbolic leaders Leaders who articulate a vision for an organization and reinforce the culture through slogans, symbols, and ceremonies.

A key strategy that big businesses use to compete in the global environment is to take part in mergers and acquisitions. However, many mergers never live up to expectations—**DaimlerChrysler** and **Pharmacia & Upjohn** are prime examples. One of the major reasons for failure is the inability to integrate the two organizational cultures. To successfully change or merge cultures, a strong symbolic leader is needed.[22] The new or merged cultural vision must generate excitement that employees can share. The leader must also continue to give public statements and speeches about the new slogan and use symbols and ceremonies to reinforce implementation of the new or merged culture.

Learning Organizations

A **learning organization** *has a culture that values sharing knowledge so as to adapt to the changing environment and continuously improve.* Solving problems and identifying and exploiting opportunities is critical to continuous improvement in learning organizations.[23] The learning organization is not a program with steps to follow. The learning organization is a philosophy or attitude about what an organization is and about the role of employees; it is part of the organizational culture.[24]

Learning organizations use information technology (IT) to manage knowledge, but IT is only part of what contributes to making them learning organizations. Through IT, knowledge, rather than being hoarded, is shared across the organization to increase the performance of business units and the entire organization.[25]

Creating a learning organization requires changes in many areas and demands strong leadership, a team-based structure, employee empowerment, open information, a participative strategy, and a strong adaptive culture.[26] A strong adaptive culture is created through effective leadership, often by a symbolic leader; however, everyone helps to create learning by participating in open sharing of information. Teams are empowered to create and share knowledge.[27]

Amazon.com's (Case Question 2) is a learning organization with an informal but serious culture—even serious about having fun. It is data driven with a bias for action. Amazon.com is obsessed with customers and continuous improvement of its website and sophisticated fulfillment systems to get orders to customers reliably and quickly. Amazon.com strives to maintain a culture that allows people to create innovative solutions to the challenges it faces. It celebrates its success with informal and formal ceremonies, including picnics on the company lawn. Jeff Bezos is a hero, with stories often told about him.

THE EXTERNAL ENVIRONMENT

The organization's **external environment** *includes the factors outside its boundaries that affect its performance.* Although managers can control the internal environment, they have very limited influence over what happens outside the organization. They need to continually align their internal environment with changes in the external environment, which can result in changing the mission and organizational culture and shifting priorities and goals.

External Environmental Factors

The nine major external factors are customers, competition, suppliers, labor force/unions, shareholders, society, technology, the economy, and governments. The first five are known as *task factors,* and the other four are known as *general factors.* Here, we briefly discuss each factor:

LO 2-4

Describe how the nine external environmental factors—customers, competitors, suppliers, labor force, shareholders, society, technology, the economy, and governments—can affect the internal business environment.

learning organization An organization with a culture that values sharing knowledge so as to adapt to the changing environment and continuously improve.

external environment The factors outside of an organization's boundaries that affect its performance.

- **Customers.** Customers have a major effect on the organization's performance through their purchase of products. Without customers, there is no need for an organization. Therefore, companies must continually improve products to create value for their customers.[28]

- **Competition.** Organizations must compete for customers. Competitors' changing strategic moves affect the performance of the organization. An important area of customer value is pricing. When a competitor changes prices, firms tend to match prices to keep customers.

Technological advances such as smartphones and tablets are changing the way we communicate and conduct business. Photo from Squaredpixels/iStockphoto.

- **Suppliers.** Organizations buy resources from suppliers. Therefore, a firm's performance is affected by suppliers. The **Boeing** Dreamliner 787 plane was delayed seven times due to suppliers.[29] Therefore, it is important to develop close working relationships with your suppliers.

- **Labor Force.** The employees of an organization have a direct effect on its performance. Management recruits human resources from the available labor force outside its boundaries. Unions also provide employees for the organization, and they are considered an external factor because they become a third party when dealing with the organization.

- **Shareholders.** The owners of a corporation, known as *shareholders*, influence management. Most shareholders of large corporations are generally not involved in the day-to-day operation of the firm, but they do vote for the directors of the corporation, who hire and fire top management.

- **Society.** Our society, to a great extent, determines what are acceptable business practices. Individuals and groups have formed to pressure business for changes. **Monsanto** was pressured because of its bioengineered agricultural products.

- **Technology.** Technology has changed the speed and the manner in which organizations conduct and transact business, and they are often a major part of a firm's systems process, including **Frito-Lay** using handheld computers to track real-time inventory.

- **The Economy.** No organization has control over economic growth, inflation, interest rates, foreign exchange rates, and so on. In general, as measured by gross domestic product (GDP), businesses do better when the economy is growing than during times of decreased economic activity, or recession. Thus, the economy has a direct impact on a firm's performance—profits.

- **Governments.** National, state, and local governments all set laws and regulations that businesses must obey. The **Occupational Safety and Health Administration (OSHA)** sets safety standards and the **Environmental Protection Agency (EPA)** sets pollution standards that must be met. **Merck** cannot market drugs without **Food and Drug Administration (FDA)** approval. In other words, to a large extent, businesses may not do whatever they want to do; the government tells businesses what they can and cannot do.

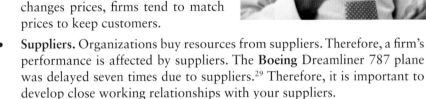

WORK
APPLICATION 2-6

Give an example of how one firm's competitors have affected that business.

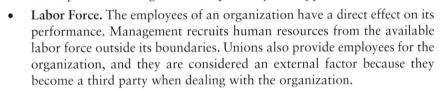

WORK
APPLICATION 2-7

Give an example of how technology has affected one or more organizations, preferably one you work for or have worked for.

2-3 APPLYING THE CONCEPT

The External Environment

Identify which external environmental factor is referred to in each statement.

A. customers
B. competition
C. suppliers
D. labor force
E. shareholders
F. society
G. technology
H. the economy
I. governments

_____ 11. "Management was going to sell our company to PepsiCo, but the government said that would be in violation of antitrust laws. What will happen to our company now?"

_____ 12. "Procter & Gamble has developed a new biodegradable material to replace the plastic liner on its diapers so that they don't take up landfill space for so long."

_____ 13. "At one time, AT&T was the only long-distance company, but then MCI, Sprint, and others came along and have taken away some of its customers."

_____ 14. "I applied for a loan to start my own business, but I might not get it because money is tight these days, even though interest rates are high."

_____ 15. "The owners of the company have threatened to fire the CEO if the business does not improve this year."

Dynamic Environments and Interactive Management

In many industries, the environment is changing at an incredibly fast pace.[30] Operating in such an environment is commonly referred to as being "in a dynamic or turbulent environment"[31] or "in chaos." Today's managers need to adapt to changing conditions.[32] There is always the opportunity that someone will come out of nowhere and crush you. Organizations must be able to thrive in a dynamic environment to maintain competitiveness.[33] Management does so through *environmental scanning*—searching the environment for important events or issues that might affect the firm.[34] But at the same time, change should be interactive.

According to Russell Ackoff, unlike reactive managers (who make changes only when forced to by external factors) and responsive managers (who try to adapt to the environment by predicting and preparing for change before they are required to do so), interactive managers design a desirable future and invent ways of bringing it about.[35] They believe they are capable of creating a significant part of the future and controlling its effects on them. They try to prevent threats, not merely prepare for them, and to create opportunities, not merely exploit them. Rather than reacting or responding, interactive managers make things happen for their benefit and for that of their stakeholders. **Apple** was interactive when it created the PC and changed how we listen to and buy music.

Amazon.com (Case Question 3) is customer driven. Selling products it doesn't make requires good suppliers. Amazon.com is a corporation with stockholders, and it has a global workforce. It has invested billions in technology. Amazon.com is affected by economic growth, inflation, interest rates, and foreign exchange rates in more than 100 countries, and it must meet their laws and regulations. As a business grows, the complexity of its internal and external environments increases, especially in the global world we live in today.[36] In the next chapter, we will discuss conducting business in a global environment. For a review of the organizational environment, see Exhibit 2-5.[37]

EXHIBIT 2-5 THE ORGANIZATIONAL ENVIRONMENT

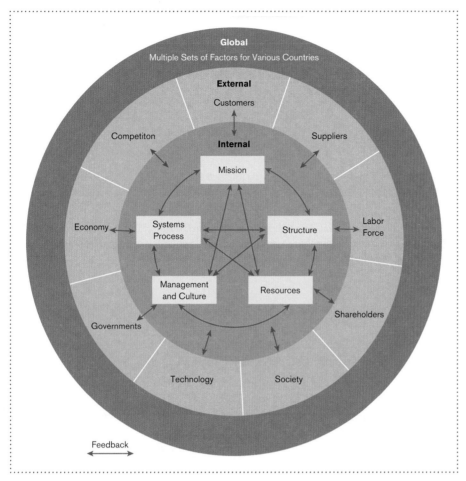

Source: R. Ackoff, *Creating the Corporate Future* (New York: Wiley, 1981).

BUSINESS ETHICS

Many Americans' trust in corporations has been strained because of criminal and unethical behavior by executives at numerous firms. The loss of public trust threatens the integrity of business.[38] To help restore confidence, the Sarbanes-Oxley Act of 2002 was passed to tighten the laws affecting business ethics. Also, business schools doubled the number of ethics-related courses to help students prepare to face ethical dilemmas during their careers.[39]

2-2 JOIN THE DISCUSSION ETHICS & SOCIAL RESPONSIBILITY

Auto Fuel Efficiency

The **National Highway Traffic Safety Administration (NHTSA)** is responsible for setting fuel efficiency standards for cars and light trucks. The miles per gallon (MPG) standards have been increasing over the years. Some people believe the standards should be higher, and others think they should not be increased so quickly. The auto makers have tried to fight the increases, stating that it is too expensive to increase fuel efficiency so quickly.

1. Are the automakers being ethical and socially responsible by fighting new higher MPG standards?
2. Should society be concerned about fuel efficiency? Should people use fuel efficiency as a major criterion when buying a car?
3. Should the government be involved in setting fuel efficiency standards? If yes, should it change the current standards? How?

2-1 | SELF ASSESSMENT

How Ethical Is Your Behavior?

For this exercise, you will respond to the same set of statements twice. The first time you read them, focus on your own behavior and the frequency with which you behave in certain ways. On the line before each statement number, place a number from 1 to 4 that represents how often you do that behavior (or how likely you would be to do it):

1	2	3	4

Frequently   Never

The numbers allow you to determine your level of ethics. You can be honest, as you will not tell others in class your score. *Sharing ethics scores is not part of the exercise.*

Next, go through the list of statements a second time, focusing on other people in an organization that you work for now or one you have worked for. Place an O on the line after the number of each statement if you have observed someone doing this behavior; place an R on the line if you reported this behavior within the organization or externally: O = observed, R = reported.

In College

_____ 1. _____ Cheating on homework assignments
_____ 2. _____ Cheating on exams
_____ 3. _____ Submitting as your own work papers that were completed by someone else

On the Job

_____ 4. _____ Lying to others to get what you want or to stay out of trouble
_____ 5. _____ Coming to work late, leaving work early, taking long breaks/lunches and getting paid for them
_____ 6. _____ Socializing, goofing off, or doing personal work rather than doing the work that you are getting paid to do
_____ 7. _____ Calling in sick to get a day off when you are not sick
_____ 8. _____ Using an organization's phone, computer, Internet access, copier, mail, or car for personal use
_____ 9. _____ Taking home company tools or equipment without permission for personal use
_____10. _____ Taking home organizational supplies or merchandise
_____11. _____ Giving company supplies or merchandise to friends or allowing them to take them without saying anything
_____12. _____ Applying for reimbursement for expenses for meals, travel, or other expenses that weren't actually incurred
_____13. _____ Taking spouse or friends out to eat or on business trips and charging their expenses to the organizational account
_____14. _____ Accepting gifts from customers/suppliers in exchange for giving them business
_____15. _____ Cheating on your taxes
_____16. _____ Misleading a customer to make a sale, such as promising rapid delivery dates
_____17. _____ Misleading competitors to get information to use to compete against them, such as pretending to be a customer/supplier
_____18. _____ Taking credit for another employee's accomplishments
_____19. _____ Selling more of a product than the customer needs in order to get the commission
_____20. _____ Spreading rumors about coworkers or competitors to make yourself look better, so as to advance professionally or to make more sales
_____21. _____ Lying for your boss when asked or told to do so
_____22. _____ Deleting information that makes you look bad or changing information to make yourself look better
_____23. _____ Allowing yourself to be pressured, or pressuring others, to sign off on documents that contain false information
_____24. _____ Allowing yourself to be pressured, or pressuring others, to sign off on documents you haven't read, knowing they may contain information or describe decisions that might be considered inappropriate
_____25. _____ If you were to give this assessment to a coworker with whom you do not get along, would she or he agree with your answers? If your answer is yes, write a 4 on the line before the statement number; if your answer is no, write a 1 on the line.

After completing the second phase of the exercise (indicating whether you have observed or reported any of the behaviors), list any other unethical behaviors you have observed. Indicate if you reported the behavior, using R.

26. _____

27. _____

28. _____

Note: This self-assessment is not meant to be a precise measure of your ethical behavior. It is designed to get you thinking about ethics and about your behavior and that of others from an ethical perspective. All of these actions are considered unethical behavior in most organizations.

Another ethical aspect of this exercise is your honesty when rating your behavior. How honest were you?

Scoring: To determine your ethics score, add up the numbers for all 25 statements. Your total will be between 25 and 100. Place the number that represents your score on the continuum below. The higher your score, the more ethical your behavior.

25	30	40	50	60	70	80	90	100

Unethical   Ethical

Ethics *are the standards of right and wrong that influence behavior.* Right behavior is considered ethical, and wrong behavior is considered unethical. Honesty is ethical, which means lying, cheating, and stealing are unethical. We constantly have to make decisions that are ethical or unethical.[40] Every culture endorses an ethical way to live.[41]

Government laws and regulations are designed to govern business behavior. However, ethics go beyond legal requirements. What is considered ethical in one country may be unethical in another. It is not always easy to distinguish between ethical and unethical behavior, such as accepting a gift (ethical) versus taking a bribe (unethical). In this section, you will learn that ethical behavior does pay; how personality traits and attitudes, moral development, and the situation affect ethical behavior; how people justify unethical behavior; some simple guides to ethical behavior; and about properly managing ethics. First, complete the Self-Assessment that follows to determine how ethical your behavior is.

Does Ethical Behavior Pay?

Ethical behavior *is* worthwhile. Research studies have reported a positive relationship between ethical behavior and leadership effectiveness.[42] Most highly successful people are ethical.[43] Being ethical may be difficult, but it has its rewards.[44] It actually makes you feel better.[45] Honest people have fewer mental health and physical complaints, like anxiety and back pain, and better social interactions.[46] Mahatma Gandhi called business without morality a sin. On the reverse side, unethical behavior is costly.

Unethical behavior is damaging on many levels. Unethical behavior contributed to the financial crisis that resulted in the world economies going into recession.[47] This was costly to society as people lost money. It has long-term negative consequences to companies, including hurt reputation, legal fees, and fines,[48] as well as sales declines, increasing cost of capital, market share deterioration, and network partner loss.[49] Some companies have gone out of business. Unethical behavior often has personal negative consequences,[50] such as getting into trouble at work, being fired, and even going to jail. If you get away with unethical behavior, it can be contagious and lead to more and larger transgressions.[51] It's the lies and cover-up, not the initial unethical behavior, that take people down.[52]

ethics Standards of right and wrong that influence behavior.

The truth will eventually catch up with you.[53] And when it does, you will lose the trust of people and hurt your relationships.[54]

How Personality Traits and Attitudes, Moral Development, and the Situation Affect Ethical Behavior

LO 2-5

Compare the three levels of moral development.

Personality Traits and Attitudes. In Chapter 10, you will learn more about personality. For now, you probably already realize that because of their personalities, some people have a higher level of ethics than others, as integrity is considered a personality trait. Unfortunately, a culture of lying and dishonesty is infecting American business and society as these behaviors have become more common and accepted.[55] Some people lie deliberately, based on the attitude that lying is no big deal; some people don't even realize that they are liars.[56]

Moral Development. A second factor affecting ethical behavior is *moral development*, which refers to distinguishing right from wrong and choosing to do the right thing.[57] People's ability to make ethical choices is related to their level of moral development.[58] One percent of people will always be honest, 1 percent will always be dishonest, and 98 percent will be unethical at times, but just a little.[59]

There are three levels of personal moral development, as outlined in Exhibit 2-6. At the first level, the *preconventional* level, a person chooses right and wrong behavior based on self-interest and the likely consequences of the behavior (reward or punishment). Those whose ethical reasoning has advanced to the second, *conventional* level seek to maintain expected standards and live up to the expectations of others. Those at the third level, the *postconventional* level, make an effort to define moral principles for themselves; regardless of leaders' or the group's ethics, they do the right thing. People can be on different levels for different issues and situations.[60]

WORK
APPLICATION 2-8

Give an example from an organization where you work or have worked of behavior at each of the three levels of moral development.

The Situation. A third factor affecting ethical behavior is the situation. In certain situations, it can be tempting to be unethical,[61] such as when you are negotiating.[62] Unsupervised people in highly competitive situations are more likely to engage in unethical behavior. Unethical behavior occurs more often when there is no formal ethics policy or code of ethics and when unethical behavior is not punished. In other words, people are more unethical when they believe they will not get caught.[63] Unethical behavior is also more likely when performance falls below aspiration levels.

People are also less likely to report unethical behavior (blow the whistle) when they perceive the violation as not being serious or when they are friends of the offender. It takes high moral responsibility to be a *whistle-blower*.

How People Justify Unethical Behavior

Most people understand right and wrong behavior and have a conscience. So why do good people do bad things? Most often, when people behave unethically, it is not because they have some type of character flaw or were born bad. Most people aren't simply good or bad. Just about everyone has the capacity to be dishonest.[64] We respond to "incentives" and can usually be manipulated to behave ethically or unethically if we find the right incentives.[65] The incentive can be personal gain or avoiding getting into trouble.[66]

Few people see themselves as unethical. We all want to view ourselves in a positive manner, and our mind echoes whatever we want to believe; this is called the "confirmation bias." Therefore, when we do behave unethically, we often justify the behavior to protect our *self-concept* so that we don't have to feel bad.[67] If we only cheat a little, we can still feel good about our sense of integrity.[68] Let's discuss several thinking processes used to justify unethical behavior.

EXHIBIT 2-6 LEVELS OF MORAL DEVELOPMENT

Level	Description of Behavior	Examples
3. Postconventional level	Behavior is motivated by universal principles of right and wrong, regardless of the expectations of leaders or one's group. A person seeks to balance self-interest with the interests of others and the common good. People at this level will follow ethical principles even if doing so violates the law and risks social rejection, economic loss, or physical punishment. Leaders at this level of moral development tend to be visionary and committed to serving others while empowering followers to also attain this level of morality.	"I don't lie to customers because it's wrong to do so." Martin Luther King Jr. broke what he considered to be unjust laws and spent time in jail in his quest for universal dignity and justice.
2. Conventional level	Behavior is motivated by the desire to live up to others' expectations. It is common to copy the behavior (ethical or otherwise) of leaders or of those in one's group. Peer pressure is used to enforce group norms. Lower-level managers at this level of moral development tend to use a leadership style similar to that of higher-level managers.	"I lie to customers because the other sales reps do it, too."
1. Preconventional level	Self-interest motivates behavior; a person acts to meet his or her own needs or gain rewards and follows rules or obeys authority only to avoid punishment. Leaders at this level often are autocratic toward others and use their position to gain personal advantages.	"I lie to customers to sell more products and get bigger commission checks."

Moral Justification is the process of reinterpreting immoral behavior in terms of a higher purpose. "It's for a greater good."69 The terrorists who struck the United States on September 11, 2001, killed innocent people, as do suicide bombers in Israel, Iraq, and elsewhere—yet such extremists believe their killing is for the good and that they will go to heaven for their actions. People who behave unethically say that they do so for the good of the organization or its employees.

Other Justifications. People at the preconventional and conventional levels of moral development more commonly use the following justifications:

- *Displacement of responsibility* is the process of blaming one's unethical behavior on others. "I was only following orders; my boss made me do it."70

- *Diffusion of responsibility* occurs when those in a group behave unethically and no one person is held responsible. "It isn't my decision."71 "Everyone does it."72 "We all take bribes/kickbacks; it's the way we do business." "We all take merchandise home (steal)." If you hear others are doing something, you will tend to be tempted to be unethical to.73 Peer pressure is used to enforce group norms.

- *Advantageous comparison* is the process of comparing oneself to others who are worse. "I'm only fudging a little."74 "I only call in sick when I'm not a few times a year; Tom and Ellen do it all the time." "We pollute less than our competitors do."

- *Disregard* or *distortion of consequences* is the process of minimizing the harm caused by the unethical behavior.[75] "No one will be hurt if I inflate the figures, and I will not get caught. And if I do, I'll just get a slap on the wrist anyway."
- *Attribution of blame* is the process of claiming the unethical behavior was caused by someone else's behavior. "It's my coworker's fault that I repeatedly hit him. He called me a [blank]—so I had to hit him."
- *Euphemistic labeling* is the process of using "cosmetic" words to make the behavior sound acceptable. "Terrorist group" sounds bad, but "freedom fighter" sounds justifiable. "Misleading" or "covering up" sounds better than "lying to others."

It is important to understand the subtlety of how unethical behavior can take hold of you. Being pragmatic by changing the rules or truth to simply what "works for you" or "makes you feel good" often leads to unethical behavior. Unethical behavior that you justify might give you some type of short-term gain, but in the long run, you've sabotaged yourself.[76]

Simple Guides to Ethical Behavior

Every day in your personal and professional lives, you face decisions in which you can make ethical or unethical choices. You make your choices based on your past learning experiences with parents, teachers, friends, managers, coworkers, and so forth. These experiences together contribute to what many refer to as the conscience, which helps you choose right from wrong in a given situation. You can develop your ethical character.[77] Following are some guides that can help you make the right decisions.

Golden Rule. Are you familiar with the Golden Rule: "Do unto others as you want them to do unto you," or "Don't do anything to anyone that you would not want someone to do to you"? It is a lesson that our body knows, and when we follow it, we feel an immediate reward.[78] Most successful people live by the Golden Rule.[79]

Four-Way Test. **Rotary International** developed a four-way test to guide one's thoughts and behavior in business transactions. The four questions are, (1) Is it the truth? (2) Is it fair to all concerned? (3) Will it build goodwill and better friendship? (4) Will it be beneficial to all concerned? When making a decision, if you can answer yes to these four questions, your potential course of action is probably ethical.

Stakeholders' Approach to Ethics. Under the stakeholders' approach to ethics, *when making decisions, you try to create a win-win situation for all relevant stakeholders so that everyone benefits from the decision.* You can ask yourself one simple question to help you determine if your decision is ethical from a stakeholders' approach: "Would I be proud to tell relevant stakeholders my decision?" If you would be proud to tell relevant stakeholders your decision, it is probably ethical. If you would not be proud to tell others your decision or you keep rationalizing it, the decision may not be ethical. You can't always create a win for everyone, but you can try.

Codes of Ethics. Also called *codes of conduct*, codes of ethics state the importance of conducting business in an ethical manner and provide guidelines for ethical behavior. Most large businesses have written codes of ethics you should follow.

WORK
APPLICATION 2-9

Give at least two organizational examples of unethical behavior and the justification that was used in each instance.

LO 2-6

Explain the stakeholders' approach to ethics.

stakeholders' approach to ethics Creating a win-win situation for all relevant stakeholders so that everyone benefits from the decision.

Discernment and Advice. Research shows that making a decision without using an ethical guide leads to less ethical choices.[80] Using ethical guides at the point of making a decision helps keep you honest.[81] If you are unsure whether a decision is ethical, talk to your boss, higher-level managers, and other people with high ethical standards. If you are reluctant to ask others for advice on an ethical decision because you may not like their answers, the decision may not be ethical.

Managing Ethics

An organization's ethics are based on the collective behavior of its employees. If each individual is ethical, the organization will be ethical. The starting place for ethics is you. Are you an ethical person? The Self-Assessment earlier in this chapter will help you answer this question. From the management perspective, managers should establish guidelines for ethical behavior, set a good example, and enforce ethical behavior.

Top Management Support and Example. Management is ultimately responsible for the ethical or unethical behavior of its employees.[82] Management from the top down needs to develop codes of ethics and an ethical culture, to ensure that employees are instructed on what is and what is not considered ethical behavior, and to enforce ethical behavior.[83] Employees tend to follow the example of ethical or unethical behavior of top management, and following management's lead is directly linked to bottom-line performance.[84] Thus, the primary responsibility is to lead by example.

Enforcing Ethical Behavior and Whistle-Blowing. If employees are rewarded rather than punished for their unethical behavior, or if managers know about it and do nothing, both employees and managers are more likely to engage in unethical business practices.[85] Many organizations have established ethics offices and developed ethics committees that act as judges and juries to determine if unethical behavior has occurred and what the punishment should be for violating company policy.

As a means of enforcing ethical behavior, employees should be encouraged to become internal whistle-blowers.[86] *Whistle-blowing* occurs when employees expose what they believe to be unethical behavior by their fellow employees. Whistle-blowing should begin internally, and information should go up the chain of command. If nothing is done, then the whistle-blower can go outside the organization as a last resort. According to the law and ethics, whistle-blowers should not suffer any negative consequences.

The Foreign Corrupt Practices Act (FCPA). The FCPA law bars U.S.-based or U.S.-listed companies from bribing foreign officials in exchange for business and requires them to keep accurate books and records. But it is sometimes hard to tell the difference between a legitimate business expense and a bribe.[87] Thus, global companies need to clarify the difference in their code of ethics, top managers must set the example, and unethical and penalties for illegal behavior must be enforced.

WORK
APPLICATION 2-10

Select a business and identify how it manages ethics.

SOCIAL RESPONSIBILITY AND SUSTAINABILITY

Ethics and social responsibility are closely related, as being socially responsible is going beyond legal and economic obligations to do the right things and acting in ways that benefit society. Engaging in sustainability is part of a business's social responsibility, as firms voluntarily act in ways to address social issues and environmental sustainability.[88] In this section, we discuss social responsibility to stakeholders, why it pays to be socially responsible, and sustainability.

TV Sex, Profanity, and Violence

The **Federal Communications Commission (FCC)** has the power to regulate television broadcasts. Advocates for more regulation (**Parents Television Council** and the **National Viewers and Listeners Association**) state that TV shows with violent acts, profanity, and sexual content should be shown later at night while children should not be watching. For example, many *Seinfeld* episodes have sexual themes, and the show was not aired until 9:00 P.M., but now it's shown at all hours of the day. *Sex in the City, Jersey Shore,* and other shows with sexual content and violence are also shown at all hours. However, advocates against regulation (**National Coalition Against Censorship**) don't want censorship at all, on the grounds that it violates free speech. They claim it's up to the parents to restrict viewing they don't approve of.

1. How does TV influence societal values? (Consider that many children watch as many as five hours of TV per day.)
2. Do TV shows that include sex and violence reflect religious and societal values?
3. Is it ethical and socially responsible to air TV shows with sexual content, profanity, and violence during hours when children are watching?
4. Is it ethical and socially responsible to portray women as sex objects?
5. Should the FCC regulate television, and if yes, how far should it go? Should it make networks tone down the sex and violence, or take shows off the air?

Social Responsibility to Stakeholders

Social responsibility is often called *corporate social responsibility,* or CSR, an umbrella term for exploring the responsibilities of business and its role in society.[89] Meeting social needs is a core aspect of every business.[90] **Social responsibility** *is the conscious effort to operate in a manner that creates a win-win situation for all stakeholders.* Companies must provide employees with safe working conditions and with adequate pay and benefits. For customers, the company must provide safe products and services with customer value. For society, the company should improve the quality of life, or at least not destroy the environment. The company must compete fairly with competitors. The company must work with suppliers in a cooperative manner. It must abide by the laws and regulations of government. The company must strive to provide equal employment opportunities for the labor force. The company must provide shareholders with a reasonable profit.

Virtually all of the *Fortune* 500 companies have formal CSR programs, and 90 percent of them allow employees to take time off from work to do volunteer work.[91] If you are attending a nonprofit college or university, the odds are that it receives money or other resources from companies as part of its CSR. Visit your favorite large corporation's website and you will most likely find a link stating how the firm engages in CSR; it is even included in most of their annual reports, often called a *social audit* as its measure of social behavior.

Does It Pay to Be Socially Responsible?

If it didn't, why would virtually all large corporations have CSR programs? CSR can improve stock returns.[92] With a choice of two products of similar price and quality, 80 percent of customers are willing to buy the more sustainable option.[93] Being socially irresponsible has negative consequences as it gives the company a negative reputation that leads to more difficulty to attracting customers, investors, and employees; and it can lead to costly lawsuits.[94] Money can be made again, but a negative reputation can take years to improve, and a good reputation may be lost forever.[95]

There is growth in the number of *social entrepreneurs* that combine their concern for social issues with their desire for financial rewards.[96] Blake Mycoskie

social responsibility The conscious effort to operate in a manner that creates a win-win situation for all stakeholders.

founded his fourth business **TOMS** shoes at age 29 to make money and help solve a social problem of children having no shoes to wear, resulting in blisters, sores, and infections. His business model is "With every pair you purchase, TOMS will give a pair of new shoes to a child in need. One for One." He wrote *Start Something That Matters* to guide others in helping society.[97] With a social mission, TOMS received lots of free publicity and sales have increased, resulting in Mycoskie making lots of money for being socially responsible.

Sustainability

Sustainability *is meeting the needs of the present world without compromising the ability of future generations to meet their own needs.*[98] It is the process of assessing how to design products that will take advantage of the current environmental situation and how well a company's products perform with renewable resources. Sustainability is now a business buzzword,[99] and based on the gravity of environmental problems, it is an important topic for all countries.[100] Countries and businesses are realizing that economic growth and environmental sustainability can work together.[101]

Society expects sustainability and for managers to use resources wisely and responsibly; protect the environment; minimize the amount of air, water, energy, minerals, and other materials used to produce the final goods we consume; recycle and reuse these goods to the extent possible rather than drawing on nature to replenish them; respect nature's calm, tranquility, and beauty; and eliminate toxins that harm people in the workplace and communities.[102] Thus, including sustainability in managing the business is being socially responsible.

Sustainability Practices and Green Companies. Sustainability issues influence activities in the business world.[103] A *green company* acts in a way that minimizes damage to the environment. With the environmental problems such as air, water, and other forms of pollution, many new ventures have been created in green management.[104] Social entrepreneurs are taking advantage of sustainability. Bob Shallenberger and John Cavanaugh launched **Highland Homes** in St. Louis to build environmentally friendly condos and houses.[105]

Large corporations are engaging in sustainability practices in a big way. A new corporate title has emerged—chief sustainability officer (CSO). CSOs are in charge of the corporation's environmental programs. Nearly all of the world's 150 largest companies have a sustainability officer with the rank of vice president or higher.[106] Some examples of organizations that have CSOs include **AT&T**, **DuPont**, **Google**, and **Sun Microsystems**. Many companies, including **Intel**, are giving annual sustainability reports.[107]

Walmart is a leader in sustainability. Back in 2010, it stated that it would cut some 20 million metric tons of greenhouse gas emissions from its supply chain by the end of 2015.[108] Walmart requirements of reduced waste from packaging have created industry-wide reforms.[109] It essentially pressures all of its thousands of suppliers to meet its sustainability standards. Even the greenest companies tout their close ties to Walmart in their promotional materials.[110] **Google** has a zero-carbon quest and has a goal of becoming the world's most energy-efficient company.[111]

Businesses today are becoming increasingly concerned about their impact on the environment and are moving toward using sustainable resources to ensure the well-being of our planet for generations to come. Photo from Stocknadia/iStockphoto.

WORK
APPLICATION 2-11

Select a business and identify how it is socially responsible on a specific issue.

sustainability Meeting the needs of the present world without compromising the ability of future generations to meet their own needs.

Amazon.com (Case Question 4) is considered to be an ethical company with a code of ethics. One of the many things it does to be socially responsible is to support and offer grants for more than 30 not-for-profit author and publisher groups that foster the creation, discussion, and publication of books. **Amazon** is also a green company that has reduced packaging and makes sure it is made from recycled materials that can be recycled again, and its headquarters was built to have eco-friendly buildings with **LEED (Leadership in Energy and Environmental Design)**–certified interiors and exteriors.

Organizations That Promote Sustainable Development. One of the leaders in the global effort to promote sustainable business practices is the **World Business Council for Sustainable Development (WBCSD)**. The WBCSD is a CEO-led, global association. Among its members are well-known companies such as **Coca-Cola, Deutsche Bank, Sony,** and **Walmart**.[112] For more information on the WBCSD, visit its website at http://www.wbcsd.org. Another organization is the **International Institute for Sustainable Development (IISD)**, which champions sustainable development around the world through innovation, partnerships, research, and communications.[113] To learn more about the IISD, visit its website at http://www.iisd.org.

The message of this chapter boils down to this: As a manager, you are going to have to manage the organization's internal environment (including its organizational culture) while interacting with its global external environment to create a win-win situation for stakeholders through ethical and socially responsible leadership, while creating long-term sustainability.

WORK APPLICATION 2-12

Select a business and identify its sustainability practices.

● ● ● CHAPTER SUMMARY

2-1   Explain the five internal environmental factors.

Management refers to the people responsible for an organization's performance. Mission is the organization's purpose or reason for being. The organization has human, physical, financial, and informational resources to accomplish its mission. The systems process is the method of transforming inputs into outputs as the organization accomplishes its mission. Structure refers to the way in which the organization groups its resources to accomplish its mission.

2-2   List and explain the need for the two primary principles of total quality management (TQM).

The two primary principles of TQM are (1) focusing on delivering customer value and (2) continually improving the system and its processes. To be successful, businesses must continually offer value to attract and retain customers. Without customers, you don't have a business.

2-3   Describe the three levels of organizational culture and their relationship to each other.

Level 1 of culture is behavior—the actions employees take. Level 2 is values and beliefs. Values represent the way people believe they ought to behave and beliefs represent if–then statements. Level 3 is

assumptions—values and beliefs that are deeply ingrained as unquestionably true. Values, beliefs, and assumptions provide the operating principles that guide decision making and behavior.

2-4   Describe how the nine external environmental factors—customers, competitors, suppliers, labor force, shareholders, society, technology, the economy, and governments—can affect the internal business environment.

Customers decide what products the business offers, and without customer value, there are no customers or business. Competitors' business practices often have to be duplicated in order to maintain customer value. Poor-quality inputs from suppliers result in poor-quality outputs without customer value. Without a qualified labor force, products and services will have little or no customer value. Shareholders, through an elected board of directors, hire top managers and provide directives for the organization. Society, to a great extent, determines what are acceptable business practices and can pressure business for changes. The business must develop new technologies, or at least keep up with them, to provide customer value. Economic activity affects the organization's ability to provide customer value.

For example, inflated prices lead to lower customer value. Governments set the rules and regulations that business must adhere to.

2-5 Compare the three levels of moral development.

At the lowest level of moral development, the preconventional level, behavior is motivated by self-interest and people seek rewards and attempt to avoid punishment. At the second level, the conventional level, behavior is motivated by a desire to maintain expected standards and live up to the expectation of others. At the highest level, the post-conventional level, behavior is motivated by a desire to do the right thing, at the risk of alienating the group. The higher the level of moral development, the more ethical is one's behavior.

2-6 Explain the stakeholders' approach to ethics.

Managers who use the stakeholders' approach to ethics create a win-win situation for the relevant parties affected by the decision. If you are proud to tell relevant stakeholders about your decision, it is probably ethical. If you are not proud to tell stakeholders or you keep rationalizing it, the decision may not be ethical.

• • • KEY TERMS

customer value, 38
ethics, 47
external environment, 42
internal environment, 36
learning organization, 42
levels of culture, 40

mission, 36
organizational culture, 37
quality, 38
social responsibility, 52
stakeholders, 36
stakeholders' approach to ethics, 50

sustainability, 53
symbolic leaders, 41
systems process, 37
total quality management (TQM), 38

• • • KEY TERM REVIEW

Complete each of the following statements using one of this chapter's key terms:

1. The organization's _____ includes the factors that affect the organization's performance from within its boundaries.

2. The organization's _____ is its purpose or reason for being.

3. _____ are people whose interests are affected by organizational behavior.

4. An _____ consists of the values, beliefs, and assumptions about appropriate behavior that members of an organization share.

5. The _____ is the technology used to transform inputs into outputs.

6. Customers determine _____ by comparing a product's actual functioning to their requirements to determine value.

7. _____ is the perceived benefit of a product, used by customers to determine whether to buy the product.

8. _____ is a process that involves everyone in an organization focusing on the customer to continually improve product value.

9. The three _____ are behavior, values and beliefs, and assumptions.

10. _____ articulate a vision for an organization and reinforce the culture through slogans, symbols, and ceremonies.

11. A _____ has a culture that values sharing knowledge so as to adapt to the changing environment and continuously improve.

12. The organization's _____ includes the factors outside its boundaries that affect its performance.

13. _____ are the standards of right and wrong that influence behavior.

14. Using the _____, when making decisions, you try to create a win-win situation for all relevant stakeholders so that everyone benefits from the decision.

15. _____ is the conscious effort to operate in a manner that creates a win-win situation for all stakeholders.

16. _____ is meeting the needs of the present world without compromising the ability of future generations to meet their own needs.

• • • REVIEW QUESTIONS

1. What are the factors within the internal environment?

2. What are the components of the systems process?

3. How is quality determined, and why do people buy products?

4. What are the five artifacts of organizational culture?

5. What are the levels of culture?

6. What is a learning organization?

7. What is the external environment?

8. What are the levels of moral development?

9. How do people justify unethical behavior?

10. What is the stakeholders' approach to ethics?

11. What is social responsibility?

12. What are some ways in which businesses are going "green"?

••• COMMUNICATION SKILLS

The following critical-thinking questions can be used for class discussion and/or as written assignments to develop communication skills. Be sure to give complete explanations for all questions.

1. Do you believe that most organizations focus on creating customer value?

2. Do you think that all organizations should use total quality management (TQM)? Explain your answer.

3. What is the relationship among management and mission, resources, the systems process, and structure? Which of these internal factors are ends, and which are means?

4. Which of the five artifacts, or important ways that employees learn about organizational culture, is the most important?

5. What is the difference between a strong and weak organizational culture, and which is preferable?

6. What is symbolic leadership? Is it important?

7. What is a learning organization? Should a manager create one?

8. If you can't control the external environment, why be concerned about it anyway?

9. Do you believe that ethical behavior will pay off in the long run?

10. Do you have your own guide to ethical behavior that you follow now? Will you use one of the guides from the text? If yes, which one and why?

11. Can ethics be taught and learned?

12. Do you believe that companies benefit from being socially responsible? Why or why not?

13. Do you believe that all businesses should go "green"? Why or why not?

••• CASE: LEGO LEARNS TO MAKE SUSTAINABLE ENVIRONMENTAL DECISIONS

Every kid loves to play with LEGO bricks. But even LEGO, the Danish company for which "LEGO" is an abbreviation of the two Danish words "leg godt," meaning "play well," still can learn how to make profits and be environmentally friendly.

The LEGO Group was founded in 1932 by Ole Kirk Kristiansen. The company has passed from father to son and is now owned by Kjeld Kirk Kristiansen, a grandchild of the founder. It has come a long way over the past 80-plus years—from a small carpenter's workshop to a modern, global enterprise that is now, in terms of sales, the world's fourth-largest manufacturer of toys.

The first LEGO automatic binding brick, the LEGO brick, is the company's important product. LEGO has been named Toy of the Century. Its products have undergone extensive development over the years—but the foundation remains the traditional LEGO brick.[114]

The manufacturing of bricks used to occur at the manufacturing plant in Enfield, CT, but has since moved to Mexico. The Enfield location now focuses only on marketing.

However, in 2011, LEGO learned its focus on developing great products meant it might have slipped up in making sure the company was environmentally compliant. The social activist group Greenpeace applied some pressure to LEGO (it also pressured HASBRO) to be more aware of the conditions of how and where its suppliers provide its packaging material.[115] Greenpeace wanted LEGO to use suppliers that used sustainable practices.

LEGO top managers could have stalled and used tactics to discredited the complaints Greenpeace had with LEGO sourcing of packaging made from unsustainable forests. LEGO customers would most likely never hear or be aware of where the paper packaging material originated.

Instead, to be more environmentally aware, LEGO agreed to not use its supplier Asia Pulp and Paper (APP) but to use packaging material certified by the

Forest Stewardship Council (FSC) instead. Greenpeace considers APP the worst forest offender in Indonesia. Greenpeace has also called on companies to start new sustainable procurement policies for purchase of all pulp and paper products.

LEGO has plans to reduce the amount of all types of packaging (not just paper products) and to use recycled products as often as possible. As part of Planet Promise, LEGO has set its overall strategic ambitions to have zero product recalls, to be in the top 10 companies globally on employee safety, to support learning for 101 million children by 2015, to use 100 percent renewable energy by 2020, and to reach a goal of zero waste. According to a 2012 sustainability report, LEGO has reduced its packaging by 18 percent and has continued to work with suppliers that are part of the Forest Stewardship Council.[116]

You can watch a video (http://green.tv/videos/lego-and-sustainability/) of CEO Jorgen Vig Knudstorp, LEGO Group CEO, who presents his company's approach to sustainable business. He discusses how LEGO has become very concerned about its footprint in the history of business. LEGO has invested in wind power, continues to work on reducing all manufacturing waste, and even is looking for ways to reduce product packaging. But, on that account, the company found that people do not tend to throw away LEGO products; instead, they save them for future generations.[117]

Case Questions

1. Which internal environmental factor is the major reason for LEGO's success?

2. LEGO's new program using recycled supplies reflects what level of culture? Refer to Chapter 2 for a refresher on the three levels of culture.

3. Which external environmental factor in this case is least important to LEGO's success?

4. Which external environmental factor, in this case, is most important to LEGO's continuing success?

5. Is LEGO engaged in socially responsible behavior?

6. Would LEGO be considered a "green" company?

7. Does LEGO have a strong or weak culture?

8. Can you think of any other ways LEGO could improve its sustainability practices?

Cumulative Case Questions

9. Which manager's resources have given LEGO a competitive advantage over its competitors? (Chapter 1)

10. How does LEGO's new recycling program highlight the four management functions? (Chapter 1)

• • • SKILL BUILDER 2–1: ETHICS AND WHISTLE-BLOWING

Objective

To determine your level of ethics.

Skills

The primary skills developed through this exercise are:

1. Management skill—interpersonal

2. AACSB competencies—ethical understanding and reasoning abilities and reflective thinking skills

3. Management function—leading

Preparing for Skill Builder 2–1

For this exercise, first complete Self-Assessment 2–1 in the chapter (page xx).

Discussion Questions

1. Who is harmed and who benefits from the unethical behaviors in items 1 through 3?

2. For items 4 through 24, select the three (circle their numbers) you consider the most unethical. Who is harmed by and who benefits from these unethical behaviors?

3. If you observed unethical behavior but didn't report it, why didn't you report the behavior? If you did blow the whistle, what motivated you to do so? What was the result?

4. As a manager, it is your responsibility to uphold ethical behavior. If you know employees are doing any of these unethical behaviors, will you take action to enforce compliance with ethical standards?

5. What can you do to prevent unethical behavior?

6. As part of the class discussion, share any of the other unethical behaviors you observed and listed.

You may be asked to present your answers to the class or share them in small groups in class or online.

Apply It

What did I learn from this experience? How will I use this knowledge in the future?

••• SKILL BUILDER 2-2: THE ORGANIZATIONAL ENVIRONMENT AND MANAGEMENT PRACTICES ANALYSIS

Objective

To determine an organization's environment, culture, ethics, social responsibility, and sustainability.

Skills

The primary skills developed through this exercise are:

1. Management skill—decision making
2. AACSB competencies—dynamics of the global economy, ethical understanding and reasoning abilities, and multicultural and diversity understanding
3. Management function—planning

Preparing for Skill Builder 2-2

For this exercise, you will select a specific organization, preferably one you work for or have worked for, and answer the questions as they relate to the business you have selected. You may contact people in the organization to get your answers. Write your answers to all questions.

The Internal Environment

1. Identify the top managers and briefly discuss their leadership style.
2. State the organization's mission.
3. Identify some of the organization's major resources.
4. Explain the organization's systems process. Discuss how the organization ensures quality and customer value.
5. Identify the organization's structure by listing its major departments.

The External Environment

In answering this section's questions, be sure to state how each of these external factors affects the organization.

6. Identify the organization's target customers.
7. Identify the organization's major competitors.
8. Identify the organization's major suppliers.
9. What labor force does the organization primarily recruit from?

10. Does the organization have shareholders? Is its stock listed on one of the three major stock exchanges? If yes, which one?
11. How does the organization affect society and vice versa?
12. Describe some of the past, present, and future technologies of the organization's industry. Is the organization a technology leader?
13. Identify the governments that affect the organization. List some of the major laws and regulations affecting the business.
14. Explain how the economy affects the organization.

Culture

15. Does the organization use all five artifacts to teach culture? Explain which are used and how.
16. Describe the culture at all three levels. Is it a strong or a weak culture?
17. Is the firm creating a learning organization? Explain why or why not.

Ethics

18. Does the organization have any guides to ethical behavior? If yes, explain.
19. How does the organization manage ethics? Does it have a code of ethics? If so, what does the code cover? Does top management lead by good ethical example? Are ethical behaviors enforced? If so, how?

Social Responsibility

20. Is the organization socially responsible? If so, how?

Sustainability

21. Does the organization use any sustainability practices? If yes, explain.

You may be asked to present your answers to the class or share them in small groups in class or online.

Apply It

What did I learn from this experience? How will I use this knowledge in the future?

••• STUDENT STUDY SITE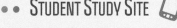

Visit the Student Study Site at **www.sagepub.com/lussier6e** to access to these additional study tools:

- Mobile-compatible self-assessment quizzes
- Mobile-compatible key term flashcards
- Video Links

- SAGE Journal Articles
- Web Links

3

Managing Diversity in a Global Environment

• • • Learning Outcomes

After studying this chapter, you should be able to:

3-1. Contrast the classification of businesses in the global village. PAGE 62

3-2. Differentiate the common barriers to trade. PAGE 64

3-3. List the six activities that make a business a global one, in order from lowest to highest cost and risk. PAGE 69

3-4. Discuss diversity and why it is important. PAGE 76

3-5. Describe the four major types of diversity groups and practices of managing diversity. PAGE 78

3-6. Compare and contrast the Hofstede national culture dimensions with Project GLOBE. PAGE 83

IDEAS ON MANAGEMENT at ExxonMobil

It is fitting that we have **ExxonMobil** as the opening case because it is the largest company in the world by market value, followed by **Apple, Google, Berkshire Hathaway,** and **Walmart** to top off the five largest companies. It is the most profitable *Fortune* 500 company, with a net income of close to $45 billion and assets valued at around $334 billion, and it employs close to 77,000 people globally. ExxonMobil is an oil and gas company that provides energy globally.

One thing is certain: even with growing efficiency, the current 7 billion people in the world and the 9 billion people by 2040 are going to need more affordable and reliable supplies of energy to realize their hopes and aspirations. To meet this challenge, ExxonMobil is headquartered in Irving, Texas, United States, but it has operating facility subsidiaries or market products in most of the world's countries and explores for oil and natural gas on six continents.

1. How is ExxonMobil's business classified in the global village? PAGE 62
2. How is ExxonMobil's business global? PAGE 73
3. What global business practices does ExxonMobil use? PAGE 74
4. Does ExxonMobil promote workplace diversity in the United States and globally? PAGE 78, 81

You'll find answers to these questions throughout the chapter. To learn more about ExxonMobil, visit its website at www.exxonmobil.com.

Source: Information for this case was taken from: "Largest U.S. corporations—Fortune 500," *Fortune* (May 20, 2013), 1–20; U.S. companies regain the top five spots," *Business Week* (April 29–May 5, 2013), 40–41; and ExxonMobil website, accessed on June 1, 2013.

• • • Chapter Outline

THE GLOBAL ENVIRONMENT

As the title implies, we are expanding the external environment from the last chapter to be global. We live in a world that is dynamically globally interconnected.[1] The major factor increasing the complexity of the environment is the globalization of markets,[2] buying and selling goods and services worldwide. Think about the complexity of **FedEx**'s environment, delivering to more than 220 countries and territories worldwide.[3] Therefore, it has to follow the rules and regulations of different governments in countries with different economies, labor forces, societies, and so on. Refer to Chapter 2, Exhibit 2-5, for a review of the environment. Clearly, to be successful, companies need global leaders.[4] For example, Carlos Ghosn is the CEO of two companies, **Renault** (France) and **Nissan** (Japan), on two different continents conducting business globally. Today's managers—and students of management—cannot afford to underestimate the importance of the global environment to business.[5] In this section, we classify businesses in the global village, discuss ethnocentrism, and present practices of global companies.

LO 3-1

Contrast the classification of businesses in the global village.

Classifying Businesses in the Global Village

Let's begin with defining *global business* as the buying and selling of goods and services among different countries. The **global village** *refers to companies conducting business worldwide without boundaries*. The word *village* implies something small and emphasizes that the world, although very large, is becoming smaller through technology. Technology has changed the way business is conducted in the global village, and the Internet enabled **eBay** and other companies to go global in a stunningly quick time.[6] In its first 30 days, **Amazon.com** recorded sales in all 50 U.S. states and 45 other countries.[7]

Domestic and International Businesses. A *domestic business* conducts business in only one country. Most small businesses, like **Anthony's Pizza Place**, are domestic businesses. But most domestics will get equipment, material, supplies, and so forth that are made in other countries. An **international company** *is based primarily in one country but transacts business in other countries*. International companies commonly buy and sell products through importing and exporting. **Ferrari** cars are made in Italy and imported for sale by car dealers in other countries.

Multinational Corporations (MNCs). A **multinational corporation (MNC)** *has ownership in operations in two or more countries*. The MNC can have partial or full ownership of the operations—a separate independent business facility (factories or offices) in another country. Partial ownership comes commonly though buying stock in a foreign company or through a strategic alliance. Italian **Fiat Spa** bought the majority of **Chrysler** stock to have controlling interest, with its CEO running both companies.[8] The MNC can also have full or 100 percent ownership of the foreign company called *wholly owned*. **ExxonMobil (Case Question 1)** is an MNC.

The foreign company is commonly referred to as *foreign subsidiaries or affiliates;* in essence, a *subsidiary* is a company owned and controlled by another company, making up a combined company, called the *holding company* or *parent company.* When going to a new country, MNCs often buy part or all of an existing business to establish its operations. **FedEx** expanded globally by acquiring several other companies to deliver its packages to other countries globally. To come to America, **Shuanghui International Holdings** acquired **Smithfield Foods** and plans to export more pork to China.[9] But companies can also have same-country subsidiaries. The parent company **PepsiCo**'s primary businesses include **Frito-Lay**, **Quaker**, **Pepsi-Cola**, **Tropicana**, and **Gatorade**, with operations in the United States and globally.[10]

global village Refers to companies conducting business worldwide without boundaries.

international company An organization based primarily in one country but transacts business in other countries.

multinational corporation (MNC) An organization that has ownership in operations in two or more countries.

3-1 JOIN THE DISCUSSION ETHICS & SOCIAL RESPONSIBILITY

Buy American

You most likely have heard the slogan "Buy American." Many labor unions urge Americans to buy products made in the United States, because that helps retain jobs for American workers. On the other hand, some Americans ask why they should buy American products if they cost more or their quality or style is not as good as that of foreign-made products. But as you've seen, it isn't always easy for consumers to know the country of ownership of many products they buy.

1. Is it ethical and socially responsible to ask people to buy American?
2. Is it ethical and socially responsible to buy foreign products?

There is also a *transnational company,* a type of MNC that eliminates artificial geographical barriers without having a real single national headquarters. **IBM** changed its structure from a country-based structure to industry groups to transcend bounders A new form of global company is one that starts with a global strategy and sales in multiple countries at the same time. They are commonly MNCs that are called a *global new ventures* or *global start-ups.* **Logitech,** a leading transnational manufacturer of the computer mouse, was started by one Swiss and two Italian people who wanted a global company from the start. The company began with headquarters, manufacturing, and engineering in California and Switzerland.

WORK
APPLICATION 3-1

Classify a business you work for or have researched as domestic, international, or multinational. If the business is international or an MNC, list some of the countries in which it does business.

Ethnocentrism Is Out and "Made in America" Is Blurred

Parochialism means having a narrow focus, or seeing things solely from one's own perspective. **Ethnocentrism** *is regarding one's own ethnic group or culture as superior to others.* Thus, a parochial view is part of ethnocentrism. Successful managers of large companies headquartered in the United States (including **Coca-Cola, FedEx, GE,** and **3M,** to name just a few) are not ethnocentric; they don't view themselves simply as American companies but rather as companies conducting business in a global village. If they can buy or make better or cheaper materials, parts, or products and make a profit in another country, they do so. **British Petroleum (BP)** has been doing business in the United States for more than 100 years and employs close to 250,000 workers across America.[11]

Many consumers subscribe to the idea behind "buy American," but few know the country of origin of the products they regularly buy. Look at the labels in your clothes and you will realize that most clothing is not made in America; 76.5 percent are made in Asia, with close to 40 percent coming from China.[12] Did you know that although **Nike** is an American company, its clothes and sneakers are not made in the United States? Some **GM** cars are made in America, with more than 60 percent of the parts coming from foreign companies. **Toyota** makes some cars in America, with around 25 percent of the parts coming from foreign companies. So which is "really" made in America? The **Made in America** store has a challenge stocking the store with fashionable only-American merchandise and hasn't been able to find any electric or electronic products because they are all made abroad.[13]

In addition to not knowing products are foreign, some people don't care where the products they buy come from; price is more important to them. Plus, some people prefer products, such as cars, made by foreign companies. Test your global knowledge of company and product country of ownership by completing Self-Assessment 3–1.

WORK
APPLICATION 3-2

Do you try to buy American products? Should you?

ethnocentrism Regarding one's own ethnic group or culture as superior to others.

3-1 SELF ASSESSMENT

Country of Origin Ownership of Products

For each item, determine the country of origin. If your answer is the United States, place a check in the left-hand column. If it's another country, write the name of the country in the right-hand column.

Product	United States	Other (list country)
1. Shell gasoline		
2. Nestlé hot cocoa		
3. Unilever Dove soap		
4. Nokia cell phones		
5. L'Oreal cosmetics		
6. Johnson & Johnson baby powder		
7. Burger King fast food		
8. Samsung televisions		
9. Bayer aspirin		
10. Anheuser-Busch InBev beer		
11. Volvo cars		
12. AMC theaters		

1. Shell is owned by Royal Dutch Shell of the Netherlands. 2. Nestlé is headquartered in Switzerland. 3. Unilever is British. 4. Nokia was a Finnish company but was acquired by US Microsoft in September 2013. 5. L'Oreal is French. 6. Johnson & Johnson is a U.S. company. 7. Burger King is Brazilian owned. 8. Samsung is South Korean. 9. Bayer is German. 10. Anheuser-Busch InBev is Belgian owned. 11. Volvo and 12. AMC are both Chinese owned.

How many did you get correct?

FOREIGN TRADE

Foreign trade is about conducting business with other countries. Like it or not, businesses compete in a global environment.[14] China has the largest population in the world with 1.343 billion people, followed by India with 1.205 billion people; that is 36 percent of the global population of more than 7 billion. Comparatively, the United States is small with only 314 million people, or consumers to sell products and services to.[15] By 2050, the world population is expected to grow to 9 billion people, with little growth from the United States and Europe.[16] The United States currently has the biggest economy, but China will eventually take the number one spot.[17] In this section, we discuss trade barriers, the World Trade Organization (WTO), trade agreements, and exchange rates and balance of trade.

LO 3-2

Differentiate the common barriers to trade.

Trade Barriers

Foreign trade benefits companies, but it can also hurt. For example, it is difficult for the United States to compete against China because of the large difference in labor costs. Also, some companies don't play fair through *dumping*. They sell products in one country at a high profit and sell in another country at a loss with the intention of driving out the competition. Thus, to help the domestic businesses compete with foreign companies at home, governments use *protectionism*—trade barriers to protect domestic companies and their workers from foreign competition. The first three are nontax barriers and the last is a tax method. See Exhibit 3-1 for an illustration and below for definitions.

EXHIBIT 3-1   TRADE BARRIERS

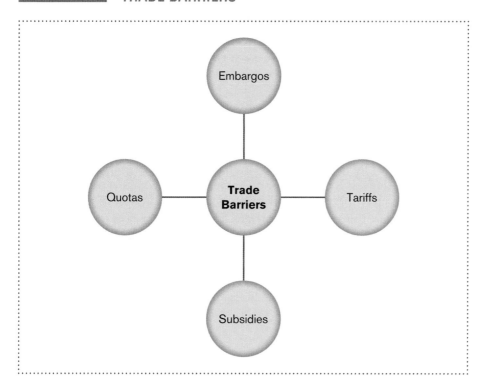

Embargos. An **embargo** is *a total ban on the importing of a product from one or more countries.* This protects domestic companies and employees, as it stops foreign products from entering the home country. *Import standards* are often set to protect the health and safety of citizens, but they are also used like an embargos to ban imports. The standards are often set higher than required of domestic companies. India bans imported chicken, meat, and eggs from the United States, claiming the embargo is to protect the health of its domestic livestock from bird flu.[18] For political and security reasons, the U.S. government has embargos on imports of all or some goods from certain countries, including Afghanistan, Iran, and Iraq. It also bans the export sale of all or certain products to some foreign countries, such as military weapons.

Quotas. A **quota** *sets a limit on the number or volume of a product that can be imported or exported during a set period.* This tends to decrease the supply of products, which results in higher prices of the imported products. China only allows 20 foreign films to be released in its movie theaters each year.[19]

Subsidies. Subsidies *include government grants, loans, and tax breaks given to domestic companies.* A grant is a gift that doesn't have to be paid back. Loans are usually set at below-market interest rates. Tax breaks allow the company to retain more of its revenues. Subsidies tend to lower the cost and price of domestic products to compete with foreign companies. Jet manufacturers **Boeing** (U.S.) and **Airbus** (European Union) complain about government subsidies creating unfair advantages for the other company.

Tariffs. A **tariff** *is a direct tax on imports to make them more expensive.* This tends to increase the price of exports, making them closer to the price of domestic products. The U.S. import tariff on trucks is 25 percent. Thus, a $20,000 imported truck will tend to sell for $25,000, with the $5,000 in taxes going to the U.S.

embargo A total ban on the importing of a product from one or more countries.

quota Sets a limit on the number or volume of a product that can be imported or exported during a set period.

subsidies Form of financial support, including government grants, loans, and tax breaks given to domestic companies.

tariff A direct tax on imports to make them more expensive.

government.[20] Some companies, including **Yingli Green Energy**, voluntarily raise prices and limit exports to avoid tariffs that would be more costly.[21]

For more information on U.S. trade barriers, visit www.usa.gov. Although most countries use protectionism, the trend is to decrease protectionism through dropping barriers to free trade.[22] Our next two topics discuss how countries are facilitating global free trade with the help of the WTO.

World Trade Organization (WTO)

Organizations and governments are working together to develop free trade among countries. Replacing the **General Agreement on Tariffs and Trade (GATT)**, the **World Trade Organization (WTO)** is an international organization dedicated to global free trade. It is a forum for governments to negotiate trade agreements. The WTO is a place for countries to settle trade disputes. It operates and enforces a system of trade rules. Essentially, the WTO is a place where its 159 member governments try to sort out the trade problems they face with each other. A WTO panel can order unfair practices stopped or allow the country claiming unfair practices to retaliate. The WTO also provides technical assistance and training for developing countries.[23] Visit http://www.wto.org for updated information about the World Trade Organization. Virtually all 159 WTO countries are members of one or more trade agreements administered by the WTO, our next topic.

Trade Agreements

There are efforts mapping the way to a global free-trade agreement.[24] But until then, here are six major trade agreements around the globe.

The Americas. The **North American Free Trade Agreement (NAFTA)** was implemented in 1994, with the United States–Canada Free Trade Agreement of 1998 being expanded to include Mexico. NAFTA called for immediately eliminating duties on the majority of tariffs on products traded among the United States, Canada, and Mexico and gradually phasing out other tariffs. MNCs, including **Volkswagen, Delphi, Home Depot**, and **Campbell Soup** are taking advantage of favorable tax and trade agreements with direct investments in operations in Mexico, and benefits start to flow back to the United States.[25]

The United States is also a member of the **Dominican Republic-Central American Free Trade Agreement (CAFTA-DR)** with the DR and five Central American countries.[26] For more information on CAFTA-DR, visit http://www.caftadr.net. There is also a trading block **Union of South American Nations (UNASUR)** with 12 South American countries.

Europe. The largest European trade alliance is the **European Union (EU)**, formerly called the European Community, which consists of 27 member states as of 2013. Other countries have applied to become members. Since 1993, the EU has been a single market without national barriers to travel, employment, investment, and trade. EU members have developed a single currency (the euro) to create an Economic and Monetary Union (EMU). Europeans in 17 EU countries and five others use the euro currency.[27] The euro makes conducting business and traveling much easier in this trading bloc. For more about the EU and its members, visit http://europa.eu.

Asia. Asia and the Pacific Rim comprise an important trade area. The **Association of Southeast Asian Nations (ASEAN)** is a trade agreement among 10 countries.[28] For updated information, visit http://www.aseansec.org. The **Asia-Pacific Economic Cooperation (APEC)** is a forum for 21 Pacific Rim countries (formally Member

EXHIBIT 3-2   TRADE AGREEMENTS

Agreement	Members	Website
North American Free Trade Agreement (NAFTA)	3 North American countries	http://www.naftanow.org/
Dominican Republic-Central American Free Trade Agreement (CAFTA-DR)	United States, Dominican Republic, and 5 Central American countries	http://www.caftadr.net
Union of South American Nations (UNASUR)	12 South American countries	http://www.unasursg.org/
European Union (EU)	21 European member states	http://europa.eu
Association of Southeast Asian Nations (ASEAN)	10 Asian and Pacific Rim countries	http://www.aseansec.org
Asia-Pacific Economic Cooperation (APEC)	21 Pacific Rim countries	http://www.apecsec.org

Economies) that seeks to promote free trade and economic cooperation throughout the Asia-Pacific region.

Exchange Rates and the Balance of Payments

Here we discuss these two topics and how they affect foreign trade.

Exchange Rates. The *exchange rate* is how much of one country's currency you get for that of another country. Your own currency is considered strong when you get more of another country's currency than you give up in the exchange and weak when you get less. If you are an American traveling to other countries, a strong dollar gives you greater buying power, as you get more for your money.

However, when a U.S. business conducts foreign trade, the opposite is true. When the dollar is weak, foreign goods are generally priced higher to cover exchange-rate losses, making them more expensive in the United States, but when it is strong, foreign goods are less expensive. See Exhibit 3-3 for an example. Thus, a weak dollar helps to create opportunities for American global businesses. However, a weak currency doesn't help domestic businesses, and some say it hurts them. As I was writing this, the Japanese yen was weak, allowing **Toyota**, **Honda**, and the other automakers the opportunity to have to price advantage over U.S. manufacturers **GM** and **Ford**.[29] So exchange rates generally affect the prices of products and services in foreign trade. For current exchange rates, visit http://www.x-rates.com.

Balance of Trade. The total country exchange results in the balance of trade. The *balance of trade* is the difference between the value of the products (including services) it exports and the value of the products it imports. A country importing more than it exports runs a trade deficit, and a country exporting more than it imports runs a trade surplus. For several years, the United States has run a trade deficit with most other countries, while China has run trade surpluses. With a trade deficit, assets flow out of the country, whereas with a surplus, assets flow into the country. The balance of trade is affected by trade barriers that can be used to stop deficits, the **WTO** through global trade rules, and currency exchange rates through giving countries the advantage in foreign trade. For more information on U.S. trade policies, visit www.usa.gov.

EXHIBIT 3-3   EXCHANGE RATES

Suppose you are selling a product in China for 8,000 yuan. With an exchange rate of 8 yuan to 1 dollar, you get $1,000 (8,000 [yuan selling price] divided by 8 [8 yuan = $1]) for each product you sell. Suppose that this price and exchange rate give you a 25-percent profit margin. Now let's see what happens with the extreme fluctuations in exchange rates that sometimes occur:

- If the exchange rate becomes 6 yuan to 1 dollar, the yuan is strong (and the dollar is weak). When you exchange the yuan for dollars, you get $1,333.33 (8,000 [yuan selling price] divided by 6 [6 yuan = $1]) for each product you sell.
- Now let's make the dollar strong (and the yuan weak). If the exchange rate goes to 10 yuan to the dollar, you get $800 (8,000 [yuan selling price] divided by 10 [10 yuan = $1]).

You can either change your yuan selling price to maintain your 25 percent profit margin or make more or less based on the exchange rate. Now think about the complexity of FedEx doing business in more than 100 currencies.

Standard of Living and the Effects of Foreign Trade

Our standard of living is based on foreign trade, so let's discuss how it affects us next.

Standard of Living. *Standard of living* refers to the level of wealth, comfort, material goods, and necessities available to a certain socioeconomic class in a certain geographic area. People in developed countries have a higher standard of living because they get paid more and have greater *purchasing power*—the relative cost of a product in different countries. The *Economist* magazine produces the Big Mac index yearly to show the differences in purchasing power (how much you get for your money) across countries. Americans pay an average of $4.20 for a Big Mac versus $4.73 in Canada, $5.68 in Brazil, and $6.81 in Switzerland, so diners in those countries get less for their money than do Americans. Conversely, it cost $3.54 in Turkey, $2.55 in Russia, $2.44 in China, and only $1.62 in India, so those buyers get more for their money.[30]

Coca-Cola is one of the best-known global brands; although it has saturated the U.S. market, it continues to grow by selling Coke globally, adjusting its pricing strategy for different cultures. Photo from Laura Chiesa/Demotix/Corbis.

It sounds great to say, "Let's sell our products in the most populated countries—China and India." However, the majority of the people can't afford many of the products produced in the developed countries, even what we call inexpensive items like Coke. How many Cokes would you buy if you made less than $1 an hour? Indians only drink 12 eight-ounce bottles of **Coca-Cola** a year compared to 240 in Brazil and 90 bottles globally.[31] Prices also have to be lower. But of course with high volume, and with increasing global standards of living, global business can be very profitable.

The Effects of Foreign Trade. Foreign trade is generally agreed to be beneficial to developing countries. Although advocacy groups complain that MNCs take advantage of cheap labor and have employees working in sweat shops, these people are willing to work in these conditions because it does in fact increase their standard of living. With time, wages and working conditions do improve. America once faced the same situation during the Industrial Revolution. Some complain about jobs being moved overseas. But others say total jobs are not lost; it is the type of jobs the country specializes in that change.[32] Protecting inefficient jobs only raises the cost of the products and services and increases the prices to customers.

Clearly free trade increases choices, competition, and purchasing power while at the same time decreasing the cost of housing, food, clothing, other necessities, and luxury products and services—increasing virtually everyone's standard of living. The fact is that most people are concerned about the price of the product and don't really care where a product is made. Some organizations and people complain about **Walmart** and other MNCs contributing to jobs going overseas to low-cost workers in sweat shops, but millions of people buy Walmart's lower-priced products and services.

As foreign trade increases business opportunities, it also creates challenges, as managers have to be effective in competing not only at home with domestic companies but also all over the globe with internationals and MNCs. In the next section, we discuss the forms of global business, and throughout this book, you will learn how to be an effective manager to help you meet the challenge of globalization.

Taking a Business Global

Businesses sell their products and services globally because they can make more money than they can selling in only their home countries.[33] Businesses such as **Pfizer**, **Kraft**, and **GE** get a big portion of their sales from overseas. **KFC** gets roughly half of all its sales overseas and twice as much revenue from China as from the United States.[34] **GM** gets 33 percent of its sales in North America (NAFTA), 17 percent from Europe, 11 percent from South America, and 39 percent from the rest of the world.[35] Sales are growing globally; in China in 2012, 46 million credit cards were issued, and global banks, including **Citigroup** and **Deutsche Bank**, are competing for the business.[36] This is why **Coca-Cola** and other companies are aggressively growing globally, especially in China and India.[37] A domestic business can become a global one through any of six activities discussed here. Exhibit 3-4 presents these methods in order by cost and risk and indicates what types of companies tend to use them.

WORK
APPLICATION 3-4

Would you be willing to pay more for the same product made domestically than abroad? For example, if Nike made sneakers in American and sold them for $125 and made them abroad and sold them for $100, which would you buy?

LO 3-3

List the six activities that make a business a global one, in order from lowest to highest cost and risk.

EXHIBIT 3-4   TAKING A BUSINESS GLOBAL

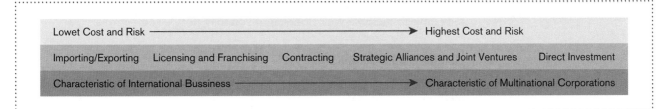

Note that global sourcing can be used alone (at low cost/risk), but is commonly used in tandem with other global strategies.

Global Sourcing

Global sourcing *is hiring others outside the firm to perform work worldwide.* It is also called *outsourcing* and *offshoring*. Global managers look worldwide for the best deal on materials/parts, labor, and so forth and a location (any country in the

global sourcing Hiring others outside the organization to perform work worldwide.

world) for producing their products and services. Outsourcing saves money and better allocates global resources, as it benefits everyone because countries specialize in what they can do better than others.[38] **Ford** and other automakers get their parts from all over the globe. **Paper Converting Machine Company (PCMC)** has some design work done by engineers in India that are paid less than its American workers for the same job. There is a saying: "Do what you do best and outsource the rest." As a global-minded manager, you will need to scan the world, not just your country, for the best deal. The other six methods of going global usually encompass global sourcing. Your college may use a global source to run its bookstore and dining hall.

Global sourcing also has some disadvantages. The company is dependent on the outsourcer to deliver the requested quantity of the product when it is needed. The contractor may not make the product to the company's specifications; products can be of poor quality and even faulty. In either case, the company, not the external outsource firm, gets the blame and lost sales. The **Boeing** 787 Dreamliner was behind scheduled delivery seven times because of suppliers, and the jet was grounded because of a battery made by another company.[39]

Importing and Exporting

When *importing,* a domestic firm *buys* products from foreign firms and sells them at home. **Pier 1 Imports'** business revolves around searching the globe for foreign goods to sell at home. When *exporting,* a domestic firm *sells* its products to foreign buyers. In 2013, **Hershey**, in its first launch beyond the U.S. market, sold its Lancaster candy under the name Yo-man in China.[40] One myth about small businesses is that it is too difficult for them to go global, but in reality they account for a large percentage of exports. The U.S. Export-Import Bank (Ex-Im Bank) helps businesses of all sizes go global. For more information, visit its website at www .exim.gov. **FedEx** and **UPS** both offer a variety of services to help any size business use global sourcing and importing and exporting.

One big advantage of exporting is that manages have complete control over the operations of the company at home, but there is also a potential disadvantage of having to work with an importer who may not give your product the sales promotion you would like to have. It is more difficult to work with others abroad because of language and cultural differences. The major disadvantage is that the target importing country may institute barriers to trade—embargos—and stop you from selling in the country, they can impose quotas to limit your sales, they can give your competitors subsidies to keep their costs and prices lower than yours, or they can put tariffs on your products, making them more expensive and hurting your sales. A third disadvantage to exporting is the cost transportation adds to the cost of your product, and the price may not be competitive in other countries. Last, you are subject to exchange rates. If your currency is strong, you may have to increase your prices, and you may not be competitive.

Licensing and Franchising

Also known as *cooperative contracts,* internationals and MNCs use these two methods to go global.

Licensing. In licensing, a licensor agrees to give a licensee the right to make its products or services or use its intellectual property in exchange for a royalty. Under a global licensing agreement, the domestic individual or company licensor allows another foreign company licensee to make its product, sell its service, or use its intellectual property—brand name, trademark, a particular technology, a patent, or a copyright—in exchange for a royalty in a particular foreign market. **Fantastics** has a license to sell college and professional sports team (NBA,

WORK
APPLICATION 3-5

Select a business and identify how it uses global sourcing and/or importing and exporting.

licensing The process of a licensor agreeing to licensee the right to make its products or services or use its intellectual property in exchange for a royalty.

MLB, NHL, NFL) apparel and accessories.[41] **Disney** allows other companies to make its cartoon characters into all kinds of products. When Disney comes out with a new movie, **McDonald's** and other companies can get a license to make characters that are given in Happy Meals. Athletes, including Michael Jordan and, more recently, Kevin Durant, license their names to be placed on **Nike** products sold globally.[42]

McDonald's has been very successful in franchising globally. Pictured here is a McDonald's in St Petersburg, Russia. Photo from Alex Segne/Alamy.

Franchising. In **franchising,** *the franchisor licenses the entire business to the franchisee for a fee and royalties.* The franchiser provides a combination of trademark, equipment, materials, training, managerial guidelines, consulting advice, and cooperative advertising to the franchisee for an initial fee and a percentage of the revenues. There are more **Subway** restaurants in the world than any other restaurant chain (39,441 in 102 countries as of this writing), making it a leader in the global development of the quick-service restaurant industry.[43] **McDonald's** has more than 32,000 locations in more than 100 countries as of this writing.[44]

Cooperative arrangements also have disadvantages, as it is difficult to oversee franchises in other countries. Some franchisees have reported lower sales to avoid paying the franchisor royalties. The licensee can also poorly manage the franchise and hurt the franchisor's reputation. The franchised product can also be culture bound. **Yum! Brands KFC** is more successful in China than is **McDonald's** largely because it offers foods tailored to the local culture's preferences, such as the Dragon Twister.

WORK
APPLICATION 3-6

Select a business you buy from that has a global license or franchise.

Contracting

Contracting is similar to global sourcing, but it tends to be on a large scale. Global product sourcing commonly includes using materials and parts from other companies in the firm's product. Conversely, contracting is having the foreign company actually make the product for you. Like with global sourcing, the contracting company is dependent on the outsourcer to deliver the requested quantity and quality of the products and services when they are needed. All kinds of products and services can be contracted.

With global **contract manufacturing,** *a company has a foreign firm manufacture the products that it sells as its own.* Many supermarkets and warehouse clubs use contract manufactures, including **Costco Kirkland** brand, to sell products to compete with national and international brands. **Nike** focuses on designing and marketing its products; it doesn't own any manufacturing facilities; virtually all of its products are made in foreign countries. **Foxconn** is a multinational Taiwanese electronics contract manufacturing company. It is the world's largest electronics contract manufacturer measured by revenues. Its clients include **Amazon.com, Apple, Cisco, HP,** and **Visio** (America), Nintendo, **Sony,** and **Toshiba** (Japan), and **Nokia** (Finland). Notable products that the company manufactures include the Kindle, iPad, iPhone, iPod, PlayStation 3, and Wii U.[45] Jamaican Olympic gold metal sprinter Usain Bolt contracted with software developer **RockLive** to launch a branded app to expand his marketing reach. Bolt's app has been downloaded more than 3 million times.[46]

All kinds of services can also be contracted to other companies. There is global *management contracting,* in which a company provides management services for

franchising An entrepreneurial venture in which a franchisor licenses a business to the franchisee for a fee and royalties.

contract manufacturing Contracting a foreign firm to manufacture products a company will sell as its own.

a foreign firm. **Hilton** manages hotels and resorts for other companies globally. As stated, global sourcing and contact manufacturing have the same disadvantages. Customer-service call centers is also a management contract that some firms have used in India. There are also global cleaning and food service providers.

Strategic Alliances and Joint Ventures

Two similar ways to go global with partners are through strategic alliances and joint ventures.

Strategic Alliances. A **strategic alliance** *is an agreement to share resources that does not necessarily involve creating a new company.* The two (or more) companies remain separate and independently controlled but share resources to sell products and services in other countries, to develop new or improved products, and/or to build production facilities. Your college may have global strategic alliances, such as study abroad programs. **Springfield College** offered its master's degree through an alliance with the **Health and Behavioral Science College**, using its facilities and some of its faculty in Israel. **Garmin** (land navigation) and **Volvo Penta** (commercial boat engines and propulsions systems) created a strategic alliance to jointly develop and sell marine navigation, instrumentation, and communication equipment.[47] **Honda** and **GE** developed a new jet engine. **GM** and **Toyota** built a factory in California, and both made cars for the U.S. market. French **Renault** (with its Leaf) helped Israeli **Better Place** develop an electric car battery, but it went out of business.[48]

Joint Ventures. The joint venture is considered to be most common strategic alliance. A **joint venture** *is created when two or more firms share ownership of a new company.* The two (or more) companies remain separate and independently controlled but share the ownership and control of the new company created through the partnership. The business model created and enforced in China is for foreign companies to have a Chinese partner. None of the top 10 car models sold in China are made by domestic companies, such as **Chery, Geely,** and **Great Wall**. U.S. manufacturer **GM** and its joint-venture partners created a new brand—**Baojun**.[49] **Daimler AG**, German automaker of **Mercedes-Benz**, has a joint venture with **Beiqui Forton Motor Company** that sells large trucks in China. Daimler gets access to Beiqui's existing network of manufacturing and selling its trucks, and Beiqui gets to use Daimler's technology, especially diesel engines and exhaust systems.[50] **Starbucks** expanded to India through a joint venture with **Tata Global Beverages**. **Starbucks-Tata** plans to open 3,000 stores in India.[51]

It is very difficult to go to a foreign country and operate a new venture. Therefore, alliances and joint ventures are especially advantageous to smaller partners who want to go global but don't have the resources to operate on their own in a foreign country and for the partner that doesn't have the resources to expand domestically. Conversely, as with the other methods of going global, it has its disadvantages. Sharing the cost and risk and splitting the profits may result in one of the partners not living up to the expectations of the other. Chinese companies have been accused of gaining knowledge through joint ventures and then using the knowledge to compete against their partners in their own home country. For example, Chinese automakers are expected to sell cars globally in the future. Alliances are very difficult to manage because the partners have to successfully integrate four cultures: two organizational cultures and two country cultures. The failure rate of joint ventures is high, so common advice is to create a detailed contract specifying responsibilities between the partners.

strategic alliance An agreement to share resources that does not necessarily involve creating a new company.

joint venture Two or more firms sharing ownership of a new company.

Direct Investment

Direct investment *is the building or buying of operating facilities in a foreign country.* It is also called *wholly owned affiliates or subsidiaries.* **ExxonMobil (Case Question 2)** uses all of the methods for going global, but it is primarily at the highest level with direct investments in all continents. **Haier Group** based in Qingdao, Shandong, China, owns a **Haier America** subsidiary in Camden, South Carolina, manufacturing refrigerators. **Toyota, Honda, Hyundai, Mercedes-Benz,** and **BMW** own production facilities in the United States but sell their autos through American dealerships. The parent/holding company can manage the foreign subsidiary with great *centralized control,* making decisions at home for the subsidiary. Alternatively, the parent can essentially let the subsidiary have its own *decentralized local control,* making its own decisions similar to a separate company.

A direct investment gives the company full control, and it gets all of the profits from its foreign subsidiary. Conversely, as shown in Exhibit 3-5, direct investment is the highest-cost and -risk method of going global—it is very expensive and the business can lose money. Thus, only an estimated 33 percent of MNCs go global this way. As with a strategic alliance or joint venture, you still need to integrate the home organizational and national culture with the subsidiary organizational and national culture successfully to be profitable.

WORK
APPLICATION 3-8

Select a business that uses strategic alliances, joint ventures, and/or direct investments globally.

3-1 APPLYING THE CONCEPT

Taking a Business Global

Identify which activity of global businesses is described in each statement.

A. global sourcing
B. importing and exporting
C. licensing and franchising
D. contracting
E. strategic alliances and joint venture
F. direct investment

_____ 1. Whirlpool makes its kitchen appliances in its factory in Europe.

_____ 2. Dell assembles its computers in the United States and sells them online to people in Japan.

_____ 3. The Big Y supermarket chain has a Canadian company make potato chips packaged under the Big Y brand name for sale in its U.S. stores.

_____ 4. Spalding Sporting Goods buys the rubber for basketballs from Brazil.

_____ 5. Subway allows a Chinese businessperson to open a Subway in Beijing.

_____ 6. Springfield College offers its degree programs in Israel at the Health and Behavioral Sciences College, which provides the facilities and administrative support.

_____ 7. Philips in France makes TVs using speakers from Japan.

_____ 9. Tony Tarnow Tires in the United States buys tires from Bridgestone in Japan for retail sale.

_____ 10. Amazon.com buys a warehouse in Spain through which it distributes books ordered from the United States by customers in the EU.

_____ 15. The Children's Television Network gives a Mexican company the right to make its Sesame Street character puppets.

Global Business Practices

Both multinational corporations and small international companies compete in the global environment, and they have one thing in common but use different business practices based on size and resources.

Think Globally, Act Locally. One thing internationals and MNCs have in common is to think globally, but they adapt to local market needs. **McDonald's** sells the Big Mac in India, but it is not made of beef, as in India it is not culturally

direct investment The building or buying of operating facilities in a foreign country.

acceptable to eat cows. **Kraft Foods** sells Green Tea Oreos in China to satisfy local taste.[52] The small U.S. company **Alameda Machine Shop** sells custom-made parts in metric sizes in Europe.

Differences in Business Practices of Internationals and MNCs. There are six major business practices that differ between these two types of global companies. **ExxonMobil (Case Question 3)**, being the largest MNC, does think globally and act locally, but it also uses all of the business practices listed in Exhibit 3-5 and discussed in the following:[53]

- **Global Management Team.** Leading MNCs have top-level managers who are foreign nationals and subsidiaries managed by foreign nationals. Small businesses often can't afford to hire foreign managers, but some use consultants and agents.

- **Global Strategy.** In an MNC, there is one strategy for the entire company, not one per subsidiary. Worldwide coordination attains economies of scale but still allows a country manager to respond to local consumer needs and counter local competition.[54] Global strategy utilizes direct investment, joint ventures, and strategic alliances. The common small-business global strategies are outsourcing and importing and exporting. We discuss these strategies in detail later in this chapter.

- **Global Operations and Products.** MNCs have standardized operations worldwide to attain economies of scale, and they make products to be sold worldwide, not just in local markets. Unit headquarters are placed in the country with the best resources to do the job rather than in the home country. Small businesses can sell standard global products, but they commonly use contractors and exporting.

- **Global Technology and R&D.** Technology and research and development (R&D) are centralized in one country rather than duplicated at each subsidiary to develop world products. Global sourcing of technology and R&D is used. Small businesses are creative; though they have limited funds for R&D, they are often quick to adopt new technology.

EXHIBIT 3-5   BUSINESS PRACTICES OF GLOBAL COMPANIES

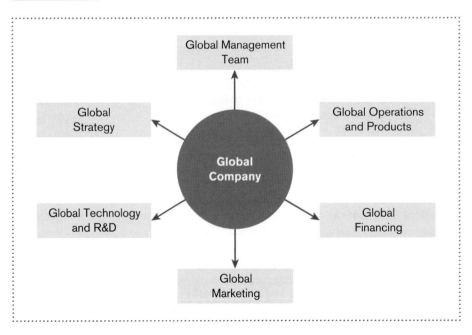

3-2 APPLYING THE CONCEPT

Global Practices

Identify each practice as more likely to be used by large or small global companies:

A. large MNCs
B. small international companies

____ 11. Use importing and exporting to operate globally.

____ 12. Include foreign nationals among their top-level managers.
____ 13. Have their own operating facilities in many countries.
____ 14. Develop the latest technology through R&D.
____ 15. Develop a product in one country and then bring the product to other countries.

- **Global Financing.** MNCs search world markets to get the best rates and terms when borrowing money for the long term; short-term financing is largely arranged in individual countries using local financial institutions. Product prices are quoted in foreign currencies rather than the home currency. MNCs sell stock in their subsidiary to the people in the country in which the subsidiary is located. Many small business owners turn to the Export-Import Bank (Ex-Im Bank) for help going global.[55] For more information on the Ex-Im Bank, visit http://www.exim.gov.

- **Global Marketing.** Global products and marketing are adapted for local markets.[56] Advertisements are often developed by local agencies. Products used to be developed in the home market and then brought to other countries later, but the trend is toward global introduction of products Small international businesses can use export management companies, agents, and distributor services to conduct their marketing. In addition, small business managers can attend trade shows, network through trade centers, and advertise in industry publications.

WORK APPLICATION 3-9

Select a company and identify as many of its global business practices as you can.

3-2 JOIN THE DISCUSSION ETHICS & SOCIAL RESPONSIBILITY

File Sharing

Since the early 2000s, some peer-to-peer (P2P) file-sharing networks and services have been targeted by music companies and an industry watch group, the **Recording Industry Association of America (RIAA),** which represents musicians, for copyright infringement and shut down. The music companies complain that they are losing profits and that musicians are losing royalties as people download music for free, which violates copyright law. The RIAA also expanded into lawsuits against individuals. Movies, software, and other copyright material are also being illegally copied through file sharing (piracy).

According to the **International Federation of the Phonographic Industry,** piracy is a real problem, as 95 percent of all music downloads violate copyrights.[57] In many countries because some governments don't have the desire or resources

to enforce copyright laws. Some governments even resist allowing companies to take legal action against companies and individuals.

1. Is it ethical and socially responsible for file-sharing companies to give people the means to download music, movies, or software for free?
2. Is it ethical and socially responsible for people to download music, movies, or software for free, which prevents recording, film, or software companies and artists from getting any royalties?
3. Is it ethical and socially responsible for countries to ignore and even resist enforcing copyright laws? Should all countries enforce copyright laws?

So, as you can see, business is global. As we have mentioned, to succeed in the global environment, the company must deal with its own organizational culture and national cultures in other countries and integrate them. To help you understand how to do this, the rest of this chapter discusses managing your organizational culture with a diverse workforce and then managing global national cultural diversity.

LO 3-4

Discuss diversity and why it is important.

WORKPLACE DIVERSITY

In this section, we will discuss what diversity is and answer the question, "Is it really important?" Next, we explain the types of diversity and end by discussing how to manage diversity.

What Is Diversity?

Let's start by stating not only what diversity is but also what it isn't, followed by how the United States is diversified, and end with a discussion of why diversity in the workplace is so important.

Diversity. When you are in class, at work, or just out in public somewhere, look around and you will most likely see that people are both the same and different. *Diversity refers to the variety of people with different group identities within the same workplace.* Diversity and work aren't separate because we tend to judge the nature of workers by the gender, race, and other diversity of the people who do it.[58] Workplace diversity includes both employees and customers. See Exhibit 3-6 for a list of four major diversity group identities, which we will discuss shortly.

EXHIBIT 3-6	TYPES OF WORKFORCE DIVERSITY

Age
Sex
Race and Ethnicity
Disability
Other

Differences Between Diversity and Affirmative Action. Diversity and affirmative action are sometimes thought to be the same—but they aren't. *Affirmative action* is purposeful steps to create employment opportunities for minorities and women, whereas diversity is broader in scope as it doesn't focus simply on not discriminating against diverse groups and helping only some of them. Most organizations have moved from affirmative action to valuing diversity,[59] as we discuss throughout this section.

diversity The variety of people with different group identities within the same workplace.

U.S. Diversity. The United States population continues to grow slowly, with around 314 million people.[60] It is rapidly diversifying.[61] The population growth is coming

---

Speaking English

The United States was once known as the "melting pot," as people from all over the world came to the country and adjusted to its culture. In the past, generally, immigrants had to learn English to get a job. Today, however, many organizations hire people who can't speak English, and they use translators and have policies written in multiple languages for these employees. Government agencies at the federal, state, and local levels are also providing translators and written materials in other languages.

1. Why are some organizations no longer requiring workers to speak English?
2. Should a worker be required to be able to speak English to get a job in the United States?
3. Is it ethical and socially responsible to (or not to) hire people who can't speak English and to provide translators and policies written in multiple languages?

EXHIBIT 3-7   U.S. POPULATION CHANGES 2012 TO 2060

Population by Race	2012 Percentage of Total Population	2060 Percentage of Total Population
Native Hawaiian and Other Pacific Islander	0.2%	0.3% ↑
American Indian and Alaska native	1.2%	1.5% ↑
Two or more races	2.4%	6.4% ↑
Asian	5.1%	8.2% ↑
Black	13%	15% ↑
Hispanic of any race	17%	31% ↑ more than double
White (non-Hispanic)	63%	43% ↓

Source: U.S. Census Bureau, reported in the *Wall Street Journal* December 13, 2012, A3.

from minorities, and Hispanics are now the largest minority group.[62] Asians are the fastest-growing, most-educated, and highest-earning immigrant population in America.[63] Today, minority births are now the majority.[64] In 10 states, white children are a minority, and in 23 states, minorities now make up more than 40 percent of the child population.[65] One in 12 children (8 percent) born in America is the offspring of illegal immigrants, making those children U.S. citizens.[66]

The Caucasian population throughout the world, including America, is decreasing, as there are more deaths than births.[67] Globally, the white population is shrinking as there are more deaths than births, and the percentage of the population that is Caucasian is decreasing.[68] By around 2040, less than half of the total U.S. population will be Caucasian.[69] By 2060, Caucasians are estimated to be 43 percent of the population, and one in three people will be Hispanic.[70] See Exhibit 3-7 for population statistics.

Is Diversity Really Important?

Yes! Discrimination is illegal, and promoting diversity creates equal opportunities for all employees, so it is the right thing to do. But diversity is also beneficial to business. Why? Think about this! Even if a company only wanted to hire and do business with Caucasians, do you really believe it could be successful or even survive? Recall that business today is conducted globally. The global white population is decreasing, making diversity an important topic within the workplace.[71] Research shows that diversity can have negative effects by increasing conflict and reducing cohesion but suggests that diversity can have positive effects on financial outcomes when managed effectively.[72] The **Executive Leadership Council (ELC)** says that there is a link between a diverse workplace and innovation, therefore maximizing profitability.[73] Diversity in groups increases creativity,[74] and minorities have sensitivity to developing new products and services that meet the needs of their diverse groups.

People unconsciously favor people of their own social groups, so having diverse employees can bring unique cultural sensitivity that appeals to a diverse customer base.[75] People may complain about having to push a button on their phone to talk in English, but if you want diverse customers, you need employees who can speak their language. **Travelers Insurance** says diversity is a business imperative, and it even advertises its diversity.[76] **ExxonMobil** (Case Question 4) promotes diversity at home in the United States and throughout the globe.

TYPES OF DIVERSITY AND MANAGING DIVERSITY

LO 3-5

Describe the four major types of diversity groups and practices of managing diversity.

WORK APPLICATION 3-10

Explain how diversity is important to your current or past workplace.

As shown in Exhibit 3-6, there are four major types of diverse groups in the workplace, but there are others as well. As you most likely already know, it is illegal to discriminate against diversity groups. **Discrimination** *is illegal because it gives unfair treatment to diversity groups in employment decisions.* Decisions that can involve discrimination include hiring, training, promoting, compensating, and terminating (layoffs/firing). *Stereotyping,* the mistaken generalization of the perceived characteristics of a diversity group to an individual, has negative consequences. Through stereotyping, discrimination has numerous negative consequences, as it threatens one's identity, leading to decreased individual performance, decreased self-esteem, a decreased desire to take on leadership positions, resistance to change efforts, conformance with company rules, conflict between individuals and groups, turnover, and sex-based harassment.[77] So discrimination is not only illegal; it also has negative consequences for the organization. We need to break down stereotypes and assess each individual's qualifications for the job.

We will discuss the legal issues of discrimination in more detail in Chapter 9, Human Resources Management. Here we focus more on the challenges of managing a diverse workforce, breaking down stereotypes, and creating equal opportunities for all individuals. Part of the challenge comes from the fact that people tend to get along better with people in their own group. Do you tend to associate with people of your own age, sex, race, disability or ability, religion, and/or the same knowledge, skills, and attitudes? As a manager, you need to get everyone to work together.

To succeed, we all need to be able to work with people of diverse ages, especially as people are living and working later in life. Photo © iStockphoto.com/GlobalStock.

discrimination An illegal practice that gives unfair treatment to diversity groups in employment decisions.

Age Diversity and Management

There is a wide range of age groups, resulting in different diverse generations in the workplace. To promote age integration, employees and especially managers should understand stereotypes about older workers that are myths. Older employees do cost more the longer they stay as the company pays for salaries, pension plans, and vacation time. But they also cost less because they have more company knowledge, show better judgment, care more about the quality of their work, and are less likely to quit, show up late, or be absent—which are very costly.[78] They also have fewer injuries on the job and cost less in health care cost than younger workers with school-aged children.[79] Other myths include, in general, that older workers can't learn new technologies, that they resist change, and that they are less productive, regardless of the type of job, than younger workers.[80]

So everyone in the organization should realize that they tend to have negative stereotypes that are not based on facts about older workers. Managers should make decisions based on the individual's qualifications for the job to be done regardless of age. Negative stereotypes tend to break down as people get to know each other on a personal level, so be sure younger and older people work together.

Generational difference can also cause conflict at work. Older baby boomers tend to prefer more face-to-face and telephone time, whereas younger Gen Y employees like texting. Baby boomers tend to focus on one task at a time, whereas Gen Ys like to multitask. Everyone needs to be flexible and understanding of individual preferences and find ways to work together effectively, and it's your job as a manager to pull everyone together.

Sex Diversity and Management

Although close to half of the entire workforce are men and half are women, and the number of managers and professional jobs are about the same,[81] women earn only around 81 percent of what men make.[82] The pay disparity has barely budged in more than a decade.[83] Women also face the **glass ceiling**—*the invisible barrier that prevents women and minorities from advancing to the top jobs in organizations.* In the United States, only 13 percent of all top managers at *Fortune* 500 companies are women, but the number is even much lower in most other countries at less than 5 percent.[84] In 2012, the United States had 18 women CEOs of *Fortune* 500 companies, or 3.6 percent.[85] Female board of directors membership was 16 percent. Italy, with 6 percent women board members, passed a law requiring that one third of board members be women.[86] There are negative stereotypes against women and minorities advancing. Complete Self-Assessment 3–2 to learn about your attitudes toward women and minorities advancing before reading on.

The **Equal Employment Opportunity Commission (EEOC)** receives between 23,000 and 28,000 charges of sex-based discrimination per year.[87] Each statement in Self-Assessment 3–2 is a negative attitude about women and minorities at work. However, research has shown all of these statements to be false; they are considered myths. Discrimination is considered the most significant factor in holding both women and minorities back from the top jobs.[88] Such statements stereotype women and minorities unfairly and prevent them from getting jobs and advancing in organizations. Thus, part of managing diversity and diversity training is to help overcome these negative attitudes and to provide equal opportunities for all. Mentoring, which we will discuss later, is a great help. We also need to make sure that male-dominated social activities, especially networks, don't unintentionally exclude women and minorities. The human resources department should also have an open-door policy so that people who feel they have been discriminated against can talk about it and have the employer conduct a fair, confidential investigation of the situation. In doing so, the company can avoid potential lawsuits.

Also, there are sex- and race-segregated occupations.[89] Some jobs are dominated by one sex or the other—for example, there are more men in military service and construction and women in nursing and elementary school teaching. Thus, we need to look at the qualifications of the individual and not discourage people and, much worse, discriminate against them by not giving them jobs they are qualified to do. COO Sheryl Sandberg of **Facebook**, who is given much of the credit for growing the company, is promoting making it safe to talk about gender in the workplace. In her book *Lean In: Women, Work, and the Will to Lead,* Sandberg suggests more women get into the higher-paying jobs in STEM (science, technology, engineering, and mathematics).[90] Warren Buffett, chairman of **Berkshire Hathaway**, says women are the key to America's prosperity and asks fellow males to get on board and fully employ the talent of all its citizens.[91]

Race and Ethnicity Diversity and Management

Race and ethnicity are similar yet different. *Race* is a biological characteristic, such as skin color, that creates diverse group identities. *Ethnicity* is a social trait, such as cultural background, customs, or allegiances, again creating diverse groups.

glass ceiling The invisible barrier that prevents women and minorities from advancing to the top jobs in organizations.

3-2 SELF ASSESSMENT

Attitudes About Women and Minorities Advancing

Be honest in this self-assessment, as your assessment will not be accurate if you don't. Also, you should not be asked to share your score with others.

Answer the 10 questions below twice, once related to women and the other related to minorities. Place the number 1, 2, 3, 4, or 5 on the line before each statement for women and at the end of the statement for minorities.

Agree				Disagree
5	4	3	2	1

Women   *Minorities*

_____ 1. Women/Minorities lack motivation to get ahead.   1. _____

_____ 2. Women/Minorities lack the education necessary to get ahead.   2. _____

_____ 3. Women/Minorities working has caused rising unemployment among white men.   3. _____

_____ 4. Women/Minorities are not strong enough or emotionally stable enough to succeed
in high-pressure jobs.   4. _____

_____ 5. Women/Minorities have a lower commitment to work than white men.   5._____

_____ 6. Women/Minorities are too emotional to be effective managers.   6. _____

_____ 7. Women/Minorities managers have difficulty in situations calling for quick and precise
decisions.   7. _____

_____ 8. Women/Minorities have a higher turnover rate than white men.   8. _____

_____ 9. Women/Minorities are out of work more often than white men.   9. _____

_____10. Women/Minorities have less interest in advancing than white men.   10. _____

Total

Women—To determine your attitude score toward women, add up the total of your answers on the lines before each statement and place it on the total line and on the following continuum.

10	20	30	40	50

Positive attitude   Negative attitude

Minorities—To determine your attitude score toward minorities, add up the total of your answers on the lines after each statement and place it on the total line and on the following continuum.

10	2	30	40	50

Positive attitude   Negative attitude

Most people identify themselves as part of a racial group; therefore, race diversity is an integral part of a country's culture. As discussed under the heading U.S. Diversity, the global white population is decreasing and the other diverse groups are growing at a fast pace, so racial equality is imperative.[92]

As also stated, like women, minorities face discrimination, but even more so. Evidence suggests that blacks are at a disadvantage when they are evaluated in terms of their leadership ability, which hurts career advancement.[93] In 2012, there were only six black CEOs of *Fortune* 500 companies, around 1 percent, including the first and only black woman CEO Ursula Burns of **Xerox**.[94] For the current list, visit www.blackentrepreneurprofile.com.

Review Self-Assessment 3–2. How is your attitude toward minority advancement? The EEOC receives more race discrimination charges than any other type of complaint, with between 26,000 and 35,000 cases per year.[95] But this is only the tip of the iceberg, as most people don't file complaints with the EEOC. Research shows that minorities are discriminated against in hiring, training, compensating, and promoting opportunities. Around 13 percent of Americans are black, but only around 7 percent are managers and 3 percent are CEOs. Hispanics make up around 17 percent of the population but only around 8 percent of managers and 5 percent of CEOs. Asians, however, are doing well with around 5 percent of the population, the managers, and the CEOs.[96] Part of the reason affirmative action became popular was to help eliminate racial discrimination and create more opportunities for minorities.

To have equal opportunities for all, a good place to start is with simple statistics. Are the hiring, promoting, and quitting rates significantly different between the sexes and between whites and minorities? Differences don't necessarily mean discrimination, but you can take action to improve the numbers. **Darden Restaurants'** workforce has 42 percent minorities and is one of the 100 best companies to work for.[97]

Make sure selection and promotion criteria are clear and objective to help avoid racial bias. Training managers that make hiring and promotion decisions to understand the problem and to be objective can help. Businesses around the world realize that a diverse supplier base with **minority business enterprises (MBEs)** is a critical competitive advantage, as MBEs better connect with their own diverse customer base, and in most cases minority suppliers offer better price, service, and value.[98] For more information on MBEs, visit the **National Minority Supplier Development Council (NMSC)** at www.nmsdc.org. **BP** has a minority member as its director of supplier diversity, and she works with the NMSC to find suppliers, as it is committed to a more inclusive supply chain.[99] **ExxonMobil (Case Question 4)** has some 160,000 suppliers and does use MBEs.

Disability Diversity and Management

Back in 1990, the Americans with Disabilities Act (ADA) defined a **disability** as *a mental or physical impairment that substantially limits one or more major life activities*. The law prohibits discrimination against people with disabilities (www.ada.gov) by treating them differently because of their disabilities. The ADA also requires companies to make reasonable accommodations so their facilities are accessible to people with disabilities to enable them to perform jobs.[100] Largely due to ADA, people with disabilities are getting more job opportunities.

However, of the four major types of diversity, they face the most discrimination. Only around 37 percent of people with disabilities have jobs, they are disproportionately employed in low-status or part-time jobs with little chance for advancement, and they are twice as likely to live in poverty.[101] Negative stereotypes are myths, as studies have found that with reasonable accommodations, people with disabilities perform their jobs just as well as people without disabilities, and they have better safety records and are no more likely to be absent or to quit their jobs.[102]

To give equal opportunities to people with disabilities, the first thing we need to do is change our mindset. Instead of looking for disabilities, look for *abilities*. For example, a person in a wheelchair is perfectly capable of most jobs that require the employee to sit. People with disabilities are good candidates for work-from-home jobs. We should actively recruit qualified workers with disabilities. Companies also need to provide reasonable accommodations; some don't cost anything and others are not expensive. At **Laser Soft Infosystems**, 15 percent of the workforce is people with disabilities.[103]

disability a mental or physical impairment that substantially limits an individual's ability.

Managers need to create and maintain an environment in which people with disabilities can feel comfortable disclosing their need for reasonable accommodations. Training can help get people without disabilities comfortable working with people who have disabilities. One thing to note is that people with disabilities are people first, so they prefer to be called people with disabilities, not disabled people.

Other Types of Diversity and Management

There are all kinds of other ways that people are diverse in the workplace, such as weight and sexual orientation, but here we limit the discussion to two of them.

Religious Diversity and Management. Although fewer people today attend organized religious services, many people identify themselves as belonging to a religion. It is illegal to discriminate against a person based on religion. To promote equal opportunity for all, we need to recognize and be aware of different religions and their beliefs, paying attention to when religious holidays fall. Companies are being flexible with schedules to accommodate religious diversity needs.

Knowledge, Skills, and Attitudes. Based on different levels of education, training, and experience, employees tend to have diverse knowledge, skills, and attitudes (KSAs). People in different functional areas of the company (operations, finance, marketing, human resources) tend to see things from their own departmental perspective and bring different contributions to the company. To maximize performance, companies are using teams and bringing in a variety of KSAs.[104] They are breaking down the barriers of departments so that everyone focuses on improving company products and services and the process to run the business. You will learn how to manage teams in Chapter 8.

Managing Diversity

We've already discussed ways to manage each of the major diverse groups by promoting diversity to create equal opportunities for all. Here we present approaches that apply to multiple diverse groups as well as all employees.

Diversity Policies and Practices. Companies need active policies and practices to promote diversity. The policies and practices should promote a diversity climate that is part of the *organizational culture* (Chapter 2).[105] Records of diverse group hiring and promoting should be kept, and efforts should be made to help these groups succeed in the workplace, often called a *diversity audit*. **Xerox** fosters a culture in which women and minorities are prepared and considered for top positions, leading to the first black woman CEO, Ursula Burns, of a major U.S. company.[106]

In promoting diversity, be sure to follow all Equal Employment Opportunity Equal Employment Opportunity (EEO)laws, treat group differences as important but not special, and tailor opportunities to individuals not groups. You should have high standards and hire and advance the most qualified candidates. But given equal qualifications for the job, the diverse candidate (which in some cases will be a white male) can be given the job to support diversity. Make sure diverse employees have access to the same job training and other practices at work to have equal opportunities to advance. Also, have diversity training for all employees. Three practices that promote diversity follow.

Diversity Training. *Diversity training* teaches people how to get along better with diverse workers. It is designed to bring about harmony and promote better

WORK
APPLICATION 3-11

First, state the types of diversity where you work(ed). Next, describe how diversity has affected you personally by being discriminated against, including being unfairly treated through being criticized or excluded in some way for being different in some way from others.

3-3 SELF ASSESSMENT

Implicit Association Test (IAT)

To complete this diversity self-assessment, go to the Project Implicit website at https://implicit.harvard.edu/implicit/demo. From there, you can select the "Go to the demonstration test" and Proceed and select one of 14 IATs to take, based on all four of our diversity types with a breakdown of several races, and other tests; or your professor will select the one for you to complete. Simply follow the instructions at the site to complete a test and get interpretations of your attitudes and beliefs about the diversity group you selected. It's free, and you can take as many as you want too.

Mentoring. *Mentors* are higher-level managers who prepare high-potential people for advancement. Mentoring is a process that enhances management skills, encourages diversity, and improves productivity. Having mentors who are willing to work with you to develop your knowledge, abilities, and skills can help you in both your professional and your personal life. Minority and women CEOs, including CEO of **Frontier Communications** Maggie Wilderotter, recommend having a mentor as an aid to career advancement.[108] Mentoring can be between people in different companies or at the same company, formal or informal. **Sun Microsystems** offers several internally developed formal mentoring programs for its employees.

Rather than providing mentors on premises, many MNCs today, such as **IBM**, are turning to online mentoring programs for global employee mentoring. With *e-mentoring,* employees typically fill out a profile and the program's software matches them up with a mentor. Instead of getting together in person, the two meet and communicate electronically, such as via email and **Skype**.

Network Diversity Groups. *Network diversity groups* have employees throughout the organization from a diverse group that share information about how to succeed in the company and how to help the company succeed. While some believe they can create division, others believe they are beneficial. **Frito-Lay** has the Latino Employee Network that provided management with very valuable feedback during the development of Doritos Guacamole Flavored Tortilla Chips by helping to ensure the taste and packaging had authenticity in the Latino community.[109]

teamwork. It helps diverse people to better understand each other by becoming aware of and more empathetic toward people different from themselves. Training breaks down negative stereotypes and builds acceptance of differences, viewing people as individuals, and realizing that diversity improves teamwork and organizational performance. Training can last for hours or days. Most large companies, including **Travelers Insurance**, offer diversity training.[107] Skill Builder 3–2 is an example diversity training exercise. For an online example of an awareness of attitudes and beliefs about diverse groups, see Self-Assessment 3–3 on this page.

GLOBAL DIVERSITY

Employees from different countries do not see the world in quite the same way because they come from different national cultures. Understanding national culture is important because it affects nearly every aspect of human behavior. National culture has a major impact on employees' work-related values and attitudes and thus should affect the way organizations are managed.[110] The capability to manage such cultural diversity, therefore, has become one of the most important skills for global leaders.[111]

We live and work in the global village, with multicultural workplaces being managed by MNCs.[112] As we move from a domestic to a global environment, global diversity becomes more complex and challenging, as a workforce composed of people from a wide range of racial and ethnic backgrounds is widely diverse.[113] So for the global business, all of the workplace diversity exists, plus national culture as well. In this section, we discuss Hofstede's cultural dimensions, Global Leadership and Organizational Behavior Effectiveness (GLOBE), and how to handle international assignments.

WORK APPLICATION 3-12

Describe a company's policies and practices for promoting diversity, preferably a business you work(ed) for.

LO 3-6

Compare and contrast the Hofstede national culture dimensions with the GLOBE initiative.

Understanding national culture is important as, regardless of the type of business, we all interactive with people from different cultures than ours. Photo from Blend Images/Alamy.

Hofstede National Cultural Diversity

Back in the 1970s and 1980s, Geert Hofstede surveyed more than 116,000 **IBM** employees in 40 countries about their work-related values. He identified five cultural dimensions on a continuum in which employees differ. (Countries in parentheses are very high or low compared to other countries on the dimension).[114]

- *Power distance inequality versus power equality*—Power distance being distributed between levels of management down to employees can be more accepted (Russia and China) or rejected as employees want to participate in decisions that affect them (Denmark and Sweden).

- *Individual versus collectivism*—Individualist cultures believe individuals should be self-sufficient with loyalty to themselves first and the group and company second (U.S. and the Netherlands), whereas collectivism places the group and company first (Indonesia and China).

- *Assertiveness versus nurturing*—Assertive cultures are more aggressive and competitive, with a focus on achievement and material possessions (Japan and Germany), whereas nurturing cultures emphasize the importance of relationships, modesty, caring, and quality of life (the Netherlands and France).

- *Uncertainty avoidance or acceptance*—Uncertainty-avoidance cultures like structure and security and are less likely to take risks (Japan and West Africa), whereas uncertainty-acceptance cultures are more comfortable dealing with the unknown and change and taking more risk (Hong Kong).

- *Long-term versus short-term orientation*—Long-term cultures look to the future and value thrift (China and Hong Kong), whereas short-term cultures focus on the past and present and immediate gratification (United States and Germany).

GLOBE

As Hofstede's research become dated, GLOBE confirmed his dimensions are still valid today and extended and expanded his five dimensions into nine, including hundreds of companies and more countries. Project GLOBE stands for Global Leadership and Organizational Behavior Effectiveness, which is an ongoing cross-cultural investigation of leadership and national culture. The GLOBE research team uses data from hundreds of organizations in more than 62 countries to identify nine dimensions in which national cultures are diverse. See Exhibit 3-8 for a list of the dimensions with examples of country ratings.[115] Notice that some of the GLOBE dimensions have the same or similar names as Hofstede's five dimensions.

International Assignments

There is a chance that you will be sent to another country to conduct business. It may be a brief visit, or it can be an international assignment as an expatriate. **Expatriates** *live and work outside their native country.* The average cost of sending an expatriate and family on a three-year international assignment is

WORK
APPLICATION 3-13

Give an example of cultural diversity you have encountered, preferably at work.

expatriates Individuals who live and work outside their native country.

EXHIBIT 3-8   GLOBE DIMENSIONS

Dimension	LOW	MODERATE	HIGH
Assertiveness People are tough, confrontational, and competitive.	Switzerland New Zealand	Ireland Philippines	Spain United States
Future Orientation People plan, delaying immediate gratification to invest in the future.	Russia Argentina	Slovenia India United States	Netherlands Canada
Gender Differences People have great gender role differences.	Sweden Denmark United States	Brazil Italy	Egypt China
Uncertainty Avoidance People are uncomfortable with the unknown/ambiguity.	Bolivia Hungary	Mexico United States	Austria Germany
Power Distance People accept power inequality differences.	South Africa Netherlands United States	England France	Spain Thailand
Societal Collectivism Teamwork is encouraged (vs. individualism).	Greece Germany	Hong Kong United States	Japan Singapore
In-Group Collectivism People take pride in membership (family, team, organization).	Denmark New Zealand	Israel Japan United States	China Morocco
Performance Orientation People strive for improvement and excellence.	Russia Venezuela	England Sweden	Taiwan United States
Humane Orientation People are fair, caring, and kind to others.	Singapore Spain	United States Hong Kong	Indonesia Iceland

3-3 APPLYING THE CONCEPT

GLOBE Dimensions

Identify the dimension of cultural diversity exemplified by each statement.

   A. assertiveness
   B. future orientation
   C. gender differences
   D. uncertainty avoidance
   E. power distance
   F. societal collectivism
   G. in-group collectivism
   H. performance orientation
   I. humane orientation

_____ 16. The people seem to prefer sports like soccer and basketball to sports like golf and track and field.

_____ 17. Managers place great importance on status symbols such as the executive dining room, reserved parking spaces, and big offices.

_____ 18. Managers provide poor working conditions.

_____ 19. Employees get nervous and stressed when changes are made.

_____ 20. Incentives motivate employees to achieve high levels of success.

$1 million.[116] It can be difficult to adjust to a different language, culture, and society. Being abruptly placed in a very different foreign country often leads to what is called *culture shock*. As a result, expatriates often unknowingly use inappropriate behaviors when they travel to foreign countries.

3-4 JOIN THE DISCUSSION ETHICS & SOCIAL RESPONSIBILITY

Bribes

An American businessperson working in a foreign country complained to a local telephone manager that the technician showed up and asked for a bribe before installing the phone. The businessperson refused, so the telephone worker left without installing the phone. The telephone company manager told the businessperson that the matter would be investigated, for a fee (bribe).

1. Is it ethical and socially responsible to pay bribes?
2. Should the businessperson have paid the bribe to get the phone installed?

Cultural values and beliefs are often unspoken and taken for granted; we tend to expect people to behave as we do. However, to be successful in the global village, you need to be sensitive to other cultures, and you need to have a global mindset.[117] In fact, companies seek employees who are aware of and sensitive to other cultures. Global companies, such as **IBM** and **EMC**, are also training managers and employees in local languages, customs, and business practices so they can be successful in the global market. How well the expatriates and their families adjust to the new foreign culture is the most important factor in determining the success or failure of the international assignment.[118] Yet not many companies provide training for family members.

Some people say that taking—or refusing—an international assignment affects career advancement, especially to top-level management. Whether you are asked to take an international assignment or not, as a global manager, you need to be flexible and adapt to other ways of behaving; you cannot expect others to change for you. So be sure to get some training for yourself and your family as part of your internal assignment to ensure you are multicultural and can have a successful assignment.

WORK
APPLICATION 3-14

How do you feel about taking an international assignment? What countries would be appealing to you?

• • • CHAPTER SUMMARY

3-1 **Contrast the classification of businesses in the global village.**

A domestic business does business in only one country. An international company is based primarily in one country but transacts business in other countries. A multinational corporation (MNC) owns operations in two or more countries. International companies are generally smaller than MNCs and are commonly importers and exporters, whereas, MNCs tend to make the products and services in or nearer to the countries they sell to.

3-2 **Differentiate the common barriers to trade.**

There are four primary barriers to trade to protect domestic companies from foreign companies. An *embargo* is a total ban on the importing of a product from one or more countries; it is often based on

import standards. A *quota* sets a limit on the number or volume of a product that can be imported or exported during a set period. *Subsidies* include government grants, loans, and tax. A *tariff* is a direct tax on imports, whereas embargos, quotas, and subsidies restrict trade without taxing the importing company.

3-3 **List the six activities that make a business a global one, in order from lowest to highest cost and risk.**

A business can become a global one by participating in: (1) *global sourcing*, hiring others outside the firm to perform work worldwide. (2) *Importing and Exporting*, buying and selling products between countries. (3) *Licensing*, the licensor agrees to give a licensee the right to make its products or services or use its intellectual property in exchange for a royalty. Or *franchising,* the franchisor licenses the entire business to the franchisee for a fee and royalties. (4) *Contract manufacturing,* a company has a foreign firm manufacture the products that it sells as its own. (5) *Strategic alliance,* an agreement to share resources that does not necessarily involve creating a new company. A *joint venture,* created when two or more firms share ownership of a new company. (6) *Direct investment,* building or buying operating facilities in a foreign country. Global sourcing is the least costly and risky of these activities, and it can be a part of any of the others.

3-4   Describe diversity and why it is important.

Diversity refers to the variety of people with different group identities within the same workplace. *Discrimination* is illegal because it gives unfair treatment to diversity groups in employment decisions. But promoting diversity creates equal opportunities for all employees, so it is the right thing to do. Diversity is also beneficial to business. The global white population is decreasing while the other races are growing at a fast pace, making developing and selling products and services to non-Caucasians critically important to survival and business growth. Diversity can have positive effects on financial outcomes, as other races are creative at innovating and selling products and services to the growing diverse population.

3-5   Describe the four major types of diversity groups and practices of managing diversity.

There is diversity in the (1) range of *ages* in the workplace, (2) a mix of male and female *sex,* (3) different *races* and *ethnic* groups, and (4) people with *disabilities* that substantially limit one or more major life activities. To manage diversity, companies cannot discriminate against any group and should promote equal opportunities for everyone. Practices that promote diversity include (1) *diversity training* to teach people how to get along better with diverse workers, (2) higher-level manager *mentors* who prepare high-potential people for advancement, and (3) *network diversity groups* of employees throughout the organization from a diverse group that share information about how to succeed in the company.

3-6   Compare and contrast the Hofstede national culture dimensions with the GLOBE initiative.

The two are similar because they both measure cultural diversity among countries. Back in the 1970s and 1980, Hofstede identified five dimensions of diversity (power distance inequality versus power equality, individuality versus collectivism, assertiveness versus nurturing, uncertainty avoidance versus uncertainty acceptance, and long-term versus short-term orientation) using employees of one company, IBM, in 40 countries. GLOBE confirmed that Hofstede's five dimensions are still valid today and extended and expanded his five dimensions into nine (assertiveness, future orientation, gender differences, uncertainty avoidance, power distance, societal collectivism, in-group collectivism, performance orientation, and humane orientation), and the sample includes hundreds of companies from more than 60 countries. GLOBE is also an ongoing study.

••• KEY TERMS

contract manufacturing, 71
direct investment, 73
disability, 81
discrimination, 78
diversity, 76
embargo, 65
ethnocentrism, 63

expatriates, 84
franchising, 71
glass ceiling, 79
global sourcing, 69
global village, 62
international company, 62
joint venture, 72

licensing, 70
multinational corporation (MNC), 62
quota, 65
strategic alliance, 72
subsidies, 65
tariff, 65

••• KEY TERM REVIEW

Complete each of the following statements using one of this chapter's key terms.

1. The _____ refers to companies conducting business worldwide without boundaries.

2. An _____ is based primarily in one country but transacts business in other countries.

3. A _____ has ownership in operations in two or more countries.

4. _____ is regarding one's own ethnic group or culture as superior to others.

5. An _____ is a total ban on the importing of a product from one or more countries.

6. A _____ sets a limit on the number or volume of a product that can be imported or exported during a set period.

7. _____ include government grants, loans, and tax breaks given to domestic companies.

8. A _____ is a direct tax on imports to make them more expensive.

9. _____ is hiring others outside the firm to perform work worldwide.

10. In _____, a licensor agrees to give a licensee the right to make its products or services or use its intellectual property in exchange for a royalty.

11. In _____, the franchisor licenses the entire business to the franchisee for a fee and royalties.

12. With global _____, a company has a foreign firm manufacture the products that it sells as its own.

13. A _____ is an agreement to share resources that does not necessarily involve creating a new company.

14. A _____ is created when two or more firms share ownership of a new company.

15. _____ is the building or buying of operating facilities in a foreign country.

16. _____ refers to the variety of people with different group identities within the same workplace.

17. _____ is illegal because it gives unfair treatment to diversity groups in employment decisions.

18. The _____ is the invisible barrier that prevents women and minorities from advancing to the top jobs in organizations.

19. A _____ is a mental or physical impairment that substantially limits one or more major life activities.

20. _____ live and work outside their native country.

• • • REVIEW QUESTIONS

1. How are businesses classified in the global village?
2. What are the four trade barriers?
3. What is the role of the World Trade Organization (WTO)?
4. What are the six major trade agreements?
5. Which country has the foreign trade advantage based on exchange rates?
6. What is the difference between a license and a franchise?
7. What is the difference between a strategic alliance, joint venture, and direct investment?
8. What do international and multinational companies have in common?
9. If you were to start your own small business, would you most likely use contracting, strategic alliances, joint ventures, or direct investment?
10. What is the difference between diversity and affirmative action?
11. What is the glass ceiling?
12. When dealing with people with disabilities, what should be the focus?
13. What are three practices used to promote diversity?
14. What are the five dimensions of Hofstede's cultural diversity?
15. What is GLOBE?
16. What are the nine dimensions of Project GLOBE?

• • • COMMUNICATION SKILLS

The following critical-thinking questions can be used for class discussion and/or as written assignments to develop communication skills. Be sure to give complete explanations for all questions.

1. How does globalization affect your life and that of your family and friends?
2. Should people in the United States make an effort to buy products made in America? If so, how should "made in America" be defined?
3. Should your home country drop all or some of its trade barriers?
4. Is the North American Free Trade Agreement (NAFTA) of more benefit or harm to the United States? Why?
5. Should there be one global trade agreement rather than the six major agreements?
6. Should countries with a trade deficit create barriers to trade to eliminate the deficit?
7. Overall, are the effects of foreign trade more positive or negative for your home country?
8. Is it too difficult and time consuming to engage in global sourcing?
9. Are smaller international companies at a disadvantage when competing with large MNCs?
10. How does diversity effect you personally? Do you really value diversity?
11. What experience have you had with each of the diverse groups?

12. How can you improve your awareness and empathy for diverse groups?

13. Identify mentors you have had in your life (relatives, friends, teachers, coaches, managers) and how they helped you to succeed. Also, will you seek out a mentor(s) to help you advance in your career?

14. Should expatriates be given global cultural diversity training; and should their families get training, too?

• • • CASE: SHERYL SANDBERG AT FACEBOOK ASKS WOMEN TO "LEAN IN"

The bar has been raised in the field of gender issues in management. Sheryl Sandberg, chief operating officer at Facebook, has published a thought-provoking book on the role of women in the office and at home. The book is Sandberg's attempt to help other women to be successful in business. It was an instant best seller and has already created meaningful discussion about the roles of men and women at work.

What is so controversial? Sandberg titled her book *Lean In: Women, Work and the Will to Lead*. The book is being sold around the world under the following different titles to reflect the meaning of "lean in" in each country. In France it is *En Avant Toutes (Forward All)*, in Italy it is *Facciamoci avanti (Step Forward)*, in Spanish it is *Vayamos Adelante (Let's Go)*, and in Brazil it is *Faça Acontecer (Make It Happen)*.[119]

What does "lean in" mean? Sandberg is calling on other women, as she puts it, to "lean in" and embrace success. Sandberg feels that "if more women lean in, we can change the power structure of our world and expand opportunities for all. More female leadership will lead to fairer treatment for *all* women."[120] She also feels that half of the companies around the world should be run by women and half of the houses run by men—which is far from the reality of the situation.[121]

Sandberg also states that her success was not just because she worked hard but because she removed internal barriers that often hold women back. These barriers that women create are a lack of self-confidence, not raising their hands, and pulling back when they should be leaning in. If women expect to crack the glass ceiling and access more powerful positions at work, they are going to have to lean in.[122]

When the book was released, many newspapers and television reports disputed the merits of her theory. The first reply was that it is easy for a woman that is wealthy and voted the fifth most powerful women in the world to say that a woman can be a leader at work and at home.

Is a woman successful if she opts to lean out and just become a stay-home mom? Or is she less successful if she just has a good middle-level job at work without the high levels of stress often associated with executive-level positions and decisions?

One of the goals of *Lean In* was to bring women together to discuss the issue. Facebook and many other social media sites already have a large number of groups formed that are meeting online and in person. You can join the *Lean In* community at www.facebook.com/leaninorg or www.leanin.org.

Although Sandberg didn't try to use the five dimensions of Hofstede's cultural diversity, she could have used them to determine if her ideas for women to "lean in" would likely be successful in different countries. The following is each of Hofstede's five dimensions with a question to consider regarding *Lean In*.

1. Power distance inequality versus power equality—Will a certain country allow women to participate at the top level more than other countries?

2. Individuality versus collectivism—Will a certain country like that women place their own career ahead of the team or group?

3. Assertiveness versus nurturing—Will a nurturing country be more likely to help a women to lean in?

4. Uncertainty avoidance or acceptance—Will a country that likes to take risks be more likely to let a woman rise to the top?

5. Long-term versus short-term orientation—Will a country that looks to the future be more willing to let women be a larger part of its future?

Case Questions

1. What group of people did Sheryl Sandberg focus on in her book?

2. How did Sheryl Sandberg break through the glass ceiling?

3. Which of the global practices is most similar to Sandberg's desire to promote diversity?

4. Which of the five dimensions of Hofstede's cultural diversity most apply to Sandberg's ideas?

5. Which dimensions of the GLOBE most apply to Sandberg's "lean in" theory?

Cumulative Case Questions

6. How do Sandberg's views on gender issues highlight the four management functions? (Chapter 1)

7. Are Sandberg's gender issues relevant in countries outside the United States? (Chapter 2).

• • • SKILL BUILDER 3-1: THE GLOBAL ENVIRONMENT, DIVERSITY, AND MANAGEMENT PRACTICES ANALYSIS

Objective

To better understand an organization's global environment, diversity, and practices that can help get a job candidate a position with the company.

Skills

The primary skills developed through this exercise are:

1. *Management skill*—conceptual decision making
2. *AACSB competencies*—dynamics of the global economy, reasoning abilities, and multicultural and diversity understanding
3. *Management function*—planning, organizing, leading, and controlling

For this exercise, select a company that does business globally, preferably one you would like to work for. You will most likely need to conduct some research to get the answers to the questions below.

1. How is the business classified in the global village?
2. What trade barriers has it had to deal with?
3. What countries does it conduct business in, and what trade agreements are these countries involved in?

4. Which of the methods for going global does the business use? Be sure to give examples of its global sources, names of any import or export partners, names of any companies that it gives licenses or franchises, any contractors, strategic allies, or joint venture partner names, and any subsidiaries it has as direct investments.
5. What are its diversity groups and its policies and practices for promoting diversity?
6. Compare the company's nine GLOBE dimensions for five countries it does business with. Make a chart similar to Exhibit 3-8 GLOBE Dimensions.
7. Does the company offer international assignments, and how does it train its expatriates and families?

You may be asked to pass in this assignment, present your answers to the class, and/or discuss your answers in small groups or online.

Apply It

What did I learn from this experience? How will I use this knowledge in the future?

• • • SKILL BUILDER 3-2: DIVERSITY TRAINING

Objective

To become more aware of and sensitive to diversity.

Skills

The primary skills developed through this exercise are:

1. *Management skill*—decision making (conceptual, diagnostic, analytical, and critical-thinking skills are needed to understand diversity)
2. *AACSB competency*—multicultural and diversity understanding
3. *Management function*—organizing

Answer the following questions.

Race and Ethnicity

1. My race (ethnicity) is _____.
2. My name, _____, is significant because it means _____. [or] My name, _____, is significant because I was named after _____.
3. One positive thing about my racial/ethnic background is _____.
4. One difficult thing about my racial/ethnic background is _____.

Religion

5. My religion is _____. [or] I don't have one.
6. One positive thing about my religious background (or lack thereof) is _____.
7. One difficult thing about my religious background (or lack thereof) is _____.

Gender

8. I am _____ (male/female).
9. One positive thing about being (male/female) is _____.
10. One difficult thing about being (male/female) is _____.

Age

11. I am _____ years old.
12. One positive thing about being this age is _____.
13. One difficult thing about being this age is _____.

Other

14. One way in which I am different from other people is _____.

15. One positive thing about being different in this way is _____.

16. One negative thing about being different in this way is _____.

Prejudice, Stereotypes, Discrimination

17. If you have, and we all have, ever been prejudged, stereotyped, or discriminated against, describe what happened.

You may be asked to discuss your answers in small groups or online to better understand people different from you.

Apply It

What did I learn from this experience? How will I use this knowledge in the future?

● ● ● Skill Builder 3-3: Cultural Diversity Awareness

Objective

To develop your awareness of cultural diversity.

Skills

The primary skills developed through this exercise are:

1. Management skill—interpersonal
2. AACSB competency—multicultural and diversity understanding
3. Management function—leading

Procedure 1 (4–6 minutes)

You and your classmates will share your international experience and nationalities. Start with people who have lived in another country, then move to those who have visited another country, and follow with discussion of nationality (e.g., I am half French and Irish but have never been to either country). The instructor or a recorder will write the countries on the board until several countries/nationalities are listed or the time is up.

Procedure 2 (10–30 minutes)

You and your classmates will share your knowledge of cultural differences between the country in which the course is being taught and those listed on the board. This is a good opportunity for international students and those who have visited other countries to share their experiences. For example, in Spain most people have a two-hour lunch break and go home for a big meal and may take a nap. In Japan, people expect to receive and give gifts. You may also discuss cultural differences within the country.

Apply It

What did I learn from this experience? How will I use this knowledge in the future?

● ● ● Student Study Site 📱

Visit the Student Study Site at **www.sagepub.com/lussier6e** to access to these additional study tools:

- Mobile-compatible self-assessment quizzes
- Mobile-compatible key term flashcards
- Video Links
- SAGE Journal Articles
- Web Links

4 Creative Problem Solving and Decision Making

● ● ● **Learning Outcomes**

After studying this chapter, you should be able to:

4-1. Explain the relationship among objectives, problem solving, and decision making. PAGE 94

4-2. Explain the relationship among the management functions, problem solving, and decision making. PAGE 95

4-3. List the six steps in the decision-making model. PAGE 96

4-4. Describe the differences between programmed and nonprogrammed decisions and among the conditions of certainty, uncertainty, and risk. PAGE 98

4-5. Describe when to use rational versus bounded rational decision making and group versus individual decision making. PAGE 99

4-6. State the difference between an objective and "must" and "want" criteria. PAGE 102

4-7. State the difference between creativity and innovation. PAGE 103

4-8. List and explain the three stages in the creative process. PAGE 104

4-9. Describe the differences among quantitative techniques, the Kepner-Tregoe method, and cost-benefit analysis for analyzing and selecting an alternative. PAGE 108

IDEAS ON MANAGEMENT at Nike

Phil Knight ran track for coach Bill Bowerman at the University of Oregon in the 1960s. From that athletic alliance, they went on together to start the **Nike** Corporation in 1972. Initially, the company imported track shoes from Japan, and Knight sold them out of his car at track meets. But the company soon began to design and market its own running shoes, and by 1980, Nike had reached a 50 percent market share in the United States athletic shoe market.

Today, **NIKE, Inc.,** based near Beaverton, Oregon, is the world's leading designer, marketer, and distributor of authentic athletic footwear, apparel, equipment, and accessories for a wide variety of sports and fitness activities. Wholly owned subsidiaries include **Cole Haan**, which designs, markets, and distributes luxury shoes, handbags, accessories, and coats; **Converse Inc.**, which designs, markets, and distributes athletic footwear, apparel, and accessories; and **Hurley International LLC**, which designs, markets, and distributes action sports and youth lifestyle footwear, apparel, and accessories. Nike was ranked 126th on the *Fortune* 500 list in 2012 with revenues of $24.1 billion and profits of $2.2 billion.

The Nike mission is to bring inspiration and innovation to every athlete in the world, reflecting a key insight that Bill Bowerman had early in the company's history—that everyone is an athlete. This idea continues to drive Nike's business decisions and inform its marketing strategies.

1. Has Nike made any bad decisions? PAGE 94
2. What type of decision does Nike make to sign large endorsement contracts with young, unproven athletes, such as NBA basketball player LeBron James back in 2003? PAGE 99
3. What objectives does Nike meet through its star athlete endorsements? PAGE 102
4. How does Nike demonstrate creativity and innovation? PAGE 103

• • • Chapter Outline

Problem Solving and Decision Making: An Overview
  Problem Solving and Decision Making Interrelationships
  Decision-Making Styles
  Decision Making in the Global Village
  The Decision-Making Model
Classify and Define the Problem or Opportunity
  Classify the Problem
  Decision Making Types
  Select the Appropriate Level of Participation
  Define the Problem
Set Objectives and Criteria
Generate Creative and Innovative Alternatives
  Creativity and Innovation

Using Information and Technology to Generate Alternatives
Using Groups to Generate Creative Alternatives
Decision Trees
Analyze Alternatives and Select the Most Feasible
  Quantitative Techniques
  The Kepner-Tregoe Method
  Cost-Benefit, Pros and Cons, and Intuition
  Ethics, Social Responsibility, and Sustainability in Decision Making
Plan, Implement the Decision, and Control
Vroom's Participative Decision-Making Model
  Using the Participative Decision-Making Model
  Participation Decision Styles

5. Does the amount of contracts given to young, unproven athletes pose a serious financial risk to Nike? Which techniques could Nike use to analyze the alternatives in contract decisions? PAGE 112

6. Which version of Vroom's participative decision-making model should Nike use to make decisions to sign young, unproven athletes to contracts? PAGE 116

You'll find answers to these questions throughout the chapter. To learn more about Nike, visit its website at www.nike.com.

Source: Case information and answers to questions within the chapter were taken from Nike's website at http://www.nikebiz.com, accessed June 4, 2013; "Largest U.S. corporations—Fortune 500," *Fortune* (May 20, 2013), 1–20.

Problem Solving and Decision Making: An Overview

Recall that decision making is one of the three critical management skills. Employees of all types and levels confront problems that require decisions on how to carry out day-to-day activities.[1] Organizational decisions are important,[2] and some decisions have significant consequences for firm performance.[3] For example, **BP** admitted to making a series of poor decisions to continue to work on an oil well in the Gulf of Mexico after a test warned that something was wrong. Poor decisions cost BP billions of dollars and fishermen their businesses, as well as destroying wildlife and ecosystems.[4] **Nike (Case Question 1)** made a poor decision in buying **Umbro** for $484 million and selling the subsidiary in 2012 for only $225 million, a 46 percent loss.

No one can say how many decisions you will make, but you should realize that your problem-solving and decision-making skills will affect your personal and career success.[5] Let's face it, we are not perfect decision makers, but you can improve your decision-making skills;[6] that is the objective of this chapter. In this section, we discuss problem solving and decision making interrelationships, as well as an exploration of your preferred decision-making style. Next is a discussion of decision making in the global village, and we end with the decision-making model steps.

LO 4-1

Explain the relationship among objectives, problem solving, and decision making.

Problem Solving and Decision Making Interrelationships

Problem solving and decision making are interrelated with each other and with objectives and the management functions. Here's how.

The Relationship Among Objectives, Problem Solving, and Decision Making. When you do not meet your objectives, you have a problem. The better you can develop plans that prevent problems before they occur, the fewer problems you will have and the more time you will have to take advantage of opportunities and respond to competitive threats. Solving problems improves the world.[7] **Google** has a focus on solving problems to improve how the world organizes information.[8]

A **problem** *exists whenever objectives are not being met.* In other words, you have a problem whenever there is a difference between what is actually happening and what you and your manager want to happen. If the objective is to produce 1,500 units per day but the department produces only 1,490, a problem exists. **Problem solving** *is the process of taking corrective action to meet objectives.* **Decision making** *is the process of selecting a course of action that will solve a problem.* Decisions must be made when you are faced with a problem.[9] Figure it out![10] When something isn't working, fix it.[11]

The first decision you face when confronted with a problem is whether to take corrective action. Some problems cannot be solved, and others do not deserve

problem The situation that exists whenever objectives are not being met.

problem solving The process of taking corrective action to meet objectives.

decision making The process of selecting a course of action that will solve a problem.

the time and effort it would take to solve them. However, your job requires you to achieve organizational objectives. Therefore, you will have to attempt to solve most problems, so fix it.[12]

The Relationship Among the Management Functions, Problem Solving, and Decision Making. All managers perform the same four functions of management. While performing these functions, you must make decisions and solve problems. For example, when planning, you must make decisions about objectives and when, where, and how they will be met. When organizing, you must make decisions about what to delegate and how to coordinate the department's resources. When staffing, you must decide whom to hire and how to train and evaluate employees. To lead, you must decide how to influence employees. To control, you must monitor progress and select methods to ensure that objectives are met.

Decision-Making Styles

How do people make decisions?[13] Experience and personality[14] contribute to a decision-making style. Before learning about the three decision-making styles, determine your preferred style by completing Self-Assessment 4–1.

Reflexive Style. A reflexive decision maker likes to make quick decisions ("shooting from the hip") without taking the time to get the information that may be needed and without considering alternatives. On the positive side, reflexive decision makers

WORK
APPLICATION 4-1

Describe a situation in which a job objective was not met. Identify the problem created and the decision made in regard to this problem.

LO 4-2

Explain the relationship among the management functions, decision making, and problem solving.

WORK
APPLICATION 4-2

Give an example of a poor decision made by a manager performing a management function. Explain the management function and the problem created by the poor decision.

4-1 SELF ASSESSMENT

Decision-Making Styles

Individuals differ in the way they approach decisions. To determine whether your decision-making style is reflexive, reflective, or consistent, evaluate each of the following eight statements using the scale below. Place a number between 1 (indicating "This behavior is common for me") and 5 (indicating "This behavior is not common for me") on the line preceding each statement.

This behavior is common for me.   This behavior is not common for me.

1	2	3	4	5

1. ____ Overall, I make decisions quickly.
2. ____ When making decisions, I go with my first thought or hunch.
3. ____ When making decisions, I don't bother to recheck my work.
4. ____ When making decisions, I gather little or no information.
5. ____ When making decisions, I consider very few alternative options.
6. ____ When making decisions, I usually decide well before any deadline.
7. ____ When making decisions, I don't ask others for advice.
8. ____ After making decisions, I don't look for other alternatives or wish I had waited longer.

____ Total score

To determine your style, add up the numbers you assigned to the statements; the total will be between 8 and 40. Note where you fall on the decision-style continuum.

Reflexive		Consistent		Reflective
8	20	30	40	

are decisive; they do not procrastinate. On the negative side, making quick decisions can lead to waste and duplication. Wally Amos, founder of **Uncle Wally's Muffin's**, admits being impulsive, leading to making some bad decisions—he says patience pays.[15] The cure is to pause for understanding.[16] If you use a reflexive style for important decisions, you may want to slow down and spend more time gathering information and analyzing alternatives.

Reflective Style. A reflective decision maker likes to take plenty of time to make decisions, gathering considerable information and analyzing several alternatives. On the positive side, the reflective type does not make hasty decisions. On the negative side, the reflective type may procrastinate, lose opportunities, and waste valuable time and other resources. The reflective decision maker may be viewed as wishy-washy and indecisive. **Cisco** CEO John Chambers said, "Without exception, all of my biggest mistakes occurred because I moved too slowly."[17] If you constantly use a reflective style, you may want to speed up your decision making.

Consistent Style. Consistent decision makers tend to make decisions without either rushing or wasting time. They know when they have enough information and alternatives to make a sound decision. Consistent decision makers tend to have the best record for making good decisions. They tend to follow the steps in the decision-making model, which we present soon.

Decision Making in the Global Village

As discussed in Chapter 3's section on GLOBE,[18] people around the globe are different, and people from different cultures don't necessarily make decisions the same way. Decision-making styles often vary based on time orientation. In some countries, decisions are made more quickly than in others. In countries that are less time conscious, such as Egypt, decision styles are more reflective than in time-conscious countries like the United States, where decision styles are more reflexive. In countries where managers use participative decision making, decisions take longer than in countries where managers use autocratic decision making. Japanese managers, for example, for whom decision making involves high levels of participation, often take longer to make decisions than U.S. managers do.

Managers in some countries (such as the United States) are more oriented to problem solving, whereas those in others (such as Thailand and Indonesia) tend to accept things the way they are. Culture influences the selection of problems to solve, the depth of analysis, the importance placed on logic and rationality, and the level of participation in decision making. Thus, in high-power-distance cultures (most Latin American countries and the Philippines), where decisions are more autocratic, participation is not acceptable. In lower-power-distance cultures (the United States, Ireland, Australia, Israel), there is greater use of participation in decision making.

The Decision-Making Model

Decision making has become more professionalized using more formal processes,[19] making the process more scientific.[20] The **decision-making model** *is a six-step process for arriving at a decision and involves (1) classifying and defining the problem or opportunity, (2) setting objectives and criteria, (3) generating creative and innovative alternatives, (4) analyzing alternatives and selecting the most feasible, (5) planning and implementing the decision, and (6) controlling the decisio*n. Notice that the steps do not simply go from start to finish. At any step, you may have to return to a prior step to make changes. For example, if

LO 4-3

List the six steps in the decision-making model.

decision-making model
A six-step process for arriving at a decision and involves (1) classifying and defining the problem or opportunity, (2) setting objectives and criteria, (3) generating creative and innovative alternatives, (4) analyzing alternatives and selecting the most feasible, (5) planning and implementing the decision, and (6) controlling the decision.

you are at step 6, controlling, and the implementation is not going as planned (step 5), you may have to backtrack to prior steps to take corrective action by generating and selecting a new alternative or changing the objective. If you have not defined the problem accurately, you may have to go back to the beginning.

Following the steps in the model will not guarantee that you will make good decisions. However, using the model will increase your chances of success in problem solving and decision making, as following a process helps lead to rational decisions.[21] Consciously use the model in your daily life, and you will improve your ability to make decisions. The remainder of this chapter discusses the details of the model so that you can develop your creative problem-solving and decision-making skills.

CLASSIFY AND DEFINE THE PROBLEM OR OPPORTUNITY

Although it may seem surprising, it's true: half the decisions made by managers fail to solve the problems they are aimed at.[22] This is often due to not classifying and defining the problem correctly. To improve your odds of successful problem solving, follow the steps in the decision-making model. The first step in the model is to classify and define the problem, which may sometimes take the form of an opportunity. In this section, we discuss how to classify problems, select the appropriate level of participation, and determine the cause of problems.

Classify the Problem

Problems may be classified in terms of the decision structure involved, the conditions under which a decision will be made, and the type of decision made using the decision-making model.

Decision-Making Structure. For **programmed decisions,** *those that arise in recurring or routine situations, the decision maker should use decision rules or organizational policies and procedures to make the decision.* Reordering inventory every time stock reaches a specified level, scheduling employees, and handling customer complaints are examples of programmed decisions.

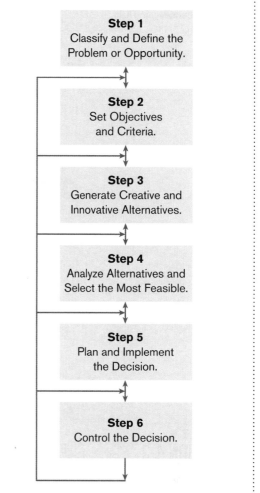

EXHIBIT 4-1   THE DECISION-MAKING MODEL

Step 1
Classify and Define the Problem or Opportunity.

Step 2
Set Objectives and Criteria.

Step 3
Generate Creative and Innovative Alternatives.

Step 4
Analyze Alternatives and Select the Most Feasible.

Step 5
Plan and Implement the Decision.

Step 6
Control the Decision.

programmed decisions Decisions that arise in recurring or routine situations, for which the decision maker should use decision rules or organizational policies and procedures.

4-1 **APPLYING** THE CONCEPT

Steps in Decision Making

Identify the step in the decision-making model represented by each statement.

step 1
step 2
step 3
step 4
step 5
step 6

_____ 1. "Andrea, is the machine still jamming, or has it stopped?"

_____ 2. "I don't understand what we are trying to accomplish."

_____ 3. "What symptoms have you observed to indicate that a problem even exists?"

_____ 4. "Probability theory should be used to help us in this situation."

_____ 5. "We will use the brainstorming technique to solve the problem."

For **nonprogrammed decisions,** *significant decisions that arise in nonrecurring and nonroutine situations, the decision maker should use the decision-making model.* To be significant, a decision must be expensive and/or have major consequences for the department or organization. Selecting a new product to sell, entering new products, and opening a new facility are examples of nonprogrammed decisions. Upper-level managers tend to make more nonprogrammed decisions than do lower-level managers do. Nonprogrammed decisions tend to take longer to make than programmed decisions do.

The decision structure continuum is illustrated in Exhibit 4-2. You must be able to differentiate between the two types of decision structures, because they provide a guideline as to how much time and effort you should expend to make effective decisions and if you should use the decision making model.

EXHIBIT 4-2 DECISION STRUCTURE CONTINUUM

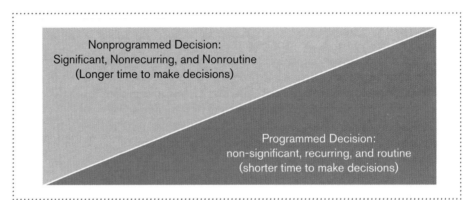

Nonprogrammed Decision:
Significant, Nonrecurring, and Nonroutine
(Longer time to make decisions)

Programmed Decision:
non-significant, recurring, and routine
(shorter time to make decisions)

Decision-Making Conditions. The three **decision-making conditions** *are certainty, risk, and uncertainty.* When making a decision under the conditions of *certainty,* you know the outcome of each alternative in advance. When making a decision under conditions of *risk,* you do not know the exact outcome of each alternative in advance but can assign probabilities to each outcome. Under conditions of *uncertainty,* lack of information or knowledge makes the outcome of each alternative unpredictable, so you cannot accurately determine probabilities.[23]

The feeling of uncertainty can be frustrating.[24] But you need to take risks to succeed in businesses.[25] Most management decisions are made between the conditions of risk and uncertainty.[26] However, upper-level managers tend to make more uncertain decisions than lower-level managers do. Although risk and uncertainty cannot be eliminated, they can be reduced with information.[27] Exhibit 4-3 illustrates the continuum of decision-making conditions.

EXHIBIT 4-3 CONTINUUM OF DECISION-MAKING CONDITIONS

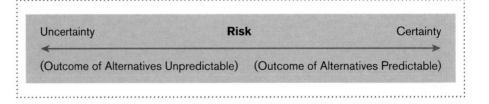

Uncertainty	Risk	Certainty
(Outcome of Alternatives Unpredictable)		(Outcome of Alternatives Predictable)

| 4-2 | **APPLYING** THE CONCEPT |

Classify the Problem

Classify the problem in each statement according to the structure and condition under which the decision must be made.

A. programmed, certainty
B. programmed, uncertainty
C. programmed, risk
D. nonprogrammed, certainty
E. nonprogrammed, uncertainty
F. nonprogrammed, risk

_____ 6. Aden has to decide if he should invest in a new company in a brand-new industry.

_____ 7. Carol, a manager in a department with high turnover, must hire a new employee.

_____ 8. When Jorge graduates from college, he will buy an existing business rather than work for someone else.

_____ 9. Sondra, a small business owner, has had a turnaround in business; it's now profitable. She wants to keep the excess cash liquid so that she can get it quickly if she needs it. How should she invest it?

_____ 10. Samir, a purchasing agent, must select new cars for the business. This is the sixth time in six years he has made this decision.

Decision-Making Types

There are two primary types of decisions that can be made using the decision-making model: rational decisions and bounded rational decisions.[28] With *rational decisions,* the decision maker attempts to use *optimizing*—selecting the best possible alternative. With *bounded rational decisions,* the decision maker uses *satisficing*—selecting the first alternative that meets the minimal criteria, which can sometimes lead to suboptimal decisions. With satisficing, only parts or none of the decision-making model presented in Exhibit 4-1 would be used, often due to time pressure and cost of information for a decision.[29] How do managers use reasoning when making decisions?[30] We tend to be what is called boundedly rational agents, attempting to maximize positive outcomes, but we are limited by our cognitive abilities.[31]

You need to remember which type of decision style to use and when. The more complex and unstructured the decision and the higher the degree of risk and uncertainty, the greater the need to spend time conducting research with the aid of the decision-making model. *Optimize* (select the best possible alternative) when you are making nonprogrammed, high-risk, or uncertain decisions. *Satisfice* (select the first alternative that meets the minimum criteria) when you are making programmed, low-risk, or certain decisions. When **Nike (Case Question 2)** signs unproven athletes, such as LeBron James's seven-year, $93 million endorsement deal, it is making a nonprogrammed decision under the condition of high risk to uncertainty. Therefore, using the rational decision making is appropriate for this decision.

Select the Appropriate Level of Participation

When a problem exists, you must decide who should participate in solving it.[32] As a rule of thumb, the key people involved with the problem should participate.[33] However, the current trend in management favors increased employee participation.[34] In the global dynamic environment, it is difficult for any one leader to figure it all out at the top.[35] Thus, the major question is not whether managers should allow employees to participate in problem solving and decision making but when and how this should be done.[36] When making decisions, you should use the management style appropriate to the situation. In the last section of this

LO 4-5

Describe when to use rational versus bounded rational decision making and group versus individual decision making.

chapter, you will learn about Vroom's participative decision-making model, and you will have a chance to practice using this model in Skill Builder 4–2.

For now, you will learn about two levels of participation: individual and group decision making. However, realize that even though the trend is toward group decision making, some people want to be involved in decision making and others do not, and not everyone has equal power to influence the group's decision.[37] Also, recall that diversity (Chapter 3) in teams can not only be problematic, but it can also lead to creative, higher-quality decisions.[38] In general, for a significant nonprogrammed decision with high risk or uncertainty, use group decision making. For a programmed decision with low risk or certainty, use individual decision making.

Exhibit 4-4 lists the potential advantages and disadvantages of involving groups in decision making. The key to success when using groups is to maximize the advantages while minimizing the disadvantages.

To be successful at decision making, you need to identify the type of problem to be solved and the level of participation to use. Exhibit 4-5 puts together the concepts from this section to help you better understand how to classify problems.

WORK
APPLICATION 4-4

Give an example of a group decision made in an organization you work for or have worked for. Identify the advantages and disadvantages encountered by the group.

EXHIBIT 4-4 POTENTIAL ADVANTAGES AND DISADVANTAGES OF USING GROUP DECISION MAKING

Potential Advantages	Potential Disadvantages
1. *Better-quality decisions.* Groups usually do a better job of solving complex problems than the best individual in the group.	1. *Wasted time and slower decision making.* It takes longer for a group to make a decision, and employees are not on the job producing.
2. *More information, alternatives, creativity, and innovation.* A group of people usually has more of these important factors.	2. *Satisficing.* Groups are more likely to satisfice than an individual, especially when group meetings are not run effectively.
3. *Better understanding of the decision.* When people participate, they understand why the decision selected was the best alternative.	3. *Domination and goal displacement.* One group member or a subgroup may control the group decision with the goal of personal gain.
4. *Greater commitment to the decision.* People involved in making a decision have increased commitment to implementing the decision.	4. *Conformity.* Group members may feel pressured to go along with the group's decision without questioning it out of fear of not being accepted.
5. *Improved morale and motivation.* Participation is rewarding and personally satisfying.	5. *Groupthink.* It occurs when members withhold different views to appear as though they are in agreement. This nullifies the advantage of diversity.
6. *Good training.* Participation trains people to work in groups.	6. *Social loafing.* Team members may withhold their effort and fail to perform their share of the work.

Define the Problem

After you have classified the problem, you or the group must define it clearly and accurately. Defining the problem accurately requires conceptual skills as part of decision making. Because of time pressures, managers often hurry to solve problems and make decisions. Rushing to solve a problem that is not correctly defined often leads to a decision that does not solve the problem—haste makes waste. An important part of defining the problem is to distinguish symptoms from cause.

EXHIBIT 4-5   CONTINUA FOR CLASSIFYING A PROBLEM

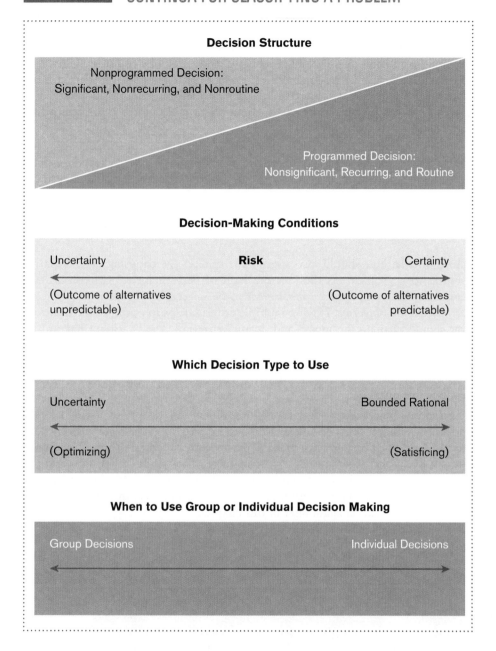

Distinguish Symptoms from the Cause of the Problem. Think of this as a cause-and-effect/symptoms relationship. Begin by listing the observable and describable occurrences (symptoms) that indicate a problem exists. Only after doing this can you determine the cause of the problem. If you eliminate the cause, the symptoms should disappear. For example, Sam has been an excellent producer. However, in the last month, Sam has been out sick or late more times than he was in the past two years. What is the problem? If you say "absenteeism" or "lateness," you are confusing symptoms and causes. They are symptoms of the problem, but they don't tell you why the problem has occurred. If you don't eliminate the cause of the problem, the symptoms will reappear. **HP** is losing money. Its not being profitable is a symptom. The real question is, "What is the cause of the decline in profits?"

WORK APPLICATION 4-5

Define a problem in an organization you work for or have worked for. Be sure to clearly distinguish the symptoms from the causes of the problem.

LO 4-6

State the difference between an objective and "must" and "want" criteria.

SET OBJECTIVES AND CRITERIA

Generally, with simple programmed decisions, the objectives and the criteria have been set. Therefore, you need not complete steps 2 through 4 of the decision-making model. However, with nonprogrammed decisions, you should follow all the steps in the decision-making model. Therefore, the second step for the individual or group facing such a decision requires setting objectives and developing criteria. **Nike's (Case Question 3)** objective in signing athletes to endorse its products is to make a profit by generating sales revenues that greatly exceed the cost of the endorsement.

Setting Objectives. Setting clear objectives helps managers to make better decisions, as it increases commitment.[39] Objectives drive decisions, and they must state what the decisions should accomplish—whether they will solve a problem or take advantage of an opportunity.[40] Teams are good at setting objectives and standards.[41] You'll learn how to set effective objectives in Chapter 5.

WORK
APPLICATION 4-5

Identify some of the qualification criteria (college degree, years of experience, etc.) for jobs at an organization you work for or have worked for. Distinguish any "must" and "want" criteria.

Setting Criteria. You should also specify the criteria for choosing an alternative solution to a problem, as they set the level of performance.[42] **Criteria** *are the standards that an alternative must meet to be selected as the decision that will accomplish the objective.* Having multiple criteria helps to optimize the decision. You should distinguish "must" and "want" criteria. "*Must*" criteria have to be met in order for an alternative to be acceptable, whereas "*want*" criteria are desirable but not necessary for the alternative to be acceptable. With satisficing, you stop with the first acceptable alternative; with optimizing, you seek to select the best possible option.

Suppose a regional manager faces the problem that a store manager has quit and a new manager must be hired. The objective is to hire a store manager by next month. The "must" criteria are that the person have a college degree and a minimum of five years' experience as a store manager. The "want" criterion is that the person should be a minority group member. The regional manager wants to hire a minority employee but will not hire one who does not meet the "must" criteria. We will discuss criteria again later in this chapter.

criteria The standards that an alternative must meet to be selected as the decision that will accomplish the objective.

4-1 | JOIN THE DISCUSSION ETHICS & SOCIAL RESPONSIBILITY

Avoiding Taxes

Many large corporations have an objective to pay less in taxes and are using corporate *tax loopholes* to avoid paying taxes. Walmart and Apple are such companies. Apple CEO Tim Cook was quoted in the press as defending Apple's tax-avoiding practices, which have saved $44 billion in offshore income from 2009 to 2012. Apple also has three Irish subsidiaries that claim to have no residence anywhere for tax purposes.[43] Some companies have moved headquarters out of the United States to countries with lower tax rates to save money.

It is not known just how many corporations are engaging in these kinds of activities. What is known, though, is that as

these corporations continue taking advantage of corporate tax loopholes, the more taxes ordinary families and small businesses pay.

1. Although it is legal, is it ethical for Apple, Walmart, and other corporations to take advantage of tax loopholes to save money?
2. If you became CEO of one of these corporations, would you continue to take advantage of the tax loopholes? Why or why not?
3. What is the government's role and responsibility regarding tax loopholes?

GENERATE CREATIVE AND INNOVATIVE ALTERNATIVES

After the problem is defined and objectives and criteria are set, you generate possible alternatives for solving the problem or exploiting the opportunity (step 3 of the decision-making model).[44] Usually, many possible ways exist to solve a problem. Without alternatives, you don't have to make a decision, and you should write your alternatives down.[45]

With programmed decision making, the alternative is usually determined by a policy. However, with nonprogrammed decision making, time, effort, and resources are needed to come up with new creative and innovative ideas.[46] In this section, you will read about creativity and innovation, as companies love to say they innovate; 43 percent of large companies have some type of a chief innovation officer.[47] We also discuss using decision trees and group methods for generating creative alternatives.

Apple has often lead the way when it comes to innovation, introducing successful products like the iPod, iPhone, and iPad. To continue to say on top Apple, like all companies, must continue to innovate. What will its next innovative product be? Photo from Kimihiro Hoshino/AFP/Getty Images.

Creativity and Innovation

Creativity *is a way of thinking that generates new ideas.* Creativity can lead to innovation. **Innovation** *is the implementation of a new idea.* Both things are critical for firm performance and survival.[48] Two important types of innovation are *product innovation* (new things goods/services) and *process innovation* (new ways of doing things).[49]

Apple is one of the most creative and innovative companies in the world. It created the PC. Its iPod and iTunes Music Store family of products revolutionized the way people listen to and buy music, and it continues to make creative changes to the iPhone and iPad.

After years of making juice and discarding the leftover cranberry skins, an employee at **Ocean Spray** came up with the idea of turning them into a consumer snack like Craisins.[50]

Nike (Case Question 4) is also considered innovative, as it continues to change the fashion looks of its sports footwear, apparel, and equipment with new materials, colors, and designs and star athletes to endorse them. Nike also offers the option of customizing your own shoes and apparel under the NIKEiD option at its website.

Creativity and Innovation Killers. There is a huge barrier to trying something different: the *fear of failure.*[51] You have to be willing to have fun and experiment and let the idea fail at first as you perfect it to success.[52] Success only comes from taking some risks.[53] To find out how much of a risk taker you are in five areas of life, see Self-Assessment 4–2.

While working with a group to come up with a decision, you'll want to be on guard against the kinds of responses that can block creativity and innovation, such as the following:[54]

- "It is impossible." "It can't be done."
- "We've never done it." "Has anyone else tried it?"
- "It won't work in our department (company/industry)."
- "It costs too much." "It isn't in the budget."
- "Let's form a committee."

LO 4-7

State the difference between creativity and innovation.

creativity A way of thinking that generates new ideas.

innovation The implementation of a new idea.

McDonald's tried to have breakfast 24/7. Its comment is "It's been tried and failed."[55] With this mentality, do you think it will ever happen? If group members say and think something is impossible, they will not try to be creative. If anyone makes such statements, your job is to remind the group to focus on generating ideas, the more offbeat the better, and to steer the discussion away from critiques of specific ideas, which are unproductive. So keep a positive, can-do attitude.

The Creative Process. Creativity can be considered the first stage in an innovative process.[56] The image of the creative type, like Steve Jobs of **Apple**, is a myth. Everyone has creative capability, and you can become more creative.[57] For example, **Coca-Cola**, **OMRON**, **Pitney Bowes**, **Shimizu**, and **Shiseido** have all developed training programs that emphasize creativity for their employees. The three stages in the **creative process** *are (1) preparation, (2) incubation and illumination, and (3) evaluation* (see Exhibit 4-6). As with the decision-making model, you may have to return to prior stages as you work through the creative process.

1. *Preparation.* First, you must define the problem by getting others' opinions, feelings, and ideas, as well as the facts. When solving a problem or seeking opportunities, look for new angles, use imagination and invention, and don't limit yourself to the boundaries of past thinking. Generate as many possible solutions as you can think of without making a judgment.

2. *Incubation and illumination.* After generating alternatives, take a break; sleep on the problem. During the incubation stage, as your subconscious works on the problem, you may gain an insight into the solution—*illumination.* Illumination can also happen while working on the problem; it is sometimes referred to as the "Aha, now I get it" phenomenon.

3. *Evaluation.* Before implementing a solution, you should evaluate the alternative to make sure the idea is practical. A good approach to use when evaluating a solution or alternative is to become the devil's advocate. With the **devil's advocate** approach, *group members focus on defending a solution while others try to come up with reasons the solution will not work.* Using the devil's advocate approach usually leads to more creativity as the idea is improved upon.

Engineer Arthur Fry of **3M** developed a new glue that was extremely weak (preparation), so the company decided not to use it. However, Fry sang in a church choir and put little pieces of paper in the hymnal to mark the songs. The problem was the paper often fell out. While listening to a sermon, he had an illumination to use his weak glue to solve the problem. The Post-it Note was evaluated and became a great success, and even today with all the electronic technology, it still sells well.[58]

LO 4-8

List and explain the three stages in the creative process.

EXHIBIT 4-6   STAGES IN THE CREATIVE PROCESS

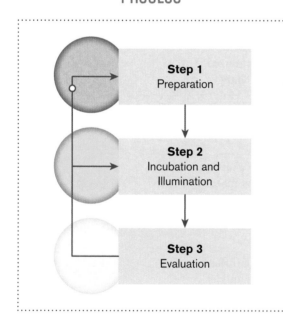

Step 1
Preparation

Step 2
Incubation and Illumination

Step 3
Evaluation

creative process The approach to generating new ideas that involves three stages (1) preparation, (2) incubation and illumination, and (3) evaluation.

devil's advocate approach Group members focus on defending a solution while others try to come up with reasons the solution will not work.

Using Information to Generate Alternatives. Successful managers use facts, information, and knowledge to make decisions.[59] Using input can lead to better decisions based on more complete information, increase employees' commitment to and perceived justice regarding those decisions, and improve employee performance.[60] However, when generating alternatives, the question for many managers is, "How much information and how many alternatives do I need, and where should I get them?" There is no simple answer. The more significant the decision, generally, the more information and/or alternatives you need. However, if you get too much information or have too many alternatives, the decision becomes too complex and the best alternative may not be selected.

Using Technology to Generate Alternatives. Technology, especially the Internet, has shown considerable potential for assisting with problem solving and decision making as it provides so much information instantly. However, when using the Internet to make decisions, one must be careful due to the amount of false information posted on the World Wide Web. Technology is also used to generate creative alternatives in groups.

Using Groups to Generate Creative Alternatives

As mentioned earlier in the chapter, there is a trend today toward group decision making.[61] A variety of methods are available for using groups to generate creative alternative solutions. Five of the more popular techniques are illustrated in Exhibit 4-7.

Brainstorming. Brainstorming *is the process of suggesting many possible alternatives without evaluation.* Brainstorming is a great way to generate creative ideas, so brainstorm ideas[62] following these guidelines. The group is presented with a problem and asked to develop as many solutions as possible. Members should be encouraged to make wild, extreme suggestions. You should also build on suggestions made by others. When selecting members for a brainstorming group, try to include diverse people;[63] 5 to 12 people make up a good-sized group. Status differences should be ignored; everyone should have an equal voice.[64] None of the alternatives should be evaluated until all possible alternatives have been presented.

Microsoft decided to rename its "Live Search" service. **Interbrand**, the firm that won the job of developing names, assigned eight people to brainstorm names around such themes as "speed" and "relevance." Over roughly six weeks, they came up with more than 2,000 choices. After whittling it down to eight choices, Microsoft chose "Bing" as the name of its new search engine.[65]

Using technology, a newer form of brainstorming is electronic *e-brainstorming*. People use computers to generate alternatives. Participants synchronously send ideas without getting together. People who are far apart geographically can brainstorm this way, and the number of participants does not have to be limited.

WORK
APPLICATION 4-7

Give an example of how you or someone else solved a problem using the stages in the creative process. Be sure to list the steps and note whether illumination came during incubation or while working on the problem.

EXHIBIT 4-7 GROUP DECISION-MAKING TECHNIQUES THAT FOSTER CREATIVITY AND INNOVATION

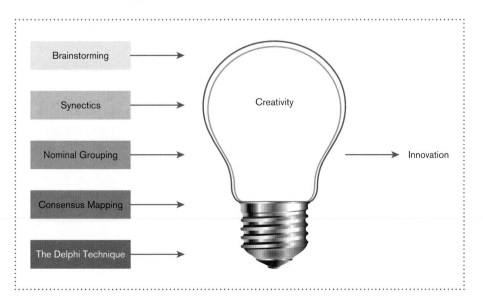

brainstorming The process of suggesting many possible alternatives without evaluation.

Synectics. Synectics *is the process of generating novel alternatives through role playing and fantasizing.* Synectics focuses on generating novel ideas rather than a large quantity of ideas. At first, the group leader does not even state the exact nature of the problem so that group members avoid preconceptions.

Nolan Bushnell, founder of **Chuck E. Cheese's**, wanted to develop a new concept in family dining, so he began by discussing leisure activities generally. Bushnell then moved to leisure activities having to do with eating out. The idea that came out of this synectic process was a restaurant–electronic game complex where families could entertain themselves while eating pizza and hamburgers.

Nominal Grouping. Nominal grouping *is the process of generating and evaluating alternatives using a structured voting method.* This process usually involves six steps:

1. *Listing.* Each participant generates ideas in writing.
2. *Recording.* Each member presents one idea at a time, and the leader records them where everyone can see them. This continues until all ideas are posted.
3. *Clarification.* Alternatives are clarified through a guided discussion, and any additional ideas are listed.
4. *Ranking.* Each employee rank-orders the ideas and identifies what he or she sees as the top three; low-ranked alternatives are eliminated.
5. *Discussion.* Rankings are discussed for clarification, not persuasion. During this time, participants should explain their choices and their reasons for making them.
6. *Vote.* A secret vote is taken to select the alternative.

Nominal grouping is appropriate to use in situations in which groups may be affected by disadvantages (Exhibit 4-4) of domination, goal displacement, conformity, and groupthink, because it minimizes these effects.

Consensus Mapping. Consensus mapping *is the process of developing group agreement on a solution to a problem.* If a consensus cannot be reached, the group does not make a decision. Consensus mapping differs from nominal grouping because there can be no competitive struggle ending in a vote that may force a solution on some members of the group. The Japanese call this approach *Ringi.* Consensus mapping can be used after brainstorming. In consensus mapping, the group categorizes or clusters ideas in the process of trying to agree on a single solution. A major benefit is that because any solution chosen is the group's, members generally are more committed to implementing it.[66] However, leaders can't always wait for consensus and must make decisions themselves.

The Delphi Technique. The *Delphi technique* involves using a series of confidential questionnaires to refine a solution. Responses on the first questionnaire are analyzed and resubmitted to participants on a second questionnaire. This process may continue for five or more rounds before a consensus emerges. Managers commonly use the Delphi technique for technological forecasting, such as projecting the next Internet breakthrough and its effect on a specific industry. By knowing what is to come, managers can make creative decisions to plan for the future.

Upper-level managers commonly use synectics and the Delphi technique for a specific decision. Brainstorming, nominal grouping, and consensus mapping techniques are frequently used at the departmental level with work groups.

WORK
APPLICATION 4-8

Give examples of organizational problems for which brainstorming, nominal grouping, or consensus mapping would be appropriate techniques.

synectics The process of generating novel alternatives through role playing and fantasizing.

nominal grouping The process of generating and evaluating alternatives using a structured voting method.

consensus mapping The process of developing group agreement on a solution to a problem.

4-3 APPLYING THE CONCEPT

Using Groups to Generate Alternatives

Identify the most appropriate group technique for generating alternatives in each situation.

A. brainstorming
B. synectics
C. nominal grouping
D. consensus mapping
E. Delphi technique

_____ 11. A manager wants to reduce waste in the production department to cut costs and increase productivity.

_____ 12. Management wants to project future trends in the banking industry as part of its long-range planning.

_____ 13. Management at a toy manufacturer wants to develop some new toys. It calls in a consultant, who is leading groups of employees and children to come up with ideas together.

_____ 14. A department is suffering from morale problems, and the manager doesn't know what to do about it.

_____ 15. A manager must choose new matching desks for the 10 employees in the office.

Decision Trees

After you come up with alternative problem solutions, you may want to make a decision tree. A *decision tree* is a diagram of alternatives. The diagram gives a visual picture of the alternatives, which makes it easier for some people to analyze them. Decision trees are also especially helpful when you face information overload.

Carolyn Blakeslee started **Art Calendar** (a business magazine for visual artists) dedicated to helping artists make a living doing what they love. Blakeslee started *Art Calendar* as a part-time business in a room in her house. But as the business grew, it became more than a full-time job. She wanted to have it all—to meet financial goals and devote time to her family and create her own artwork. Like many small business owners, she had to make a decision. Her choices are diagrammed in a decision tree in Exhibit 4-8.

EXHIBIT 4-8 DECISION TREE

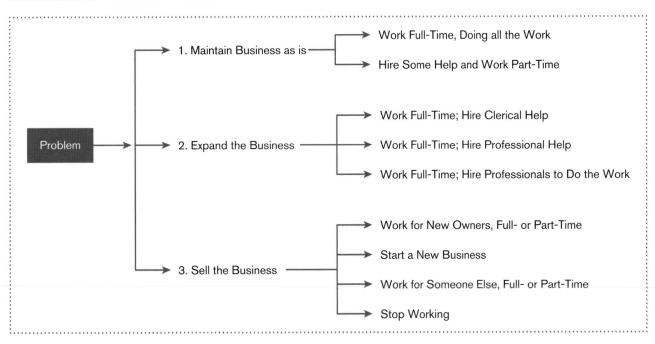

As Exhibit 4-8 shows, when creating a decision tree, you write down all the alternative solutions to a problem. After listing alternatives, you analyze them and make a decision. Blakeslee decided to expand her business—to work full-time and hire professional help. But she later decided to sell the company, now called **Professional Artist**.[67]

LO 4-9

Describe the differences among quantitative techniques, the Kepner-Tregoe method, and cost-benefit analysis for analyzing and selecting an alternative.

ANALYZE ALTERNATIVES AND SELECT THE MOST FEASIBLE

Notice that in the decision-making model in Exhibit 4-1, generating alternatives and analyzing alternatives and selecting the most feasible are two different steps (steps 3 and 4). This is because generating and evaluating alternatives at the same time tends to lead to satisficing and wasting time discussing poor alternatives rather than to optimizing.

In evaluating alternatives, think forward and try to predict the possible outcome of each. Be sure to compare alternatives to the objectives and criteria set in step 2 of the decision-making process. In addition, compare each alternative to the others.

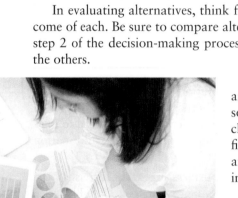

This section presents four approaches that are commonly used to analyze alternative solutions: quantitative techniques (a general class of approaches, of which we will discuss five), the Kepner-Tregoe method, cost-benefit analysis, and intuition. We also discuss making ethical decisions.

Quantitative Techniques

As you read in Chapter 1, one of the five approaches to management is management science, which uses math to aid in problem solving and decision making. Quantitative techniques professionalize decision making by using math in the objective analysis of alternative solutions.[68] Companies, including **IBM**, have analytics specialists running the numbers to improve selecting the best alternative decisions.[69]

Many companies today, including Amazon, realize that good decisions often hinge on gathering relevant data and performing good data analysis. Photo from Canstock.

The discussion that follows will make you aware of five quantitative techniques. Managers may not be expected to compute the math for all types of quantitative techniques. However, if you know when to use these techniques, you can seek help from specialists within or outside the organization. If you are interested in the actual calculations, you should take courses in quantitative analysis.

Break-Even Analysis. Break-even analysis allows calculation of the volume of sales or revenue that will result in a profit. It involves forecasting the volume of sales and the cost of production. The break-even point occurs at the level at which no profit or loss results. If a **Lowe's** store buys a carpet cleaner for $300 and rents it for $25 a day, how many times does it have to rent it in order to break even? If you said 12, you are correct.

Capital Budgeting. Capital budgeting is used to analyze alternative investments in assets, such as machines and the *make-or-buy* and rent/lease-or-buy decision. The payback approach allows the calculation of the number of years it will take to recover the initial cash invested. Another approach computes the *average rate of return*. It is appropriate when the yearly returns differ. A more sophisticated

4-4 APPLYING THE CONCEPT

Selecting Quantitative Methods

Select the appropriate quantitative method to use in each situation.

  A. break-even analysis
  B. capital budgeting
  C. linear programming
  D. queuing theory
  E. probability theory

____ 16. Carlos wants to invest money in stocks to make a profit.

____ 17. The manager of a fast-food restaurant wants to even the workload in the store. At times, employees hang around with no customers to wait on; at other times, they have long waiting lines.

____ 18. A Red Box owner wants to know how many times a DVD will have to be rented out to recoup the expense of adding it to the rental list.

____ 19. The registrar's office at the university is determining which classrooms to assign to which classes.

____ 20. Bailey must decide whether to repair her oldest machine or to replace it with a new one.

approach, *discounted cash flow*, takes into account the time value of money. It assumes that a dollar today is worth more than a dollar in the future. Organizations including **AMF, Kellogg's, Procter & Gamble,** and **3M** use discounted cash flow analysis.

Linear Programming. Optimum allocation of resources is determined using linear programming (LP). The resources that managers typically allocate are time, money, space, material, equipment, and employees. Companies primarily use LP for programmed decisions under conditions of certainty or low risk, but LP is also widely applied to product-mix decisions. **Lear Siegler** uses LP when determining work flow to optimize the use of its equipment. **Bendix** uses LP to minimize transportation (shipping) costs for its truck fleet.

Queuing Theory. Queuing theory focuses on waiting time. An organization can have any number of employees providing service to customers. If the organization has too many employees working at one time, not all of them will be waiting on customers, and the money paid to them is lost. If the organization has too few employees working at one time, it can lose customers who don't want to wait for service, which results in lost revenue. Queuing theory, which helps the organization balance these two costs, is used by retail stores to determine the optimum number of checkout clerks and by production departments to schedule preventive maintenance. **Kaiser Permanente** uses queuing theory to help doctors' offices reduce waiting times for patients.

Probability Theory. Probability theory enables the user to make decisions that take into consideration conditions of risk. You assign a probability of success or failure to each alternative. Then you calculate the expected value, which is the payoff or profit from each combination of alternatives and outcomes. The calculations are usually done on a payoff matrix by multiplying the probability of the outcome by the benefit or the cost. Probability theory is used to determine whether to expand facilities and to what size, to select the most profitable investment portfolio, and to determine the amount of inventory to stock. You could use it to choose a job. Using probability theory, hedge fund investors are providing movie financing to major film studios, such as **Walt Disney** and **Sony Pictures,** using computer-driven investment simulations to pick movies with the right characteristics to make money.

WORK
APPLICATION 4-9

Give examples from an organization you work for or have worked for of decisions that might appropriately be analyzed using the quantitative techniques of break-even analysis, capital budgeting, linear programming, queuing theory, and probability theory.

The Kepner-Tregoe Method

The Kepner-Tregoe method combines the objective quantitative approach with some subjectivity. The subjectivity comes from determining *"must" and "want" criteria* and assigning weighted values to them. As you read earlier in the chapter, "must" criteria are those attributes that an alternative solution must have if it is to be considered. "Want" criteria are desirable but not essential. Absence of certain "want" criteria does not cause an alternative to be eliminated. This method allows you to prioritize the criteria to ensure that the most important ones are given more weight through ranking them. When assigning ratings, be careful not to overweight low probabilities.[70]

The Kepner-Tregoe method is a technique for comparing alternatives using the criteria selected in step 2 of the decision-making model. It is helpful when comparing purchase options (such as when a business is considering acquiring machines, computers, or trucks) and when selecting people to be hired and promoted. Exhibit 4-9 shows an example of its use. Refer to the exhibit as you read the discussion of buying a car within two weeks. The choice of car is a nonprogrammed decision, which you will make by yourself. Exhibit 4-9 lists the "must" and "want" criteria for each alternative. (Determination of "must" and "want" criteria done for you corresponds to step 2 in the decision-making model in Exhibit 4-1. The choice of alternative cars in this example corresponds to step 3 in the decision-making model.)

1. **Step 1. Assess each alternative with regard to the "must" criteria.** Eliminate any alternative that does not meet all "must" criteria. As you can see, alternative car 4 does not meet all the "must" criteria and is eliminated.

2. **Step 2. Rate the importance of each "want" criterion on a scale from 1 to 10 (10 being most important).** Exhibit 4-9 lists these ratings in the Importance column. They range from 3 to 10.

3. **Step 3. Determine how well each alternative meets each "want" criterion.** Assign a value of 1 to 10 to each alternative for each criterion. (Some "want" criteria may be assigned the same value.) This step involves not only assessing each alternative individually on each criterion but also comparing the alternatives to each other on each criterion.

4. **Step 4. Compute the weighted score (WS) for each alternative on each criterion.** Working horizontally, multiply the number that indicates the importance of each criterion by the number indicating how well the alternative meets the criterion. Exhibit 4-9 shows a weighted score for each criterion for car 1 (as well as for car 2 and car 3). For each alternative, the eight individual weighted scores are added together to create a Total Weighted Score, shown at the bottom of each column.

5. **Step 5. Select the alternative with the highest total weighted score.** As the solution to the problem, car 2 should be selected because it has a total weighted score of 257 versus 248 and 247 for the other cars.

Cost-Benefit, Pros and Cons, and Intuition

Quantitative techniques and the Kepner-Tregoe method are objective mathematical approaches to comparing alternatives. However, there are times when management science approaches alone don't work well, as discussed here.

Cost-Benefit Analysis. Sometimes it is unclear whether the benefit to be gained from an alternative is worth its cost. For example, how do you put a price on a human

EXHIBIT 4-9 THE KEPNER-TREGOE METHOD FOR ANALYZING ALTERNATIVES

"Must" Criteria	Car 1	Car 2	Car 3	Car 4
Cost under $18,000	Yes	Yes	Yes	Yes
Available within one week	Yes	Yes	Yes	No

"Want" Criteria	Importance*	Car 1		Car 2		Car 3	
		Criterion Rating	Weighted Score	Criterion Rating	Weighted Score	Criterion Rating	Weighted Score
Good gas mileage	7	5	$7 \times 5 = 35$	6	$7 \times 6 = 42$	8	$7 \times 8 = 56$
Sporty	8	5	$8 \times 5 = 40$	7	$8 \times 7 = 56$	4	$8 \times 4 = 32$
Color (blue)	3	10	$3 \times 10 = 30$	0	$3 \times 0 = 0$	0	$3 \times 0 = 0$
AM/FM stereo/ CD Player	5	7	$5 \times 7 = 35$	8	$5 \times 8 = 40$	3	$5 \times 3 = 15$
Good condition	10	5	$10 \times 5 = 50$	6	$10 \times 6 = 60$	8	$10 \times 8 = 80$
Low mileage	6	6	$6 \times 6 = 36$	4	$6 \times 4 = 24$	5	$6 \times 5 = 30$
Relatively new	7	3	$7 \times 3 = 21$	5	$7 \times 5 = 35$	5	$7 \times 5 = 35$
TOTAL WEIGHTED SCORE (WS)			247		257		248

*Indicates importance (on a scale of 10 [high] to 1 [low]) assigned to each criterion as a weight.

life, and how should you compare the cost of adding extra safety features to the benefits of fewer "potential" accidents? In such cases, *cost-benefit analysis* is a technique for comparing the cost and benefit of each alternative course of action using subjective intuition and judgment along with math.

Pros and Cons. With pros-and-cons analysis, you identify the advantages, which can be considered the benefits, and the disadvantages, which can be considered the costs, of each alternative. Ben Franklin is said to have used pros-and-cons analysis. Franklin would draw a line down the middle of a piece of paper. On one side he would list the pros and on the other the cons of whatever he was considering. You should write them down too when using this technique for non-programmed decisions.

Intuition. *Intuition* is used when you make a decision based on experience, feeling, and accumulated judgment; it is unconscious reasoning. When you have dealt with a problem before and it comes up again, you can act quickly with what seems to be limited information when in fact it is based on your experience. Bill Gates of **Microsoft** said that Steve Jobs of **Apple** was a natural in terms of intuitive taste for both people and products.[71] Intuition is commonly used with non-programmed decisions with low risk, but it is also used with the decision-making model to complement the other techniques; Exhibit 4-10 compares the three major approaches to analyzing and selecting alternatives.

EXHIBIT 4-10 CONTINUUM OF ANALYSIS TECHNIQUES

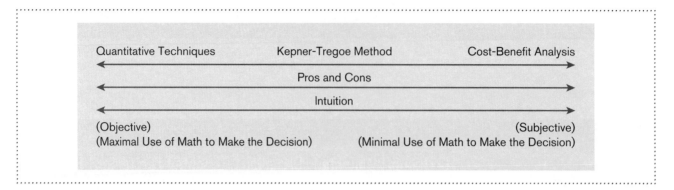

WORK
APPLICATION 4-10

Give examples from an organization where you work or have worked of decisions that might appropriately be analyzed using the Kepner-Tregoe method and cost-benefit analysis.

As shown in Exhibit 4-10, cost-benefit analysis, pros and cons, and intuition are more subjective than management science techniques and the Kepner-Tregoe method. Therefore, when using this approach with a group, the group should do a realistic critical evaluation of all alternatives when making nonprogrammed decisions. Using a method such as the devil's advocate approach can help the group avoid the potential problems of satisficing, dominance, and groupthink.

Regardless of the method used to analyze alternatives, the one selected must meet the criteria established in step 2 of the decision-making model. If none of the alternatives meets the criteria, you have two options: (1) return to step 2 and change the criteria for the best alternative or (2) return to step 3 and generate more alternatives.

Multimillion-dollar endorsement contracts may seem like a lot to offer to star athletes. However, contract amounts are paid over several years, and **Nike (Case Question 5)** has more than $24 billion in sales yearly. The contracts also include clauses that specify how they may be ended if things don't work out. So, relatively speaking, endorsement contracts are not a great financial risk for Nike. Nike can use quantitative break-even analysis in making contract decisions, as Nike managers know the cost and can figure the sales needed to break even on contracts. Probability theory might be used to analyze contract decisions. Cost-benefit analysis and intuition are no doubt also applied in making contract decisions, as there is a cost to having a competitor contract with the athletes, thereby causing Nike to lose sales and market share.

Ethics and Social Responsibility in Decision Making

As discussed in Chapter 2, corporations are expected to be ethical and socially responsible. **BP** made decisions to save the company time and expenses rather than doing what was ethical and socially responsible. The result was 11 workers killed and the worst oil spill in U.S. history. Doing the right thing is not only a moral issue, it invariably makes companies more competitive and reputable. BP's careless decision making not only caused loss of business but damaged its reputation tremendously.

When performing the management functions, you need to maintain high ethical standards. Even when making unpopular decisions, such as layoffs, you can still be ethical and socially responsible. For example, many companies provide advance notice of layoffs, give severance pay to those losing their jobs, and help people who lose their jobs find new ones within the company or elsewhere. As a manager, you should follow the ethical guidelines in Chapter 2 when analyzing alternatives to make sure you select one that is ethical while striving to be socially responsible and considering sustainability.

Plan, Implement the Decision, and Control

The final two steps in the decision-making model involve planning and implementing the decision (step 5) and controlling (step 6). After making a decision, you develop a plan of action with a schedule for implementation.[72] (You will learn the details of the planning process in the next chapter.)

After a decision has been made and plans developed, the plans must be implemented. This seems obvious, but one in three decisions is not implemented.[73] Communicating the plan to all employees is critical to successful implementation. (You will learn about communication in Chapter 13.) In implementing a decision, it is likely to be necessary to delegate assignments to others. (You will learn about delegating in Chapter 7.)

Control methods should be developed while planning to measure decision outcomes. Checkpoints should be established to determine whether the chosen alternative is solving the problem. If not, corrective action may be needed.[74] When we will not admit that we made a bad decision, we are in the process known as *escalation of commitment*.[75] We tend to maintain commitment to losing courses of action, even in the face of bad news, by wasting more resources.[76] Why? Because we don't like to lose something once we have it and we don't like to admit we made a mistake even to ourselves. The pain of losing outweighs the joy of winning. It's called *loss aversion*.[77] When you make a poor decision, you should admit the mistake and try to rectify it quickly.[78] Go back over the steps in the decision-making model. You also need to learn from your mistakes by building intuition so you don't repeat them.

Cutting corners to save on expenses can result in being socially irresponsible and much more costly in the long run. The 2010 Deepwater Horizon Spill illustrated just how catastrophic poor decision making can be. Photo from United States Coast Guard.

Vroom's Participative Decision-Making Model

Earlier in the chapter, we discussed some of the advantages of group decision making. Today's managers need a way of determining not only when to use groups to arrive at decisions and when to make decisions alone but also, when a group is used, what level of participation to use. The model is based on research by Victor Vroom and his colleagues at Yale University on leadership and decision-making processes, involving more than 100,000 managers.[79] (Note that the model does not take the place of the decision-making model; it tells you when to use a group and what level of participation you should use with the decision-making model.) In this section, you will learn how to use the model, and in Applying the Concept 4–5 and Skill Builder 4–2, you can develop your skill at using the model to make decisions.

Using the Participative Decision-Making Model

The **participative decision-making model** *is a time-driven or development-driven decision tree that assists a user in selecting one of five leadership styles (decide, consult individuals, consult group, facilitate, and delegate) to use in a given situation (based on seven questions/variables) to maximize a decision.*

Vroom's model is called a normative model because it provides a sequential set of questions that are rules (norms) to follow to determine the best decision style

participative decision-making model A time-driven or development-driven decision tree that assists a user in selecting one of five leadership styles to use in a given situation to maximize a decision.

Selling Stocks

Assume you are a stockbroker for an investment company. Your manager has encouraged you to sell a specific company stock, the XYZ Company, and your company pays a higher commission rate on the sale of the XYZ stock than it does for others. You have done an analysis of the XYZ stock and do not think it is the best recommendation for your investors.

1. Is it ethical for the company to pay a higher commission on some stocks?
2. Is it ethical for you to recommend a stock that you don't believe is the best stock even though you will earn a higher commission if you do?
3. What would you do if you didn't sell the stock and your boss had a meeting with you to encourage you to sell the stock?

for the given situation. To use the participative model, you must have a specific decision to make, have the authority to make the decision, and have specific group members who may participate in the decision. As you read this section, be sure to refer to Exhibit 4-11. As you can see, there are two versions of the model and questions to answer.

Select the Time-Driven or Development-Driven Decision. First you must choose one of the two versions of the model. The choice is determined by whether timeliness or group development is more important in the given situation.

- Use the *time-driven model* when it is more important to make a decision relatively quickly.
- Use the *development-driven model* when it is more important to gain group commitment and support by giving group members decision-making practice.

Answer Questions That Determine the Appropriate Participative Decision Style. To determine which of the five leadership styles is the most appropriate for a given situation, you answer a series of diagnostic questions based on seven variables. Note that the questions are the same on both models. The seven questions are numbered 1 through 7 and are found at the top of the model. As stated in Exhibit 4-11, you rate each questions as high (H) or low (L) in importance.

Here we explain each question in more detail by its number: (1) How important is the decision to the success of the project or organization? (2) How important is group commitment to implementing the decision? (3) How much knowledge and expertise does the leader have with respect to this decision? (4) If the leader were to make the decision alone, is the certainty that the group would be committed to the decision H or L? (5) Does the group show H or L support for the team or organizational goals to be attained? (6) How much knowledge and expertise do individual group members have with respect to this decision? and (7) Is group members' competence in working together as a team to solve the problem H or low L?

Not all seven questions are relevant to all decisions. In some situations, as few as two questions are needed to select the most appropriate leadership style. As questions 3 and 6 imply, for important decisions, it is critical to include the leader and/or group members with the expertise to solve the problem. The issue of commitment (questions 2 and 4) is also important. And as questions 5 through 7 imply, a leader should not delegate decisions to groups with low support for objectives, low group expertise, and low team competence.

EXHIBIT 4-11 PARTICIPATIVE DECISION-MAKING MODEL

The model is a decision tree used for making a specific decision. First, select one of the two models based on whether timeliness or group development is more important in the given situation. Next, answer going from left to right, answer the questions as being either high (H) or low (L) in importance to the decision, skipping those are not relevant and avoiding crossing any horizontal lines. The last column gives you the leadership style to use to make the decision.

Time Driven (PROBLEM STATEMENT)

1 Decision Significance?	2 Importance of Commitment?	3 Leader Expertise?	4 Likelihood of Commitment?	5 Group Support?	6 Group Expertise?	7 Team Competence?	Time-Driven Decision
H			H	–	–	–	Decide
						H	Delegate
		H	L		H	L	Consult (Group)
			H	L	–		
			L	–	–		
						H	Facilitate
					H	L	Consult (Individuals)
	L		H	L	–		
	H		H	L	–		
						H	Facilitate
					H	L	Consult (Group)
			L	H	L	–	
				L	–	–	
		H	–	–	–	–	Decide
						H	Facilitate
		L			H	L	Consult (Individuals)
		L	–	H	L	–	
				L	–	–	
L	H		H	–	–	–	Decide
						H	Delegate
						L	Facilitate
	L	–	–	–	–	–	Decide

Development Driven (PROBLEM STATEMENT)

1 Decision Significance?	2 Importance of Commitment?	3 Leader Expertise?	4 Likelihood of Commitment?	5 Group Support?	6 Group Expertise?	7 Team Competence?	Development-Driven Decision
H						H	Delegate
					H	L	Facilitate
				H	L	–	Consult (Group)
				H	L	–	
	H					H	Delegate
					H	L	Facilitate
			L	H	L	–	
		–		L	–	–	Consult (Group)
						H	Delegate
					H	L	Facilitate
	L			H	L	–	Consult (Group)
					L	–	–
L	H		H	–	–	–	Decide
					L	–	–	Delegate
	L	–	–	–	–	–	Decide

Source: Reprinted from *Organizational Dynamics,* Volume 28 (4), Victor H. Vroom, "Leadership and the Decision-Making Process," p. 87, Copyright 2000 with permission from Elsevier.

Participation Decision Styles

After answering the questions on the model, you end by finding out which decision style to use in the given situation. Here are Vroom's five leadership styles to use based on the level of participation of group members in the decision:

- **Decide.** You, as the leader of the group, make the decision alone and announce it, or sell it, to the group. You may get information from others outside the group and within the group without specifying the problem.

- **Consult Individuals.** You describe the problem to individual group members, get information and suggestions, and then make the decision.
- **Consult Group.** You hold a meeting and describe the problem to the group, get information and suggestions, and then you make the decision.
- **Facilitate.** You hold a group meeting and act as a facilitator as the group works to define the problem and the limits within which a decision must be made. As the leader, you seek participation, debate, and concurrence on the decision without pushing your ideas. However, you have the final say on the decision.
- **Delegate.** You let the group diagnose the problem and make the decision within stated limits. Your role as the leader is to answer questions and provide encouragement and resources.

4-5 APPLYING THE CONCEPT

The Participative Decision-Making Model

Refer to the time-driven model in Exhibit 4–11 and select the appropriate decision style for each situation.

A. decide
B. consult individuals
C. consult group
D. facilitate
E. delegate

_____ 21. Things are going okay in your department, but you know that performance could be better. The workers are knowledgeable, have positive work norms, and work well together. You are thinking about having a one-time brainstorming session. You've never led one.

_____ 22. You are a new manager, and you find that someone in your department has been making lots of personal photocopies. The extra expense is affecting your budget. You want the copying to stop. You are pretty sure you know who is doing it.

Refer to the development-driven model in Exhibit 4–11 and select the appropriate decision style for each situation.

F. decide
G. consult individuals
H. consult group
I. facilitate
J. delegate

_____ 23. You oversee a self-directed team, which requires very little supervision. One of the seven team members has retired and needs to be replaced.

_____ 24. You supervise five part-time employees who are high school students. You know that your store has been losing customers, but you don't know why. You want to find out and improve the situation.

_____ 25. You work in purchasing and have to buy five new cars for the sales staff within a set budget.

WORK
APPLICATION 4-11

Give an example of a specific decision that you or your boss have had to make. Was the decision time driven or development driven? Using Exhibit 4–11, select the appropriate decision style for the situation. Be sure to state the questions you answered and how (H or L) you answered each.

Vroom has developed a *computerized version* of his model that is more complex and more precise yet easier to use than the version just described. It combines the time-driven and development-driven versions into one model, includes 11 variables/questions (rather than 7), and has five possible levels for each variable (not simply H or L). In addition, the computerized version guides the user through the process of analyzing the situation with definitions, examples, and other forms of help. Although the computerized model is beyond the scope of this course, you will have a chance to practice using the time-driven and development-driven models in Skill Builder 4–2.

Nike (Case Question 6) managers don't want to make a quick decision and the decision has a long-term orientation because contracts last for years and advertising is ongoing. Therefore, Nike should use the development-driven version of Vroom's model.

Having read this chapter, you should understand the importance of problem solving and decision making; how to use the decision-making model (and when not to use it); the importance of creativity and quantitative techniques in analyzing alternatives; and the need to plan, implement the decision, and control it. Finally, it is important to be ethical and socially responsible in your decision making and make sure that the employees you supervise are too in order to ensure sustainability.

• • • CHAPTER SUMMARY

4-1. **Explain the relationship among objectives, problem solving, and decision making.**

Managers are responsible for setting and achieving organizational objectives. When managers do not meet objectives, a problem results. When a problem exists, decisions must be made about what, if any, action must be taken.

4-2. **Explain the relationship among the management functions, problem solving, and decision making.**

When managers perform the functions of planning, organizing, leading, and controlling, they make decisions and solve problems.

4-3. **List the six steps in the decision-making model.**

The steps in the decision-making model are (1) classifying and defining the problem or opportunity, (2) setting objectives and criteria, (3) generating creative and innovative alternatives, (4) analyzing alternatives and selecting the most feasible, (5) planning and implementing the decision, and (6) controlling the decision.

4-4. **Describe the differences between programmed and nonprogrammed decisions and among the conditions of certainty, uncertainty, and risk.**

Programmed decisions are recurrent, routine, and nonsignificant. Nonprogrammed decisions are non-recurring, nonroutine, and significant. The difference in decision-making conditions is based on the degree of certainty of the outcome of the decision. Under conditions of certainty, you know the outcome of alternatives. Under conditions of risk, you can assign probabilities to the outcomes, but you do not know the outcomes of alternatives. Under conditions of uncertainty, lack of information or knowledge makes the outcome of each alternative unpredictable, so you cannot determine probabilities.

4-5. **Describe when to use rational versus bounded rational decision making and group versus individual decision making.**

Use rational decision making with a group when faced with a nonprogrammed decision with high risk or uncertainty. Use bounded rational decision making and make an individual decision when faced with a programmed decision with low risk or certainty. However, this is a general guide; there may be exceptions to the rule.

4-6. **State the difference between an objective and "must" and "want" criteria.**

An objective is the result you want to achieve when making the decision. "Must" criteria are the requirements that an alternative must meet to be selected. "Want" criteria are desirable but are not necessary for an alternative to be selected.

4-7. **State the difference between creativity and innovation.**

Creativity is a way of thinking that generates new ideas. Innovation is the implementation of new ideas for products and processes.

4-8. **List and explain the three stages in the creative process.**

The three stages are (1) preparation—developing familiarity with the problem, (2) incubation and illumination—taking a break from the problem and perhaps getting an idea for the solution, and (3) evaluation—making sure the idea will work.

4-9. **Describe the differences among quantitative techniques, the Kepner-Tregoe method, and cost-benefit analysis for analyzing and selecting an alternative.**

Quantitative techniques and the Kepner-Tregoe method are management science approaches; cost-benefit analysis is not. Quantitative methods use math to objectively select the alternative with the highest value. The Kepner-Tregoe method uses math, with some subjectivity in selecting and weighting criteria, to select the alternative with the highest value. Cost-benefit analysis is primarily based on subjective analysis; it can use some math, but alternatives do not have a final number value to compare.

• • • KEY TERMS

brainstorming, 105
consensus mapping, 106
creative process, 104
creativity, 103
criteria, 102
decision making, 94

decision-making conditions, 98
decision-making model, 96
devil's advocate approach, 104
innovation, 103
nominal grouping, 106
nonprogrammed decisions, 98

participative decision-making
   model, 113
problem, 94
problem solving, 94
programmed decisions, 97
synectics, 106

• • • KEY TERM REVIEW

Complete each of the following statements using one of this chapter's key terms.

1. A _____ exists whenever objectives are not being met.

2. _____ is the process of taking corrective action to meet objectives.

3. _____ is the process of selecting a course of action that will solve a problem.

4. The steps of _____ include (1) classifying and defining the problem or opportunity, (2) setting objectives and criteria, (3) generating creative and innovative alternatives, (4) analyzing alternatives and selecting the most feasible, (5) planning and implementing the decision, and (6) controlling the decision.

5. For _____, which are recurring or routine, the decision maker should use decision rules or organizational policies and procedures.

6. For _____, which are significant, nonrecurring, and nonroutine, the decision maker should use the decision-making model.

7. The three _____ are certainty, risk, and uncertainty.

8. _____ are the standards that an alternative must meet to be selected as the decision that will accomplish the objective.

9. _____ is a way of thinking that generates new ideas.

10. _____ is the implementation of a new idea.

11. The three stages in the _____ are (1) preparation, (2) incubation and illumination, and (3) evaluation.

12. With the _____, group members focus on defending a proposed solution to a problem while others try to come up with criticisms of why the solution will not work.

13. _____ is the process of suggesting many possible alternatives without evaluation.

14. _____ is the process of generating novel alternatives through role playing and fantasizing.

15. _____ is the process of generating and evaluating alternatives using a structured voting method.

16. _____ is the process of developing group agreement on a solution to a problem.

17. The _____ is a time-driven or development-driven decision tree that assists users in selecting one of five leadership styles to use in a given situation to maximize a decision.

• • • REVIEW QUESTIONS

1. What is the relationship among the management functions, problem solving, and decision making?

2. Why is it necessary to determine the decision structure and decision-making conditions?

3. What is the current trend concerning the use of groups to solve problems and make decisions?

4. Is a decrease in sales and/or profits a symptom or a cause of a problem?

5. Would a maximum price of $1,000 to spend on a stereo be an objective or a criterion?

6. Is there really a difference between creativity and innovation?

7. What is the major difference between nominal grouping and consensus mapping?

8. Why are generating and analyzing alternatives separate steps in the decision-making model?

9. What quantitative techniques are commonly used to compare alternatives?

10. When is the cost-benefit analysis commonly used?

11. For what is Vroom's participative decision-making model primarily used?

• • • COMMUNICATION SKILLS

The following critical-thinking questions can be used for class discussion and/or as written assignments to develop communication skills. Be sure to give complete explanations for all questions.

1. Are problem solving and decision making really all that important? How do you rate your decision-making ability?

2. Which potential advantage and disadvantage of group problem solving and decision making do you think arises most frequently?

3. Are creativity and innovation really important to all types of businesses? Is it important to evaluate a creative idea before it becomes an innovation?

4. What is the role of intuition in decision making? Should managers use more objective or subjective intuition techniques when making decisions?

5. Have you ever used any of the techniques for analyzing and selecting an alternative? If so, which one(s)?

6. Should managers be ethical in their decision making? If so, how should ethics be used in decision making?

7. Have you or someone you know experienced escalation of commitment? If so, explain.

8. Do men and women make decisions differently?

9. Have you ever made a decision with information that was not timely, of good quality, complete, and/or relevant? If so, was the decision a good one? Why or why not?

• • • CASE: THE COCA-COLA COMPANY

Coca-Cola was created by Dr. John Stith Pemberton, a pharmacist in Atlanta, Georgia. It went on sale in a drugstore for five cents a glass as a soda fountain drink on May 8, 1886. Today, the Coca-Cola Company is the largest beverage company in the world. It has grown to become the world's most recognized brand, with more than 3,500 products sold in 200 countries. Coca-Cola is ranked in the top 60 Fortune 500 Companies, top 210 Fortune Global 500 Companies, top 5 of the Fortune World's Most Admired Companies, and its CEO Muhtar Kent is ranked in the Fortune top 10 Businessperson of the Year.

Coke was one of the first U.S. companies to go international. The company began building its global network in the 1920s. One of the first countries the company expanded to was China, opening its first bottling plants in Tianjin and Shanghai in 1927. In recent years, it has spent more than $2 billion expanding operations in China. In the late 2000s, the Coca-Cola Company was looking for new ways to expand in China. Coca-Cola announced a bid for Huiyuan, one of China's top local brands and the country's largest maker of 100-percent fruit juice. The deal would have been the largest for the Coca-Cola Company in Asia and the second-largest acquisition overall for the company in its history. However, the Chinese government found Coca-Cola's bid to be in violation of the country's new antimonopoly law and blocked the company's acquisition bid. Coke still wants to grow in China, so what should it do at this point?

Case Questions

1. Explain the relationship between Coca-Cola's objective, decision, and problem in this case.

2. What is the classification of the problem/opportunity and which decision-making model should have been used in the acquisition decision in this case?

3. Which quantitative techniques could have been used in the acquisition decision in this case?

4. After having its bid for Huiyuan rejected, should Coca-Cola have continued to focus on acquisitions by trying to acquire another company in an attempt to expand in China?

5. After having its bid for Huiyuan rejected, what other alternatives did Coca-Cola have to expand in China? Faced with this problem, what should Coke do?

6. Do you drink Coca-Cola Company beverages? If so, which products? How many of the 3,500+ Coca-Cola brands can you name?

Cumulative Case Questions

7. Describe the role of the manager's resources in Coca-Cola's success. (Chapter 1)

8. Which management functions, skills, and management levels are more important in developing the growth strategy for Coca-Cola? Which are more important for making and delivering Coca-Cola beverages? (Chapter 1)

9. Coca-Cola has been a highly successful company over the years. Which internal and external

environmental factors were most instrumental in its long-term success? (Chapter 2)

10. How is Coca-Cola's business classified in the global village? Which approach to taking a business global is it using today? (Chapter 3)

Source: Information for this case was taken from the Coca-Cola Company's website at http://www.thecoca-colacompany.com, accessed September 17, 2013. Fortune Global 500 (July 22, 2013), F3; Fortune 500 (May 20, 2013), F3; Fortune Businessperson of the Year (December 12, 2011), 91. Fortune The World's Most Admired Companies (March 18, 2013), 138.

••• SKILL BUILDER 4-1: MAKING A DECISION USING THE DECISION-MAKING MODEL

Select a problem or opportunity that you now face. Remember, a problem exists when objectives are not being met—when there is a difference between what is happening and what you want to happen. The problem or opportunity may be from any facet of your life—work, college, sports, a relationship, a purchase to be made in the near future, where to go on a date, and so on. Use the decision-making model outline that follows to solve your problem or take advantage of the opportunity.

Objective

To improve your ability to make decisions.

Skills

The primary skills developed through this exercise are:

Management skill—decision making (conceptual, diagnostic, analytical, critical thinking, and quantitative reasoning)

AACSB competency—analytic skills

Management function—primarily planning (but decisions are made when organizing, leading, and controlling)

Step 1. Classify and Define the Problem or Opportunity

Decision structure. Do you need to make a programmed or a nonprogrammed decision?

Decision condition. Are you facing a condition of uncertainty, of risk, or of certainty?

Decision-making type. Is a rational or bounded rational decision appropriate? (Continue to follow all steps in the decision-making model even if a bounded rational decision is appropriate.)

Select the appropriate level of participation. Should the decision be made by an individual or a group? (If a group decision is appropriate, use a group for the following steps in the model. But remember to maximize the advantages and minimize the disadvantages of group decision making.)

Define the problem. List the symptoms and causes of the problem (or opportunity); then write a clear statement of it.

Step 2. Set Objectives and Criteria

Write down what is to be accomplished by the decision and the standards that any alternative must meet to be selected as the decision that will accomplish the objective. (Specify "must" and "want" criteria if appropriate for the decision.)

Objective: Criteria: (must) and (want)

Step 3. Generate Creative and Innovative Alternatives

What information do you need? (Remember that information must be timely, of good quality, complete, and relevant to be useful.) Will you use any technology?

If you are working with a group, will brainstorming, nominal grouping, or consensus mapping be used?

List your alternatives (at least three); number them. If a decision tree will be helpful, make one.

Step 4. Analyze Alternatives and Select the Most Feasible

Is a quantitative, Kepner-Tregoe, or cost-benefit (pros and cons) analysis appropriate? Choose a method and complete your analysis.

Step 5. Plan and Implement the Decision

Write out your plan for implementing the decision. Be sure to state the controls you will use to make sure you know if the decision is working. How can you avoid escalation of commitment?

Step 6. Control the Decision

After implementing the decision, make notes about progress in solving the problem or taking advantage of the opportunity. Indicate any need for corrective action, and if you need to, return to prior steps in the decision-making model.

Apply It

What did I learn from this experience? How will I use this knowledge in the future?

Your instructor may ask you to do this Skill Builder in class in a group. If so, the instructor will provide you with any necessary information or additional instructions.

••• SKILL BUILDER 4-2

Using the Vroom Model

You read about the Vroom participative decision-making model in this chapter. Using the appropriate version of the model (time-driven or development-driven), determine which leadership style to use for each situation below. Note that this skill builder is based on leadership and can be used with Chapter 12.

Objective

To determine the appropriate leadership style.

Skills

The primary skills developed through this exercise are:

1. *Management skill*—decision making (conceptual, diagnostic, analytical, critical thinking, and quantitative reasoning)

2. *AACSB competency*—analytic skills

3. *Management function*—primarily planning (but decisions are made when organizing, leading, and controlling)

Situation 1

You are the manager of the production department for a company that manufactures a mass-produced product. You have two production machines in your department with 10 people working on each. You have an important order that needs to be shipped first thing tomorrow. Your boss has made it very clear that you must meet this deadline. It's 2:00 P.M., and you are right on schedule to meet the order deadline. At 2:15, an employee tells you that one of the machines is smoking a little and making a noise. If you keep running the machine, it may make it until the end of the day and you will deliver the important shipment on time. If you shut down the machine, the manufacturer will not be able to check it until tomorrow and you will miss the deadline. You call your boss, but there is no answer; there is no telling how long it will take for the boss to get back to you if you leave a message. There are no higher-level managers to consult, and no one with more knowledge of the machine than you. Which leadership style should you use?

Step 1. Which version of the model should you use? (_____ time-driven _____ development-driven)

Step 2. How did you answer the model's questions? Did you skip any questions?

Step 3. Which leadership style is the most appropriate?

__ Decide __ Consult individuals __ Consult group __ Facilitate __ Delegate

Situation 2

You are the leader of your church, with 125 families (200 members). You have a doctor of religious studies degree with just two years' experience as the head of a church; you have not taken any business courses. The church has one paid secretary, three part-time program directors for religious instruction, music, and social activities, plus many volunteers. The paid staff members serve on your advisory board with 10 other church members who are primarily business leaders in the community. You develop a yearly budget, which is approved by the advisory board. The church's source of income is weekly member donations. The advisory board doesn't want the church to operate in the red, and the church has very modest surplus funds. Your volunteer accountant, who is a board member, asks to meet with you. During the meeting, she informs you that weekly collections are down 20 percent below budget and that the cost of utilities has increased 25 percent over the yearly budget figure. You are running a large deficit, and at this rate your surplus will be gone in two months. Which leadership style will you use to address these problems?

Step 1: Which version of the model should you use? (_____ time-driven _____ development-driven)

Step 2: How did you answer the model's questions? Did you skip any questions?

Step 3: Which leadership style is most appropriate?

__ Decide __ Consult individuals __ Consult group __ Facilitate __ Delegate

Situation 3

You are the new dean of the school of business at a small private university. The faculty consists of 20 professors, only 2 of whom are nontenured; on average, these faculty members have been at the university for 12 years. You expect to leave this job for one at a larger school in three years. Your primary goal is to start an advisory board for the business school to improve community relations and alumni relations and to raise money for financial aid. As you are new to the area and have no business contacts, you need help to develop a network of alumni and other community leaders fairly quickly if you are to show results at the end of your three years on the job. Members of the faculty get along well and are generally talkative, but when you approach small groups of them, they tend to become quiet and disperse. Which leadership style would you use to achieve your objective?

Step 1: Which version of the model should you use? (_____ time-driven _____ development-driven)

Step 2: How did you answer the model's questions? Did you skip any questions?

Step 3: Which leadership style is most appropriate?

__ Decide__ Consult individuals __ Consult group __ Facilitate __ Delegate

Situation 4

You are the president of a dotcom company that has been having financial problems for a few years. As a result, your top two managers left for other jobs, one four months ago and the other two months ago. With your networking contacts, you replaced both within a month, but the new managers don't have a lot of time on the job and haven't worked together for very long. They currently have their own individual approaches to getting their jobs done. However, they are both very bright, hardworking, and dedicated to your vision of what the company can be. To turn the company around, you and your two managers will have to work together, with the help of all your employees. Virtually all the employees are high-tech specialists who want to be included in decision making. Your business partners have no more money to invest. If you cannot turn a profit in four to five months, you will most likely go bankrupt. Which primary leadership style would you use to achieve your objective?

Step 1: Which version of the model should you use? (____ time-driven ____ development-driven)

Step 2: How did you answer the model's questions? Did you skip any questions?

Step 3: Which leadership style is most appropriate?

__ Decide __ Consult individuals __ Consult group __ Facilitate __ Delegate

Apply It

What did I learn from this experience? How will I use this knowledge in the future?

Your instructor may ask you to do this Skill Builder in class in a group. If so, the instructor will provide you with any necessary information or additional instructions.

• • • STUDENT STUDY SITE 📱

Visit the Student Study Site at **www.sagepub.com/lussier6e** to access to these additional study tools:

- Mobile-compatible self-assessment quizzes
- Mobile-compatible key term flashcards
- Video Links
- SAGE Journal Articles
- Web Links

5 Strategic and Operational Planning

Learning Outcomes

After studying this chapter, you should be able to:

5-1. Describe how strategic planning differs from operational planning. PAGE 127

5-2. Explain the reason for conducting an industry and competitive situation analysis. PAGE 129

5-3. Explain the reason for conducting a company situation analysis. PAGE 130

5-4. List the parts of an effective written objective. PAGE 133

5-5. Describe the four grand strategies. PAGE 136

5-6. Describe the three growth strategies. PAGE 137

5-7. Describe the three adaptive strategies. PAGE 140

5-8. State the difference between standing plans and single-use plans. PAGE 143

IDEAS ON MANAGEMENT at Starbucks

Howard Schultz was working in a local **Starbucks,** named after the quiet and right-minded character from Herman Melville's *Moby Dick*. Its logo is also inspired by the sea, featuring a twin-tailed siren from Greek mythology. The idea that transformed the local coffee retailer into a global brand came to Schultz on a visit to Italy. Observing the popularity of espresso bars there, he thought of introducing the coffee bar concept back in the United States. Schultz later bought Starbucks' assets, and the company now serves millions of customers every day in nearly 18,000 retail stores in 60 countries with profits exceeding $1.3 billion annually, and it become ranked in the top half of the *Fortune* 500. Starbucks was also named the World's Most Ethical Company. Starbucks Corporation founder Schultz continues to be president, CEO, and chairman of the board and is one of the Forbes Richest People in America with wealth greater than $1.5 billion. He is such a great CEO that he was named Business Person of the Year by *Fortune*.

1. What are some of Starbucks's strategic and operational plans? PAGE 127
2. What are Starbucks's mission statement and competitive advantage? PAGES 129, 132
3. What long-range goals has Starbucks established? PAGE 133
4. What is the corporate grand strategy and primary growth strategy at Starbucks? PAGES 136, 137, 138
5. What types of adaptive and competitive strategies does Starbucks currently employ? PAGES 140, 141
6. What type of functional and operational plans does Starbucks have? PAGE 145

You'll find answers to these questions throughout the chapter. To learn more about Starbucks, visit its website at www.starbucks.com.

Sources: Information for this case was taken from http://www.starbucks.com, accessed June 13, 2013; "Largest U.S. corporations—Fortune 500," *Fortune* (May 20, 2013): 1–20; R. M. Murphy, "The 2011 Business Person of the Year," *Fortune* (December 12, 2011): 87–95; "The Richest People in America: The Forbes 400," *Forbes* (October 8, 2012): 129–136.

• • • Chapter Outline

Strategic and Operational Planning
Planning Dimensions
Strategic versus Operational Planning and Strategies
The Strategic Planning Process
Developing the Mission
Analyzing the Environment
Situation Analysis
Competitive Advantage
Setting Objectives
Writing Effective Objectives
Criteria for Objectives
Management by Objectives (MBO)
Corporate Strategies
Grand Strategy

Growth Strategies
Portfolio Analysis
Business Strategies
Adaptive Strategies
Competitive Strategies
Operational Planning
Functional Strategies
Standing Plans versus Single-Use and Contingency Plans
Time Management
Multitasking
Implementing and Controlling Strategies

STRATEGIC AND OPERATIONAL PLANNING

There is an old saying: "When you fail to plan, you plan to fail." Research supports this saying.[1] However, some critics warn that in a dynamic environment, planning can lead to pitfalls.[2] Some managers complain that they don't have time to plan, yet research shows that planners do better and make faster decisions than nonplanners. To be successful, you need to set objectives and plan how to achieve them.[3]

This chapter focuses on improving your planning skills. In this section, we explore planning dimensions, strategic versus operational planning and strategies, and the strategic planning process. Before we begin, complete the Self-Assessment to determine how well you plan.

Planning Dimensions

Planning has several dimensions. Exhibit 5-1 summarizes the five planning dimensions: management level, type of plan, scope, time, and repetitiveness. Note that upper-level and some middle-level managers spend more time developing strategic, broad/directional, long-range, single-use plans for the organization.

5-1   SELF ASSESSMENT

Effective Planning

Indicate how well each statement describes your behavior by placing a number from 1 to 5 on the line before the statement.

Describes me   Does not describe me

5	4	3	2	1

_____ 1. I have a specific result to accomplish whenever I start a project of any kind.

_____ 2. When setting objectives, I state only the result to be accomplished; I don't specify how the result will be accomplished.

_____ 3. I have specific and measurable objectives; for example, I know the specific grade I want to earn in this course.

_____ 4. I set objectives that are difficult but achievable.

_____ 5. I set deadlines when I have something I need to accomplish, and I meet the deadlines.

_____ 6. I have a long-term goal (what I will be doing in 3–5 years) and short-term objectives to get me there.

_____ 7. I have written objectives stating what I want to accomplish.

_____ 8. I know my strengths and weaknesses, am aware of threats, and seek opportunities.

_____ 9. I analyze a problem and alternative actions rather than immediately jumping right in with a solution.

_____ 10. I spend most of my day doing what I plan to do rather than dealing with emergencies and trying to get organized.

_____ 11. I use a calendar, appointment book, or some form of "to do" list.

_____ 12. I ask others for advice.

_____ 13. I follow appropriate policies, procedures, and rules.

_____ 14. I develop contingency plans in case my plans do not work out as I expect them to.

_____ 15. I implement my plans and determine if I have met my objectives.

Add up the numbers you assigned to the statements to see where you fall on the continuum below.

Effective Planner   Ineffective Planner

75	65	55	45	35	25	15

Don't be too disappointed if your score isn't as high as you would like. All of these items are characteristics of effective planning. Review the items that did not describe you. After studying this chapter and doing the exercises, you can improve your planning skills.

EXHIBIT 5-1   PLANNING DIMENSIONS

Management Level	Type of Plan	Scope	Time	Repetitiveness
Upper and Middle	Strategic	Broad/directional	Long Range	Single-Use Plan
Middle and Lower	Operational	Narrow/specific	Short Range	Standing Plan

Other middle-level and all lower-level managers, in contrast, spend more time specifying how the strategic plans will be accomplished by developing operational, narrow/specific, short-range plans and implementing standing plans (policies, procedures, and rules). Throughout this chapter, we explore these five planning dimensions.

Strategic versus Operational Planning and Strategies

Strategic versus Operational Planning. There are two types of plans. **Strategic planning** is the process of developing a mission and long-range objectives and determining in advance how they will be accomplished. **Operational planning** is the process of setting short-range objectives and determining in advance how they will be accomplished.

The differences between strategic planning and operational planning are primarily the time frame and management level involved. Long term generally means that it will take longer than one year to achieve the objective. Strategic plans are commonly developed for five years and reviewed and revised every year so that a five-year plan is always in place. Upper-level managers develop strategic plans.[4] Operational plans have short-term objectives that will be met in one year or less. Middle- and lower-level managers develop operational plans. However, upper-level managers are involved in both day-to-day and strategic decision making based on research and intuition.[5]

At **Starbucks (Case Question 1)**, the decisions to expand by opening new stores, going into overseas markets, and selling its products in grocery stores are all examples of strategic, long-term planning. Operational plans at Starbucks include short-term objectives developed for individual stores, such as an annual sales forecast or marketing plan for a specific location developed by a store manager or regional manager.

Strategic and Operational Strategies. A *strategy is a plan for pursuing a mission and achieving objectives.* Strategic and operational types of plans include three *planning levels:* corporate, business, and functional. Each of these levels of planning requires strategies. The corporate and business levels are part of strategic planning, and the functional level is part of operational planning.

A *corporate strategy* is the strategic plan for managing multiple lines of business. In essence, there is more than one business within the corporation. A *business strategy* is the strategic plan for managing one line of business. Functional strategies are part of operational planning. A *functional strategy* is the operational plan for managing one area of a business.

Exhibit 5-2 illustrates the relationship between strategic and operational planning and their three planning levels. We will discuss the various types of corporate, business, and functional strategies in separate sections later. The plans at the three levels must be coordinated through the strategic planning process.

LO 5-1

Describe how strategic planning differs from operational planning.

WORK
APPLICATION 5-1

Give an example of a strategic objective and an operational objective from an organization you work for or have worked for.

WORK
APPLICATION 5-2

Does a business you work for or have worked for have one or multiple lines of business? List the line(s).

strategic planning The process of developing a mission and long-range objectives and determining in advance how they will be accomplished.

operational planning The process of setting short-range objectives and determining in advance how they will be accomplished.

strategy A plan for pursuing a mission and achieving objectives.

EXHIBIT 5-2   STRATEGIC AND OPERATIONAL PLANNING AND STRATEGIES

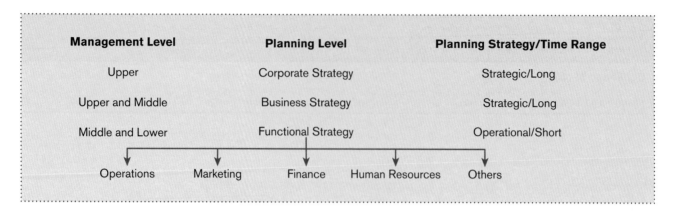

Management Level	Planning Level	Planning Strategy/Time Range
Upper	Corporate Strategy	Strategic/Long
Upper and Middle	Business Strategy	Strategic/Long
Middle and Lower	Functional Strategy	Operational/Short

Operations   Marketing   Finance   Human Resources   Others

The Strategic Planning Process

The steps in the *strategic planning process* are (1) developing the mission, (2) analyzing the environment, (3) setting objectives, (4) developing strategies, and (5) implementing and controlling strategies. Developing strategies takes place at all three levels of management. An important part of this process is strategic decisions on how to use company resources.[6] Exhibit 5-3 illustrates the strategic planning process. Notice that the process is not simply linear; it does not proceed through steps 1 through 5 and then end. As the arrows indicate, you may need

EXHIBIT 5-3   THE STRATEGIC PLANNING PROCESS

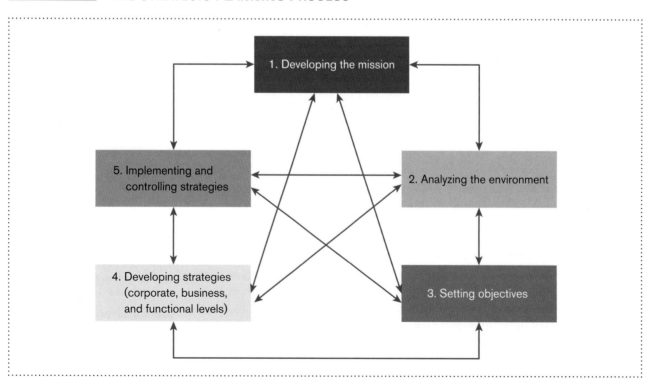

to return to prior steps and make changes as part of an ongoing process. Research shows that companies that change strategies regularly outperform those that change irregularly.[7] The major headings throughout the rest of this chapter list the steps in the strategic planning process.

DEVELOPING THE MISSION

Recall our discussion of the mission statement in Chapter 2, and we'll be brief here. Developing the mission is the first step in the strategic planning process. However, after analyzing the environment, managers should reexamine the mission and values to see if they need to be changed.[8] The mission is the foundation of the other four steps in the strategic planning process. The organization's mission is its purpose or reason for being. The mission provides an organization's identity by answering the question, "Who are we as an organization?"[9] It includes the values supporting the organizational culture.[10] Since 1998, when **Google** started, its mission has been to organize the world's information.[11] The **Starbucks (Case Question 2)** corporate mission is "to inspire and nurture the human spirit—one person, one cup and one neighborhood at a time."

A mission is often based on or also creates a *vision* that defines where the company is headed in inventing its future and why. It contains the expectations the organization strives to achieve. Successful people are visionaries.[12] Top management needs to articulate a compelling vision.[13] However, the firm is only successful when the stakeholders share the vision of the future.[14]

The organization's mission should provide its employees with a sense of unified purpose that brings everyone in the organization together to achieve it. Photo from Vetta Stock Photo/iStockphoto.

ANALYZING THE ENVIRONMENT

The second step of the strategic planning process is analyzing the environment, also known as situation analysis. A **situation analysis** *focuses on those features in a company's environment that most directly affect its options and opportunities.* This analysis has three parts: industry and competitive situation analysis, company situation analysis, and identification of a competitive advantage. It is important to do a good analysis because managers tend to misestimate, misunderstand, and mis-specify what they think they face.[15] Keep in mind that companies with multiple lines of business must conduct an environmental analysis for each line of business.

Situation Analysis

Industry and Competitive Situation Analysis. In the global village, you need to understand the competitive environment.[16] Industries vary widely in their makeup, competitive situation, and growth potential. Determining the position of an industry requires answering questions such as these: "How large is the market?" "What is the growth rate?" "How many competitors are there?" According to Michael Porter, competition in an industry is a composite of five competitive forces that should be considered in analyzing the competitive situation.[17] Exhibit 5-4 shows a competitive analysis for Starbucks explaining each of the five forces. Note that you start in the middle.

LO 5-2

Explain the reason for conducting an industry and competitive situation analysis.

WORK APPLICATION 5-3

Conduct a simple five-force competitive analysis for a company you work for or have worked for. Use Exhibit 5–4 as an example.

situation analysis An analysis of those features in a company's environment that most directly affect its options and opportunities.

EXHIBIT 5-4 STARBUCKS'S FIVE-FORCE COMPETITIVE ANALYSIS

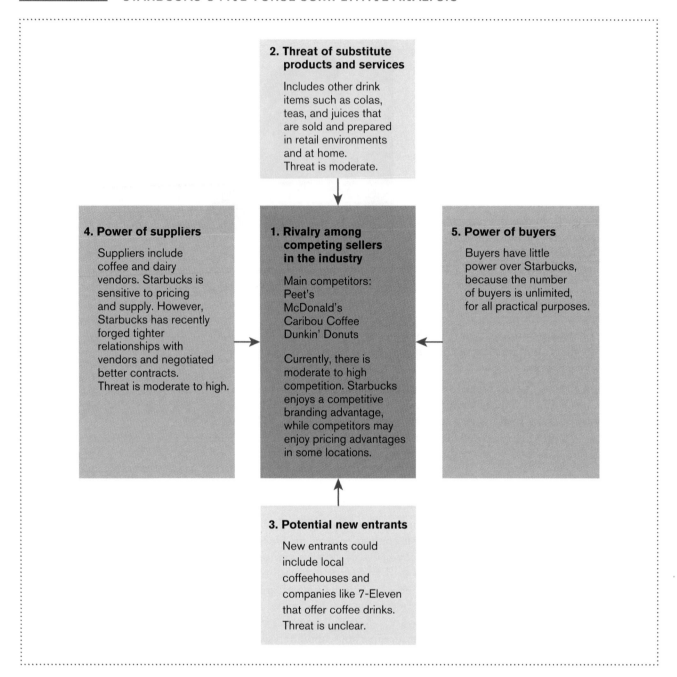

2. Threat of substitute products and services

Includes other drink items such as colas, teas, and juices that are sold and prepared in retail environments and at home.
Threat is moderate.

4. Power of suppliers

Suppliers include coffee and dairy vendors. Starbucks is sensitive to pricing and supply. However, Starbucks has recently forged tighter relationships with vendors and negotiated better contracts.
Threat is moderate to high.

1. Rivalry among competing sellers in the industry

Main competitors:
Peet's
McDonald's
Caribou Coffee
Dunkin' Donuts

Currently, there is moderate to high competition. Starbucks enjoys a competitive branding advantage, while competitors may enjoy pricing advantages in some locations.

5. Power of buyers

Buyers have little power over Starbucks, because the number of buyers is unlimited, for all practical purposes.

3. Potential new entrants

New entrants could include local coffeehouses and companies like 7-Eleven that offer coffee drinks.
Threat is unclear.

LO 5-3

Explain the reason for conducting a company situation analysis.

Company Situation Analysis. A company situation analysis is used at the business level to determine the strategic issues and problems that need to be addressed through the next three steps of the strategic planning process. A complete company situation analysis has five key parts, listed in Exhibit 5-5:

1. *Assessment of the present strategy based on performance.* Performance must be evaluated.[18] This assessment can be a simple statement or a more complex comparison of performance indicators (market share, sales, net profit, return on assets, and so on) over the last five years.

2. *SWOT analysis. An organization's internal environmental strengths and weaknesses and external environmental opportunities and threats*

EXHIBIT 5-5   PARTS OF A COMPANY SITUATION ANALYSIS

1. Assessment of the present strategy based on performance → 2. SWOT analysis → 3. Assessment of competitive strength and identification of competitive advantage → 4. Conclusions concerning competitive position → 5. Determination of the issues and problems that need to be addressed through the strategic planning process

are determined through a **SWOT analysis.** (SWOT stands for strengths, weaknesses, opportunities, and threats.) In a SWOT analysis, the internal environmental factors analyzed for *strengths* and *weaknesses* are management and culture, mission, resources, systems process, and structure. The external environmental (Chapter 2) factors analyzed for *opportunities* and *threats* are customers, competitors, suppliers, and so on. Exhibit 5-6 outlines a SWOT analysis for **Starbucks.**

SWOT analysis A determination of an organization's internal environmental strengths and weaknesses and external environmental opportunities and threats.

EXHIBIT 5-6   SWOT ANALYSIS FOR STARBUCKS

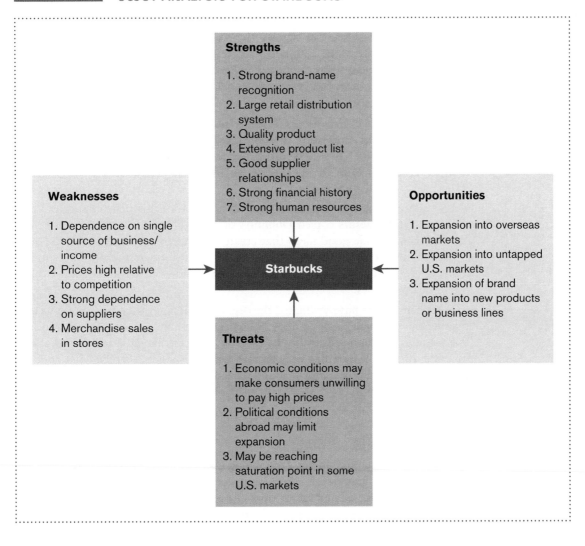

Strengths

1. Strong brand-name recognition
2. Large retail distribution system
3. Quality product
4. Extensive product list
5. Good supplier relationships
6. Strong financial history
7. Strong human resources

Weaknesses

1. Dependence on single source of business/income
2. Prices high relative to competition
3. Strong dependence on suppliers
4. Merchandise sales in stores

Starbucks

Opportunities

1. Expansion into overseas markets
2. Expansion into untapped U.S. markets
3. Expansion of brand name into new products or business lines

Threats

1. Economic conditions may make consumers unwilling to pay high prices
2. Political conditions abroad may limit expansion
3. May be reaching saturation point in some U.S. markets

List a couple of the major strengths and weaknesses of an organization you work for or have worked for.

1. *Assessment of competitive strength and identification of competitive advantage.* In assessing competitive strength, you compare the *critical success factors* for their business to those of each major competitor. Critical success factors are the few major things that the business must do well to be successful. We will discuss competitive advantage shortly.

2. *Conclusions concerning competitive position.* How is the business doing compared to its competition? Are things improving or slipping?

3. *Determination of the issues and problems that need to be addressed through the strategic planning process.* Based on the results of the first four parts of the company situation analysis, what needs to be done in the future to improve the business's competitive position?

Competitive Advantage

A **competitive advantage** *specifies how an organization offers unique customer value.* It answers the questions, "What makes us different from and better than the competition?" and "Why should a person buy our products or services rather than those of our competitors?"[19] A company has to have answers to these questions to have a competitive advantage and succeed in business. A firm may identify a competitive advantage in the process of assessing its competitive strength. **Starbucks's (Case Question 2)** competitive advantage is its relaxed coffee house environment where friends can meet that offers free Wi-Fi, high-quality coffee, and other products.

Two aspects of a company's competitive advantage are core competency and benchmarking. A *core competency* is what a firm does well. By identifying core competencies, managers can oversee the creation of new products and services that take advantage of the company's strengths. **Honda** has a core competency in engines. Honda went from producing only cars and motorcycles to also producing garden tillers, lawn mowers, snowblowers, snowmobiles, power generators, and outboard motors.

Benchmarking *is the process of comparing an organization's products or services and processes with those of other companies.* In benchmarking, you try to find out about other products and processes, through *competitive intelligence,* and copy them or improve upon them legally and ethically. Most benchmarking takes place within an industry.

The Internet is an excellent source of information for benchmarking. **Pizza Hut** and **Little Caesars** copied **Domino's** delivery. However, looking at noncompetitors can provide good ideas that create a competitive advantage. Drive-thru windows have typically been associated with fast-food restaurants but, today, banks, liquor stores, coffee shops, pharmacies, and even wedding chapels have drive-thru windows.

After managers have evaluated the organization and the competition by completing the situation analysis, they should go back and review the mission and its vision to see if it needs to be changed. Remember that situation analysis is an ongoing process, referred to as *scanning the environment*. It tells what is going on in the external environment that may require change to continually improve customer value.

SETTING OBJECTIVES

After developing a mission and completing a situation analysis, you are ready for the third step in the strategic planning process: setting objectives that flow from the mission to take advantage of opportunities and address problems identified through the situation analysis. Goal orientation is about setting objectives and

competitive advantage Specifies how an organization offers unique customer value.

benchmarking The process of comparing an organization's products and services and processes with those of other companies.

5-1   JOIN THE DISCUSSION ETHICS & SOCIAL RESPONSIBILITY

Crop Genetic Structure

Monsanto is a U.S.-based agricultural biotechnology MNC. It produces leading seed brands, such as corn, cotton, and wheat. Using biotechnology to change the characteristics of crop plants (i.e., genetic modification) seemed like a good *opportunity* to create beneficial new food products, such as foods that are lower in cholesterol. However, there is an ongoing debate about the safety of genetically modified food for people and feed for animals, with some opposition to genetic modification. In terms of SWOT analysis, this opposition represents a *threat* to Monsanto.

1. Do you feel eating food that has been genetically altered is safe?
2. Is it ethical and socially responsible to genetically alter food crops?
3. How should Monsanto try to convince people that genetically modified food is safe?

achieving them.[20] Objectives answer the question, "What do you want to do?"[21] They are results; they do not state how they will be accomplished—that's the plan. In this section, you will learn about goals and objectives, writing objectives, criteria for effective objectives, and management by objectives (MBO).

You should be able to distinguish between goals and objectives. *Goals* state general, broad targets to be accomplished. **Objectives** *state what is to be accomplished in specific and measurable terms with a target date.* **Google** has a goal to become the world's most energy-efficient company.[22] **Starbucks's (Case Question 3)** long-range goal is to continue to expand globally; it also has a goal of being environmentally responsible, with more eco-conscious stores on a global scale from the design stage right through to construction and operations. Can you see how goals should be translated into objectives so that you can determine if the goal and objective have been achieved?

Writing Effective Objectives

Successful people are *goal oriented.*[23] What are your objectives? Setting objectives directs your efforts.[24] To help ensure that you will meet your objectives, it is a good idea to write them down and keep them someplace where they are constantly visible. You will practice setting objectives in Skill Builder 5–1.

Max E. Douglas developed a model that is helpful in writing effective objectives.[25] One variation on Douglas's model, shown in Model 5–1, includes (1) the word *to* followed by (2) an action verb, (3) a statement of the specific and measurable result to be achieved, and (4) a target date. Some examples of corporate strategic objectives are shown following the model.

WORK APPLICATION5-5

State one or more goals of an organization you work for or have worked for.

LO 5-4

List the parts of an effective written objective.

MODEL 5-1   OBJECTIVE WRITING MODEL

(1) To + (2) Action Verb + (3) Specific and Measurable Result + (4) Target Date

IBM: (1) To (2) double (3) revenue in Africa to $1 billion (4) by 2115[1]

Chevron: To increase oil output 20% by 2017[2]

Porsche (subsidiary of Volkswagen): To quadruple sales to 500,000 cars a year by 2020[3]

1. Staff, "Things Fall Apart. IBM Is Here to Help," *BusinessWeek* (February 25–March 3, 2013): 28–29.
2. Staff, "The Oil Industry," *Wall Street Journal* (March 13, 2013): A1.
3. V. Fuhrmans, "Porsche to Pick Up Speed Under VW," *Wall Street Journal* (July 6, 2012): B3.

objectives Statements of what is to be accomplished that is expressed in singular, specific, and measurable terms with a target date.

Criteria for Objectives

As the model for writing objectives implies, an effective objective conforms to three "must" criteria: it expresses a *specific* and *measurable* result, and it sets a *date* for achieving that result. It should also have a single result—or don't put multiple objectives together. Another similar way of writing objectives is called *S.M.A.R.T. goals*—specific, measurable, attainable, realistic, and timely. Let's discuss the parts of Model 5–1, or the criteria that needed to be meet in the model.

Specific. The objective should state the exact level of performance desired.[26] People with specific goals achieve higher levels of performance than those with general goals.

Ineffective Objective	To maximize profits in 2016 (How much is "maximize"?)
Effective Objective	To earn a net profit of $1 million in 2016

Measurable. You are what you measure.[27] If you are to achieve objectives, you must be able to observe and measure progress regularly to determine if the objectives have been met.

Ineffective Objective	Perfect service for every customer (How is "perfect service" measured?)
Effective Objective	To attain an "excellent" satisfaction rating from 90 percent of customers surveyed in 2016

Target Date. A specific date should be set for accomplishing the objective. When people have a deadline, they usually try harder to get a task done on time than when they are simply told to do it when they can.[28]

Ineffective Objective	To become a multimillionaire (By when?)
Effective Objective	To become a multimillionaire by December 2020

It is also more effective to set a specific date than to give a time span, because it's too easy to forget when a time period began and should end.

Somewhat Effective	To double international business to $5 billion annually within five years
Effective Objective	To double international business to $5 billion annually by the end of 2019

EXHIBIT 5-7   CRITERIA THAT OBJECTIVES SHOULD MEET

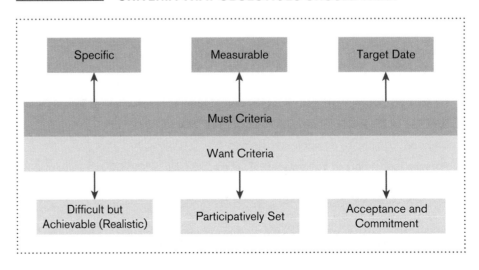

5-1 APPLYING THE CONCEPT

Objectives

For each objective, state which "must" criteria is not met.

   A. single result
   B. specific
   C. measurable
   D. target date

_____ 1. To be perceived as the best hotel in the Nashville area by the end of 2014

_____ 2. To write objectives within two weeks

_____ 3. To double the sales of iPods in the United States

_____ 4. To sell 2 percent more mufflers and 7 percent more tires in 2013

_____ 5. To increase revenue in 2014

In addition to the three "must" criteria, objectives should meet three "want" criteria when possible. Note that the want criteria, unlike must, are not known if they exist by just reading the objective. For a list of the criteria that objectives should meet, see Exhibit 5–7.

Note, however, that some objectives are ongoing and do not require a stated date. The target date is indefinite until it is changed.

Effective Objective	To have 25 percent of sales coming from products that did not exist five years ago
Somewhat Effective	To be number one or two in world sales in all lines of business

Difficult but Achievable (Realistic). A number of studies show that individuals perform better when given difficult but achievable objectives[29] rather than objectives that are too difficult or too easy.

Participatively Set. Groups that participate in setting their objectives generally outperform groups with assigned objectives; participation helps members feel they have a shared destiny.[30] You should use the appropriate level of participation for the employees' capabilities (Chapters 1 and 4).

Acceptance and Commitment. If objectives are to be met, people must accept them and be committed to achieve them.[31] If employees do not commit to an objective, then even if it meets all the other "must" and "want" criteria, it may not be accomplished.

Management by Objectives (MBO)

Management by objectives (MBO) _is the process in which managers and their employees jointly set objectives for the employees, periodically evaluate performance, and reward according to the results._ MBO is also referred to as work planning and review, goals management, goals and controls, and management by results.

MBO has three steps:

Step 1. Set individual objectives and plans. You set objectives with each individual employee. The objectives are the heart of the MBO process and should meet the "must" and "want' criteria.

Step 2. Give feedback and evaluate performance. Communication is the key factor in determining MBO's success or failure. Thus, you and your employees must meet frequently to review progress.[32] The frequency of evaluations depends on the individual and the job performed.

WORK APPLICATION 5-6

Using the model for writing objectives, write one or more objectives for an organization you work for or have worked for, making sure they meet the "must" criteria.

management by objectives (MBO) The process in which managers and their employees jointly set objectives for the employees, periodically evaluate performance, and reward according to the results.

Step 3. Reward according to performance. Employees' performance should be measured against their objectives.[33] Employees who meet their objectives should be rewarded through recognition, praise, pay raises, promotions, and so on. We will discuss motivating employees with rewards in Chapter 11 and measuring performance in Chapter 14.

CORPORATE STRATEGIES

After the mission has been developed, the situation analysis has been completed, and objectives have been set, you move on to the fourth step of the strategic planning process: developing strategies at the corporate, business, and functional levels. In this section, we discuss corporate strategies, which are shown in Exhibit 5-8. Recall that to have a corporate strategy, the parent corporation must have subsidiary companies. So a corporate strategy is a means to add value to its different business units.[34]

EXHIBIT 5-8   GRAND AND GROWTH STRATEGIES

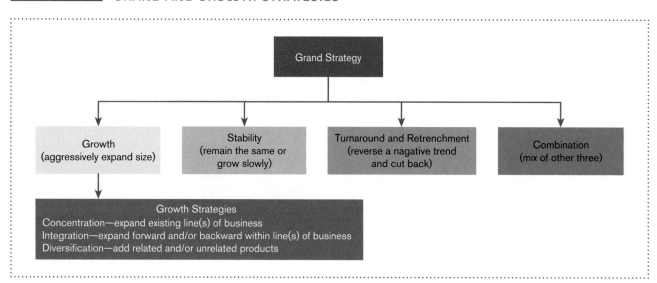

LO 5-5

Describe the four grand strategies.

grand strategy An overall corporate strategy for growth, stability, or turnaround and retrenchment, or for some combination of these.

Grand Strategy

Multibusiness corporations are the most prevalent form of business around the globe, and they need a grand strategy.[35] A **grand strategy** *is an overall corporate strategy for growth, stability, or turnaround and retrenchment, or for some combination of these.* Each grand strategy aligns with different objectives. Let's discuss each separately.

Growth. With a *growth strategy*, the company makes aggressive attempts to increase its size through increased sales. **Google** is on an aggressive growth strategy, as it bids to be everything to everyone with its growing number of services and, more recently, products.[36] **Starbucks (Case Question 4)** has a growth strategy.

Stability. With a *stability strategy*, the company attempts to hold and maintain its present size or to grow slowly. Many companies are satisfied with the status quo. Rather than increasing its size aggressively, the company attempts to balance growth and profits. The **WD-40 Company** produces WD-40 lubricant. The company pursues a strategy of stability as it has "slowly" added products over the years.[37]

Turnaround and Retrenchment. A *turnaround strategy* is an attempt to reverse a declining business as quickly as possible. A *retrenchment strategy* is the divestiture or liquidation of assets. These strategies are listed together because most turnarounds include retrenchment. Turnaround strategies generally attempt to improve cash flow by increasing revenues, decreasing costs, reducing assets, or combining these strategies. **Procter & Gamble** is pursuing a turnaround strategy, as it lost brand-loyal consumer-products customers during the recession to no-name or local brands.[38] Swiss **UBS** is retrenching by eliminating as many as 15 business units and a third or more of the jobs (10,000) at its investment-banking division.[39] Likewise, German **Siemens** is cutting underperforming businesses.[40]

A *spinoff* is a form of retrenchment in which a corporation sets up one or more of its business units as a separate company rather than selling it. British **Cadbury Schweppes plc** split itself into two companies—one selling candy (Cadbury, now owned by **Kraft**[41]) and the other soda (Schweppes, now **Dr Pepper Snapple Group**[42]).

Combination. A corporation may pursue growth, stability, and turnaround and retrenchment for its different lines of business or areas of operations. **Ford** is pursuing a growth strategy by building its fifth factory in China, with its Chinese joint venture partner **Chongqing Changan**, to double its production and sales outlets by 2015 in the world's largest car market by sales.[43] But at the same time, Ford is ending production in Australia by 2016 and closing factories in Europe due to high costs and stagnant economies. Costs in Australia are double those in Europe and nearly four times Ford in Asia.[44]

Growth Strategies

Most large MNCs have growth strategies, and that is a major reason they are global companies. A company that wants to grow has three major options. These **growth strategies** *are concentration, backward and forward integration, and related and unrelated diversification.*

Concentration. With a *concentration strategy,* the organization grows aggressively in its existing line(s) of business. **Starbucks (Case Question 4)** has a concentration strategy to continue to open new stores globally, as does **Walmart, Subway,** and **McDonald's.**

Integration. With an *integration strategy,* the organization enters a new line or lines of business related to its existing one(s). *Forward integration* occurs when the organization enters a line of business closer to the final customer. For example, **Apple** has engaged in forward integration by opening Apple stores, thus bypassing traditional retailers and selling its products directly to the customer, and **Google** and **Microsoft** are following its lead.[45] *Backward integration* occurs when the organization enters a line of business farther away from the final customer. **ArcelorMittal,** corporate headquarters in Luxembourg, pursued a backward integration strategy with its purchases of iron-ore and coal mines to help lower the cost of producing steel, making it the world's leading steel and mining company.[46] **Delta** bought a refinery to lower its jet-fuel costs.[47] **Starbucks** has important alliances with its coffee suppliers globally.

WORK
APPLICATION 5-7

State the grand strategy for an organization you work for or have worked for.

LO 5-6

Describe the three growth strategies.

growth strategies Strategies a company can adopt in order to grow: concentration, backward and forward integration, and related and unrelated diversification.

5-2 **APPLYING** THE CONCEPT

Growth Strategies

Identify the type of growth strategy described by each statement.

A. concentration
B. related diversification
C. forward integration
D. unrelated diversification
E. backward integration

_____ 6. Gateway, a computer manufacturer, produces printers.

_____ 7. Sears buys a tool manufacturer to make its Craftsman tools.

_____ 8. Nike buys the Holiday Inn hotel chain.

_____ 9. Abercrombie & Fitch opens a new retail store in a mall.

_____ 10. Levi Strauss & Co. opens stores to sell its jeans and casual wear.

As part of its growth strategy, **Facebook** has bought several companies including **FriendFeed** for $50 million and **Instagram** for $1 billion. Photo from David Paul Morris/Bloomberg via Getty Images.

merger Occurs when two companies form one corporation.

acquisition Occurs when one business buys all or part of another business.

Diversification. With a *diversification strategy,* the organization goes into a related or unrelated line of products. **Nike** used *related (concentric) diversification* when it diversified from sports shoes to sports clothing and then to sports equipment. **Starbucks (Case Question 4)** selling its products in grocery stores was a related diversification strategy. The **Virgin Group** has pursued an *unrelated (conglomerate) diversification* since its existence, owning more than 55 companies categorized as lifestyles, media and mobile, money, music, and travel.[48]

Merger and Acquisition Growth Strategy. As discussed in Chapter 3, companies can grow through strategic alliances and joint ventures.[49] Companies can also pursue a growth strategy by means of mergers and acquisitions,[50] commonly referred to as M&As.[51] Companies engage in M&As to decrease competition, to compete more effectively with larger companies, to realize economies of size, to consolidate expenses, and to achieve access to markets, products, technology, resources, and management talent.[52]

A **merger** *occurs when two companies form one corporation.* **Anheuser-Busch** and **InBev** merged to create **Anheuser-Busch InBev,** creating the leading global beer brewer. **AOL** and **Time Warner** also merged to combine online and print media.

An **acquisition** *occurs when one business buys all or part of another business.* One business becomes a part of an existing business. **Google** acquired more than 125 businesses between 2010 and 2012.[53] It bought **Motorola** for $12.5 billion to get into mobile devices and hardware, including the Droid line of smartphones, to promote its Android software to compete against **Apple.**[54] **Facebook** has bought several companies, including **FriendFeed** for $50 million and **Instagram** for $1 billion.[55] Recent acquisitions of **Starbucks (Case Question 4)** comprise many companies over the years; recent ones include **La Boulange** and **Evolution Fresh.**

5-2 JOIN THE DISCUSSION ETHICS & SOCIAL RESPONSIBILITY

Insider Trading

Insiders are people who have confidential information about upcoming events that will affect the price of a stock. It is common for the price of a stock to go up when investors learn that the company is negotiating a merger or acquisition of another company. Insiders are not supposed to buy or sell any stock they have confidential information about or to tell anyone this information to avoid illegal profit from stock dealing. This process, known as "tipping," is illegal.

1. If you were "tipped" by an insider, would you buy/sell the stock?
2. What are the implications of using insider information? Is anyone hurt by the practice? If yes, who is hurt and how are they hurt?
3. Without using insider information, some speculators try to predict which companies are likely to merge or be acquired and buy stock options. This is a legal way of making money, but is it ethical?

Portfolio Analysis

Business portfolio analysis *is the corporate process of determining which lines of business the corporation will be in and how it will allocate resources among them.* A business line, also called a strategic business unit (SBU), is a distinct business having its own customers that is managed independently of other businesses within the corporation. What constitutes an SBU varies from company to company, but it can be a division, a subsidiary, or a single product line.

The primary objective of *corporate portfolio management (CPM)* is to make strategic decisions about the allocation of resources among SBU.[56] A popular approach to CPM is to create a **Boston Consulting Group (BCG)** Growth-Share Matrix for each line of business or product line as a business strategy. A BCG matrix contains four cells: *Cash cows* generate more resources than they need, so the profits are used to fund question marks and starts (**GE Capital**[57]). *Question marks* are entries into new businesses (**Google's** acquisition of **YouTube**[58]). *Stars* are question marks that succeed (**Diet Coke**[59]). *Dogs* are doing poorly and are usually sold or liquidated (**Nike** sold **Umbro**[60]). Exhibit 5-9 shows a BCG matrix for **Starbucks**.

A company in a single line of business cannot conduct a business portfolio analysis. However, it should perform a *product portfolio analysis.* **McDonald's** started by offering a simple hamburger and fries. Over the years, the company introduced new products, such as the Big Mac, that started as a question mark, became a star, and then joined the hamburger and fries as a cash cow. McDonald's introduced pizza and the Angus Burger as question marks, but rather than becoming stars, they became dogs and were dropped from most restaurants.

BUSINESS STRATEGIES

Each line of business must develop its own mission, analyze its own environment, set its own objectives, and develop its own strategies. For the organization with a single line of products, corporate and business strategies are the same, so we are still in the fourth step of the strategic planning process. In this section, we discuss adaptive and competitive strategies.

WORK
APPLICATION 5-8

Identify any growth strategies used by an organization you work for or have worked for. Be sure to identify the type of growth strategy and note if any mergers, acquisitions, joint ventures, or strategic alliances were used.

business portfolio analysis The corporate process of determining which lines of business the corporation will be in and how it will allocate resources among them.

EXHIBIT 5-9   BCG GROWTH SHARE MATRIX FOR STARBUCKS

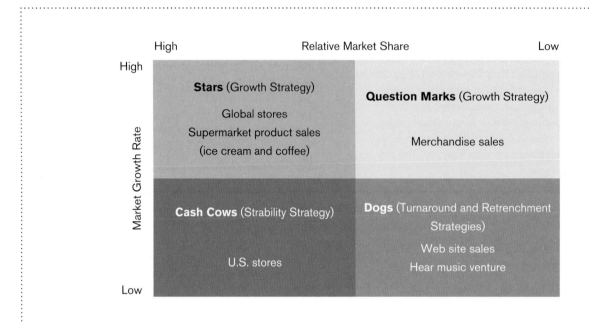

Adaptive Strategies

LO 5-7

Describe the three adaptive strategies.

Adaptive strategies emphasize adapting to changes in the external environment and entering new markets as means of increasing sales.[61] The **adaptive strategies** *are prospecting, defending, and analyzing.* Each adaptive strategy reflects a different objective. Exhibit 5-10 indicates the different rates of environmental change, potential growth rates, and corresponding grand strategy for each adaptive strategy.

Prospecting Strategy. The *prospecting strategy* calls for aggressively offering new products and services and/or entering new markets. The prospecting strategy resembles the grand strategy of growth. It is often used by smaller companies that want to grow fast,[62] like **Groupon**, which was one of the fastest-growing start-up prospectors of all times.[63] **Google** started small as a prospector and continues to be a prospector as a large *Fortune* 500 company, ranked 55.[64] **Nissan** was a prospector when it unveiled the LEAF, the world's first battery-powered car. **Starbucks** (**Case Question 5**) continues to open new stores globally to enter new markets as a prospector.

Defending Strategy. The *defending strategy* calls for staying with the present product line and markets and maintaining or increasing customers in new markets. It is often used by large established companies that want to protect their dominance,[65] like **Coca-Cola** keeping its number one position against archrival **Pepsi**. The defending strategy resembles the grand strategy of stability. **Wilson** has successfully defended its position for almost 100 years as the world's leading manufacturer of ball sports equipment.[66]

adaptive strategies Overall strategies for a line of business, including prospecting, defending, and analyzing.

Analyzing Strategy. The *analyzing strategy* calls for a midrange approach between prospecting and defending. Placing the three strategies on a continuum

EXHIBIT 5-10 ADAPTIVE STRATEGIES

Adaptive Strategy	Rate of Environmental Change	Potential Growth Rate	Corresponding Grand Strategy
Prospecting	Fast	High	Growth
Analyzing	Moderate	Moderate	Combination
Defending	Slow	Low	Stability

(Exhibit 5-10), the analyzer is between the two extremes and tends to outperform both prospectors and defenders as it simultaneously achieves efficiency and adaptiveness.[67] Analyzing resembles the combination grand strategy. Analyzing involves moving into new market areas at a cautious, deliberate pace and/or offering a core product group and seeking new opportunities.[68] Analyzers commonly match their rivals' prospecting actions through the use of benchmarking. Based on **Apple's** iPhone, iPad, and Apple TV, **Google** acquired Motorola to offer its Droid smartphones,[69] and **Microsoft** came out with the Surface tablet and Xbox One, combining TV with games for an all-in-one home entertainment system.[70]

WORK
APPLICATION 5-9

Identify the adaptive strategy used by an organization you work for or have worked for. Be sure to describe how it used the strategy.

5-3 APPLYING THE CONCEPT

Adaptive Strategies

Identify the type of strategy represented in each statement.

A. prospecting
B. defending
C. analyzing

___ 11. This is the primary strategy of industry leader Coca-Cola in the saturated U.S. cola market.

___ 12. McDonald's comes out with a new Angus Burger to compete with Burger King's Angus Burgers.

___ 13. Red Lobster goes international by opening restaurants in the UK.

___ 14. Dell pioneers a computer that can be folded up and put in your pocket.

___ 15. This is the strategy used by Domino's when Pizza Hut started to copy delivering pizza.

COMPETITIVE STRATEGIES

Michael Porter identified three effective business *competitive strategies:* differentiation, cost leadership, and focus.[71]

Differentiation Strategy. With a *differentiation* strategy, a company stresses its competitive advantage over its competitors.[72] **Nike, Ralph Lauren, Calvin Klein,** and others place their names on the outside of their products to differentiate them from those of the competition. Differentiation strategy somewhat resembles the prospecting strategy. **Coca-Cola** uses differentiation, which it achieves with its scripted name logo and contour bottle.[73] **Starbucks's (Case Question 5)**

Asics may not offer the wide range of athletic shoes and clothing items that its competitors Nike and Adidas do, but its focused strategy to target only the running shoe market has been very successful. Photo from AP Photo/Damian Dovarganes.

competitive strategy is differentiation, as it focuses on coffee houses with upscale buyers willing to pay higher prices than at Dunkin' Donuts and McDonald's.

Cost Leadership Strategy. With a *cost leadership* strategy, the company stresses lower prices to attract customers. To keep its prices down, it must have tight cost control and an efficient systems processes. Growth demands high volume and high volume demands low prices. **Walmart** and **Target** have had success with this strategy. **Nissan** planned to offer a low-priced **Datsun** new car for $3,000 to $5,000.[74] Cost leadership somewhat resembles the defending strategy.

Focus Strategy. With a focus strategy, the company targets a specific regional market, product line, or buyer group. Within a particular target segment, or market niche, the firm may use a differentiation or cost leadership strategy. With a focus strategy, smaller companies can often compete with MNC.[75] **Asics** successfully competes with much larger **Nike** and **Adidas** in the running shoe market; more than half the runners in the New York Marathon wore Asics.[76] *Ebony* and *Jet* magazines target African Americans, **MTV** focuses on young people, and **Rolex** watches have a market niche of upper-income people. **Henkel** Right Guard deodorant is aimed at men and **P&G** Secret at women.

Porter doesn't recommend trying to combine differentiation and cost leadership because it is rarely successful, as the company gets stuck in the middle.[77] Remember that the various grand and adaptive strategies complement one another. Managers select the appropriate strategy based on the mission, situation analysis, and objectives.

OPERATIONAL PLANNING

So far in this chapter, you have learned about long-range, external, competitive strategic planning; we are at the last part of the fourth step of the planning process. In this section, we discuss short-range operational planning, including functional strategies, standing and single-use plans, and contingency plans.

Functional Strategies

The functional departments of a company must develop internal strategies for achieving the mission and objectives. **Functional strategies** *are strategies developed and implemented by managers in marketing, operations, human resources, finance, and other departments of a company.*

Marketing Strategy. The marketing department has the primary responsibility for knowing what the customer wants, or how to add customer value, and for defining the target market. Marketing focuses on the four Ps: product, promotion, place, and price. In other words, the marketing department makes decisions about which products to provide, how they will be packaged and advertised, where they will be sold and how they get will there, and how much they will be sold for.

functional strategies Strategies developed and implemented by managers in marketing, operations, human resources, finance, and other departments.

Operations Strategy. The operations (or production) department is responsible for systems processes that convert inputs into outputs. Operations focuses on quality and efficiency in producing the products that marketing determines will provide customer value. (You will learn more about operations in Chapter 15.)

Finance Strategy. The finance department has at least two functions: (1) financing the business activities by raising money through the sale of stock (equity) or bonds or through loans (debt), deciding on the debt-to-equity ratio, and paying off the debt and dividends (if any) to shareholders and (2) keeping records of transactions, developing budgets, and reporting financial results (income statement and balance sheet). A third function of the finance department in many organizations is making the optimum use of cash reserves, in particular, investing as a means of making money. (You will learn more about finance in Chapter 14.)

Human Resources Strategy. The HR department is responsible for working with all the other functional departments in the areas of recruiting, selecting, training, evaluating, and compensating employees. (You will learn more about human resources in Chapter 9.)

Other Functional Strategies. Based on the type of business, any number of other departments will also need to develop a strategy. One area that varies in importance is research and development (R&D). Businesses that sell a product usually allocate greater resources (budgets) for R&D than do businesses that provide a service. **Amazon.com** invested in R&D to develop the Kindle e-reader.[78]

Standing Plans versus Single-Use and Contingency Plans

Depending on how repetitive they are, plans may be either *standing plans,* which are made to be used over and over again (repeated), or *single-use plans,* which are made to be used only once (nonrepetitive). Most strategic plans are single use, whereas operational plans are more often standing plans. Exhibit 5-11 illustrates the different types of standing and single-use plans.

WORK
APPLICATION 5-10

Identify one functional area of an organization you work for or have worked for. What was its operational strategy?

LO 5-8

State the difference between standing plans and single-use plans.

EXHIBIT 5-11   STANDING PLANS VERSUS SINGLE-USE PLANS

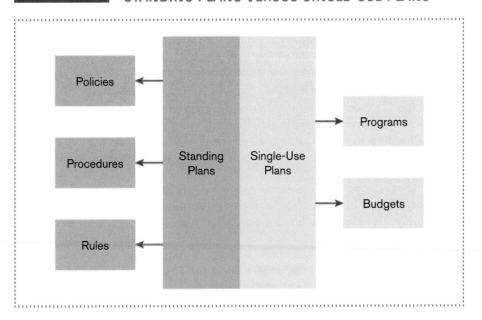

Standing Plans. Operational objectives may be accomplished by following standing plans, which save planning and decision-making time. **Standing plans** *are policies, procedures, and rules developed for handling repetitive situations.* Their purpose is to guide employees' actions in decision making.

Policies provide general guidelines to be followed when making decisions. Here are a few examples of policy statements: "The customer is always right." "We produce high-quality goods and services." "We promote employees from within." Notice that policy statements are intentionally general guides; you use your discretion in implementing them. As a manager, your daily decisions will be guided by policies. It will be your job to interpret, apply, and explain company policies to employees. Policies can change,[79] and you may develop your own policies for your employees.

A **procedure** *is a sequence of actions to be followed in order to achieve an objective.* Procedures may also be called *standard operating procedures (SOPs)* or *methods.* Procedures can be formal or informal and are more specific than policies.[80] They entail a series of decisions rather than a single decision and may involve more than one functional area. Procedures ensure that all recurring, routine situations are handled in a consistent, predetermined manner. Many organizations have procedures for purchasing, taking inventory, settling grievances, and so forth.

Rules state exactly what should or should not be done. Employees have no discretion on how to implement rules and regulations.[81] These are examples of rules: "No smoking or eating in the work area." "Everyone must wear a hard hat on the construction site." "Stop at a red light." Violating rules usually subjects a person to penalties that vary in severity according to the seriousness of the violation and the number of offenses. Managers are responsible for establishing and enforcing rules in a uniform manner.[82]

Single-Use Plans. **Single-use plans** *are programs and budgets developed for handling nonrepetitive situations.* Single-use plans, unlike standing plans, are developed for a specific purpose and probably will not be used again in the same form. However, a single-use plan may be used as a model for a future version of the program or budget. A growth strategy is a single-use plan.

A *program* describes a set of activities and is designed to accomplish an objective over a specified time period. Programs are not meant to exist over the life of the organization. A program may have its own policies, procedures, budget, and so forth. It might take several years or less than a day to complete a given program. Examples include the development of a new product or expansion of facilities.

When developing a program, managers typically (1) set project objectives, (2) break the project down into a sequence of steps, (3) assign responsibility for each step, (4) establish starting and ending times for each step, and (5) determine the resources needed for each step.

A *budget* is the funds allocated to operate a unit for a fixed period. When that time has passed, a new budget is needed. Developing a budget requires planning skills rather than accounting and mathematical skills. When developed, a budget is a planning tool, and when implemented, it is a control tool. We discuss budgeting in Chapter 14.

Contingency Plans. No matter how effectively you plan, there will be times when events prevent you from achieving your objectives. Things that go wrong are often beyond your control in a dynamic environment.[83] When the uncontrollable occurs, you should be prepared with a backup, or contingency, plan. **Contingency plans** *are alternative plans to be implemented if uncontrollable events occur.* If a key employee calls in sick, another employee fills in to do the job. Construction work is usually contingent on the weather. If it's nice, employees work outside; if it is not, they work indoors.

WORK
APPLICATION 5-11

Give an example of a policy, a procedure, and a rule from an organization you work for or have worked for.

WORK
APPLICATION 5-12

Give an example of a program you were involved in at work.

standing plans Policies, procedures, and rules developed for handling repetitive situations.

policies General guidelines to be followed when making decisions.

procedure A sequence of actions to be followed in order to achieve an objective.

rules Statements of exactly what should or should not be done.

single-use plans Programs and budgets developed for handling nonrepetitive situations.

contingency plans Alternative plans to be implemented if uncontrollable events occur.

5-4 APPLYING THE CONCEPT

Identifying Plans

Identify the type of plan exemplified by each statement.

A. policy
B. procedure
C. rule
D. program
E. budget

____ 16. How much will it cost to operate your department next month?

____ 17. Everyone must wear safety glasses while operating the machine.

____ 18. Forms for maternity leave must be approved by the manager and submitted to the personnel office one month in advance of the planned leave.

____ 19. "Quality is job one."

____ 20. President Barack Obama's economic stimulus plan

To develop a contingency plan, answer three questions:

1. What might go wrong?
2. How can I prevent it from happening?
3. If it does occur, what can I do to minimize its effect?

The answer to question 3 is your contingency plan. With good contingency plans, you can prevent problems and solve them quickly and effectively. **BP** was criticized for not having an effective contingency plan in place after one of its oil rigs in the Gulf of Mexico exploded, ultimately resulting in the worst oil spill in history. BP could have saved billions of dollars in fixing a disaster that could have been avoided in the first place with an effective contingency plan.

When developing contingency plans, ask everyone involved what can go wrong and what should be done if it does go wrong. Also ask others within and outside the organization who have implemented similar plans. They may have encountered problems you haven't thought of, and they may have good contingency plans to suggest.

Starbucks's (Case Question 6) functional strategies are critical to its success. The marketing department works on improving and developing new products and promoting the Starbucks brand. To pursue international expansion, marketing will have a lot to do in determining locations throughout the globe. The operations department has two primary functions: to create new stores and to operate existing stores effectively and efficiently. The human resources department plays a major role in training employees to increase operating efficiency and customer satisfaction. It will also have to recruit, select, train, evaluate, and compensate thousands of employees as Starbucks continues to grow. In addition, growth requires an effective finance strategy to raise money and keep track of accounting and budgeting. Opening each new Starbucks store requires a single-use plan; each store is somewhat different. However, standing plans for the store-opening process, which take advantage of organizational learning, are also in place. Starbucks also has extensive policies, procedures, and rules to operate each store in a consistent manner. Finally, opening stores and operating them require contingency plans.

Time Management

Time management refers to techniques that enable people to get more done in less time with better results. Companies have discovered that poor productivity and inadequate customer service are related to poor time management,[84] as a recent

WORK
APPLICATION 5-13

Describe a situation in which a contingency plan is appropriate. Explain the plan.

survey found that employees waste about 20 percent of their time at work.[85] Time management skills will have a direct effect on your productivity and career success.[86]

Analyzing Time Use With a Time Log. The first step to successful time management requires using a time log. A *time log* is a daily diary that tracks your activities and enables you to determine how you spend (and waste) your time each day. Exhibit 5-11 gives an example you can use as a template to develop your own time logs. You should keep track of your time every day over a period of one or two typical weeks. Try to keep the time log with you throughout the day. Fill in the Description column for each 15-minute time slot, if possible, describing what you did.

After completing your time logs, analyze the information and find time-consumers you can eliminate.[87] Write notes in the Evaluation of Time Use column of the log, using the following abbreviations:

- Determine how much time you are spending on your high-priority (HP) and low-priority (LP) responsibilities. How do you spend most of your time?
- Identify areas where you spend too much time (TT) and where you do not spend enough time (NT).
- Identify major interruptions (I), distractions (D) like **Facebook**,[88] and crisis situations (C) that keep you from doing what you want to get done. How can you eliminate them? Do you have effective contingency plans?

A Time Management System. Do you sometimes find yourself looking at your schedule and wondering when you'll find the time to do everything you need to do? If so, a time management system may help. The time management system you will read about in this section has a proven record of success and is used by thousands. Try it for three weeks; after that, you can adjust it to meet your own needs.

There are four key components of the time management system: (1) *Priorities*. People waste time doing the wrong thing.[89] Assign a priority to each task,[90] and do the most important thing first—make it a rule.[91] (2) *Objectives*. Set weekly objectives using the objectives model (3) *Plans*. Develop operational plans to meet your objectives. (4) *Schedules*. Schedule each week and workday. Time management systems all boil down to developing a plan and sticking to it as much as possible. The *time management system* involves planning each week, scheduling each week, and scheduling each day. Refer to Exhibit 5-11 for the template for each step.

Step 1. **Plan each week.** Fill in a plan for the upcoming week. Start by setting nonroutine objectives then list major activities necessary to accomplish each objective. Indicate the priority level of each activity: high, medium, or low. Then complete the "Time Needed" and "Day to Schedule." One caution: planning too much is frustrating and causes stress when you cannot get everything done, so be realistic.[92]

Step 2. **Schedule each week.** Scheduling has been called the most critical task.[93] Start scheduling by filling in already committed time slots, such as regular weekly meetings. Then schedule controllable events. Most managers should leave about 50 percent of the week unscheduled to accommodate unexpected events. Your job or schoolwork may require more or less unscheduled time.

Step 3. **Schedule each day.** Your schedule is in essence a to-do-list. Leave your daily schedule flexible. Watch out for procrastination[94] and perfectionism.[95] Remember that if you are working on a high-priority item and you find yourself facing a lower-priority task, let it wait unless it is a true emergency. This will help you control interruptions and distractions.[96]

To-Do Lists. The time management system described here works well for managers who have to plan for a variety of nonrecurring tasks. For managers and

WORK
APPLICATION 5-14

Review your time log to identify your three biggest time wasters. How can you cut down or eliminate these time wasters?

EXHIBIT 5-12   TIME MANAGEMENT TOOLS

DAILY TIME LOG

Daily Time Log for Day _____ Date _____		
Starting Time	Description	Evaluation of Time Use
8:00		
8:15		
8:30		
8:45		
9:00		
9:15		
9:30		
9:45		
10:00		
(etc., to ending time)		

WEEKLY PLANNER

Plan for the week of _____

Objectives:

Activities	Priority	Time Needed	Day to Schedule

Total time for the week

WEEKLY SCHEDULE

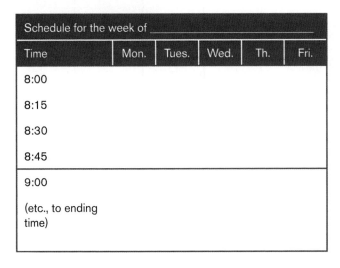

Schedule for the week of _____					
Time	Mon.	Tues.	Wed.	Th.	Fri.
8:00					
8:15					
8:30					
8:45					
9:00					
(etc., to ending time)					

DAILY SCHEDULE

Schedule for the day of _____
Time
8:00
8:15
8:30
8:45
9:00
(etc., to ending time)

employees who deal primarily with routine tasks, a to-do list that prioritizes items may work quite well. We will discuss using a to-do list in Chapter 7.

Forms similar to those in Exhibit 5-12 and can be purchased in any number of formats, including in electronic form such as your email, websites, and apps. Some are free and some charge, such as **Remember the Milk, Life Balance, Getting Things Done, Action Method,** and **Any.Do.** Or you can make your own forms.

Time Management Techniques. Self-Assessment 5–2 contains 49 time management techniques arranged by management function. Planning and controlling are placed together because they are so closely related. Organizing and leading

| 5-2 | **SELF** ASSESSMENT |

Time Management Techniques

Following is a list of 49 ideas that can be used to improve your time management skills. Place a checkmark in the appropriate box for each item.

Planning and Controlling Management Functions	1 = should do	2 = could do	3 = already doing	4 = doesn't apply to me
1. Use a time management system.	☐	☐	☐	☐
2. Use a to-do list and prioritize the items on it. Do the important things rather than the seemingly urgent things.	☐	☐	☐	☐
3. Get an early start on top-priority items.	☐	☐	☐	☐
4. Do only high-priority items during your best working hours (prime time); schedule unpleasant or difficult tasks during prime time.	☐	☐	☐	☐
5. Don't spend time performing unproductive activities to avoid or escape job-related anxiety. It doesn't really work; get the job done.	☐	☐	☐	☐
6. Throughout the day ask yourself, "Should I be doing this now?"	☐	☐	☐	☐
7. Plan before you act.	☐	☐	☐	☐
8. Plan for recurring crises to eliminate crises (contingency planning).	☐	☐	☐	☐
9. Make decisions. It is better to make a wrong decision than to make none at all.	☐	☐	☐	☐
10. Schedule enough time to do the job right the first time. Don't be too optimistic about the amount of time it takes to do a job.	☐	☐	☐	☐
11. Schedule a quiet hour to be interrupted only by true emergencies. Have some-one take messages or ask people who call then to call you back.	☐	☐	☐	☐
12. Establish a quiet time for the entire organization or department. The first hour of the day is usually the best time.	☐	☐	☐	☐
13. Schedule large blocks of uninterrupted (emergencies-only) time for projects and so forth. If this doesn't work, hide somewhere.	☐	☐	☐	☐
14. Break large (long) projects into parts (periods).	☐	☐	☐	☐
15. Before abandoning a scheduled item to do something unscheduled, ask yourself, "Is the unscheduled event more important than the scheduled event?" If not, stay on schedule.	☐	☐	☐	☐
16. Do related activities (for example, making and returning calls, writing letters and memos) in the same time slot.	☐	☐	☐	☐

Organizing Management Function	1 = should	2 = could do	3 = already do	4 = doesn't apply to me
17. Schedule time for unanticipated events and let people know the time. Ask people to see or call you only during this time, unless it's an emergency. Answer mail and do routine things while waiting for people to contact you. If people ask to see you—"Got a minute?"—ask whether it can wait until your scheduled time.	☐	☐	☐	☐
18. Set a scheduled time, agenda, and time limit for all visitors, and keep on topic.	☐	☐	☐	☐
19. Keep a clean, well-organized work area/desk.	☐	☐	☐	☐

Organizing Management Function	1 = should	2 = could do	3 = already do	4 = doesn't apply to me
20. Remove all non-work-related or distracting objects from your work area/desk.	☐	☐	☐	☐
21. Do one task at a time.	☐	☐	☐	☐
22. When paperwork requires a decision, make it at once; don't read through the paperwork again later and decide.	☐	☐	☐	☐
23. Keep files well arranged and labeled with an active and inactive file section. When you file an item, pur a throwaway date on it.	☐	☐	☐	☐
24. Call rather than write or visit, when appropriate.	☐	☐	☐	☐
25. Delegate someone else to write letters, memos, and so forth.	☐	☐	☐	☐
26. Use form letters and form paragraphs is word processing software.	☐	☐	☐	☐
27. Answer letters (memos) on the letter itself.	☐	☐	☐	☐
28. Have someone read and summarize things for you.	☐	☐	☐	☐
29. Divide reading requirements with others and share summaries	☐	☐	☐	☐
30. Have calls screened to be sure the right person handles each call.	☐	☐	☐	☐
31. Plan before calling. Have an agenda and all necessary information ready; take notes on the agenda.	☐	☐	☐	☐
32. Ask people to call you back during your scheduled unexpected time. Ask about the best time to call them.	☐	☐	☐	☐
33. Have a specific objective or purpose for every meeting you conduct. If you cannot think of an objective, don't have the meeting.	☐	☐	☐	☐
34. Invite to meetings only the necessary participants and keep them only as long as needed.	☐	☐	☐	☐
35. Always have an agenda for a meeting and stick to it. Start and end as scheduled	☐	☐	☐	☐
36. Set objectives for travel. List everyone you will meet with. Call or send them agendas, and have a file folder for each with all necessary data for your meeting.	☐	☐	☐	☐
37. Combine and modify activities to save time.	☐	☐	☐	☐

Leading Management Function	1 = should	2 = could do	3 = already do	4 = doesn't apply to me
38. Set clear objectives for subordinates and make sure they know what they are accountable for; give them feedback and evaluate results often.	☐	☐	☐	☐
39. Don't waste others' time. Don't make subordinates wait idly for decisions, instructions, or materials, at meetings, and so on. Conversely, wait for a convenient time to speak to subordinates or others, rather than interrupting them and wasting their time.	☐	☐	☐	☐
40. Train your subordinates. Don't do their work for them.	☐	☐	☐	☐
41. Delegate activities in which you do not need to be personally involved, especially nonmanagement functions.	☐	☐	☐	☐
42. Set deadlines earlier than the actual deadline.	☐	☐	☐	☐
43. Use the input of your staff. Don't reinvent the wheel.	☐	☐	☐	☐
44. Teach time management skills to your subordinates.	☐	☐	☐	☐
45. Don't procrastinate; do it.	☐	☐	☐	☐
46. Don't be a perfectionist—define "acceptable" and stop there.	☐	☐	☐	☐
47. Learn to stay calm. Getting emotional only causes more problems.	☐	☐	☐	☐
48. Reduce socializing, but don't become antisocial.	☐	☐	☐	☐
49. Communicate well. Don't canfuse employees.	☐	☐	☐	☐

WORK
APPLICATION 5-15

From the time management techniques listed in the Self-Assessment, choose the three most important ones you should be using. Explain how you will implement each technique.

Most of us are not as good at multitasking as we think we are. How long can you go without checking your smartphone or another device? When doing tasks that require concentration, like studying, avoiding distractions and turning off devices will improve productivity. Photo from Big Cheese Photo/Thinkstock.

WORK
APPLICATION 5-16

How would you assess your use of multitasking in your personal life? In your professional life? How can you improve?

are separated. Select and, more importantly, implement the items that will help you get more done in less time.

Multitasking

Multitasking is the practice or capability of handling more than one task at a time. In our e-world, people are multitasking more today than ever.[97] Complete Self-Assessment 5–3 to get an idea of your use of multitasking and how it affects you.

Multitasking, the Brain, and Decreased Productivity. Although you may not want to believe it, research has shown that the human brain is not actually capable of doing two things at once. Think of it as a single-screen TV. You can't watch two shows at once, but you can flip back and forth, missing some of each show; the more shows you watch, the more you miss of each one. Time is lost when switching between tasks, and the time loss increases with the complexity of the task. When people multitask things that require thinking, either at the same time or alternating rapidly between them, errors go way up, and it takes far longer—often double the time or more—to get the jobs done than if they were done sequentially.[98] A study found that productivity dropped as much as 40 percent when subjects tried to do two or more things at once.[99]

Research has shown that most people, even those who think they are good at it, are not good at multitasking. One of the problems with high levels of multitasking is that it undermines our attention spans by decreasing our ability to concentrate for any length of time. With things binging and bonging and tweeting at you, you don't think.[100] Daily workplace interruptions, such as text, phone calls or the arrival of email, consume more than two hours of the average professional's workday.[101]

Effective Multitasking. So how can you multitask effectively? The first step is to recognize that the entire process is, essentially, a form of time management[102] and that many of the time management techniques listed in Self-Assessment 5–2 can be applied to multitasking. Effective multitasking can also be accomplished.[103] Here are some suggestions.

- *Know when it is appropriate.* Realize that certain thinking tasks, like reading, require your undivided attention. When your full attention should be on a single complex or important task, multitasking is not appropriate and will likely affect the quality of your work. Save multitasking for nonurgent, noncomplex tasks.

- *Limit distractions and interruptions.* You can save time by shutting off these interruptions and distractions.[104] Office workers are interrupted around every three minutes. Once off track, it can take 23 minutes to return to the original task.[105] Stay on track for a set amount of time, such as a half or full hour. Only after the set time can you check for texts, emails, and so forth.[106] Music and especially TV are distracting and can overtax the brain.[107] If you need background sounds to overcome

5-3 SELF ASSESSMENT

Multitasking

Identify how frequently you experience each statement.

Not frequently   Frequently

1	2	3	4	5

_____1. I have a hard time paying attention; my mind wanders when I'm listening to someone or reading.

_____2. I have a hard time concentrating; I can't do just one work/homework task for an hour or longer.

_____3. I continually check my texts, phone, email, online/Facebook, etc. while doing work/homework.

_____4. I feel stress if I'm not checking screens regularly.

_____5. I'm easily bored, distracted, or interrupted while doing work/homework.

Add up your score (5 to 25) and place it here _____. On the continuum below, mark the point that represents your total score.

Multitasking not an issue   Possible over multitasking

1	5	10	15	20	25

distracting noise, try music that you don't really like or dislike, so you can ignore it, like classical music or ocean sounds, or you can wear noise-canceling headphones.

IMPLEMENTING AND CONTROLLING STRATEGIES

The fifth and final step of the strategic planning process involves implementing and controlling strategies to ensure that the mission and objectives, at all three levels, are achieved. Top and middle managers are more involved with the planning, whereas the lower-level functional managers and employees implement the strategies on a day-to-day basis. Successful implementation of strategies requires effective and efficient support systems throughout the organization. Although strategic planning usually goes well, implementation is often a problem. One reason is that strategic plans often end up buried in bottom drawers; no action is taken to implement the strategy. Throughout Chapters 6 through 13, you will learn how to organize and lead so as to implement strategies.

As strategies are being implemented, they must also be controlled. *Controlling* is the process of monitoring progress and taking corrective action when needed to ensure that objectives are achieved (Chapter 1). Another important part of controlling is staying within the budget when appropriate or changing it when necessary to meet changes in the dynamic environment.[108] Strategic change is difficult,[109] but failure to change strategies can lead to severe consequences.[110] You will develop your change management skills in the next chapter and controlling skills in Chapters 14 and 15.

Having read this chapter, you should understand the importance of effective planning and recognize the five planning dimensions and the differences between standing plans and single-use plans and between strategic and operational plans. You should know how to use a time management system, have techniques to improve your time management, and know when and when not to multitask. You should be able to develop a mission, analyze the environment, and set effective objectives using a model. You should also understand the need to coordinate strategies and the importance of implementing and controlling strategies.

• • • CHAPTER SUMMARY

5-1. **Describe how strategic planning differs from operational planning.**

The primary differences concern the time frame and the level of management involved. Strategic planning involves developing a mission and long-range objectives and plans; operational planning involves short-range objectives and plans. Upper-level managers develop strategic plans, and middle- and lower-level managers develop operational plans.

5-2. **Explain the reason for conducting an industry and competitive situation analysis.**

The industry and competitive situation analysis is used to determine the attractiveness of an industry. It is primarily used at the corporate level to make decisions regarding which lines of business to enter and exit and how to allocate resources among lines of business.

5-3. **Explain the reason for conducting a company situation analysis.**

The company situation analysis is used at the business level to determine the issues and problems that need to be addressed through the strategic planning process.

5-4. **List the parts of an effective written objective.**

The parts of the objective are (1) *to* + (2) action verb + (3) singular, specific, and measurable result to be achieved + (4) target date.

5-5. **Describe the four grand strategies.**

With a growth strategy, the firm aggressively pursues increasing its size. With a stability strategy, the firm maintains the same size or grows slowly. With a turnaround strategy, the firm attempts a comeback; with retrenchment, it decreases in size. With a combination strategy, two or more of the three strategies are used for different lines of business.

5-6. **Describe the three growth strategies.**

With a concentration strategy, the firm grows aggressively in its existing line(s) of business. With integration, the firm grows by entering forward or backward line(s) of business. With diversification, the firm grows by adding related or unrelated products.

5-7. **Discuss the three adaptive strategies.**

With the prospecting strategy, the firm aggressively offers new products or services and/or enters new markets. With the defending strategy, the firm stays with its product line and markets. With the analyzing strategy, the firm moves into new markets cautiously and/or offers a core product group and seeks new opportunities.

5-8. **State the difference between standing plans and single-use plans.**

The major difference is the repetitiveness of the situation the plan is intended to address. Standing plans are policies, procedures, and rules developed for handling repetitive situations. Single-use plans are programs and budgets developed for handling nonrepetitive situations.

• • • KEY TERMS

acquisition, 138
adaptive strategies, 140
benchmarking, 132
business portfolio analysis, 139
competitive advantage, 132
contingency plans, 144
functional strategies, 142
grand strategy, 136

growth strategies, 137
management by objectives (MBO), 135
merger, 138
objectives, 133
operational planning, 127
policies, 144
procedure, 144

rules, 144
single-use plans, 144
situation analysis, 129
standing plans, 144
strategic planning, 127
strategy, 127
SWOT analysis, 131

• • • KEY TERM REVIEW

Complete each of the following statements using one of this chapter's key terms:

1. _____ is the process of developing a mission and long-range objectives and determining in advance how they will be accomplished.

2. _____ is the process of setting short-range objectives and determining in advance how they will be accomplished.

3. A _____ is a plan for pursuing a mission and achieving objectives.

4. A _____ focuses on those features in a company's environment that most directly affect its options and opportunities.

5. Through a _____, the organization's internal environmental strengths and weaknesses and external environmental opportunities and threats are determined.

6. _____ specifies how an organization offers unique customer value.

7. _____ is the process of comparing the organization's products or services and processes with those of other companies.

8. _____ state what is to be accomplished in specific and measurable terms with a target date.

9. _____ is the process in which managers and their employees jointly set objectives for the employees, periodically evaluate performance, and reward according to the results.

10. _____ is the overall corporate strategy of growth, stability, or turnaround and retrenchment, or for some combination of these.

11. _____ include concentration, backward and forward integration, and related and unrelated diversification.

12. A _____ occurs when two companies form one corporation.

13. An _____ occurs when one business buys all or part of another business.

14. _____ is the corporate process of determining which lines of business the corporation will be in and how it will allocate resources among them.

15. _____ include prospecting, defending, and analyzing.

16. _____ are developed and implemented by managers in marketing, operations, human resources, finance, and other departments.

17. _____ are policies, procedures, and rules developed for handling repetitive situations.

18. _____ provide general guidelines to be followed when making decisions.

19. A _____ is a sequence of actions to be followed in order to achieve an objective.

20. _____ state exactly what should or should not be done.

21. _____ are programs and budgets developed for handling nonrepetitive situations.

22. _____ are alternative plans to be implemented if uncontrollable events occur.

••• REVIEW QUESTIONS

1. What are the five planning dimensions?
2. What are the two types of plans?
3. Is there a difference between a plan and a strategy?
4. Which planning levels and their strategies are part of strategic planning?
5. What are the steps in the strategic planning process?
6. What is the relationship between the mission statement and developing strategies?
7. Why is a company situation analysis part of the strategic planning process?
8. What is the writing objectives model?
9. What criteria should an objective meet?
10. What are the grand strategies?
11. What is the difference between a merger and an acquisition?
12. What are the adaptive strategies?
13. What is the relationship between grand strategies and adaptive strategies?
14. What are the competitive strategies?
15. What are the common functional strategy areas?
16. What is the difference between standing plans and single-use plans?
17. Explain the use of a time log.
18. List and briefly describe the three steps in the time management system.
19. Explain what multitasking is and how to practice it effectively.

••• COMMUNICATION SKILLS

The following critical-thinking questions can be used for class discussion and/or as written assignments to develop communication skills. Be sure to give complete explanations for all questions.

1. Why are strategic and operational planning important?
2. Should all businesses have corporate, business, and functional strategies?

3. Should a mission statement be customer focused?

4. Should all businesses formally analyze the environment?

5. Should all businesses have a competitive advantage?

6. Is it ethical to copy other companies' ideas through benchmarking?

7. Are both goals and objectives necessary for a business?

8. Is it important to write objectives?

9. As a manager, would you use management by objectives (MBO)?

10. Which growth strategy would you say is the most successful?

11. Why would a business use a focus strategy rather than trying to appeal to all customers?

12. Give examples of functional departments other than those mentioned in the text.

• • • CASE: BLACKBERRY TRIES TO NAVIGATE A TURNAROUND STRATEGY

Remember when BlackBerry was so popular that it was just about the only cell phone that people bought? Well, with the soaring popularity of Apple iPhones and Samsung smartphones with Android operating systems, BlackBerry is quickly losing market share.

In 2003, BlackBerry introduced the first of what the company feels was the beginning of the modern smartphone. This was a device that not only functioned as a telephone but also allowed for the sending and receiving of email and text messages as well as web browsing. One of the main focuses of the early BlackBerry was to allow for mobile email. Clearly people who were on the go needed a way to access their email without having to find a computer—and BlackBerry was an early entrant into the marketplace.[111]

The phone was very popular with businesspeople. It could be stated that every businessperson with a cell phone before 2005 or so had a BlackBerry phone. At the time, the company name was Research in Motion (known as RIM). The stock price for RIM was one of the most watched prices by investors on a daily basis.

The name BlackBerry was chosen for the phones after a thorough search for just the right name to fit the little cell phone with a small screen and little black buttons. Eventually, the name BlackBerry was chosen since the little buttons used to make calls and send emails on the phone looked like blackberries. The name was successful, and many people started to consider the word *blackberry* a cell phone from a company called RIM— and not a fruit. By 2013, RIM changed its name to the more commonly known BlackBerry name. By then the name change had little influence on sales.[112]

However, the problems started when Apple developed a strategy to enter the cell phone industry. BlackBerry wasn't large enough to block Apple from entering the market it controlled. The birth of the iPhone meant that BlackBerry would have to compete against Apple's well-known reputation for designing new-to-the-world products that were beautifully crafted and functioned like no other product in the marketplace. For example, Apple was fresh from launching the iPod, which overnight changed the music industry by allowing customers to download songs from the Apple website for about $1.00.

Many cell phones from companies such as Samsung soon flooded the cell phone market, and BlackBerry's cell phone was lost in the crowd. The final straw might have been phones run by the Android operating system (which is owned by Google). For example, Samsung's Galaxy S4 cell phone model, which uses the Android technology, was one of the most anticipated cell phone releases in 2013.[113]

In response, BlackBerry is trying to execute a turnaround strategy that can save its remaining market share and loyal business customers. BlackBerry's board of directors and CEO Thorsten Heins, who recently stepped down as CEO of BlackBerry, considered the idea of making BlackBerry a private company.[114] Becoming a private company would mean that anyone considering buying or funding BlackBerry would help to buy back their own stock.

Although this would allow BlackBerry to control its own destiny, it is hard to believe that it would protect the company from the Apple and Android cell phone products.

Unfortunately, the latest product, the BlackBerry 10, did not go over well with buyers. The lack of sales was frustrating considering the phones looked sleek, with a larger screen much like the rest of the phones in the modern cell phone marketplace.

Since the BlackBerry 10 did not sell well, the company has since laid off 4,500 employees and reported a quarterly loss of almost a billion dollars. The loss is mainly a write-off of the unsold phones and the restructuring charges.[115]

On September 23, 2013, Fairfax Financial Holdings Ltd., a Canadian insurance firm, signed a letter of intent with the BlackBerry board under which it could pay $9 a share in cash for the 90% of BlackBerry shares it doesn't already own. In November 2013, however, the deal collapsed. Can BlackBerry survive?[116]

The problem at BlackBerry is that it lost its competitive advantage of being a differentiated product that appealed to the business market. The company used to have a top-notch management team, the coolest name on the market for a smartphone, and the best-designed and -operating phone in the industry. Those are a lot of competitive advantages to lose in one decade.

Case Questions

1. Is BlackBerry's decision to lay off 4,500 employees is an example of strategic or operational planning?

2. How could BlackBerry have benefited from conducting industry and company (SWOT) situational analysis?

3. Which grand strategy was BlackBerry considering to use in the case?

4. If Blackberry considered opening up its retail stores, would that be considered a forward or backward integration strategy?

5. Has BlackBerry's primary adaptive strategy of the past few years been prospecting, defending, or analyzing?

6. Has BlackBerry's primary competitive strategy against its competitors been product differentiation, cost leadership, or focus?

7. Is the functional operational strategy of finding more customers the responsibility of marketing, human resources, operations, or finance?

8. Explain BlackBerry's strategic and operational plans.

9. Does BlackBerry have a core competency? If so, what is it?

Cumulative Case Questions

10. Which management functions, skills, and management levels are most important in implementing the growth strategy for BlackBerry? (Chapter 1)

11. Which environmental factors were most instrumental in BlackBerry's competition with Apple, Samsung, and Google during the late 2000s? (Chapter 2)

12. Use the Internet to find an article that discusses the forecast for smartphone usage across the globe. (Chapter 3)

• • • SKILL BUILDER 5-1: WRITING OBJECTIVES

For this exercise, you will first work at improving ineffective objectives. Then you will write nine objectives for yourself.

Objective

To develop your skill at writing objectives.

Skills

The primary skills developed through this exercise are:

1. *Management skill*—decision making (setting objectives is the first step to planning)

2. *AACSB competencies*—communication abilities and analytic skills

3. *Management function*—planning (both strategic and operational)

Part 1

Indicate which of the "must" criteria each of the following objectives fails to meet and rewrite the objective so that it meets all those criteria. When writing objectives, use the following model:

To + action verb + specific and measurable result + target date

1. To improve our company image by the end of 2016

Criteria not met:

Improved objective:

2. To increase the number of customers by 10 percent

Criteria not met:

Improved objective:

3. To increase profits during 2016

Criteria not met:

Improved objective:

4. To sell 5 percent more hot dogs and soda at the baseball game on Sunday, June 14, 2015

Criteria not met:

Improved objective:

Part 2

Write three educational, three personal, and three career objectives you want to accomplish using the Objectives Model 5–1. Your objectives can be short term (something you want to accomplish today) or long term (something you want to have accomplished 20 years from now) or in between those extremes. Be sure your objectives meet the criteria for effective objectives.

Apply It

What did I learn from this experience? How will I use this knowledge in the future?

• • • SKILL BUILDER 5-2

The Strategic Planning Process at Your College

This exercise enables you to apply the strategic planning process to your college or university as an individual and/or group.

Objective

To develop your planning skills.

Skills

The primary skills developed through this exercise are:

1. *Management skill*—decision making (conceptual, diagnostic, analytical, and critical thinking)
2. *AACSB competencies*—communication abilities, analytic skills, and reflective thinking skills
3. *Management function*—planning (strategic)

Step 1. Developing the Mission

1. What is the mission statement of your university/college or school/department?
2. Is the mission statement easy to remember?
3. How would you improve the mission statement?

Step 2. Analyzing the Environment

1. Conduct a five-force competitive analysis, like that in Exhibit 5-4 (page 130).
2. Complete a SWOT analysis, like that in Exhibit 5-6.
3. Determine the competitive advantage of your university/college or school/department.

Step 3. Setting Objectives

What are some goals and objectives of your university/college or school department?

Step 4. Developing Strategies

1. Identify your university/college's or school/department's grand, adaptive, and competitive strategies.

_____

_____

2. Where would you place your program/major on the BCG growth-share matrix?

_____

_____

_____

_____

Step 5. Implementing and Controlling Strategies

How would you rate your university/college's or school/department's strategic planning? How could it be improved?

Apply It

What did I learn from this experience? How will I use this knowledge in the future?

• • • STUDENT STUDY SITE

Visit the Student Study Site at **www.sagepub.com/lussier6e** to access to these additional study tools:

- Mobile-compatible self-assessment quizzes
- Mobile-compatible key term flashcards
- Video Links
- SAGE Journal Articles
- Web Links

6 Managing Change, Innovation, and Entrepreneurship

● ● ● **Learning Outcomes**

After studying this chapter, you should be able to:

6-1. Identify the forces for change, the types of change, and the forms of change. PAGE 160

6-2. Explain the differences in managing innovation during incremental and discontinuous change in terms of approach, goals, and strategy. PAGE 165

6-3. List the reasons employees resist change and suggest ways of overcoming such resistance. PAGE 167

6-4. Identify the steps in the Lewin and comprehensive change models. PAGE 171

6-5. State the difference in the use of forcefield analysis and survey feedback. PAGE 174

6-6. Explain the difference between an entrepreneur and an intrapreneur. PAGE 175

IDEAS ON MANAGEMENT at Xerox

Xerox is the world's leading enterprise for business process and document management. It provides true end-to-end solutions, from back-office support to the printed page, to help companies operate their business and manage information. Xerox technology, expertise and services enable workplaces—from small businesses to large global enterprises—to simplify the way work gets done so they operate more effectively and focus more on what matters most: their real business. Xerox continues its growth strategy, doing business in 160 countries with 140,000 employees with revenues exceeding $22.3 billion. It's a *Fortune* Global 500 company.

Ursula M. Burns started as a summer intern and worked her way up to the top of the corporate ladder to her present job as chairman and CEO of Xerox. She is the first African-American woman CEO to head a *Fortune* 500 company (it's in the top 150) and the first woman to succeed another woman as head of a Fortune 500 company. Just weeks after taking over as CEO, Burns announced the biggest deal in Xerox's history—the $6.4 billion acquisition of outsourcing firm **Affiliated Computer Services.** By the end of 2009, Xerox's net income had doubled from its 2008 total.

Burns is leading a major transformation of Xerox from its prior focus on selling printers and copiers to a service business. Long and best known for its success in innovative document technology, Burns has taken the company into some places people never expected to find Xerox, doing things they probably didn't know Xerox could do. Burns is ranked in the top 20 of the *Forbes* 100 Most Powerful Women.

1. What types of change did Ursula Burns make as she worked her way up the corporate ladder at Xerox? PAGE 162

2. How is Xerox committed to innovation? PAGE 165

3. How does Xerox use organizational development (OD)? PAGE 174

4. Is Xerox entrepreneurial? PAGE 175

You'll find answers to these questions throughout the chapter. To learn more about Xerox, visit its website at www.xerox.com.

Sources: Information for this case and answers within the chapter are taken from Xerox's website at http://www.xerox.com, accessed June 21, 2013; "Largest U.S. corporations—*Fortune* 500," *Fortune* (May 20, 2013): 1–20; "Global 500: The World's Largest Corporations; The 100 Most Powerful Women," *Forbes* (September 10, 2012): 90.

• • • Chapter Outline

INNOVATION AND CHANGE

Innovation and change are critical for firm performance and survival.[1] So your ability to be flexible enough to change with the diversifying global environment will affect your career success.[2] In this section, we discuss the innovation and change interrelationship and risk, the forces for change, and types and forms of change.

The Innovation and Change Interrelationship and Risk

Creativity, Innovation, and Change. Recall from Chapter 4 that *creativity* is a way of thinking that generates new ideas and that creativity can lead to innovation. *Innovation* is the implementation of a new idea. So employee creativity is crucial for innovation.[3] Two important types of innovation are *product innovation* (new things goods/services) and *process innovation* (new ways of doing things).[4] Thus, all innovations require some changes to be made in the organization. Change happens at the individual, team, or organizational level and impacts all aspects of organizational life.[5] **Organizational change** *is alternations of existing work routines and strategies that affect the whole organization.*[6] John Chambers, **Cisco** CEO, said that his most important decisions are about adjusting to change.[7]

Taking Risk. When implementing innovative changes, you face risk.[8] Change can result in worse or better performance. The innovator can reap the profits, like **Apple**.[9] So top managers are inclined to take risks and innovate in order to obtain a competitive advantage.[10] Adapting to dynamic environments has been identified as a major element in maintaining competitiveness.[11] However, partly due to the last recession and slow-growing economy in the United States, some companies have become more risk averse.[12] So some CEOs are encouraging employees to take more risks.[13]

Failing to Take Risk. Unfortunately, failing to take risks and change with the dynamic environment can lead to a decline in business. Research supports that companies that change regularly outperform those that change irregularly.[14] There is always the risk that some company will come out of nowhere and crush you.[15] **Research in Motion (RIM)** dominated the cell phone markets with its BlackBerry. But the **Apple** iPhone and **Google** Android phones have taken away many of its customers. **GM** also lost market share to foreign competitors and even went bankrupt and needed a government bailout to continue in business. With a major change in top managers, they had a turnaround.

Forces for Change

There are driving patterns of change.[16] Here are three forces that lead to changes in business; businesses must adapt to these changing conditions.[17]

The Environment. The high rate of changing business environment presents many challenges.[18] As you saw in Chapter 2, an organization interacts with its external and internal environments, and these factors require change in an organization. An important external factor includes keeping up with competitors' innovations.[19] **Microsoft** came out with the Xbox One to compete with **Apple** TV, and **Amazon** responded with the Kindle TV Set-Top Box.[20] A second factor includes keeping up with customer taste and changes in buying patterns.[21]

Technology Cycles. A *technology cycle* begins with the birth of a new technology and ends when it is replaced by a newer, substantially better technology. The **Ford** Model T car replaced the horse-drawn carriage. The vinyl record (**RCA** record

---

WORK
APPLICATION 6-1

Give an example of an innovation from an organization you work for or have worked for. Be sure to specify whether it was a product innovation or a process innovation.

LO 6-1

Identify the forces for change, the types of change, and the forms of change.

organizational change Alterations of existing work routines and strategies that affect the whole organization.

player) was replace by the cassette (**Sony** Walkman), then the CD (**GPX** CD player/boom box), and now we transition to online purchasing, including **Apple** iTunes (MP3-iPod to iPhone) and to streaming. It takes time to go through a technology cycle, but through the transition, there are usually many improvements that change the performance of the product, often going through generations.

Next Generation. The technology cycle is different from the *next generation,* such as 3G to 4G, because it allows the old technology to still work with the new technology. **Microsoft** updates its Office software and Xbox, but it allows the older-generation documents and games to be used with the new generation. People often prefer the next generation to a new technology cycle because there is less need to change, as they don't like to have to lose the old technology and pay for the new technology.

The Management Functions and Change. Most plans that managers develop require changes. When managers organize and delegate tasks, they often require employees to make some changes in their regular routine. When managers hire, orient, train, and evaluate performance, change is required. Leadership calls for influencing employees, often to change in some way, and control may require the use of new methods or techniques to ensure the objective is met.

Types of Change

Types of change refer to what actually changes within the organization. The four **types of change** are *changes in strategy, in structure, in technology, and in people.* Because of the systems effect, you need to consider the repercussions of a change in one variable (type of change) on the others and plan accordingly. As you read about each type of change, you will understand the interrelationship of the systems effect. See Exhibit 6-1 for a list of the changes.

WORK
APPLICATION 6-2

Give an example of a force that resulted in a change in an organization you work for or have worked for.

EXHIBIT 6-1 TYPES OF CHANGES

Strategy	Structure	Technology	People
The corporate, business, and functions strategies (Chapter 5) change over time.	How the organization as a whole and its departments and jobs change over time (Chapter 7).	How the firm transforms inputs into outputs can change (Chapter 13–15).	Employees can change their attitudes and behavior and develop skills that change their performance (Chapters 8–14).

Changes in Strategy. Changes in the environment often require changes in strategy.[22] You'll recall from Chapter 5 that an organization may change its strategy (at the corporate, business, and/or functional level), but it can take years to drive major strategy changes through a company like **Cisco**.[23] During the recent economic recession, **GE, Sony,** and **Unilever** all made changes to their strategy from making premium, more-expensive products to some less-complex, better-value products in order to retain customers. **Apple** came out with a lower-priced iPhone.

Changes in Structure. Structure referrers to how the organization is departmentalized into work units. Structure commonly follows strategy. In other words, a change in strategy often results in a change in structure.[24] **Microsoft** has changed its structure multiple times over the years as it added new lines of business products.[25] We will discuss structure in Chapter 7. With the trend to adopt structures that rely on small groups to perform critical tasks,[26] people changes are also needed.

types of change Changes in strategy, in structure, in technology, and in people.

6-1 APPLYING THE CONCEPT

Types of Change

Identify the type of change in each statement:

- A. strategy
- B. structure
- C. technology
- D. people

_____ 1. "We are laying off some middle and lower-level managers to increase the number of people reporting to one boss."

_____ 2. "The new software we purchased requires fewer people to make the tools."

_____ 3. "With the increasing number of competitors, we are going to have to spend more time and effort to keep our existing customers."

_____ 4. "Anna, I'd like you to consider getting a college degree if you are serious about a career in management with us."

_____ 5. "We are switching suppliers so that we can get a higher-quality component to put into our product."

WORK
APPLICATION 6-3

Give one or more examples of a type of change you experienced in an organization you work for or have worked for.

Changes in Technology. Advances in technology increase the need for effective and efficient routine change.[27] Recall from Chapter 2 that the *systems process* is the technology used to transform inputs into outputs, and the technology doesn't have to be high tech. So *technology* is the essential part of the systems process,[28] and how we do our jobs does change. New machines and equipment, information processing, and automation are examples of changes based on technology. With the fast pace of technology changes, you need to be flexible and adapt and learn quickly.[29] New technologies sometimes replace people, just as **U.S. military** drones can,[30] and can increase productivity.

Changes in People. Organizations can't change without changes in people. Tasks change with technology and structural changes. A change in team membership is a common type of people change.[31] When tasks change, people's *skills* and *performance* must change. Organizations often attempt to change employees' *attitudes* and *behavior*. A change in organizational *culture* (Chapter 2) is also considered a people change. People develop and implement strategy and structure. People also create, manage, and use technology; therefore, people are the most important resource.[32] Change in other variables will not be effective without people.

While working her way up the corporate ladder at **Xerox (Case Question 1)**, Burns has helped the company make radical changes in strategy, structure, technology, and people. The strategy change she is making is transitioning the company from being a manufacturer of printers and copiers to a service business process and document-management company. With acquisitions came new services that changed the structure of Xerox, such as new innovative products, including helping clients switch from standard copier machines to ones that could be integrated with computer networks. Xerox had people changes by hiring 10,000 more employees.

Forms of Change

Change also takes one of two broad forms: incremental or discontinuous.

Incremental Change. Incremental change *is continual improvement that takes place within the existing technology cycle.* Companies innovate by lowering costs and improving performance of existing products and services. You need to change at the right pace.[33] Adjusting to slow, incremental change is like canoeing in calm water. By contrast, coping with a dynamic environment filled with uncertainty and requiring rapid change in order to react to unexpected improvements is like white-water rafting. **IBM CEO** Virginia Rometty's message to employees is that

incremental change Continual improvement that takes place within the existing technology cycle.

6-1 | JOIN THE DISCUSSION ETHICS & SOCIAL RESPONSIBILITY

Online High School

There are high schools, including National High School, offering online courses and diplomas. They tend to be attractive to individual-sport athletes, such as tennis players, golfers, and skaters because they allow flexibility to train, travel long distances to compete, and do course work in between. Online courses also allow student to work at their own pace. Unlike public school, students pay to earn credits and don't have face-to-face, in-person contact with peers and teachers. Some of the online high schools are for-profit businesses making lots of money.

1. How do you feel about high school students missing the experience of attending traditional classes and socializing with their peers?
2. How do you feel about students paying to earn a high school diploma online when they can earn one for free at a public school?
3. Is it ethical and socially responsible to offer a for-profit online high school?

IBM hasn't transformed rapidly enough, and they step up and deal with that at all levels—think fast and move fast.[34]

Intel (and other companies) continues to cut the cost of its computer chips and increase the speed during each technology cycle or with each next-generation chip. Incremental changes continue to the point of *technological discontinuity* with advances or unique combinations of existing technologies creating a significant breakthrough in performance or function. **Microsoft** stepped up the technology innovation with its Xbox One going ahead of Apple TV.[35] **Apple** unveiled the biggest redesign in iPhone software.[36]

Discontinuous Change. Discontinuous change *is a significant breakthrough in technology that leads to design competition and a new technology cycle.* During the breakthrough in technology, companies often fight for *design dominance* to set the market standard. **Toshiba** had HD DVD technology and **Sony** had Blu-ray. **Warner Brothers** went with Blu-ray only, and Blu-ray became the market standard. **Samsung** and **LG** are fighting for the dominant 3-D TV design.[37] Dominant designs can also be set by independent standard bodies. The **International Telecommunication Union (ITU)** agreed on the new standard for 4G (fourth-generation) service on smartphones, replacing 4G LTE. 4G makes your smartphone at least 500 times faster than 3G.[38]

NCR (original name National Cash Register) is an excellent example of a company that has been able to make incremental changes for 125 years as it has moved from technology cycles of offering mechanical cash registers to electronic ones and now digital computing. NCR has also moved into other fields of consumer interaction with a variety of software and hardware, most recently including a cloud-based point-of-sale system for small businesses.[39]

MANAGING INNOVATION

Innovation is a business buzzword. Companies use it constantly; **Apple** and **Google** mentioned innovation 22 and 14 times, respectively, in their annual reports. Many companies have innovation officers.[40] In this section, we discuss organizational structures and cultures that stimulate innovative change and how to manage innovation during incremental and discontinuous change.

Innovative Organizational Structures and Cultures

Innovative Structures. Organizations that stimulate innovation are commonly structured as flat organizations with limited bureaucracy, have a generalist

discontinuous change A significant breakthrough in technology that leads to design competition and a new technology cycle.

A Google self-driving car maneuvers through the stress of Washington, DC. The system on this modified Toyota Prius combines information gathered from Google Street View with artificial intelligence software. Despite its growing size, Google remains committed to fostering an innovative culture. Photo from Karen Bleier/AFP/Getty Images.

division of labor, coordinate with cross-functional teams, and are flexible. They use small team structures.[41] Use of informal authority is common, and authority is decentralized. We will discuss these structures in Chapter 7. They don't stress following standing plans (Chapter 5).[42]

Many innovative organizations set up *skunkworks projects*. A skunkworks project is one typically developed by a small and loosely structured group of people who research and develop a project primarily for the sake of radical innovation. A skunkworks project often operates with a high degree of autonomy and is often undertaken in secret with the understanding that if the development is successful, then the product will be designed in the usual process. **Apple, Lexus,** and **Michelin** are just a few companies that successfully use skunkworks projects to develop new products. At **Google X** (its secretive lab), incremental changes aren't good enough; they really strive to innovate for discontinuous technology breakthroughs, such as **Google** Glasses and its driverless car.[43]

Innovative Cultures. The successful organizations encourage creativity and innovation. Organizations known to have strong innovative cultures include **3M, Amazon.com, Google,** and **LG Electronics. Apple** CEO Tim Cook brags about its culture of innovation.[44] Such organizations develop structures that match and become a part of their innovative cultures. Innovative firms tend to have similar cultures that encourage experimentation. Such cultures commonly have the following characteristics:

- *Encouragement of Risk Taking.* Encouragement for risk taking comes from the organization, supervisors, and group members. Getting employees to voice ideas helps change the status quo.[45] Managers are asking employees to express opinions, concerns, or ideas for innovation.[46] Innovative cultures encourage and reward employees for taking risks without fear of punishment if they fail.[47] Failure is viewed as a learning experience. Former **Procter & Gamble** (P&G) CEO A. G. Lafley stated, "You learn more from failure than you do from success."[48] Indian **Tata Group** gives an annual award for the best failed idea, and **Intuit** and **Eli Lilly** have failure parties.[49]

A method of encouraging risk taking is through encouraging *intrapreneurs*, people who start a new line of business for an existing company. We discuss the difference between entrepreneurs and intrapreneurs later in this chapter.

- *Flexibility.* Managers work to overcome barriers to change.[50] Employees are more innovative when they are empowered to do things their own way.[51] Employees don't have narrow job descriptions. They have a sense of ownership and control over their ideas and work, and they can make changes to their work without having to get permission, as they are not micromanaged.

Part of being flexible is letting employees work on ideas that don't seem practical or related to the business. **P&G** first developed a material that could absorb a lot of water; then it decided to develop Pampers disposable diapers. **Google** is working on stretchable electronics and proposed an invisible helmet and medical-supply delivery drones.[52]

WORK
APPLICATION 6-4

Does an organization you work for or have worked for have any of the characteristics of innovative structure and cultures? Overall, does the organization have a creative culture?

6-2 APPLYING THE CONCEPT

Innovative and Noninnovative Cultures

Identify the type of organizational culture described in each statement.

A. innovative culture
B. noninnovative culture

____ 6. "When I'm delegated a task, my boss always tells me the details of how to do the job. Why can't I meet the objective my way for a change?"

____ 7. "This company emphasizes following its policies, procedures, and rules."

____ 8. "Our jobs are broad in scope with a lot of autonomy to do the jobs the way the team wants to do them."

____ 9. "We have a very tall organization."

____ 10. "I tried to develop a faster rotating blade, but it didn't work. However, my boss gave me a very sincere thank-you for trying."

- *Open systems.* With an open system, you seek innovation from within and outside the firm.[53] Many companies today are turning to their customers, suppliers, and others in their supply chain for innovation. **Starbucks** sponsored an online contest in which customers could submit ideas on how to reduce paper cup consumption. Starbucks provided $20,000 in cash prizes to customers with the most innovative ideas.[54]

Managing Innovation During Incremental and Discontinuous Change

Let's discuss the difference in managing these two forms of change, which also are presented in Exhibit 6-2.

Managing Innovation During Incremental Change: The Compression Approach. It is called the *compression approach* because it is used in more certain environments during incremental change. The goal is to lower costs and incrementally improve performance and functions of the existing dominant design. The general strategy is to continue to improve the existing technology as rapidly as possible, moving to the *next-generation* technology while still allowing the use of the old technology; this is called *generational change.* The compression approach uses as series of planned steps to avoid wasted time and delays between steps of generational change. **Apple** continues to incrementally improve its iPod and iPhone.

Managing Innovation During Discontinuous Change: The Experimental Approach. It is called the *experimental approach* because it is used in more uncertain environments during discontinuous change. The goal is to make significant improvements in performance and to establish a new dominant design, creating the next technology cycle. The general strategy is to build something new, different, and substantially better, causing a breakthrough in technology to begin a new technology cycle that leaves the old technology obsolete. With the uncertainty, companies compete to establish the new dominant design to become the market leader. **Apple** essentially began slowly making the music CD obsolete when it created a new technology cycle with its iPod to iPhone and iTunes store.

Xerox (Case Question 2) is committed to innovation, with six research centers and 5,000 scientists and engineers worldwide. Altogether, Xerox Group invests $1.4 billion in R&D each year. It has been issued more than 50,000 patents worldwide and is issued 2 patents each and every day. At its website, in the company information, there is an "Innovation" link, where you can find the slogan, "Something is only an innovation if it makes a difference to our clients or to the world." It also has a brochure (PDF) titled **Xerox Innovation** Creating the Future

LO 6-2

Explain the differences in managing innovation during incremental and discontinuous change in terms of approach, goals, and strategy.

WORK APPLICATION 6-5

Does an organization you work for or have worked compete in a more incremental or discontinuous change environment?

EXHIBIT 6-2   MANAGING INNOVATION

	Incremental Change	Discontinuous Change
Approach	Compression	Experimental
Environment	More certain	Uncertain
Goals	To lower costs and incrementally improve performance and functions of the existing dominant design	To make significant improvements in performance and to establish a new dominant design, creating the next technology cycle
Strategy	To continue to improve the existing technology as rapidly as possible, moving to the next-generation technology while still allowing the use of the old technology	To build something new and different, a substantially better breakthrough in technology, to begin a new technology cycle that leaves the old technology obsolete

Today." Informed by a deep understanding of technology trends, Xerox has four innovation themes emerge in its research portfolio: automating manual processes, transforming data into decisions, making personalization pervasive, and enabling the sustainable enterprise.

Managing Change

As we've discussed, innovation is essential to business success, and it requires change. Unfortunately, managing change is difficult, as an estimated 50 to 66 percent of all changes fail to deliver expected results.[55] Need we say that managing change is a critical skill to develop? In this section, we discuss stages in the change process and resistance to change and how to overcome it, and we present a model for identifying and overcoming resistance to change.

Stages in the Change Process

People tend to go through four distinct stages when facing change. The four **stages of the change process** *are denial, resistance, exploration, and commitment.*

1. *Denial.* Changes are often difficult to understand or accept.[56] So when people first hear that change is coming, they may deny that it will affect them. Managers at **RIM** most likely denied that BlackBerry would lose its cellphone market leadership position.

2. *Resistance.* Once people get over the initial shock and realize that change is going to be a reality, they often resist the change. People, including managers at **RIM**, often doubt there really is a need for change.

3. *Exploration.* When the change begins to be implemented, employees explore the change, often through training, and ideally they begin to better understand how it will affect them. Managers at **RIM** realized they were behind in smartphone technology and worked on innovations to catch up with competitors.

4. *Commitment.* Through exploration, employees determine their level of commitment to making the change a success. Commitment is necessary to implement the change, but some employees continue to resist the change.[57] Some of the managers at **RIM** realized the actual threat to its BlackBerry too late, and only time will tell if RIM's turnaround strategy will work.

stages of the change process Denial, resistance, exploration, and commitment.

Exhibit 6-3 illustrates the four-stage change process. Notice that the stages are in a circular formation because change is an ongoing process, not a linear one. People can regress, as the arrows show.

EXHIBIT 6-3   STAGES IN THE CHANGE PROCESS

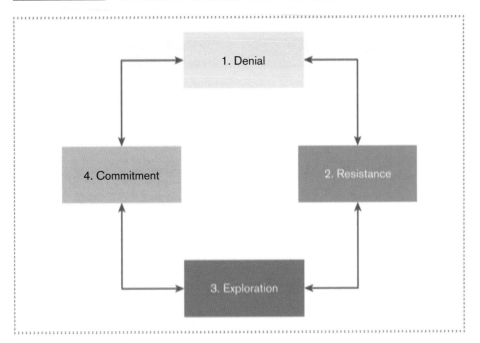

Resistance to Change

Some people deliberately attempt to block change efforts.[58] Most change programs fail because of employee resistance to change.[59] Why do employees resist change, and how do managers overcome resistance to change? As shown in Exhibit 6-4, employees resist change for five major reasons:

- *Uncertainty.* Uncertainty tends to make us react defensively by denying the need for change and allows us to rationalize that we don't really need to change. Fear of the unknown outcome of change often brings fear of potential failure.[60] We often get anxious and nervous and resist change in order to cope with these feelings.[61] But don't be afraid to try new things.[62]

- *Learning anxiety.* For many of us, the prospect of learning something new produces anxiety—*learning anxiety*. We realize that new learning may make us temporarily incompetent and may expose us to rejection by valued groups.

- *Self-interest.* We tend to resist change that threatens our own self-interest. We are commonly more concerned about our best interests than about the interests of the organization even when failure to change can have severe consequences.[63]

- *Fear of loss.* With change, jobs may possibly be lost. Change may involve an economic loss as a result of a pay cut. A change in work assignments or schedules may create a loss of social relationships.

- *Fear of loss of control.* Change can also result in an actual or perceived loss of power, status, security, and especially control. We may resent the feeling that our destiny is being controlled by someone else.

Successful Habits. When we are successful, we tend to think change is not needed. Even when we do change, we can fall back into old habits that have worked in the past. **Microsoft** Windows for PCs was highly successful for some 25 years, but it was too slow to develop mobile cell phone software like **Google's** Android, and the **Apple** iPad is taking sales away from laptops sales that use Windows.[64]

LO 6-3

List the reasons employees resist change and suggest ways of overcoming such resistance.

WORK
APPLICATION 6-6

Give an example of a situation in which you resisted a change. Be sure to specify which of the five reasons fueled your resistance to change.

EXHIBIT 6-4 RESISTANCE TO CHANGE AND WAYS TO OVERCOME RESISTANCE

Resistance to Change	Overcoming Resistance
Uncertainty	Develop trust climate for change
Learning anxiety	Plan
Self-interest	State why change is needed and how it will affect employees
Fear of loss	Create a win-win situation
Fear of loss of control	Involve employees Provide support and evaluation Create urgency

How to Overcome Resistance to Change

You need to overcome resistance to implement change.[65] Seven major things you can do to help overcome resistance to change are discussed in the following:

- *Develop a positive trust climate for change.* Develop and maintain good human relations. Make employees realize you have their best interests in mind and develop mutual trust. Encouraging employees to suggest changes and implementing their ideas are important parts of continuous improvement.

- *Plan.* Implementing changes successfully requires good planning. You need to identify the possible resistance to change and plan how to overcome it. View change from the employees' position. Set clear objectives so employees know exactly what the change is.[66] The next four tips should be part of your plan.

- *Clearly state why the change is needed and how it will affect employees.* Changes can be difficult to understand, so employees want and need to know why the change is necessary and how it will affect them, both positively and negatively.[67] So you need to communicate clearly what you want to do.[68] Employees need to understand why the new, changed method is more legitimate than the existing method of doing things.[69] Be open and honest with employees. Giving employees the facts as far in advance as possible helps them to overcome fear of the unknown.[70]

- *Create a win-win situation.* We have a desire to win.[71] The goal of human relations is to meet employee needs while achieving departmental and organizational objectives. Be sure to answer the other parties' unasked question, "What's in it for me?" When people can see how they benefit, they are more willing to change. If the organization is going to benefit by the change, so should the employees when possible.

- *Involve employees.* To create a win-win situation, involve employees. A commitment to change is usually critical to its successful implementation.[72] Employees who participate in developing changes are more committed to them than employees who have changes dictated to them. To get involvement and a commitment to change, phrase your own ideas as if someone else said them.[73]

- *Provide support and evaluation.* Employees need to know that managers are there to help them cope with the changes. You need to make the learning process as painless as possible by providing training and other support. Managers must also provide feedback and evaluation during the learning process to increase the employees' efficiency and effectiveness in implementing the change.

- *Create urgency.* When you decide on a change, you have to move fast.[74] Many people procrastinate making changes. A feeling of urgency is the primary driver toward taking action. If something is perceived as urgent, it is given a high priority and is usually done immediately. It appears that **RIM** managers were too late in creating urgency to improve the BlackBerry and that management didn't implement the other six tips effectively to make the necessary changes to maintain its market leadership.

A Model for Identifying and Overcoming Resistance to Change

Before making changes, you should anticipate how others will react. Resistance to change varies in its intensity, source, and focus.[75]

Intensity. People have different attitudes toward change. Some thrive on it; some are upset by it; many resist it at first but gradually accept it. As a manager of change, you must anticipate whether resistance will be strong, weak, or somewhere in between. Intensity will be lower if you use the seven methods for overcoming resistance to change.

Sources. There are three major sources of resistance to change:

1. *Facts.* The facts (provable statements) about an impending change are often circulated through the grapevine—but people tend to use facts selectively to prove their point. Facts used correctly help to overcome fear of the unknown.

2. *Beliefs.* Facts can be proved; beliefs cannot. Beliefs are subjective opinions that can be shaped by others. Our beliefs lead us to think that a change is correct or incorrect or good or bad. Differences in perception can cause resistance to change.

3. *Values.* Values are what people believe are worth pursuing or doing. What we value is important to us and influences our behavior.[76] Values pertain to right and wrong and help establish priorities. Values are also related to religion and ethics.

Focus. There are three major focuses of resistance to change:

1. *Self.* People naturally want to know "What's in it for me? What will I gain or lose?" When the facts of change have a negative effect on employees, creating a perceived loss, employees resist the change.

2. *Others.* After considering what's in it for them and concluding that a change does not affect them, people tend to consider how the change will affect their friends, peers, and colleagues. If employees analyze the facts and believe that a change will affect others negatively, they may be resistant to the change.

3. *Work environment.* The work environment includes the physical setting, the work itself, and the climate. People like to be in control of their environment, and they resist changes that take away their control.

Exhibit 6-5 is a resistance matrix with examples of each area of resistance. Once you have identified the probable resistance to change, you can work at overcoming it. Note that the intensity of resistance can be strong, moderate, or weak for each of the nine matrix boxes. In Skill Builder 6–1, you will use the resistance matrix to identify the source and focus of change.

EXHIBIT 6-5   RESISTANCE MATRIX

Sources of Resistance: Facts, Beliefs, and Values		
1. Facts about self	**4. Beliefs about self**	**7. Values pertaining to self**
• I have never done the task before. • I failed the last time	• I'm too busy to learn it. • I'll do it, but don't blame me if it's wrong.	• I like the way I do my job now. Why change? • I like working in a group.
2. Facts about others	**5. Beliefs about others**	**8. Values pertaining to others**
• She has the best performance record in the department. • Other employees told me it's hard to do.	• He just pretends to be busy to avoid extra work. • She's better at it than I am; let her do it.	• Let someone else do it; I do not want to work with her. • I like working with him. Don't cut him rom our department.
3. Facts about the work environment	**6. Beliefs about the work environment**	**9. Values pertaining to the work environment**
• We are only paid $7 an hour. • It's over 100 degrees.	• This is a lousy job. • The pay here is too low.	• I don't care if we meet the goal or not. • The new task will make me work inside. I'd rather be outside.
Intensity (high, medium, or low for each box)		

ORGANIZATIONAL DEVELOPMENT

Understanding the processes and mechanisms of managing change is a central theme in management.[77] Organizational development is the commonly used method of managing planned change.[78] **Organizational development (OD)** *is the ongoing planned process of change used as a means of improving performance through interventions.* The human resources management department (discussed in Chapter 9) is usually responsible for OD throughout an organization. The **change agent** *is the person responsible for implementing an organizational change effort.* So the change agent often runs an OD program.[79] The change agent may be a member of the organization or a hired consultant. In this section, we discuss change models and OD interventions.

Change Models

Models are a mechanism to help implement planned organizational change.[80] Two popular change models used by organizations today are Lewin's change model and a more comprehensive model for change. Based on the environment, you need to change, or move through the model, at the right pace.[81]

Lewin's Change Model. In the early 1950s, Kurt Lewin developed a technique that is still used today for changing people's behavior, skills, and attitudes.[82] The model presents a change–stability paradox,[83] going from unfreezing to refreezing. Lewin's change model consists of the three steps listed in Exhibit 6-6.

LO 6-4

Identify the steps in the Lewin and comprehensive change models.

1. *Unfreezing.* This step usually involves reducing the forces that are maintaining the status quo.[84] Organizations sometimes accomplish unfreezing by introducing information that shows discrepancies between desired performance and actual performance.

2. *Moving.* This step is the change process in which employees learn new, desirable behaviors, skills, values, and attitudes.

3. *Refreezing.* The desirable performance becomes the permanent way of doing things, or the new status quo, that employees conform to.[85] Refreezing often takes place through reinforcement and support for the new behavior.

EXHIBIT 6-6   CHANGE MODELS

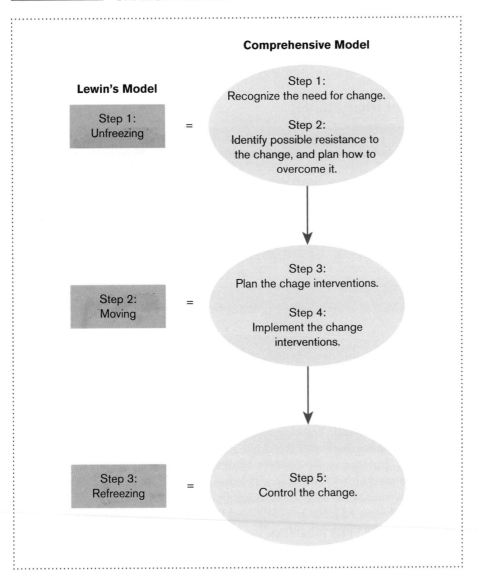

A Comprehensive Change Model. Lewin's general change model requires a more detailed reformulation for today's rapidly evolving business environment. The model consists of five steps, as shown in Exhibit 6-6:

1. *Recognize the need for change.* Clearly state the change needed—set objectives. Don't forget to consider how the change will affect other areas of the organization through the system effect.
2. *Identify possible resistance to the change, and plan how to overcome it.*
3. *Plan the change interventions.* Based on the diagnosis of the problem, the change agent must select the appropriate intervention.
4. *Implement the change interventions.* The change agent or someone he or she selects conducts the intervention to bring about the desired change.
5. *Control the change.* Follow up to ensure that the change is implemented and maintained. Make sure the objective is met. If not, take corrective action.

Organizational Development Interventions

OD is about making organizational change,[86] through a change agent.[87] **OD interventions** *are specific actions taken to implement specific changes.* Although there are many types, we discuss the nine OD interventions listed in Exhibit 6-7.

EXHIBIT 6-7   OD INTERVENTIONS AND THEIR FOCUS

OD Intervention	Individual Focus	Group Focus	Organization Focus
1. Training and Development	X		
2. Sensitivity Training	X		
3. Team Building		X	
4. Process Consultation		X	
5. Forcefield Analysis		X	
6. Survey Feedback			X
7. Large-Group Intervention			X
8. Work Design	X	X	X
9. Direct Feedback	X	X	X

Training and Development. Training and development are listed first because they focus on the individual, and the other interventions often include some form of training. Training is the process of developing skills, behaviors, and attitudes to be used on the job. You will learn about training in the next chapter. Recall that training is used in valuing diversity. Many companies, including **GE, Shell, Johnson & Johnson (J&J)**, and **IBM**, are highly committed to quality leadership-development programs.[88]

Sensitivity Training. Sensitivity training takes place in a group of 10 to 15 people. The training sessions have no agenda. People learn about how their behavior affects others and how others' behavior affects theirs. So the focus is on individual

OD interventions Specific actions taken to implement specific changes.

behavior in a group. Although popular in the 1960s, it is not commonly used in business today.

Team Building. Team building is probably the most widely used OD technique today, and its popularity will continue as more companies use work teams.[89] **Team building** *is an OD intervention designed to help work groups increase structural and team dynamics and performance.* It is widely used as a means of helping new or existing groups improve their effectiveness in setting objectives, planning, problem solving and decision making, and developing open, honest working relationships based on trust and an understanding of group members. Team-building programs vary in terms of agenda and length, also depending on team needs and the change agent's skills.

Teamwork can accomplish great things. Some organizations take team-building activities outside of the office to help team members develop trust and improve communication. Photo from Jupiter Images/Thinkstock.

Process Consultation. Process consultation is often part of team building, but it is commonly used as a separate, more narrowly focused intervention. **Process consultation** *is an OD intervention designed to improve team dynamics.* Team building may focus on the process of getting a job itself done, but process consultation focuses on how people interact as they get the job done. Team dynamics (or processes) include how the team communicates, allocates work, resolves conflict, handles leadership, solves problems, and makes decisions.[90] The ultimate objective is to train the group so that process consultation becomes an ongoing team activity. You will learn more about team dynamics in Chapter 8.

Forcefield Analysis. Forcefield analysis is particularly useful for small-group (4 to 18 members) problem solving. **Forcefield analysis** *is an OD intervention that diagrams the current level of performance, the forces hindering change, and the forces driving toward change.* Exhibit 6-8 represents a possible forcefield analysis for **Dell's** corporate computing division, which has recently been losing market share. The process begins with an appraisal of the current level of performance, which appears in the middle of the diagram. The hindering forces holding back performance are listed on the left. The driving forces keeping performance at this level are listed on the right. After viewing the diagram, group members develop strategies for maintaining or increasing the driving forces and for decreasing the hindering forces.

Survey Feedback. Collecting feedback is one of the oldest and most popular OD techniques at the department, division, and organizational levels. **Survey feedback** *is an OD intervention that uses a questionnaire to gather data to use as the basis for change.* If you ever filled out a professor/course assessment form or a restaurant or any service form in person, by phone, or online, you have participated in survey feedback. The change agent develops a survey designed to identify problems and areas for improvement and, based on the survey results, recommends planned change improvements.

Large-Group Intervention. **Large-group intervention** *is an OD technique that brings together participants from all parts of the organization, and often key outside stakeholders, to solve problems or take advantage of opportunities.* Large-group interventions often include 50 to 500 people and may last for

team building An OD intervention designed to help work groups increase structural and team dynamics and performance.

process consultation An OD intervention designed to improve team dynamics.

forcefield analysis An OD intervention that diagrams the current level of performance, the forces hindering change, and the forces driving toward change.

survey feedback An OD intervention that uses a questionnaire to gather data to use as the basis for change.

large-group intervention An OD technique that brings together participants from all parts of the organization, and often key outside stakeholders, to solve problems or take advantage of opportunities.

EXHIBIT 6-8 FORCEFIELD ANALYSIS

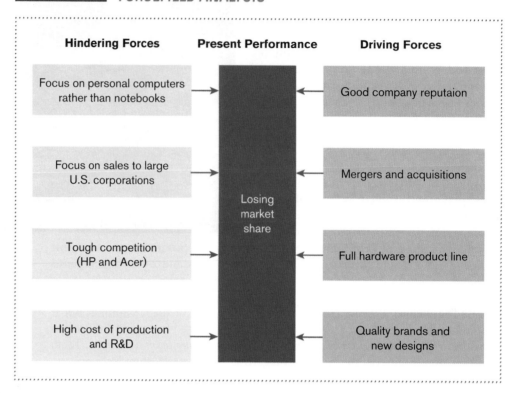

Hindering Forces	Present Performance	Driving Forces
Focus on personal computers rather than notebooks		Good company reputaion
Focus on sales to large U.S. corporations	Losing market share	Mergers and acquisitions
Tough competition (HP and Acer)		Full hardware product line
High cost of production and R&D		Quality brands and new designs

LO 6-5

State the difference in the use of forcefield analysis and survey feedback.

days. A major difference between large-group interventions and the other OD interventions is the focus on functional diversity and inclusion of key stakeholders. For example, when developing a new product, a company might convene a large group of people in product development, engineering and R&D, marketing, production, and service from within the firm and also customers and suppliers, who would meet to analyze the new product in an effort to ensure its success. **GE** uses large-group intervention, which it calls GE WorkOuts, in each of its business units to solve problems and increase productivity for continuous improvement.[91]

Work Design. As we will discuss in Chapter 7, work design refers to organizational structure. Work can be designed as an individual job, as a job for a group to perform, or by departmentalization. Job enrichment is commonly used to change jobs to make them more interesting and challenging, which leads to innovation.

WORK APPLICATION 6-8

Give an example of one or more OD interventions used in an organization that you work for or have worked for.

Direct Feedback. **Direct feedback** *is an OD intervention in which the change agent makes a direct recommendation for change.* In certain situations, especially those involving technology changes, the most efficient intervention is to have a change agent make a direct recommendation for a specific change. Often such a change agent is an outside consultant.

Xerox (Case Question 3) uses OD interventions. For new employees, Xerox provides many robust learning opportunities through training and development and in-depth mentoring programs. Employees also have unlimited access to "Learning at Xerox," which includes thousands of online courses and digital books and reference aids that help develop skills and knowledge. It also uses team building with its employees and feedback from both employees and customers. Xerox is an OD change agent offering direct feedback to its clients.

direct feedback An OD intervention in which the change agent make sa direct recommendation for change.

6-3 APPLYING THE CONCEPT

OD Interventions

Identify the appropriate OD intervention for the change described in each statement.

A. training and development
B. sensitivity training
C. team building
D. process consultation
E. forcefield analysis
F. survey feedback
G. large-group intervention
H. work design
I. direct feedback

_____ 11. "We have outgrown our present inventory system, which is also dated. What intervention should we use to develop a new one?"

_____ 12. "The new copying machine is installed. Who are we going to teach to run it and what intervention should we use?"

_____ 13. "What intervention should we use to prepare our employees to put the product together as a group rather than each person continuing to produce one part of it?"

_____ 14. "Things are going well, but I think we could benefit from an organization-wide intervention to solve our slow delivery problem."

_____ 15. "Morale and motivation have fallen throughout the division in recent months. We need an intervention that can identify the problems so we can change the situation."

ENTREPRENEURSHIP

Entrepreneurs are a driving force for innovation and change worldwide. Park Geun Hye, president of South Korea, recently urged her citizens to become more entrepreneurial.[92] *Entrepreneurship activities* include creating new products or processes, entering new markets, or creating new business ventures and organizations.[93] Clearly, **Xerox (Case Question 4)** as a company is entrepreneurial. Complete the Self-Assessment 6–1 to discover whether you have entrepreneurial qualities. In this section, we discuss new venture creation by entrepreneurs and intrapreneurs and how they select and plan new ventures.

New Venture Entrepreneurs and Intrapreneurs

When people think of entrepreneurship, they often tend to think of small businesses. However, in the global business environment, organizations of all types and sizes are becoming more entrepreneurial.[94] A **new venture** *is a new business or a new line of business.* When Jeff Bezos started **Amazon.com** to sell books, it was a new business venture; when it offered customer cloud computing services, it was a new line of business. In either case, all new ventures bring about innovation and change.

Entrepreneurs versus Intrapreneurs and Franchisees. **Entrepreneurs** *commonly start new small-business ventures.* Entrepreneurs turn resources into new businesses.[95] They tend to think differently about economic opportunity from nonentrepreneurs.[96] Entrepreneurs identify, evaluate, and exploit opportunities.[97]

Intrapreneurs *commonly start a new line of business within a larger organization.* Intrapreneurs are also called *corporate entrepreneurs.* In essence, intrapreneurs commonly start and run small businesses within large organizations, often as separate business units.[98] *Franchisees* (Chapter 3), such as **Subway** shop owners, are important in entrepreneurship, as they create new ventures. However, they are under the direction of a franchisor. So they are not considered real entrepreneurs or intrapreneurs by some,[99] as they are kind of an external intrapreneur creating a duplicate business.

LO 6-6

Explain the difference between an entrepreneur and an intrapreneur.

new venture A small business or a new line of business

entrepreneur Someone who starts a small-business venture

intrapreneur Someone who starts a new line of business within a larger organization

6-1 SELF ASSESSMENT

Entrepreneurial Qualities 1–2

Have you ever thought about starting your own business? This exercise gives you the opportunity to determine whether you have entrepreneurial qualities. Each item below presents two statements describing opposite ends of a spectrum of attitudes or behavior. Below each pair of statements is a 6-point scale, with each end corresponding to one of the given statements and several positions in between. After reading the two statements for each item, place a check mark on the point on the scale that best represents where you see yourself on the spectrum. Answer the questions honestly; you will not be required to share your answers during class.

1. I have a strong desire to be independent, to do things my way, and to create something new.
I like following established ways of doing things.

| 6 | 5 | 4 | 3 | 2 | 1 |

2. I enjoy taking reasonable risks.
I avoid taking risks.

| 6 | 5 | 4 | 3 | 2 | 1 |

3. I avoid making the same mistakes twice.
I often repeat my mistakes.

| 6 | 5 | 4 | 3 | 2 | 1 |

4. I can work without supervision.
I need supervision to motivate me to work.

| 6 | 5 | 4 | 3 | 2 | 1 |

5. I seek out competition.
I avoid competition.

| 6 | 5 | 4 | 3 | 2 | 1 |

6. I enjoy working long, hard hours.
I enjoy taking it easy and having plenty of personal time.

| 6 | 5 | 4 | 3 | 2 | 1 |

7. I am confident in my abilities.
I lack self-confidence.

| 6 | 5 | 4 | 3 | 2 | 1 |

8. I need to be the best and to be successful.
I'm satisfied with being average.

| 6 | 5 | 4 | 3 | 2 | 1 |

9. I have a high energy level.
I have a low energy level.

| 6 | 5 | 4 | 3 | 2 | 1 |

10. I stand up for my rights.
I let others take advantage of me.

| 6 | 5 | 4 | 3 | 2 | 1 |

Scoring: Add up the numbers below your check marks. The total will be between 10 and 60. Note where your score fits on the continuum of entrepreneurial qualities below.

Strong					Weak
60	50	40	30	20	10

Entrepreneurship is clearly not for everyone. Generally, the higher/stronger your entrepreneurial score, the better your chance of being a successful entrepreneur. However, simple paper-and-pencil surveys are not always good predictors. If you had a low score but really want to start a business, you may be successful. But realize that few people have all the typical entrepreneurial qualities.

Small-Businesses Entrepreneurs. The legal definition of "small" varies by country and by industry. In the United States, the **Small Business Administration (SBA)** establishes small-business size standards on an industry-by-industry basis.[100] According to the U.S. **Department of Labor (DOL)**, a small business employs fewer than 100 workers, and a *small to medium-size enterprise (SME)* employs fewer than 500 workers. [101] For our purposes, a **small business** *is a business that is independently owned and operated, with a small number of employees and relatively low volume of sales.* Small business is important because more than 90 percent of U.S. businesses are small businesses. Entrepreneurs make major contributions to society.[102] They are central to economic growth,[103] as entrepreneurs provide new innovations,[104] new jobs,[105] and products and services to large businesses.

Small businesses fuel the economy. Have you thought about being an entrepreneur and starting your own business someday? Photo from Monkey Business Images/ Thinkstock.

Don't forget that almost all large businesses started small. Steve Jobs and Steve Wozniak started **Apple** in the Jobs family garage, and today it is ranked sixth on the *Fortune* 500 list and second for profits at around $42 billion and assets exceeding $176 billion.[106]

Large Businesses Intrapreneurs. Both the **SBA** and the **DOL** define a large business as employing 500 or more workers. Large businesses are clearly trying to be more entrepreneurial by taking advantage of innovate opportunities.[107] So large businesses that innovate and change have an *entrepreneurial orientation.*[108] Major corporations spend billions of dollars on intrapreneurship, which is often call *internal corporate ventures.*[109] **3M** and **GE** are well known for encouraging *entrepreneurship activities and intrapreneurship.* One of 3M's goals is to have 25 percent of sales coming from products that did not exist five years ago. Thus, 3M and GE are constantly seeking new intrapreneurial ventures. Plus, people are leaving their jobs to become entrepreneurs of small businesses to pursue their own goals, dreams, and desires to start their own business.[110]

Risk Taking by Entrepreneurs and Intrapreneurs. To be successful at anything requires taking calculated risks.[111] Staring a new business is risky, as there is a high failure rate.[112] So clearly, staring a new venture involves risk taking,[113] and the risk of entrepreneurship is much greater than that of intrapreneurship. Entrepreneurs pursue opportunities without regard to the resources they currently own and take risks acquiring resources from external sources.[114]

Entrepreneurs don't get a real paycheck; they get profits or losses. They commonly risk personal assets, as they finance part or all of their business and run the risk of losing their investment.[115] Some entrepreneurs have lost their life savings, retirement investments, homes, cars, and other assets. Often, they quit their jobs to start their new businesses and cannot go back if the business fails; they risk a dependable salary for potential profits, which usually take a few years to earn and may never come.

On the other hand, intrapreneurs commonly have no risk of personal investment, as the large business provides the financing, and if the venture fails, they can usually return to their prior job or a similar one. Intrapreneurs also maintain their salary and often get a raise and/or part of the profits. However, like entrepreneurs, intrapreneurs usually work long hours. Because entrepreneurs take greater risks than intrapreneurs, their reward (like their loss) is usually greater, as all the profits are theirs.

WORK
APPLICATION 6-9

Are you interested in being an entrepreneur or an intrapreneur? What business would you like to start?

small business A business that is independently owned and operated with a small number of employees and relatively low volume of sales

6-2 JOIN THE DISCUSSION ETHICS & SOCIAL RESPONSIBILITY

Virtual Internships

You are familiar with the traditional internship model, in which a student works at an organization to gain experience and perhaps a full-time job after graduation. With today's Internet technology, more and more companies are hiring virtual interns, who work from their college computers. Virtual interns do a variety of tasks, including secretarial work, software and website development, and information technology (IT) projects. Most virtual interns never even set foot inside the organization's facilities.

Entrepreneurs Nataly Kogan and Avi Spivack cofounded Natavi Guides, a New York small business, in 2002, to publish guidebooks for students. Natavi hires virtual interns to write stories and locates people by posting openings with career offices at more than 30 universities nationwide. Kogan estimates that Natavi saved $100,000 in overhead during the first year in business by not having to furnish office space, computers, and other equipment to interns.

1. What are the benefits of virtual internships to employers and to interns?
2. Should a student be given college credit for a virtual internship, or should he or she receive only pay without credit—a part-time job?
3. Is it ethical and socially responsible to use interns instead of regular employees?
4. Will the use of virtual interns become the norm, or will the practice fade?

Selecting the New Venture and Business Planning

The first step to entrepreneurship is usually to select the new venture or the industry in which the business will compete. Successful entrepreneurs select ventures with good growth potential (many buyers, few strong competitors) and profit opportunities.[116] Great opportunities come from helping consumers save time or money or more fully enjoy the time spent on a given project or activity.[117]

Completive Advantage. Recall from Chapter 5 that a **competitive advantage** *specifies how an organization offers unique customer value*. It answers the questions What makes us different from the competition? Why should a person buy our product rather than the products of our competitors?[118] If you don't have answers to these questions, you may not be able to get enough customers to have a successful business. Sir Richard Branson's advice is don't start a business unless you are radically different from the competition.[119] You develop a sustainable competitive advantage through your valuable resources,[120] including low prices (**Walmart**), location (local **Andrea Day-Care** center), convenience (**Amazon.com**), or brand (**Coca-Cola**).

First-Mover Advantage. A related concept to competitive advantage is **first-mover advantage**, which refers to *offering a unique customer value before competitors do so*. **Pizza Hut** had a competitive advantage for chain pizza restaurant dining. When **Domino's** started, it did not compete directly with restaurants; it made free delivery its competitive advantage, gaining the first-mover advantage over competitors. But free delivery was easily duplicated, so Domino's lost its unique competitive advantage. **Jiffy Lube** also lost some of its first-mover competitive advantage through duplication. **Sony** was the first to come out with a SmartWatch with a touch screen, but it isn't selling/moving well. Only time will tell if it will turn into a first-mover advantage, will continue to struggle, or will be discontinued.[121]

Through marketing research, you investigate the competition and select products based on your competitive advantage. You also need to forecast sales to determine growth and profit potential. In Skill Builder 6–3 at the end of the chapter, you will select a new venture.

competitive advantage specifies how an organization offers unique customer value

first-mover advantage Offering a unique customer value before competitors do so

The Business Plan. After you select a new business venture, you need to plan to start it. A **business plan** *is a written description of a new venture—its objectives and the steps for achieving them.* Writing a business plan forces you to crystallize your thinking about what you must do to start your new venture before investing time and money in it, but it must be based on realistic evidence. You usually need a business plan to borrow money.[122] The U.S. **Small Business Administration** (**SBA**—www.sba.gov) is an excellent source of help with selecting a new business, planning it, and growing it.

From this chapter, you should understand the importance of managing change and how to manage change using OD interventions, as well as the importance of innovation and diversity, which need to be part of the organizational culture.

business plan Written description of a new venture, describing its objectives and the steps for achieving them

••• CHAPTER SUMMARY

6-1. **Identify the forces for change, the types of change, and the forms of change.**

The external environments, new technology cycles, and the internal management functions are forces for change. The four types of changes include strategy, structure, technology, and people. Two major forms of change are incremental and discontinuous change.

6-2. **Explain the differences in managing innovation during incremental and discontinuous change in terms of approach, goals, and strategy.**

The *compression approach* is used in more certain environments during incremental change, whereas the *experimental approach* is used in more uncertain environments during discontinuous change. The *goal* during incremental change is to lower costs and incrementally improve performance and functions of the existing dominant design, whereas the goal during discontinuous change is to make significant improvements in performance and to establish a new dominant design, creating the next technology cycle. The general *strategy* used during incremental change is to continue to improve the existing technology as rapidly as possible, moving to the next-generation technology while still allowing the use of the old technology, whereas the strategy during discontinuous change is to build something new and different, a substantially better breakthrough in technology, to begin a new technology cycle that leaves the old technology obsolete.

6-3. **List the reasons employees resist change, and suggest ways of overcoming such resistance.**

Employees resist change because of fear of the unknown, learning anxiety, self-interest, and fear of economic loss or loss of power, status, security, or control. These forms of resistance can be overcome by establishing a positive trust climate for change, planning, clearly explaining the need for the change, pointing out how individual employees will benefit from the change, involving employees, and providing support and evaluation for employees during the change and creating urgency.

6-4. **Identify the steps in the Lewin and comprehensive change models.**

The Lewin model steps are (1) unfreezing, (2) moving, and (3) refreezing. The steps in the comprehensive model are (1) recognize the need for change, (2) identify possible resistance to the change and plan how to overcome it, (3) plan the change interventions, (4) implement the change interventions, and (5) control the change.

6-5. **Explain the difference between team building and process consultation.**

Team building is broader in scope than process consultation. Team building is an OD intervention designed to improve both how the work is done and how team members work together as they do the work (team dynamics). Process consultation is designed to improve team dynamics.

6-6. **State the difference in the use of forcefield analysis and survey feedback.**

Forcefield analysis is used by a small group to diagnose and solve a specific problem. Survey feedback uses a questionnaire filled out by a large group to identify problems; the group does not work together to solve a problem. Forcefield analysis can be used to solve a problem identified through survey feedback.

• • • KEY TERMS

business plan, 179
change agent, 170
competitive advantage, 178
direct feedback, 174
discontinuous change, 163
entrepreneur, 175
first-mover advantage, 178
forcefield analysis, 173

incremental change, 162
intrapreneur, 175
large-group intervention, 173
new venture, 175
OD interventions, 172
organizational change, 160
organizational development
    (OD), 170

process consultation, 173
small business, 177
stages of the change process, 166
survey feedback, 173
team building, 173
types of change, 161

• • • KEY TERM REVIEW

Complete each of the following statements using one of this chapter's key terms.

1. _____ is alternations of existing work routines and strategies that affect the whole organization.

2. The _____ are changes in strategy, structure, technology, and people.

3. _____ is continual improvement that takes place within the existing technology cycle.

4. _____ is a significant breakthrough in technology that leads to design competition and a new technology cycle.

5. The _____ are denial, resistance, exploration, and commitment.

6. _____ is the ongoing planned process of change used as a means of improving performance through interventions.

7. The _____ is the person responsible for implementing an organizational change effort.

8. _____ are specific actions taken to implement specific changes.

9. _____ is an OD intervention designed to help work groups increase structural and team dynamics and performance.

10. _____ is an OD intervention designed to improve team dynamics.

11. _____ is an OD intervention that diagrams the current level of performance, the forces hindering change, and the forces driving toward change.

12. _____ is an OD intervention that uses a questionnaire to gather data to use as the basis for change.

13. _____ is an OD technique that brings together participants from all parts of the organization, and often key outside stakeholders, to solve problems or take advantage of opportunities.

14. _____ is an OD intervention in which the change agent makes a direct recommendation for change.

15. A _____ is a new business or a new line of business.

16. _____ commonly start a new small business venture.

17. _____ commonly start a new line of business within a large organization.

18. A _____ is a business that is independently owned and operated for profit, with a small number of employees and relatively low volume of sales.

19. A _____ specifies how the organization offers unique customer value.

20. The _____ is offering a unique customer value before competitors do so.

21. A _____ is a written description of the new venture—its objectives and the steps for achieving them.

• • • REVIEW QUESTIONS

1. How do the management functions relate to change?

2. What is the difference between a change in strategy and a change in structure?

3. List the four areas of technology change.

4. What are the two forms of change?

5. What are the characteristics of an innovative culture?

6. What are the two approaches to managing innovation?

7. What are the four stages in the change process?

8. What are the five major reasons employees resist change?

9. What are the three major sources and focuses of resistance to change?

10. Explain the difference between team building and process consultation.

11. State the difference in the use of forcefield analysis and survey feedback.

12. What is a new venture, and who starts it?

13. How do you define small business?

14. What are competitive and first-mover advantages?

••• COMMUNICATION SKILLS

The following critical-thinking questions can be used for class discussion and/or as written assignments to develop communication skills. Be sure to give complete explanations for all questions.

1. How does the systems effect relate to the four types of change?

2. Which type of change is the most important?

3. Do you believe that organizational change today is more slow/incremental (calm-water canoeing) or radical (white-water rafting)?

4. Do you consider yourself to be a creative and innovative person? Why or why not?

5. Would you prefer to work during a time of incremental or discontinuous change?

6. Which stage of the change process is the most difficult to overcome?

7. Which of the five reasons for resisting change do you believe is most common?

8. Which of the seven ways to overcome resistance to change do you believe is the most important?

9. Does creating urgency really help to get people to change? Give at least one example to support your position.

10. As a manager, which, if any, OD interventions would you use?

11. Would you rather work for a small or large business? Why?

••• CASE: RICHARD BRANSON (VIRGIN AIRLINES) ON MANAGING A GROWING ENTREPRENEURIAL BUSINESS

Sir Richard Branson is the slightly eccentric founder of U.K.-based Virgin Group, which consists of more than 400 companies around the world, including the airlines Virgin Atlantic and Virgin America, wireless company Virgin Mobile, and international health club Virgin Active.[123]

Richard Branson is well known as a guru of entrepreneurship. You could call him a change agent in his own company since he is always inspiring everyone who works for him to look for industries they can enter and provide the spark for a discontinuous change on the way business is done in that industry.

Branson started his first business when he was 16 and, in 1972, opened a chain of record stores, Virgin Records, that kick-started his Virgin brand globally. His business ventures have ranged from a vodka line to financial services to a private 74-acre island for rent.

Branson often writes about what it was like when he started his business. But, in an interesting twist, he recently wrote about what he learned as a small entrepreneur and how those lessons are still being applied to his modern-day business empire.

So what are the lessons he learned that he still applies? What are the similarities between managing one business and managing 400 businesses?

1. Surround yourself with good people no matter what size your business.

2. If you treat your employees right, they will treat your customers right, and sustained profits will follow.

3. Launch a new business with the same energy and enthusiasm as you did with your first business—it will help create momentum.

4. You have to win customers away from your competitors. You have to surprise and delight customers by offering something different.

5. You have to experience failures changing your business along the way. It takes experience to properly change your internal management structure to match external opportunities to work with new partners and start new businesses.

6. Although making decisions with your gut is important, Branson now uses teams of people to analyze data about economic, consumer, and population trends while looking for new products and opportunities. He believes that the education and health care industries are looking for opportunities to work with successfully branded companies.[124]

Branson believes his man goal is to change industries—not just keep them the same. He feels that trying to change industries makes all the employees want to achieve more than what other competitors ever achieved in their industry.

If you read enough of Branson's books and articles in entrepreneurship magazines, you will realize he brings his eccentric behavior to classic organizational change concepts such as building teams, managing the change process, creating discontinuous change in industries, being willing to take a risk, and developing your organization. He just does it a little like your eccentric uncle who comes over to your house to visit once a year and sounds crazy—until you realize he runs 400 companies and is one of the richest men in the world. Things have changed since Branson started in business. Global competition is pressuring Virgin to change.

Case Questions

1. Is the pressure for Sir Richard Branson to change Virgin's business strategy coming from the internal or external environment?

2. In order to better compete with its rivals, should Virgin focus on a change in strategy, structure, technology, or people?

3. Is Virgin in the denial, resistance, exploration, or commitment stage when it enters new industries?

4. Is Virgin an innovative company?

5. Is Virgin currently at the unfreezing, moving, or refreezing stage of Lewin's model?

6. Which of the following organizational development interventions could Virgin most benefit from? Training and development, sensitivity training, team building, process consultation, forcefield analysis, survey feedback, large-group intervention, work design, or direct feedback

7. Use the five steps of the comprehensive change model to explain Virgin's business strategy.

Cumulative Case Questions

8. Discuss Sir Richard Branson's management functions in implementing Virgin's strategy. (Chapter 1)

9. What external environmental factors were most influential in Virgin changing its business strategy? (Chapter 2).

10. What type of grand strategy is Virgin pursuing? (Chapter 4)

• • • SKILL BUILDER 6-1: IDENTIFYING RESISTANCE TO CHANGE

Objective

To improve your skill at identifying resistance to change.

Skills

The primary skills developed through this exercise are:

1. *Management skill*—decision making (conceptual, diagnostic, analytical, and critical-thinking skills are needed to understand resistance to change)

2. *AACSB competency*—analytic skills

3. *Management function*—organizing

Preparing for Skill Builder 6-1

Below are 10 statements made by employees who have been asked to make a change on the job. Identify the source and focus of their resistance using Exhibit 6-4. Because it is difficult to identify intensity of resistance on paper, skip the intensity factor. However, when you deal with people on the job, you need to identify the intensity. Place the number of the box (1–9) that best represents the resistance on the line in front of each statement.

_____ 1. "But we never did the job that way before. Can't we just do it the same way as always?"

_____ 2. The tennis coach asked Jill, the star player, to have Rashida as her doubles partner. Jill said, "Come on, Rashida is a lousy player. Ria is better; don't break us up." The coach disagreed and forced Jill to accept Rashida.

_____ 3. The manager, Winny, told Marco to stop letting everyone in the department take advantage of him by sticking him with extra work. Marco said, "But I like my coworkers and I want them to like me, too. If I don't help people, they may not like me."

_____ 4. "I can't learn how to use the new computer. I'm not smart enough to use it."

_____ 5. The police sergeant asked Chris, a patrol officer, to take a rookie cop as her partner. Chris said, "Do I have to? I broke in the last rookie. He and I are getting along well."

_____ 6. An employee asked Loc, the manager, if she could change the work-order form. Loc said, "That would be a waste of time; the current form is fine."

_____ 7. Diane, an employee, is busy at work. Her supervisor tells her to stop what she is doing and begin a new project. Diane says, "The job I'm working on now is more important."

_____ 8. "I don't want to work with that work team. It has the lowest performance record in the department."

_____ 9. A restaurant worker tells the restaurant manager, "Keep me in the kitchen. I can't work in the bar because drinking is against my religion."

_____ 10. "But I don't see why I have to stop showing pictures of people burning in a fire to help get customers to buy our smoke detector system. I don't think it's unethical. Our competitors do it."

Apply It

What did I learn from this experience? How will I use this knowledge in the future?

• • • SKILL BUILDER 6-2: MANAGING CHANGE AT YOUR COLLEGE

Objective

To better understand the need for change, resistance to change, and how to overcome resistance.

Skills

The primary skills developed through this exercise are:

1. *Management skill*—decision making (organizing requires conceptual skills)
2. *AACSB competencies*—analytic skills and reflective thinking skills
3. *Management function*—organizing

Preparing for Skill Builder 6–2

As an individual, group, or class, select a change you would like to see implemented at your college. Answer the following questions and conduct a forcefield analysis.

1. State the change you would like to see implemented.
2. State which of the four types of change it is.
3. Identify any possible resistance(s) to the change.
4. Select strategies for overcoming the resistance(s).
5. Conduct a forcefield analysis for the change. Write the present situation in the center and the forces that hinder the change and the forces that can help get the change implemented, using Exhibit 6-8 as an example.

Hindering Forces   Present Situation   Driving Forces

Apply It

What did I learn from this experience? How will I use this knowledge in the future?

• • • SKILL BUILDER 6–3: SELECTING A NEW VENTURE

Objective

To develop a simple business plan idea.

Skills

The primary skills developed through this exercise are:

1. *Management skill*—decision making
2. *AACSB competency*—analytic
3. *Management function*—planning

Select Your New Venture

Would you like to be your own boss? Have you given any thought to running your own business someday? For this exercise, you will think of a new venture you would like to start someday. The new venture can be entrepreneurial or intrapreneurial. With either approach, don't be concerned about financing the business. At this stage, you are only selecting a new venture. If you select intrapreneurship, you don't have to be working for the organization for which you would like to start a new venture. Provide information about your potential business in the following list. Give all of the topics some thought before writing down your final answers.

1. Company name (or line of business)
2. Products (goods and/or services)
3. Target market (potential customer profile)
4. Mission statement (Chapter 2 and 5)
5. Environment competitive analysis (Chapter 5, five forces, and SWOT)
6. Competitive advantage (Will you have a first-mover advantage?)
7. Possible location of business (home, mall, downtown, near college, etc.)
8. Determine the issues and problems that need to be addressed through strategic planning.

Apply It

What did I learn from this skill-building experience? How will I use this knowledge in the future?

Your instructor may ask you to do this Skill Builder in class in a group. If so, the instructor will provide you with any necessary information or additional instructions.

• • • STUDENT STUDY SITE

Visit the Student Study Site at **www.sagepub.com/lussier6e** to access to these additional study tools:

- Mobile-compatible self-assessment quizzes
- Mobile-compatible key term flashcards
- Video Links
- SAGE Journal Articles
- Web Links

Photo from Oversnap/iStockphoto.

7 Organizing and Delegating Work

• • • **Learning Outcomes**

After studying this chapter, you should be able to:

7-1. Explain the difference between mechanistic and organic organizations and the environments in which they are more effective. PAGE 186

7-2. Discuss the difference between formal and informal authority and centralized and decentralized authority. PAGE 189

7-3. List and briefly explain the four levels of authority. PAGE 189

7-4. Explain what an organization chart is and list the four aspects of a firm that it shows. PAGE 192

7-5. Discuss the difference between internal and external departmentalization. PAGE 193

7-6. Explain the difference between job simplification and job expansion. PAGE 198

7-7. Explain how to set priorities by answering three priority questions and determining whether activities have high, medium, or low priority. PAGE 201

7-8. List the four steps in the delegation process. PAGE 205

IDEAS ON MANAGEMENT at Volkswagen Group

Volkswagen means "people's car." The German MNC Volkswagen Group is one of the world's leading automobile manufacturers and the largest carmaker in Europe. The Group comprises 12 brands from seven European countries: Volkswagen Passenger Cars, Audi, SEAT, ŠKODA, Bentley, Bugatti, Lamborghini, Porsche, Ducati, Volkswagen Commercial Vehicles, Scania, and MAN. Each brand has its own character and operates as an independent subsidiary. In Western Europe, almost one in four new cars (24.4 percent) is made by the Volkswagen Group. Volkswagen activities may focus on the automobile, but the Volkswagen Group is far more than just a carmaker, as a wide variety of mobility-related services round out its portfolio.

Volkswagen Group has a goal of becoming the world's largest automaker. To that end, it continues to be innovative. Group Research has its headquarters in Wolfsburg and researches for all Group brands. International trend scouting and technology scouting form part of its strategic orientation, and it also operates from research bases in the U.S., Japanese, and Chinese markets.

Uniting a wide variety of brands and companies with all their individual characteristics and focuses under one umbrella is a great challenge, especially as the Volkswagen Group is committed to maintaining their individual identities. But this is the only way all the brands and companies can make their own contributions to the common value stream and form cornerstones of the Group.

1. Where is Volkswagen Group on the mechanistic and organic continuum? PAGE 186
2. What are the important organizational principles guiding Volkswagen in achieving its goal of becoming the world's largest automaker? PAGE 188
3. Is Volkswagen more centralized or decentralized? PAGE 190
4. What is Volkswagen Group's organizational design? PAGE 195
5. What prioritization issues does Volkswagen face? PAGE 201

You'll find answers to these questions throughout the chapter. To learn more about the Volkswagen Group, visit its website at www.volkswagenag.com.

Sources: Information for this case was taken from Volkswagen's website at http://www.volkswagenag.com, accessed June 26, 2013.

• • • Chapter Outline

Organizational Considerations and Principles
    Organizational Considerations
    Principles of Organization
Authority
    Formal and Informal Authority and Scope and
      Levels of Authority
    Centralized and Decentralized Authority
    Line and Staff Authority
Organizational Design
    Organization Chart
    Departmentalization

    Multiple Departmentalization
    Reengineering Contemporary Organizational
      Designs
Job Design
    Job Simplification
    Job Expansion
    Work Teams
    The Job Characteristics Model
Organizing Yourself and Delegating
    Setting Priorities
    Delegating

ORGANIZATION CONSIDERATIONS AND PRINCIPLES

Why do firms that seem equal execute at different levels of efficiency? The answer is in how their resources are organized and managed.[1] Organizing, the second function of management, is defined as the process of delegating and coordinating tasks and resources to achieve objectives. The four resources managers organize are human, physical, financial, and information (Chapter 1). So you manage resources by organizing activities.[2] When designing an entire organization, there are some things to consider and principles to follow. These are the topics of this section.

Organizational Considerations

Here are some things to consider and questions to answer when organizing the entire company.

Mechanistic versus Organic Organization and the Environment. Overall there are two major forms of organization that are more effective in different environments (Chapter 2). **Mechanistic organizations** *are bureaucratic, focusing on following procedures and rules through tight controls and having specialized jobs, with decisions being made by top managers.* This model tends to work well in stable environments. Conversely, **organic organizations** *are flexible, with minimal focus on procedures and rules, broadly defined jobs, and decisions made at lower levels.* This model tends to work well in dynamic environments.

Although there are two forms, they are really on a continuum between being mechanistic or organic. Many companies are organized somewhere between the two extremes but can be more identified overall with one form or the other. It is also common for some parts like manufacturing to be mechanistic, whereas as research, design, and marketing are organic; this is the case at **Volkswagen Group (Case Question 1).**

Strategy, Size, and Technology. As discussed in Chapter 5, companies develop strategies and, thus, company organizational structure must be designed to achieve the strategies.[3] As companies change strategies, they tend to change their structure. With innovative growth strategies in a dynamic environment, organic structures tend to work well, whereas with stability strategy in a stable environment, mechanistic tends to work well (Burns and Stalker, Chapter 1). Generally, the larger the firm, the more mechanistic it becomes, but highly innovative companies can be organic. Companies that use mass-production technology tend to use a more mechanistic organization, whereas firms with more custom-made products tend to be organic (Woodward, Chapter 1).

Organization Questions. There are at least six questions that you need to answer when organizing. The questions are listed in Exhibit 7-1. The answers are discussed in more detail in the indicated topic sections of this chapter.

Principles of Organization

Exhibit 7-2 lists the organizational principles generally followed by companies that we discuss in this section. Note that not all companies follow all of the guidelines. You will learn that there is a difference in their use by organic and mechanistic organizations.

Unity of Command and Direction. The principle of *unity of command* requires that each employee report to only one boss. When there are two bosses, you can often get two conflicting messages. The principle of *unity of direction* requires that all activities be directed toward the same objectives. Unity of command and direction

LO 7-1

Explain the difference between mechanistic and organic organizations and the environments in which they are more effective.

mechanistic organizations Bureaucratic organizations, focusing on following procedures and rules through tight controls and specialized jobs, with top managers making decisions.

organic organizations Flexible organizations with minimal focus on procedures and rules, broadly defined jobs, and decisions made at lower levels.

EXHIBIT 7-1 ORGANIZING QUESTIONS

Questions for Managers	Chapter Topic
Who should departments and individuals report to?	Chain of command; organization chart
How many individuals should report to each manager?	Span of management
How should we subdivide the work?	Division of labor; departmentalization
How do we get everyone to work together as a system?	Coordination
At what level should decisions be made?	Centralization vs. decentralization of authority
How do we organize to meet our mission and strategy?	Departmentalization

EXHIBIT 7-2 PRINCIPLES OF ORGANIZATION

- Unity of command and direction
- Chain of command
- Span of management (flat and tall organizations)
- Division of labor (specialization, departmentalization, integration)
- Coordination
- Balanced responsibility and authority
- Delegation
- Flexibility

is more closely enforced in mechanistic organizations than in organic ones, which are more flexible, with decisions being made at lower levels.

Chain of Command. *Chain of command*, also known as the Scalar Principle, is the clear line of authority from the top to the bottom of an organization. The chain of command forms a hierarchy,[4] which is illustrated in the organization chart. All members of the firm should know whom they report to and who, if anyone, reports to them. The chain of command is clearer and more closely followed in mechanistic organizations.

Span of Management. The **span of management** (or span of control) *refers to the number of employees reporting to a manager.* The fewer employees supervised, the smaller or narrower the span of management. The more employees supervised, the greater or wider the span.

The span of management in an organization is related to the number of its organizational levels, which determines its organizational height. In a *tall organization*, there are many levels with narrow spans of management. In a *flat organization*, there are few levels with wide spans of management. In recent years, many organizations have flattened. **Shell** cut 20 percent of its top management.[5] Mechanistic organizations tend to be taller.

Division of Labor. With *division of labor*, employees have specialized jobs. Related functions are grouped together under a single boss. Employees generally have specialized jobs in a functional area such as accounting, production, or sales. Mechanistic organizations have a greater division of labor.

WORK APPLICATION 7-1

Follow the chain of command from your present position (or one you held in the past) to the top of the organization. Start by identifying anyone who reported to you, then list your boss's title, your boss's boss's title, and on up to the top manager's title.

WORK APPLICATION 7-2

Identify your boss's span of management, or your own if you are or were a manager. How many levels of management are there in your organization? Is it a flat or a tall organization?

span of management The number of employees reporting to a manager.

Coordination. *Coordination* ensures that all departments and individuals within an organization work together to accomplish strategic and operational objectives.[6] Coordination is the process of integrating tasks and resources to meet objectives. Paul Lawrence and Jay Lorsch coined the terms *differentiation* and *integration*.[7] Differentiation refers to the need to break the organization into departments, and integration refers to the need to coordinate the departmental activities. Coordination is generally easier in mechanistic organizations.

Start-up organizations often use organic structures that allow for more flexibility. Photo from Vetta Stock Photo/iStockphoto.

responsibility The obligation to achieve objectives by performing required activities.

authority The right to make decisions, issue orders, and use resources.

delegation The process of assigning responsibility and authority for accomplishing objectives.

Balanced Responsibility and Authority. With balanced responsibility and authority, the responsibilities of each individual in the organization are clearly defined. Mechanistic employees have more clearly defined responsibilities. Each individual is also given the authority necessary to meet these responsibilities and is held accountable for meeting them. When you delegate, you do not give responsibility and authority away; you share them.

Responsibility *is the obligation to achieve objectives by performing required activities.* When strategic and operational objectives are set, the people responsible for achieving them should be clearly identified. Managers are responsible for the performance of their units.

Authority *is the right to make decisions, issue orders, and use resources.* As a manager, you will be given responsibility for achieving unit objectives. You must also have the authority to get the job done. Authority is delegated. The CEO is responsible for the results of the entire organization and delegates authority down the chain of command to the lower-level managers, who are responsible for meeting operational objectives.

Accountability is the evaluation of how well individuals meet their responsibilities. All members of an organization should be evaluated periodically and held accountable for achieving their objectives, which is being done at **Shell**.[8] Managers are accountable for everything that happens in their departments. As a manager, you delegate responsibility and authority to perform tasks, but you should realize that you can never delegate your accountability.

Delegation. Delegation is *the process of assigning responsibility and authority for accomplishing objectives.* Responsibility and authority are delegated down the chain of command. Delegation will be covered in detail later in this chapter. But for now, you should realize that delegation only takes place when you give an employee a new task. If a task is already part of the job and you ask them to do a task, it's not delegation. Delegating tends to be used more often in organic organizations, as jobs are not as clearly defined and employees are expected to do a wider variety of tasks.

Flexibility. Employees in mechanistic organizations focus on following company rules; they fear getting into trouble for breaking or bending the rules. Organic organization employees are allowed to be more flexible and make exceptions to the procedures and rules to create customer satisfaction.

Because each of the 12 brands in the **Volkswagen Group (Case Question 2)** is managed separately, the most important organizational principles guiding it toward the goal of being the world's largest automaker are unity of direction, coordination, delegation, and flexibility. All 12 subsidiaries need a unity of

7-1 **APPLYING** THE CONCEPT

Principles of Organization

Identify which organizational principle or principles are represented by each statement.

    A. unity of command and direction
    B. chain of command
    C. span of management
    D. division of labor
    E. coordination
    F. balanced responsibility and authority
    G. delegation
    H. flexibility

____ 1. "Sometimes my department manager tells me to do one thing but my project manager tells me to do something else at the same time. Therefore, I often wonder which task I should do."

____ 2. "I want an employee to do a special report but, as a middle manager, I can't give anyone a direct order to do it. I have to have one of my supervisors give the order."

____ 3. "There has been an accident, and the ambulance is on the way. Juan, call Doctor Rodriguez and have her get to emergency room C in 10 minutes. Pat, get the paperwork ready. Karen, prepare emergency room C."

____ 4. "Sara told me to pick up the mail. When I got to the post office, I did not have a key to the box, so the postal worker wouldn't give me the mail."

____ 5. Players on a football team are on either the offensive or the defensive squad.

direction to achieve the objective. Coordination at headquarters between the 12 subsidiaries is critical (differentiation and integration), and because they are independent brands, authority must be delegated to them, as they are responsible for their own results and held accountable, and each subsidiary has the flexibility to operate as a separate company.

AUTHORITY

In this section, you will learn about formal and informal authority, levels of authority, centralized and decentralized authority, and line and staff authority.

Formal and Informal Authority and Scope and Levels of Authority

It is helpful to distinguish between formal and informal authority[9] and to understand the scope and level of your authority for a given task.

Formal and Informal Authority. *Formal authority* (or structure) is based on the specified relationships among employees. It is the sanctioned way of getting the job done. The organization chart illustrates formal authority and shows the lines of authority. *Informal authority* (or structure) arises from the patterns of relationships and communication that evolve as employees interact and communicate. It is the unsanctioned way of getting the job done. Formal authority is common in mechanistic organizations, whereas informal authority is more accepted in organic organizations.

Scope of Authority. The *scope of authority* is a hierarchy that narrows as it flows down the organization.[10] The president has more authority than a vice president, who has more authority than a manager. Responsibility and authority are delegated and flow down the organization, whereas accountability flows up the organization, as Exhibit 7-3 illustrates.

Levels of Authority. The **levels of authority** are *the authority to inform, the authority to recommend, the authority to report, and full authority.*

LO 7-2

Discuss the difference between formal and informal authority and centralized and decentralized authority.

LO 7-3

List and briefly explain the four levels of authority.

levels of authority The authority to inform, the authority to recommend, the authority to report, and full authority.

EXHIBIT 7-3 SCOPE OF AUTHORITY

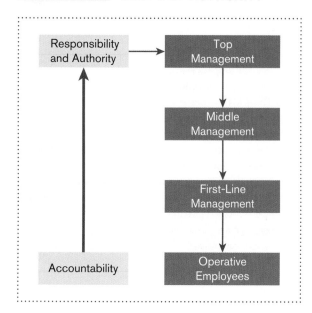

1. *The authority to inform.* You inform your supervisor of possible alternative actions. The supervisor has the authority to make the decision.

2. *The authority to recommend.* You list alternative decisions/actions, analyze them, and recommend one action. However, you may not implement the recommendation without the boss's okay. The boss may require a different alternative if he or she does not agree with the recommendation. Committees are often given authority to recommend.

3. *The authority to report.* You may freely select a course of action and carry it out. However, afterward you must report the action taken to the boss.

4. *Full authority.* You may freely make decisions and act without the boss's knowledge. However, even people with full authority may consult their bosses for advice.

Centralized and Decentralized Authority

The major distinction between centralized and decentralized authority lies in who makes the important decisions. With **centralized authority**, *important decisions are made by top managers.* With **decentralized authority**, *important decisions are made by middle and first-line managers.* Decentralization pushes authority and accountability further down the line.[11] **Volkswagen Group (Case Question 3)** lets each of its 12 brands operate as separate business units; therefore, it is decentralizing authority.

Which type of authority works best? There is no simple answer, as it depends on the situation.[12] The major advantages of centralization are control and reduced duplication of work. The major advantages of decentralization are efficiency and flexibility. Mechanistic organizations tend to use centralized authority, whereas organic ones tend to use decentralized authority. **General Electric** and **Toyota** have successfully used decentralized authority, and **General Dynamics** and **McDonald's** have successfully used centralized authority.

Authority is a continuum, with centralized authority at one end and decentralized authority at the other. Most organizations lie somewhere between the two extremes but can be classified overall. The key to success seems to be having the right balance between the two extremes.

Micromanagement. Micromanagement is *a management style generally used as a negative term for when a manager closely observes or controls the work of his or her employees.* Rather than giving general instructions on tasks and then devoting time to supervising larger concerns, the micromanager monitors and assesses every step of a business process and avoids delegation of decisions. A micromanager tends to require constant and detailed performance feedback and tends to be excessively focused on procedural trivia rather than on overall performance, quality, and results. This often delays decisions, clouds overall goals and objectives, restricts the flow of information between employees, and guides the various aspects of a project in different and often opposed decisions.[13] Micromanaging is more common with centralized authority.

Line and Staff Authority

There are differences between line and staff authority, and staff can be generalist or specialist.

WORK APPLICATION 7-4

Identify and explain your level of authority for a specific task in an organization.

WORK APPLICATION 7-5

Describe the type of authority (centralized or decentralized) used in an organization you work for or have worked for.

centralized authority Important decisions are made by top managers.

decentralized authority Important decisions are made by middle and first-line managers.

7-1 **JOIN THE DISCUSSION** ETHICS & SOCIAL RESPONSIBILITY

Breaking the Rules

Suppose you are a sales rep for a major pharmaceutical company. You get paid by commission, so the more drugs you sell to doctors, the more money you make. You know that sales reps in your company have been visiting doctors and telling them that if they prescribe your company's medication, they will receive 5 percent of the sales revenues. This arrangement can bring in thousands of dollars each year for both the sales reps and the doctors. You know the names of a few sales reps who are allegedly giving these kickbacks, but you are not sure how many sales reps are involved. You also don't know if sales managers know about the kickbacks or are receiving payments from the reps.

1. Is it unethical to be flexible and break the law against kickbacks?
2. Why are kickbacks illegal? Who benefits from kickbacks, who gets hurt by them, and how?
3. What would you do in this situation? (Would you start giving kickbacks yourself? Blow the whistle on sales reps to their managers? Blow the whistle to an outside source like the government or the media? Do nothing?)

Line versus Staff Authority. *Line authority* is *the responsibility to make decisions and issue orders down the chain of command.* *Staff authority* is *the responsibility to advise and assist other personnel.* Line managers are primarily responsible for achieving the organization's objectives and directly bringing revenue into the organization, and staff people provide them with services that help them do that. Operations, marketing, and finance are usually line departments. Human resources management, public relations, and data processing are almost always staff departments. The line departments are internal "customers" of the staff departments.

General and Specialist Staff. *General staff* work for only one manager and help the manager in any way needed. *Specialist staff* help anyone in the organization who needs it. Human resources, accounting, public relations, and maintenance offer specialized advice and assistance. Line managers and division managers use the services of staff departments such as printing and human resources. Exhibit 7-4 reviews types and levels of authority. Mechanistic organizations tend to have more specialized staff than do organic organizations.

WORK APPLICATION 7-6

Identify one or more line and staff positions in an organization you work for or have worked for. Also, indicate whether the staff positions are general staff or specialist staff.

EXHIBIT 7-4	**TYPES AND LEVELS OF AUTHORITY**

Authority			
• Formal: sanctioned	• Line: issue orders	• Inform: present alternatives	• Centralized: top managers
• Informal: unsanctioned	• Staff: assist line	• Recommend: present alternatives and suggest one	• Decentralized: meddle and first-line managers
		• Full: do and don't tell	

micromanagement A management style generally used as a negative term for when a manager closely observes or controls the work of his or her employees.

line authority The responsibility to make decisions and issue orders down the chain of command.

staff authority The responsibility to advise and assist other personnel.

ORGANIZATIONAL DESIGN

Organizational design is important,[14] as it refers to the internal structure of an organization, or the arrangement of positions in the organization into work units

7-2 APPLYING THE CONCEPT

Authority

Identify the type of authority referred to in each statement.

A. formal
B. informal
C. centralized
D. decentralized
E. line
F. staff

_____ 6. "Managers here have the autonomy to run their departments in the way they want to."

_____ 7. "Here is a list of cars and my recommendation on which one to replace the current company car."

_____ 8. "That is a great idea. I'll talk to the boss, and if he likes it, he'll let us present the idea to his boss."

_____ 9. "I get frustrated when I recommend good job candidates to the production manager and he does not hire them."

_____ 10. "It is great working here. I have developed great relationships with people throughout the organization and we are encouraged to share information with everyone else to get the job done."

LO 7-4

Explain what an organization chart is and list the four aspects of a firm that it shows.

or departments and the interrelationships among these units or departments. As you'll learn in this section, organizational design is illustrated in the organization chart and is determined by the type of departmentalization.

Organization Chart

The formal authority or structure within an organization defines the working relationships between the organization's members and their jobs and is illustrated by an organization chart. It helps to see your organizational structure in a chart.[15] An **organization chart** *is a graphic illustration of the organization's management hierarchy and departments and their working relationships.* Each box represents a position within the organization, and each line indicates the reporting relationships and lines of communication. (An organization chart does not show the day-to-day activities performed or the structure of the informal organization.)

Exhibit 7-5, an adaptation of **General Motors's** organization chart,[16] illustrates four major aspects of such a chart:

- *The level of management hierarchy.* The hierarchy shows the levels of management.[17] At GM, the CEO and division presidents are top management, the vice presidents and managers are middle management, and the supervisors are first-line management.

- *Chain of command.* By following the vertical lines, you can see who reports to whom, as the GM division presidents report to the CEO. Within each division, vice presidents report to a president. The managers report to a vice president, and supervisors report to a manager. The assistant to the CEO is a general staff person, and the finance and human resources departments include specialist staff.

- *The division and type of work.* GM divides work by type of automobile: Buick, Cadillac, Chevrolet, and GMC (trucks). Each vice president within a division is responsible for a function.

- *Departmentalization.* An organization chart shows how the firm is divided into permanent work units. GM is organized primarily by product divisional departmentalization.

To better focus on the customer, some organizations, including **Dana Corporation, FedEx, Nordstrom,** and **Walmart,** have developed an upside-down organization chart with the customer at the top of the chart and management at the

organization chart A graphic illustration of an organization's management hierarchy and departments and their working relationships.

EXHIBIT 7-5 ORGANIZATION CHART

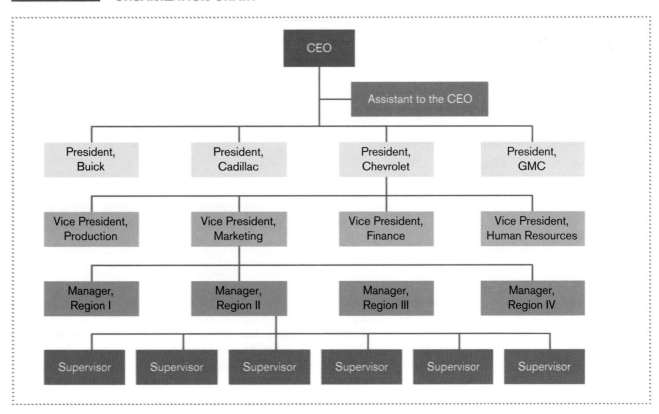

bottom. The upside-down chart reminds everyone in the organization that the ultimate goal is to provide customer value and emphasizes to managers that their role is to support employees in providing customer value.

Departmentalization

Departmentalization *is the grouping of related activities into units.* Departments may have either an internal or an external focus. Departmentalization based on the internal operations or functions that the employees perform and the resources needed to accomplish that work is called *functional departmentalization*. External, or output, departmentalization is based on activities or factors outside the organization; it is referred to more specifically as *product, customer,* or *territory departmentalization.*

Functional Departmentalization. Functional departmentalization involves organizing departments around essential input activities, such as production, sales, and finance, which are managerial or technological functions. Functional departmentalization is illustrated in the top left portion of Exhibit 7–6. The functional approach is the form most widely used by small organizations. Large organizations that have a diversity of products or types of customers or that cover a wide territory cannot departmentalize effectively simply around functions. Instead, they focus on factors external to the company.

Product (Service) Departmentalization. Product (service) departmentalization involves organizing departments around goods (or services). Companies with multiple products commonly use product departmentalization. Retail chains like **Sears** use product departmentalization. The organization chart at the bottom left in Exhibit 7-6 illustrates product departmentalization.

LO 7-5

Discuss the difference between internal and external departmentalization.

departmentalization The grouping of related activities into units.

EXHIBIT 7-6   TYPES OF DEPARTMENTALIZATION

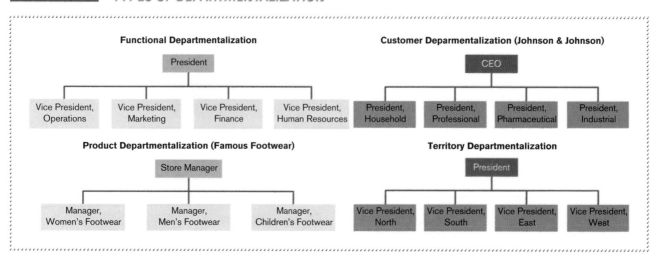

Customer Departmentalization. Customer departmentalization involves organizing departments around the needs of different types of customers. The product or service may be the same or slightly different, but the needs of the customer warrant different marketing approaches. **Motorola** restructured to merge about a half dozen business units into two huge divisions—one geared to retail consumers and the other to industrial customers. **Haier Group** in China reorganized into 4,100 self-managed units with each devoted to a customer or group of customers.[18] Some not-for-profit organizations use it, such as, a counseling center offering drug counseling, family counseling, and so on. The organization chart at the top right in Exhibit 7–6 illustrates customer departmentalization.

Territory (Geographic) Departmentalization. Territory (geographic) departmentalization involves establishing separate units in each area in which the enterprise does business. The federal government uses this structure. For example, the **Federal Reserve System** is divided into 12 geographic areas, and each one has a similar central bank. The organization chart at the bottom right in Exhibit 7–6 illustrates departmentalization by territory.

Multiple Departmentalization

Many organizations, particularly large, complex ones, use several types of departmentalization to create a hybrid structure.[19] Any mixture of types can be used. For example, some organizations have functional departments within a manufacturing facility, but sales are departmentalized by territory with separate sales managers and salespeople in different areas.

Matrix Departmentalization. *Matrix departmentalization* combines functional and product departmentalization. With matrix departmentalization, an employee works for a functional department and is also assigned to one or more products or projects. The major advantage of matrix departmentalization is flexibility. It allows the enterprise to temporarily organize for a project. The major disadvantage is that each employee has two bosses—a functional boss and a project boss—which violates the unity-of-command principle. Coordination can also be difficult.[20] **Xerox** and **Boeing** use matrix departmentalization. Exhibit 7-7 illustrates a matrix structure.

EXHIBIT 7-7 MATRIX DEPARTMENTALIZATION

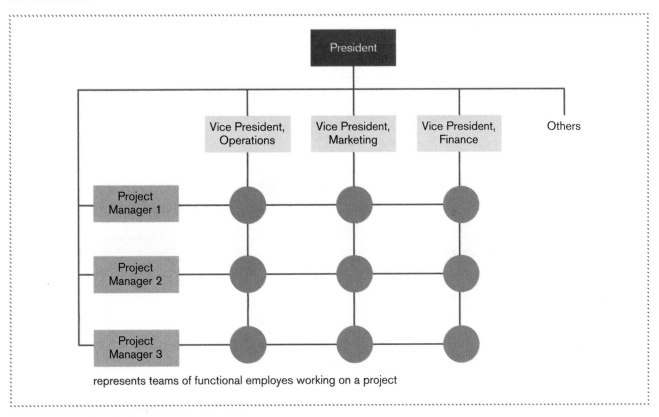

represents teams of functional employes working on a project

Divisional Departmentalization. As part of the corporate grand strategy (Chapter 5), a divisional structure is *based on semiautonomous strategic business units*. In essence, this structure creates coordinated companies within a company. Divisional structure is common for large, complex global businesses that offer related goods and services. **PepsiCo** uses divisional departmentalization for its **Pepsi** soda, **Gatorade** sport drinks, **Frito-Lay** snacks, and **Quaker Oats** cereal and granola bars.[21]

Within the divisional structure, any mixture of the other forms of departmentalization may also be used. **Volkswagen Group (Case Question 4)** is one company with 12 separate independent brands, so it overall uses a divisional departmentalization. However, selling vehicles in 153 countries, it is also departmentalized by territory. Each of the 12 brand subsidiaries also has a variety of product models that can be organized into product departmentalization, and they each have to perform their own functions that can be departments. The brands also use matrix departmentalization when designing new car models.

The *conglomerate* (holding company) *structure* is based on autonomous profit centers.[22] Companies with unrelated diversified business units use the conglomerate structure. Top management focuses on business portfolio management to buy and sell lines of business without great concern for coordinating divisions. **The Walt Disney Company** and **Time Warner** use the conglomerate structure.

Reengineering Contemporary Organizational Designs

Companies are reengineering their business processes. Some of the new approaches to organizational design are horizontal team, network, modular, virtual, and learning organizations. Reengineering and new organizational designs are more common in organic than in mechanistic organizations.

WORK
APPLICATION 7-7

Draw a simple organization chart for an organization you work for or have worked for. Identify the type of departmentalization and staff positions, if any.

divisional structure Departmentalization based on semiautonomous strategic business units.

7-3 APPLYING THE CONCEPT

Departmentalization

Identify the type of departmentalization illustrated by each organization chart.

a. functional   d. territory (geographic)

b. product (service)   e. matrix

c. customer   f. divisional

____ 11. Dallas Consulting Company

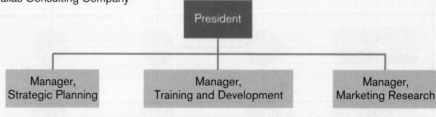

____ 12. Wood Publishing Company

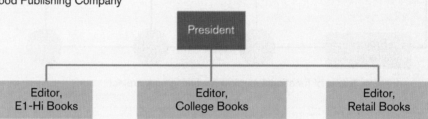

____ 13. Worldwide Marriage Encounter—USA

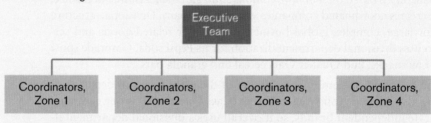

____ 14. Best Company International

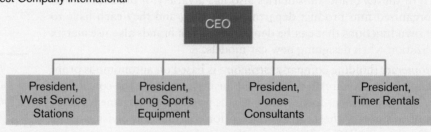

____ 15. Production department of metal toys company

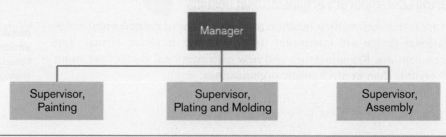

Reengineering. *Reengineering* is the fundamental rethinking and radical redesign of business processes to achieve dramatic improvements in critical, contemporary measures of performance, such as cost, quality, service, and speed.[23] As defined, it's about radical big improvement, not incremental change. You start by throwing out the old methods and reengineer new, radically better ways of getting the work done. Michael Porter says we need to reengineer health-care organizations, including how doctors and nurses work together.[24] An entire company, department, or job can be reengineered. Here we focus on the company and department levels; we focus on reengineering the job in the next major section—Job Design.

Horizontal Team Organization. Many companies are moving away from a vertical, hierarchical, top-down focus to a horizontal, team-based structure.[25] Teams increase speed of response, individual accountability, flexibility, knowledge sharing, and coordination throughout the organization. Teams often create innovative routines that benefit other groups in the company.[26] You will learn about work teams later in the chapter. **Cummins, General Foods, Procter & Gamble**, and **Sherwin-Williams** have all developed team structures.

Network, Modular, and Virtual Organizations. *Networks* are *boundaryless* interrelationships among different organizations.[27] Networks have a positive impact on performance,[28] and modular and virtual organizations are types of networks. A network firm may be viewed as a central hub surrounded by a network of outside specialists that change as needed. Network *modular* firms focus on what they do best, outsource the rest to other companies, and coordinate their activities. **Nike** and **Reebok** design and market their footwear and outsource manufacturing to contractors that change over time. Some companies, including **Dell** and **RCA**, either purchase products ready made or buy all the parts and only assemble the product.

A *virtual organization* is a continually evolving network of companies that unite temporarily to exploit specific opportunities or to attain strategic advantages and then disband when objectives are met. The virtual organization has no central hub; it's more like a potluck dinner, as each independent company selects which companies it wants to network with to meet a specific objective. E-commerce is increasing the use of virtual organizations.

The Learning Organization. As discussed in Chapter 2, in a learning organization, everyone in the firm is engaged in identifying and solving problems to continuously improve and achieve the firm's objectives. There is no agreement about how the learning organization looks or operates. However, it does use the horizontal team structure with open information and knowledge sharing.[29] Learning organizations are also characterized by decentralized decision making, participative strategy, empowered employees who share responsibility, and a strong adaptive nature.[30]

As discussed in this section, firms are changing the way they organize. Complete the Self-Assessment to determine your organizational preference. Knowing your preference can help in job searching.

JOB DESIGN

Tasks or activities to be performed by organizations are grouped into functional departments,[31] and the tasks are further grouped into jobs for each employee. **Job design** *is the process of identifying tasks that each employee is responsible for completing.* Job design is crucial because it affects job satisfaction and productivity.[32] So companies are redesigning and reengineering work process and jobs.[33] Many organizations, including **GE** and **Pizza Hut**, are asking employees to suggest ways to redesign their work. Empowering employees to be involved in designing their own jobs motivates them to increase productivity.

job design The process of identifying tasks that each employee is responsible for completing.

7-1 SELF ASSESSMENT

Organizational Preference

Individuals differ in the type of organizations in which they prefer to work. To determine your organizational preference, evaluate each of the following 12 statements, using the scale below. Place a number from 1 to 5 that represents your level of agreement with the statement.

I agree				I disagree
5	4	3	2	1

_____ 1. I prefer having just one boss telling me what to do rather than multiple people.

_____ 2. I prefer to just perform my job rather than being concerned about organizational objectives and being involved in setting them.

_____ 3. I prefer knowing the reporting relationship, who is whose boss, and working through proper channels rather than just working directly with a variety of people based on the situation.

_____ 4. I prefer to get information from my boss rather than multiple sources.

_____ 5. I prefer having a clear job description so I know just what I need to do at work rather than the ambiguity of not being sure and doing whatever needs to be done.

_____ 6. I prefer being a specialist rather than a generalist.

_____ 7. I prefer doing my own thing that contributes to the organization rather than coordinating the work I do with that of others in teams.

_____ 8. I prefer to make excuses and blame others rather than accept responsibility for my shortcomings.

_____ 9. I prefer having my boss make decisions for me at work rather than making my own decisions.

_____ 10. I prefer routine at work rather than being delegated new tasks to perform.

_____ 11. I prefer having job security rather than knowing I could be let go.

_____ 12. I prefer that people get promoted based primarily on seniority rather than based on performance.

_____ Total

Scoring: To determine your preference, add up the numbers you assigned to the statements; the total will be between 12 and 60.

The higher your score, the more you prefer to work in a traditional organizational structure, often referred to as mechanistic. The lower your score, the more you prefer to work in a contemporary organizational structure, often called organic. Review your answers knowing that the opening statement applies to traditional organizations and the opposite statement (after "rather than") applies to contemporary organizations. Most firms tend to be organized somewhere between the two extremes.

As we will discuss in this section, jobs may be simplified or they may be expanded. You can use work teams and a job characteristics model to design jobs.

LO 7-6

Explain the difference between job simplification and job expansion.

Job Simplification

Job simplification is the process of eliminating or combining tasks and/or changing the work sequence to improve performance. Job simplification makes jobs more specialized. It is based on the organizing principle of division of labor and Taylor's scientific management (Chapter 1). The idea behind job simplification is to work smarter, not harder. A job is broken down into steps (flowchart), and employees analyze the steps to see if they can eliminate, combine, or change the sequence of activities.

- _Eliminate._ Does the task, or parts of it, have to be done at all? If not, don't waste time doing it.

- _Combine._ Doing similar things together often saves time. However, save multitasking for nonurgent, noncomplex tasks.

- _Change sequence._ Often, a change in the order of doing things results in a lower total time.

Intel managers decided that it was not necessary to fill out a voucher for expenses amounting to less than $100. Thus, fewer vouchers were filled out, saving time and paperwork. At **IBM Credit**, for loans given to companies buying its computers, approval took six days as it went through five people in five different departments. IBM reengineered the job so that only one person approved the credit and cut the approval time down to four hours.[34]

Job Expansion

Job expansion is the process of making jobs less specialized. Jobs can be expanded through rotation, enlargement, and enrichment.

Job Rotation. Job rotation involves performing different jobs in some sequence, each one for a set period. For example, employees making cars on a GM assembly line might rotate so that they get to work on different parts of the production process for a set period. Many organizations develop conceptual skills in management trainees by rotating them through various departments. **Target, Ford, Motorola,** and **Prudential Financial** use job rotation.

Related to job rotation is *cross-training*. With cross-training, employees learn to perform different jobs so they can fill in for those who are not on the job. As skills increase, employees become more valuable to the organization.

Target uses job rotation to help management trainees broaden their skills. The more jobs an employee can perform, the more valuable he or she is to the organization. Photo from Dawn Villella/AP Photo.

Job Enlargement. Job enlargement involves adding tasks to broaden variety. For example, rather than rotate jobs, the car workers could combine tasks into one job. **AT&T, Chrysler, GM,** and **IBM** have used job enlargement. Unfortunately, adding more tasks to an employee's job is often not a great motivator.

Job Enrichment. Job enrichment *is the process of building motivators into the job itself to make it more interesting and challenging.* Job enrichment works for jobs of low motivation potential and employees who are ready to be empowered to do meaningful work.[35] A simple way to enrich jobs is for the manager to delegate more responsibility to employees to make a job satisfying. **Monsanto, Motorola,** and **the Travelers Companies** have successfully used job enrichment.

Work Teams

The traditional approach to job design has been to focus on individual jobs. Recently, there has been a trend toward designing jobs for work teams—or, to be more accurate, teams are redesigning members' jobs.[36] The development of work teams is a form of job enrichment. Teams develop innovative routines that get passed on to other teams.[37] Two common types of work teams are integrated teams and self-managed teams.

Integrated Work Teams. *Integrated work teams* are assigned a number of tasks by a manager, and the team in turn gives specific assignments to members and is responsible for rotating jobs. Unlike members of self-managed work teams, most members have no input in each other's work. Integrated work teams are frequently used in areas such as building maintenance and construction.

WORK APPLICATION 7-8

Describe how a job at an organization you work for or have worked for could be simplified. Be sure to specify if you are eliminating, combining, or changing the sequence of the job.

WORK APPLICATION 7-9

Describe how a job at an organization you work for or have worked for could be expanded. Be sure to specify if you are using job rotation, job enlargement, or job enrichment and to be explicit about how the job is changed.

job enrichment The process of building motivators into a job to make it more interesting and challenging.

WORK
APPLICATION 7-10

Self-Managed Work Teams. *Self-managed work teams* are assigned a goal, and the team plans, organizes, leads, and controls to achieve the goal. Usually, self-managed teams operate without a designated manager; the team is both manager and worker. Teams commonly elect their own members and evaluate each other's performance. **General Mills, Aetna, W. L. Gore and Associates**, and **3M** have successfully used self-managed work teams.

Exhibit 7-8 reviews the job design options we have discussed so far. In designing jobs, managers can use the job characteristics model, to be discussed next.

EXHIBIT 7-8 JOB DESIGN OPTIONS

Job Simplification	Eliminate tasks
	Combine tasks
	Change task sequence
Job Expansion	Rotate jobs
	Add tasks
	Job enrichment (increase task variety and employee responsibility)
Work Teams	Integrated
	Self-managed

job characteristics model A conceptual framework for designing or enriching jobs that focuses on core job dimensions, psychological states of employees, and the strength of employees' need for growth.

The Job Characteristics Model

The job characteristics model, developed by Richard Hackman and Greg Oldham, provides a conceptual framework for designing or enriching jobs.[38] The model can be used by individual managers or by members of a team. Exhibit 7-9 illustrates the **job characteristics model**. Use of job characteristics improves employees' motivation and job satisfaction[39] and can increase performance.[40]

Five core dimensions can be fine-tuned to improve the outcomes of a job in terms of employees' productivity and their quality of working life:

1. *Skill variety* is the number of diverse tasks that make up a job and the number of skills used to perform the job.
2. *Task identity* is the degree to which an employee performs a whole identifiable task. For example, does the employee put together an entire television or just place the screen in the set?
3. *Task significance* is an employee's perception of the importance of the task to others—the organization, the department, coworkers, and/or customers.
4. *Autonomy* is the degree to which the employee has discretion to make decisions in planning, organizing, and controlling the task performed.
5. *Feedback* is the extent to which employees find out how well they perform their tasks.
6. Note that if employees are not interested in enriching their jobs, the job characteristics model will fail. You will learn more about needs and motivation in Chapter 11.

EXHIBIT 7-9 THE JOB CHARACTERISTICS MODEL

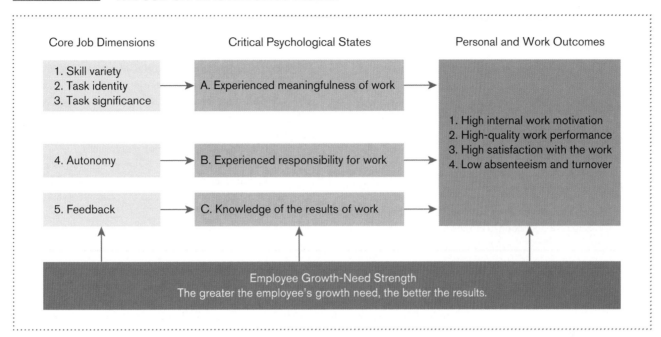

Core Job Dimensions

1. Skill variety
2. Task identity
3. Task significance

4. Autonomy

5. Feedback

Critical Psychological States

A. Experienced meaningfulness of work

B. Experienced responsibility for work

C. Knowledge of the results of work

Personal and Work Outcomes

1. High internal work motivation
2. High-quality work performance
3. High satisfaction with the work
4. Low absenteeism and turnover

Employee Growth-Need Strength
The greater the employee's growth need, the better the results.

ORGANIZING YOURSELF AND DELEGATING

Successful managers are effective at setting priorities and delegating work.[41] Recall that planning entails setting objectives and that organizing is the process of delegating and coordinating resources to achieve objectives. Thus, prioritizing objectives is important, because some objectives are more important than others;[42] as a manager, you get the work done by delegating it to employees.[43]

Now that you understand how organizations and jobs are designed, it's time to learn how to organize yourself by setting priorities and delegating work. Start by completing the Self-Assessment 7–2 on prioritizing to determine what is important to you personally (your values).

The higher the total in any area, the higher the value you place on that particular area. The closer the totals are in all eight areas, the more well rounded you are.

Think about the time and effort you put into your top three values. Are you putting in enough time and effort to achieve the level of success you want in each area? If not, what can you do to change?

Today's employees want to know how they are doing. Giving feedback is an important part of the manager's job because it helps employees continually improve their performance. Photo from Stocknroll/iStockphoto.

Setting Priorities

Let's begin by briefly discussing setting priorities for the entire organization, followed by a more detailed discussion focusing on teaching you how to set your own day-to-day priorities.

Many of today's companies are spotlighting fewer high priorities to make sure the most important ones are accomplished.[44] **eBay** made going mobile its top priority, and it was an early mover.[45] **Volkswagen Group (Case Question 5)** has a grand strategy goal to become the world's largest automaker. At the corporate

LO 7-7

Explain how to set priorities by answering three priority questions and determining whether activities have high, medium, or low priority.

7-4 APPLYING THE CONCEPT

Job Designs

Identify which job-design technique is exemplified in each statement.

A. job simplification
B. job rotation
C. job enlargement
D. job enrichment
E. work teams
F. job characteristics model

____ 16. "Sales reps who have business lunches that are under $30 no longer need to provide a sales receipt."

____ 17. "I'd like to change your job so that you can develop new skills, complete entire jobs by yourself so that the job is more meaningful, do the job the way you want to, and know how you are doing."

____ 18. "To make your job less repetitive, I am going to add three new tasks to your job responsibility."

____ 19. "I'd like you to learn how to run the cash register so that you can fill in for Jack while he is on vacation."

____ 20. "I am delegating a new task to you to make your job more challenging."

---

level, it has to prioritize the allocation of resources among the 12 brand subsidiaries. It also has to prioritize which global markets it will allocate resources to compete in. China is now the world's largest auto market, so Volkswagen is investing heavily in China to gain global market share to help reach its goal.

As a manager, you'll be required to carry out several tasks at any given time.[46] How you select the priority order in which these tasks will be completed will affect your success.[47] To prioritize successfully, make a to-do list of tasks that you must perform and then assign each task a priority.[48] After prioritizing tasks, focus on accomplishing only one task at a time. Recall from our discussion on multitasking in Chapter 5 that when you focus on more than one important thinking task at a time, error rates go way up and it takes much longer to get the jobs done.

Priority-Determination Questions.[49] Answer "yes" or "no" to the following three **priority-determination questions** *about each task that needs to be completed:*

1. *Do I need to be personally involved because of my unique knowledge or skills?* Often, you are the only one who can do the task; if so, then you must be involved.

2. *Is the task my responsibility, or will it affect the performance or finances of my department?* You must oversee the performance of your department and keep finances in line with the budget.

3. *When is the deadline—is quick action needed?* Should you work on this activity right now, or can it wait? The key is to start the task soon enough so that you will meet the deadline.

Assigning Priorities. After answering the three questions, you can assign a high, medium, or low priority to each activity:

- *Delegate (D) priority:* If the answer to question 1 is no, the task is delegated and it is not necessary to answer questions 2 and 3. However, planning how to delegate the task now becomes a priority.

- *High (H) priority:* Assign the task a high priority if you answer yes to all three questions.

- *Medium (M) priority:* Assign the task a medium priority if you answer yes to question 1 but no to one of the remaining two questions.

- *Low (L) priority:* Assign the task a low priority if you answer yes to question 1 but no to both questions 2 and 3.

priority-determination questions Questions that help determine the priority of tasks to be completed.

7-2	**SELF** ASSESSMENT

Personal Priorities

Rate how important each of the following is to you on a scale from 0 (not important) to 100 (very important). Write the number you choose on the line to the left of each item.

Not Important   Somewhat Important   Very Important

0 _____ 10 _____ 20 _____ 30 _____ 40 _____ 50 _____ 60 _____ 70 _____ 80 _____ 90 _____ 100

_____ 1. An enjoyable, satisfying job
_____ 2. A high-paying job
_____ 3. A good marriage
_____ 4. Meeting new people, attending social events
_____ 5. Involvement in community activities
_____ 6. My relationship with God, my religion
_____ 7. Exercising, playing sports
_____ 8. Intellectual development
_____ 9. A career with challenging opportunities
_____ 10. Nice cars, clothes, home, etc.
_____ 11. Spending time with family
_____ 12. Having several close friends
_____ 13. Volunteer work for not-for-profit organizations
_____ 14. Meditation, quiet time to think, pray, etc.
_____ 15. A healthy, balanced diet
_____ 16. Educational reading, self-improvement TV programs, etc.

Below, copy the number you assigned to each of the 16 items in the space next to the item number; then add the two numbers in each column.

Professional	Financial	Family	Social	Community	Spiritual	Physical	Intellectual
1. _____	2. _____	3. _____	4. _____	5. _____	6. _____	7. _____	8. _____
9. _____	10. _____	11. _____	12. _____	13. _____	14. _____	15. _____	16. _____
Totals _____	_____	_____	_____	_____	_____	_____	_____

The Prioritized To-Do List. Exhibit 7-10 is a prioritized to-do list that you can copy and use on the job. Follow these steps when using the prioritized to-do list:

1. *Write the task* that you must perform on the task line.

2. *Answer the three priority questions* by placing a Y (yes) or N (no) in the relevant column. Also place the deadline and time needed to complete the task in the relevant column. The deadline and time needed are used with lower-level priorities that change into high priorities as the deadline approaches. You may want to write in the deadline for starting the task rather than the completion deadline.

3. *Assign a priority* to the task by placing the letter D (delegate), H (high), M (medium), or L (low) in the priority column. The top left of the prioritized to-do list shows how to determine priority based on the answers to the priority-determination questions. If you write D, set a priority on when to delegate the task.

EXHIBIT 7-10   PRIORITIZED TO-DO LIST

Assigning a Priority		Priority-Determination Questions				
		#1	#2	#3	4	5
D Delegate priority	(N) No to question 1	1. Do I need to be personally involved?	2. Is it my responsibility, or will it affect the performance or finances of my department?	3. Is quick action needed?	4. Deadline/ time needed	5. Priority
H High priority	(YYY) Yes to all three questions					
M Medium priority	(YNY or YYN) Yes to question 1 and No to questions 2 and 3					
L Low priority	(YNN) Yes to question 1 and No to questions 2 and 3					
	Task					

4. *Determine which task to complete now.* You may have more than one high-priority task, so follow the rule of "Do the most important thing first."[50] When all high priorities are completed, go to medium-priority tasks, followed by low-priority tasks.

Update the prioritized to-do list and add new tasks. As time passes, the medium- and low-priority tasks become high-priority tasks. There is no set rule for how often to update, but do it at least daily. As new tasks come up, be sure to add them to your to-do list and prioritize them. In doing so, you will avoid the tendency to put off a high-priority task to work on a lower-level task.

If you have a management job with a large variety of changing tasks that require long-range planning, you may want to use the time-management system described in Chapter 5. You can use the prioritized to-do list with the time-management system for daily scheduling. If you have a job with a small variety of changing tasks that require short-range planning, you may simply use the prioritized to-do list to keep yourself organized and focused on high-priority tasks. Complete Skill Builder 7–1 at the end of this chapter to develop your skill at setting managerial priorities using a prioritized to-do list.

WORK APPLICATION 7-11

List three to five tasks you must complete in the near future and prioritize them using Exhibit 7–10.

Delegating

Delegation is the process of assigning responsibility and authority for accomplishing objectives. Telling employees to perform tasks that are part of their job design is issuing orders, not delegating. Delegating refers to giving employees new tasks. The new task may become part of a redesigned job, or it may simply be a onetime assignment.

Benefits of and Obstacles to Delegating. When managers delegate, they benefit by having more time to perform high-priority tasks.[51] Delegation trains employees and improves their self-esteem; it is a means of enriching jobs and can result in improved personal and work outcomes.

Unfortunately, there are some obstacles to delegation, as managers become used to doing things themselves. They fear that employees will fail to accomplish the task or will show them up. Managers believe that they can perform the task more efficiently than others. You should realize that delegating is an important management skill; don't let these or other obstacles stop you from delegating.

Delegation Decisions. Successful delegation is often based on selecting what to delegate and to whom to delegate. Exhibit 7-11 suggests what to delegate and what not to delegate.

WORK APPLICATION 7-12

Describe an obstacle to delegation or a sign of delegating too little that you have observed.

| EXHIBIT 7-11 | WHAT TO DELEGATE AND WHAT NOT TO DELEGATE |

What to Delegate	What Not to Delegate
• Paperwork	• Anything that you need to be involved with because of your unique knowledge or skill
• Routine tasks	• Personnel matters (evaluating, disciplining, firing)
• Technical matters	• Confidential matters
• Tasks that develop employees	• Projects or tasks in crisis
• Tasks associated with solving employees' problems	• Activities delegated to you personally

The Delegation Process. After determining what to delegate and to whom, you must plan for and delegate the tasks. Following the four steps in the delegation process can increase your chances of delegating successfully:

LO 7-8

List the four steps in the delegation process.

Step 1. **Explain the need for delegating and the reasons for selecting the employee.** It is helpful for an employee to whom you delegate a task to understand why the assignment must be completed and to realize the importance of the task. Telling employees why they were selected should make them feel valued. Don't use the "it's a lousy job but someone has to do it" approach. Be positive; make employees aware of how they may benefit from the assignment. If step 1 is completed successfully, employees should be motivated, or at least willing, to do the assignment.

Step 2. **Set objectives that define responsibility, level of authority, and deadline.** The objectives should clearly state the result the employee is responsible for achieving by a specific deadline. Define the level of authority the employee has.

Step 3. **Develop a plan.** Once the objectives and deadline are set, a plan is needed to achieve them. The level of autonomy for developing the plan to accomplish the task should be based on the employee's capability level. (Refer to Skill Builder 1–4 in Chapter 1 for details on selecting the management style appropriate for the employee's capability level.) Make sure instructions for completing the task are clear; writing them down helps.

7-2   JOIN THE DISCUSSION ETHICS & SOCIAL RESPONSIBILITY

Delegating Destroying Documents

Arthur Andersen, a consulting company, was taken to court for destroying evidence that could have been used in court to support allegations of illegal activities. Arthur Andersen destroyed evidence related to the auditing of Enron to protect both companies from being found guilty of engaging in illegal business practices. Arthur Andersen claimed that it was not trying to destroy incriminating evidence, that it was simply destroying records, which is done periodically. Destroying documents is, in fact, routine. The key question is this: "What is being destroyed and why is it being destroyed?"

1. Is it ethical and socially responsible to delegate the task of destroying documents that may potentially be used as evidence of wrongdoing?

2. What would you do if your boss asked you to destroy documents and you thought the goal was to cover up evidence of wrongdoing by the firm? (Would you just do it? Say nothing but neglect to do it? Question your boss's motives? Look closely at what you were asked to destroy? Check with your boss's boss to make sure it's okay to do it? Tell the boss you will not do it? Tell the boss to do it him- or herself? Blow the whistle to an outside source?)

3. If you were charged with destroying evidence, do you believe it would be a good defense to say, "I was only following orders"?

WORK
APPLICATION 7-13

Select a manager you work for or have worked for and analyze how well he or she implements the four steps of delegation. Which steps does the manager typically follow and not follow?

Step 4. Establish control checkpoints and hold employees accountable. For simple, short tasks, a deadline without control checkpoints is appropriate. However, when tasks have multiple steps and/or will take some time to complete, it is often advisable to check progress at predetermined times (control checkpoints). This approach builds information flow into the delegation system from the start. You and the employee should agree on how (phone call, visit, memo, or detailed report) and when (daily, weekly, or after specific steps are completed but before going on to the next step) the employee will provide information regarding the assignment. When establishing control, consider the employee's capability level. The lower the capability, the more frequent the checks; the higher the capability, the less frequent the checks. All parties involved should note the control checkpoints on their calendars.

MODEL 7-1   THE DELEGATION PROCESS

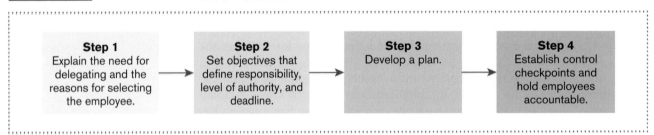

Step 1 Explain the need for delegating and the reasons for selecting the employee.

Step 2 Set objectives that define responsibility, level of authority, and deadline.

Step 3 Develop a plan.

Step 4 Establish control checkpoints and hold employees accountable.

The four steps of the delegation process are summarized in Model 7–1. In Skill Builder 7–3 at the end of this chapter, you will practice using the delegation process so you can develop your delegation skills.

Having completed this chapter, you should understand the differences between mechanistic and organic organizations and the principles of organization, authority, departmentalization, job design, and how to set priorities and delegate tasks.

• • • CHAPTER SUMMARY

7-1. Explain the difference between mechanistic and organic organizations and the environments in which they are more effective.

Mechanistic organizations are bureaucratic, focusing on following procedures and rules through tight controls, and have specialized jobs, with decisions being made by top managers. Conversely, *organic organizations* are flexible, with minimal focus on procedures and rules, and have broadly defined jobs, with decisions being made at lower levels. Mechanistic organization tends to be effective in stable environments, whereas organic organization tends to work well in dynamic environments.

7-2. Discuss the difference between formal and informal authority and centralized and decentralized authority.

Formal authority involves sanctioned relationships and ways of getting the job done, whereas informal authority involves unsanctioned relationships and ways of getting the job done. With centralized authority, top managers make important decisions; with decentralized authority, middle and first-line managers make important decisions.

7-3. List and briefly explain the four levels of authority.

(1) *The authority to inform*—the person simply presents alternatives. (2) *The authority to recommend*—the person presents alternatives and suggests one. (3) *The authority to report*—the person takes action and then tells the boss. (4) *Full authority*—the person takes action and does not have to tell the boss about it.

7-4. Explain what an organization chart is and list the four aspects of a firm that it shows.

An organization chart is a graphic illustration of the organization's management hierarchy and departments and their working relationships. It shows the level of management hierarchy, chain of command, division and type of work, and departmentalization.

7-5. Discuss the difference between internal and external departmentalization.

Internal departmentalization focuses on functions performed within the organization and the resources needed to accomplish the work; this type is also known as functional departmentalization. External departmentalization can be based on the organization's product(s), its customers, or the territories in which the organization does business.

7-6. Explain the difference between job simplification and job expansion.

Job simplification is used to make jobs more specialized by eliminating or combining tasks and/or changing the sequence of work. Job expansion is used to make jobs less specialized by rotating employees, enlarging the job, and/or enriching the job to make it more interesting and challenging.

7-7. Explain how to set priorities by answering three priority questions and determining whether activities have high, medium, or low priority.

A manager first answers yes or no to the three priority questions: (1) Do I need to be personally involved because of my unique knowledge or skills? (2) Is the task my responsibility, or will it affect the performance or finances of my department? (3) When is the deadline—is quick action needed? Depending on the answers to these questions, the manager delegates the task or assigns it a high, medium, or low level of priority.

7-8. List the four steps in the delegation process.

The steps in the delegation process are (1) explain the need for delegating and the reasons for selecting the employee; (2) set objectives that define responsibility, level of authority, and deadline; (3) develop a plan; and (4) establish control checkpoints and hold employees accountable.

• • • KEY TERMS

authority, 188
centralized authority, 190
decentralized authority, 190
delegation, 188
departmentalization, 193
divisional structure, 195
job characteristics model, 200

job design, 197
job enrichment, 199
levels of authority, 190
line authority, 191
mechanistic organizations, 186
micromanagement, 191
organic organizations, 186

organization chart, 192
priority-determination questions, 202
responsibility, 188
span of management, 187
staff authority, 191

••• Key Term Review

Complete each of the following statements using one of this chapter's key terms.

1. _____ are bureaucratic, focusing on following procedures and rules through tight controls, and have specialized jobs, with decisions being made by top managers.

2. _____ are flexible, with minimal focus on procedures and rules, and have broadly defined jobs, with decisions being made at lower levels.

3. The _____ refers to the number of employees reporting to a manager.

4. _____ is the obligation to achieve objectives by performing required activities.

5. _____ is the right to make decisions, issue orders, and use resources.

6. _____ is the process of assigning responsibility and authority for accomplishing objectives.

7. The _____ are the authority to inform, the authority to recommend, the authority to report, and full authority.

8. With _____, important decisions are made by top managers.

9. With _____, important decisions are made by middle and first-line managers.

10. _____ is a management style generally used as a negative term for when a manager closely observes or controls the work of his or her employees.

11. _____ is the responsibility to make decisions and issue orders down the chain of command.

12. _____ is the responsibility to advise and assist other personnel.

13. An _____ is a graphic illustration of an organization's management hierarchy and departments and their working relationships.

14. _____ is the grouping of related activities into units.

15. A _____ departmentalizes based on semiautonomous strategic business units.

16. _____ is the process of identifying tasks that each employee is responsible for completing.

17. _____ is the process of building motivators into a job to make it more interesting and challenging.

18. The _____ is a conceptual framework for designing or enriching jobs that focuses on core job dimensions, psychological states of employees, and the strength of employees' need for growth.

19. _____ are questions that help determine the priority of tasks to be completed.

••• Review Questions

1. What is the difference between unity of command and unity of direction?

2. What is the relationship between the chain of command and the span of management?

3. What do the terms *differentiation* and *integration* mean?

4. What is the difference between responsibility and authority?

5. Can accountability be delegated?

6. How does the scope of authority change throughout an organization, and what is the flow of responsibility, authority, and accountability?

7. What is the difference between general staff and specialist staff?

8. What type of authority is needed to make decisions and issue orders down the chain of command?

9. What does an organization chart show? What doesn't it show?

10. What is the difference between product and customer departmentalization?

11. What type of organizations commonly use functional departmentalization?

12. What is the difference between a network structure and a virtual organization?

13. What is job design, and why is it necessary?

14. What is the difference between an integrated work team and a self-managed work team?

15. Why is the strength of employees' need for growth important to the job characteristics model?

16. Why is it important to update priorities on a to-do list?

17. As a simple guide, what one question can a manager ask to determine what and what not to delegate?

18. Why is each of the four steps in the delegation process necessary?

••• COMMUNICATION SKILLS

The following critical-thinking questions can be used for class discussion and/or as written assignments to develop communication skills. Be sure to give complete explanations for all questions.

1. Does formal organizational structure really matter? In other words, shouldn't management just focus on getting the work done?

2. How is division of labor (specialization of jobs) used in the medical profession and in schools? How does the restaurant industry use specialization?

3. Is centralized or decentralized authority better?

4. As firms grow, should they have division of labor and add staff positions? Give examples with your answer.

5. Historian Alfred Chandler suggested that structure should follow strategy. Should a firm develop the strategy first and then develop the organization structure? Why or why not?

6. Matrix departmentalization violates the unity-of-command principle. Should companies not use matrix departmentalization?

7. What impact does technology have on organizational structure?

8. Why has there been a trend toward more team, network, virtual, and learning organizations? Is this a fad, or will it last?

9. When focusing on jobs, is it better to use job simplification or job expansion?

10. Are setting priorities and delegating really all that important?

••• CASE: ORGANIZATION AT COSTCO WAREHOUSES

Does your family shop at Costco? If so, it is quite an exciting experience! $1.50 will buy you a long hot dog and all the soft drink you desire. The products are in jumbo-sized boxes that seem to scream for the customer to buy everything. Product is piled up high into the rafters and stored for future sales. Product demonstrations and samples appear around every corner. It is sort of like having the fun of Disney World without all the expenses.

But how does Costco perform so well in such a tough retail environment? It stays focused and keeps everything organized. The employees become more like your friends since they stay with Costco because they are treated so well by the company.

But doesn't the competition do the same thing? What is Costco's secret? Here are a few possible answers.

First, 88 percent of Costco employees have company-sponsored health insurance; Walmart says that only "more than half" of its employees have company-sponsored health insurance. Costco workers with coverage pay premiums that amount to less than 10 percent of the overall cost of their plans. Costco treats its employees well in the belief that a happier work environment will result in a more profitable company. "I just think people need to make a living wage with health benefits," says CEO Craig Jelinek. "It also puts more money back into the economy and creates a healthier country. It's really that simple."[52]

Second, Costco is very frugal. You are not going to find plush offices either at their headquarters or at the stores. Their stores are fun to shop at—but they still look like traditional warehouses. It can be quite cold eating a hot dog and drinking a soda while there is a cold breeze coming through the open warehouse doors.

A key turning point came when Costco merged with the Price Club in 1993.[53] Although Price Club was around before Costco, the image and performance of Costco were so positive that it was worth combining the two organizational structures into one larger organization. Although the management teams conflicted at first, they quickly realized both companies liked building stripped-down warehouses to win over customers with bulk purchases.

Third, the CEO receives a fair pay—but not excessive compared to Walmart. Costco's CEOs have been true leaders in their desire to also have a higher pay then normal for their employees at the lower levels of the organizational structure. Costco employees earn $20.00 an hour, which dramatically reduces employee turnover versus their competitors.[54]

Last, Costco charges about $100 a membership to shop at its stores. Customers enjoy their Costco experience so much that they do not even complain about having to buy a membership!

You can watch a video of Costco's success at http://www.businessweek.com/videos/2013-05-30/what-is-costcos-secret-to-success.

Case Questions

1. Does Costco appear to follow the unity-of-command principle of organization?

2. Did the organizational change of buying the Price Club affect the chain of command by making it a flat organization?

3. Why was coordination probably the most important principle of organization in Costco's merger with Price Club?

4. Does Costco's organizational structure reflect centralized or decentralized authority?

5. Based on Chandler's theory, how has strategy at Costco affected its structure?

6. Would Costco be considered a learning organization? Why or why not?

7. How can Costco use the job characteristics model?

Cumulative Case Questions

8. Which environmental forces affected Costco's decision to change its strategy and structure? (Chapter 2)

9. Is the use of the decision-making model appropriate in deciding how to change Costco? (Chapter 3)

10. What are Costco's strategies at the corporate and business levels? (Chapter 4)

• • • SKILL BUILDER 7–1: SETTING PRIORITIES

Objective

To improve your skill at setting priorities.

Skills

The primary skills developed through this exercise are:

1. *Management skill*—decision making (setting priorities is based on conceptual skills)

2. *AACSB competencies*—analytic skills and reflective thinking skills

3. *Management function*—organizing (resources and time)

Preparing for Skill Builder 7–1

For this exercise, assume that you are the first-line manager of a production department in a large company. Read the to-do list containing 10 tasks that accompanies this exercise and assign priorities to each task by following the steps below. (Note: The 10 tasks have been numbered for you. When you make a to-do list for your own tasks, we recommend that you not number them.)

1. Answer the three priority-determination questions by placing a Y for yes or N for no in the columns labeled 1, 2, and 3. Because you are not the top manager of this department, do not fill in the deadline/time-needed column.

2. Assign a priority to the task by placing the letter D (delegate), H (high), M (medium), or L (low) in the priority column. Use the list at the top left to determine the priority based on the answers to the priority questions.

3. Determine which task to complete first. You may have more than one high priority, so select the most important one to do first.

Apply It

What did I learn from this experience? How will I use this knowledge in the future?

Prioritized To-Do List		Priority-Determination Questions				
		#1	#2	#3	4	5
D Delegate priority	(N) No to question 1	Do I need to be personally involved?	Is it my responsibility, or will it affect the performance or finances of my department?	Is quick action needed?	Deadline/time needed	Priority
H High priority	(YYY) Yes to all three questions					
M Medium priority	(YNY or YYN) Yes to question 1 and No to question 2 or 3					
L Low priority	(YNN) Yes to question 1 and No to questions 2 and 3					
Task						
1. Tom, the sales manager, tells you that three customers stopped doing business with your company because your products have decreased in quality. As production manager, it is your job to meet with the production crew and determine how to solve this problem.						

Prioritized To-Do List	Priority-Determination Questions				
	#1	#2	#3	4	5
2. Your secretary, Michele, tells you that there is a salesperson waiting to see you. He does not have an appointment. You don't do any purchasing.					
3. Molly, a vice president, wants to see you to discuss a new product to be introduced in one month.					
4. Tom, the sales manager, sent you a memo stating that the sales forecast was incorrect. Sales are expected to increase by 20 percent starting next month. Inventory must be increased to meet the unexpected sales forecast.					
5. Dan, the personnel director, sent you a memo informing you that one of your employees has resigned. Your turnover rate is one of the highest in the company.					
6. Michele tells you that someone named Bob Furry called while you were out. He asked you to return his call but wouldn't state why he was calling. You don't know who he is or what he wants.					
7. Phil, one of your best workers, wants an appointment to tell you about an incident that happened in the shop.					
8. Tom calls and asks you to meet with him and a prospective customer for your product. The customer wants to meet you.					
9. John, your boss, calls and asks to see you about the decrease in the quality of your product.					
10. In the mail you got a note from Randolf, the president of your company, and an article from *The Wall Street Journal*. The note says FYI (for your information).					

• • • SKILL BUILDER 7–2: ORGANIZATIONAL STRUCTURE AT YOUR COLLEGE

This exercise enables you to apply the organizing concepts discussed in the chapter to your college or university as an individual and/or group.

Objective

To better understand organizational structures.

Skills

The primary skills developed through this exercise are:

1. *Management skill*—decision making (organizing requires conceptual skills)

2. *AACSB competencies*—analytic skills and reflective thinking skills

3. *Management function*—organizing (at all levels of the organization)

Preparing for Skill Builder 2

Your professor will select the university, college, school, or department level of analysis for this exercise. Based on the level, answer the following questions to analyze the organization. You may need to interview some administrators or faculty members to get answers.

1. Refer to Exhibit 7–2. How are the principles of organization followed? (Be sure to include the span of management and division of labor.)

2. Identify line and staff positions. Is authority centralized or decentralized? Identify line and staff positions.

3. What type of departmentalization is used? Draw a simple organizational chart.

4. Describe the job design of faculty members.

5. Identify some of the current priorities and types of assignments delegated.

_____

_____

Apply It

What did I learn from this experience? How will I use this knowledge in the future?

• • • SKILL BUILDER 7–3: DELEGATING

Objective

To develop delegating skills.

Skills

The primary skills developed through this exercise are:

1. *Management skill*—decision making (organizing requires assigning work through delegation)

2. *AACSB competencies*—analytic skills and reflective thinking skills

3. *Management function*—organizing

Preparing for Skill Builder 7–3

Before beginning this exercise, review the text material on delegating.

Procedure

Work in groups of three. Each person in the group will role play delegating one of the following three tasks to another member of the group, following the steps described in the text (explaining, setting objectives, and developing a plan). The third group member will observe and evaluate the delegation of the task; an evaluation form appears at the end of this exercise. Members then switch roles for the second task and again for the third. By the end of the exercise, each person in the group will have delegated a task, received an assignment, and observed the delegation of a task. (Note that in the real world, the process would not end with the delegation of the task. As a manager, you would establish control checkpoints to ensure that the task was completed as required.) After each person in the group has delegated a task, the group should discuss how effectively he or she delegated.

Delegation Task 1

Delegator: You are a college student with a paper due in three days. You have handwritten 20 pages, but they must be typed. You don't type well, so you have decided to hire someone to do it for you. The going rate is $1.50 per page. Be sure to include the course name, paper title, special typing instructions, and so on. Assume that you are meeting the typist for the first time and that he or she doesn't know you.

Receiver of the assignment: Assume that you are willing to do the job.

Delegation Task 2

Delegator: You are the manager of a fast-food restaurant. In the past, you have set workers' schedules, and your policy has been to continually vary them. You have decided to delegate the scheduling to your assistant manager. This person has never done any scheduling but appears to be very willing and confident about taking on new responsibility.

Receiver of the assignment: Assume that you are interested in doing the scheduling if the manager delegates the task.

Delegation Task 3

Delegator: You own and manage your own business. You have eight employees, one of whom is the organization's secretary. The secretary presently uses an old desktop computer, which needs to be replaced. You can afford to spend up to $1,000 for a new computer. Because the secretary will use the new machine, you believe that this employee should be involved in, or maybe even make, the decision. The secretary has never purchased equipment for the company, and you believe the person will be somewhat insecure about the assignment.

Receiver of the assignment: Assume that you are able to do the job but are somewhat insecure.

Evaluation Form

Each group should use three copies of this form: one for the observer, one for the person filling the role of delegator, and one for the person filling the role of receiver of the assignment. (The three forms should be labeled somehow, perhaps with O for observer, D for delegator, and R for receiver.) As one person in the group is delegating a task, the observer checks the steps that the delegator accomplishes. On another copy of the form, the delegator of the task checks those steps he or she believes are accomplished. On the third copy of this form, the receiver of the assignment checks those steps the delegator accomplishes. (When group members change roles for the next delegation task, they should exchange evaluation forms so that each person has the form appropriate to his or her role.) Discuss the questions below after each delegation situation. (The discussion should focus on any discrepancies between the evaluations of the three group members.)

Did the delegator follow these steps in the delegation model 7.1?	Task		
	1	2	3
Step 1. Explain the need for delegating and the reason for selecting the employee.			
Step 2. Set an objective that defines responsibility and level of authority, and set a deadline.			
Step 3. Develop a plan—was it effective?			
Step 4. Where there any checkpoints and was the person held accountable?			

Did the receiver of the assignment clearly understand what was expected and how to follow the plan?

How could the delegation be improved?

Apply It

What did I learn from this experience? How will I use this knowledge in the future?

• • • SKILL BUILDER 7-4: JOB SIMPLIFICATION

Objective

To improve your skills at job simplification.

Skills

The primary skills developed through this exercise are:

1. *Management skill*—decision making (organizing requires designing jobs)
2. *AACSB competencies*—analytic skills and reflective thinking skills
3. *Management function*—organizing

Preparing for Skill Builder 7-4

For this exercise, you will use job simplification for your morning routine by following the steps below.

1. Make a flowchart by listing exactly what you do every morning from the time you get out of bed until the time you get to school/work in step-by-step order. Be sure to number each step and to list each activity separately. (For example, don't just write "Go to the bathroom," but list each activity you do while in the bathroom to prep for the day—shower, shave, brush teeth, comb hair, etc.)

2. At the end of the day (or whenever you have some free time), do a job simplification analysis of your flowchart to see if there are any activities you can eliminate, combine, and/or change the sequence of.

3. Based on your analysis, develop a new flowchart that eliminates, combines, and/or changes the sequence of the tasks you typically perform every morning.

4. Consciously follow the steps of your new flowchart until it becomes routine.

Apply It

What did I learn from this experience? How will I use this knowledge in the future?

• • • STUDENT STUDY SITE

Visit the Student Study Site at **www.sagepub.com/lussier6e** to access to these additional study tools:

- Mobile-compatible self-assessment quizzes
- Mobile-compatible key term flashcards
- Video Links
- SAGE Journal Articles
- Web Links

8 Managing Team Work

• • • Learning Outcomes

After studying this chapter, you should be able to:

IDEAS ON MANAGEMENT at W. L. Gore & Associates

W. L. Gore & Associates is a uniquely inventive, technology-driven enterprise focused on discovery and product innovation. Its best-known product is GORE-TEX® (a waterproof, breathable, windproof fabric), but by using proprietary technologies with the versatile polymer polytetrafluoroethylene (PTFE), Gore has created numerous products for electronic signal transmission, fabric laminates, and medical implants, as well as membrane, filtration, sealant, and fiber technologies for diverse industries. You may use Glide® dental floss, you most likely have heard music played on its Elixir® guitar strings, and you may have enjoyed static-free cell phone calls courtesy of the Gore SnapSHOT® electromagnetic-interference shield.

The company was founded in Newark, Delaware, by Wilbert L. (Bill) and Genevieve (Vieve) Gore. Gore remains a privately held company, with sales now exceeding $3 billion. It was ranked eighth on the World's Best Multinational Workplaces list by the Great Place to Work® Institute. Gore has been repeatedly named among the 100 Best Companies to Work For by *Fortune* magazine, and its culture is a model for contemporary organizations seeking growth by unleashing creativity and fostering teamwork. Much of Gore's innovative success comes from the power of its small, self-managing teams' organizational structure.

1. How does W. L. Gore & Associates benefit from the use of groups and teams? PAGE 218
2. How does W. L. Gore's group structure facilitate teamwork? PAGE 222
3. How is group process managed at W. L. Gore? PAGE 227
4. What programs are in place at W. L. Gore to foster group development? PAGE 231
5. How does W. L. Gore ensure productive meetings? PAGE 236

••• Chapter Outline

Teams and the Lessons of the Geese

Groups and Teams and Performance

    Groups and Teams

    The Group Performance Model

Group Structure

    Group Types

    Group Size

    Group Composition

    Group Leadership and Objectives

Group Process

    Group Roles

    Group Norms

    Group Cohesiveness

    Status Within the Group

    Decision Making and Conflict Resolution

Stages of Group Development and Management Styles

    Stage 1. Forming—Autocratic

    Stage 2. Storming—Consultative

    Stage 3. Norming—Participative

    Stage 4. Performing—Empowerment

    Stage 5. Termination

    Changes in Group Development and Management Style

Developing Groups Into Teams

    Training and the Management Functions

    Team Rewards and Recognition

Managing Meetings

    Planning Meetings

    Conducting Meetings

    Handling Problem Members

You'll find answers to these questions about groups and teams at W. L. Gore throughout the chapter.

To learn more about W. L. Gore, visit its website at www.gore.com.

Source: Information for this case was taken from the W. L. Gore & Associates website at http://www.gore.com, accessed July 6, 2013; R. E. Silverman, "Who's the Boss? There Isn't One," *Wall Street Journal* (June 20, 2012): B1, B8.

TEAMS AND THE LESSONS OF THE GEESE

Refer to Chapter 4, Exhibit 4-4 for the list of advantages and disadvantages of using groups and when it is appropriate to use a group to make decisions. In this chapter, we focus on using teamwork. As discussed in the last chapter, companies are adopting team-based organizational designs[1] and relying on small teams to perform critical tasks.[2] Therefore, having teamwork skills is important to your career as a team member,[3] and to succeed in management, you have to be able to build great teams.[4] Teamwork skills are based on your ability to develop relationships. So through this chapter and the rest of the book, you can improve your teamwork skills and your ability to manage teams. But first, let's learn the lessons of the geese that can help us.

You've no doubt seen geese heading south for the winter flying in a V formation, and so you might be interested in knowing what scientists have discovered about why they fly that way:

1. As each bird flaps its wings, it creates uplift for the bird following. By flying in a V formation, the flock's flying range is 71 percent greater than if each bird flew on its own.

   Lesson: People who share a common direction and sense of community can get where they are going quicker and easier because they are easing the trip for one another.

2. Whenever a goose falls out of formation, it suddenly is affected by the drag and resistance of trying to go it alone and quickly gets back into formation to take advantage of the lifting power of the bird immediately in front.

   Lesson: Traveling in the same direction as others with whom we share a common goal provides strength, power, and safety in numbers.

3. When the lead goose gets tired, it falls back into the formation and another goose flies point.

   Lesson: It pays to take turns doing the hard jobs.

4. The geese toward the back honk to encourage those up front to keep up their speed.

   Lesson: We all need to be encouraged with active support and praise.

5. When a goose gets sick or is wounded and falls out, two geese fall out of formation and follow the first one down. They stay with the downed goose until the crisis resolves, and then they launch on their own to catch up with their group or join another formation.

   Lesson: We must stand by each other in times of need.

GROUPS AND TEAMS AND PERFORMANCE

AACSB's (Chapter 1) necessary competencies include team skills,[5] so colleges are developing teamwork skills.[6] Teams are the backbone of organizations because of

WORK
APPLICATION 8-1

Consider your present job or a past job. Did you work in a group or a team? Explain, using each of the six characteristics in Exhibit 8–1. Note: You may want to select one job and use it to answer the work applications throughout this chapter.

8-1 SELF ASSESSMENT

Are You A Team Player?

Rate each of the following statements by placing a number from 1 to 5 on the line. Use the scale below.

Describes me				Does not describe me
5	4	3	2	1

_____ 1. I focus on what I accomplish during team projects.
_____ 2. I don't like to compromise.
_____ 3. I depend on myself to get ahead.
_____ 4. I prefer to work alone rather than in a group when I have a choice.
_____ 5. I like to do things my way.
_____ 6. I do things myself to make sure the job gets done right.
_____ 7. I know that teams do better when each member has a particular contribution to make.
_____ 8. I'm more productive when I work alone.
_____ 9. I try to get things done my way when I work with others.
_____ 10. It bothers me if I can't get the group to do things my way.

Add the numbers you assigned to the statements, and place the total on the continuum below.

Individual							Team Player	
50	45	40	35	30	25	20	15	10

the systems effect: each group/department is affected by at least one other group and each department affects the performance of the total organization. In this section, we discuss the differences between groups and teams, some factors that affect group performance, and the effects of organizational context on performance. First, complete Self-Assessment 8–1 to determine if you are a team player.

Groups and Teams

Although the terms *group* and *team* are used interchangeably, a distinction can be made between them. A **group** *has two or more members with a clear leader who perform independent jobs with individual accountability, evaluation, and rewards.* A **team** *has a small number of members with shared leadership who perform interdependent jobs with individual and group accountability, evaluation, and rewards.* So teams are interdependent individuals who share responsibility for outcomes.[7] The team sets the standards.[8]

Distinctions between groups and teams and their levels of autonomy are presented in Exhibit 8-1. As shown at the bottom of the exhibit, groups and teams are on a continuum; it's not always easy to make a clear distinction. The terms *management-directed, semiautonomous,* and *self-managed* (or *self-directed*) are commonly used to differentiate along the continuum. Management-directed is clearly a group, self-directed is clearly a team, and semiautonomous is between the two. With management-directed groups, there is a clear boss, but with self-directed teams, there is no one boss or everyone is the boss.[9] **Haier Group** in China uses self-managed units.[10] All teams are groups, but not all groups are teams.

LO 8-1

Describe the major differences between groups and teams.

group Two or more members with a clear leader who perform independent jobs with individual accountability, evaluation, and rewards.

team A small number of members with shared leadership who perform interdependent jobs with both individual and group accountability, evaluation, and rewards.

EXHIBIT 8-1   GROUPS VERSUS TEAMS

Characteristics	Group	Team
Size	Two or more; can be large	Small number, often 5 to 12
Leadership	One clear leader making decisions	Shared leadership
Jobs	Members perform one clear job individual members do one independent part of a process and pass it on to next person to do the next part.	Members share job responsibility by performing many interdependent tasks with complementary skills; the team completes an entire process.
Accountability and Evaluation	Leader evaluates individual members' performance	Members evaluate each other's individual performance and group performance
Rewards	Members are rewarded based on individual performance only	Members are rewarded for both individual and group performance
Objectives	Organizational	Organizational and those set by the team

Level of Autonomy

Group Management-Directed	Semiautonomous	Team Self-Directed

$\longleftrightarrow$

8-1   APPLYING THE CONCEPT

Group or Team

Identify each statement as characteristic of a group or a team.

A. a group
B. a team

____ 1. "There are about 30 people in my department."
____ 2. "Only my boss conducts my performance appraisals, and I get good ratings."
____ 3. "We don't have any departmental goal; we just do the best we can to accomplish the mission."
____ 4. "Most of my compensation is paid in bonuses that are based primarily on my department's performance."
____ 5. "I get the assembled product from Jean; then I paint it and send it to Tony for packaging."

LO 8-2

Explain the group performance model.

group performance model Group performance is a function of organizational context, group structure, group process, and group development stage.

The Group Performance Model

The performance of groups is based on four major factors. According to the **group performance model**, *group performance is a function of organizational context, group structure, group process, and group development stage.* The group performance model is illustrated in Exhibit 8-2. A number of overall organizational and environmental factors affect how groups function and their level of performance. These organizational context factors have been discussed in prior chapters and are listed in the exhibit. The other three factors affecting group performance are covered in detail in the following sections.

The organizational structure at **Gore (Case Question 1)** is team based. Teams set objectives and are responsible for achieving them. Team members select new members, and twice each year team members rank each other based on who is adding the most value to the company, which affects individual pay raises. In addition, Gore rewards all associates (they are not called employees) with profit sharing and stock options.

EXHIBIT 8-2   GROUP PERFORMANCE MODEL

Group Performance Is a Function of			
Organizational Context	**Group Structure**	**Group Process**	**Group Developmental Stage**
Environment	Type	Roles	Forming
Mission	Size	Norms	Storming
Strategy	Composition	Cohesiveness	Norming
Culture	Leadership	Status	Performing
Structure	Objectives	Decision making	Terminating
Systems and processes		Conflict resolution	

GROUP STRUCTURE

Group structure dimensions include *group type, size, composition, leadership,* and *objectives.* Each of these five components of group structure is described in this section.

Group Types

There are different types of groups.[11] **Group types** *are formal or informal, functional or cross-functional, and command or task.*

Formal or Informal Groups. *Formal groups,* such as departments and their smaller subparts, are created by an organization as part of its formal structure. All employees have formal group membership and the higher in the organization, the more formal groups the manager is a member of.[12] Some large companies have formal top management teams.[13] *Informal groups* are not created by the organization as part of the formal structure. They are created spontaneously when members join together voluntarily because of similar interests.

Functional or Cross-Functional Groups. The members of *functional,* or vertical, *groups* perform jobs within one limited area. A work unit or department is a functional group. Marketing, finance, operations, and human resources departments are functional groups. The members of *cross-functional,* or horizontal, *groups* come from different areas and possibly different levels of an organization, and they are on the increase, including at **Haier Group.**[14] Generally, the higher the management level, the more cross-functional the responsibility.

Each manager in the organization serves as the link to other groups. Ideally, all functional groups coordinate their activities through the aid of the managers, who are responsible for linking the activities together. Rensis Likert calls this the *linking-pin role.* It is also called *intergroup leadership.*[15] Exhibit 8-3 illustrates functional and cross-functional groups with managers acting as linking pins.

Command or Task Groups. **Command groups** *consist of managers and the employees they supervise.* People are usually hired to be a part of a command group. Command groups are distinguished by department membership as functional or cross-functional. In Exhibit 8-3, the president and the vice presidents are a cross-functional command group, whereas each vice president and the managers reporting to him or her form a functional command group.

LO 8-3

List and explain the three dimensions of group types.

WORK APPLICATION 8-2

Identify task groups used in an organization you work for or have worked for. Specify whether each group is a task force or a standing committee.

group structure dimensions Group type, size, composition, leadership, and objectives.

group types Formal or informal, functional or cross-functional, and command or task.

command groups Groups that consist of managers and the employees they supervise.

EXHIBIT 8-3 FUNCTIONAL AND CROSS-FUNCTIONAL GROUPS

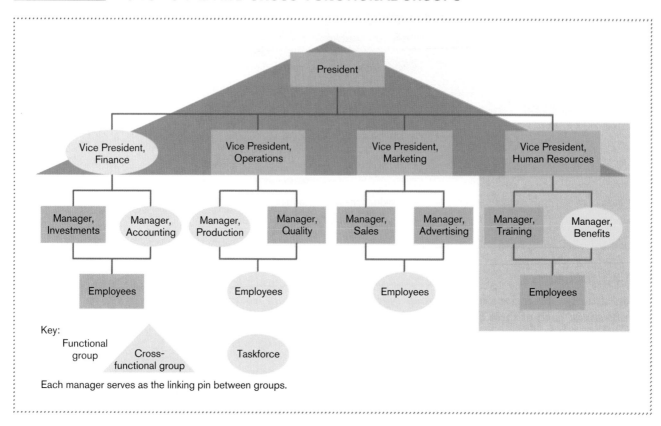

Key:

Functional group

Cross-functional group

Taskforce

Each manager serves as the linking pin between groups.

Task groups *consist of employees selected to work on a specific objective.* There are two primary types of task groups: task forces and standing committees.

A *task force,* or *ad hoc committee,* is a temporary group formed for a specific purpose. *Project teams,* which use a matrix structure (Chapter 7), are a form of task group in which employees have a functional boss and work with cross-functional departments as needed. The purpose of the task force highlighted in Exhibit 8-3 is to select three top candidates to present to the board of directors as potential replacements for the current president, who will retire in six months. This task force has members from all the functional areas in the company.

A *standing committee* is a permanent task group that works on continuing organizational issues. Membership on standing committees is often rotated every year so that new ideas are brought to the group. For example, membership may be for three years, with one third of the committee replaced every year.

There are a couple of major differences between a command group and a task group. Command group members tend to be from the same functional area, whereas task groups are often cross functional. In addition, everyone in an organization belongs to a command group, but employees may work for an organization for many years without ever being a member of a cross-functional task group. Generally, the higher the level of management, the more time is spent in task groups and their meetings.

Global Virtual Teams. The trends toward globalization and teamwork have led to the emergence of global virtual teams. The members of **global virtual teams** *are*

task groups Employees selected to work on a specific objective.

physically located in different places but work together as a team. Advances in information and telecommunications technologies are allowing new ways of structuring, processing, and distributing work and overcoming the barriers of distance and time. Team members anywhere in the world in any time zone can work together on projects. However, distance and time zones can cause coordination issues because of differing work schedules, holidays, and vacations. Billie Williamson, a partner at **Ernst & Young**, has been managing virtual teams for more than a decade.

Technology makes it easier for virtual teams to work together effectively. Globalization means that the need for global virtual teams will increase, especially for multinational corporate employees. Photo from Comstock/ Thinkstock.

Group Size

There Is No Ideal Group Size. The ideal number varies depending on the purpose, situation, and type of work performed. Groups tend to be larger than teams. At **Titeflex**, teams of 6 to 10 people manufacture fluid and gas-holding systems. **EDS** has project teams of 8 to 12 members. **Johnsonville Foods** uses self-managed teams of around 12.

A group that is too small limits ideas and creativity. It tends to be too cautious, and the workload is not distributed over enough members. On the other hand, a group that is too large tends to be too slow, and not everyone gets to participate. With 20 or more members, there are too many members to reach consensus on many decisions, and members tend to form subgroups. In large groups, *free-riding* (also called *social loafing*) is also a problem. Free-riding occurs when members rely on others to carry their share of the workload.

How Size Affects Management. The appropriate leadership style may depend on group size. The larger the size, the more formal or autocratic the leadership needs to be to provide direction. Managers tend to be more informal and participative when they have smaller teams. Group members are more tolerant of and, at times, even appreciative of autocratic leadership in large groups. Larger groups tend to inhibit equal participation. Generally, participation is more equal in groups of around five. This is why teams are small. The larger the group (department), the greater the need for formal and structured plans, policies, procedures, and rules.

Management Implications. Usually, managers have no say in the size of their command groups. However, if you have a large department, you can break this larger group into teams. As the chair of a committee, you may be able to select the group size. Remember that people are more willing to express their opinions, concerns, and ideas in smaller groups.[16] In doing so, keep the group size appropriate for the task and be sure to get the right group composition.

Group Composition

Group composition *is the mix of members' skills and abilities.* Regardless of type and size, group or team performance is affected by the composition.[17] Without the right mix of skills and abilities, a group will not perform at high levels.[18] Recall from Chapter 3 that diversity provides group benefits.[19]

group composition The mix of members' skills and abilities.

global virtual teams Teams whose members are physically located in different places but work together as a team.

Management Implications. One of the most important group leadership functions is to attract, select, and retain the best people for the job. When selecting group or team members, be sure to include diverse individuals. You want members with

8-1 JOIN THE DISCUSSION ETHICS & SOCIAL RESPONSIBILITY

Team Players

JetBlue Airways is not structured around teams. However, teamwork skills and attitudes are important to the success of JetBlue. In fact, JetBlue screens job candidates extensively to make sure that they are team players.

1. Is it necessary to be a team player to be a successful employee at JetBlue?
2. Is it ethical and socially responsible of JetBlue to reject job candidates because they are considered not to be team players?

complementary skills rather than people with the same skills. Cross-functional teams are likely to provide diversity and complementary skills.

Group Leadership and Objectives

Leadership. To a large extent, the leader determines group structure. Exhibit 8-1 pointed out that the leadership style is different in groups and teams. The quality of team leadership, whether from the formal leaders or other team members (like you), is becoming increasingly important as it affects team performance.[20] You will learn more about group and team leadership and managing teams throughout this chapter.

Objectives. In Chapter 5, you learned the benefits of setting objectives; they apply to both individuals and groups, and teams set their own objectives. In groups, however, the objective is commonly very broad—usually to fulfill the mission.

Management Implications. Part of a leader's responsibility is to be sure the size and composition of a group or team is appropriate for the situation. As a group or team leader or as a member with leadership skills, be sure that the group or team has clear objectives.

In summary, group structure dimensions include group type, size, composition, leadership, and objectives. Exhibit 8-4 reviews group structure dimensions.

How associates work at **Gore (Case Question 2)** sets them apart. It is a *team-based, flat lattice organization*. There are no traditional organizational charts, no chains of command, and no predetermined channels of communication. It's been called the bossless company. How does this work? Associates are hired for general work areas. With the guidance of their sponsors (not bosses), associates commit to projects that match their skills. Everyone can earn the credibility to define and drive projects. Sponsors help associates chart a course in the organization that will offer personal fulfillment while maximizing their contribution to the enterprise. Leaders may be appointed, but more often, leaders emerge naturally by demonstrating special knowledge, skill, or experience that advances a business objective.

GROUP PROCESS

Group process *refers to the patterns of interactions that emerge as members perform their jobs.* Group process is also called *group dynamics*. In Chapter 7, we discussed process consultation as an OD intervention, and here we describe group process as it affects team performance.[21] Bill Gates, cofounder of **Microsoft**, advises young people to learn to work with people—to develop group dynamics skills.[22] **Group process dimensions** *are roles, norms, cohesiveness, status, decision making, and conflict resolution.* These components are discussed in this section.

WORK
APPLICATION 8-3

Identify a group or team you belong to and describe its size, composition, leadership, and objectives.

group process The patterns of interactions that emerge as members perform their jobs.

group process dimensions Roles, norms, cohesiveness, status, decision making, and conflict resolution.

EXHIBIT 8-4 DIMENSIONS OF GROUP STRUCTURE

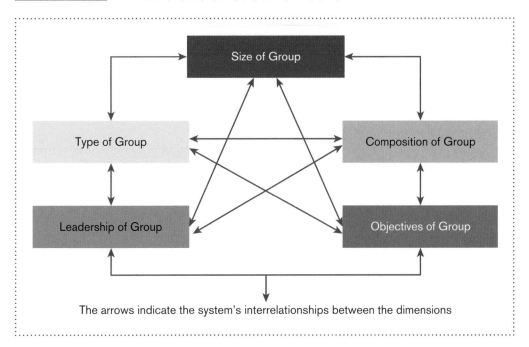

The arrows indicate the system's interrelationships between the dimensions

Group Roles

We have individual roles in groups,[23] and role structures emerge.[24] However, job and group roles are different. *Job roles* are shared expectations of how group members will fulfill the requirements of their position—what you do to get the job done—whereas group roles are the roles used through group process—how you interact as you work.

Classifying Group Roles. The three primary **group roles** *are group task roles, group maintenance roles, and self-interest roles.*

Group task roles are played by members who do and say things that directly aid in the accomplishment of the group's objectives. Task roles are often said to be structuring, job centered, production oriented, task oriented, or directive.

Group maintenance roles are played by members who do and say things to develop and sustain the group process. Terms used to describe maintenance roles include employee centered, relationship oriented, and supportive.

Self-interest roles are played by members who do and say things that help themselves.[25] Usually when group members put their own needs before those of the group, the performance of the group suffers.[26] Playing self-interest roles often is unethical behavior.[27] As a team member, watch for self-interest roles and hidden agendas and transcend your own self-interest for the sake of the team.[28] Learn to distinguish between self-interest that benefits both the individual and the organization (a win-win situation) and self-interest that benefits the individual and hurts the organization (a win-lose situation).

How Roles Affect Group Performance. To be effective, a group must have members who play task roles and maintenance roles while minimizing self-interest roles. Groups that have only task role players may suffer performance problems because they do not deal with conflict effectively and because the job will be boring if there is no maintenance. On the other hand, groups that have a great time but do not have members playing task roles will not get the job done. Any group whose members are mostly playing self-interest roles will not produce to its fullest potential.

LO 8-4

Define the three major roles played in groups.

group roles Group task roles, group maintenance roles, and self-interest roles.

WORK
APPLICATION 8-4

Identify members of a group or team you have been on and state the primary role each played in the group.

Management Implications. If you are a manager or team member, you should be aware of the roles the group members play. If no member is playing the task or maintenance role required at a given time, you should play the role. As the manager, you should also make the group aware of the need to play these roles and the need to minimize self-interest roles. Later in the chapter, you will learn about group development and how the leader should use task and maintenance roles to help the group develop.

8-2 | **APPLYING** THE CONCEPT

Roles

Identify the type of role exemplified in each statement.

A.   task
B.   maintenance
C.   self-interest

____ 6. "We tried that before you came to work here; it did not work. My idea is much better. So let's do it my way."

____ 7. "What does this have to do with the problem we are working on? We are getting sidetracked."

____ 8. "I like Tolo's idea better than mine. Let's go with his idea instead."

____ 9. "Wait. We can't make the decision because we haven't heard Karin's idea yet."

____ 10. "I don't understand. Could you explain why we are doing this again?"

LO 8-5

State the differences between rules and norms and how norms are enforced.

WORK
APPLICATION 8-5

Identify at least two norms that developed in a group/team of which you were a member. Explain how you knew they were norms and how the group enforced those norms.

norms Expectations about appropriate behavior that are shared by members of a group.

Group Norms

In addition to policies, procedures, and rules, all groups form their own unwritten norms that determine what is socially accepted as appropriate behavior.[29] Rules are formally established by management or by the group itself. Norms are not developed by management or explicitly agreed to by a group; they develop as members interact. Norms are also called unspoken rules of a group that shape behavior and attitudes.[30] **Norms** *are expectations about behavior that are shared by members of a group.*

How Norms Develop. Norms develop spontaneously as the members of a group interact and compare themselves to the other members.[31] For example, the group decides, without ever actually talking about it, what is an acceptable level of work. If the group members develop a shared expectation that a certain level is desirable, members will produce it. Or, for example, norms develop about whether the use of certain words (such as swear words) or unethical behavior is considered acceptable.[32] Norms can change over time to meet the needs of the group.

How Groups Enforce Norms. Breaking norms usually results in conflict.[33] If a group member does not follow a norm, the other members try to enforce compliance—in other words, *peer pressure*.[34] As we have all faced group pressure, we can understand how it is a powerful influence over our behavior.[35] For example, if Sal works at more than the accepted level of performance, other members may kid or ridicule him. If Sal continues to break the norm, members might ostracize him to enforce compliance with the norm. Members could also damage his work or take his tools or supplies to slow down his production. Sal could be considered an outsider of the group.[36]

8-2 JOIN THE DISCUSSION ETHICS & SOCIAL RESPONSIBILITY

Norms

Group members influence each other's behavior through the development and enforcement of norms—that is, essentially through peer pressure. In general, this process is positive, as it helps get the job done. On the other side, complying with illegal or unethical norms can lead to disasters, as it did at Enron.

1. Should employees be able to "do their own thing" without group enforcement of norms?
2. Is it ethical and socially responsible for groups to develop and enforce norms? If yes, what type of ethical standards should a group have?

Management Implications. Be aware that we tend to adjust our behaviors to try to match that of our team norms,[37] so be careful not to be lead into illegal or unethical behavior. Group norms can be positive, helping the group meet its objectives, or they can be negative, hindering the group from meeting its objectives. For example, if a company's production standard is 110 units per day, a group norm of 100 is a negative norm. However, if the standard were 90, it would be a positive norm. You should be aware of group norms and work toward maintaining and developing positive norms and try to eliminate negative norms. Managers should confront groups with negative norms and try to work out solutions to make them positive.

Group Cohesiveness

The extent to which members of a group abide by and enforce the group norms depends on the degree of loyalty and cohesiveness.[38] **Group cohesiveness** *is the extent to which members stick together.* The more cohesive the group, the more it sticks together—bonds—as a team.[39]

LO 8-6

Describe cohesiveness and explain why it is important to teams.

Factors Influencing Cohesiveness. Six factors influence group cohesiveness:

1. *Objectives.* The stronger the agreement with and commitment to the achievement of the group's objectives, the higher the cohesiveness of the group.
2. *Size.* Generally, the smaller the group, the higher the cohesiveness. Three to nine members seems to be a good group size for optimum cohesiveness.
3. *Homogeneity.* Generally, the more similar the group members are, the higher the cohesiveness. Although diverse groups have advantages (Chapter 3), differences can cause more conflict and reduce cohesion.[40]
4. *Participation.* Generally, the more equal the level of participation among members, the higher the group's cohesiveness.
5. *Competition.* Generally, if the group focuses on internal competition, its members will try to outdo each other and low cohesiveness results. If the group focuses on external competition, its members tend to pull together as a team.
6. *Success.* The more successful a group is at achieving its objectives, the more cohesive it tends to become.[41] Success tends to breed cohesiveness, which in turn breeds more success. People want to be on a winning team.

WORK
APPLICATION 8-6

Identify the level of cohesiveness in a group or team of which you are or have been a member.

How Cohesiveness Affects Group Performance. Cohesive groups tend to have a higher level of success at achieving their objectives with greater satisfaction. Members of

group cohesiveness The extent to which members stick together.

cohesive groups tend to miss work less often, are more trusting and cooperative, and have less tension and hostility. Cohesiveness is associated with performance in the following ways:

- Groups with the highest levels of productivity were highly cohesive and accepted management's level of productivity.
- Groups with the lowest levels of productivity were also highly cohesive but rejected management's level of productivity; they set and enforced their own level below that of management. This can happen in organizations where employees and managers have an "us against them" attitude.
- Groups with intermediate levels of productivity were low in cohesiveness irrespective of their acceptance of management's level of productivity. The widest variance of individual group members' performance was among the groups with lower cohesiveness. Members of such groups tended to be more tolerant of nonconformity to group norms.

Management Implications. As a team member or leader, you should strive to develop cohesive groups that exhibit a high level of productivity.[42] Encouraging group members' participation helps the group develop cohesiveness and builds agreement and commitment toward the group's objectives. Some intragroup competition may be helpful, but you should focus primarily on intergroup competition. Recall the advantages of managing a diverse group, and make efforts to develop a cohesive yet diversified group.

Status Within the Group

Ideally, as group members interact, they develop respect for one another on numerous dimensions. The more respect, prestige, influence, and power a group member has, the higher his or her status within the group.[43] **Status** *is the perceived ranking of one member relative to other members in the group.*

The Development of Status. Status is based on several factors, including members' performance, job title, wage or salary, seniority, knowledge or expertise, interpersonal skills, appearance, education, race, age, sex, and so on. Members who conform to the group's norms tend to have higher status than members who do not. A group is more willing to listen to a high-status member and to overlook such a member's breaking of the norms. High-status members also have more influence on the development of the group's norms and the decisions made by the group. Lower-status members' ideas are often ignored, and they tend to copy high-status members' behavior and to agree with their suggestions in order to be accepted.[44]

How Status Affects Group Performance. High-status members have a major impact on a group's performance.[45] In a command group, the boss is usually the member with the highest status. The leader's ability to manage affects the group performance. Other high-status members also affect performance. If high-status members support positive norms and high productivity, chances are the rest of the group will, too.

Another important factor influencing group performance is status congruence. *Status congruence* is the acceptance and satisfaction members receive from their group status. Members who are not satisfied with their status may not be active participants of the group. They may physically or mentally escape from the group and not perform to their full potential. Or they may cause group conflict as they fight for a higher status level.

status The perceived ranking of one member relative to other members in a group.

8-3 APPLYING THE CONCEPT

Group Process

Identify the dimension of the group process exemplified in each statement.

A. roles
B. norms
C. cohesiveness
D. status
E. decision making
F. conflict resolution

_____ 11. "When you need advice on how to do things, go see Carlos; he knows the ropes around here better than anyone."

_____ 12. "I'd have to say that Aden is the peacemaker around here. Every time there is a disagreement, he tries to get the members to work out the problem."

_____ 13. "Kennedy, you're late for the meeting. Everyone else was on time, so we started without you."

_____ 14. "What does this have to do with solving the problem? We are getting sidetracked."

_____ 15. "Although we do have occasional differences of opinion, and we have trouble agreeing on decisions, we really get along well and enjoy working together."

Management Implications. To be effective, you need to have high status within a command group. As the manager, maintain good human relations with the group, particularly with the high-status informal leaders, to be sure that they endorse positive norms and objectives. Be aware of and try to prevent conflicts that may be the result of lack of status congruence.[46] Ideally, status should be about equal among group members. But in reality, be sure to listen to and include low-status members in the group process so they are not outsiders of the group.[47]

Decision Making and Conflict Resolution

The decisions made by groups and teams have a direct effect on performance. In groups, decision-making authority is held by the manager. However, in teams, decision-making authority is held by the members through empowerment.[48] But try not to let the team make any decisions based on individual self-interest that may hurt the organization.[49] Also, for group decisions to succeed, the group must unify behind the decision, even if some members vigorously disagreed with it.

Conflict is common in groups and teams, and unresolved conflicts can have a negative effect on performance.[50] Unresolved conflict often leads to members' withdrawal from the group process and hurts cohesiveness.[51] So you need to prevent disruptive conflicts[52] and resolve conflicts to maintain productive working relationships.[53] In Chapter 10, you will develop your skills at resolving conflict.

At **Gore (Case Question 3)**, sponsors help new associates understand and carry out their roles within the team, learn the norms, fit in, gain status, handle conflict, and be an active part of team decision making. Gore plays down status differences with its philosophy that "we have no managers and employees; we are _all_ associates working as a team."

If you understand and develop group process skills, you will be a more effective member, leader, and manager. Exhibit 8-5 summarizes the six dimensions of group process.

WORK
APPLICATION 8-7

Recall a group of which you were a member. List each member, including you, and identify each person's level of status within the group. Explain why each member had the level of status you identified.

EXHIBIT 8-5 DIMENSIONS OF GROUP PROCESS

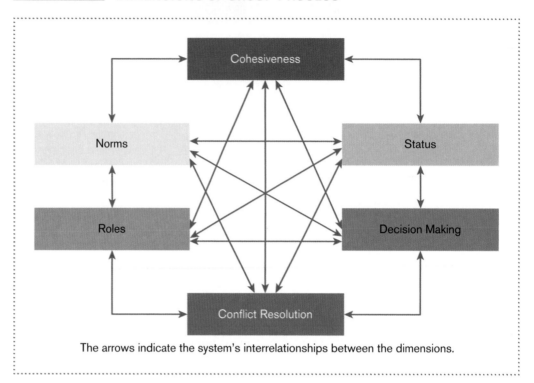

The arrows indicate the system's interrelationships between the dimensions.

STAGES OF GROUP DEVELOPMENT AND MANAGEMENT STYLES

All groups have unique organizational contexts, group structure, and group processes that change over time, and changes affect group performance.[54] However, it is generally agreed that all groups go through the same stages as they emerge, develop, grow, or terminate over time.[55] The **stages of group development** are *forming, storming, norming, performing, and termination.*

As groups grow and change, so should the ways in which they are managed.[56] In this section, we discuss the five stages of group development and an appropriate management style for each stage, which are illustrated in Model 8–1.

Stage 1. Forming—Autocratic Management Style

The *forming stage,* also known as the *orientation stage,* is characterized by a low development level. When people first form a group, they tend to have moderate to high commitment to group goals and tasks. However, because they have not worked together, they often do not have the competence to do the job as a team.

During forming, members have concerns about the structure, leadership, and objectives of the group. Note that command groups are rarely started with all new members but that a change in membership generally does change group process and can affect group development and performance.[57] This stage is more characteristic of task groups that have clear beginnings. Group process issues include anxiety over how members will fit in (status), what will be required of them (roles and norms), what the group will be like (cohesiveness), how decisions will be made, and how members will get along (conflict). These structure and process issues must be resolved if the group is to progress to the next stage of development.

stages of group development Forming, storming, norming, performing, and termination.

| MODEL 8-1 | STAGES OF GROUP DEVELOPMENT AND MANAGEMENT |

Stage of Group Development	Forming	Storming	Norming	Performing
Level of Group Development High / Low	Low	Moderate	High	Outstanding
Management Style	Autocratic	Consultative	Participative	Empowering
Management Behavior	High Directive[1] Low Supportive[2]	High Directive High Supportive	Low Directive High Supportive	Low Directive Low Supportive

[1] Directive behavior is using a group task role.

[2] Supportive behavior is using a group maintenance role.

Autocratic Management Style. During the forming stage of group development, the appropriate management style is usually autocratic; that is, a manager tells group members what to do and how to do it and closely oversees their performance. When a group first comes together, you need to spend most of the time directing the group by playing a task role of helping the group clarify its objectives, providing clear expectations of members. But also allow some time for group members to start to get to know one another with a lower focus on being supportive playing the maintenance role.

Stage 2. Storming—Consultative Management Style

The *storming stage,* also known as the *dissatisfaction stage,* is characterized by a moderate development level. As members work together for some time, they tend to become dissatisfied with the group. Members start asking such questions as these: "Why am I a member?" "Is the group going to accomplish anything?" "Why don't other group members do what is expected?" Often the task is more complex and difficult than anticipated; members become frustrated and have feelings of incompetence. However, the group does develop some competence to perform the task.

During the dissatisfaction stage, the group needs to work on resolving its structure and process issues before it can progress to the next stage of development. Groups can get stuck in this stage of development by not developing a workable group process; in that case, members may never progress to being satisfied with the group and performing as a team.

Consultative Management Style. During the storming stage, the appropriate management style is usually consultative; that is, you as the manager are highly directive and oversee group members' performance playing the task role, but at the same time, you are highly supportive, including their input, playing the maintenance role and encouraging members to continue to work toward objectives.

Stage 3. Norming—Participative Management Style

The *norming stage,* also called the *resolution stage,* is characterized by high development. With time, members often resolve the differences between their initial expectations and the realities of objectives, tasks, skills, and so forth. As members develop competence, they often become more satisfied with the group as they develop friendships. Members learn to work together as they attain a group structure and process with acceptable leadership, norms, status, cohesiveness, and decision making. During periods of conflict or change, the group needs to resolve these issues.[58]

Commitment can vary from time to time as the group interacts. If the group does not deal effectively with group process issues, the group may regress to stage 2 or continue fluctuating in commitment and competence. If the group is successful at developing a workable group structure and process, it will move to the next stage.

Participative Management Style. During the norming stage, the appropriate management style is usually participative: you and the group members share decision making. Once group members know what to do and how to do it, there is little need to model and encourage task behavior. The group needs you to play a maintenance role.

When commitment varies, it is usually because there is some problem in the group's process, such as a conflict. You need to focus on maintenance behavior to get the group through the issue(s) it faces. If you continue to provide task directives that are not needed, the group can either become dissatisfied and regress or remain at this level.

Stage 4. Performing—Empowerment Management Style

The *performing stage,* also called the *production stage,* is characterized by outstanding development. At this stage, commitment and competence do not fluctuate much. The group works as a team with high levels of satisfaction. The group maintains its effective group structure and process. The fact that members are very productive helps lead to positive feelings. The group structure and process may change with time, but the issues are resolved quickly and easily; members are open with each other.

Empowerment Management Style. During the performing stage, the appropriate management style is usually empowering—you give group members the authority to do their task in their own way and to make decisions on their own. Groups that develop to this stage have members who play the appropriate task and maintenance roles; you do not need to play either type of role unless there is a problem, because the group has effective shared leadership, though not all have equal power.[59]

Stage 5. Termination

Command groups do not usually reach the *termination stage,* also called the *adjourning stage,* unless there is some drastic reorganization. However, task

WORK
APPLICATION 8-8

Recall a group from a present or past job. Identify the group's stage of development and the leadership style. Did the leader use an appropriate style? Explain what could be done to improve the group's structure and/or process.

groups do terminate. During this stage, members experience feelings about leaving the group, but there is no need for a management style.

Different groups make it to different levels of development. However, to help ensure that groups develop, employees can be trained in group process skills. Teams tend to develop to higher levels than groups. As a leader or member of a group or team, be aware of the development stage and use the appropriate management style to help it develop to the desired productivity level.

Changes in Group Development and Management Style

As a manager, you need to change your leadership behavior to help the group progress through all stages of development. Two key variables in each stage of group development are competence (work on the task) and commitment. These two variables do not progress in the same manner. Competence tends to continue to increase over time, whereas commitment tends to start high, drop off, and then rise. This pattern is illustrated in Model 8–1; the appropriate leadership style and leadership behavior for each stage of development is shown at the bottom. In Skill Builder 8–2 at the end of this chapter, you will develop your ability to identify group development stages and to match appropriate management style to various real-world situations.

Gore (Case Question 4) has ongoing teams that need to take in new members, so new hires get a sponsor responsible for newcomers' success. Associates serve on multiple teams; thus, Gore seeks associates who are good team players and leaders who play the needed task and maintenance roles for group success. So the team, not the manager, takes the team through the stages of group development.

DEVELOPING GROUPS INTO TEAMS

As Exhibit 8-1 pointed out, groups and teams are different. Among businesses today, the trend is toward the empowerment of teams, because teams are more productive than groups.[60] As a manager, it's your job to build great teams.[61] In this section, we discuss training, explore the difference between a group manager and a team leader, and using recognition and rewards for teams.

Training and Team Leadership

Training. People can be trained to become better team players. If they are to function as a team, the manager and members need training in group process skills,[62] as you are being trained in this chapter. That is why AACSB encourages developing team building skills.[63] **Hudson Trail Outfitters** retailer gives employees incentives for completing training.[64] An OD team-building program (Chapter 6) is also very helpful in turning groups into teams with the help of a change agent.[65] **Sabre Holdings** uses teams and trains employees to be team players through team building.[66] Part of the training is to understand the difference between being a group manager and being a team leader.

Group Managers versus Team Leaders. The roles of the group manager and team leader are different. The group manager takes responsibility for performing the four functions of management (Chapter 1). **Team leaders** *empower members to take responsibility for performing the management functions and focus on developing effective group structure and group process and on furthering group development.* Sometimes team managers are not designated as the official leaders.

LO 8-8

Explain the difference between a group manager and a team leader.

team leaders Empower members to take responsibility for performing the management functions and focus on developing effective group structure and group process and on furthering group development.

WORK
APPLICATION 8-9

Think about the leadership style of a present or past boss. Did that person behave as a group manager or as a team leader? What made you classify the person this way?

The Management Functions. Let's discuss team leadership, realizing that a group doesn't develop into a team overnight; it takes training by the leader over time.

- *Leading.* Most teams do identify a specific person as the leader, but the leader shares this responsibility.[67] You don't focus on telling employees what to do and assigning individuals to do it. You focus on developing group structure and process. Bring the team up to the performing stage of development, changing management styles with the level of development. Use the appropriate management style based on the team and its need for your leadership.[68]

- *Planning.* To convert a group into a team, you must empower the members to set objectives, develop plans, and make decisions. Involve members and make sure that they know the objectives, accept them, and are committed to achieving them.[69]

- *Organizing and Staffing.* The important part of organizing and staffing a team is the participation of its members in selecting, evaluating, and rewarding members. Jobs on a team are interchangeable and are assigned by the members as they perform dependent parts of the entire process.

- *Controlling.* You help the team set the standards and develop positive norms.[70] As you move from being a group to being a team, members are responsible for monitoring progress, taking corrective action, and performing quality control.

Team Rewards and Recognition

Individuals should be rewarded and recognized, but for teams to succeed, the organizational structure needs to reward and recognize team cooperation rather than focusing on internal competition between individuals. Good team players should get praise, pay raises, promotions, and other rewards and recognition for their work. Incentives need to be tied to performance.[71] The challenge is to correctly balance individual and teamwork compensation and recognition with the level of individual and team performance. Here are three ways that employees can be rewarded and recognized for teamwork.

Nonfinancial. Being part of a successful team is satisfying, as it provides opportunity for personal development and to help teammates grow, as well as providing enjoyable relationships. So being part of a satisfying team helps motivate employees to be good team players. The company can also have formal and informal meetings or awards ceremonies to recognize team accomplishments with lunches/dinners, cookouts/barbeques, plaques/certificates, T-shirts/jackets/coffee mugs, and so forth. Nonfinancial rewards work well in any team provided the team progresses to the performing stage of group development.

WORK
APPLICATION 8-10

Give examples of team rewards and recognition where you work(ed).

Skill-Based Pay. Employees are paid for learning additional skills or knowledge they need to perform multiple jobs within a team and to share knowledge with other team members. Skill-based pay works well with self-managing teams performing complex tasks. Employees at **Patience and Nicholson** can increase their pay by $6 an hour over three to four years by learning to operate multiple drill bit machines.[72]

Gainsharing. Employees share the financial gains through increasing productivity, decreasing costs, and improving quality. Gainsharing tends to work well in stable environments with mechanistic organizational designs (Chapter 7).

MANAGING MEETINGS

CEOs spend an estimated one third of their work time in meetings.[73] As businesses use more teams, meetings are taking up an increasing amount of time for all employees. However, the number-one time waster is too many meetings, as office workers average around four hours a week in meetings and consider more than half of it wasted time.[74] Committees have been called a body that keeps minutes and wastes hours. **Microsoft's** Paul Betts says he grew frustrated by the number of meetings he had to attend, estimating the average meeting cost and wasted around $500.[75] Some employees find meetings irritating.[76] Some of the best managers can't seem to run effective meetings.[77] Therefore, the need for skills at attending and managing meetings is stronger than ever. In this section, we discuss how to plan and conduct a meeting and how to handle problem group members as a manager, but you can also improve meetings by suggesting improvements that you will learn now.

Like many CEOs, Indra Nooyi, the CEO of Pepsi, likely spends much of her time in meetings. Managing effective meetings is an essential part of the manager's job. Photo from Graham Crouch/Bloomberg via Getty Images.

Planning Meetings

Before we get into planning and running a meeting, let's discuss some of the things companies are doing regarding wasted meetings. **Facebook, Dropbox,** and **Square** are reshaping the daily routine of thousands of office workers, with a special emphasis on fewer meetings. Facebook has a lose policy called No-Meeting Wednesday. **Twitter** and **Microsoft** are reducing the number of manager-led meetings by empowering employees to make more decisions. Others are keeping meetings short and making attendees stand during the meeting.[78] Others are limiting the time for presentations.[79] Companies, including **Intel**, are training their employees on how to be effective members and managers of meetings.

The quality of both leaders' and members' preparation for a meeting has a direct effect on the meeting; in other words, planning pays off. Unprepared managers tend to conduct unproductive meetings. There are at least six areas in which planning is needed. A written copy of the plan should be sent to members prior to the meeting. See Exhibit 8-6 for a sample meeting plan.

Objectives. People complain that too little is accomplished in meetings.[80] This is often due to the fact that those who call meetings often have no clear idea of the purpose for the meeting. **Google** CEO Larry Page pushes managers to outline clear goals before scheduling a meeting. So the first thing to ask yourself is, Do we need this meeting, and why? You need everyone to understand what they're trying to accomplish in a meeting. So, before calling a meeting, clearly define its purpose and set objectives to be accomplished during the meeting.

Participants and Assignments. Decide who should attend the meeting. Too many people at a meeting can slow things down. Does the full group or team need to attend? **Google** CEO Larry Page limits most meetings to 10 attendees.[81] Should a specialist who is not part of the team be invited to provide input? With controversial issues, the leader may find it wiser to talk with the key members before the meeting.

EXHIBIT 8-7 MEETING PLAN

Meeting Element	Description	Example
Time	List meeting date, meeting place (unless the team always meets in the same place), and time (both beginning and ending times).	November 22, 2010, Gold Room, 9–10 a.m.
Objectives	State the objective or purpose of the meeting (Note: Objectives may be listed with agenda items, as shown in agenda item 1 below, rather than as a separate section, but wherever they are listed, they should be specific.)	
Participation and assignments	List the assignment for the entire team or, if individual members have different assignments, list each person's name and assignment. (Assignments may be listed as agenda items, as shown in agenda items 2 and 3.)	All members should have read the six enclosed brochures about computer systems before the meeting. Be ready to discuss your preferences.
Agenda	List each item to be covered in the meeting, in order of importance, with an approximate time limit.	1. Discussion of new computer systems; narrow down the choices to two out of six possibilities; 45 minutes 2. Venus Project report (Ted); 5 minutes 3. Presentation on proposed change in production process (Karen); 5 minutes. (Discussion will take place at our next meeting, after team members have had a chance to give the proposal some thought.)

Meetings run longer when people haven't prepared well for them. So participants should know in advance what is expected of them at the meeting. Think about each person attending the meeting and ask, What can each one contribute? If any preparation is expected (read material, do some research, make a report, and so forth), attendees should have adequate advance notice to prepare.

Agenda. Every formal meeting needs an agenda distributed beforehand. The agenda tells the members what is expected and how the meeting will progress. It should identify the activities that will take place in order to achieve the objective. Team members may also submit agenda items. Having a set time limit for each agenda item helps keep the group on target; needless discussion and getting off the subject are common at meetings.[82] However, you may need to be flexible and allow more time. Agenda items that require action should have objectives listed with them.

Place agenda items in order of priority. Then, if the group does not have time to cover every item, the least important items will be carried forward to the next meeting.

Date, Place, and Time. Get team members' input on which days of the week and times of the day are best for meetings. When members are close, it is better to have more frequent, shorter meetings focusing on one or a few items. However, when members have to travel, fewer, longer meetings are needed.

Be sure to select an adequate place for the meeting and plan for the physical comfort of the group. Seating should allow eye contact for small discussion groups, and enough time should be allocated so that the members do not have to rush. If reservations are needed for the meeting place, make them far enough in advance to get a proper meeting room.

Meetings are typically scheduled for 30 to 90 minutes, but they shouldn't run for longer than it takes to accomplish the objectives. Meetings are about discipline, so stick with the time limit.[83]

Leadership. The leader should determine the appropriate management style for the meeting. Different agenda items may need to be handled differently. For example, some items may simply call for disseminating information, but others may require a discussion, vote, or a consensus; still other items may require a report from a member. An effective way to develop group members' ability is to rotate the role of the group moderator/leader for each meeting. At **Rubicon Oil & Gas** company, employees take turns running meetings.

Technology. Email has eliminated the need for some meetings. Some companies, including **McDonald's**, are having more conference telephone calls. Other companies, including **Johnson & Johnson**, are using more videoconferencing/**Skype**, as the meeting software is getting better and costs are dropping. These techniques save travel costs and time, and they may result in better and quicker decisions. **Asana** is the shared task list for teams; the place to plan, organize and stay in sync.[84] Ongoing chat rooms can also take the place of meetings and are especially useful with virtual teams with members from around the globe in different time zones. **GitHub** stores programmers' source codes, avoiding in-person meeting by replacing them with a freewheeling chat room.[85]

Personal computers have been called the most useful tool for running meetings since Robert's Rules of Order. Group members can use their laptops or tablets to take notes on what took place during a meeting and distribute a hard copy or email of the notes at the end of the meeting.

Unfortunately, some employees bring tech gadgets (such as smartphones) to meetings, but they use them to do other things not related to the meeting, such as checking emails, sending personal texts, and actually taking calls. This can distract members and reduce the effectiveness of the meeting—or class. Some organizations are banning their use during meetings (class)—but some will take a tech break during the meeting.[86]

Conducting Meetings

The First Meeting. It is important to carry yourself with confidence in meetings.[87] At its first meeting, a team is in the forming stage. Members should be given the opportunity to spend some time getting to know one another. Introductions set the stage for subsequent interactions. A simple technique is to start with introductions, then move on to the group's purpose, objectives, and members' job roles. During or following this procedure, schedule a break that enables members to interact informally. If members find that their social needs will not be met, dissatisfaction may occur quickly.

The Three Parts of Meetings. Meetings should have the following three parts:

1. *Identify objectives.* Begin the meeting on time; waiting for late members penalizes the members who are on time and develops a norm for coming late. Begin by reviewing progress to date, the group's objectives, and the purpose or objective for the specific meeting. Recorded minutes are usually approved at the beginning of the meeting. For most meetings, a secretary should be appointed to take minutes.

LO 8-9

Discuss the three parts of meetings.

2. *Cover agenda items.* Stick to the agenda and keep the discussion on track to ensure you achieve the objectives.[88] Be sure to cover agenda items in priority order. Try to keep to the approximate times, but be flexible. If the discussion is constructive and members need more time, give it to them.

3. *Summarize and review assignments.* End the meeting on time. The leader should summarize what took place during the meeting and review all of the assignments given during the meeting. The secretary and/or leader should record all assignments. If there is no accountability and follow-up on assignments, members may not complete them.

JetBlue uses a team structure, and teams have meetings, but employees make a conscious effort to avoid unproductive meetings and to be respectful of each other's time. At every meeting, there is a "*time cop*" who makes sure that the meeting does not last any longer than necessary. The time cop keeps the meeting on topic, allows each agenda item only its allotted time, and ends the meeting on time.

At **Gore (Case Question 5)**, every associate is part of one or more teams, so all associates attend team meetings scheduled as needed. Sponsors also make sure that newcomers have opportunities to sit in on important meetings with other teams to better understand the systems effect of their projects and products and to learn how Gore operates.

Handling Problem Members

Employees help the team and organization through "*voice*"—the expression of constructive opinions, concerns, or ideas about work-related issues that lead to improved work and group processes and innovation.[89] However, certain personality types can cause the group to be less efficient than it could be. So let's identify six problem types you will most likely encounter in meetings and how to keep them productive.

Silent Type. Some employees choose silence over voice, and for others, it's part of their personality.[90] In either case, to be fully effective, all group members should participate. If members are silent, the group does not get the benefit of their input. You need to hear from everyone to make sure the team is moving ahead together.

It is your responsibility to encourage silent members to participate without being obvious or overdoing it. You can draw them out by asking them in advance for a specific contribution and/or use the "*round robin*" rotation method, in which all members take turns giving their input.[91] These methods are generally less threatening than being called on directly. However, the rotation method is not appropriate all the time. To build up silent members' confidence, call on them with questions they can easily answer.

If you are a silent type, try to participate more often. Realize that speaking up is hard to do for many people, and that women may be more likely to be silent at meetings because they are more attentive to what people are feeling or thinking and more sensitive to group dynamics. Come to meetings prepared, knowing what you want to say (you can practice your delivery), and bring notes. This will help prevent you from being distracted by what others are saying and wondering how you should respond. You can also have the leader or a talkative person bring up your idea and turn the conversation over to you. Know when to stand up for your views and be assertive; trust yourself, and take risks.[92]

Talker. Talkers have something to say about everything, and they tend to ramble. They like to dominate the discussion.[93] However, if they do, the other members do not get to participate. The talker can cause intragroup problems such as low cohesiveness and conflicts. A second type of talker is the people who have a private conversation during the meeting.

It your responsibility to slow talkers down, not to shut them up. Do not let them dominate the group. Interrupt people talking to each other to keep it a team meeting. You can gently interrupt the talker and present your own ideas or call on other specific members to present their ideas. The rotation method can be effective with talkers because they have to wait their turn.

If you tend to be a talker, try to slow down. Give others a chance to talk and do things for themselves. Good leaders develop others' ability in these areas.

Managers must strive to engage all employees so that there are no social loafers. Photo from Monkey Business Images/Getty Images.

Wanderer. Wanderers distract the group from the agenda items; they tend to change the subject and often like to complain.

It's your responsibility to keep the group on track. Don't let them wander; stay focused on the agenda.[94] Be kind, thank each member for the contribution, then throw a question out to the group to get it back on track.

If you tend to be a wanderer, try to be aware of your behavior and stay on the subject at hand.

Bored Member. Your group may have one or more members who are not interested in the job. The bored person may be preoccupied with other issues and not pay attention or participate in the group meeting. Bored members may also feel superior and overestimate their value to the team.[95]

Look for nonverbal clues of boredom and engage them. Assign the bored member a task such as recording ideas on the board or recording the minutes. Call on bored members; bring them into the group. If you allow them to sit back, things may get worse and others may decide not to participate either.

If you tend to be bored, try to find ways to help motivate yourself. Work at becoming more patient and in control of behavior that can have negative effects on other members.

Arguer. Like the talker, the arguer likes to be the center of attention. Arguers enjoy arguing for the sake of arguing rather than helping the group. They turn things into a win-lose situation, and they cannot stand losing. They can also be negative, arguing that others' ideas will not work.[96]

Resolve conflict, but not in an argumentative way. Do not get into an argument with arguers; that is exactly what they want to happen. If an argument starts, bring others into the discussion. If an argument becomes personal, cut it off. Personal attacks only hurt the group. Keep the discussion moving on target.

If you tend to be an arguer, strive to convey your views in an assertive, positive way rather than in a negative, aggressive manner. Challenge ideas, not the people themselves; don't make it personal. Listen to others' views and be willing to change if they have better ideas.

Social Loafer. As stated in Chapter 4, one of the disadvantage of using groups is social loafing. Social loafers are slackers that withhold their effort and fail to perform their share of the work. Social loafers try to blend into the background, where their lack of effort and doing their fair share of the work isn't easily

8-4 APPLYING THE CONCEPT

Problematic Group Members

Identify the problem type described in each statement.

A. silent type
B. talker
C. wanderer
D. bored member
E. arguer
F. social loafer

____ 16. Tam is usually reluctant to give his ideas. When asked to explain his position, he often changes his answers to agree with others in the group.

____ 17. Sherrie enjoys challenging members' ideas and getting them emotional. She likes getting her own way. When a group member does not agree with Sherrie, she makes sarcastic comments about the member's prior mistakes.

____ 18. Clarita is always first or second to give her ideas. She is always elaborating on ideas. Because she is so quick to respond, others sometimes make comments to her about it.

____ 19. Sonia, one of the usually active group members, is sitting back quietly today for the first time. The other members are doing all the discussing and volunteering for assignments.

____ 20. As the group is discussing a problem, Liam asks if they heard about the company owner and the mailroom clerk.

spotted. If you have done any team-based class projects, you likely have seen slackers who contribute poor, little, or no work but want the same grade as everyone else that did the work.

Following all the previously mentioned meeting guidelines helps, especially giving clear individual assignments. Don't let the group develop norms that allow social loafing, and use peer pressure to get them to do their work. Confront social loafers assertively; you will learn how to using the conflict resolution model in Chapter 10. When necessary, threaten to go to the boss. If these methods do not work, go to the supervisor (professor or boss) and explain the situation, stating the specific behavior and that you and the group have tried to resolve the problem, but the social loafer refuses to perform to standards.

If you have tendencies toward a social loafing, realize that everyone wants to be on a successful team and that success comes from everyone doing their share of the work. So if you want to be on a good team with high levels of performance, you need to pitch in and help develop positive norms of equal participation.

Working With Group Members. Whenever you work in a group, do not embarrass, intimidate, or argue with any members, no matter how much they provoke you. Don't belittle others in meetings and don't let members belittle others. If you do, the group will perceive them as martyrs and you as a bully. If problem members do not respond to the preceding techniques, confront them individually outside of the group. Get them to agree to work in a cooperative way.

As we bring this chapter to a close, you should understand the growing use of teams in business settings and how to develop groups into teams. You should know that team performance is based on organizational context, group structure (type, size, composition, leadership, and objectives), group process (roles, norms, cohesiveness, status, decision making, and conflict resolution), and group development (orientation, dissatisfaction, resolution, production, and termination). You should also know how to run and participate in effective meetings and how to handle problem members.

WORK
APPLICATION 8-11

Recall a meeting you have recently attended. Did you receive an agenda prior to the meeting? How well did the leader conduct the meeting? Give ideas on how the meeting could have been improved. Did the group have any problem members? How well did the leader handle them?

• • • CHAPTER SUMMARY

8-1. **Describe the major differences between groups and teams.**

The major areas of difference are size, leadership, jobs, accountability and evaluation, rewards, and objectives. A group is two or more members with a clear leader who perform independent jobs and experience individual accountability, evaluation, and rewards. A team has a small number of members with shared leadership who perform interdependent jobs and experience both individual and group accountability, evaluation, and rewards.

8-2. **Explain the group performance model.**

According to the group performance model, group performance is a function of organizational context, group structure, group process, and group development stage.

8-3. **List and explain the three dimensions of group types.**

Groups are formal or informal, functional or cross-functional, and command or task groups. Formal groups are created as part of the organizational structure; informal groups are not. Functional group members come from one area, whereas cross-functional members come from different areas. Command groups include managers and their employees, whereas task groups include selected employees who work on a specific objective. A task force is temporary, whereas a standing committee is ongoing.

8-4. **Define the three major roles played in groups.**

Group task roles are played by members who do and say things that directly aid in the accomplishment of the group's objectives. Group maintenance roles are played by members who do and say things that develop and sustain the group process. Self-interest roles are played by members who do and say things that help themselves but hurt the group.

8-5. **State the differences between rules and norms and how groups enforce norms.**

Rules are formally established by management or by the group itself. Norms are the group's shared expectations of its members' behavior. Norms are not developed by management or explicitly agreed to by the group; they develop as members interact. Groups enforce their norms through peer pressure to conform to the expected behavior.

8-6. **Describe cohesiveness and explain why it is important to teams.**

Group cohesiveness is the extent to which members stick together. Group cohesiveness is important because highly cohesive groups have a higher level of productivity than groups with low levels of cohesiveness.

8-7. **List the four major stages of group development and describe the appropriate management style usually associated with each.**

(1) *Forming* is characterized by a low development level. The appropriate management style is generally *autocratic*. (2) *Storming* is characterized by a moderate development level. The appropriate management style is generally *consultative*. (3) *Norming* is characterized by a high development level. The appropriate management style is generally *participative*. (4) *Performing* is characterized by an outstanding development level. The appropriate management style is generally *empowerment*.

8-8. **Explain the difference between a group manager and a team leader.**

The group manager takes responsibility for performing the four functions of management. The team leader empowers team members to take responsibility for performing the management functions and focuses on developing effective group structure, group process, and group development.

8-9. **Discuss the three parts of meetings.**

Meetings should begin with a review of the purpose and objectives for the meeting. During the meeting, agenda items should be covered in priority order. The meeting should end with a summary of what took place and assignments to be completed for future meetings.

• • • KEY TERMS

• • • KEY TERM REVIEW

Complete each of the following statements using one of this chapter's key terms.

1. A _____ is two or more members with a clear leader who perform independent jobs with individual accountability, evaluation, and rewards.

2. A _____ is a small number of members with shared leadership who perform interdependent jobs with both individual and group accountability, evaluation, and rewards.

3. In the _____, group performance is a function of organizational context, group structure, group process, and group development stage.

4. _____ are group type, size, composition, leadership, and objectives.

5. _____ include formal or informal, functional or cross-functional, and command or task.

6. _____ consist of managers and the employees they supervise.

7. _____ consist of employees selected to work on a specific objective.

8. Members of _____ are physically located in different places but work together as a team.

9. _____ is the mix of members' skills and abilities.

10. _____ is the patterns of interactions that emerge as members perform their jobs.

11. _____ include roles, norms, cohesiveness, status, decision making, and conflict resolution.

12. _____ include group task roles, group maintenance roles, and self-interest roles.

13. _____ are expectations about behavior that are shared by members of a group.

14. _____ is the extent to which members stick together.

15. _____ is the perceived ranking of one member relative to other members in a group.

16. The _____ are, forming, storming, norming, performing, and termination.

17. _____ empower members to take responsibility for performing the management functions and focus on developing effective group structure and group process and on furthering group development.

• • • REVIEW QUESTIONS

1. Which are usually larger, groups or teams?

2. Which level of management has the most influence over organizational context?

3. Is there an ideal group size?

4. Why is diversity important to group composition?

5. Why are objectives important to groups?

6. How do groups enforce norms?

7. Which type of group tends to terminate and which does not?

8. Are the four functions of management important to both groups and teams?

9. Why is it important to keep records of meeting assignments?

10. Describe the six types of problem members in meetings. How does each cause a problem to the group?

• • • COMMUNICATION SKILLS

The following critical-thinking questions can be used for class discussion and/or as written assignments to develop communication skills. Be sure to give complete explanations for all questions.

1. Which lesson of the geese do you think is most lacking and needed in teams today? Why?

2. Is it really worth making a distinction between groups and teams? Why or why not?

3. Which part of the group performance model is the most important to high levels of performance? Why?

4. Select any type of group (work, school, sports) you belong or have belonged to. Explain how each of the group's five structure components affects or did affect its performance.

5. Select any type of group (work, school, sports) you belong or have belonged to. Explain how each of the group's six group process components affects or did affect its performance.

6. Are most team leaders really capable of determining the stage of group development and using the appropriate leadership style for the situation? Why or why not?

7. Based on your experience with meetings and what you have read and heard from others, which part of planning a meeting is most lacking?

8. Which type of group problem member is most annoying to you? Why? How can you better work with this type of group member in the future?

• • • CASE: THE TEAMWORK APPROACH AT TARGET

Do you like to shop at Target? Does it appear that all the employees enjoy working together? There is a reason that you probably answered "yes." The CEO of Target Corporation, Gregg Steinhafel, believes there is no "I" in TEAM.

The mission of Target is as follows:

Our mission is to make Target your preferred shopping destination in all channels by delivering outstanding value, continuous innovation and exceptional guest experiences by consistently fulfilling our Expect More. Pay Less.® brand promise.[97]

How did Target develop its team atmosphere? In 1902, after becoming a partner in the Goodfellows Dry Good company, George Dayton took ownership of the company and renamed it the Dayton Dry Goods Company. Headquartered in Minneapolis, the company passed on to many other Dayton family members until the time in the 1960s when most of the United States started to have a Target store open up in there area.

Along the way, each generation of the Dayton family became more active in giving money to charity to help lift the level of humanity in the world. In 1946, the company announced it would give 5% of pretax dollars to charity.

In the last few years, along with increasing revenues and profits, the company can be found all around the world. A complete slide show of the history of Dayton Goods (which opened the first Target in 1962) can be found at https://corporate.target.com/about/history.

One can assume the history and the mission of Target is one of the reasons there is a team focus instead of an "I" mentality. Current CEO George Steinhafel worked his way up at Target from being a regular employee—so he knows the importance of collaboration as part of the Target culture. He works equally well using email or face-to-face interactions to communicate with his employees. He supports his team members to use Facebook and other social media applications to communicate with each other. He believes that using social media helps employees to keep in touch and exchange information on new products and merchandise.[98]

Teams need to work together when designing clothing. It's a collaborative team effort that requires coordination across many areas, including teams in merchandising, marketing, design, communications, presentation, supply chain, and stores. "All of them must be engaged in bringing this concept to life," says Steinhafel.[99]

Target offices in India are full of amenities to enhance team members' time at the office. Team members play table tennis or chess in a spacious recreation room and enjoy a free lunch at the indoor/outdoor café. Teams can gather in comfortable areas to work or have some fun. Team activities such as watching movies and fashion shows are held to build team unity.[100]

Target has developed opportunities to grow with the company. For example, Target has identified more than 120 different career paths that exist for team members to explore. Employees are encouraged to volunteer for their favorite charity. Along with having four performance reviews each year, employees are provided Information on what skills and abilities are needed to prepare for a career in management.[101]

Case Questions

1. Would the norms of Target match the norms of a typical company?

2. Do the teams at Target appear to be in the orientation, dissatisfaction, resolution, production, or termination stage of group development?

3. Do you think team decisions are typically made by the CEO, a manager, or a team member at Target?

4. Does the comment "There is no I in Team" indicate strong cohesiveness or strong roles as part of the group process?

5. Does encouraging managers and employees to spend time online using social media to exchange ideas create formal or informal group discussion?

6. How does a company like Target create and maintain a sense of cohesiveness?

Cumulative Case Questions

7. Which principles of organization best apply to this case? Why? (Chapter 5)

8. How does the issue of managing change apply in this case? (Chapter 6)

9. How does Target use the three levels of culture to produce a strong culture? (Chapter 2)

• • • SKILL BUILDER 8–1: COMPARING TEAMS

Objectives

To use your experience to better understand what makes teams successful and to better contribute to team performance.

Skills

The primary skills developed through this exercise are:

1. *Management skill*—interpersonal (teamwork)
2. *AACSB competency*—analyzing—within groups)
3. *Management function*—leading (in groups)

Preparation

Select the best and worst group (work, school, sports, club, etc.) of which you are/were a member and answer the following questions:

1. What was it about the best group that made you select it? Be sure to incorporate the chapter's discussion on groups and teams in your answer.

2. What was it about the worst group that made you select it? Be sure to incorporate the chapter's discussion of teams and groups in your answer.

Procedure

In groups of five to seven, share your answers to the Preparation questions, and identify the three major factors making a group the best and worst.

Apply It

What did I learn from this exercise? How will I use this knowledge in the future?

• • • SKILL BUILDER 8-2: MANAGEMENT STYLES IN GROUP SITUATIONS

Objective

To determine appropriate leadership styles in group situations.

Skills

The primary skills developed through this exercise are:

1. *Management skill*—interpersonal (teamwork)
2. *AACSB competency*—analyzing (preferred group leadership style)—teamwork
3. *Management function*—leading (in groups)

Assess Your Preferred Team Management Style

Following are 12 situations. Select the one alternative that most closely describes what you would do in each situation. Don't be concerned with trying to select the right answer; select the alternative you would really use. Circle a, b, c, or d. (Ignore the D ____ and the S ____ following each answer choice; these will be explained later.)

1. Your group works well together; members are cohesive and have positive norms. They maintain a fairly consistent level of production that is above the organizational average, as long as you continue to play a maintenance role. You have a new assignment for them. To accomplish it, you would: D ____

   a. Explain what needs to be done and tell them how to do it. Oversee them while they perform the task. S ____

   b. Tell the group how pleased you are with its past performance. Explain the new assignment, but let them decide how to accomplish it. Be available if they need help. S ____

   c. Tell the group what needs to be done. Encourage them to give input on how to do the job. Oversee task performance. S ____

   d. Explain to the group what needs to be done. S ____

2. You have been promoted to a new supervisory position. The group you supervise appears to have little talent to do the job, but the members do seem to care about the quality of the work they do. The last supervisor was fired because of the group's low productivity level. To increase productivity, you would: D ____

   a. Let the group know you are aware of its low production level, but let the members decide how to improve it. S ____

   b. Spend most of your time overseeing group members as they perform their jobs. Train them as needed. S ____

   c. Explain to the group that you would like to work together to improve productivity. Work together as a team. S ____

   d. Tell the group how productivity can be improved. With their ideas, develop methods and make sure they are implemented. S ____

3. Your department continues to be one of the top performers in the organization. The members work well as a team. In the past, you generally let them take care of the work on their own. You decide to: D ____

   a. Go around encouraging group members on a regular basis. S ____

   b. Define members' roles and spend more time overseeing performance. S ____

   c. Continue things the way they are; leave them alone. S ____

   d. Hold a meeting. Recommend ways to improve and get members' ideas as well. After agreeing on changes, oversee the group to make sure it implements the new ideas and does improve. S ____

4. You have spent much of the past year training your employees. However, they do not need you to oversee production as much as you used to. Several group members no longer get along as well as they

did in the past. You've played referee lately. You: D ____

a. Have a group meeting to discuss ways to increase performance. Let the group decide what changes to make. Be supportive. S ____

b. Continue things the way they are now. Supervise them closely and be the referee when needed. S ____

c. Leave the group alone to work things out for themselves. S ____

d. Continue to supervise closely as needed, but spend more time playing a maintenance role; develop a team spirit. S ____

5. Your department has been doing such a great job that it has increased in size. You are surprised at how fast the new members were integrated. The team continues to come up with ways to improve performance on its own. Because it has grown so large, the department will be moving to a larger location. You decide to: D ____

a. Design the new layout and present it to the group to see if the members can improve on it. S ____

b. Allow the group to design the new layout. S ____

c. Design the new layout and put a copy on the bulletin board so employees know where to report for work after the move. S ____

d. Hold a meeting to get employee ideas on the layout of the new location. After the meeting, think about their ideas and finalize the layout. S ____

6. You are appointed to head a task group. Because of the death of a relative, you had to miss the first meeting. At the second meeting, the group seems to have developed objectives and some ground rules. Members have volunteered for assignments that have to be accomplished. You: D ____

a. Take over as a strong leader and change some ground rules and assignments. S ____

b. Review what has been done so far and keep things as they are. However, you take charge and provide clear direction from now on. S ____

c. Take over the leadership, but allow the group to make the decisions. Be supportive and encourage them. S ____

d. Given the group is doing so well, leave and do not attend any more meetings. S ____

7. Your group was working at, or just below, standard. There has been a conflict within the group, and as a result, production is behind schedule. You: D ____

a. Tell the group how to resolve the conflict. Then closely supervise to make sure people do what you say and production increases. S ____

b. Let the group work it out. S ____

c. Hold a meeting to work as a team to come up with a solution. Encourage the group members to work together. S ____

d. Hold a meeting to present a way to resolve the conflict. Sell the members on its merits, ask for their input, and follow up. S ____

8. Your organization allows flextime. Two of your employees have asked if they can change work hours. You are concerned because the busy work hours need adequate coverage. The department is very cohesive with positive norms. You decide to: D ____

a. Tell them things are going well; we'll keep things as they are now. S ____

b. Hold a department meeting to get everyone's input, then reschedule their hours. S ____

c. Hold a department meeting to get everyone's input; then reschedule their hours on a trial basis. Tell the group that if there is any drop in productivity, you will go back to the old schedule. S ____

d. Tell them to hold a department meeting. If the department agrees to have at least three people on the job during the busy hours, they can make changes, giving you a copy of the new schedule. S ____

9. You have arrived ten minutes late for a department meeting. Your employees are discussing the latest assignment. This surprises you because, in the past, you had to provide clear direction and employees rarely would say anything. You: D ____

a. Take control immediately and provide your usual direction. S ____

b. Say nothing and just sit back. S ____

c. Encourage the group to continue but also provide direction. S ____

d. Thank the group for starting without you and encourage them to continue. Support their efforts. S ____

10. Your department is consistently very productive. However, occasionally the members fool around and someone has an accident. There has never been a serious injury. You hear a noise and go to see what it was. From a distance you can see Sue sitting on the floor, laughing, with a ball made from company material in her hand. You: D ____

a. Say and do nothing. After all, she's OK, and the department is very productive; you don't want to make waves. S ____

b. Call the group together and ask for suggestions on how to keep accidents from recurring. Tell them you will be checking up on them to make sure the behavior does not continue. S ____

c. Call the group together and discuss the situation. Encourage them to be more careful in the future. S ____

d. Tell the group that's it; from now on you will be checking up on them regularly. Bring Sue to your office and discipline her. S ____

11. You are at the first meeting of an ad hoc committee you are leading. Most of the members are second- and third-level managers from the marketing and financial areas; you are a supervisor from production. You decide to start by: D ____

a. Working on developing relationships. Get everyone to feel as though they know each other before you talk about business. S ____

b. Going over the group's purpose and the authority it has. Provide clear directives. S ____

c. Asking the group to define its purpose. Because most of the members are higher-level managers, let them provide the leadership. S ____

d. Providing both direction and encouragement. Give directives and thank people for their cooperation. S ____

12. Your department has done a great job in the past. It is getting a new computer system. You have been trained to operate the computer, and you are expected to train your employees to operate it. To train them, you: D ____

a. Give the group instructions and work with people individually, providing direction and encouragement. S ____

b. Get the group together to decide how they want to be instructed. Be very supportive of their efforts to learn. S ____

c. Tell them it's a simple system. Give them a copy of the manual and have them study it on their own. S ____

d. Give the group instructions. Then go around and supervise their work closely, giving additional instructions as needed. S ____

Scoring

To determine your preferred leadership style, follow these steps:

1. Circle the letter you selected for each situation.

	Autocratic	Consultative	Participative	Empowerment
1.	a	c	b	d
2.	b	d	c	a
3.	b	d	a	c
4.	b	d	a	c
5.	c	a	d	b
6.	a	b	c	d
7.	a	d	c	b
8.	a	c	b	d
9.	a	c	d	b
10.	d	b	c	a
11.	b	d	a	c
12.	d	a	b	c
Totals	____	____	____	____

2. Add up the number of circled items per column. The column with the most circled items represents your preferred style.

The more evenly distributed the numbers are among the four styles, the more flexible you are at leading groups. A total of 0 or 1 in any column may indicate a reluctance to use that style. Is your preferred leadership style the same as your preferred management style (Chapter 1)?

••• SKILL BUILDER 8-3: ASSIGNING APPROPRIATE MANAGEMENT STYLES TO GROUP SITUATIONS

Objectives

To help you understand the stages of group development and to select the appropriate leadership styles for group situations.

Preparation

You should understand the stages of group development and have completed assessment of your leadership style.

Step 1. Determine the level of development of the group in each of the 12 situations. Place the number (1, 2, 3, or 4) on the line marked D at the end of the situation.

1 = forming stage

2 = storming stage

3 = norming stage

4 = performing stage

Step 2. Identify the leadership style described in each answer choice. Place the letter A, C, P, or E on the line marked S following each answer choice.

A = autocratic

C = consultative

P = participative

E = empowering

Step 3. Now circle the letter of the answer choice that represents the leadership style that is most appropriate for the level of development for the group in each situation.

See Model 8–1 for an illustration of the four levels of development and their leadership styles.

Apply It

What did I learn from this experience? How will I use this knowledge in the future?

Your instructor may ask you to do part of this Skill Builder in class as a group. You may be instructed, for example, to break into teams to assign stages of development and leadership styles to each situation, or you may be asked to discuss the reasons behind your stage and style decisions.

••• SKILL BUILDER 8-4: GROUP PERFORMANCE

Note: This exercise is designed for class groups that have worked together for some time. (Five or more hours of prior work are recommended.)

Objectives

To gain a better understanding of group structure, process, and development and of meetings and how they affect group performance.

Skills

The primary skills developed through this exercise are:

1. *Management skill*—interpersonal (teamwork)

2. *AACSB competency*—analyzing a group—teamwork

3. *Management function*—leading (in groups)

Answer the following questions as they apply to your class group/team.

1. Using Exhibit 8-1, would you classify your members as a group or a team? Why?

Group Structure

2. What type of group/team are you (formal/informal, functional/cross-functional, command/task)?

3. Assess the size of your group/team (too large, too small, ideal).

4. What is the group/team composition?

5. Is there a clear leader or leaders? If so, who is or are the leaders?

6. Does your group/team have clear objectives?

7. List some ways in which group structure could be improved to increase group performance.

Group Process

8. List each group member, including yourself, and the major role(s) each plays.

9. Identify at least three group norms. Are they positive or negative? How does the group enforce them?

10. How cohesive is your group (very cohesive, moderately cohesive, minimally cohesive)?

11. List each group member, including you, in order of status.

12. How are decisions made in your group/team?

13. How is conflict resolved in your group/team?

14. List some ways in which group process could be improved to increase group performance.

Group Development Stage

15. At what stage of development is your group/team? Explain.

16. List some ways in which your group/team can move to a higher level of development to increase group performance.

Meetings

17. List some ways in which your meetings could be improved to increase group performance.

18. Does your group have any problem members? What can be done to make them more effective?

Apply It

What did I learn from this experience? How will I use this knowledge in the future?

Your instructor may ask you to continue this Skill Builder in class by discussing your answers to the questions with other members of your class group. You may also be asked to do a team-building exercise by jointly making specific recommendations about ways in which your team can improve its performance.

••• STUDENT STUDY SITE

Visit the Student Study Site at **www.sagepub.com/lussier6e** to access to these additional study tools:

- Mobile-compatible self-assessment quizzes
- Mobile-compatible key term flashcards
- Video Links

- SAGE Journal Articles
- Web Links

9 Human Resources Management

● ● ● **Learning Outcomes**

After studying this chapter, you should be able to:

9-1. List the four parts of the human resources management process. PAGE 250

9-2. Explain why job analysis is needed, and distinguish between a job description and job specifications. PAGE 255

9-3. Describe recruiting sources for candidates for jobs and the selection process. PAGE 256

9-4. Explain what orientation and training and development of employees involve. PAGE 262

9-5. List the steps in job instructional training. PAGE 263

9-6. Explain the two types of performance appraisal. PAGE 265

9-7. Explain the concept "You get what you reinforce." PAGE 265

9-8. Describe the difference between job analysis and job evaluation. PAGE 269

IDEAS ON MANAGEMENT at Costco Wholesale

Costco began operations in 1983. In October 1993, Costco merged with Price Club, which had pioneered the concept of membership warehouses, to form **PriceCostco**. In 1997, the company changed its name to **Costco Wholesale** and all Price Club locations were rebranded Costco. Costco became the first company ever to grow from zero to $3 billion in sales in less than six years. Today, Costco is ranked 22nd on the *Fortune* 500 list with more than 600 stores and 68 million members worldwide, revenue exceeding $99 billion, and profits greater than $1.7 billion.

In the United States, Costco's main competition is **Sam's Club** (subsidiary of **Walmart**) and **BJ's Wholesale Club**. It is the second-largest retailer and the largest membership warehouse club chain in America and the seventh-largest retailer in the world and is ranked 79th on the *Fortune* Global 500.

Cofounder Jim Sinegal points to his employees as the key to Costco's success. Based on this philosophy, Costco is one of the most impressive employers in the world when it comes to the treatment of its retail employees, with higher pay and better benefits through its human resource management process for its 147,000 employees. This helps keep Costco's employee turnover rate at around 12 percent, remarkably low for the retail industry.

1. How does Costco view its human resources management process? PAGE 250
2. What types of recruiting methods does Costco use? PAGE 258
3. How does Costco use its compensation and benefits package to retain employees? PAGE 271
4. What is Costco's attitude toward organizational labor? PAGE 273

You'll find answers to these questions throughout the chapter. To learn more about Costco, visit its website at www.costco.com.

Source: Information for this case was taken from Costco's website at http://www.costco.com, accessed July 11, 2013; Wikipedia's entry on Costco at http://en.wikipedia.org/wiki/Costco, accessed July 11, 2013; "Largest U.S. corporations—Fortune 500," *Fortune* (May 20, 2013): 1–20; "Fortune Global 500: The world's largest corporations," *Fortune* (July 23, 2012): F1.

● ● ● Chapter Outline

The Human Resources Management Process

    The Human Resources Department

    The Legal Environment

    Harassment and Sexual Harassment

Human Resources Planning

    Strategic Human Resources Planning

    Job Analysis

Attracting Employees

    Recruiting

    The Selection Process

    Selection Interviewing

Developing Employees

    Orientation

    Training and Development

    Performance Appraisal

Retaining and Terminating Employees

    Compensation

    Health and Safety

    Unions and Labor Relations

    Terminating Employees

LO 9-1

List the four parts of the human resources management process.

THE HUMAN RESOURCES MANAGEMENT PROCESS

There have been many studies globally to determine the relationship between human resources management (HRM) and performance.[1] Here are the results of a few of the studies. MNCs need effective HRM to remain globally competitive.[2] The importance of people to business success is undisputed, as the organizational practice that has a major impact on this dimension is HRM.[3] Effective HRM gives a company a competitive advantage[4] and greater survival chances, lower employee turnover rates, and higher revenue growth.[5] Companies achieve their objectives through effective HRM practices, resulting in higher productivity and quality and better service, safety, and financial performance.[6] With the uncertain economy, many companies are hiring temporary and part time employees rather than full-time workers.[7] But in either case, the HRM process is the same.

The **human resources management process** *involves planning for, attracting, developing, and retaining employees.* It is also known as the *staffing process.* Exhibit 9-1 illustrates the process; each of the four parts of the process is discussed in this chapter. Notice the arrows used to illustrate the systems effect. For example, planning and compensation affect the kinds of employees an organization can attract; labor relations affect planning; job analysis affects training; and so on.

Costco (Case Question 1) cofounder Jim Sinegal knew from the start that if employees were treated right, including being offered good pay and benefits and chances for promotion, the company's HRM costs would easily be recouped. Its satisfied employees are motivated to work hard and produce more, and the increased productivity more than exceeds the cost of attracting, developing, and compensating new employees. This explains why Costco's turnover rate is one of the lowest in the retailing industry.

EXHIBIT 9-1   THE HUMAN RESOURCES MANAGEMENT PROCESS

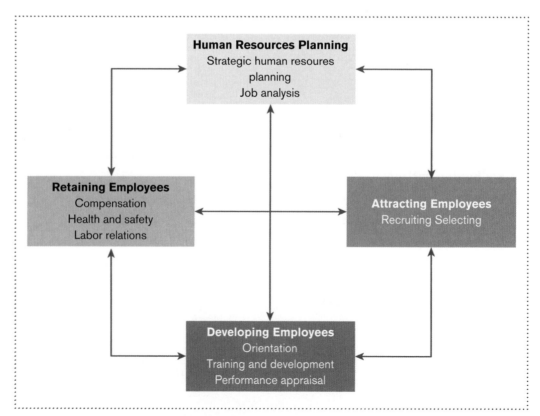

human resources management process Planning for, attracting, developing, and retaining employees.

We'll begin our examination of the HRM process with a discussion of the HRM department, which is responsible for carrying out the HRM process, and of the legal environment, as the law affects all four functions of the HRM process.

The Human Resources Department

Human resources is one of the four major functional departments in an organization. It is a staff department that advises and assists all the other departments in the organization. In organizations large enough (usually about 100 or more employees) to have a separate human resources department, the department performs each of the four functions of the HRM process

As discussed in Chapter 3, outsourcing is becoming more common in business. Many firms, especially small businesses, are outsourcing most or parts of their HRM functions. Companies that outsource part of their HRM functions include **Nokia Solutions and Networks**, and **Unilever**.

A major challenge to HRM departments is record keeping. HR professionals in low-performing organizations spend almost one third of their time maintaining records, auditing, or controlling. Even in high-performing companies, they spend almost one quarter of their time of these tasks. Much of this record keeping is needed to be in compliance with government laws and regulations that require regular reports.[8] More than one half of business owners and executives ranked regulatory burden among their top five concerns, and there is no relief in sight, as the Obama administration will continue its aggressive regulatory philosophy that frequently draws criticism from the business community and conservatives.[9]

WORK
APPLICATION 9-1

Describe the kinds of interactions you have had with the human resources department of an organization you work for or have worked for.

The Legal Environment

The external environment, especially the competitive and legal environment, has a major impact on HRM practices. Organizations are not completely free to hire, promote, or fire whomever they want. The HRM department usually has the responsibility of seeing that the organization complies with the law.

Federal Laws Related to HRM. Some of the major federal laws and regulations affecting employment in U.S. companies are presented in Exhibit 9-2 and discussed in the following.

Major laws affecting employment are the Equal Employment Opportunity Act of 1972, which is an amendment to the Civil Rights Act of 1964 that prohibits employment discrimination on the basis of sex, religion, race or color, or national origin and applies to virtually all private and public organizations that employ 15 or more employees. The **Equal Employment Opportunity Commission (EEOC)** minority guidelines identify Hispanics, Asians, African Americans, Native Americans, and Alaskan natives as minorities protected under the act; the act also protects disadvantaged young people, disabled workers, and persons older than 40 years of age. Although the law protects women from discrimination in employment, they are not considered to be a statistical minority because they make up half of the population; in some work situations, women are a majority.[10]

The EEOC is responsible for enforcing equal opportunity laws. It has 53 district, field, area, and local offices across the nation, and it operates a toll-free line

When interviewing job candidates, managers need to be careful to obey the law by not asking any illegal discriminatory questions. Photo from Digital Vision/Thinkstock.

EXHIBIT 9-2   FEDERAL LAWS RELATED TO HRM

Law	Description
Equal Employment Opportunity	
Equal Employment Opportunity (EEOC) Act of 1972 (Title VII of the Civil Rights Act of 1964)	Prohibits discrimination on the basis of race, religion, color, sex, or national origin in all areas of the employment relationship
Civil Rights Act of 1991	Strengthened civil rights by providing for possible compensation and punitive damages for discrimination
Age Discrimination in Employment (ADEA) Act of 1967 (amended 1978, 1984)	Prohibits age discrimination against people older than 40 and restricts mandatory retirement
Vocational Rehabilitation Act of 1973	Prohibits discrimination based on physical or mental disability
Americans with Disabilities Act (ADA) of 1990	Strengthened the Vocational Rehabilitation Act to require employers to provide "reasonable accommodations" to allow disabled employees to work
Compensation and Benefits	
Equal Pay Act of 1963	Requires that men and women be paid the same for equal work
Family and Medical Leave Act of 1993	Requires employers with 50 or more employees to provide up to 12 weeks unpaid leave for family (childbirth, adoption) or medical reasons
Health and Safety	
Occupational Safety and Health Act (OSHA) of 1970	Establishes mandatory safety and health standards in organizations; regulated by the Occupational Safety and Health Administration (OSHA)

(1-800-669-4000) around the clock to provide information on employee rights. For more information, visit its website www.eeoc.gov.

Violation of the law can lead to being investigated by the EEOC or to becoming a defendant in a lawsuit. Courts find discrimination when employee selection criteria are vague, elusive, unstructured, undefined, or poorly conceived. As a manager, you should be familiar with your organization's EEO guidelines.

Preemployment Inquiries. The EEOC is currently putting extra focus on hiring.[11] On a job application or during an interview, no member of an organization can ask discriminatory questions. The two major rules of thumb to follow include: (1) Every question asked should be job related. When developing questions, you should have a purpose for using the information. Only ask questions you plan to use in the selection process. (2) Any general question that you ask should be asked of all candidates.

Exhibit 9-3 lists what can and cannot be asked during the selection process. In all cases, the assumption is that the information asked for must be related to a bona fide occupational qualification for the job. A **bona fide occupational qualification (BFOQ)** *is one that is reasonably necessary to normal operation of a particular organization.* For example, a BFOQ for a job teaching Jewish religion classes could require that the person selected be a practicing Jew, but it could not be a BFOQ to teach math or English in a Jewish school.

The trend today is to hire the most qualified person for the job without consideration of the diversity groups they belong too. However, when candidates are equal in qualifications, minorities and women tend to get the job when they are underrepresented in the workplace. But white males may also be underrepresented such as nursing and elementary school teaching.

bona fide occupational qualification (BFOQ) An occupational qualification that may be discriminatory but that is reasonably necessary to normal operation of a particular organization.

EXHIBIT 9-3 PREEMPLOYMENT INQUIRIES

Topic	Can Ask...	Cannot Ask...
Name	Current legal name and whether the candidate has ever worked under a different name	Maiden name or whether the person has changed his or her name
Address	Current residence and length of residence there	Whether the candidate owns or rents his or her home, unless one or the other is a bona fide occupational qualification (BFOQ)
Age	Whether the candidate's age is within a certain range (if required for a particular job; for example, an employee must be 21 to serve alcoholic beverages); if hired, can ask for proof of age	How old are you? What is your date of birth? Can you provide a birth certificate? How much longer do you plan to work before retiring?
Sex	Candidate to indicate sex on an application if sex is a BFOQ	Candidate's sexual identity
Marital and Family Status	Whether candidate can adhere to the work schedule; whether the candidate has any activities, responsibilities, or commitments that may hinder him or her from coming to work	Specific questions about marital status or any question regarding children or other family issues
National Origin, Citizenship, or Race	Whether the candidate is legally eligible to work in the United States, and whether the candidate can provide proof of status if hired	Specific questions about national origin, citizenship, or race
Language	What languages the candidate speaks and/ or writes; can ask candidate to identify specific language(s) if these are BFOQs	What language the candidate speaks when not on the job or how the candidate learned the language
Criminal Record	Whether the candidate has been convicted of a felony; if the answer is yes, can ask other information about the conviction if the conviction is job-related	Whether the candidate has ever been arrested (an arrest does not prove guilt); for information regarding a conviction that is not job-related
Height and Weight	Whether the candidate meets BFOQ height and/or weight requirements and whether the candidate can provide proof of height and weight if hired	Candidate's height or weight if these are not BFOQs
Religion	If candidate is of a specific religion, if religious preference is a BFOQ	Candidate's religious preference, affiliation, or denomination if not a BFOQ
Credit Rating	For information if a particular credit rating is a BFOQ	Unless a particular credit rating is a BFOQ
Education and Work Experience	For information that is job related	For information that is not job related
References	For names of people willing to provide references or who suggested the candidate apply for the job	For a reference from a religious leader
Military Record	For information about candidate's military service that is job related	Dates and conditions of discharge from the military; draft classification; National Guard or reserve unit of candidate
Organizations	About membership in job-related organizations, such as unions or professional or trade associations	About membership in any non-job-related organization that would indicate candidate's race, religion, or the like
Disabilities	Whether candidate has any disabilities that would prevent him or her from performing the job being applied for	General questions about disabilities

9-1   APPLYING THE CONCEPT

Legal or Illegal Questions

Using Exhibit 9–3, identify whether each question can or cannot be asked during a job interview.

    A. legal (can ask)

    B. illegal (cannot ask during preemployment)

_____ 1. Have you ever belonged to a union?

_____ 2. How old are you?

_____ 3. Have you been arrested for stealing on the job?

_____ 4. Do you own your own car?

_____ 5. Do you have any form of disability?

_____ 6. Are you a member of the Knights of Columbus, Jewish Community Center, Rotary, or other organizations?

_____ 7. Can you prove you are legally eligible to work?

_____ 8. What languages do you speak?

_____ 9. Are you married or single?

_____ 10. How many children do you have?

_____ 11. So you want to be a truck driver. Are you a member of the Teamsters?

_____ 12. Are you straight or homosexual?

_____ 13. Have you ever filed a lawsuit against an employer?

_____ 14. What is your residence and how long have you lived there?

_____ 15. Do you have AIDS or HIV?

WORK APPLICATION 9-2

Have you or has anyone you know been asked discriminatory questions during the preemployment process? If yes, please explain the situation in language acceptable to all.

Harassment and Sexual Harassment

As discussed in Chapter 3 with diversity, sex discrimination is illegal,[12] and so is sexual harassment.[13] The EEOC is currently putting extra focus on harassment.[14] It is illegal, so let's discuss two types here.

Harassment. Harassment is a form of employment discrimination that violates Title VII of the Civil Rights Act, ADEA, and ADA. *Harassment* is unwelcome conduct that is based on race, color, religion, sex (including pregnancy), national origin, age (40 or older), disability, or genetic information. Petty slights, annoyances, and isolated incidents (unless extremely serious) will not rise to the level of illegality. Harassment becomes unlawful where (1) enduring the offensive conduct becomes a condition of continued employment or (2) the conduct is severe or pervasive enough to create a work environment that a reasonable person would consider intimidating, hostile, or abusive.[15] The HR department is responsible for helping ensure that no one is harassed at work and for keeping records.

Sexual Harassment. It is a real problem, as the EEOC gets more than 11,000 sexual harassment lawsuits filed a year, and settlements amount to more than $52 million. Women file around 83 percent of the cases, so men (17 percent) have fewer complaints.[16]

According to the EEOC, sexual harassment is a form of sex discrimination that violates Title VII of the Civil Rights Act of 1964. Unwelcome sexual advances, requests for sexual favors, and other verbal or physical conduct of a sexual nature constitute sexual harassment when this conduct explicitly or implicitly affects an individual's employment, unreasonably interferes with an individual's work performance, or creates an intimidating, hostile, or offensive work environment.[17]

Keeping it simple, *sexual harassment* is any unwelcomed behavior of a sexual nature. There are two major types. *Quid pro quo sexual harassment* occurs when sexual consent affects job outcomes, such as getting a job or assignment or promotion, or keeping one's job. *Hostile work environment* sexual harassment occurs when unwelcomed sexual behavior creates an intimidating and offensive workplace for anyone.

Sexual Harassment

Indicate which kind of behavior is described in each statement.

   A. sexual harassment (1) quid pro quo or (2) hostile work environment
   B. not sexual harassment

____ 16. Helene tells her assistant Jean that he will have to go to a motel with her if he wants to be recommended for a promotion.

____ 17. Joe and Kate have each hung up pictures of nude men and women on the walls near their desks, in view of other employees who walk by.

____ 18. Gary tells his coworker Sandra an explicitly sexual joke, even though twice before Sandra expressed her distaste for such humor.

____ 19. Asif typically puts his hand on his secretary's shoulder as he talks to her, and she is perfectly comfortable with the way he treats her.

____ 20. Tomas, the supervisor of the production department, tells Marisol, the department's current student intern, that he thinks she is sexy and that he'd like to take her out.

Verbal Warning. Some behavior is clearly harassment the first time, such as unwelcome requests for quid pro quo and touching in private areas. But other behaviors are not clearly harassment, such as telling racial, religious, or sexual jokes and being asked out on a date that are welcomed. Therefore, if someone does something that offends you, you should tell him or her that you find it offensive harassment and not to do it again. Repeated unwelcomed offensives become sexual harassment that you should report, even if you are not the victim.

HUMAN RESOURCES PLANNING

In this section, we discuss strategic human resources planning and job analysis.

Strategic Human Resources Planning

The job of strategic human resource management (strategic HRM) is to provide the right kinds of people in the right quantity with the right skills at the right time.[18] It should be based on the mission, goals, and strategy of the organization.[19] There needs to be a direct link between strategic HRM and company strategy (Chapter 4).[20] If the strategy is growth, then you need a plan to hire employees. If the strategy is retrenchment, then there will be layoffs. **Strategic human resources planning** *is the process of staffing the organization to meet its objectives.* MNCs globally are working to develop a set of "universal" best strategic HRM practices.[21]

At retailers like **Lands' End,** the staffing needs increase during the Christmas holiday season. More than 2,000 seasonal and temporary workers are required to fill these jobs. Staffing is done according to a plan formulated as early as January of that year.[22]

Job Analysis

Strategic HRM determines the number of people and skills needed, but it does not specify how each job is performed. Thus, workforce planning is important,[23] including job analysis, because it serves as a basis for attracting, developing, and retaining employees. *Job analysis* is the process of determining what the position entails and the qualifications needed to staff the position. It puts your strategic HRM plans into action.[24] As the definition implies, job analysis is the basis for the job description and the job specifications.

WORK
APPLICATION 9-3

Have you or has anyone you know been harassed at work? If yes, please explain the situation in language acceptable to all.

LO 9-2

Explain why job analysis is needed, and distinguish between a job description and job specifications.

strategic human resources planning The process of staffing the organization to meet its objectives.

The **job description** *identifies the tasks and responsibilities of a position*. The trend is to organic organizations describing jobs more broadly in order to design enriched jobs (Chapter 7). Exhibit 9-4 shows a sample job description.

EXHIBIT 9-4   JOB DESCRIPTION

DEPARTMENT: Plant Engineering

JOB TITLE: Lead Sheet Metal Specialist

JOB DESCRIPTION:

Responsible for the detailed direction, instruction, and leading of sheet metal department personnel in the construction and repair of a wide variety of sheet metal equipment. Receives verbal or written instructions from foreperson as to sequence and type of jobs or special methods to be used. Allocates work to members of the group. Directs the layout, fabrication, assembly, and removal of sheet metal units according to drawings or sketches and generally accepted trade procedures. Obtains materials or supplies needed for specific jobs according to standard procedures. Trains new employees, as directed, regarding metal-working procedures and safe working practices. Checks all work performed by the group. Usually makes necessary contacts for the group with supervision or engineering personnel. May report irregularities to higher supervision but has no authority to hire, fire, or discipline other employees.

WORK
APPLICATION 9-4

Complete a job analysis for a job you hold or held; write a simple job description and job specifications.

WORK
APPLICATION 9-5

Were you given a realistic job preview during a job interview? Explain.

LO 9-3

Describe recruiting sources for candidates for jobs and the selection process.

Part of the job analysis should be to develop a *realistic job preview (RJP)*. The RJP provides the candidate with an accurate, objective understanding of the job. Research indicates that employees who feel that they were given accurate descriptions are more satisfied with the organization, believe the employer stands behind them and is trustworthy, and express a lower desire to change jobs than do those who feel that they were not given an accurate job description.[25]

Based on the job description, the second part of job analysis is to determine job specifications. **Job specifications** *identify the qualifications needed by the person who is to fill a position*. The job specifications identify the types of people needed.

Attracting Employees

After hiring needs have been determined and jobs analyzed, the HR department generally recruits people to fill positions and presents potential employees for line managers to select from. You need to recruit and select qualified job searchers.[26] In this section, you will learn about recruiting, the selection process, and how to conduct an interview.

Recruiting

Recruiting *is the process of attracting qualified candidates to apply for job openings*. To fill an opening, possible candidates must first be made aware that the organization is seeking employees, and you have to compete with other companies that are also recruiting.[27] They must then be persuaded to apply for the jobs. Recruiting should be an ongoing process[28] so that you will hire the best people.[29] Recruiting good candidates leads to job satisfaction and improved firm value.[30] Recruiting can be conducted internally and externally; Exhibit 9-5 lists possible recruiting sources.

Internal Recruiting. *Internal recruiting* involves filling job openings with current employees or people they know. More firms are opting to recruit from within, including **Cisco Systems** with its Talent Connect program, and it is useful for team-based projects.[31] There are two common types of internal recruiting:

job description Identifies the tasks and responsibilities of a position.

job specifications Identify the qualifications needed by the person who is to fill a position.

recruiting The process of attracting qualified candidates to apply for job openings.

EXHIBIT 9-5 RECRUITING SOURCES

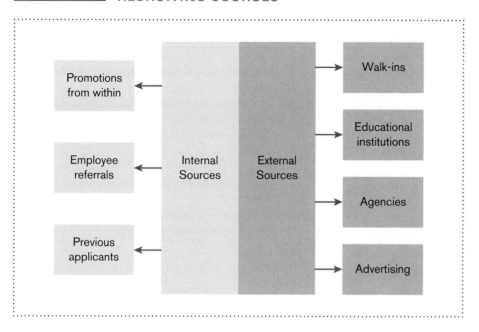

- *Promotions From Within.* Many organizations post job openings on bulletin boards, in company newsletters, and so on. Current employees may apply or bid for the open positions. **Procter & Gamble** uses a promotion-from-within program called Build From Within.[32]

- *Employee referrals.* Employees may be encouraged to refer friends and relatives for positions. For hard-to-recruit jobs, some firms pay a bonus to employees when their referred applicant is hired.

- *External Recruiting. External recruiting* involves filling job openings with applicants outside the organization. Many companies are recruiting using social media, such as **LinkedIn** and **Facebook**. The following are external recruiting sources:

- *Walk-Ins.* Without actually being recruited, good candidates may come to an organization "cold" and ask for a job. Those seeking management-level positions generally tend to send a résumé and cover letter asking for an interview.

- *Educational institutions.* Recruiting takes place at high schools, vocational/technical schools, and colleges. Many schools offer career planning and placement services to aid students and potential employers. Educational institutions are good places to recruit people who have no prior experience.

- *Agencies.* There are three major types of agencies: (1) *Temporary agencies,* such as **Kelly Services**, provide part- or full-time help for limited periods. (2) *Public agencies* are nationwide state employment services. They generally provide job candidates to employers at no cost or very low cost. (3) *Private employment agencies* are privately owned and charge a fee for their services. *Executive recruiters* are sometimes referred to as "headhunters." They specialize in recruiting managers and/or those with specific high-level technical skills, such as engineers and computer experts, charging the employer a large fee.

- *Advertising.* A simple help-wanted sign in the window is an advertisement. Newspapers are good places to advertise most positions, but professional and trade magazines may be more suitable for specific professional recruiting. Many employers and people look for work online. Several websites, such as **Monster.com** and **CareerBuilder.com**, provide job listing opportunities.

WORK
APPLICATION 9-6

Identify the recruiting source used to hire you for your current job or one of your previous jobs.

Recruiting Sources

Select the major recruiting source(s) that should be used for each of the job openings described.

Internal Sources

   A. promotions from within
   B. employee referrals

External Sources

   A. walk-ins
   B. educational institutions
   C. advertising
   D. agencies

_____ 21. One of your workers is taking a six-week maternity leave and needs to be replaced.

_____ 22. One of the first-line supervisors is retiring in two months.

_____ 23. You will have a secretary position available at the end of the month and you would like to get the word out now so as to reach as many qualified candidates as possible.

_____ 24. Your sales manager likes to hire young people without experience in order to train them to sell using a unique approach.

_____ 25. Your maintenance department needs a person to perform routine cleaning services.

Costco (Case Question 2) is committed to internal recruiting and promoting from within the company, but it also uses external recruiting by hiring walk-ins for primarily entry-level positions. The majority of its managers started out at entry-level positions in Costco's warehouses, learned the business, and moved up within the company. While Costco uses some external candidates, all other job openings are filled by internal recruiting. Costco is committed to promoting from within the company. Costco believes that promoting from within ensures equal promotional opportunities for motivated individuals, and this is one of the reasons Costco has such a loyal workforce.

The Selection Process

Selection *is the process of choosing the most qualified applicant recruited for a job.* Selection is important because bad hires can be costly.[33] We discuss six parts of the selection process next. Note that not all parts of the selection process are used for some jobs and that there is no set sequence of steps to be followed in the selection process. However, you can think of the parts as a set of hurdles to get through to get the job.

Application Form. The recruited candidates are typically asked to complete an application or, for professional jobs, a résumé, but in either case, today online applications are often required so that the information is stored in the company's *human resource information system (HRIS)*. Your first step is usually screening applications to select the top candidates to proceed to the following parts of the selection process.

Screening Interviews. Specialists in the HR department often conduct screening interviews to select the top candidates who will continue in the selection process. This step helps save line managers' time when there are large numbers of job applicants. Many organizations, including **Nike** and **PricewaterhouseCoopers**, use computers to conduct screening interviews. **Google** is known for having between 4 and 12 grueling screening interviews.[34]

selection The process of choosing the most qualified applicant recruited for a job.

9-1 **JOIN THE DISCUSSION** ETHICS & SOCIAL RESPONSIBILITY

Homeless Workers

Andre Jehan, Pizza Schmizza founder of the Northwest chain, has an unusual way of recruiting and selecting workers. Homeless people are given pizza slices and soda and sometimes a couple of dollars to carry a sign that reads "Pizza Schmizza paid me to hold this sign instead of asking for money." Jehan believes he is helping the homeless, saying that carrying the signs has been a win-win situation, as the homeless, many of whom have mental illness or other problems that keep them from being able to hold a job, don't

feel embarrassed or exploited; they look forward to the work and food. However, Donald Whitehead, National Coalition for the Homeless, says Jehan is exploiting the homeless.

1. Is Andre Jehan exploiting the homeless?
2. Is it ethical and socially responsible to give homeless people food for carrying signs?

Source: G. Williams, "Will Work for Pizza," *Entrepreneur* (October 2003), http://www.entrepreneur.com/article/65058. Retrieved October 29, 2013.

Testing. Tests can be used to predict job success, as long as the tests meet EEOC guidelines for *validity* (people who score high on the test do well on the job and those who score low do not do well on the job) and *reliability* (if people take the same test on different days, they will get approximately the same score each time).[35] Some of the major types of tests include achievement tests, aptitude tests, personality tests, interest tests, and physical exams. Most midsize and large companies use some form of testing, with a focus on testing for skills, including **Starbucks**.[36] One new trend in testing is to have candidates perform actual work for the company for free as part of the selection process.[37]

Candidates for open job positions are often tested through assessment centers. **Assessment centers** *are places job applicants undergo a series of tests, interviews, and simulated experiences to determine their potential.* At **Great Western Bank**, job candidates for a teller job sit before a computer, which asks them to make change, respond to tough customers, and sell products that customers don't ask for. These tests and simulated experiences help the narrow down the number of candidates.

Background and Reference Checks. Organizations should help prevent poor hires and the negative effects of negligent hiring by instituting a reference-checking system to verify the information on a candidate's application form and/or résumé.[38] Many applications contain false or erroneous material,[39] such as stating candidates have earned college degrees when they have never even attended college. Many candidates also lie during a job interview.[40]

Interviewing. The interview is usually the most heavily weighted and the last of the steps in the selection process. The interview gives the candidate a chance to learn about the job and organization and you a chance to assess things about a candidate that can't be obtained from an application, test, or references, such as the candidate's ability to communicate and his or her personality, appearance, and motivation. The best fit includes if the person will fit with the organizational culture. More than half of HR professionals ranked culture fit as the most important criterion at the interview stage.[41] Because job interviewing is so important, you will learn how to prepare for and conduct a job interview in this section.

Hiring. Based on the preceding, you compare the candidates and decide who is the best suited for the job. Diversity should be considered when selecting a candidate. The candidate is contacted and offered the job. If the candidate does not accept the job or accepts but leaves after a short time, the next-best candidate is offered the job.

To maintain your reputation with job searchers and customers, once a person accepts the job, all the other candidates should be informed that they didn't get

WORK
APPLICATION 9-7

Identify which selection methods were used in the process of selecting you for a job you have now or one you held in the past. If a test was used, specify the type of test.

assessment centers Places job applicants undergo a series of tests, interviews, and simulated experiences to determine their potential.

9-1 **SELF** ASSESSMENT

Career Development

Indicate how accurately each statement describes you by placing a number from 1 to 5 on the line before the statement.

Describes me				Does not describe me
5	4	3	2	1

____ 1. I know my strengths, and I can list several of them.

____ 2. I can list several skills that I have to offer an employer.

____ 3. I have career objectives.

____ 4. I know the type of full-time job that I want next.

____ 5. My written job objective clearly states the type of job I want and the skills I will use on the job.

____ 6. I have analyzed help-wanted ads or job descriptions and determined the most important skills I will need to get the type of full-time job I want.

____ 7. I have or plan to get a part-time job, summer job, or internship related to my career objectives.

____ 8. I know the proper terms to use on my résumé to help me get the full-time job, part-time job, or summer internship I want.

____ 9. I understand how my strengths and skills are transferable, or how they can be used on jobs I apply for, and I can give examples on a résumé and in an interview.

____ 10. I can give examples (on a résumé and in an interview) of suggestions or direct contributions I made that increased performance for my employer.

____ 11. My résumé focuses on the skills I have developed and on how they relate to the job I am applying for rather than on job titles.

____ 12. My résumé gives details of how my college education and the skills I developed in college relate to the job I am applying for.

____ 13. I have a résumé that is customized to each part-time job, summer job, or internship I apply for rather than one generic résumé.

Add up the numbers you assigned to the statements and place the total on the continuum below.

Career ready				In need of career development	
65	55	45	35	25	15 or less

Career planning and networking to get jobs are discussed in the appendix to the chapter.

---

the job in a timely manner along with thanks for applying. If an applicant asks why he or she didn't get the job, be careful with your answer, because the person may start an argument, think you weren't fair, and may even proceed to sue your company for discrimination based on your answer. The recommended legal advice is to simply say something like "although you are qualified, we selected another person who is a better match with our company."[42]

The focus of this chapter is on hiring others. But take a few minutes to determine how ready you are to progress in your own career by completing the Career Development Self-Assessment.

Selection Interviewing

To get a job, you need to be able to ace the interview,[43] but as a manager, you will need to know how to conduct a job interview. So this part of the section can help you do both well. You can practice this skill in Skill Builder 9–1.

Types of Interviews and Questions. Exhibit 9-6 shows the types of interviews and questions. One thing to keep in mind is the need to develop a set of consistent questions to ask all candidates so that you can objectively compare them to select the most qualified.[44]

WORK APPLICATION 9-8

What types of job interviews have you experienced?

WORK APPLICATION 9-9

Identify the types of questions you were asked during a job interview.

EXHIBIT 9-6 TYPES OF INTERVIEWS AND QUESTIONS

Interviews
Structured interview: all candidates are asked the same list of prepared questions
Unstructured interview: has no planned questions or sequence of topics
Semistructured interview: the interviewer has a list of questions but also asks unplanned questions
Questions
Closed-ended questions: "Do you have a class-one license?"
Open-ended questions: "Why do you want to be a computer programmer for our company?"
Hypothetical questions: "What would the problem be if the machine made a ringing sound?"
Probing questions: the probe is not planned; it is used to clarify the candidate's response to an open-ended or hypothetical question. "What do you mean by 'it was tough'?" "What was the dollar increase in sales you achieved?"

Preparing for and Conducting the Interview. Completing the interview preparation steps shown in Model 9–1 and following the five steps of the interview in Model 9–2 will help you improve your interviewing skills.

MODEL 9-1 INTERVIEW PREPARATION STEPS

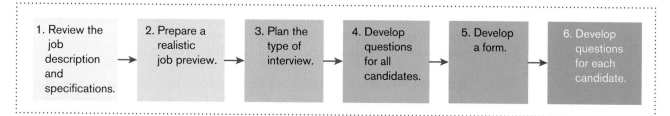

1. Review the job description and specifications. → 2. Prepare a realistic job preview. → 3. Plan the type of interview. → 4. Develop questions for all candidates. → 5. Develop a form. → 6. Develop questions for each candidate.

MODEL 9-2 INTERVIEWING STEPS

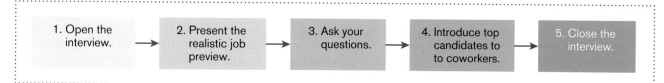

1. Open the interview. → 2. Present the realistic job preview. → 3. Ask your questions. → 4. Introduce top candidates to to coworkers. → 5. Close the interview.

Problems to Avoid. Avoid the following problems during the selection process:

- *Rushing.* Try not to be pressured into hiring just any candidate. Find the best person available.
- *Stereotyping.* Don't judge or leap to conclusions. Match the candidate to the job based on analysis rather than instinct.
- *"Like me" syndrome.* Don't look for a candidate who is your clone. People who are not like you may do an excellent job. Remember the benefits of diversity (Chapter 3).
- *Halo and horn effect.* Do not judge a candidate on the basis of one or two favorable characteristics (the "halo effect") or one or two unfavorable characteristics (the "horn effect"). Make the selection on the basis of the total qualifications of all candidates.

WORK
APPLICATION 9-10

Identify the steps that were used when you were interviewed for a job.

- *Premature selection.* Don't make your selection based only on a candidate's application or résumé or after interviewing a candidate who impressed you. Do not compare candidates after each interview. The order in which you interview applicants can influence you. Be open-minded during all interviews, and make a choice only after you have finished all interviews. Compare each candidate on each job specification.

Selecting the Candidate. After all interviews are completed, compare each candidate's qualifications to the job specifications to determine who would be the best fit for the job. Be sure to get coworkers' impressions of each candidate, because they will have to work with them, and recall that best fit includes fitting in with the organizational culture.[45]

Developing Employees

LO 9-4

Explain what orientation and training and development of employees involve.

After employees have been hired, they must be oriented, trained, and evaluated—all of which are part of developing employees, as they enhance employee knowledge, skills and abilities, motivation, and opportunity to contribute positive outcomes.[46] In this section, we discuss orienting, training, and evaluating employees.

Orientation

Orientation *is the process of introducing new employees to the organization and their jobs.* Orientation gives new employees a chance to "learn the ropes." They are often called newcomers in organizational entry,[47] and newcomer socialization done effectively increases new employee job satisfaction and performance.[48] Most orientations emphasize corporate values, culture, and strengths.[49]

Orientation Programs. Although orientation programs vary in formality and content, five important elements should be included: (1) description of organization and department functions, (2) specification of job tasks and responsibilities, (3) explanation of standing plans, (4) a tour, and (5) introduction to coworkers. Organizations that have developed innovative orientation programs include **Rover.com, Wipro, Rackspace, Bazaarvoice,** and **Google.**[50]

Orientation and training may and often do take place simultaneously. During the orientation and training period, organizations tell employees the firm's personnel policies, such as how many sick days are allowed. Many organizations have some form of personnel policy handbook, which they give to employees or have online.

WORK
APPLICATION 9-11

Recall an orientation you experienced. Which elements did it include and exclude? Briefly describe the orientation.

Training and Development

Employees have to be taught how to perform a new job, and that is what we discuss here.

Training versus Development. Training and development are different processes. **Training** *is the process of teaching employees the skills necessary to perform a job.* Training typically addresses the technical skills of nonmanagers. **Development** *is ongoing education to improve skills for present and future jobs.* Development is less technical and is aimed at improving human, communication, conceptual, and decision-making skills primarily in managerial and professional employees.

Effective training and development are an investment, not an expense, as they pay for themselves through competitive advantage and increased performance.[51] This is why companies worldwide are investing heavily in training and long-term employee development.[52] **Hudson Trail Outfitters** even rewards employees

training The process of teaching employees the skills necessary to perform a job.

development Ongoing education to improve skills for present and future jobs.

orientation The process of introducing new employees to the organization and their jobs.

for completing training programs.[53] As managers' skills should be developed,[54] leadership programs and courses are currently popular.[55] This is why best-practice companies (e.g., **GE, IBM,** and **Johnson & Johnson**) provide leadership programs.[56]

Off-the-Job and On-the-Job Training. As the name implies, *off-the-job training* is conducted away from the work site, often in some sort of classroom setting. A common method is vestibule training. **Vestibule training** *develops skills in a simulated setting.* It is used when teaching job skills at the work site is impractical. For example, many large retail stores have training rooms where new employees learn how to run cash registers and other equipment. The training is usually conducted by a training specialist.

On-the-job training (OJT) is done at the work site with the resources the employee uses to perform the job. The manager or an employee selected by the manager usually conducts the training. Providing mentors is an ongoing training method.[57] Most large organizations conduct some training off the job, whereas small companies tend to use OJT. Because of its proven record of success, job instructional training (JIT) is a popular training method used worldwide.

Job Instructional Training. JIT has four steps, presented in Model 9–3 and described here.

A company's success is based on developing its leaders to continually improve organizational performance. IBM is an example of one company investing in leadership programs.

LO 9-5

List the steps in job instructional training.

MODEL 9-3 JOB INSTRUCTIONAL TRAINING STEPS

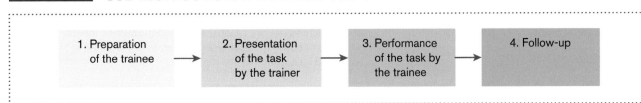

Step 1. Preparation of the trainee. Put the trainee at ease as you create interest in the job and encourage questions. Explain the task objectives and quantity and quality requirements, and discuss their importance.

Step 2. Presentation of the task by the trainer. Perform the task yourself slowly, explaining each step several times. Once the trainee seems to have the steps memorized, have him or her explain each step as you perform the task. Prepare a written list of the steps in complex tasks and give a copy to the trainee.

Step 3. Performance of the task by the trainee. Have the trainee perform the task slowly while explaining each step. Correct any errors and be willing to help the trainee perform any difficult steps. Continue until the employee can perform the task proficiently.

vestibule training Training that develops skills in a simulated setting.

WORK
APPLICATION 9-12

Identify which steps of JIT your trainer used to train you for a present or past job. Was the training conducted on or off the job?

WORK
APPLICATION 9-13

Explain the training methods used to teach you how to perform your present job or a past job.

Step 4. Follow-up. Inform the trainee of those who are available to provide help with any questions or problems. Gradually leave the trainee alone. Begin by checking quality and quantity frequently, then decrease the amount of checking based on the trainee's skill level. Watch the trainee perform the task and be sure to correct any errors or faulty work procedures before they become habits. Be patient and encouraging.

Training and Development Methods. Exhibit 9-7 lists various commonly used training methods, many of which can be used as part of JIT. The training methods are grouped on the basis of the primary skills developed (Chapter 1). However, some of the technical methods can be combined. The trend is to have more active involvement of participants and offer online simulation training and development.[58] You should realize that people within your company and throughout the global village have different learning styles, so you need to use cultural sensitivity in selecting the most appropriate training method.[59]

EXHIBIT 9-7 TRAINING AND DEVELOPMENT METHODS

Skills Developed	Methods	Description
Technical skills	Written material, lectures, videotapes, question-and-answer sessions, discussions, demonstrations Programmed learning	Questions or problems related to previously presented material are presented to the trainee in a booklet or on a computer screen. The trainee is asked to select a response to each question or problem and is given feedback on the response. Depending on the material presented, programmed learning may also develop interpersonal and communication skills.
	Job rotation	Employees are trained to perform different jobs. Job rotation also develops trainees' conceptual skills.
	Projects	Trainees are given special assignments, such as developing a new product or preparing a report. Certain projects may also develop trainees' interpersonal skills and conceptual skills.
Interpersonal skills	Role playing	Trainees act out situations that might occur on the job, such as handling a customer complaint, to develop skill at handling such situations on the job.
	Behavior modeling	Trainees observe how to perform a task correctly (by watching either a live demonstration or a videotape). Trainees role-play the observed skills and receive feedback on their performance. Trainees develop plans for using the observed skills on the job.
Decision-making skills	Cases	The trainee is presented with a simulated situation and asked to diagnose and solve the problems involved. The trainee usually must also answer questions about his or her diagnosis and solution.
	In-basket exercises	The trainee is given actual or simulated letters, memos, reports, and so forth that would typically come to the person holding the job. The trainee must determine what action each item would require and must assign priorities to the actions.
	Management games	Trainees work as part of a team to "manage" a simulated company over a period of several game "quarters" or "years."
	Interactive videos	Trainees can view videotapes that present situations requiring conceptual skills or decision making.

9-4 APPLYING THE CONCEPT

Training and Development Methods

Select the appropriate training method(s) for each situation.

Technical Skills

A. written material
B. lecture
C. videotape
D. question-and-answer session
E. discussion
F. demonstration
G. programmed learning
H. job rotation
I. project

Interpersonal Skills

J. role playing
K. behavior modeling

Decision-Making Skills

L. case
M. in-basket exercise

N. management game
O. interactive video

_____ 26. In our strategy course, we are running a company by filling out these forms and getting quarterly results.

_____ 27. Your supervisors need to do a better job of handling employee complaints.

_____ 28. You have a large department with a high turnover rate. Employees must learn several rules and regulations in order to perform their jobs.

_____ 29. You occasionally have new employees whom you must train to handle the typical daily problems they will face on the job.

_____ 30. You need employees to prepare a special report.

_____ 31. You want to be sure that employees can cover for each other if one or more of them is absent.

_____ 32. You need to teach employees how to handle customer complaints.

Performance Appraisal

After you have hired and trained employees, you must evaluate how well employees perform their jobs so they know how they are doing, so it is an important part of the manger's job.[60] **Performance appraisal** *is the ongoing process of evaluating employee performance.* In a mechanistic organization, managers perform the evaluation, but in organic structures, each team member does a self-evaluation[61] and peers also evaluate each other.[62] In some cases, the evaluation is expanded to everyone the employees comes into contact with, including other departments, customers, and suppliers through *360-degree feedback*.[63]

The Performance Appraisal Process. Exhibit 9-8 illustrates the performance appraisal process. Note the connection between the organization's mission and vision and objectives and the performance appraisal process. Performance should be measured in terms of the mission and objectives that are based on the firm's strategy.[64]

Performance appraisal should not be simply a once- or twice-a-year formal interview. As its definition states, performance appraisal is an ongoing process. Employees need regular feedback on their performance,[65] so give routine and candid assessments.[66] Coaching involves ongoing giving of praise for a job well done to maintain performance or taking corrective action when standards are not met.[67] In Chapter 14, we will discuss coaching and discipline.

You Get What You Reinforce. One of the important things you should learn in your study of the management process is that people will generally do what they are rewarded for doing (good work) and avoid what they are punished for doing (breaking rules). People seek information concerning what activities are rewarded and then seek to do those things, often to the exclusion of activities not rewarded, including doing good work. The extent to which this occurs depends on the attractiveness of the rewards or severity of the punishment. So if you want employees to do a good job, you need to reward the ones who do a good job and not reward

LO 9-6
Explain the two types of performance appraisal.

LO 9-7
Explain the concept "You get what you reinforce."

performance appraisal The ongoing process of evaluating employee performance.

EXHIBIT 9-8 THE PERFORMANCE APPRAISAL PROCESS

or punish those that do a poor job. Reinforcement is a motivation theory that we will discuss in detail in Chapter 11.

Standards and Measurement Methods. To effectively assess performance, you need to have clear standards and methods to measure performance.[68] The **American National Standards Institute (ANSI)** has outlined the minimum elements of a performance management system for goal setting, performance review, and performance improvement plans.[69] For details, visit its website at www.ansi.org.

The formal performance appraisal often involves the use of a standard form developed by the human resources department to measure employee performance. Exhibit 9-9 explains the commonly used performance appraisal measurement methods and displays them on a continuum based on their use in administrative and developmental decisions. Determining the best appraisal method to use depends on the decision. A combination of the methods is usually superior to any one method used by itself.

The success of performance appraisal does not lie in the method or form used; it depends on your interpersonal coaching skills. An important part of your job is to make sure that your employees know what the standards are and how they are performing through ongoing coaching. If you give an employee an average rather than a good rating, you should be able to clearly explain why. The employee

EXHIBIT 9-9 PERFORMANCE APPRAISAL MEASUREMENT METHODS

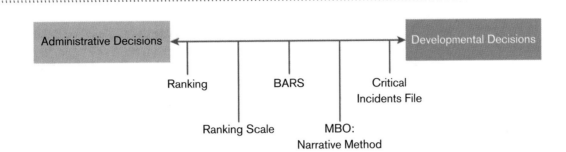

- The **Critical Incidents File** is a performance appraisal method in which a manager keeps a written record of positive and negative performance of employees throughout the performance period.
- **Management by Objectives (MBO)** is a process in which managers and employees jointly set objectives for the employees, periodically evaluate performance, and reward according to the results.
- The **Narrative Method** requires a manager to write a statement about the employee's performance. The system can vary. Managers may be allowed to write whatever they want, or they may be required to answer questions about the employee's performance. The narrative method is often combined with another method.
- **Behaviorally Anchored Rating Scale (BARS)** is a performance appraisal method combining the rating scale and the critical incidents file. It is more objective and accurate than either method used separately. Rather than having ratings of excellent, good, average, and so forth, the form has several statements that describe the employee's performance, from which the manager selects the best one. Standards are clear when a good BARS is developed.
- The **Rating Scale** is a performance appraisal checklist on which a manager simply rates the employee's quantity of work, quality of work, dependability, judgment, attitude, cooperation, and initiative.
- **Ranking** is a performance appraisal method that is used to evaluate employee performance from best to worst. Under the ranking method, the manager compares an employee to other employees, rather than to a standard measurement. An offshoot of ranking is the forced distribution method, which is similar to grading on a curve. Predetermined percentages of employees are placed in various performance categories, for example: excellent, 5%; above average, 15%; average, 60%; below average, 15%; and poor, 5%.

9-5 APPLYING THE CONCEPT

Performance Appraisal Methods

Select the performance appraisal method that is most appropriate for the given situation.

A. critical incidents file
B. MBO
C. narrative method
D. BARS
E. rating scale
F. ranking

_____ 33. One of your employees has applied for a better job at another company and asked you for a letter of recommendation.

_____ 34. You recently started a small company with 10 employees. You are overworked, so you want to develop one performance appraisal form that you can use with all employees.

_____ 35. You have been promoted from a supervisory position to a middle-management position. You have been asked to select your replacement.

_____ 36. Winnie is not performing up to standard. You decided to talk to her in order to improve her performance.

_____ 37. You want to create a system for developing each employee.

_____ 38. Your small business has grown to 50 employees. Employees have complained that the one existing appraisal form does not work well for different types of employee jobs. You have decided to hire a professional to develop a performance appraisal system that is more objective and job specific, with forms for various employee groups.

should understand what exactly needs to be done during the next performance period to get the higher rating. With clear standards and coaching, you can minimize disagreements over performance during the formal performance appraisal.

Developmental and Evaluative Performance Appraisal Interviews. Extending Exhibit 9–9, there two types of performance appraisal (PA): developmental and evaluative. A *developmental performance appraisal* is used to make decisions and plans for performance improvements. An *evaluative performance appraisal* is used to make administrative decisions about such issues as pay raises, transfers and promotions, and demotions and terminations. The evaluative PA focuses on the past, whereas the developmental PA focuses on the future. They are related because a developmental PA is always based on an evaluative PA. However, the primary purpose of performance appraisal should be to help employees continuously improve their performance.[70]

When a developmental and an evaluative PA are conducted together (which they commonly are), the appraisal is often less effective, especially when the employee disagrees with the evaluation. Most managers are not good at being a judge and a coach at the same time. Therefore, separate meetings make the two uses clear and can help you be both a judge and a coach. To help you prepare for and conduct an evaluative PA interview, see Model 9–4; see Model 9–5 for developmental PA interviews.

MODEL 9-4   THE EVALUATIVE PERFORMANCE APPRAISAL INTERVIEW

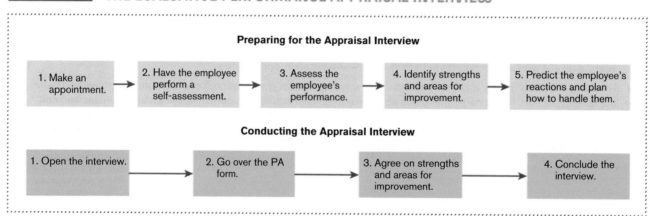

MODEL 9-5   THE DEVELOPMENTAL PERFORMANCE APPRAISAL INTERVIEW

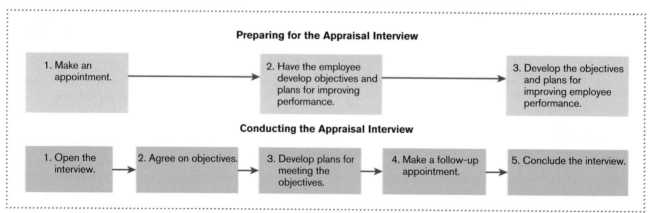

RETAINING AND TERMINATING EMPLOYEES

After planning, attracting, and developing employees, an organization must have HR systems to retain good and terminate poor employees. Discussions of retention and termination commonly use the term *turnover*. *Turnover*, in short, is employees leaving the firm, but the collective quantity and quality of depletion of employee knowledge, skills, abilities, and other characteristics (KSAOs) is a loss to the company.[71] Employee turnover can negatively impact morale, job satisfaction, and performance.[72] Job satisfaction is important because employees who are not happy with their jobs are generally more likely to leave.[73] Thus, employers are offering incentives to stay with the company,[74] such as **Enterprise** car rental offering fast-track promotions.[75] In this section, we discuss compensation, health and safety, labor relations, and terminating employees, all of which affect retention and termination.

Compensation

Compensation *is the total of an employee's pay and benefits.* Compensation is an important part of the HRM process because it affects both attracting and retaining employees.[76] An important overall compensation decision is pay level. *Pay level* reflects top management's choice to be a high-, medium-, or low-paying organization. Low-paying firms may save money on pay, but the savings can be lost to the high cost of turnover as employee leave for better jobs.

Pay Systems. There are three general pay methods, and an organization can use all three. (1) *Wages* are paid on an hourly basis. (2) *Salary* is based on time—a week, a month, or a year. A salary is paid regardless of the number of hours worked. (3) *Incentives* are pay for performance. Incentives include piece rate (pay based on production), commissions (pay based on sales), merit raises (the more productive workers get paid more), and bonuses. Common types of bonuses are a specific reward for reaching an objective, profit sharing in which employees get a part of the profits, and company stock and options to buy the stock at below market value.[77] The use of pay for performance is the trend today. The HR department develops pay systems and pay determination and keeps records in compliance with wage and hour laws.[78]

LO 9-8

Describe the difference between job analysis and job evaluation.

9-2   JOIN THE DISCUSSION ETHICS & SOCIAL RESPONSIBILITY

College Sports Agents

The National Collegiate Athletic Association (NCAA) continues to penalize college sports teams because their athletes receive cars, cash, clothing, and other gifts from sports agents. NCAA rules allow agents to meet with college athletes. However, they forbid these students from entering into contracts—including oral deals—with agents or accepting gift incentives to sign contracts later. The idea is to ensure fair play and to shield amateurs until they are done with school.

The amount of hours that student athletes put into collegiate sports, however, coupled with the millions of dollars that some

major universities earn from the performance of their student athletes, has sparked a debate as to whether these student athletes deserve monetary compensation, despite the fact that they are still students and are playing at an amateur (not professional) level.

1. Is it ethical and socially responsible for college athletes to accept gift incentives from sports agents?
2. Do you think the NCAA should change its rules and allow college athletes to get paid?

Pay Determination. A difficult decision is how much to pay each employee. It is very important to determine an amount that is within your budget but at the same time high enough to retain your current and future employees. An external approach is to find out what other organizations pay for the same or similar jobs and set pay levels that are comparable. An internal approach is to use job evaluation. **Job evaluation** *is the process of determining the worth of each job relative to the other jobs within the organization.* Organizations commonly group jobs into pay grades, creating a pay dispersion.[79] The higher the grade of the job, the higher the pay. The external and internal approaches are often used together.

compensation The total of an employee's pay and benefits.

job evaluation The process of determining the worth of each job relative to the other jobs within the organization.

A controversial issue related to job evaluation is comparable worth. *Comparable worth* is the principle that jobs that are distinctly different but that entail similar levels of ability, responsibility, skills, working conditions, and so on are of equal value and should have the same pay scale. It stems from the fact that traditionally female-dominated jobs generally pay less than traditionally male-dominated jobs (Chapter 3), so comparable worth would help close the pay gap between men and women. Several times legislation has been proposed to make comparable worth a law, but it has been defeated, largely due to the difficulty in comparing very different jobs.

Benefits. *Benefits* are various nonwage compensations provided to employees in addition to their normal wages or salaries. Legally required benefits include *workers' compensation* to cover job-related injuries, *unemployment compensation* to provide for employees who are laid off or terminated, and *Social Security* for retirement. The employer generally pays all of the workers' and unemployment compensation and matches the amount the government takes out of each employee's pay for Social Security. Employers are also required to provide up to 12 weeks of job-protected, unpaid leave during any 12-month period due to a serious health condition that makes the employee unable to perform his or her job, to care for a sick family member, or to care for a new child under the *Family and Medical Leave Act.*

Google employees receive time during the day to play in the game room at the New York Headquarters of Google, where it was just named the best place to work in America. Photo from Yana Paskova/For the Washington Post via Getty Images.

Offering health insurance benefits helps to attract and retain employees, and it is a major concern for both employees and employers, especially with the unknown affects of the Affordable Care Act (ACA), called Obamacare. A **MetLife** study found that 60 percent of employees are concerned about having access to affordable health insurance and worry about how they will pay for the out-of-pocket medical costs. Employers are concerned about the rising cost of health care and how the ACA will affect their health care benefits as it is implemented over the next few years.[80]

Commonly offered optional benefits include health insurance; paid sick days, holidays, and vacations; and pension plans. Optional benefits can be paid in full by employers or split between employee and employer. Other benefits less commonly offered include dental and life insurance, membership in fitness centers, membership in credit unions, and tuition reimbursement for education.

Some companies offer creative optional benefits for their employees. For example, many companies have on-site wellness centers and extend the benefit to families,[81] and some offer on-site day care and elder care. **Google** is known for its crazy free perks like free meals and comfortable places to take breaks and relax.[82] **BMW** in Greer, South Carolina, has an on-site health clinic.[83]

Many corporations offer "cafeteria-style," or flexible, benefit plans to their employees. These plans let employees select the benefits that best meet their needs up to a preset dollar value. In most instances, these plans are funded by both the employee and employer. The portion paid by the employee is deducted from their gross pay before federal and state taxes are applied.

A word of advice for the young; start saving for retirement in your 20s. If you employer offers a retirement account, such as a 401(k) plan, start one as soon as you can. Ask the HR staff if the company will match the money you put into your retirement plan and go to the max to take advantage of free money. Matching dollar for dollar is a 100 percent return on your investment.[84] Would you like to be a millionaire? If you start putting away $2,000 a year (with or without a match) in your early 20s, with competent professional help, you can be a millionaire by the time you retire at age 67.

Work–Life Balance and Benefits. In analyzing the needs of the workforce, work–life balance is high on the list of issues facing both employers and employees.[85] In fact, recent research shows that work–life balance now ranks second only to compensation as the most important driver of employee attraction, commitment, and retention.[86] Some companies, including Campbell Soup and Lowe's, are providing employee assistance programs, seminars, and workshops on how to better balance work and life.

Businesses are increasing using *flexible work practices (FWPs)*, allowing employees control over when, where, or how much they work because it improves work-life balance and job satisfaction and lowers stress.[87] More than 13 million, or around 10 percent, of U.S. employees *telecommute*—work from home—at least one day a week because it can lower costs and boost productivity.[88]

Costco (Case Question 3) is able to retain employees with a low turnover rate of around 12 percent by offering its workers higher-than-average wages and better benefits with opportunities for advancement through promotion from within. In 2013, 85 percent of its U.S. employees, including part-time workers, received health care and other benefits (compared to less than 50 percent at **Walmart** and **Target**), prior to the implementation of the Affordable Care Act (ACA).

WORK
APPLICATION 9-14

Describe the compensation package offered by your present or past employer.

Health and Safety

Safety performance affects recruitment and retention,[89] and it is a major problem globally, as hundreds of employees die on the job each year.[90] To help protect employees, companies must meet safety standards set by the U.S. Occupational Safety and Health Administration (OSHA), maintain records of injuries and deaths due to workplace accidents, and submit to on-site inspections. Those who do not comply are subject to citations and penalties, usually in the form of fines.[91] **BP** had to pay $50.6 million for safety violations found by OSHA regulators at one of its refineries.[92]

The HR department commonly has responsibility for ensuring the health and safety of employees. It works closely with the other departments and maintains health and safety records. A growing area of safety concern is workplace incivility and violence.[93] As a manager, you should know the safety rules, be sure your employees know them, and enforce them to prevent accidents.

9-3 JOIN THE DISCUSSION ETHICS & SOCIAL RESPONSIBILITY

Sweatshops

Nike and many other companies have been criticized for using contract manufacturing with sweatshops that employ workers for very low wages and in poor working conditions. In many countries where much of today's manufacturing takes place, there are few or no health and safety regulations. Some employees get hurt and die on the job. People complain that the United States is losing jobs overseas to companies that are exploiting people.

However, others argue that most Americans don't want these jobs and that U.S. companies are helping people in other countries by giving them jobs. Thus, these companies are raising the standard of living in other countries and keeping prices down at home.

1. In your opinion, are companies that hire sweatshop workers helping these workers or exploiting them?
2. Should a global company compensate all employees at the same rates, or should compensation be based on the cost of doing business and the cost of living in a given country?
3. Is it possible for a company to apply the same health and safety standards that it follows in the United States to its operations in other countries and still compete globally with companies that don't apply such standards?
4. Is it ethical and socially responsible to contract work with sweatshops?
5. What, if anything, should be done about sweatshops?

Unions and Labor Relations

A *labor union* is an organization that represents employees in collective bargaining with the employer over wages, benefits, and working conditions. **Labor relations** *are the interactions between management and unionized employees.* Labor relations are also called *union–management relations* and *industrial relations.* Unions are a source of recruitment and retention. Union membership has been steadily declining in the U.S. for several decades. In 2012, only 11.3 percent, or 14.4 million workers, were union members.[94] Therefore, most businesses do not have labor relations as part of their HR process.

The National Labor Relations Act (also known as the Wagner Act after its sponsor) established the **National Labor Relations Board (NLRB)**, which oversees labor relations in the United States by conducting unionization elections, hearing unfair labor practice complaints, and issuing injunctions against offending employers. For more information about the NLRB, visit its website at http://www.nlrb.gov.

The Union-Organizing Process. There are typically five stages in forming a union, as shown in Exhibit 9-10.

Collective Bargaining. **Collective bargaining** *is the negotiation process resulting in a contract between employees and management that covers employment conditions.* The most common employment conditions covered in contracts are compensation, hours, and working conditions, but a contract can include any condition that both sides agree to. Job security is a major bargaining issue for unions today.[95]

labor relations The interactions between management and unionized employees.

collective bargaining The negotiation process resulting in a contract between employees and management that covers employment conditions.

EXHIBIT 9-10 **THE UNION-ORGANIZING PROCESS**

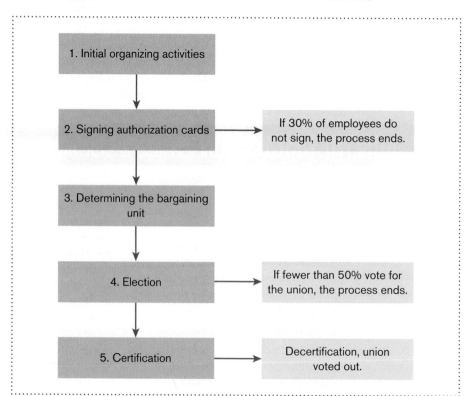

To avoid a strike or a lockout (a refusal by management to let employees work) and to handle *grievances* by either side, collective bargainers sometimes agree to use neutral third parties, called mediators, from the **Federal Mediation and Conciliation Service (FMCS)**. (For more information about the FMCS, visit its website at http://www.fmcs.gov.) A *mediator* is a neutral party that helps management and labor settle their disagreements. In cases in which management and employees are not willing to compromise but do not want to call a strike or a lockout, they may call in an arbitrator. An *arbitrator* is different from a mediator in that the arbitrator makes a binding decision, one to which management and labor must adhere. The services of an arbitrator are more commonly used to settle employee grievances than to deal with impasses in collective bargaining.

The majority of **Costco (Case Question 4)** locations are not unionized, but some former Price Club locations in California and the northeastern United States are staffed by Teamsters union members. The nonunion locations have revisions to their Costco Employee Agreement every three years concurrent with union contract ratifications in locations with collective bargaining agreements. Only remotely similar to a union contract, the Employee Agreement sets forth such things as benefits, compensations, wages, disciplinary procedures, paid holidays, bonuses, and seniority. The employee "agreement" is subject to change by Costco at any time and offers no absolute protection to the workers.

Terminating Employees

When employment stops, the firm has turnover.[96] Employment is terminated for three primary reasons: (1) attrition, (2) firings, and (3) layoffs. Attrition is voluntary turnover, but firing and layoffs are not.[97]

Attrition. It occurs when employees leave for other jobs, elect to stop working for a time, or retire. Employees lost through attrition often need to be replaced. **Groupon** faced a retention problem, as it has a high turnover rate of its sales staff.[98] Child care and elder care are two common reasons for attrition. Retirement is an ongoing issue that the HR staff needs to anticipate, and some companies are retaining employees by offering retirees part-time positions.[99] Employees who leave voluntarily are often interviewed so that managers can find out their reasons for leaving. The *exit interview,* usually conducted by someone from the HR department, can help identify problem areas that lead to turnover.

Firing. Employees who do not perform to standards or violate serious rules should be fired. Firings should be done by you as the manager and should be the last resort. You should coach the employee to improve performance up to an acceptable level. Reasons for termination should be spelled out in the company's employee manual. Employees should know the grounds for firing and how the termination procedure works. You should go by the book and have documentation—build a written record that includes any warnings issued to the employee and performance reviews—in case there is future litigation.[100]

Layoffs/Downsizing. Employees can also lose their jobs due to company layoffs or downsizing based on a retrenchment strategy (Chapter 5). Layoffs usually occur because of poor economic conditions, organizational problems, or mergers and acquisitions. Most large companies try to be ethical and socially responsible during layoffs, and the HR department offers *outplacement services* to help employees find new jobs and give *severance pay* to provide some money while the person conducts a job search.[101]

Downsizing, although a popular practice in the corporate world, has been called one of the most ineffective and expensive methods of reducing a workforce.

Morale usually drops, and companies tend to end up losing more employees than they bargained for due to a surge in voluntary turnover after the downsizing initiative begins, and it is usually the better employees who voluntarily leave for other jobs.

Having read this chapter, you should understand the human resources management process of (1) obeying the law and planning for: (2) attracting—recruiting and selecting; (3) developing—orientation, training and development, and performance appraisals; and (4) retaining and terminating employees.

• • • CHAPTER SUMMARY

9-1. List the four parts of the human resources management process.

The four parts of the human resources management process are (1) planning for, (2) attracting, (3) developing, and (4) retaining employees.

9-2. Explain why job analysis is needed, and distinguish between a job description and job specifications.

Job analysis is necessary because it is the basis for attracting, developing, and retaining employees. The job description identifies the tasks and responsibilities of a position, whereas job specifications identify the qualifications needed by the person who is to fill the position.

9-3. Describe recruiting sources of candidates for jobs and the selection process.

Recruiting can be either internal or external. Internal sources of job candidates are promotions and employee referrals. External sources include walk-ins, educational institutions, agencies, and advertising. The selection process can include having candidates complete application forms, be interviewed, take tests, and submit to background and reference checks.

9-4. Explain what orientation and training and development of employees involve.

Orientation is the process of introducing new employees to the organization and their jobs. Training is the process of teaching employees the skills necessary to perform a job. Development is ongoing education to improve skills for present and future jobs.

9-5. List the steps in job instructional training.

The steps in job instructional training are (1) preparation of the trainee, (2) presentation of the task by the trainer, (3) performance of the task by the trainee, and (4) follow-up.

9-6 Explain the two types of performance appraisal.

The two types of performance appraisal are the developmental performance appraisal and the evaluative performance appraisal. A developmental performance appraisal is used to make decisions and plans for performance improvements. An evaluative appraisal is used to make administrative decisions, including decisions about pay raises, transfers, promotions, demotions, and terminations.

9-7. Explain the concept "You get what you reinforce."

People will generally do what they are rewarded for doing (good work) or avoid what they are punished for doing (breaking rules). People seek information concerning what activities are rewarded and then seek to do those things, often to the exclusion of activities not rewarded. So to get employees to do a good job, managers need to reward the ones who do a good job and not reward or punish those that do a poor job.

9-8. Describe the difference between job analysis and job evaluation.

A job analysis is used to determine what the job entails and the qualifications needed to staff the position. Job evaluation is used to determine the worth of each job to the other jobs within the organization.

• • • KEY TERMS

••• Key Term Review

Complete each of the following statements using one of this chapter's key terms.

1. The _____ consists of planning for, attracting, developing, and retaining employees.

2. A _____ allows discrimination where it is reasonably necessary to normal operation of a particular organization.

3. _____ is the process of staffing the organization to meet its objectives.

4. The _____ identifies the tasks and responsibilities of a position.

5. _____ identify the qualifications needed by a person who is to fill a position.

6. _____ is the process of attracting qualified candidates to apply for job openings.

7. _____ is the process of choosing the most qualified applicant recruited for a job.

8. _____ are places job applicants undergo a series of tests, interviews, and simulated experiences to determine their potential.

9. _____ is the process of introducing new employees to the organization and their jobs.

10. _____ is the process of teaching employees the skills necessary to perform a job.

11. _____ is ongoing education to improve skills for present and future jobs.

12. _____ develops skills in a simulated setting.

13. _____ is the ongoing process of evaluating employee performance.

14. _____ is the total of an employee's pay and benefits.

15. _____ is the process of determining the worth of each job relative to the other jobs within the organization.

16. _____ are the interactions between management and unionized employees.

17. _____ is the negotiation process resulting in a contract between employees and management that covers employment conditions.

••• Review Questions

1. List the two major rules of thumb to follow during preemployment inquiries.

2. What is a bona fide occupational qualification (BFOQ)?

3. What is a job analysis?

4. What are the types of internal recruiting?

5. What are the stages in developing employees?

6. What is the difference between training and development?

7. What is vestibule training?

8. How often should performance appraisals be conducted?

9. How is compensation used to both attract and retain employees?

10. What types of organizations have labor relations?

11. What is the difference between a mediator and an arbitrator?

••• Communication Skills

The following critical-thinking questions can be used for class discussion and/or as written assignments to develop communication skills. Be sure to give complete explanations for all questions.

1. Why do you think that most organizations do not employ state-of-the-art human resources management (HRM) practices?

2. What is your opinion of the use of bona fide occupational qualifications (BFOQs)?

3. What is your opinion of using promotions from within as a recruiting source?

4. Do you agree that the job interview should be the primary criterion for selection?

5. What is the most common problem to avoid during interviewing?

6. If you work as a manager for a company with a human resources department, does this mean that you don't have to orient and train employees? Explain.

7. What is your view of performance appraisals? How can they be improved?

8. What pay system do you prefer? Why is this your preference?

9. Why don't most employees realize how expensive benefits are and how much they contribute to compensation cost?

10. Are unions greedy because they expect workers to receive more than they are worth, or is management greedy because it takes excessive salaries and gives too large a share of the profits to the owners?

• • • CASE: GOOGLE'S HUMAN RESOURCE MANAGEMENT

Do you think it would be easy to work in the human resource department at Google? Do you think people are always looking to work at Google? Or is it possible that people actually want to leave Google?

It turns out that a lot of women were leaving Google. Google, the place that is known for happy employees, asked why.

Instead of Human Resources, Google calls the department People Operations. The mission of People Operations is as follows:

> In People Operations (you probably know us better as "Human Resources"), we "find them, grow them, and keep them"—bringing the world's most innovative people to Google and building programs that help them thrive. Whether recruiting the next great Googler, refining our core programs, developing talent or simply looking for ways to inject more fun into the lives of our Googlers, we bring a data-driven approach that is reinventing the human resources field.[102]

So, why did women want to leave Google? It turned out that Google used their analytical skills to study the problem and found that the maternity leave plan did not match what the women needed. So Google created a more flexible plan that would allow a new mother to take a reasonable amount of time off as necessary. Although the old benefit favored women in the Google headquarters with 12 weeks off for maternity, it only allowed for 7 weeks off for women that worked for Google in the rest of the world. The new maternity plan also offered the same benefit to all the company's workers around the world. Plus a woman could take time off for having her baby, work for a few months, and then take off the rest of the time she had left on her maternity leave.[103]

Google is often rated the best company in the world to work for by *Fortune* magazine.[104] Why does that occur? Does Google know something that the rest of the world has missed? Does your company offer free gourmet food or on-site laundry? Does your company have long tables at lunch to encourage a variety of people to talk to each other?

Human resources for any company has thousands of decisions to make about their people every day. As Prasad Setty from People Operations said, "We make thousands of people decisions every day—who we should hire, how much we should pay them, who we should promote, who we should let go of. What we try to do is bring the same level of rigor to people decisions that we do to engineering decisions. Our mission is to have *all* people decisions be informed by data."

Or, to put it into a less data-driven context, "if you like your job, but for all that it should be—and it could be—something more. So why isn't it?"[105] Hopefully, every human resources department can help its employees to become all they can be.

Case Questions

1. Which human resources management process was most likely the least important for Google?

2. Which human resource management process was the problem with Google's female employees?

3. Does Google practice effective strategic human resources planning?

4. From reading the case, does it seem that Google gets most of its employees from internal or external recruiting?

5. How did Google change its human resources management process regarding maternity leave?

Cumulative Case Questions

6. Explain how changes in the external environment resulted in changes in the internal environment at Google (Chapter 2).

7. What type of strategy is Google currently pursuing? (Chapter 4)

8. How did Google manage diversity in the case? (Chapter 6)

• • • SKILL BUILDER 9-1: SELECTING A TENNIS COACH

Objectives

To perform a job analysis and to develop skills in employment interviewing

Skills

The primary skills developed through this exercise are:

1. *Management skill*—decision making (conceptual, diagnostic, analytical, and critical-thinking skills are needed to select an employee)

2. *AACSB competencies*—communication abilities and analytic skills

3. *Management function*—organizing (staffing)

Recruiting

You are in your first year as athletic director at a high school. The tennis coach position is open, and you must fill it. The compensation for the job is set in the budget; the coach is to be paid in one lump sum at the end of the season. The salary is competitive with the pay of other tennis coaches in the area.

Because you have no recruiting budget, you do some internal recruiting and contact some athletic directors in your area to spread the word about the opening. You recruit three candidates for the coaching position. Following are descriptions of their qualifications:

- *Candidate A* has been a history teacher at your school for 10 years. This person was the tennis coach for two years. It's been five years since this person coached the team. You don't know why the candidate stopped coaching or how good a job was done. Candidate A never played competitive tennis. However, someone told you that the candidate plays regularly and is pretty good. You guess the teacher is about 35 years old.

- *Candidate B* works as a supervisor on the 11 P.M. to 7 A.M. shift for a local business. This candidate has never coached before. However, the person was a star player in high school and college. Candidate B still plays in local tournaments, and you see the name in the local newspaper now and then. You guess this candidate is about 25 years old.

- *Candidate C* has been a basketball coach and physical education teacher at a nearby high school for the past five years. The person has a master's degree in physical education. You figure it will take the person 20 minutes to get to your school. Candidate C has never coached tennis but did play on the high school team. The candidate plays tennis about once a week. You guess the person is about 45 years old.

Preparing for the Interviews

Follow the six interview preparation steps in Model 9–1. (You can skip step 1, as there is no job description or specifications.) Because there are only three candidates, you have decided to interview them all.

Conducting the Interviews

During the in-class part of this exercise, you will conduct a job interview. Be sure to bring your written list of questions to class.

- *Procedure 1* (5–10 minutes). Break into groups of five or six, pass the lists of questions around to the other members, and discuss them. You may make changes to improve your list. For example, you may want to add some questions you had not thought of.

- *Procedure 2* (30–80 minutes). Each person elects to play the role of one of the three job candidates. While playing the role, you may use your real name but assume that you have the qualifications described earlier. Ad lib as necessary. Another member of the group plays the role of interviewer, and the third person is the observer. The interviewer uses the questions devised earlier to conduct the interview. The observer gives feedback at the end of the interview, and the group members discuss how the interview could be improved. After the discussion, group members switch roles: A different group member plays another job candidate, and another group member acts as interviewer. Again, discuss the interview once it is completed before switching roles for a third time.

- *Procedure 3.* Each member of the group selects the candidate for the job; members of the other groups will do the same. The class can discuss the reasons for choosing a particular candidate.

Apply It

What did I learn from this experience? How will I use this knowledge in the future?

• • • SKILL BUILDER 9-2: JOB INSTRUCTIONAL TRAINING

Objective

To improve your skill at conducting training using the JIT model.

Skills

The primary skills developed through this exercise are:

1. *Management skills*—technical (to do the task) and interpersonal (to communicate and motivate the person to do the task)

2. *AACSB competency*—communication abilities

3. *Management function*—organizing (training and development)

Preparing for Skill Builder 2

For this Skill Builder, you will prepare to conduct a training session in which you will use the steps of the job instructional training (JIT) process outlined in the text and illustrated in Model 9–3.

Select a task: Begin by selecting a task or a skill that you are familiar with but that other class members may not know how to do. It should be a task or a skill that you can teach someone else in about 10 minutes (for example, how to knit, an athletic technique, the basics of some computer software, the rules of a card game, how to perform a magic trick, or the like).

Set objectives: Write down your objectives for the training session.

Prepare for training: Write a description of your training session, making sure that it follows the steps in the JIT process. Your plan should include a description of how you will measure and evaluate your training results. The training itself will be conducted in class. Plan to bring to class anything you'll need for your training (knitting needles and yarn, a deck of cards, or whatever).

Apply It

What did I learn from this experience? How will I use this knowledge in the future?

• • • SKILL BUILDER 9–3: HIRING A PROFESSOR AT YOUR COLLEGE

Objective

To develop your understanding of the hiring process.

Skills

The primary skills developed through this exercise are:

1. *Management skill*—decision making (conceptual, diagnostic, analytical, and critical-thinking skills are needed to select an employee)
2. *AACSB competencies*—analytic skills and reflective thinking skills
3. *Management function*—organizing (staffing)

Preparing for Skill Builder 9–3

For this Skill Builder, you will use the concepts discussed in the chapter to answer the following questions on how you would go about hiring a new professor to teach at your college. You should do some research to help you do the following four things.

1. Write a brief job description and job specifications for an opening to teach this and other related courses full time.
2. Write a list of questions that you will ask the candidates during the job interview.
3. What methods would you use to evaluate the professor's teaching performance?
4. How much does the position pay, and what are the benefits?

Apply It

What did I learn from this experience? How will I use this knowledge in the future?

• • • STUDENT STUDY SITE 📱

Visit the Student Study Site at **www.sagepub.com/lussier6e** to access to these additional study tools:

- Mobile-compatible self-assessment quizzes
- Mobile-compatible key term flashcards
- Video Links
- SAGE Journal Articles
- Web Links

Appendix
Career Management and Networking

• • • **Learning Outcomes**

After studying this appendix, you should be able to:

A-1. List the steps in career planning. PAGE 281

A-2. List the steps in the networking process. PAGE 285

A-3. Describe a one-minute self-sell. PAGE 287

CAREER MANAGEMENT

Career success is probably on your mind, as it is important to both work and life satisfaction.[106] A **career** is a sequence of related job positions, involving increasing responsibility and increased compensation and held over a lifetime. Career success depends on hard work and planning. Today people no longer spend their entire career with the same company. Remember that you must take the responsibility for managing your career; you can't simply rely on others to give you jobs, raises, and promotions. This appendix will help you with your career by discussing career planning and development and getting a job. If you have not completed the Career Development Self-Assessment in Chapter 9, do so now.

Career Planning and Development

There is a difference between career planning and career development. **Career planning** *is the process of setting career objectives and determining how to accomplish them.* **Career development** *is the process of gaining skill, experience, and education to achieve career objectives.*

In order to be successful, you need a career plan. Most colleges offer career-planning services that can help you. The career-planning counselor's role is not to find you a job but to help you set realistic career objectives and plans. The *career-planning model* steps below can help you develop your own career plan. Skill Builder A-1 will guide you in the use of these steps to develop your own career plan.

Step 1. Self-assessment. The starting point in career planning is the self-assessment inventory: Who are you? What are your interests, values, needs, skills, experience, and competencies? What do you want to do during your career? The key to career success is to determine what you do well, what you enjoy doing, and how to find a job that combines your interests and skills. The right career for you will give you work-life balance. If you aren't sure what your interests are, your college career center may have test to help match you with a job. You can also take test online at some websites.

Step 2. Career preferences. Others can help you get a job, but you are responsible for selecting your career. Based on your self-assessment, you must decide what you want from your job and career and prioritize these preferences. It is not enough simply to determine what you want to do. It is also important to determine why you want to do these things. What motivates you? How much do you want it? What is your commitment to your career? Without the appropriate level of motivation and commitment to your career objectives and plans, you will not be successful in attaining them.[107]

Some of the things you should consider as you think about your career preferences are (1) what industry you want to work in, (2) what size organization you want to work for, (3) what type of job(s) you want in your career and which

---

LO A-1

List the steps in career planning.

**WORK
APPLICATION A-1**

What career development efforts are you making?

career planning The process of setting career objectives and determining how to accomplish them.

career development The process of gaining skill, experience, and education to achieve career objectives.

• • • **Appendix Outline**

functional areas interest you (production/operations, marketing, finance, human resources, and so on), (4) what city, state, or country you want to work in, and (5) how much income you expect when you start your career and 5 years and 10 years after that.

Once you have thought about these preferences, read about the career areas that interest you. Talk to people in your school's career-planning office and to people who hold the types of jobs you are interested in. (This is called networking, and we discuss networking in more detail later in this appendix.) Determine the requirements and qualifications you need to get a job in the career that interests you. Participating in an internship or fieldwork and taking on a part-time job and/or a summer job in your field of interest can help you land the job you want after graduation.

Step 3. Career objectives. You need to set goals and act on them. Set short- and long-range objectives, using the planning guidelines discussed in Chapter 5.

Step 4. Plan. Develop a plan that will enable you to attain your objectives. This is where career development fits in. You must determine what skills, experience, and education you need in order to progress from your current level to your career goal. You should write out your career plan—but just because it's written down doesn't mean it can't be changed. You should be open to unplanned opportunities and be willing to take advantage of them.

Step 5. Control. Review your objectives, check your progress at least every few months, and change and develop new objectives and plans. Update your résumé as you improve your skills and experience. Having good career coach or mentors can help you get a job and advance through career stages.

Getting a Job

It has been said that getting a good job is a job in itself. If you want to land a good job, you should develop a career plan before you begin your job search. Then you prepare a résumé and cover letter for each job, research the organization, and prepare for the interview. But let's start with some pre–job search considerations.

Pre–Job Search Considerations. These ideas can help you.

- *Search Yourself.* Many employers will look you up on the Internet, so before you start looking for a job, research your online reputation. Enter your name into search engines to see what employers might find. Go to your social-networking sites (**Facebook, MySpace**) and be sure to remove any inappropriate photos (not fully dressed, drinking, etc.) and comments.

- *Phone Message.* You may also get calls from employers, so make sure your phone messages are businesslike; skip the music and sound professional.

- *Job Selection.* Make sure you get a job that is in your field that will add experience you need to progress in your career. Avoid taking any job just to have a job, because your experience can move you in a direction with experience you don't want that can even actually hurt your chances of getting into your career.

- *Jobs While Searching.* If you are thinking, "well, I need money," here are three options to help get you to the job you really want. (1) Work for a temporary agency. This can give you some experience and get you into some organizations you may want to work for that could lead to networking and a full-time job. Agency staff commonly help improve resumes. (2) Be a substitute teacher. In most states you don't need to be a certified teacher, and in some states you don't even need to have completed your college degree. Temping and subbing can be tough, but you can earn money and you can easily take days off from temping, and when subbing, you are done with work early enough to get to job interviews as you search for the job in your field that you really want to progress to in your career. (3) If you know you want to work for a specific organization, do an internship or take an entry-level job to get your foot into the door. If you do a good job, you may be able to move up through a promotion from within to the job you really want.

- *Target Your Search Using Keywords.* Don't simply send out hundreds of generic resumes. Select jobs you want and customize your resume and cover letter to match the job. In the objective, state the company name and title of the job you want. Most large companies scan resumes for keywords. To increase your chances of being in the interview pile, you need to carefully read the job description and use the exact words in your resume, and don't vary the term for variety. After selecting the targeted job, your entire resume should focus on letting the employer know that you can do the job.

Résumé and Cover Letter. According to one recruiting executive at **Xerox**, the résumé is about 40 percent of getting a job. Your résumé and the cover letter you send with it are your introduction to the organization you wish to work for. If the résumé is messy or contains mistakes, you may not get an interview. The cover letter should be short—one page or less. Its purpose is to introduce your résumé and to request an interview. The résumé should also be short; one page is recommended, unless you have extensive education and experience. Exhibit A provides a sample résumé. Note that the objective lists a specific job and company, so again target your search by listing the job and the company for each and every job you apply for. Skill Builder A-2 will give you practice in preparing a résumé.

- *Accomplishments.* When listing internships and other work experience, volunteer work, and sports on your résumé, be sure to focus on accomplishments and skills that can be used on the job you are applying for. Show leadership skills and initiative. Also, explain what value you added in detail with metrics—how many people did you supervise? How did the organization benefit by having you as an employee? If you offered ideas on how to improve performance or developed a new way of doing things, say so.

- *Transferable Skills.* When you are applying for a professional job unrelated to prior jobs, no one cares that you mowed lawns or bused tables. Describe the skills you learned that can be used to do the job you are applying for, such as communication and leadership skills. Explain how you dealt with customers.

- *Critique.* Have your resume reviewed for improvements by multiple people, such as the career center staff, professors, family and friends, and especially people in your career field. But realize that there is no one best resume format. People will give you different suggestions for improvements, so correct any errors, but use your best judgment on how to improve it.

- *Use resumes for All Jobs.* Note that presenting a résumé when you are applying for part-time or summer employment or an internship can give a positive impression that makes you stand out from the competition to get the job.

- *Research.* Without doing research, you may not get the job.

- *Finding Jobs.* Research shows that most jobs are filled through networking,[108] so we will discuss how to network in detail in the next major section. But in setting your career objectives, you may have done some research into particular organizations you might want to work for. Larger company websites have a link for "careers"—opportunities and job listings and you can apply online. Many colleges offer seminars in job-search strategies. Help-wanted ads in newspapers and online job-search services (such as http://www. monster.com and www.careerbuilder.com) are common places to research jobs and, www.CollegeRecruiter.com focuses on internships and entry-level jobs for recent college grads. You can also post your resume online and create a profile on career-related networking sites, such as **LinkedIn**, and participate in discussion boards to develop online relationships that can lead to a job. Many people credit LinkedIn with helping them get job and advance in their careers.[109]

- *Employer Information.* Once you have been invited to an interview, but before you go to it, you should research the organization in more detail—let the interviewer know you are really interested in the job through doing your homework. You want to determine as much about the organization as you can. For example, you should know something about the products and/or services it offers, the industry and its trends, and the organization's profits and future plans. One place to find this information is the organization's website. Essentially all employer websites will give detail on their products and services, and corporations should have an annual report providing the other information you want to bring up in the interview.

The Interview—Tips. In most hiring decisions, the interview is given the most weight—usually about 60 percent. Your résumé and your references can get you an interview, but how you perform during the interview usually determines whether you get the job. During the interview, you need to convince the person that you can do the job and that you are a good fit to the job, department, and firm. It pays to be polite to everyone.[110] Here are some tips related to interviewing that can help you get the job, and there are more tips in the follow-up section:

- Don't show up more than 10 minutes early; respect the interviewer's time.
- It is vital to make a very positive first impression, so your attire and appearance should be appropriate for the job.
- Offer a firm handshake and make direct contact, and use eye contact throughout the interview.
- Answer the questions directly with details but without long-winded, useless information.
- Your best bet is to wait until you're offered the job before talking about compensation. And you should have done your research to know what the salary range is, because they may ask you how much you expect. But you can try to avoid making the first offer by asking them what the salary range is or what the company has budgeted for the position.
- After the interview, evaluate your own performance; make some notes on what you did and did not do well.
- Send a thank-you letter/email to the interviewer, adding anything you forgot to say, stating your interest and the most important reasons you should get the job, and closing by saying that you look forward to hearing from the interviewer. Enclose/attach a copy of your résumé.

- Wait at least a week before checking on your candidacy.
- Only call the person at the office, and leave a message if you get voicemail.
- If you know that you did not get the job, ask the interviewer why and how you can improve. You may or may not be told, but an honest answer can be helpful in preparation for future interviews.

Career Services. Many college career-planning services offer workshops on job searching, resume writing, and how to interview for a job. Some provide the chance to go through a mock interview that is videotaped so that you can evaluate yourself afterward. If your career-planning office offers this service, take advantage of it.

Helpful Websites. The **Riley Guide** (www.rileyguide.com) is an independent online free directory of career and job search resources.[111] **ProvenResumeS.com** has an excellent website with free information to help you write your resume.

WORK
APPLICATION A-2

Which specific ideas on getting a job do you plan to use?

Networking

We'll begin by discussing the importance of networking, and then we'll outline the five steps of the networking process.

The Importance of Networking

Networking is important to your career success,[112] but it is not just about you, as others should benefit in your network.[113] **Networking** *is the process of building relationships for the purpose of career building and socializing.* In other words, networking is marketing yourself; through networking you are being responsible for your career and the exposure of your talents and skills. You have most likely heard the statement "It's not what you know, it's who you know that's important." Networking is more important than sending resumes that end up getting you nowhere. Even today with social media sites like **Facebook**, word of mouth is the best way to find a job.[114]

There are many reasons, in addition to getting a job, to develop your networking skills:

- To get a job
- To learn how to perform better at your job
- To advance within an organization
- To stay current in your field
- To maintain mobility
- To get advice and resources to start and to grow a business
- To develop personal and professional relationships

The Networking Process

When you need any type of help, who do you turn to? Networking sounds easy, and people tend to think that it should come naturally. However, the reality is that networking is a learned skill that just about everyone struggles with at one time or another. In this section, we'll discuss a process that will enhance your career development.[115] Although the same networking process is used for both job searches and broad career development, this discussion focuses more on the job search. So when you are looking for a job, get the word out. Tell everyone you know you are looking for work—in person, by phone, and online.

LO A-2

List the steps in the networking process.

networking The process of developing relationships for the purpose of career building and socializing.

EXHIBIT A RÉSUMÉ

Will Smith

10 Oak Street

Springfield, MA 01118

(413) 555–3000 / wsmith@aol.com

Objective

Hardworking self-starter seeks sales position at New England Wholesale Foods

Education

B. S. Marketing, GPA: 3.4, May 2014

Springfield College, Springfield, MA

Experience

Big Y Supermarket

100 Cooley St. Springfield, MA 01118, supervisor Fred Fry (413) 782–8273

Marketing Internship Spring Semester 2014

- Helped with the weekly newspaper ad inserts and suggested a layout change that is currently being used

- Worked directly for the store manager on a variety of tasks and projects including research to better understand customers

Eblens

732 Boston Rd, Springfield, MA 01118, supervisor Julie DeSata (413) 783–0982

Salesperson May–August 2012

- Sold clothing and footwear to a diverse mix of customers

- July Employee of the Month for having the highest sales volume

Eastern Landscaping

10 Center St. Springfield, MA 01109, supervisor John Fotier (413) 782–7439

Landscaper May 2009–August 2011

- Developed communication skills by interacting with customers and resolving complaints

- Helped get two new customers, which resulted in a 5 percent increase in sales

Honors and Interests

- **Dean's Scholarship:** Recipient of academic scholarship for academic achievement excellence

- **Kappa Delta Pi Honor Society**

- **NCAA Division III Basketball:** Member of the Springfield College basketball team; captain senior year

Step 1. Perform a self-assessment and set objectives. You conduct the same kind of self-assessment for networking as you do when planning for career development. However, in networking, you set narrower objectives. For example, your own networking objectives might include "get a mentor," "determine the expertise, skills, and requirements needed for [a specific job]," and "get feedback on my résumé and job and/or career preparation so that I can be ready to move into [a specific job]." Again, focus on your skills and accomplishments and tie them to the job you want.

WORK
APPLICATION A-3

Write a networking objective.

Step 2. Create your one-minute self-sell. Create a brief statement about yourself to help you accomplish your goal. A **one-minute self-sell** *is an opening statement used in networking that quickly summarizes your history and career plan and asks a question.* If it is to take 60 seconds or less, your message must be concise, but it also needs to be clear and compelling. It gives the listener a sense of your background, identifies your career field and a key result you've achieved, and it tells the listener what you plan to do next and why. It also should stimulate conversation.

LO A-3

Describe a one-minute self-sell.

- *History.* Start with a summary of the highlights of your career to date. Briefly describe the jobs or internships you've held and any relevant courses, certification, and other qualifications you have.
- *Plans.* Identify the career you are seeking, the industry you prefer, and a specific function or role. You can also mention names of organizations you are targeting and state why you are looking for work.
- *Question.* Finally, ask a question to encourage two-way communication. The question will vary, depending on the person you hope to network with and the goal of your one-minute self-sell. For example, you might ask one of the following questions:

"What areas might offer opportunities for a person with my experience?" "In what other fields can I use these skills or this degree?" "Are there other positions in your organization where my skills could be used?" "What do you think of my career goals? Are they realistic, given my education and skills?" "Do you know of any job openings in my field?"

In your one-minute self-sell, be sure to clearly separate your history, your plans, and your question, and customize your question based on the contact you are talking to. Consider the following example:

WORK
APPLICATION A-4

Write a one-minute self-sell to achieve the networking objective you wrote for Work Application A-3.

Hello. My name is Will Smith. I am a senior at Springfield College, graduating in May with a major in marketing, and I have completed an internship in the marketing department at the Big Y supermarket. I'm seeking a job in sales in the food industry. Can you give me some ideas of the types of sales positions available in the food industry?

Practice delivering your self-sell to family members and friends, and get feedback from them to improve it. The more opportunities you find to use this brief introduction, the easier it becomes. Skill Builder A-3 will give you the opportunity to practice your one-minute self-sell.

Step 3. List your potential network contacts. You should build a network before you need it, so start today. Chances are you have already involved in networking with **Facebook** or other websites (and don't forget to develop a profile at **LinkedIn** and/ or another professional website), so use it along with other networking methods to get a job. Begin with who you know, your primary contacts; look through your address book or your Rolodex. Your goal is to create a list of professional and personal contacts. Professional contacts include colleagues (past and

one-minute self-sell An opening statement used in networking that quickly summarizes your history and career plan and asks a question.

present); members of trade or professional organizations and alumni associations; vendors, suppliers, or managers from current or past jobs; and mentors. On a personal level, your network includes relatives, neighbors, friends, and even personal service providers (your doctor, dentist, insurance agent, stock broker, accountant, or hairstylist).

Ask your primary contacts for secondary contacts you can network with. You'll want to continually update and add to your list as you get referrals from others. You will discover that your network grows exponentially.

Next, expand your list to include people you don't know. How do you do this? Make a point to go where people gather: meetings of the Chamber of Commerce or college alumni clubs, college reunions, trade shows, and career fairs. There are e-groups and chat rooms for all types of interests; seek these out and participate. Get more involved with professional associations; many have special student memberships, and some even have college chapters. To develop your career reputation, become a leader, not just a member, in whatever civic/social/religious organizations you join. Volunteer to be on committees or boards, to give presentations, and so on. When you give a speech, you are instantly networking with everyone in the audience.

Step 4. Conduct networking interviews. Consult your list of potential network contacts and set up a networking interview to begin meeting your objective. It may take many interviews to meet a goal, such as getting a job. You may have to begin with an informational interview—a phone call or (preferably) a meeting that you initiate to gain information from a contact who has hands-on experience in your field of interest. In such a situation (in contrast to a job interview), you are the interviewer, so you need to be prepared with specific questions to ask the contact regarding your targeted career or industry.

You'll find that if you ask, many people will agree to talk to you for 15 or 20 minutes. These meetings can be most helpful, especially if you can talk to someone within an organization you'd like to join or in an industry you are targeting. Leave a business card and résumé so that the person can contact you in case something comes up. During the interview, be sure to do the following:

- Establish rapport—thank the person for talking with you.
- Deliver your one-minute self-sell.
- Ask your prepared questions, such as "What do you think of my qualifications for this field?" "With your knowledge of the industry, what career opportunities do you see in the future?" "What advice do you have for me as I begin my career?"
- Get additional contacts for your network. You might ask a question like "If you were exploring this field, who else would you talk with?" Most people can give you three names; if you are offered only one, ask for others.[116] Add the new contacts to your network list and plan to interview them. (When contacting new people, be sure to mention who referred you to them.)
- Ask your contact how you might help him or her.

Follow up the interview with a thank-you note and a status report, and enclose your résumé.

Step 5. Maintain your network. It is important to keep members of your network informed of your career progress. Saying thank you to those who helped you along the way will strengthen your business relationships; providing updated information about yourself will increase the likelihood of getting help in the future. It is also a good idea to notify everyone in your network that you are in a new position and to provide contact information. Networking doesn't stop once you've made a career change. Make a personal commitment to continue networking in order to be in charge of your career development. Go to trade shows and conventions, make business contacts, and continue to update, correct, and add to your network list. Computer software is available that can help you manage your networking.

Networking is not only about getting help; it's also about helping others, especially those in your network. You will be amazed at how helping others can help you. Try to contact everyone on your network list at least once a year and find out what you can do for him or her. Send congratulations on recent achievements.

Reid Hoffman, founder of **LinkedIn,** is the guru of networking, and he is in constant contact with his network he calls his tribe.[117] He wrote the book on networking, with Ben Casnocha, *The Start-Up of You* (Crown, 2012), and there are great excerpts in "The Real Way to Network" in *Fortune* (February 6, 2012, pp. 23–32).

Appendix Summary

A-1. **List the steps in career planning.**

The steps in the career planning model are (1) completing a self-assessment, (2) determining your career preferences, (3) setting objectives, (4) developing a plan, and (5) controlling the plan.

A-2. **List the steps in the networking process.**

The steps in the networking process are (1) performing a self-assessment and setting objectives,

(2) creating a one-minute self-sell, (3) developing a list of potential network contacts, (4) conducting networking interviews, and (5) maintaining the network.

A-3. **Describe a one-minute self-sell.**

A one-minute self-sell is an opening statement used in networking that quickly summarizes a person's history and career plan and asks a question.

Key Terms

career development, **281**   networking, **285**   one-minute self-sell page, **287**
career planning, **281**

Key Term Review

Complete each of the following statements using one of this appendix's key terms.

1. A _____ is a sequence of related job positions, involving increasing responsibility and increased compensation and held over a lifetime.

2. _____ is the process of setting career objectives and determining how to accomplish them.

3. _____ is the process of gaining skill, experience, and education to achieve career objectives.

4. _____ is the process of building relationships for the purpose of career building and socializing.

5. The _____ is an opening statement used in networking that quickly summarizes your history and career plan and asks a question.

Skill Builder A-1: Career Planning

Objective

To develop a career plan.

Skills

The primary skills developed through this exercise are:

1. *Management skill*—decision making (developing career plans)

2. *AACSB competency*—reflective thinking (as you take charge of your career)

3. *Management function*—planning

Preparing for Skill Builder A-1

Answering the following questions will help you develop a career plan. Use additional paper if needed. If your instructor asks you to do this exercise in class, do not reveal anything about yourself that you prefer not to share with classmates.

Step 1. Self-Assessment

A. Write two or three statements that answer the question, "Who am I?"

B. Write about two or three of your major accomplishments. (They can be in school, work, sports, or hobbies.) List the skills it took to accomplish each one.

C. Identify skills and abilities you already possess that you can use in your career (for example, skills related to planning, organizing, communicating, or leading).

Step 2. Career Preferences

A. What type of industry would you like to work in? (List as many as interest you.)

B. What type and size of organization do you want to work for?

C. List in priority order, beginning with the most important, the five factors that will most influence your job/career decisions (examples are opportunity for advancement, challenge, security, salary, hours, location of job, travel involved, educational opportunities, recognition, prestige, environment, coworkers, boss, responsibility, and variety of tasks).

D. Describe the perfect job.

E. What type of job(s) do you want during your career (marketing, finance, operations, personnel, and so forth)? After selecting a field, select a specific job (for example, salesperson, manager, or accountant).

Step 3. Career Objectives

A. What are your short-term objectives for the first year after graduation?

B. What are your intermediate-term objectives (the second through fifth years after graduation)?

C. What are your long-range objectives?

Step 4. Develop an Action Plan to Help You Achieve Your Objectives.

Be sure to state deadlines for each action you plan to take.

SKILL BUILDER A-2: RÉSUMÉ

Objective

To develop a resume.

Skills

The primary skills developed through this exercise are:

1. *Management skill*—interpersonal (as you communicate your job qualifications)

2. *AACSB competency*—reflective thinking skills (as you take charge of your career), communication (of your qualifications)

3. *Management function*—leading (communication)

Preparing for Skill Builder A-2

Now that you have a career plan, create a résumé that reflects your plan. For help, visit your college career center and/or the ProvenResumes website at http://www.provenresumes.com. Before finalizing your résumé, improve it by using the following assessment procedure.

Résumé Assessment

1. Could a reader understand, within 10 seconds, what job you are applying for and that you are qualified for the position on the basis of skills, experience, and/or education?

2. Does the résumé include an objective that clearly states the position being applied for (such as sales rep)?

3. Does the résumé list skills or experience that support the claim that you can do the job? (For example, if you don't have sales experience, does the résumé list skills developed on other jobs, such as communication skills? Or does it indicate that you have product knowledge or point out that you enjoy meeting new people and that you are able to easily converse with people you don't know?)

4. If education is a major qualification for the job, does the résumé list courses you've taken that prepared you for the position applied for?

5. Does the résumé clearly list your accomplishments and contributions you made during your job experiences to date?

Skill Builder A-3: Networking Skills

Objective

To develop your networking skills.

Skills

The primary skills developed through this exercise are:

1. *Management skill*—interpersonal (as you communicate your job qualifications)

2. *AACSB competency*—Reflective thinking skills (as you take charge of your career), communication (of your qualifications)

3. *Management function*—leading (communication)

Preparing for Skill Builder A-3

Review the appendix section on the networking process, and complete the following steps.

1. Perform a self-assessment and set objectives. List two or three of your accomplishments, and set an objective—for example, to learn more about career opportunities in your major or to get an internship or a part-time, summer, or full-time job.

2. Practice the one-minute self-sell that you wrote for Work Application A–4.

3. Develop your network. List at least five people to be included in your network, preferably individuals who can help you achieve your objective.

4. Conduct a networking interview. To help meet your objective, select one person from your network list to interview (by phone if it is not possible to meet in person) for about 20 minutes. Write questions to ask during the interview.

Source: This exercise was developed by Andra Gumbus, Associate Professor, College of Business, Sacred Heart University. © Andra Gumbus, 2002. It is used with Dr. Gumbus's permission.

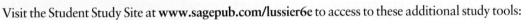

● ● ● Student Study Site

Visit the Student Study Site at **www.sagepub.com/lussier6e** to access to these additional study tools:

- Mobile-compatible self-assessment quizzes
- Mobile-compatible key term flashcards
- Video Links
- SAGE Journal Articles
- Web Links

Photo from Scott Gries/Invision for Malaria No More/AP Photo.

10 Organizational Behavior
Power, Politics, Conflict, and Stress

• • • Learning Outcomes

After studying this chapter, you should be able to:

10-1. Describe each of the Big Five personality dimensions. PAGE 297

10-2. Explain the perception process, and identify the two factors that influence it. PAGE 297

10-3. Describe the interrelationship among personality, perception, and attitudes, and explain the contribution of each to a manager's behavior. PAGE 298

10-4. Explain what job satisfaction is and why it is important. PAGE 299

10-5. Define power, and explain the difference between position and personal power. PAGE 302

10-6. Identify the differences among reward, legitimate, and referent power. PAGE 303

10-7. Discuss how power and politics are related. PAGE 305

10-8. Describe how money and politics have similar uses. PAGE 305

10-9. Explain what networking, reciprocity, and coalitions have in common. PAGE 305

10-10. List and define five conflict management styles. PAGE 313

10-11. List the steps in initiating and using the collaborative conflict resolution model. PAGE 316

10-12. Explain the stress tug-of-war analogy. PAGE 321

IDEAS ON MANAGEMENT at the RLJ Companies

Robert L. Johnson was the founder and chairman of **Black Entertainment Television (BET)**, the first cable television network aimed at African Americans. In 2003, Johnson sold BET to **Viacom** for $3 billion. His 63 percent stake made Johnson worth more than a billion dollars after taxes, making him the first African American billionaire. He went on to become the founder and chairman of the **RLJ Companies,** an innovative business network that provides strategic investments in a diverse portfolio of 13 companies, of which he is full or part owner. He and **Michael Jordan** led the group that acquired the **Charlotte Bobcats National Basketball Association (NBA)** expansion franchise, making him the first African American to be the principal owner of a North American major-league sports franchise. Johnson sold majority ownership to Michael Jordan and MJ Basketball Holdings for $275 million, but Johnson retains a minority ownership interest and serves as the Bobcats' governor to the NBA.

1. How would you describe Robert Johnson's personality? PAGE 297
2. How have perception and attitudes affected Robert Johnson's career? How did he deal with discrimination? PAGE 302
3. What types of power does Johnson have? How does he use his power? PAGE 304
4. How does Johnson effectively use organizational politics at the RLJ Companies? PAGE 308
5. What types of negotiating and collaborating does Johnson do? PAGE 316

You'll find answers to these questions throughout the chapter. To learn more about RLJ Companies, visit its website at www.rljcompanies.com.

Source: Information for this case was taken from RLJ Companies' website at http://www.rljcompanies.com, accessed July 25, 2013.

• • • Chapter Outline

Organizational Behavior (OB) Foundations
   Personality
   Perception
   Attitudes
Changing OB Foundations
   Power
   Sources of Power
   Types of Power and How to
     Increase Your Power
Organizational Politics
   Political Behavior
   Guidelines for Developing
     Political Skills

Negotiation
   Negotiating
   The Negotiation Process
Managing Conflict
   The Psychological Contract and Functional and
     Dysfunctional Conflict
   Conflict Management Styles
   Conflict Resolution
   Initiating Conflict Resolution
   Responding to and Mediating Conflict Resolution
Stress
   Job Stress Causes
   The Stress Tug-of-War

ORGANIZATIONAL BEHAVIOR (OB) FOUNDATIONS

Have you ever wondered why people do and say (actions/behavior) the things they do at work? **Organizational behavior** (OB) *is the study of actions that affect performance in the workplace.* The *goal of OB theorists* is to explain and predict actions and how they will affect performance. Our behavior influences our performance,[1] which in turn influences others' performance,[2] and their behavior influences our behavior and performance.[3] Recall (Chapter 1) that interpersonal skills are important to management success; how we behave with others determines our OB skills.

The foundations of individual behavior that affect behavior and performance include personality, perception, and attitudes—the topics of this section. However, these foundations are not observable. You can only observe individuals' actions and try to explain and predict their behavior based on your understanding of the foundations. It's about reading people.[4] So the better you understand OB, the better you can interact with others.[5]

Personality

Why are some people outgoing and others shy, some loud and others quiet, some warm and others cold, some aggressive and others passive?[6] The answer: personality characteristics.[7] **Personality** *is a combination of behavioral, mental, and emotional traits that define an individual.* We all have our own personality,[8] and our personality is the primary influence on how we behave.[9] Your personality even affects your weight.[10]

Personality is based on genetics and environmental factors. Your personality dimensions are influenced by genes you received before you were born. Your basic personality is developed by age five, thus making parents and child-care providers important in the early years of life, but your personality can change. Your family, friends, school, and work relationships influence your personality.

To be successful, you must be prepared to work well with people with a variety of personality types. Understanding people's personalities is important because personality affects behavior as well as perceptions and attitudes.[11] Knowing about people's personalities helps you explain and predict their behavior and job performance.[12] Therefore, many organizations, including **Six Flags, Best Buy,** and **Target,** give personality tests to ensure a proper match between the worker and the job, and some MBA programs are requiring personality tests.[13]

There are many personality classification methods. Two widely recognized methods are classification on the basis of single traits and classification on the basis of the Big Five personality dimensions.

Single Traits of Personality. Here are some of the single traits that make up one's personality.

- *Locus of control* is a trait that lies on a continuum between believing that control over one's destiny is external and believing that it is internal. *Externalizers* believe that they have no control over their fate and that their behavior has little to do with their performance. *Internalizers* believe that they control their fate and that their behavior has a direct effect on their performance. Internalizers have been shown to have higher levels of performance. Who do you believe is responsible for your destiny?[14]

- *Optimism* also lies on a continuum whose opposite end is pessimism. Optimistic people believe that things will go well, and they tend to be generally happier and more confident.[15] Positive expectations lead to higher levels of performance.[16] Pessimistic people believe that things will not go well. They

organizational behavior The study of actions that affect performance in the workplace.

personality A combination of behavioral, mental, and emotional traits that define an individual.

tend to be unhappy much of the time and experience more stress than optimistic people. Are you an optimist or pessimist? Remember that what you think determines what happens to you. So be an optimistic positive thinker.

- *Risk propensity* lies on a continuum from risk taking to risk avoiding. Entrepreneurs are risk takers.[17] Successful organizations look for managers who will take risks based on research. Organizations with risk-avoiding managers often go out of business because they do not keep up with changes in their industries.

- *Machiavellianism* is a trait based on the belief that the ends can justify the means and power should be used to reach desired ends. *High Machs* are generally considered effective in situations in which bargaining and winning are important, such as jobs involving negotiation and sales. However, high Machs tend to be more concerned about meeting their own needs (self-interest role, Chapter 8) than helping the team and organization. Thus, they tend to create win-lose situations and may use unethical behavior to win.

Personalities help explain behavior. Pictured here is Susan Cain, author of *Quiet: The Power of Introverts in a World that Can't Stop Talking*, who argues that introverts bring a unique perspective to organizations. Photo from Rex Features via AP Photo.

The Big Five Personality Dimensions. The use of the Big Five personality dimensions, or traits, is the most widely accepted way to study personality.[18] Before reading about the Big Five, complete the Self-Assessment Personality Profile to better understand your own personality.

10-1 | SELF ASSESSMENT

Personality Profile

Using the scale below, rate each of the 25 statements according to how accurately it describes you. Place a number from 1 to 7 on the line before each statement. There are no right or wrong answers, so be honest and you will really increase your self-awareness.

Like me	Somewhat like me	Not like me

7_____6_____5_____4_____3_____2_____1

_____ 1. I enjoy meeting new people.

_____ 2. I am concerned about getting along well with others.

_____ 3. I have good self-control; I don't get emotional and get angry and yell.

_____ 4. I'm dependable; when I say I will do something, it's done well and on time.

_____ 5. I try to do things differently to improve my performance.

_____ 6. I feel comfortable speaking to a diverse mix of people (different ages, races, genders, religions, intelligence levels, etc.).

_____ 7. I enjoy having lots of friends and going to parties.

_____ 8. I perform well under pressure.

_____ 9. I work hard to be successful.

_____ 10. I go to new places and enjoy traveling.

_____ 11. I am outgoing and initiate conversations rather than shy and hesitant to approach others.

_____ 12. I try to see things from other people's points of view.

_____ 13. I am an optimistic person who sees the positive side of situations (the cup is half full).

_____ 14. I am a well-organized person.

_____ 15. When I go to a new restaurant, I order foods I haven't tried.

_____ 16. I am willing to go talk to people to resolve conflicts rather than say nothing.

_____ 17. I want other people to like me and view me as very friendly.

_____ 18. I give people lots of praise and encouragement; I don't put people down and criticize.

_____ 19. I conform by following the rules of an organization.

_____ 20. I volunteer to be the first to learn and do new tasks at work.

_____ 21. I try to influence other people to get what I want.

_____ 22. I enjoy working with others more than working alone.

_____ 23. I view myself as being relaxed and secure rather than nervous and insecure.

_____ 24. I am considered to be credible because I do a good job and come through for people.

_____ 25. When people suggest doing things differently, I support them and help bring change about; I don't make statements like, "It won't work," "We never did it this way before," "No one else ever did this," or "We can't do it."

To determine your personality profile, (1) in the blanks below, place the number from 1 to 7 that represents your score for each statement. (2) Add up each column—your total should be a number from 5 to 35. (3) On the number scale, circle the number that is closest to your total score. Each column in the chart represents a specific personality dimension.

Extraversion		Agreeableness		Adjustment		Conscientiousness		Openness to Experience	
	35		35		35		35		35
	30		30		30		30		30
_____ 1.	25	_____ 2.	25	_____ 3.	25	_____ 4.	25	_____ 5.	25
_____ 6.	20	_____ 7.	20	_____ 8.	20	_____ 9.	20	_____ 10.	20
_____ 11.	15	_____ 12.	15	_____ 13.	15	_____ 14.	15	_____ 15.	15
_____ 16.	10	_____ 17.	10	_____ 18.	10	_____ 19.	10	_____ 20.	10
_____ 21.	5	_____ 22.	5	_____ 23.	5	_____ 24.	5	_____ 25.	5
_____ Total		_____ Total		_____ Total		_____ Total		_____ Total	

The higher the total number, the stronger the dimension that describes your personality. What are your strongest and weakest dimensions? To better understand the Big Five, read each of the five statements describing each dimension consecutively— read 1, 6, 11, 16, and 21, then do the same for the other four dimensions.

- *Extroversion* is measured along a continuum between extrovert and introvert. *Extroverts* tend to be social, talkative, and assertive and willing to take charge.[19] *Introverts* tend to be less social, quiet, nonassertive, and less willing to take charge.

- *Agreeableness* lies on a continuum between easy and difficult to work with. *Agreeable* people are considered to be nice and good natured—cooperative, flexible, polite, tolerant, forgiving, and trusting. *Disagreeable* people are the opposite making them difficult to work with.

- *Emotionalism* (also called neuroticism or emotional stability) is on a continuum between stability and instability. Emotionally *stable* people are calm and in control of their behavior; they are secure and positive. *Unstable* people are angry, depressed, anxious, nervous, insecure, and excitable—they can get out of control and display their emotions negatively, such as by yelling. They don't cope well with pressure.[20] Emotions are important, but we should try to maintain stable behavior.[21]

- *Conscientiousness* continuum goes between responsible/dependable and irresponsible/undependable. *Conscientious* people are responsible/dependable, hardworking, persistent, organized, and achievement oriented. *Unconscientious* people are irresponsible, so you can't depend on them.

- *Openness to experience* lies on a continuum between being willing to try new things and not being willing to do so. People who are *open to experience* tend to be receptive to new ideas and willing to change; they are curious and broad minded, with a tolerance for ambiguity. People *closed to experience* want to stay with the status quo.

Robert Johnson of the **RLJ Companies (Case Question 1)** clearly has an internal locus of control, is optimistic, and is a risk taker. Without these personality traits, he would never have overcome prejudice and discrimination to climb the corporate ladder to the level of vice president of a cable company, nor would he have started BET and the RLJ Companies. However, he is not a high Mach, as he strives to create win-win situations. In terms of the Big Five, he is an extrovert, usually agreeable, emotionally stable, responsible/dependable, and open to new experiences.

Perception

Why do some people view a behavior or decision you made as fair and just while others do not? The answer often lies in perception.[22] Perception refers to a person's interpretation of reality. It is important to realize that perceptions, right or wrong, affect behavior and performance because behavior is the product of or is based on perception. So what people know or don't know isn't important—all that really matters is their perception.[23]

The Perception Process. Perception *is the process of selecting, organizing, and interpreting environmental information.* No two people ever perceive—and thus ever experience—anything exactly the same way. One factor that determines how you select, organize, and most importantly interpret information is your own internal environment, including your personality, self-esteem, attitudes, intelligence, needs, values, and so on. *Self-esteem,* or self-concept, is your perception of yourself. Self-esteem is a personality trait; it lies on a continuum between positive and negative or between high and low. A related concept, *self-efficacy,* is the perceived belief in your own capability to perform in a specific situation.

A second factor that influences the perception process is the information available from the external environment. The more accurate the information that is received, the more close the perception may be to reality. If a good employee quits because he or she is mistreated or if he or she only preceives mistreatment, the result is still the lost of a good employee.

The Attribution Process. One factor that affects people's attitudes and expectations is their attributions. **Attribution** *is the process of determining the reason for someone's behavior and whether that behavior is situational or intentional.* Situational behavior is either accidental or out of the control of the individual, whereas intentional behavior is done on purpose. Your response to someone else's behavior will be determined in part by whether you attribute the behavior to situational factors or intentional factors.[24] The attribution process is illustrated in Exhibit 10-1.

LO 10-1

Describe each of the Big Five personality dimensions.

LO 10-2

Explain the perception process, and identify the two factors that influence it.

WORK
APPLICATION 10-1

Identify a present or past boss's personality; refer to the personality traits in the Self-Assessment.

EXHIBIT 10-1   THE ATTRIBUTION PROCESS

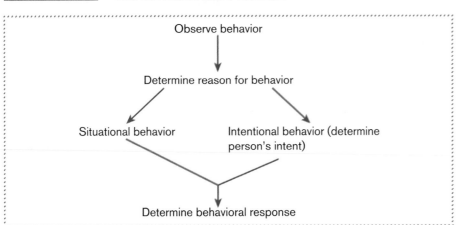

Observe behavior

Determine reason for behavior

Situational behavior → Intentional behavior (determine person's intent)

Determine behavioral response

perception The process of selecting, organizing, and interpreting environmental information.

attribution The process of determining the reason for someone's behavior and whether that behavior is situational or intentional.

WORK
APPLICATION 10-2

Give three examples of how you (or a manager you know) have used the attribution process at work.

WORK
APPLICATION 10-3

Give an example of a situation that you and someone else experienced together but perceived differently. Which of the biases in perception might explain the difference in perception?

For example, suppose that Eduardo, a manager, observes an employee, Pat, coming to work late. If Eduardo has observed that Pat is often late, he might conclude that Pat's lateness is intentional and that she doesn't care about being on time. In that case, Eduardo would probably decide to discipline Pat. However, if Pat is late only once, Eduardo might determine that her lateness was situational—the result of car problems, traffic, or the like—and take no action.

Bias in Perception. Different people may perceive the same behavior differently because of perception biases listed:

- *Selectivity* refers to people's tendency to screen information in favor of their desired outcome. People will sometimes make great efforts to find information that supports their point of view and ignore information that does not. In other words, people only see and hear what they want to.

- *Frame of reference* refers to seeing things from your own point of view. Employees often view management decisions differently than managers do. Managers and employees commonly use the same data during contract negotiations; however, managers perceive that employees want more pay and are not willing to increase productivity, whereas employees perceive managers as greedy and not willing to share the wealth that employees create. Remember that it is not your perception but others' perceptions that will influence their behavior and performance.[25] Try to see things from others' perspective and create a win-win situation so that all parties get what they want, based on their perceptions.

- *Stereotyping* is the process of making generalizations about the behavior of a group and then applying the generalities to one individual. People form stereotypes about race/nationality, religion, sex, age, and so forth. Stereotyping a person can lead to perception errors, because not all individuals from a particular group possess the same traits or exhibit the same behaviors. Negatively stereotyping an individual can also affect that person's self-perception in a negative way. Try not to negatively stereotype employees; get to know them as individuals.

- *Expectations* refers to seeing or hearing what we anticipate. Read the phrase in the triangle shown:

Bird
in the
the hand

Did you read the word *the* twice? Or, like most people, did you read what you expected, only one *the?* Many people, especially those who know each other well, often do not really listen to each other. They simply hear what they expect to hear.

- *The "like me" assumption* is the process of believing others perceive things as you do because they are similar to you or that your behavior makes sense. Remember to value diversity. What you believe to be logically the best way to do something may not be perceived as being logical from others' perspective. Don't expect others to accept your ideas and behave as you do, and don't judge others' behavior as wrong just because it is different from yours.

LO 10-3

Describe the interrelationship among personality, perception, and attitudes, and explain the contribution of each to a manager's behavior.

How closely do you think your self-perceptions would match those of your coworkers and family? Would you be interested in being coached so that you could change your behavior? As suggested in the Self-Assessment Personality Profile, have others give you their perception of your personality traits.

Attitudes

Attitudes *are positive or negative evaluations of people, things, and situations.* They are judgments and are based on perceptions. Most attitudes are the result of either direct experience or observational learning from the environment.

Attitude Formation and Behavior. Family, friends, teachers, coworkers, the mass media, and so on affect your attitude formation. Before you signed up for this course, you may have read the course description, talked to students who completed it to find out more about the course, and thought about your interest in the course. Based on what you read and heard and your interest in the subject, you may have started this course with a particular attitude. People generally find what they are looking for, so if you had a positive attitude coming into the course, you probably like it—and vice versa. However, attitudes can be changed.[26] Has your attitude toward this course become more positive or negative? What were the primary factors that formed your present attitude toward this course?

Attitudes often affect behavior. Negative attitudes toward change tend to lead to behavioral resistance to the change, and vice versa.[27] People with opposite attitudes toward a person, job, course, event, or situation often behave differently. People's attitudes toward you may affect your behavior. Do you behave differently with people who like you than with those who don't?

How Employees' Attitudes Affect Performance. Attitude is a major factor in determining performance. Conscientiousness is a good predictor of job performance, so companies recruit employees with good attitudes because they are more conscientious. J. W. Marriott, Jr., president of **Marriott International**, stated, "We have found that our success depends more upon employee attitude than any other single factor."

Not only can employees' attitudes have an effect on their own performance, but they can also have an effect on the performance of their coworkers. Since employees may have to work in cooperation with each other, other employees may pick up on negative attitudes of coworkers and adopt them as their own. Therefore, having a positive attitude is an important determinant of both individual and organizational performance. What is your attitude toward working? To succeed, develop and maintain a positive work attitude.[28]

How Managers' Attitudes Affect Employee Performance. The **Pygmalion effect** *is the theory that managers' attitudes toward and expectations and treatment of employees largely determine their performance.* Various studies have supported this theory, as managers have the ability to affect employee attitudes.[29] Happy leaders tend to have happy employees.[30] The basic premise of the theory is that people fulfill expectations about themselves. Thus, if managers expect employees to be productive and successful and treat them accordingly, employees react by being productive, or vice versa.

LO 10-4
Explain what job satisfaction is and why it is important.

WORK
APPLICATION 10-4
Give an example of how your attitude affected your performance at work.

WORK
APPLICATION 10-5
Think of someone who really expected you to perform well (or poorly) and treated you as if you would do well (or poorly), which strongly affected your success (or failure). Explain how the Pygmalion effect influenced your performance.

attitudes Positive or negative evaluations of people, things, and situations.

Pygmalion effect The theory that managers' attitudes toward and expectations and treatment of employees largely determine their performance.

10-2 SELF ASSESSMENT

Job Satisfaction

Select a present or past job. Identify your level of satisfaction by placing a check mark at the appropriate position on the continuum for each determinant of job satisfaction.

Personality

I have positive self-esteem.   ___ ___ ___ ___ ___ ___   I *do not* have positive self-esteem.

Work itself

I enjoy doing the tasks I perform.   ___ ___ ___ ___ ___ ___   I *do not* enjoy doing the tasks I perform.

Compensation

I am fairly compensated.   ___ ___ ___ ___ ___ ___   I am *not* fairly compensated.

Growth and upward mobility

I have the opportunity to learn new   ___ ___ ___ ___ ___ ___   I have *no* opportunity to learn new
things and get better jobs.   things and get better jobs.

Coworkers

I like and enjoy working with my   ___ ___ ___ ___ ___ ___   I *do not* like and enjoy working
coworkers.   with my coworkers.

Management

I believe that managers are doing a   ___ ___ ___ ___ ___ ___   I *do not* believe that managers
good job.   are doing a good job.

Overall Job Satisfaction

When determining your overall job satisfaction, you cannot simply add up a score based on the above six determinants, because they are most likely of different importance to you. Thus, think about your job and the above factors, and rate your overall satisfaction with your job.

I am satisfied with my job (high level   ___ ___ ___ ___ ___ ___   I am dissatisfied with my job (low level of
of satisfaction).   satisfaction).

Unfortunately, some managers negatively stereotype their employees as having low ability or willingness to work. This negative attitude leads to low expectations and not treating employees with respect. Their employees see and do as their managers expect. These managers' expectations lead to the *self-fulfilling prophecy* of low-performing employees. As a manager, if you create win-win situations by expecting high performance and treating employees as capable, you will get the best performance from them.

Attitudes and Job Satisfaction. *Job satisfaction* is a person's attitude toward the job. It is beneficial for firm value.[31] Although there has long been a debate over the expression that a happy worker is a productive worker, there is support for the idea of a positive relationship between job satisfaction and **citizenship behavior**— *employee efforts that go above and beyond the call of duty.*[32] Studies have also found that dissatisfied employees are more apt to break the rules and sabotage performance.[33] **Google** strives to keep employees happy because it helps productivity.[34] Also, job satisfaction can affect satisfaction off the job, as people tend to take their jobs home with them, which affects their behavior.

Job satisfaction is generally measured along a continuum from satisfied/positive/high to dissatisfied/negative/low. Unfortunately, a survey found that

citizenship behavior Employee efforts that go above and beyond the call of duty.

10-1 JOIN THE DISCUSSION ETHICS & SOCIAL RESPONSIBILITY

Smoking

Concerns about the impact of secondhand smoke and the comfort of nonsmokers have prompted many states to enact laws that severely restrict smoking in the workplace, such as only permitting smoking in designated areas outside the building. In addition to state laws, many cities and counties have enacted ordinances against smoking in the workplace. Beyond what is required by state or local law, any employer is free to ban smoking in the workplace, even if state and local laws allow it.

1. Should employees be allowed to smoke wherever and whenever they want to at work?

2. How did your perceptions of and attitude toward smoking affect your answer to the previous question?
3. Might limiting employees' smoking change their behavior on the job? How so?
4. What kinds of personality traits might make employees resist management's efforts to restrict their smoking during working hours?
5. Is it ethical and socially responsible to restrict employees' smoking?

around 53 percent of Americas are unsatisfied with their jobs, and only 15.4 percent said they are very satisfied.[35] Six major determinants of job satisfaction are presented in Self-Assessment 10–2 on job satisfaction. Complete it to find out your own level of job satisfaction. You can have an overall high level of job satisfaction and not like some aspects of your job; this is common.

Changing OB Foundations

As stated, you can change your own personality, perceptions, and attitudes and those of your employees. But it is not easy; it takes a conscious effort and work, and it is usually easier to change yourself than others.

Changing Your OB Foundations. Would you like to be happier and have better relationships? You can train your brain to be positive and feel happier every day.[36] Happiness is based largely on *attitudes*. A simple technique is to constantly focus on the positives at work and in your personal life and be optimistic. Spend less time thinking about problems and complaining to others—do you like to be around a negative person who is always complaining? If you catch yourself being negative, stop and change your attitude using positive affirmations, such as I can do this, I'm conscientious, I will meet the deadline, I enjoy work/school, I'm a happy person. You can also complete Skill Builder 10–3 Improving Your OB Foundations.

For personality, go back to Self-Assessment 10–1. To succeed in management, you generally need to be an *extrovert* willing to take charge, *agreeable* but still the boss, in control of your behavior with *stable emotions, conscientious* to get the job done, and *open to experiences* to keep up with the changes in your field. Are there any dimensions of the Big Five you can work on to improve?

For perception, do you have positive *self-esteem*? With *attribution,* do you consider others intentionally against you? How frequently do you see and hear things differently than others? Do you avoid biases of selectivity, frame of reference, stereotyping, expectations, and the like me assumption? Do you try to see things from the other person's perception? How can you improve?

Changing Employees' OB Foundations. As a manager, assess your employees' personality dimensions. Can you coach them be more agreeable, stable, conscientious, and open to experiences? Remember that it's not reality that matters, it's employees' perceptions. Do a good job of seeing things from the employees' side and do a good job of communicating the facts to help them to perceive the situation as you do. It is easier to hire a person with a good attitude than to change employee attitudes, so select employees carefully considering attitudes. If employees have a negative attitude about something, point it out to them and help them realize that it is having a negative effect on their and others' behavior and performance and coach them to change. In Chapter 14 you will learn how to use a coaching model that can help maintain and improve performance.

Research has shown that African Americans face prejudice and discrimination, often based on stereotyped negative perceptions of their competence (Chapter 3). **Robert Johnson (Case Question 2)** overcame prejudice and discrimination because he realized that they were part of the landscape. He knew he was going to face them, but he didn't let that stop him from achieving his goals. He looked for commonalities of interest. Johnson proved that he was competent, and he overcame negative perceptions and attitudes to break the glass ceiling. Johnson believes in himself, has a positive attitude, and knows there are very few things that can stop him from achieving his goals.

Power

LO 10-5

Define power, and explain the difference between position and personal power.

Based on an internal focus of OB foundations, we move to a more external focus of OB topics including major sections on power, organizational politics, negotiation, conflict, and stress. In this section, we discuss the importance of power in organizations and its sources, the types of power, and how to increase your power.

Sources of Power

Some people view power as the ability to make other people do what they want them to do or the ability to do something to people or for people. These definitions may be true, but they tend to give power a manipulative, negative connotation. Within an organization, power should be viewed in a positive sense. Without power, managers could not achieve organizational objectives. Leadership and power go hand in hand. Although power is not equal,[37] top managers are giving more power to employees (*empowerment*).[38] For our purposes, **power** *is the ability to influence others' behavior*. You don't have to be a manager to have power, as some employees actually have more influence over other employees than the manager does. You do not actually have to use power to influence others. Often it is the perception of your power rather than actual power that influences others.

There are two sources of power influencing behavior: one's position and one's person.[39] *Position power* is derived from top management and is delegated down the chain of command. *Personal power* is derived from followers, based on an individual's behavior. Charismatic people tend to be leaders and have personal power.[40] Therefore, personal power can be gained or lost. It is best to have both position power and personal power.

Types of Power and How to Increase Your Power

power The ability to influence others' behavior.

There are different types of power. The seven types of power are presented in Exhibit 10-2. You can increase your power without taking power away from others. Increasing your power builds your career and helps you get ahead.

EXHIBIT 10-2   SOURCES AND TYPES OF POWER

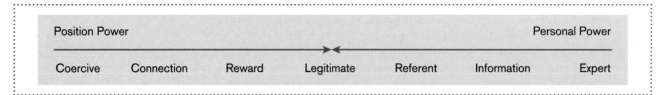

Position Power						Personal Power
Coercive	Connection	Reward	Legitimate	Referent	Information	Expert

Coercive Power. The use of *coercive power* involves threats and/or punishment to influence compliance. Out of fear of reprimands, probation, suspension, or dismissal, employees often do as their boss requests. Other examples of the use of coercive power include verbal abuse, humiliation, and ostracism. Group members may use coercive power to enforce norms. Coercive power is appropriate to use in maintaining discipline when enforcing rules.

Generally, to have coercive power, you need to have a management job that enables you to gain and maintain the ability to hire, discipline, and fire your employees. However, some people can pressure others to do what they want without position authority.

Connection Power. *Connection power* is based on the user's relationship with influential people. You rely on the use of contacts or friends who can influence the person you are dealing with.[41] The right connections can give power, or at least the perception of power. If people know you are friendly with people in power, they are more apt to do as you request.

Networking (see the Appendix to Chapter 9) means developing connections. To increase your connection power, expand your network of contacts with important managers who have power. When you want something, identify the people who can help you attain it, make alliances, and win them over to your side. Connections are developed through political networking, the topic of the next section.

Reward Power. *Reward power* is based on the user's ability to influence others by providing something of value to them. In a management position, reward power involves the use of positive reinforcement or incentives, such as praise, recognition, pay raises, and promotions, to influence others' behavior. With peers, you can exchange favors or give them something of value. Let people know what's in it for them when you need their help by creating a win-win situation.

To increase your reward power, you must be in a position in which you have some control over evaluating employees' performance and determining their raises and promotions. Find out what others value and try to reward them in that way. Using praise can help increase your power. Employees who feel they are appreciated rather than being used will give you more power.

Legitimate Power. *Legitimate power* is based on the user's position power in the organization. Legitimacy is important so that employees will tend to feel that they ought to do what the boss says.[42] Day-to-day manager–employee interactions are based on legitimate power.

To increase your legitimate power, you need to attain a management position.

LO 10-6

Identify the differences among reward, legitimate, and referent power.

10-2 JOIN THE DISCUSSION ETHICS & SOCIAL RESPONSIBILITY

Following Orders

Officers in the armed forces tend to use legitimate power with troops. Military recruits are conditioned to follow orders without questioning authority. In fact, it is a crime for a military member to willfully disobey any lawful order. However, many military officers issue unlawful orders to recruits and expect them to obey them.

1. Is it ethical and socially responsible to teach people in the military or any other organization to follow orders without questioning authority?
2. What would you do if your boss gave you an unethical/unlawful order?
3. Is following orders a good justification for conducting unethical/unlawful practices?

Referent Power. *Referent power* is based on the user's personal source of power relationships with others. When asking another person to do something, you would express it as a request rather than as an order. Referent power is often used by people who have little or no position power; it is also used in teams where leadership is shared.

To increase your referent power, develop your interpersonal skills and make efforts to gain others' confidence and trust.

Information Power. *Information power* is based on others' need for data. Managers rely on information, which is usually but not always related to the job. Some assistants have more information and are more helpful in answering questions than the managers they work for. An important part of the manager's job is to convey information. Employees often come to managers for information on what to do and how to do it.

To increase your information power, know what is going on in the organization. Having information gives you power.[43] Provide service and information to other departments. Serve on committees, because doing so gives you a chance to increase both information power and connection power.

Expert Power. *Expert power* is based on the user's skill and knowledge. Being an expert gives you power.[44] Being an expert makes other people more convinced to trust and respect you. When your expertise is valued, so are your ideas and leadership. Thus, employees with expert power are often promoted to management positions.

To increase your expert power, participate in all the training and educational programs your organization provides. Keep up with the latest technology. Volunteer to be the first to learn something new. Be willing to take on the more complex, hard-to-evaluate tasks.

10-1 APPLYING THE CONCEPT

Using Power

Identify the appropriate type of power to use in each situation.

A. coercive
B. connection
C. reward or legitimate
D. referent
E. information or expert

_____ 1. You have to get an important customer order shipped today, and Amita, who usually needs some direction and encouragement from you to maintain production, is not working to standard today. As she does occasionally, she claims that she does not feel well but cannot afford to take time off.

_____ 2. Laxmi, one of your best workers, usually needs little direction from you. However, recently her performance level has dropped. You are quite sure Laxmi has a personal problem affecting her work.

_____ 3. You want a new personal computer to help you do a better job. Computer purchases must be approved by a committee, and its decisions are very political in nature.

_____ 4. One of your best workers, Carlos, wants a promotion. Carlos has talked to you about getting ahead and has asked you to help prepare him for when the opportunity comes.

_____ 5. Ari, one of your worst employees, has ignored one of your directives again.

As founder and chairman of **the RLJ Companies (Case Question 3)**, Robert Johnson clearly has position power. He is well respected and thus also has personal power. Because of his expert power, Johnson has won several awards. Johnson primarily relies on his referent power. He used his referent power to get the resources necessary to achieve BET's vision of becoming the world's preeminent African American entertainment media company, and for turning the RLJ Companies into a multimillion-dollar company. Johnson's employees are motivated, well rewarded, and empowered, not coerced, to pursue Johnson's vision.

ORGANIZATIONAL POLITICS

In this section, we discuss the nature of organizational politics, political behavior in organizations, and guidelines for developing political skills. Begin by determining your own political behavior by completing Self-Assessment 10–3.

LO 10-7

Discuss how power and politics are related.

10-3 SELF ASSESSMENT

Use of Political Behavior

Beside each statement, write the number of the choice that best describes how often you use the particular behavior on the job (or how often you imagine you will use it once you are employed).

1 = rarely	2 = seldom	3 = occasionally	4 = frequently	5 = usually

_____ 1. I get along with everyone, even those considered to be difficult to get along with.

_____ 2. I avoid giving my personal opinions on controversial issues, especially when I know others don't agree with them.

_____ 3. I try to make people feel important by complimenting them.

_____ 4. I compromise when working with others and avoid telling people they are wrong.

_____ 5. I try to get to know the key managers and find out what is going on in all the organizational departments.

_____ 6. I dress the same way as the people in power and take on the same interests (watch or play sports, join the same clubs, etc.).

_____ 7. I purposely seek contacts with higher-level managers so that they will know my name and face.

_____ 8. I seek recognition and visibility for my accomplishments.

_____ 9. I get others to help me get what I want.

_____ 10. I do favors for others and ask them for favors in return.

To determine your level of political behavior, add the 10 numbers you selected as your answers. The total will range from 10 to 50. The higher your score, the more political behavior you use. Place your score on the continuum below.

Nonpolitical					Political
60	50	40	30	20	10

Like power, politics is often viewed negatively, because people sometimes abuse political power. A positive way to view politics is to realize that it is simply a medium of exchange.[45] Like money, politics in and of itself is neither good nor bad. It is simply a means of getting what we want. In most economies, money is the medium of exchange; in an organization, politics is the medium of exchange.

Political skills come into play when using power. Politics *is the process of gaining and using power.* Whether you have a positive or negative attitude toward politics, politics is a reality of organizational life, and it pays.[46] You cannot meet your objectives without the help of others, including people and departments over which they have no authority, so you need to use political skills. The amount and importance of politics vary from organization to organization. However, larger organizations tend to be more political, and the higher the level of management, the more important politics becomes.[47]

Political Behavior

Networking. As you'll recall from the Appendix to Chapter 9, **networking** *is the process of developing relationships for the purpose of career building and socializing.* Networking implies connecting with others and developing relationships.[48] Since relationships are the lifeblood of organizations, networking skills are needed

LO 10-8

Describe how money and politics have similar uses.

LO 10-9

Explain what networking, reciprocity, and coalitions have in common.

politics The process of gaining and using power.

networking The process of developing relationships for the purpose of career building and socializing.

to succeed. Therefore, successful managers spend more time networking than do average managers.[49]

Using Reciprocity. *Reciprocity* *involves the mutual exchange of favors and privileges to accomplish objectives.* When people do something for you, you incur an obligation, and they may expect to be repaid—you owe them. When you do something for someone else, you create a debt that you may be able to collect at a later date when you need a favor—they owe you. People expect reciprocity.[50] The process of reciprocity is also referred to as *social exchange theory.*[51] You can get what you want if you help enough people get what they want.

Coalition Building. A **coalition** *is a network of alliances that help achieve an objective.* Reciprocity is used to achieve ongoing objectives, whereas coalitions are developed for achieving a specific objective. Many decisions made in organizations are actually made by coalitions before a formal meeting and approval. For example, Rajesh has an idea for a new service to be offered by his company. By himself, Rajesh has no authority to offer a new service. To begin building a coalition, he might first go to his boss or bosses. Rajesh would present the idea to his boss and get approval to gain wider support. He would then try to get peers and people at other levels as allies. Walking into the meeting to make the decision, Rajesh knows he has management support and that the service will be offered.

Guidelines for Developing Political Skills

It is natural, especially for young people, to take a purely rational approach to a job, without considering politics. But many business decisions are nonrational, based primarily on power and politics. If you want to climb the corporate ladder, you should develop your political skills. Review the 10 statements in Self-Assessment 10–3 on political behavior and the three political behaviors just discussed, and consciously increase your use of any or all of these behaviors. The guidelines in Exhibit 10-3 and discussed here can also help you develop your political skills.

EXHIBIT 10-3   POLITICAL BEHAVIORS AND GUIDELINES FOR DEVELOPING POLITICAL SKILLS

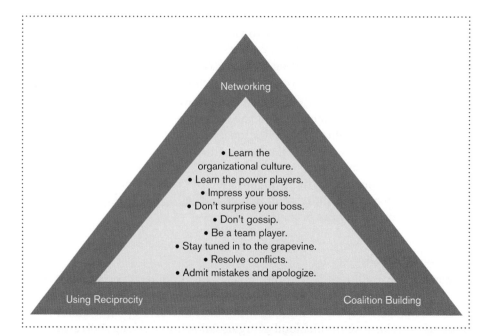

networking The process of developing relationships for the purpose of career building and socializing.

reciprocity The mutual exchange of favors and privileges to accomplish objectives.

coalition A network of alliances that help achieve an objective.

Learn the organizational culture. Learn how the organization operates, both formally and informally, as you are socialized into the organization.[52] Find out what it takes to succeed in your job and to advance, and read between the lines. Use political behavior to get noticed and to promote yourself, but be sure to use methods that are considered appropriate and ethical within the organizational culture.

Learn the power players—your boss. Decisions affecting you are made by "power players," so your relationship with them is important.[53] Find out who those people are in your organization and find opportunities to get to know them using political behavior.[54] And always remember that your boss is a key player for you, regardless of your personal feelings toward him or her. Your manager's *perception* of you will shape your career success.[55] To get raises and promotions, you need to have a good working relationship with your boss.[56] If you are not getting top performance evaluations, talk to your boss and develop a plan to get them.

Impress your boss. If you want to get ahead, you should try to impress your boss by delivering more than you are asked to do. Beating deadlines, arriving at work early and staying later, and volunteering for more work are all ways to impress a boss and get top performance evaluations (Chapter 9). Get to know what your boss expects from you and do it. Set objectives and goals with your boss.[57]

Don't surprise your boss. It's common to put off telling the boss bad news, but if you are having a work problem, let your boss know early. If you are behind schedule to meet an important deadline and your boss finds out about it from others, you'll be embarrassed—especially if your boss finds out from his or her boss.

Don't gossip. One unfortunate fact of life in many organizations is that some workers and managers are "backstabbers"—people who like to make others look bad by spreading gossip about them. Workplace gossip is unproductive.[58] It breeds resentment and can wreak havoc on company morale and efficiency. Do not partake in gossiping. Follow the old rule "If you can't say something nice about somebody, don't say anything at all." And if others are gossiping, establish that you are not interested in listening. Forgive? Forget? Not likely.[59] If you gossip about your boss, he or she may find out and you can lose trust, and it will most likely hurt your relationship and chances for a top performance evaluation.

Be a team player. There are very few, if any, jobs in which organizational objectives can be achieved without the support of a group or team. Therefore, being a team player is crucial not only to your success as an individual employee but also to the success of the organization as well. In order to be a team player, you must earn others' respect, confidence, and trust through loyalty to your boss and peers.[60] This can be accomplished by getting along well with your coworkers and helping them succeed.

Stay tuned in to the grapevine. Find out what is going on through the grapevine. The grapevine can help you to learn the organizational culture and identify key players to include in your coalitions. Your grapevine should include a network of people within and outside your organization. Avoid secrecy, as it can breed negative political behavior.[61]

Resolve conflicts. Following the preceding guidelines can help you avoid a political fight. However, if you are suddenly left out of the information loop or if your coworkers or boss start treating you differently, find out why. Confront individuals or groups suspected of instigating conflict. Managing and resolving conflict is discussed in more detail later in the chapter.

WORK
APPLICATION 10-8

Give an example of how you used political behavior to achieve an organizational objective.

Admit mistakes and apologize. We all make mistakes, so admit them, especially to your boss. Defending and justifying mistakes and behavior that hurt others damages relationships. Justifying mistakes leads to not learning from them and repeating mistakes[62] and possibly to lower performance evaluations. Research has shown that a sincere apology can go a long way in repairing damaged relationships.[63]

10-2 | APPLYING THE CONCEPT

Political Behavior

Identify the political behavior in each situation as

  A. effective
  B. ineffective

____ 6. Carly avoids socializing so that she can be more productive on the job.

____ 7. Hoang sent copies of a very positive performance report that his supervisor wrote about him to three higher-level managers to whom he does not report. They did not request copies.

____ 8. Ron has to drop off daily reports at a certain office by noon. He brings them in around 10:00 on Tuesdays and Thursdays so that he can run into some higher-level managers who meet at that time near the office. On the other days, Ron drops the reports off around noon on his way to lunch.

____ 9. Juanita is taking golf lessons so that she can join the Saturday golf group that includes some higher-level managers.

____ 10. Pavel told his boss's boss about a mistake his boss made yesterday.

WORK APPLICATION 10-9

Which of the suggestions for developing political skills is the most relevant to you?

Robert Johnson (Case Question 4) has lots of experience with organizational politics. Johnson is a big believer in networking, having started and expanded the RLJ Companies through networking. He has done favors for others who have done favors for him (reciprocity). Johnson communicates the company's vision and effectively builds consensus among broad-based coalitions of people who will achieve the vision. Johnson is able to resolve conflict effectively through consensus building. Johnson realizes that when employees observe unethical politics, they don't feel like they are part of the vision, and they won't perform as effectively. By giving employees trust and support, Johnson gets them to do their best.

NEGOTIATION

You have to negotiate in both your personal and your professional life. OB behavior of power and politics is often used during negotiations, and negotiating is an essential career skill.[64] So in this section, you will learn how to negotiate.

Negotiating

Negotiating is a process in which two or more parties in conflict attempt to come to an agreement—a deal. If there is a set "take it or leave it" deal, such as retail prices, there is no negotiation. Also, not all negotiations end with an agreement. There are times when contracts are negotiated,[65] such as in management–union collective bargaining, when buying and selling goods and services, when setting standards,[66] and when discussing a job compensation offer.[67] Acquisitions require sophisticated negotiating,[68] and **Facebook** cofounder Mark Zuckerberg is a good negotiator and personally handled the **Instagram** acquisition.[69]

Negotiation is often a *zero-sum game* in which one party's gain is the other party's loss. For example, every dollar less that you pay for a car is your gain and the seller's loss. Like power and politics, negotiating is not about taking advantage of others but instead about building relationships and helping each other get what we want.[70] Ideally, all parties should believe they got a good deal. Not everyone is born a great negotiator, but the skill can be developed. Following the steps in the negotiation process can help you develop your negotiation skills.

The Negotiation Process

The negotiation process has three, possibly four, steps: plan, negotiate, possibly postpone, and finally, come to an agreement or no agreement.[71] These steps are summarized in Model 10.1 and discussed in this section. In the course of actual negotiations, you may have to make slight adjustments to the steps in the process, as there can be three or four steps.

Plan. Success or failure in negotiating is usually based on preparation. Planning has four steps:

MODEL 10-1   THE NEGOTIATION PROCESS

Reach Resolution Agreement
Close the deal.

Plan ⟶ Negotiate ⟶ Postpone

No Agreement
Find out why there is no agreement, so as to improve in the future.

Plan
1. Research the other party or parties to the negotiation.
2. Set objectives.
3. Try to develop options and trade-offs.
4. Anticipate questions and objection, and prepare answers.

Negotiate
1. Develop rapport and focus on obstacles, not on the person.
2. Let the other party make the first offer.
3. Listen and ask questions to focus on meeting the other party's needs.
4. Don't be too quick to give in, and ask for something in return.

Postpone
1. If you postpone, the other party may create urgency.
2. If the other party postpones, you may create urgency.

Step 1. Research the other party or parties to the negotiation. Know the key power players. Try to find out what the other parties want, what they will and will not be willing to give up, and what you and/or your deal are really worth before you negotiate.[72] The more you know about the other party, the better your chances are of reaching an agreement.

With international negotiations, Americans need to realize that in many countries, especially Asian countries, negotiators are more ceremonial and are much slower to reach a deal. They often want to get to know and trust you over time. So you may need to be patient in order to close a foreign deal.

Step 2. Set objectives. Based on your research, what can you expect—what is your objective? You have to identify the one thing you must come away with. In some negotiations, your objective will be to change someone's behavior;

Negotiating is not just about getting what you want; it's also about giving the other person what he or she wants so you both get a good deal. Photo from Svetikd/iStockphoto.

at other times, you may be negotiating salary or benefits or a better price from a supplier. In any case, you want to set three objectives, or levels:[73]

- A specific lower limit that you are unwilling to give up (say, a certain behavior on the part of your peer in the department or a minimum price from your supplier). You must be willing to walk away from negotiations if this lower limit is not agreed to.
- A target objective that represents what you believe is fair.
- An opening objective that is more than you actually expect but that you may achieve. The first number on the table influences the rest of the negotiation.[74] A higher price makes a lower price seem reasonable, even when it isn't.[75]

Remember that the other party is probably also setting these kinds of objectives. The key to successful negotiation is for each person or party to achieve something between their minimum objective and their target objective. This creates fair deal or a win-win situation.

Step 3. Try to develop options and trade-offs. In some negotiating situations, you may find that you are in a position of power to achieve your target objective. For example, when negotiating prices with a supplier or applying for jobs, you may be able to quote other prices or salary offers and get the other person to beat them. If you have to give up something or cannot get exactly what you want, be prepared to ask for something in return.

Step 4. Anticipate questions and objections, and prepare answers. Very likely the other party to negotiations will want an answer to the unasked question, "What's in it for me?" Focus on how the negotiations will benefit the other party;[76] speak in terms of "you" and "we" rather than "I."

There is a good chance that the other person will raise objections. Unfortunately, not everyone will be open about his or her real objections. Thus, you need to listen and ask questions to find out what is preventing an agreement.[77] It will also help to project positive self-esteem, enthusiasm, and confidence. If the other person does not trust you, you will not reach an agreement.

Negotiate. After you have planned, you are ready to negotiate the deal. Face-to-face negotiations are generally preferred because you can see the other person's nonverbal behavior (discussed in Chapter 13) and better understand objections. However, negotiations by telephone and written negotiations work, too. It will help to keep the following four steps in mind as you negotiate.

Step 1. Develop rapport and focus on obstacles, not on the person. Use the other party's name as you greet him or her. Open with small talk. How long you wait before getting down to negotiations will depend on the particular situation and the other party's style.

Never attack the other party's personality or use negative statements such as "You're being unfair to ask for such a price." Statements like these will make the other party defensive, which will make it harder to reach an agreement. During negotiations, people look for four things: inclusion, control, safety, and respect. If people perceive that you are pushing them into something, threatening them, or belittling them, they will not trust you and will be unlikely to come to an agreement with you.

Step 2. Let the other party make the first offer—most of the time. Letting the other party make the first offer often gives you the advantage, because if the other party offers you more than your target objective, you can close the agreement. Of course, the other party may pressure *you* to make the first offer. For example, the other party may say, "Give us your best price, and we'll decide whether to take it." If so, you can counter with a question such as "What do you expect to pay?" or "What is a reasonable price?" When this does not work, say something like "Our usual price is XXX. However, if you make me a proposal, I'll see what I can do for you."

If you have work experience, when negotiating salary, it is often better to ask for a high salary first; recall it influences the rest of the negotiation,[78] and a lower price, still in your target and attainable, seems more reasonable.[79]

Step 3. Listen and ask questions to focus on meeting the other party's needs. Create an opportunity for the other party to disclose reservations and objections. When you ask questions and listen, you gather information that will help you overcome the other party's objections. Search for common ground.[80] Determining whether the objection is a "want" criterion or a "must" criterion (Chapter 4) will help you decide how to proceed.

When meeting the other party's needs, you don't want to be taken advantage of. Negotiations do tend to leave room for unethical or iffy gamesmanship. To protect yourself, you can ask questions to which you already know the answers and straight up ask them to come clean. Ask, "Is there something important that you know about this deal you haven't told me?

Step 4. Don't be too quick to give in, and remember to ask for something in return. Those who ask for more often get more.[81] You want to satisfy the other party without giving up too much yourself. Remember not to go below your minimum objective, and be prepared to walk away if that minimum can't be met. When you are not getting what you want, having other options can help give you bargaining power.

Though you don't want to be quick to give in, you might want to be the first to make a concession, particularly when you are negotiating complex deals. A concession makes the other party feel obligated, which gives you negotiating power. Being nice or selflessness helps.[82]

Avoid unilateral concessions. Recall your planned trade-offs. For example, if the other party asks for a lower price, ask for a concession such as a large-volume sale to get it, or a longer delivery time, a less popular color, and so on. If you can't get your salary, ask for extra vacation time or a lower medical payment or larger retirement matching benefit.

Postpone. When there doesn't seem to be any progress, it may be wise to postpone negotiations.

If the other party is postponing, you can try to create urgency. In doing so, remember that people will do more to avoid a loss than to score a win.[83] Suppose the other party says, "I'll get back to you." You may try to create urgency by saying, for example, "This product is on sale and the sale ends today." However, honesty is the best policy. The primary reason people will negotiate with you is that they trust and respect you. Establishing a relationship of trust is the necessary first step in closing a deal. Or, if you have other options, you can use them to create urgency, such as by saying, "I have another job offer pending. When will you let me know if you want to offer me the job?"

If you want to postpone, the other party may try to create urgency. If you are not satisfied with the deal or want to shop around, tell the other party you want to think about it. You may also need to check with your manager or someone else, which simply may be for advice, before you can finalize the deal. If the other party is creating urgency, be sure the urgency is real; don't be pressured into agreeing to something you are not satisfied with or may regret later. If you do want to postpone, give the other party a specific time that you will get back to them.

Agreement. Once you have come to an agreement, put things in writing, if appropriate. It is common to follow up an agreement with a letter/email of thanks that restates the agreement. Also, after the deal is reached, stop selling it. Change the subject to a personal one and/or leave, depending on the other party's preferred negotiation style.

No Agreement. There will be times when you simply will be unable to come to an agreement, or make a sale. Rejection, refusal, and failure happen to us all; in negotiating, you need to be thick skinned. The difference between the "also-rans" and the "superstars" lies in how they respond to the failure. If you cannot close a deal, analyze the situation and try to determine how you can improve in the future.

MANAGING CONFLICT

A **conflict** *exists whenever people are in disagreement and opposition.* You are in conflict when someone does something that bothers you, so conflict is part of everyday life.[84] With globalization and increasingly team-based structures, the frequency and intensity of conflict will only continue to increase.[85] To have good human relations, you need strong conflict resolution skills.[86] In this section, we discuss the psychological contract, functional and dysfunctional conflict, and five conflict management styles.

The Psychological Contract and Functional and Dysfunctional Conflict

All human relations rely on the psychological contract. The *psychological contract* is composed of the implicit expectations of each party. You have a set of expectations about what you will contribute to the organization and what it will provide to you. Often we are not aware of our expectations until they have not been met. **Conflict** *arises when the psychological contract is broken, which happens for two primary reasons:* (1) We fail to make explicit our own expectations and fail to inquire into the expectations of others. (2) We assume that others have the same expectations that we hold. As long as people meet our expectations, everything is fine; when they don't meet our expectations, we are in conflict. Thus, it is important to share information and communicate expectations assertively.

conflict A situation in which people are in disagreement and opposition.

After all, how can you expect others to meet your expectations when they don't know what they are?

People often think of conflict as "fighting" and view it negatively. However, conflict can be positive.[87] **Functional conflict** *exists when disagreement and opposition support the achievement of organizational objectives.* Functional conflict can decrease complacency and reveal inefficiencies. This, in turn, can lead to a more positive work environment, increase employee creativity, and enhance motivation, morale, and performance.

On the other hand, conflict that prevents the achievement of organizational objectives is negative, or *dysfunctional,* conflict.[88] Dysfunctional conflict is often personal and can bring about many negative outcomes within an organization, including damaged relationships, decreased productivity, revenge, avoidance, and aggression.[89]

The key to successful conflict resolution is to focus on the specific behavior or issue at hand, not the person. Photo from Michael Jung/iStockphoto.

Conflict Management Styles

When you are faced with conflict, you have five conflict management styles to choose from. The five styles, along with concern for your own and others' needs; passive, aggressive, and assertive behavior; and win-lose combinations, are presented in Exhibit 10-4 and are discussed below. The advantages and disadvantages and the appropriate use of each conflict management style (there is no one best style) are also discussed.

LO 10-10

List and define five conflict management styles.

EXHIBIT 10-4   CONFLICT MANAGEMENT STYLES

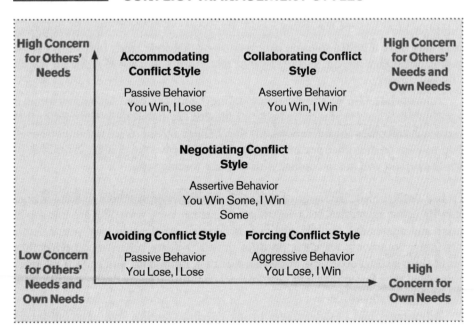

High Concern for Others' Needs

Accommodating Conflict Style

Passive Behavior
You Win, I Lose

Collaborating Conflict Style

Assertive Behavior
You Win, I Win

High Concern for Others' Needs and Own Needs

Negotiating Conflict Style

Assertive Behavior
You Win Some, I Win Some

Avoiding Conflict Style

Passive Behavior
You Lose, I Lose

Forcing Conflict Style

Aggressive Behavior
You Lose, I Win

Low Concern for Others' Needs and Own Needs

High Concern for Own Needs

functional conflict A situation in which disagreement and opposition support the achievement of organizational objectives.

Avoiding Conflict Style. The user of an *avoiding conflict style* attempts to passively ignore conflict rather than resolve it. When you avoid a conflict, you are being unassertive and uncooperative. People avoid conflict by refusing to take a stance, by mentally withdrawing, or by physically leaving. A lose-lose situation results because the conflict is not resolved.

Advantages and Disadvantages of the Avoiding Conflict Style. The advantage is that it may maintain relationships that would be hurt through conflict resolution. The disadvantage is the fact that conflicts do not get resolved. Avoiding problems usually does not make them go away; the problems often get worse. The longer you wait to confront others, the more difficult the confrontation usually is.

Appropriate Use of the Avoiding Conflict Style. It is appropriate to use when (1) the conflict is trivial, (2) your stake in the issue is not high, (3) confrontation will damage an important relationship, (4) you don't have time to resolve the conflict, or (5) emotions are high—wait until later.

It is *inappropriate* to repeatedly avoid confrontation until you get so angry and upset that you end up yelling at other people. This passive-aggressive behavior tends to make the situation worse by hurting human relations. So don't let emotions build up; confront others early when calm.[90]

Accommodating Conflict Style. The user of an *accommodating conflict style* attempts to resolve conflict by passively giving in to the opposing side. When you use this style, you are being unassertive but cooperative. You attempt to satisfy the needs of others but neglect your own needs by letting others get their own way. A win-lose situation is created.

Differences Between the Avoiding and Accommodating Conflict Styles. A difference between the avoiding and the accommodating style is based on behavior. When avoiding, you don't have to do anything you really don't want to do; when accommodating, you do. If you and another person are working on a project together and you go along with that person's way of doing a particular task even though you disagree with it, you are using the accommodating style because you end up doing something you don't really want to do.

Advantages and Disadvantages of the Accommodating Conflict Style. The advantage of accommodating is that you maintain relationships by doing things other people's way. The disadvantage is that giving in may be counterproductive. You may have a better solution. An overuse of this style tends to lead to people taking advantage of you, and the type of relationship you try to maintain is usually lost anyway.

Appropriate Use of the Accommodating Conflict Style. Accommodating is appropriate when (1) you enjoy being a follower, (2) maintaining the relationship outweighs all other considerations, (3) the changes agreed to are not important to you but are to the other person, (4) the time to resolve the conflict is limited, or (5) the person you are in conflict with uses the forcing style.

Forcing Conflict Style. The user of a *forcing conflict style* attempts to resolve conflict by using aggressive behavior to get his or her own way. You are uncooperative and aggressive; you do whatever it takes to satisfy your own needs. Some managers commonly use their position power to force others to do what they want them to do. Forcers use authority, threaten, intimidate, and call for majority rule when they know they will win. Forcers commonly enjoy dealing with avoiders and accommodators.

Advantages and Disadvantages of the Forcing Conflict Style. The advantage of forcing is that better organizational decisions will be made when the forcer is

10-3 APPLYING THE CONCEPT

Conflict Management Styles

Identify the most appropriate conflict management style to use in each situation.

    A.   avoiding style
    B.   accommodating style
    C.   forcing style
    D.   negotiating style
    E.   collaborating style

_____ 11. You have joined a committee in order to make contacts. You have little interest in what the committee actually does. At a committee meeting, you make a recommendation that is opposed by another member. You realize that you have the better idea, but the other party is using a forcing style.

_____ 12. You are on a task force that has to select a new copying machine. The four alternatives will all do the job, but team members disagree about the brand, price, and service.

_____ 13. You are a sales manager. Bonnie, one of your competent salespeople, is trying to close a big sale. The two of you are discussing the sales call she will make. You disagree on the strategy to use to close the sale.

_____ 14. You're on your way to an important meeting and running a little late. As you leave your office, at the other end of the work area you see Liang, one of your employees, goofing off instead of working.

_____ 15. You're over budget for labor this month. At the moment, the work load is light, so you ask Ken, a part-time employee, to leave work early. Ken tells you he doesn't want to go because he needs the money.

correct. The disadvantage is that overuse of this style leads to hostility and resentment toward its user. Forcers tend to have poor human relations.

Appropriate Use of the Forcing Conflict Style. Forcing is appropriate when (1) unpopular action must be taken on important issues, (2) commitment by others to a proposed action is not crucial to its implementation, (3) maintaining relationships is not critical, or (4) a resolution of the conflict is urgently needed.

Negotiating Conflict Style. The user of the *negotiating conflict style*, also called the *compromising style*, attempts to resolve conflict through assertive give-and-take concessions. When you use the negotiating style, you are moderate in assertiveness and cooperation. An "I win some, you win some" situation is created through compromise.

Advantages and Disadvantages of the Negotiating Conflict Style. The advantages of negotiating are that the conflict is resolved relatively quickly and working relationships are maintained. The disadvantage is that compromise often leads to counterproductive results, such as suboptimum decisions. An overuse of this style leads to game playing in which people ask for twice as much as they need in order to get what they want.

Appropriate Use of the Negotiating Conflict Style. Negotiating is appropriate to use when (1) the issues are complex and critical and there is no simple and clear solution, (2) parties have about equal power and are interested in different solutions, (3) a solution will be only temporary, or (4) time is short.

Collaborating Conflict Style. The user of a *collaborating conflict style*, also called the *problem-solving style*, assertively attempts to resolve conflict by working together with the other person to find an acceptable solution. When you use the collaborating approach, you are being assertive and cooperative. Whereas avoiders and accommodators are concerned about others' needs and forcers are concerned about their own needs, collaborators are concerned about finding the best solution to the problem that is satisfactory to all parties. Unlike forcers, collaborators

WORK
APPLICATION 10-10

Think of one of your present or past bosses and give several examples of the conflict management style that person used most often.

are willing to change if a better solution is presented. This is the only style that creates a true win-win situation.

Differences Between the Negotiating and Collaborating Conflict Styles. A difference between the two styles is in the solution each leads to. Again, suppose you and another person are working on a project, and he or she wants to do a task in a way that you disagree with. With the negotiating style, you might do this task his or her way and the next task your way; you each win some and lose some. With the collaborating style, you work to develop an approach to the task that you can both agree on. The key to collaboration is agreeing that the solution picked is agreeable to both parties. Thus, a win-win situation is achieved.

Advantages and Disadvantages of the Collaborating Conflict Style. The advantage of collaborating is that it tends to lead to the best solution to the conflict using assertive behavior. It offers the most benefit to the individual, group, and organization. The disadvantage is that it takes more skill, effort, and time to resolve conflict using this style than it does using the other styles. There are situations in which it is difficult to come up with an agreeable solution, or when a forcer prevents its use.

Appropriate Use of the Collaborating Conflict Style. Collaborating is appropriate when (1) you are dealing with an important issue that requires an optimal solution and compromise would result in suboptimizing, (2) people are willing to place the group goal before self-interest, (3) maintaining relationships is important, (4) time is available, or (5) the conflict is between peers.

Of the five styles, avoiding, accommodating, and forcing are generally the easiest to learn. If you have problems using the avoiding and accommodating styles when appropriate, work at giving in to others by saying or doing nothing or by going along with others' way of doing things. For most people, the two most difficult styles to develop are the negotiating and collaborating styles. Thus, you already learned how to negotiate and in the next section you will learn how to resolve conflicts using the collaborative style. Skill Builders 10–1 and 10–2 also develop negotiation and conflict resolution skills.

Robert Johnson (Case Question 5) had to negotiate to get the resources to start BET and the RLJ Companies, expand, and continue to operate the company. He uses the collaborating conflict style to get his employees to buy into his vision and to get them to work hard to achieve the vision. Johnson also negotiated joint venture partnerships and collaborated with **Western Asset Management** to form and operate an asset management company, with **McLarty–Landers Automotive Group** to form an automobile dealership group, and the **Weinstein Company** to create an urban entertainment company.

Conflict Resolution

Confronting problems helps to resolve them.[91] This section provides a model that helps you develop your skill at resolving conflicts without damaging interpersonal relationships. The model contains steps you can follow when initiating, responding to, and mediating a conflict resolution, as shown in Model 10–2.

Initiating Conflict Resolution

An initiator is a person who confronts another person(s) in order to resolve conflict. When initiating a conflict resolution, you may want to use the **collaborative conflict resolution model** illustrated in Model 10–2 and discussed below. Timing is important. If others are busy, see them later to discuss the conflict in private.[92] In addition, the statement should deal with only a single issue and not several unrelated issues at once.

WORK
APPLICATION 10-11

Which one of the five conflict management styles do you tend to use most often? Explain.

LO 10-11

List the steps in initiating and using the collaborative conflict resolution model.

collaborative conflict resolution model A conflict resolution model that calls for (1) stating the problem in a BCF statement, (2) getting the other party to acknowledge the problem or conflict, (3) asking for and/or presenting alternative resolutions to the conflict, and (4) coming to an agreement.

MODEL 10-2   THE COLLABORATIVE CONFLICT RESOLUTION MODEL

INITIATOR	RESPONDER	MEDIATOR
Step 1. State the problem in terms of behaviors, consequences, and feelings (in a BCF statement).	*Step 1.* Respond as appropriate to the initiator's statement of the problem, using your own BCF statements.	*Step 1.* Bring the conflicting parties together and help them resolve the conflict by coaching them as they follow the steps in the model.
Step 2. Get the other person to acknowledge the problem or conflict.	*Step 2.* Acknowledge the problem or conflict.	*Step 2.* Remain neutral, focusing on how the conflict is affecting work.
Step 3. Ask for and/or present alternative resolutions to the conflict.	*Step 3.* Discuss alternative resolutions to the conflict.	*Step 3.* Address behavior, not personalities.
Step 4. Come to an agreement.	*Step 4.* Come to an agreement.	*Step 4.* Encourage the parties to clarify their statements and responses.
		Step 5. Follow up to make sure the parties carry out the actions they agree to in step 4.

Step 1. State the problem in terms of behaviors, consequences, and feelings (in a BCF statement). The **BCF statement** *describes a conflict in terms of behaviors (B), consequences (C), and feelings (F), in a way that maintains ownership of the problem.* Let's begin by stating what "maintaining ownership of the problem" means. Think about it: If you don't smoke and a smoker lights a cigarette, who has the problem? Since the smoker enjoys it, the problem is yours. Be nice.[93] Maintaining ownership of the problem means expressing it without

- *judging* the behavior as right or wrong, and *assigning blame* about who is right or wrong.
- *threatening* the other person. Threats should be a last, not first, option.

Remember that you don't want to hurt your relationship.[94] Judging, fixing blame, and threats only make people defensive, which is counterproductive.[95] You should also not open by presenting your solution; notice that is steps 3 and 4.

Now that you know what "maintaining ownership of the problem" means, you can construct a BCF statement, keeping it short. For example, you could say, "When you smoke around me (B), I have trouble breathing and become nauseous (C), and I feel ill and stressed (F)." Note that you can vary the sequence if the situation warrants it.

After planning your BCF statement, think of some possible solutions you might suggest in step 3. Be sure your ideas take into consideration the other person's point of view. Put yourself in his or her position—use empathy.[96] If you were the other person, would you like the solutions you have thought of?

BCF statement A statement that describes a conflict in terms of behaviors, consequences, and feelings, in a way that maintains ownership of the problem.

WORK
APPLICATION 10-12

Describe a conflict in which you used (or should have used) a BCF statement.

Step 2. Get the other person to acknowledge the problem or conflict. After stating your BCF, let the other person respond. If the other person doesn't understand or acknowledge the problem, you'll need to be persistent. Repeat your statement in different terms, if necessary.

Step 3. Ask for and/or present alternative resolutions to the conflict. Next, ask the person how the conflict might be resolved. If he or she acknowledges the problem but seems unwilling to resolve it, appeal to common goals. Try to make the other person realize how he or she, the team, the department, or the company might also benefit from a solution to this conflict.

Step 4. Come to an agreement. Determine what specific actions you will each take to resolve the conflict. Perhaps the person will agree not to smoke in your presence now that he or she knows how it affects you. Clearly state whatever actions you each agree to. Skill Builder 10–2 will give you a chance to practice initiating a conflict resolution using the model.

Responding to and Mediating Conflict Resolution

Responding to Conflict Resolution. In the role of responder, you have a responsibility to contribute to successful conflict resolution when someone confronts you with a problem. You should keep in mind the steps in the collaborative conflict resolution model center "Responder" in Model 10–2. Carry out whatever specific actions you and the initiator have agreed to.

Mediating Conflict Resolution. Frequently, parties in conflict cannot resolve their dispute alone. In these cases, a mediator may be used. A **mediator** *is a neutral third party who helps resolve a conflict.* As a manager, you may be called upon to serve as a mediator between two or more employees or groups of employees.[97] In this case, remember that you should be a mediator, not a judge. Get the employees to resolve the conflict themselves, if possible. Remain impartial unless one party is violating company policies, and follow the "Mediator" steps on the right in Model 10–2.

When bringing conflicting employees together, focus on how the conflict is affecting their work. Discuss the issues by addressing specific behavior, not personalities. If a person says, "We cannot work together because of a personality conflict," ask him or her to identify the specific behavior that is the root of the conflict. The discussion should make the employees aware of their behavior and of how its consequences are causing the conflict.

If the conflict cannot be resolved by mediation, an arbitrator may be used as a follow-up. An **arbitrator** *is a neutral third party who resolves a conflict by making a binding decision.* The arbitrator is like a judge whose decision must be followed. However, the use of arbitration should be kept to a minimum because it is not a collaborative conflict style.

STRESS

Dealing with different personality types, varying perceptions and attitudes, power, politics, and conflict can be very stressful. People often have internal reactions to external environmental stimuli. **Stress** *is the body's reaction to environmental demands.* This reaction can be emotional and/or physical. In this section, we discuss functional and dysfunctional stress, causes of job stress, how to manage stress, and the stress tug-of-war analogy.

Stress levels are on a continuum:[98]

low stress————optimal stress————burnout

mediator A neutral third party who helps resolve a conflict.

arbitrator A neutral third party who resolves a conflict by making a binding decision.

stress The body's reaction to environmental demands.

With no or low stress, people tend to just take it easy and waste time and performance is lower, which is *dysfunctional.* An optimal level of stress, like a deadline, is *functional* because it helps improve performance. However, beyond a certain point, stress stops being helpful and becomes *dysfunctional* because it hurts performance. It can also lead to *burnout,* a constant lack of interest and motivation to perform one's job causing mental and physical health problems.[99] But stress is an individual matter. Some people are better at handling stress than others.[100] In the same situation, one person may be very comfortable and stress free while another feels stressed to the point of burnout.

Job Stress Causes and Management

Let's begin with identifying common causes of job stress and then discussing how to manage stress.

Causes of Job Stress. Here are six common causes of job stress:

- *Personality Type.* The *Type A personality* is characterized as fast moving, hard driving, time conscious, competitive, impatient, and preoccupied with work. The *Type B personality* is the opposite of Type A. In general, people with Type A personalities experience more stress than people with Type B personalities. Complete Self-Assessment 10–4 to determine your personality type as it relates to stress.
- *Organizational Culture.* The amount of cooperation and support one experiences and the level of organizational morale effects stress levels.
- *Organizational Change.* Changes can be stressful, especially if they are major and continuous.
- *Management Behavior.* The manager (bad boss) is often a cause of stress put on employees. The better managers are at supervising employees, the less stress there is.
- *Type of Work.* Some types of work are more stressful than others.[101] People who have jobs they enjoy derive satisfaction and handle stress better than those who do not.
- *Interpersonal Relations.* Conflicts among coworkers who do not get along can be very stressful.

Stress Management. Stress management is the process of eliminating or reducing stress. Many organizations today are making stress a priority through training employees in stress management because it improves the bottom line.[102] Here are six stress management techniques you can use to decrease stress:

- *Time Management.* Generally, people with good time management skills experience less job stress. Refer to Chapter 5 for details on time management.
- *Relaxation.* It is important that you relax to help yourself unwind. Finding a hobby or activity you enjoy, taking a vacation, getting an adequate amount of sleep, laughing, and performing relaxation exercises (See Exhibit 10-5) are all ways in which you can relax.
- *Nutrition.* Good health is essential to everyone's performance, and nutrition is a major factor in health. Eating a well-balanced breakfast provides the body with nutrients to help cope with stress all day. Too often people turn to cigarettes, alcohol/drugs, caffeine (coffee/energy drinks), junk food, and too much sleep to "manage" stress. While these may provide short-term relief, they often create other long-term problems.

WORK
APPLICATION 3-13

If you are currently experiencing stress at school or work, identify which of the stress management techniques you believe you can put into practice.

10-4 SELF ASSESSMENT

Personality Type and Stress

Identify how frequently each item applies to you at work or school. Place a number from 1 to 5 on the line before each statement.

5 = usually   4 = often   3 = occasionally   2 = seldom   1 = rarely

_____ 1. I enjoy competition, and I work/play to win.

_____ 2. I skip meals or eat fast when there is a lot of work to do.

_____ 3. I'm in a hurry.

_____ 4. I do more than one thing at a time.

_____ 5. I'm aggravated and upset.

_____ 6. I get irritated or anxious when I have to wait.

_____ 7. I measure progress in terms of time and performance.

_____ 8. I push myself to work to the point of getting tired.

_____ 9. I work on days off.

_____ 10. I set short deadlines for myself.

_____ 11. I'm not satisfied with my accomplishments for very long.

_____ 12. I try to outperform others.

_____ 13. I get upset when my schedule has to be changed.

_____ 14. I consistently try to get more done in less time.

_____ 15. I take on more work when I already have plenty to do.

_____ 16. I enjoy work/school more than other activities.

_____ 17. I talk and walk fast.

_____ 18. I set high standards for myself and work hard to meet them.

_____ 19. I'm considered a hard worker by others.

_____ 20. I work at a fast pace.

_____ Total

Add up the numbers you assigned to all 20 items. Your score will range from 20 to 100. Indicate where your score falls on the continuum below.

Type A								Type B
100	90	80	70	60	50	40	30	20

The higher your score, the more characteristic you are of the Type A personality. The lower your score, the more characteristic you are of the Type B personality.

- *Exercise.* Physical exercise is an excellent way to improve health while releasing stress. Virtually any form of exercise can act as a stress reliever, such as fast walking or jogging, biking, swimming, weight lifting, and playing sports. You are more likely to stick with it if you perform an exercise you enjoy. Exercising with a partner helps.

EXHIBIT 10-5   RELAXATION TECHNIQUES

Head and Neck	Back and Core	Legs and Feet	Shoulders and Arms
Forehead: Wrinkle forehead by trying to make eyebrows touch hairline; hold for 5 seconds.	Back: Lie on back on the floor or a bed and arch back up off the floor, while keeping shoulders and buttocks on the floor; tighten for 5 seconds.	Thighs: Press thighs together and tighten for 5 seconds.	Shoulders: Lift shoulders up to ears and tighten for 5 seconds.
Eyes, nose: Close eyes tightly for 5 seconds.	Stomach: Suck in and tighten stomach muscles for 5 seconds.	Feet, ankles: Flex feet with toes pointing up as far as possible and hold position for 5 seconds.	Upper arms: Bend elbows and tighten upper arm muscles for 5 seconds.
Lips, cheeks, jaw: Draw corners of mouth back tightly in a grimace; hold for 5 seconds.	Hips, buttocks: Tighten buttocks for 5 seconds.	Toes: Curl toes under and tighten for 5 seconds; then wiggle toes to relax them.	Forearms: Extend arms out against an invisible wall and push forward with hands for 5 seconds.
Neck: Drop chin to chest; then slowly rotate head without tilting it back.			Hands: Extend arms to front; then clench fists tightly for 5 seconds.

10-3   JOIN THE DISCUSSION ETHICS & SOCIAL RESPONSIBILITY

Obesity

Being overweight places stress on the body, and poor nutrition contributes to obesity. Obesity is on the increase, and it is a major contributor to the rising cost of health care. Health officials are trying to persuade Americans to lose weight. The government has released public service ads to convince people to get in shape and eat right.

1. Is there prejudice and discrimination against obese people at work?
2. Is it ethical and socially responsible for the government to try to get people to lose weight through ads and other methods?
3. What is the reason for the increase in obesity in the United States? Are restaurant owners and other food marketers responsible for the obesity problem, or are consumers at fault?

- *Positive Thinking.* People with an optimistic personality and attitude generally have less stress than pessimists. As discussed, you become what you think, and you can become more positive and optimistic.
- *Support Network.* Talking to others in a support network can help reduce stress. Develop a network of family, friends, and peers you can go to for help with your problems.

The Stress Tug-of-War

Think of stress as a tug-of-war with you in the center, as illustrated in Exhibit 10-6. On the left are causes of stress trying to pull you away from functional stress

WORK
APPLICATION 3-14

At which of the stress management techniques are you best and worst? What can you do to improve your stress management skills?

LO 10-12

Explain the stress tug-of-war analogy.

10-4   APPLYING THE CONCEPT

Stress Management Techniques

Identify each statement by the technique being used.

A.   time management
B.   relaxation
C.   nutrition
D.   exercise
E.   positive thinking
F.   support network

_____ 16. "I've been getting up earlier and eating breakfast."

_____ 17. "I've been talking to my partner about my problems."

_____ 18. "I've taken up gardening in my spare time."

_____ 19. "I've been repeating statements to myself to be more optimistic."

_____ 20. "I've started using a to-do list."

EXHIBIT 10-6   THE STRESS TUG-OF-WAR

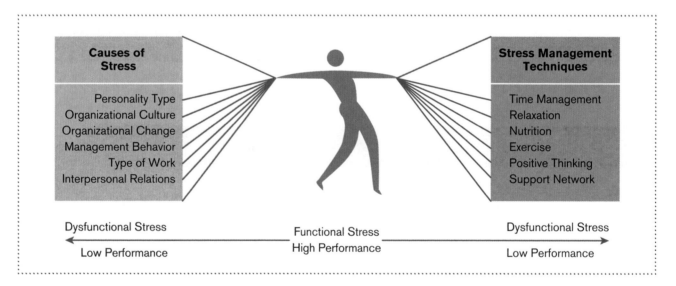

toward dysfunctional stress. On the right are stress management techniques you use to keep yourself in the center. If the stress becomes too powerful, it will pull you off center. The functional stress turns into dysfunctional stress and, as a result, your performance suffers. The stress tug-of-war is an ongoing game. On easy days, you move to the right, and on overly tough days, you move to the left. Your main objective is to stay in the center.[103]

Having read this chapter, you should understand the foundations of individual behavior: personality, perception, and attitude. You should also understand the role that power and politics play in organizations. You should be able to negotiate and manage and resolve conflicts properly. Finally, you should understand the causes of stress and how to minimize it.

• • • CHAPTER SUMMARY

10-1. **Describe each of the Big Five personality dimensions.**

Extroversion lies on a continuum between extrovert and introvert; *agreeableness* between easy and difficult to work with; *emotionalism* between stability and instability; *conscientiousness* between responsible/dependable and irresponsible/undependable; and *openness to experience* between willing to try new things and not being willing to do so.

10-2. **Explain the perception process, and identify the two factors that influence it.**

Perception is the process of selecting, organizing, and interpreting environmental information. How you select, organize, and interpret information is based on both internal individual factors, including your personality and attitudes, and the information available from the external environment.

10-3. **Describe the interrelationship among personality, perception, and attitudes, and explain the contribution of each to a manager's behavior.**

Personality affects perception and attitudes. Perception also affects attitudes, and attitudes affect perception. Thus, all three are interrelated and are important because, combined, they are the foundations of organizational behavior directly affecting behavior and performance.

10-4. **Explain what job satisfaction is and why it is important.**

Job satisfaction is a person's attitude toward the job. Job satisfaction is important because it affects behavior and performance. There is a positive relationship between job satisfaction and citizenship behavior—employee efforts that go above and beyond the call of duty.

10-5. **Define *power*, and explain the difference between position and personal power.**

Power is the ability to influence others' behavior. Position power is derived from top management and delegated down the chain of command, whereas personal power is derived from followers based on an individual's behavior.

10-6. **Identify the differences among reward, legitimate, and referent power.**

The different types of power are based on how the person with power influences others. Reward power is based on the user's ability to influence others by providing something of value to them. Legitimate power is based on the user's position power in the organization. Referent power is based on the user's personal power relationships with others.

10-7. **Discuss how power and politics are related.**

Power is the ability to influence the behavior of others. Politics is the process of gaining and using power. Therefore, political skills are a part of power.

10-8. **Describe how money and politics have similar uses.**

Money and politics have similar uses because they are mediums of exchange. In our economy, money is the medium of exchange. In an organization, politics is the medium of exchange.

10-9. **Explain what networking, reciprocity, and coalitions have in common.**

Networking, reciprocity, and coalitions are all political behaviors. Networking is the process of developing relationships for the purpose of career building and socializing. Reciprocity involves the mutual exchange of favors and privileges to accomplish objectives. Coalitions are networks of alliances that help achieve an objective.

10-10. **List and define five conflict management styles.**

(1) The user of the *avoiding conflict style* attempts to passively ignore conflict rather than resolve it. (2) The user of the *accommodating conflict style* attempts to resolve conflict by passively giving in to the other party. (3) The user of the *forcing conflict style* attempts to resolve conflict by using aggressive behavior to get his or her own way. (4) The user of the *negotiating conflict style* attempts to resolve conflict through assertive give-and-take concessions. (5) The user of the *collaborating conflict style* assertively attempts to resolve conflict by working together with the other party to find an acceptable solution.

10-11. **List the steps in initiating and using the collaborative conflict resolution model.**

The steps in the collaborative conflict resolution model are (1) state the problem in a BCF statement, (2) get the other person to acknowledge the conflict, (3) ask for and/or present alternative resolutions to the conflict, and (4) come to an agreement.

10-12. **Explain the stress tug-of-war analogy.**

In the stress tug-of-war, you are in the center, where stress is functional and performance is high. On your left are the causes of stress trying to pull you off center. On your right are the stress management techniques you use to keep yourself in the center. If the causes of stress pull you off center, the stress turns dysfunctional and, as a result, your performance decreases. If there is an absence of stress, performance is also decreased.

••• Key Terms

arbitrator, 318
attitudes, 299
attribution, 297
BCF statement, 317
citizenship behavior, 300
coalition, 306
conflict, 312

collaborative conflict resolution
    model, 316
functional conflict, 313
mediator, 318
networking, 305
organizational behavior, 294
perception, 297

personality, 294
politics, 305
power, 302
Pygmalion effect, 299
reciprocity, 306
stress, 318

••• Key Term Review

Complete each of the following statements using one of this chapter's key terms.

1. _____ is the study of actions that affect performance in the workplace.

2. _____ is a combination of behavioral, mental, and emotional traits that define an individual.

3. _____ is the process of selecting, organizing, and interpreting environmental information.

4. _____ is the process of determining the reason for someone's behavior and whether that behavior is situational or intentional.

5. _____ are positive or negative evaluations of people, things, and situations.

6. The _____ is the theory that managers' attitudes toward and expectations and treatment of employees largely determine their performance.

7. _____ refers to employee efforts that go above and beyond the call of duty.

8. _____ is the ability to influence others' behavior.

9. _____ is the process of gaining and using power.

10. _____ involves the mutual exchange of favors and privileges to accomplish objectives.

11. A _____ is a network of alliances that help achieve an objective.

12. A _____ exists whenever people are in disagreement and opposition.

13. _____ exists when disagreement and opposition support the achievement of organizational objectives.

14. A _____ describes a conflict in terms of behaviors, consequences, and feelings in a way that maintains ownership of the problem.

15. A _____ is a neutral third party who helps resolve a conflict.

16. An _____ is a neutral third party who resolves a conflict by making a binding decision.

17. _____ is the body's reaction to environmental demands.

••• Review Questions

1. What are the Big Five personality dimensions?

2. What are four biases in perception?

3. What are the determinants of job satisfaction? Are they of equal importance to everyone?

4. What are the seven types of power?

5. Can management order that power and politics in an organization be abolished? If yes, should they?

6. Why should you learn the organizational culture and identify power players where you work?

7. How do you know when you are in conflict?

8. What is the difference between functional and dysfunctional conflict, and how does each affect performance?

9. What does it mean to "maintain ownership of a problem"?

10. What is the difference between a mediator and an arbitrator?

11. What are the characteristics of a Type A personality?

12. What are six stress management techniques?

••• Communication Skills

The following critical-thinking questions can be used for class discussion and/or as written assignments to develop communication skills. Be sure to give complete explanations for all questions.

1. Does personality really play a part in your personal and professional happiness and success? Can you change your personality? If so, how?

2. Why do most people use attribution rather than ask people why they do and say the things they do? How often do you use attribution rather than asking people? Why?

3. Does the Pygmalion effect really work? Why or why not?

4. What is your attitude toward power and politics in organizations? Should power and politics be changed, and if so, how?

5. Which of the guidelines for developing political skills do you think is most important? Why?

6. What are the most relevant points you learned about negotiation that you didn't already know and use? Will you follow the steps in the negotiation process in future negotiations?

7. Which of the conflict management styles do you tend to use most often? Why?

8. How much stress do you have in your life? When do you tend to have more stress, and what is or are the major cause or causes of the stress?

9. Which of the stress management techniques listed in the text do you use currently? Can you think of or do you use any other stress management techniques that are not listed in the text?

• • • CASE: COLLEGE POLITICS

There is a small college in the Midwest with a Department of Management (DM) with nine faculty members. It is one of 12 departments in the School of Arts and Sciences (SAS). The chair of the Department of Management, Frank Polito, is in his first year as chair. Six faculty members, including Latoya Washington, have been in the department longer than Polito.

When Polito asked the dean of the SAS about the college's policy on task descriptions for graduate assistants, the dean stated that there was no formal collegewide policy, but he would speak to the vice president (VP) for academic affairs. The VP and the dean discussed the matter and decided to let individual departments develop their own policies about graduate assistants and their responsibilities. Since Polito believed faculty members should have guidelines to follow, he made developing a policy for graduate assistants an agenda item for the next department meeting.

During the meeting, Polito asked for members' views on what graduate assistants should and should not be allowed to do. Polito was hoping the department would come to a consensus on a policy. Washington was the only faculty member who was using graduate assistants to grade exams. One of the other faculty members spoke out against this use of graduate assistants. Other faculty members agreed, stating that it was the professor's job to grade exams. Washington stated that since her exams were objective, requiring clear correct answers, it was not necessary for her to grade them personally. She pointed out that faculty members in other departments and across the country were using graduate assistants to teach entire courses and to grade subjective papers and exams; therefore, she did not think it would be fair to forbid her to use graduate assistants to grade objective exams. Washington also stated that the department did not need a policy, and she requested that the department not set one. However, Polito, as the department chair, insisted that they set a policy. Washington was the only person who expressed an opposing view during the meeting. However, after the meeting, another faculty member, Nigel Weston, who had said nothing during the meeting, told Washington that he agreed that forbidding her to use graduate assistants for grading exams would not be fair.

There was no department consensus as Polito had hoped there would be. Therefore, Polito said he would draft a department policy, which would be discussed at a future meeting. The next day, Washington sent a memo to department members asking if it was ethical and legal to deny her the use of the same resources as others across the campus. Washington also stated that if the department set a policy against using graduate assistants to grade objective exams, she would appeal the policy decision to the dean, VP, and president.

Case Questions

1. Which Big Five personality dimension is affecting Latoya Washington's behavior? Washington is disagreeing with a policy changes and is trying to stop it. She may also be somewhat emotional about losing help that will require her to do more work herself.

2. What role are perception bias and attitudes playing in this case, and which determinant of job satisfaction would influence Washington? The perception bias is *frame of reference*. Polito and Washington have different views of the need for a policy. The two of them also have different attitudes about the use of grad assistants—Polito negative and Washington positive. If Washington can't use grad assistants, it will have a negative effect on her job satisfaction because of the work itself—she will have to do more work, which she doesn't want to do.

3. What type of power do Polito and Washington appear to be using during the meeting?

4. Which political behavior seems to be stopping Washington from getting what she wants, and which political behavior could be of most help to her if she wants to continue to use graduate assistants for grading exams?

5. What does the psychological contract have to do with this case?

6. In sending her memo to the department, Washington used which conflict management style?

7. Was sending the memo a wise political move? What might Washington have gained or lost by sending it?

8. What would you do if you were Polito? (a) Would you talk to the dean and let him know that Washington said she would appeal the policy decision? If so, which kind of political behavior would this approach represent? (b) Would you draft a policy directly stating that graduate assistants cannot be used to grade objective exams? (c) Would your answer to (b) be influenced by your answer to (a)?

9. If you were Washington, once you saw that you had no support during the meeting, would you have continued to defend your position or agreed to stop using graduate assistants to grade exams? Would your answer be different if you were not a tenured faculty member?

10. If you were Washington and Polito drafted a policy that department members agreed with, would you appeal the decision to the dean? Would your answer be different if you were not a tenured faculty member?

11. If you were the dean of SAS, knowing that the VP did not want to set a college wide policy, and

Washington appealed to you, what would you do? Would you develop a schoolwide policy for SAS?

12. (a) Should Jim Weston have spoken up in defense of Washington during the meeting? If you were Weston, would you have taken Washington's side against the other seven members? (b) Would your answer be different if you were friends with Washington or if you were a tenured professor?

Cumulative Case Questions

13. What are the ethical issues in this case, and how do perception and attitudes influence ethics? (Chapter 2)

14. At what level (collegewide, by schools, or by departments within each school) should a graduate assistant policy be set? (Chapter 5)

15. What type of change is Polito making? (Chapter 6)

16. Which of the major reasons for resistance to change is Washington exhibiting? (Chapter 6)

• • • SKILL BUILDER 10-1: CAR DEALER NEGOTIATION[104]

Preparing for Skill Builder 10-1

Before beginning this Skill Builder, read and be sure you understand the text discussion of the negotiation process.

Objective

To develop your understanding of power and to build negotiation skills.

Skills

The primary skills developed through this exercise are:

1. *Management skill*—interpersonal (negotiation)

2. *AACSB competencies*—communication abilities and analytic skills

3. *Management function*—leading (through influencing others)

Experience

You will be the buyer or seller of a used car.

Procedure 1 (1–2 minutes)

Pair off and sit facing your partner so that you cannot read each other's confidential sheet. Pairs should be as far apart as possible so they cannot overhear other pairs' conversations. If there is an odd number of students in the class, one student will be an observer or work with the instructor. Decide who will be the buyer and who will be the seller of the used car.

Procedure 2 (1–2 minutes)

The instructor will give a confidential sheet to each buyer and seller. (These do not appear in this book.)

Procedure 3 (5–6 minutes)

Buyers and sellers read their confidential sheets and jot down some plans (what your basic approach will be, what you will say) for the negotiation.

Procedure 4 (3–7 minutes)

Negotiate the sale of the car. You do not have to buy or sell the car. After you make the sale or agree not to sell, read your partner's confidential sheet and discuss the experience.

Integration (5–7 minutes)

Answer the following questions:

1. What type of plan was appropriate for this situation?

2. Which type of power was most relevant in helping you to negotiate the car deal?

3. Did you experience any stress as a result of this exercise (faster heart rate, perspiration, anxiety, tension, or pressure)?

4. Did you set a lower limit, target, and opening price?

5. Did you imply that you had other options and/or develop trade-offs?

6. Did you anticipate questions and objections, and prepare answers?

7. Did you develop rapport and focus on obstacles rather than the person?

8. Did you let the other party make the first offer?

9. Did you listen and ask questions to focus on meeting the other party's needs?

10. Were you quick to settle for less than your target price and/or ask for something in return for giving concessions?

11. Did you reach a sales agreement?

12. If you did reach a sales agreement, which price did you receive?

Apply It

What did I learn from this experience? How will I use this knowledge in the future?

• • • SKILL BUILDER 10-2: INITIATING CONFLICT RESOLUTION

Objective

To develop your skill at initiating conflict resolution.

Skills

The primary skills developed through this exercise are:

1. *Management skill*—interpersonal (conflict management)

2. *AACSB competencies*—communication abilities and analytic skills

3. *Management function*—leading (through influencing others)

During class, you will be given the opportunity to role play a conflict you are facing or have faced in order to develop your conflict resolution skills. Students and workers have reported that this exercise helped prepare them for successful initiation of conflict resolution with roommates or coworkers. Fill in the following information:

1. Other party/parties (you may use fictitious names):

_____

_____

2. Describe the conflict situation: List pertinent information about the other party (i.e., relationship to you, knowledge of the situation, age, and background):

_____

_____

3. Identify the other party's possible reaction to your confrontation. (How receptive will he or she be to collaborating? What might he or she say or do during the discussion to resist change?)

_____

_____

4. How will you overcome the resistance to change?

_____

_____

5. Following the steps in the collaborative conflict resolution model, write out your BCF statement.

_____

_____

Apply It

What did I learn from this experience? How will I use this knowledge in the future?

• • • SKILL BUILDER 10-3: IMPROVING YOUR OB FOUNDATIONS

Objective

To develop a plan for improving your OB foundations of personality and attitudes.

Skills

The primary skills developed through this exercise are:

1. *Management skill*—interpersonal (personal motivation)

2. *AACSB competency*—reflective thinking skills

3. *Management function*—leading

We can all improve certain aspects of our personalities and attitudes. Review your responses to the Self-Assessment Personality Profile (pages 295–296). Of the traits listed, choose one you'd like to work on improving, or a negative attitude, as a way of increasing your job performance and satisfaction. For example, suppose you decided that you needed to develop a more optimistic and positive attitude

and that to do so, you would work on thinking and talking more positively. You might write the following specific steps for accomplishing your plan:

- I will be aware of what I say and will focus on the positive rather than the negative. I will tell myself, for example, "I'm getting a lot done today, I can do it" rather than "I'll never meet this deadline," or "I'm losing weight," not "I'm too fat," or "I need to lose weight."

- If I do find myself saying something negative to myself or to someone else, I will immediately stop and rephrase the statement in a positive manner.

- I will let friends and coworkers know that I am working on being more positive and ask for their help. I will ask them not only to point out when I'm being negative but also to reinforce me when they observe a more positive attitude from me.

Zig Ziglar recommends that if you really want to be more positive about your situation (at work, in school, in your family, in a romantic relationship, etc.), you need to focus on the good side, not dwell on the negative. To do so, write out a list of everything you like about the situation. Then write down some positive affirmations, such as "I have a positive attitude"; "I enjoy my job/school"; "I like Fred." Every morning and evening, while looking in the mirror, read your list. You may also record your list and play it. Do this for a month and you and others will see a changed, more positive personality and attitudes.

Here are some specific steps you might list for yourself if you wanted to develop a more extraverted personality: I will say hi to people before they say hi to me. I will attend a party at which I don't know many people, and I will approach people first to talk to them. I will go to class early (or stay after class) once a week and approach someone I don't know, or don't know well, and talk to that person for a few minutes before (or after) class. You can also follow Zig Ziglar's recommendation and write a positive affirmation for yourself, such as "I enjoy meeting new people."

• • • STUDENT STUDY SITE

Visit the Student Study Site at **www.sagepub.com/lussier6e** to access to these additional study tools:

- Mobile-compatible self-assessment quizzes
- Mobile-compatible key term flashcards
- Video Links

- SAGE Journal Articles
- Web Links

11 Motivating for High Performance

IDEAS ON MANAGEMENT at Market America and SHOP.COM

Market America is a dynamic and innovative product brokerage and Internet marketing company specializing in one-to-one marketing and social shopping. ma was founded in 1992, and in 2011 it acquired **SHOP.COM**—a pioneer in online comparison shopping—creating a powerful, new social shopping destination poised to challenge the Internet's leading e-commerce sites. ma's mission is to provide a system for entrepreneurs to create an ongoing income while providing consumers worldwide with a better way to shop. SHOP.COM is one of the largest online retailers for consumers worldwide with 2,500 exclusive Market America–branded products/services and more than 50 million additional products/services through affiliates and direct partners.

Products and services are sold through a system of independent distributors and UnFranchise® entrepreneur owners. Each entrepreneur is equipped with a SHOP.COM website. ma provides a systemized and standardized business model, just like a franchise. It provides support, training, technology, products, and a proven business system. It's called the "UnFranchise® business" because you have all the benefits of a franchise but do not have to pay a franchise fee. Additionally, instead of paying the franchisor a royalty, ma pays you commissions and retail profits from the sales through its SHOP.COM website and referral network. ma has generated more than $4.3 billion in accumulated retail sales, and its independent entrepreneurs have earned more than $2.4 billion in commissions and retail profits. ma was founded and is still headquartered in North Carolina, but it has international operations in Australia, Canada, Hong Kong, Taiwan, the United Kingdom, and Mexico.

1. What does Market America do to motivate its distributors, and how does this affect performance? PAGE 333

2. How does Market America meet its distributors' content motivation needs? PAGE 335

3. How does Market America meet its distributors' process motivation needs? PAGE 341

• • • Chapter Outline

4. How does Market America use reinforcement theory to motivate its distributors? PAGE 346

5. Does the Market America UnFranchise® business model for motivation work in other countries? PAGE 351

You'll find answers to these questions throughout the chapter. To learn more about Market America, visit its website at www.marketamerica.com.

Source: Information for this case and answers within the chapter were taken from the Market America website at http://www.marketamerica.com, accessed August 6, 2013.

MOTIVATION AND PERFORMANCE

Executives are often frustrated and puzzled when it comes to understanding what truly motivates their employees.[1] This chapter is all about understanding how to motivate yourself and others. In this section, we discuss what motivation is and how motivation affects performance. You will also get an overview of three major classes of theories of motivation.

What Is Motivation, and How Does It Affect Performance?

Motivation and Effort. From a business perspective, **motivation** *is the willingness to achieve organizational objectives or to go above and beyond the call of duty (organizational citizenship behavior).* A fundamental task of managers is to mobilize and motivate employees,[2] to motivate them to accomplish great things,[3] including achieving objectives.[4]

Motivational *effort* is important,[5] and effort has three parts. *Initiation of effort* refers to how much effort to exert (What level of performance will I go for?). *Direction of effort* refers to where to put effort (Do I do job A or B?). *Persistence of effort* refers to how long effort will be forthcoming (Do I keep pushing or let up?) You have to motivate yourself?[6] What is your motivational effort for this course? People want to gain something for their effort.[7] Understanding that people are motivated by self-interest is key to understanding motivation.[8]

LO 11-1

Illustrate the motivation process.

The Motivation Process. Through the **motivation process**, *employees go from need to motive to behavior to consequence to satisfaction or dissatisfaction.* For example, you are thirsty (need) and have a desire (motive) to get a drink. You get a drink (behavior) that quenches your thirst (consequence and satisfaction). Satisfaction is usually short-lived. Getting that drink satisfied you, but soon you will need another drink. For this reason, the motivation process is a feedback loop:

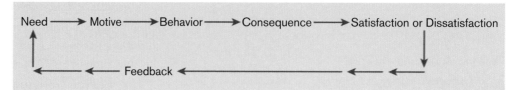

motivation The willingness to achieve organizational objectives or to go above and beyond the call of duty (organizational citizenship behavior).

motivation process The process of moving from need to motive to behavior to consequence to satisfaction or dissatisfaction.

A need or want motivates behavior. However, needs and motives are complex; people don't always know what their needs are or why they do the things they do. Understanding needs will help you understand behavior. You cannot observe motives, but you can observe behavior and infer the motive.

The Role of Expectations in Motivation and Performance. The poor performance of employees can be caused inadvertently by managers themselves and may not result from poor skills, a lack of experience, or insufficient motivation.[9] Recall the Pygmalion effect (Chapter 10): Managers' attitudes toward and expectations and treatment of employees largely determine their performance. Enthusiasm is contagious. If your employees see that you are enthusiastic about your job, they are more likely to be enthusiastic about theirs. Employees will be satisfied with doing the minimum,[10] so you need to have high expectations and treat employees as though they are high achievers to get the best from them. **Walmart** founder Sam Walton said, "High expectations are the key to everything."

In addition to managers' expectations, employees' expectations also affect performance through the *self-fulfilling prophecy*. Henry Ford, founder of **Ford Motor Company**, said that if you believe you can or believe you can't, you are right. If you think you will be successful, you will be. If you think you will fail, you will, because you will fulfill your own expectations. You will live up or down to your own expectations. You become what you think about, so be positive, confident, and optimistic.

Motivation and the Performance Formula. Generally, a motivated employee will try harder than an unmotivated one to do a good job.[11] However, performance is not simply based on motivation.[12] Three interdependent factors determine the level of performance attained: ability, motivation, and resources. The interaction of these factors can be expressed as a **performance formula**:

$$\text{performance} = \text{ability} \times \text{motivation} \times \text{resources}$$

For maximum performance, all three factors must be high. When performance is not optimum, you must determine which performance factor needs to be improved. The key to success is to figure out what you like to do (*motivation*), what you are good at doing (*ability*), and getting the *resources* to achieve your goals—such as a college degree.

Market America's (Case Question 1) primary means of affecting performance is to create self-motivation by making each distributor his or her own boss—which only succeeds with people who are interested in entrepreneurship. In terms of the performance formula, ma's UnFranchise® approach develops the ability and motivation to sell, and the company provides the management knowhow and marketing resources to create and grow your own business.

LO 11-2

Explain the performance formula and how to use it.

performance formula Performance = ability × motivation × resources.

11-1 APPLYING THE CONCEPT

The Performance Formula

Identify the factor contributing to low performance in the following five situations.

A. ability
B. motivation
C. resources

_____ 1. Tony does not produce as much as the other department members because he does not put much effort into the job.

_____ 2. "I practice longer and harder than my track teammates Malik and Usain. I don't understand why they beat me in the races."

_____ 3. "I could get all As in school if I wanted to, but I'd rather relax and have a good time."

_____ 4. The production team got behind schedule because the printing press was down for repairs.

_____ 5. Latoya went on a sales call. When she reached into her briefcase, she realized that she did not have her product display book. Trying to explain the products without being able to show them to the customer resulted in a lost sale.

An Overview of Three Major Classes of Motivation Theories

It has been said that nothing is as practical as a good theory, and motivation theories have found numerous applications in organizations. However, there is no single universally accepted theory of how to motivate people. In this chapter, we discuss three major classes of motivation theories and show how you can use them to motivate yourself and others. Exhibit 11-1 lists the major motivation theories. After studying all of these theories, you can select one theory to use, use several theories in developing your own approach, or apply the theory that best fits the specific situation.

LO 11-3

Discuss the major similarities and differences among the four content motivation theories: hierarchy of needs theory, ERG theory, two-factor theory, and acquired needs theory.

CONTENT MOTIVATION THEORIES

According to content motivation theorists, if you want high levels of performance, you must meet employee needs. When employees are asked to meet objectives, they think, but usually do not say, "What's in it for me?"[13] The key to achieving

EXHIBIT 11-1   ## MAJOR MOTIVATION THEORIES

Class of Motivation Theories	Specific Theory (Creator)
Content motivation theories focus on identifying and understanding employees' needs.	**Hierarchy of needs theory** proposes that employees are motivated by five levels of needs: physiological, safety, social, esteem, and self-actualization. (Maslow)
	ERG theory proposes that employees are motivated by three needs: existence, relatedness, and growth. (Alderfer)
	Two-factory theory proposes that employees are motivated by motivators (higher-level needs) rather than by maintenance factors (lower-level needs). (Herzberg)
	Acquired needs theory proposes that employees are motivated by their need for achievement, power, and affiliation. (McClelland)
Process motivation theories focus on understanding how employees choose behaviors to fulfill their needs.	**Equity theory** proposes that employees are motivated when their perceived inputs equal outputs. (Adams)
	Goal-setting theory proposes that achievable but difficult goals motivate employees. (Locke)
	Expectancy theory proposes that employees are motivated when they believe they can accomplish a task and the rewards for doing so are worth the effort. (Vroom)
Reinforcement theory proposes that the consequences of their behavior will motivate employees to behave in predetermined ways. (Skinner)	**Types of Reinforcement**
	Positive reinforcement is offering attractive consequences (rewards) for desirable performance to encourage the continuation of that behavior.
	Avoidance reinforcement is threatening to provide negative consequences for poor performance to encourage desirable behavior.
	Punishment is providing an undesirable consequence (punishment) for an undesirable behavior to prevent the behavior.
	Extinction is the withholding of reinforcement for a particular behavior.

organizational objectives is to meet the needs of employees. As you create a win-win situation, you need to sell the benefits that meet employees' needs to the employees.

Content motivation theories *focus on identifying and understanding employees' needs.* In this section, we describe and discuss the application of four content motivation theories: hierarchy of needs theory, ERG theory, two-factor theory, and acquired needs theory.

Hierarchy of Needs Theory

The **hierarchy of needs theory** *proposes that employees are motivated by five levels of needs: physiological, safety, social, esteem, and self-actualization.* Abraham Maslow developed this theory in the 1940s[14] based on four major assumptions: (1) Only unmet needs motivate. (2) People's needs are arranged in order of importance (in a hierarchy) from basic to complex. (3) People will not be motivated to satisfy a higher-level need unless the lower-level needs have been at least minimally satisfied. (4) People have five levels of needs, listed here in hierarchical order from lowest to highest:

- *Physiological needs.* These are people's basic needs for air, water, food, shelter, sex, and relief from or avoidance of pain.
- *Safety needs.* Once they satisfy their physiological needs, people are concerned with safety and security.
- *Social needs.* After establishing safety, people look for love, friendship, acceptance, and affection.
- *Esteem needs.* After they meet their social needs, people focus on acquiring status, self-respect, recognition for accomplishments, and a feeling of self-confidence and prestige.
- *Self-actualization needs.* The highest-level need is to develop one's full potential. To do so, people seek growth, achievement, and advancement.

Motivating Employees with Hierarchy of Needs Theory. Managers should meet employees' lower-level needs so that those needs will not dominate the employees' motivational process. So meet lower-level needs first and focus on meeting higher-level needs.[15] Exhibit 11-2 lists ways in which organizations attempt to meet the needs in Maslow's hierarchy.

Working for **Market America (Case Question 2-a)** allows people to meet many needs. Earning money allows them to satisfy physiological needs. Because the job involves a minimum of risk, people's safety needs are met. Customer contact and meetings satisfy some of people's social needs. The job itself offers great growth potential and thus may satisfy some distributors' esteem needs. Finally, being the boss allows people to have control over the work experience, which may help them meet self-actualization needs.

ERG Theory

A well-known simplification of the hierarchy of needs theory, the **ERG theory**, *proposes that employees are motivated by three needs: existence, relatedness, and growth.* Clayton Alderfer reorganized Maslow's hierarchy of five types of needs into three needs: existence (physiological and safety needs), relatedness (social), and growth (esteem and self-actualization). Alderfer agreed with Maslow that unsatisfied needs motivate individuals, and he theorized that more than one need may be active at one time.[16]

WORK APPLICATION 11-1

Describe how your needs at each of Maslow's levels are addressed by an organization you work for now or were addressed by one you worked for in the past.

content motivation theories Theories that focus on identifying and understanding employees' needs.

hierarchy of needs theory Theory that proposes that employees are motivated by five levels of needs: physiological, safety, social, esteem, and self-actualization.

ERG theory Theory that proposes that employees are motivated by three needs: existence, relatedness, and growth.

EXHIBIT 11-2   HOW MANAGERS MOTIVATE BASED ON MASLOW'S HIERARCHY OF NEEDS THEORY

Self-Actualization Needs
Organizations help employess meet their self-actualization needs by providing them with opportunities for skill development, the chance to be creative, promotions, and the ability to have complete control over their jobs.

Esteem Needs
Organizations meet employees' esteem needs with pay raises, recognition, challenging tasks, participation in decision making, and opportunity for advancement.

Social Needs
Organizations meet employees' social needs by providing them with the opportunity to interact with others, to be accepted, and to have friends. Many organizations schedule employee parties, picnics, trips, and sports teams.

Safety Needs
Organizations meet employess' safety needs by providing safe working conditions, job security. and fringe benefits (medical insurane/sick pay/pensions).

Physiological Needs
organizations meet employess' physiological needs by providing adequate salary, work breaks, and safe working conditions.

Motivating Employees with ERG Theory. To apply ERG theory, you must determine which employee needs have been met and which have not been met or have been frustrated and then must plan how to meet the unsatisfied needs.

Two-Factor Theory

In the 1950s, Frederick Herzberg classified two sets of needs that he called *factors*.[17] Herzberg combined lower-level needs into one classification he called *maintenance factors* and higher-level needs into one classification he called *motivators*. The **two-factor theory** proposes *that employees are motivated by motivators rather than by maintenance factors.* Maintenance factors are also called *extrinsic motivators*, because the motivation comes from outside the job. Motivators are called *intrinsic motivators* because the motivation comes from the work itself.[18] Complete the Self-Assessment to find out what motivates you.

Based on their research, Herzberg and his associates disagreed with the traditional view that satisfaction and dissatisfaction were at opposite ends of a single continuum. Instead, they proposed two continuums: one for maintenance factors and one for motivators. The continuum for maintenance factors runs from not dissatisfied to dissatisfied. The continuum for motivators runs from satisfied to not satisfied, as illustrated in Exhibit 11-3.

Herzberg contended that addressing maintenance factors will keep employees from being dissatisfied, but it will not make them satisfied or motivate them. For example, if employees are dissatisfied with their pay (a maintenance factor) and

WORK
APPLICATION 11-2

Recall a present or past job; were you dissatisfied or not dissatisfied with the maintenance factors? Were you satisfied or not satisfied with the motivators? Identify the specific maintenance factors and motivators, and explain your response.

two-factor theory Theory that proposes that employees are motivated by motivators rather than by maintenance factors.

they get a raise, they will no longer be dissatisfied. However, before long employees will get accustomed to the new standard of living and become dissatisfied again. They will need another raise to avoid becoming dissatisfied again. This becomes a repeating cycle.

Motivating Employees With Two-Factor Theory. Organizations need to ensure that employees are not dissatisfied with maintenance factors and then focus on motivating them through their jobs.[19] Employees are more motivated when they feel they are doing meaningful work.[20] One successful way to motivate employees is to build challenges and opportunities for achievement into their jobs.[21] *Job enrichment,* the Job Characteristics Model, and delegating (discussed in Chapter 7) can be effective motivators.

Market America (Case Question 2-b) allows people to operate their own businesses. In terms of the two-factor theory, the focus of this organization is on motivators that allow distributors to meet their high-level needs for esteem and self-actualization. Maintenance factors are not directly addressed.

Acquired Needs Theory

The **acquired needs theory** *proposes that employees are motivated by their needs for achievement, power, and affiliation.* It is also called learned needs and three-needs theory. Henry Murray developed the general needs theory.[22] This was adapted by John Atkinson and David McClelland, who developed the acquired needs theory.[23] McClelland does not have a classification for lower-level needs. His affiliation needs are the same as Maslow's social and relatedness needs, and his power and achievement needs are related to esteem, self-actualization, and growth.

Motivating employees is central to the role of the manager. Motivating employees who are frustrated or have unmet needs can be challenging. Photo from Pixland/Thinkstock.

EXHIBIT 11-3   HERZBERG'S TWO-FACTOR THEORY

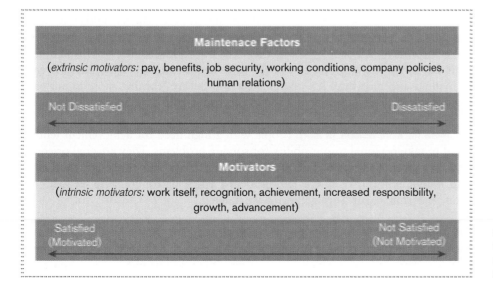

Maintenace Factors

(*extrinsic motivators:* pay, benefits, job security, working conditions, company policies, human relations)

Not Dissatisfied ←————————————————→ Dissatisfied

Motivators

(*intrinsic motivators:* work itself, recognition, achievement, increased responsibility, growth, advancement)

Satisfied (Motivated) ←————————————————→ Not Satisfied (Not Motivated)

acquired needs theory Theory that proposes that employees are motivated by their needs for achievement, power, and affiliation.

11-1 SELF ASSESSMENT

What Motivates You?

Following are 12 job factors that contribute to job satisfaction. Rate each according to how important it is to you by placing a number from 1 to 5 on the line before each factor.

Very important		Somewhat important		Not important
5	4	3	2	1

_____ 1. An interesting job I enjoy doing

_____ 2. A boss who treats everyone the same regardless of the circumstances

_____ 3. Getting praise and other recognition and appreciation for the work that I do

_____ 4. A job that is routine without much change from day to day

_____ 5. The opportunity for advancement

_____ 6. A nice job title regardless of pay

_____ 7. Job responsibility that gives me freedom to do things my way

_____ 8. Working conditions (safe environment, cafeteria, etc.)

_____ 9. The opportunity to learn new things

_____ 10. An emphasis on following company rules, regulations, procedures, and policies

_____ 11. A job I can do well and succeed at

_____ 12. Job security

Indicate below how you rated each factor.

Motivating Factors	Maintenance Factors
1. _____	2. _____
3. _____	4. _____
5. _____	6. _____
7. _____	8. _____
9. _____	10. _____
11. _____	12. _____
Total points: _____	_____

Add each column vertically. Are motivators or maintenance factors more important to you?

Unlike the other content theories, the acquired needs theory holds that needs are based on personality and are developed and learned as people interact with the environment. All people possess the needs for achievement, power, and affiliation, but to varying degrees. One of the three needs tends to be dominant in each individual and motivates his or her behavior. Before learning more about each need, complete Self-Assessment 11–2 to determine your profile.

The Need for Achievement (n Ach). People with a high need for achievement tend to want to take personal responsibility for solving problems. They are goal oriented, and they set moderate, realistic, attainable goals. They seek challenge, excellence, and individuality; take calculated, moderate risks; desire concrete feedback on their performance; and are willing to work hard.

The Need for Power (n Pow). People with a high need for power have a take-charge attitude.[24] They tend to want to control the situation, to influence or control others, to enjoy competition in which they can win (they do not like to lose), and to be willing to confront others.

11-2 SELF ASSESSMENT

Acquired Needs

Indicate how accurately each of the 15 statements describes you by placing a number from 1 to 5 on the line before each statement.

Like me		Somewhat like me		Not like me
5	4	3	2	1

_____ 1. I enjoy working hard.
_____ 2. I enjoy competing and winning.
_____ 3. I enjoy having many friends.
_____ 4. I enjoy a difficult challenge.
_____ 5. I enjoy being in a leadership role.
_____ 6. I want other people to like me.
_____ 7. I want to know how I am progressing as I complete tasks.
_____ 8. I confront people who do things I disagree with.
_____ 9. I enjoy frequently getting together socially with people.
_____ 10. I enjoy setting and achieving realistic goals.
_____ 11. I try to influence other people so that I get my way.
_____ 12. I enjoy belonging to many groups and organizations.
_____ 13. I enjoy the satisfaction of completing a difficult task.
_____ 14. In a leaderless situation, I tend to step forward and take charge.
_____ 15. I enjoy working with others more than working alone.

To determine your dominant need, write the number you assigned to each statement in the table below. Add up the total of each column, which should be between 5 and 25 points. The column with the highest score is your dominant need.

Achievement	Power	Affiliation
1. _____	2. _____	3. _____
4. _____	5. _____	6. _____
7. _____	8. _____	9. _____
10. _____	11. _____	12. _____
13. _____	14. _____	15. _____
Totals _____	_____	_____

The Need for Affiliation (n Aff). People with a high n Aff tend to seek close relationships with others, to want to be liked by others, to enjoy social activities, and to seek to belong. They like to interact with other people rather than being alone.

The Manager Acquired Needs Profile. Managers tend to have a high n Pow, followed by a high need for n Ach, and a low n Aff. People with a high n Aff tend to avoid management because they tend to have a low n Pow and like to be one of the group rather than its manager who needs to evaluate and discipline others.

Motivating Employees With Acquired Needs Theory. People have different needs profiles and must be motivated and led differently.[25] To motivate employees with a high *n Ach,* give them nonroutine, challenging tasks with clear, attainable objectives. Give them fast and frequent feedback on their performance. To motivate employees with a high n Pow, give them greater autonomy, letting them plan and control their jobs as much as possible. Try to include them in decision making, especially when the decision affects them. To motivate employees with a high n Aff, be sure

WORK
APPLICATION 11-3

Explain how your need for achievement, power, and/or affiliation has affected your motivation on the job.

to let them work as part of a team. They derive satisfaction from the people they work with more than from the task itself. Delegate responsibility for orienting and training new employees to them.

Market America (Case Question 2-d) helps distributors meet all three acquired needs. It provides support so that they can achieve their goal of successfully running their own business, they have the power to be in control, and they can develop an affiliation with customers and other distributors.

Exhibit 11-4 compares the four content motivation theories. Read left to right by row to see how each of Malsow's needs is classified under the other three theories.

EXHIBIT 11-4   A COMPARISON OF FOUR CONTENT MOTIVATION THEORIES

Hierarchy of Needs (Maslow)	ERG Theory (Alderfer)	Two-Factor Theory (Herzberg)	Acquired Needs Theory (McClelland)
Self-actualization	Growth	Motivators	Achievement and Power
Esteem	Growth	Motivators	Achievement and Power
Social	Relatedness	Maintenance factors	Affiliation
Safety	Existence	Maintenance factors	(Not addressed)
Physiological	Existence	Maintenance factors	(Not addressed)
Needs must be met in a hierarchical order.	Needs at any level can be unmet simultaneously.	Maintenance factors will not motivate employees.	Motivating needs are developed through experience.

LO 11-4

Discuss the major similarities and differences among the three process motivation theories: equity theory, goal-setting theory, and expectancy theory.

process motivation theories Theories that focus on understanding how employees choose behaviors to fulfill their needs.

equity theory Theory that proposes that employees are motivated when their perceived inputs equal outputs.

PROCESS MOTIVATION THEORIES

Process motivation theories *focus on understanding how employees choose behaviors to fulfill their needs.* Content motivation theories focus simply on identifying and understanding employees' needs. Process motivation theories go a step further and attempt to explain how and why we choose to try to satisfy needs in different ways, the mental process we go through as we understand situations, and how we evaluate our need satisfaction. In this section, we discuss equity theory, goal-setting theory, and expectancy theory.

Equity Theory

Equity theory, particularly the version of J. Stacy Adams, proposes that people are motivated to seek social equity in the rewards they receive (output) for their performance (input),[26] and the theory is still popular today.[27] **Equity theory** *proposes that employees are motivated when their perceived inputs equal outputs.*

According to equity theory, people compare their inputs (effort, experience, seniority, status, intelligence, and so forth) and outputs (praise, recognition, pay, benefits, promotions, increased status, supervisor's approval, etc.) to those of relevant others.[28] A relevant other could be a coworker or a group of employees from the same or different organizations. Employees are more motivated to achieve organizational objectives when they believe they are being treated fairly,[29] especially regarding pay equity.[30]

Notice that the definition says that employees compare their *perceived* (not actual) inputs to outputs.[31] Equity may actually exist. However, if employees believe that there is inequity, they will change their behavior, attempting to create equity. Inequity perceptions hurt attitudes, commitment, and cooperation, thereby decreasing individual, team, and organizational performance.[32] It is used as a justification for unethical behavior.[33]

Motivating Employees With Equity Theory. Using equity theory in practice can be difficult, because you don't know the employees' reference groups and their views of inputs and outcomes. However, managers can help control employee perceptions of fairness.[34] The theory does offer some useful general recommendations:

1. Managers should be aware that equity is based on perception, which may not be correct. Managers should not play favorites but instead should treat employees equally but in unique ways.

2. Rewards should be equitable. Employees producing at the same level should be given equal rewards. Employees who perceive they are working harder than others, and or for less pay, may decrease performance.

3. High performance should be rewarded, but employees must understand the inputs needed to attain certain outputs. When using incentive pay, managers should clearly specify the exact requirements to achieve the incentive. A manager should be able to state objectively why one person got a higher merit raise than another.

Market America's (Case Question 3-a) UnFranchise® business model treats all distributors with equity. Owners have unlimited potential, as the more time and effort (inputs) they put into their business, the more potential rewards (outputs) they can reap. However, not everyone is cut out for sales, and some people who start as independent distributors drop out or stay at this level rather than advancing to become UnFranchise® owners.

Goal-Setting Theory

Goal-setting theory is currently the most valid approach to work motivation.[35] It complements the two-factor and acquired needs theories, as hundreds of studies have demonstrated that setting specific, challenging goals leads to higher levels of motivation and performance.[36] The **goal-setting theory** *proposes that achievable but difficult goals motivate employees.* Our behavior has a purpose, which is usually to fulfill a need. Goals give us a target that we can commit to achieving.[37]

Lou Holtz—motivational speaker, **ESPN** college football analyst, and former football coach of the national championship winner **University of Notre Dame** and the **University of South Carolina**—stated that the three keys to success are a winning attitude, positive self-esteem, and setting a higher goal.[38] Holtz said, "Of all my experiences in managing people, the power of goal setting is the most incredible."

Motivating Employees With Goal-Setting Theory. Don't set easy goals, because most employees will just do the minimum.[39] Don't simply tell employees to do their best, because they most likely will not perform well and will use the excuse that they did their best when they really didn't. For goals to be motivational, they must be difficult but achievable with employee commitment to get employees motivated to push hard (stretch) to reach the goal.[40] Refer to Chapter 5 for how to set objectives using the model that will motivate yourself and others.

Market America (Case Question 3-b) relies heavily on goal-setting theory. One of its goals is to take on **Amazon.com** as a top location for one-stop Internet shopping. Goal setting is one of "the Basic 5" steps for success at Market

WORK APPLICATION 11-4

Give an example of how equity theory has affected your motivation or someone else's you work with or have worked with. Be sure to specify if you were underrewarded, overrewarded, or equitably rewarded.

WORK APPLICATION 11-5

Give an example of how goal(s) affected your motivation and performance or that of someone you work with or have worked with.

goal-setting theory Theory that proposes that achievable but difficult goals motivate employees.

Recall from Chapter 1 that setting goals is the starting point of the management functions. Goal-setting theory suggests that setting difficult but achievable goals can motive employees to excel. Photo from Scotto72/iStockphoto.

WORK
APPLICATION 11-6

Give an example of how expectancy theory has affected your motivation or someone else's you work with or have worked with. Be sure to specify the expectancy and the valence.

expectancy theory Theory that proposes that employees are motivated when they believe they can accomplish a task and the rewards for doing so are worth the effort.

America. Distributors are taught to set business and personal goals—both short term and long term. They are then encouraged to develop a detailed plan of what they must do each year, each month, each week, and each day to achieve their goal(s).

Expectancy Theory

Expectancy theory is based on Victor Vroom's formula: motivation = expectancy × instrumentality × valence.[41] The **expectancy theory** *proposes that employees are motivated when they believe they can accomplish a task and the rewards for doing so are worth the effort.*

Three important variables in Vroom's formula determine motivation:

1. *Expectancy* refers to the person's perception of his or her ability (probability) to accomplish an objective. Generally, the higher one's expectancy, the better the chance for motivation. When employees do not believe that they can accomplish objectives, they will not be motivated to try. What is your expectancy grade for this course?

2. *Instrumentality* refers to the perception of the relationship between performance and the outcome/reward. Generally, the higher one's expectation for a positive outcome, the better the chance for motivation. Do the low odds of winning the lottery's big prize motivate you to buy tickets?

3. *Valence* refers to the value a person places on the outcome. Generally, the higher the value (importance) of the outcome, the better the chance of motivation. Are you motivated to apply for a minimum-wage job?

Motivating Employees With Expectancy Theory. Following are some keys to using expectancy theory successfully:

1. Clearly define objectives and the performance needed to achieve them.
2. Tie performance to rewards. High performers should be rewarded more than low performers.
3. Be sure rewards have value to employees. Get to know employees as individuals.
4. Make sure employees believe that you will do what you say you will.

Market America (Case Question 3-c) focuses on attracting people who have the expectancy that they can succeed at running their own business, and it provides the business model to help them succeed. Valence does vary for these people, but most UnFranchise® owners are seeking their own business so that they can achieve financial independence and the freedom to determine how to spend their time.

Reinforcement Theory

B. F. Skinner, reinforcement motivation theorist, contended that in order to motivate employees, there is no need to identify and meet needs. Instead, you need to understand the relationship between behaviors and their consequences and

11-1 JOIN THE DISCUSSION ETHICS & SOCIAL RESPONSIBILITY

Academic Standards

The academic credit-hour system was set up many years ago to ensure that there would be some standardization across colleges throughout the country and that academics and employers had the same understanding of the workload that a college student had carried to earn a degree. The credit-hour system was based on the assumption that a student would spend 2 hours of preparation for each hour of in-class time. So, a student taking five classes should spend 15 hours per week in classes and about 30 hours preparing for classes, or a total of about 45 hours a week—which is a full-time schedule.

1. How many hours outside of class, on average, do you and other students you know spend preparing for class each week?
2. Are college professors today assigning students 2 hours of preparation for every hour in class? If not, why do you think they have dropped this standard?
3. Are students who are essentially doing part-time work (that is, attending classes but doing little academic work outside of class) during college being prepared for a career after graduation (with a 40- to 60-hour workweek)?
4. Is it ethical and socially responsible for professors to drop standards and for colleges to award degrees for doing less work than students did 5, 10, or 20 years ago?

then reinforce desirable behaviors and discourage undesirable behaviors.[42] People respond to consequences and will behave as you want them too if you find the right incentives.[43]

The **reinforcement theory** *proposes that the consequences of their behavior will motivate employees to behave in predetermined ways.* Employees learn what is and is not desired behavior as a result of the consequences for specific behaviors, which they engage in to meet their needs and self-interest. In this section, we discuss two important concepts used to modify behavior (the types of reinforcement and the schedules of reinforcement) and how to motivate using reinforcement.

Types of Reinforcement

The four types of reinforcement are positive, avoidance (negative), punishment, and extinction. The first two tend to encourage desirable behavior. Punishment is a consequence that tends to discourage undesirable behavior,[44] whereas extinction eliminates a targeted behavior.

Positive Reinforcement. Positive reinforcement generally works better than punishment,[45] especially when training employees.[46] One method of encouraging desirable behavior is to offer attractive consequences (rewards). For example, an employee who arrives on time for a meeting is rewarded by thanks from the supervisor. If desirable behavior is not positively reinforced, it may decrease or even be eliminated. (The elimination of a behavior through lack of reinforcement is called *extinction*.) For example, if employees' high performance is ignored by management, the employees may stop making extra effort, thinking, "Why should I do a good job if I'm not rewarded in some way?"

Avoidance Reinforcement. Avoidance reinforcement is also called *negative reinforcement*. Like positive reinforcement, avoidance reinforcement is used to encourage continued desirable behavior; in this case, the reinforcement occurs because the behavior prevents a negative consequence (instead of leading to a positive one). For example, an employee arrives at meetings on time to avoid the negative consequence of a reprimand. With avoidance reinforcement, it's the threat of a negative consequence that controls behavior.

Punishment. Punishment involves the actual use of a negative consequence to decrease undesirable behavior. For example, an employee who arrives late for

LO 11-5

Explain the four types of reinforcement.

reinforcement theory Theory that proposes that the consequences of their behavior will motivate employees to behave in predetermined ways.

11-2 **JOIN THE DISCUSSION** ETHICS & SOCIAL RESPONSIBILITY

Airlines

Airlines often charge more for one-way tickets and for flights ending at their hubs than for round-trip tickets and for flights through their hubs to other destinations. So to save money, some travelers buy round-trip tickets but only go one way, and some buy tickets through the hub but end their travel at the hub instead of taking the connection. The airlines call this behavior breach of contract, and they have punished travel agencies for selling tickets that aren't properly used, demanded higher fares from travelers caught using tickets improperly, and cancelled some travelers' frequent-flier miles, saying they were fraudulently obtained.

1. Not using an airline ticket fully breaks the airline's rules, not any law, so it's not illegal. But is it ethical and socially responsible of travelers to do so?
2. Is it ethical and socially responsible of airlines to charge more for less travel?
3. Is it ethical and socially responsible to punish people who break the ticket rules?

It is better to use positive reinforcement, but sometimes managers need to use punishment. Photo from Asiseeit/iStockphoto.

a meeting is reprimanded. Other means of punishment include fines, demotions, and taking away privileges. (Note that rules are for avoidance, which are designed to get employees to avoid certain behaviors, are not punishment in and of themselves; punishment is only given if a rule is broken.) Using punishment may reduce the targeted behavior, but it may also cause other undesirable behavior, such as lower productivity or theft or sabotage, and it is ineffective for motivating employees to work harder.

Extinction. Extinction (like punishment) is applied in an attempt to reduce or eliminate a behavior. Unlike punishment, however, which is the active application of a negative consequence, extinction involves withholding reinforcement when an undesirable behavior occurs. For example, a manager might ignore an employee who arrives late for a meeting. However, extinction often doesn't work because ignoring problems usually only leads to more problems, such as lateness.

Schedules of Reinforcement

An important consideration in using positive reinforcement to control behavior is when to reinforce performance. The two major reinforcement schedules are continuous and intermittent.

Continuous Reinforcement. With a continuous schedule of reinforcement, each and every desired behavior is reinforced. Examples of this approach include the use of a machine with an automatic counter that lets the employee know, at any given moment, exactly how many units have been produced; the payment of a piece rate for each unit produced; a commission for every sale; or a compliment from the manager for every positive customer report. Continuous reinforcement is better for sustaining desired behavior; however, it is not always possible or practical.

Intermittent Reinforcement. With intermittent reinforcement schedules, reinforcement is given based on the passage of time or amount of output. When the reinforcement is based on the passage of time, an *interval* schedule is being used. When reinforcement is based on output, a *ratio* schedule is being used. Ratio

11-2 APPLYING THE CONCEPT

Motivation Theories

Identify the theory behind each of the following statements on how to motivate employees.

- A. hierarchy of needs theory
- B. ERG theory
- C. two-factor theory
- D. acquired needs theory
- E. equity theory
- F. goal-setting theory
- G. expectancy theory
- H. reinforcement theory

_____ 6. "Avi would yell in the halls because he knew it bothered me. So I decided to ignore his yelling, and he stopped."

_____ 7. "I got to know all of my employees' values. Now I can offer rewards that will motivate them when they perform a task well."

_____ 8. "Our company already offers good working conditions, salaries, and benefits, so we are working at satisfying employees' need for socialization."

_____ 9. "When my employees do a good job, I thank them using a four-step model to show my appreciation for a job well done."

_____ 10. "I used to try to improve working conditions to motivate employees. But I stopped and now focus on giving employees more responsibility so they can grow and develop new skills."

_____ 11. "I tell employees exactly what I want them to do, with a tough deadline that they can achieve."

_____ 12. "I now realize that I tend to be an autocratic manager because it helps fill my needs. I will work at giving some of my employees more autonomy in their jobs."

_____ 13. "I used to try to meet needs in a five-step sequence. After I heard about this new technique, I now focus on three needs and realize that needs can be unmet at more than one level at a time."

_____ 14. "I motivate employees by making their jobs interesting and challenging."

_____ 15. "I make sure I treat everyone fairly to motivate them."

_____ 16. "I know Katya likes people, so I give her jobs in which she works with other employees."

---

schedules are generally better motivators than interval schedules. When electing to use intermittent reinforcement, you have four alternatives:

1. _Fixed-interval schedule._ Giving a paycheck every week or breaks and meals at the same time every day.
2. _Variable-interval schedule._ Giving praise only now and then.
3. _Fixed-ratio schedule._ Giving a bonus after workers produce at a standard rate.
4. _Variable-ratio schedule._ Giving praise only for exceptional performance, which is common in athletics.[47]

Motivating With Reinforcement. Following are some general guidelines for motivating employees using reinforcement:

1. Make sure employees know what behavior is expected and reinforced. Set clear, effective objectives.
2. Select appropriate rewards. A reward to one person could be considered a punishment by another. Let your employees know what's in it for them for achieving desirable behavior.
3. Select the appropriate reinforcement and schedule.
4. Do not reward mediocre or poor performance.
5. Look for the positive and give praise regularly rather than focusing on the negative and criticizing.[48] Make people feel good about themselves (the Pygmalion effect, Chapter 10).
6. Do things _for_ your employees instead of _to_ them, and you will see productivity increases.

WORK
APPLICATION 11-7

Give a few examples of the types of reinforcement and the schedules used at a present or past job.

11-3 | JOIN THE DISCUSSION ETHICS & SOCIAL RESPONSIBILITY

Using Reinforcement Theory

Reinforcement theory has been used successfully to maintain and increase performance by many companies globally. However, its use does have critics who claim that it manipulates employees and that it is the carrot-and-stick approach to motivation.

1. Does reinforcement motivate you?
2. Is reinforcement effective (does it serve to motivate) in today's global economy?
3. Is the use of reinforcement theory ethical and socially responsible or manipulative?

Market America (Case Question 4) uses positive reinforcement with a continuous schedule, as each and every sale results in compensation. There are business meetings, and distributors are reinforced with praise and other recognition for accomplishments. Distributors share success stories, testimonials, voicemail tips, audiotapes, and books.

LO 11-6

State the major differences among content, process, and reinforcement theories.

COMBINING THE MOTIVATION PROCESS AND MOTIVATION THEORIES

Motivation is important, but you may be wondering: How do these theories fit together? Is one the best? Should I try to pick the correct theory for a given situation? People want a theory of total motivation,[49] so that is what this section is all about. The groups of theories are complementary; each refers to a different stage in the motivation process or answers a different question. Content motivation theories answer this question: "What needs do employees have that should be met on the job?" Process motivation theories answer another question: "How do employees choose behavior to fulfill their needs?" Reinforcement theory answers a different question: "What can managers do to get employees to behave in ways that meet the organizational objectives?"

In the first section of this chapter, you learned that the motivation process moves from need to motive to behavior to consequence to satisfaction or dissatisfaction. The motivation process becomes a little more complex when we incorporate the motivation theories in the form of answers to the preceding questions, as illustrated in Exhibit 11-5. Note that step 4 loops back to step 3 because, according to reinforcement theory, behavior is learned through consequences. Step 4 does not loop back to steps 1 or 2 because reinforcement theory is not concerned with needs, motives, or satisfaction; it focuses on getting employees to behave in certain ways through consequences provided by managers. Also, note that step 5 loops back to step 1, because meeting needs is an ongoing and never-ending process. Finally, be aware that, according to the two-factor theory, step 5, satisfaction or dissatisfaction, is not on one continuum but on two separate continuums (satisfied to not satisfied or not dissatisfied to dissatisfied), based on the level of need being met (motivator or maintenance factor).

MOTIVATING EMPLOYEES WITH REWARDS AND RECOGNITION

To answer employees' often unasked question, "What's in it for me?," companies develop motivational systems that include rewards and recognition.[50] Recall that rewards can be internally (intrinsic) or externally (extrinsic) focused and be financial or nonfinancial. This section begins by stating how the motivation theories use rewards and recognition, followed by a discussion of reward and recognition programs and giving praise.

EXHIBIT 11-5   THE MOTIVATION PROCESS AND THE MOTIVATION THEORIES

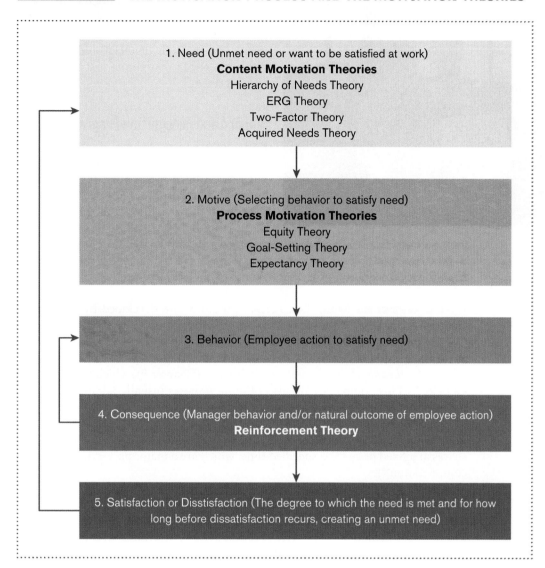

1. Need (Unmet need or want to be satisfied at work)
Content Motivation Theories
Hierarchy of Needs Theory
ERG Theory
Two-Factor Theory
Acquired Needs Theory

2. Motive (Selecting behavior to satisfy need)
Process Motivation Theories
Equity Theory
Goal-Setting Theory
Expectancy Theory

3. Behavior (Employee action to satisfy need)

4. Consequence (Manager behavior and/or natural outcome of employee action)
Reinforcement Theory

5. Satisfaction or Disstisfaction (The degree to which the need is met and for how long before dissatisfaction recurs, creating an unmet need)

How Each of the Motivation Theories Uses Rewards and Recognition

The *hierarchy of needs* and *ERG theories* use financial rewards to meet the lower-level needs but use nonfinancial rewards to meet higher-level needs. With *two-factor theory,* maintenance needs are primarily meet financially and motivators are met nonfinancially. *Acquired needs* rewards vary with need. People with high n Ach seek achievement and can be motivated to achieve goals with both types of rewards. The n Pows tend to provide both because having power is a nonfinancial reward, but as people gain power, they often get pay raises. The n Affs's needs are meet primarily though friendships.

People want *equity* in both their pay and treatment, which includes recognition. With *goal-setting theory,* people can be motivated to meet goals with both financial and nonfinancial rewards. Using *expectancy theory* effectively is based on knowing what people value as rewards, which can be either or both depending on the individual.

Many organizations use reward and recognition programs because they have been successful in motivating employees to perform at high levels. Photo from Fuse/Getty Images.

Again, *reinforcement theory* doesn't focus on meeting needs, and although the focus is on giving a positive reward, it also gives punishment instead. The rewards (or punishment) can be both financial and nonfinancial with either continuous or intermittent reinforcement.

Reward and Recognition Programs

Back in Chapter 8, we discussed team rewards and recognition. Here we expand our discussion. People work for money, so financial rewards are critical, but just as important is recognition for the work we do.[51] Employee recognition leads to profits.[52] So both financial and nonfinancial rewards and recognition are important to motivate employees to met objectives and put their ideas into practice.[53] **Yum! Brands** uses recognition programs to build teams and get results.[54]

Types of Rewards and Recognition. Formal programs are developed by the human resource department.[55] People respond to incentives,[56] and rewards and recognition are motivational incentives,[57] so they are also called *incentive systems.* Some of the many types of rewards and recognition include *good pay and benefits, flexible work schedules,*[58] and *pay for performance* (Chapter 9), which are offered at **Google**.[59] Many companies are also offering *bonuses* (usually additional money for meeting objectives), *profit sharing* (creating a pool of monies to be disbursed to employees by taking a stated percentage of a company's profits), and *stock options* (giving employees the right to buy a specified number of a company's shares at a fixed price for a specified time, which are a major part of top executive compensation[60]).

Frequency of Rewards and Recognition. As management has learned, including at **Intuit**, the older system of giving large cash awards to only the very top performers doesn't motivate employees very effectively. Motivational consulting firm **Globoforce** recommends sharing the wealth and giving small rewards. When the firm wants to reinforce certain behavior, you should give 80 to 90 percent of employees some reward every year. To show appreciation, small prizes of around $100 work as well as larger ones, such as tickets to a game/play/movie and gift certificates for dinner or to stores. The VP of HR at Intuit says, "I've never seen bigger awards get as much bang for the buck.[61]

Most firms have an annual convention or meeting of some kind that includes giving rewards. However, more companies are having monthly recognitions, including **Aflac**.[62] But **Globoforce** found that companies get the best results with weekly rewards. Five percent of employees should get an award every week so that employees don't forget about the program. Small awards all the time are a way to constantly tell employees management appreciates their efforts.[63]

Departmental Rewards and Recognition. You can even give your own rewards and recognition to your department employees. A good way to start is to give small spot rewards based on performance. When **Intuit** acquired **Paycycle**, Jennifer Lepird spent several weeks working long hours integrating the new employees into Intuit's salary structure. The acquisition team manager sent her a handwritten note of recognition with a gift certificate reward. Lepird was thrilled that somebody took the time to recognize her effort.[64] Yes people appreciate recognition even without any financial reward. So let's move on to learning how to give praise.

WORK
APPLICATION 11-8

Select an organization that you work for or have worked for and briefly describe its rewards and recognition.

Giving Praise

In the 1940s, Lawrence Lindahl conducted a survey revealing that what employees want most from a job is full appreciation for work done. Similar studies have been performed over the years, with little change in results.[65] Praise is a motivator because it meets employees' needs for esteem/self-actualization, growth, and achievement. Giving praise is simply complimenting the achievements of others,[66] and this recognition increases performance.[67] It cost you nothing to give praise,[68] involves very little effort, and produces a lot in return.[69]

Although it is the easiest and least costly motivational technique, it is underused. Unfortunately, managers often don't realize how important giving recognition is to employee motivation and performance, and they get so busy that they neglect to give praise. When was the last time your boss thanked or praised you for a job well done? When was the last time your boss complained about your work? If you are a manager, when was the last time you praised or criticized your employees? What is the ratio of praise to criticism?

Ken Blanchard and Spencer Johnson emphasized the importance of giving praise in their best-selling book *The One-Minute Manager*.[70] They developed a technique for feedback that involves giving one minute of praise; so keep praise short and look the person in the eye. Model 11–1 shows the steps in the **giving praise model**.

MODEL 11-1   GIVING PRAISE

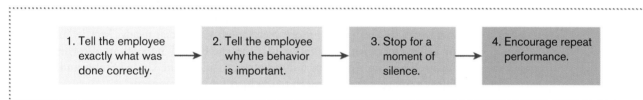

1. Tell the employee exactly what was done correctly. → 2. Tell the employee why the behavior is important. → 3. Stop for a moment of silence. → 4. Encourage repeat performance.

Step 1. Tell the employee exactly what was done correctly. Be very specific and descriptive.[71] "Mia, I just overheard you deal with that customer's complaint. You did an excellent job of keeping your cool; you were polite. That person came in angry and left happy." General statements such as "You're a good worker" are not as effective. On the other hand, don't talk for too long or the praise loses its effectiveness.

Step 2. Tell the employee why the behavior is important. Briefly state how the organization and/or person benefits from the action. Also, tell the employee how you feel about the behavior. Be specific and descriptive: "Without customers, we don't have a business. One dissatisfied customer can cause hundreds of dollars in lost sales. It really made me proud to see you handle that tough situation the way you did."

Step 3. Stop for a moment of silence. Being silent is tough for many managers. The rationale for the silence is to give the employee the chance to feel the impact of the praise.

Step 4. Encourage repeat performance. This encouragement motivates the employee to continue the desired behavior.[72] You may also make some physical gesture, if both parties feel comfortable with physical contact: "Thanks, Mia, keep up the good work" (while giving a thumbs-up or shaking hands).

giving praise model A four-step technique for providing feedback to an employee (1) Tell the employee exactly what was done correctly; (2) tell the employee why the behavior is important; (3) stop for a moment of silence; (4) encourage repeat performance.

When it is difficult to give face-to-face praise, it can also come in the form of a *phone call/Skype* and *written communication* following the giving praise model. Email works, but it is said that a *handwritten note* is worth more than a $100 gift card, but the two go well together, and a note can be as powerful as face-to-face praise.[73] **Applied Materials** CEO Mike Splinter and **Disney** CEO Bob Iger send personal handwritten notes to their employees when they have done an exceptional job.[74]

As you can see, giving praise is easy and it doesn't cost a penny. Managers trained to give praise say it works wonders and that it is a much better motivator than giving a raise or other monetary reward.

DO MOTIVATION THEORIES APPLY GLOBALLY?

The motivation theories you have studied were developed largely in North America. As organizations become global, you must be aware of the cultural impact on theoretical generalizations. Geert Hofstede recognized that motivational concerns vary globally in the 1970s,[75] and the recent GLOBE research (Chapter 3) supports these findings.[76] For example, in Sweden, there is a very high tax rate on overtime pay that makes it less likely that more money will motivate employees to work more hours.

The intrinsic motivation provided by the satisfaction of higher-level needs tends to be more relevant in developed countries than in developing countries, in which most people are on a lower level of the hierarchy of needs. The term *self-actualization* has no literal translation in some Chinese dialects. Even in developed countries, the level of needs on which people focus varies. In the United States, people tend to be motivated by higher-level needs of self-actualization and esteem; in Greece and Japan, security is more important; and in Sweden, Norway, and Denmark, people are more concerned with social needs. McClelland's need for achievement is more predominant in the United States than elsewhere. Thus, this need has limited use as a motivator outside of the United States and Canada, unless managers are willing to try to instill it in employees.

Individualistic versus Collective Cultures and Motivation

One major cultural difference that affects motivation in businesses is that between individualistic and collective societies. Individualistic societies (the United States, Canada, Great Britain, Australia) tend to value individual accomplishment. Collective societies (China, Japan, Mexico, Singapore, Venezuela, Pakistan) tend to value group accomplishment and loyalty. Cultural differences suggest that self-actualization, achievement, and esteem needs tend to be met through group membership in Japan and China and through individual accomplishments in the United States.

11-3 | APPLYING THE CONCEPT

Individual versus Collective Motivation Techniques

Identify which country each statement is more closely associated with.

A. Individual culture (United States, Great Britain, Australia)
B. Collective culture (China, Japan, Mexico)

_____ 17. Countries where managers developed a system of giving pins/stars, etc., as symbols of high achievement

_____ 18. Countries that tends to focus on motivating groups rather than individuals

_____ 19. Countries where managers would tend to get the best results with acquired needs theory

_____ 20. Countries in which companies provide greater job security

Expectancy theory holds up fairly well cross-culturally, because it is flexible. It allows for the possibility that there may be differences in expectations and valences across cultures. For example, social acceptance may be of higher value than individual recognition in collective societies.

Market America (Case Question 5) started in the United States, but it has international operations in both individual- and collective-culture countries of Australia, Canada, Hong Kong, Taiwan, the United Kingdom, and Mexico. By recognizing the need to adjust to meet diverse cultural needs, Market America is confident that its UnFranchise® approach will work with anyone who wants to be an entrepreneur anywhere in the world.

As we close this chapter, you should have a better understanding of the relationship between motivation and performance. You should also know the different content motivation theories, process motivation theories, reinforcement theory, and how these motivation theories affect the motivation process. Finally, you should have better knowledge of employee reward and recognition programs and about motivation theories in a global context.

Chapter Summary

11-1. **Illustrate the motivation process.**

Employees go through a five-step process to meet their needs beginning with a need that motives behavior that leads to a consequence and satisfaction or dissatisfaction on meeting the need, and there is feedback throughout the process. Note that this is a cyclical process, because needs recur.

11-2. **Explain the performance formula and how to use it.**

The performance formula proposes that performance is based on ability, motivation, and resources. For maximum performance, all three factors must be high. When performance is not optimum, managers need to determine which factor of the performance formula is weak and take appropriate action to correct the problem.

11-3. **Discuss the major similarities and differences among the four content motivation theories: hierarchy of needs theory, ERG theory, two-factor theory, and acquired needs theory.**

The similarity among the four content motivation theories is their focus on identifying and understanding employees' needs. The theories identify similar needs but differ in the way they classify the needs. Hierarchy of needs theory classifies needs as physiological, safety, social, esteem, and self-actualization needs. ERG theory proposes existence, relatedness, and growth needs. Two-factor theory includes motivators and maintenance factors. Acquired needs theory includes achievement, power, and affiliation needs. (See Exhibits 11-1 and 11-4 for a comparison of the four content theories of motivation.)

11-4. **Discuss the major similarities and differences among the three process motivation theories: equity theory, goal-setting theory, and expectancy theory.**

The similarity among the three process motivation theories is their focus on understanding how employees choose behaviors to fulfill their needs. However, they are very different in how they perceive employee motivation. Equity theory proposes that employees are motivated when their perceived inputs equal outputs. Goal-setting theory proposes that achievable but difficult goals motivate employees. Expectancy theory proposes that employees are motivated when they believe they can accomplish the task and the rewards for doing so are worth the effort.

11-5. **Explain the four types of reinforcement.**

Positive reinforcement is rewarding desirable behavior. Avoidance reinforcement (also called *negative reinforcement*) is the use of the threat of a negative consequence to prevent undesirable behavior; the negative consequence is not used as long as the behavior is desirable. Punishment is the actual use of a negative consequence to decrease undesirable behavior. Extinction is the withholding of reinforcement in order to reduce or eliminate (extinguish) a behavior.

11-6. **State the major differences among content, process, and reinforcement theories.**

Content motivation theories focus on identifying and understanding employees' needs. Process motivation theories go a step further to understand how employees choose behavior to fulfill their needs. Reinforcement theory is not concerned about employees' needs; it focuses on getting employees to do what managers want them to do through the consequences provided for their behavior. The use of rewards is the best means of motivating employees.

••• KEY TERMS

acquired needs theory, 337
content motivation theories, 335
equity theory, 340
ERG theory, 335
expectancy theory, 342

giving praise model, 349
goal-setting theory, 341
hierarchy of needs theory, 335
motivation, 332
motivation process, 332

performance formula, 333
process motivation theories, 340
reinforcement theory, 343
two-factor theory, 336

••• KEY TERM REVIEW

Complete each of the following statements using one of this chapter's key terms.

1. _____ is the willingness to achieve organizational objectives or to go above and beyond the call of duty (organizational citizenship behavior).

2. The _____ is the process of moving from need to motive to behavior to consequence to satisfaction or dissatisfaction.

3. The _____ is performance = ability × motivation × resources.

4. _____ focus on identifying and understanding employees' needs.

5. The _____ proposes that employees are motivated by five levels of needs: physiological, safety, social, esteem, and self-actualization.

6. _____ proposes that employees are motivated by three needs: existence, relatedness, and growth.

7. _____ proposes that employees are motivated by motivators rather than by maintenance factors.

8. _____ proposes that employees are motivated by their needs for achievement, power, and affiliation.

9. _____ focus on understanding how employees choose behaviors to fulfill their needs.

10. _____ proposes that employees are motivated when their perceived inputs equal outputs.

11. _____ proposes that achievable but difficult goals motivate employees.

12. _____ proposes that employees are motivated when they believe they can accomplish a task and the rewards for doing so are worth the effort.

13. _____ proposes that the consequences of their behavior will motivate employees to behave in predetermined ways.

14. The steps in the _____ are as follows: (1) Tell the employee exactly what was done correctly; (2) tell the employee why the behavior is important; (3) stop for a moment of silence; (4) encourage repeat performance.

••• REVIEW QUESTIONS

1. How is the performance formula used by managers?

2. What are the three major classes of motivation theories?

3. What are the four content motivation theories?

4. What do the E, R, and G stand for in ERG theory?

5. What are the two factors in Herzberg's two-factor theory?

6. What is the role of perception in equity theory?

7. Does the goal-setting theory really motivate employees?

8. What are the two variables of the expectancy theory?

9. What are the two schedules of reinforcement?

10. Is there a relationship among the three major classifications of motivation theories?

••• COMMUNICATION SKILLS

The following critical-thinking questions can be used for class discussion and/or as written assignments to develop communication skills. Be sure to give complete explanations for all questions.

1. Do people really have diverse needs?

2. What is motivation, and why is it important to know how to motivate employees?

3. Do you agree that managers' attitudes and expectations affect employee motivation and performance? Explain your answer.

4. Do you agree with the performance formula? Will you use it on the job?

5. Which of the four content motivation theories makes the most sense to you? Why?

6. Which of the three process motivation theories makes the most sense to you? Why?

7. What reinforcement methods have been used to get you to go to work and to be on time?

8. Reinforcement theory is unethical because it is used to manipulate employees. Do you agree with this statement? Explain your answer.

9. Which motivation theory makes the most sense to you? Explain why.

10. What are the major methods and techniques you plan to use on the job as a manager to increase motivation and performance?

11. Do you agree with Deming's statement that U.S. companies need to change to a group approach to compete in a global economy?

• • • CASE: FRIEDMANS APPLIANCE

Following is a conversation between Bob Lussier, this book's author, and Art Friedman, about a business technique that Friedman implemented at his business, Friedmans Appliance. At the time, Friedmans, in Oakland, California, employed 15 people.

Bob: What is the reason for your success in business?

Art: My business technique.

Bob: What is it? How did you implement it?

Art: I called my 15 employees together and told them, "From now on I want you to feel as though the company is ours, not mine. We are all bosses. From now on you decide what you're worth and tell the accountant to put it in your pay envelope. You decide which days and hours you work and when to take time off. We will have an open petty cash system that will allow anyone to go into the box and borrow money when they need it."

Bob: You're kidding, right?

Art: No, it's true. I really do these things.

Bob: Did anyone ask for a raise?

Art: Yes, several people did. Charlie asked for and received a $100-a-week raise.

Bob: Did he and the others increase their productivity to earn their raises?

Art: Yes, they all did.

Bob: How could you run an appliance store with employees coming and going as they pleased?

Art: The employees made up schedules that were satisfactory to everyone. We had no problems of under- or overstaffing.

Bob: Did anyone steal from the petty cash box?

Art: No. We actually had extra cash.

Bob: Would this technique work in any business?

Art: It did work for my business!

Although Art Friedman has now retired, Friedmans Appliance is still a successful company located at 2304 Monument Blvd, Pleasant Hill, CA. Friedmans continues to focus on sales and service with more than 80 brands and 20,000 products on display in its 25,000-square-foot showroom giving live demonstrations and a 100 Day Price Match Guarantee and 100% Customer Satisfaction Guarantee. The website (http://www.friedmansappliance.com) provides its telephone number 925–808–2950 for customers who want to speak to an appliance expert directly.

Case Questions

1. Explain how Art Friedman used the performance formula and each of the four content motivational theories.

2. Which of the three process motivation theories and type of reinforcement is the most relevant to the case?

3. Do you know of any organization that uses any unusual techniques to motivate employees? If yes, what is the organization's name? What does it do?

4. Could Friedman's technique work in all organizations? Explain your answer.

5. If you were in a position of authority, would you use Friedman's technique? Explain your answer.

Cumulative Case Questions

6. What does this case have to do with entrepreneurship? (Chapter 6)

7. When Art Friedman made the decision to change how his company was run, what was the classification of the problem? (Chapter 4)

8. What is the role of delegation and authority in this case? (Chapter 7)

9. What type of change did Friedman make? (Chapter 6)

10. How would the change affect the human resources process at Friedmans? (Chapter 9)

Source: Information for this case as stated is taken from a prior conversation and updated information is from the Friedmans Appliances website, http://www.friedman-sappliance.com, accessed September 17, 2013.

• • • SKILL BUILDER 11–1: GIVING PRAISE

Objective

To develop the skill of giving praise to motivate people to higher levels of performance.

Skills

The primary skills developed through this exercise are:

1. *Management skill*—leadership (motivating others)
2. *AACSB competency*–communication abilities
3. *Management function*—leading

Think of a job situation in which you did something well, deserving of praise and recognition. For example, you may have saved the company some money, you may have turned a dissatisfied customer into a happy one, and so on. Imagine yourself in a management position, and write out the praise you would give to an employee for doing what you did.

Briefly describe the situation:

Step 1. Tell the employee exactly what was done correctly.

Step 2. Tell the employee why the behavior is important.

Step 3. Stop for a moment of silence. (Count to 5 silently.)

Step 4. Encourage repeat performance.

Apply It

What did I learn from this experience? How will I use this knowledge in the future?

• • • SKILL BUILDER 11–2: SELF-MOTIVATION

Objective

To better understand what motivates you.

Skills

The primary skills developed through this exercise are:

1. *Management skill*—leadership (motivating yourself)
2. *AACSB competency*—reasoning abilities)
3. *Management function*—leading

Review the two Self-Assessment exercises.

What did you learn about yourself?

How can you improve your self-motivation so that you can be more successful?

• • • STUDENT STUDY SITE 📱

Visit the Student Study Site at **www.sagepub.com/lussier6e** to access to these additional study tools:

- Mobile-compatible self-assessment quizzes
- Mobile-compatible key term flashcards
- Video Links
- SAGE Journal Articles
- Web Links

Photo from Andrew Harrer/Bloomberg via Getty Images.

12 Leading With Influence

• • • Learning Outcomes

After studying this chapter, you should be able to:

12-1. Compare the trait, behavioral, situational, and contemporary leadership theories. PAGE 358

12-2. Explain why the terms manager and leader are not interchangeable. PAGE 358

12-3. Discuss the major similarity and difference between two-dimensional leadership styles and the Leadership Grid®. PAGE 362

12-4. State the primary difference between the contingency leadership model and other situational approaches to leadership. PAGE 365

IDEAS ON MANAGEMENT at American Express

American Express is in the business of making it easy for people and businesses to buy things and for merchants to sell products and services in person and online. In addition to this payment service, it also provides travel services (including travelers' checks) and expense management solutions for consumers and businesses of all sizes. The 650,000 American Express employees process millions of financial transactions every day worldwide.

Ken Chenault joined American Express in 1981 and spent 20 years working his way up the corporate ladder. He became president and COO in 1997 and, in 2001, became the third African American in history to become a CEO of a *Fortune* 500 company. During Chenault's career, he has been well liked and has become known as a tough but fair manager who demands and gets results from the people on his team. Chenault says the role of the leader is to define reality and to give hope; not only can leadership be learned, but it is also a responsibility and a privilege that must be cultivated.

Chenault's leadership skills have led American Express through two major crises in the past decade. Just nine months after being named CEO, Chenault led American Express through the crisis of the 9/11 terrorist attacks that cost the lives of 11 American Express employees, stranded thousands of customers, and closed the company headquarters across the street from the World Trade Center. Seven years later, a severe economic recession and financial meltdown hit the United States, and the banking and credit industry was particularly hit hard. However, thanks to Chenault's exceptional leadership, American Express remained profitable throughout the recession as its largest rivals, **JPMorgan Chase**, **Citigroup**, and **Bank of America** posted record losses.

1. What leadership traits does Ken Chenault have? PAGE 360
2. Which behavioral leadership styles does Ken Chenault use? PAGE 364
3. Which situational leadership styles does Ken Chenault use? PAGE 370
4. Is Ken Chenault a visionary, charismatic, and/or transformational leader? PAGE 372
5. Is handling complaints important at American Express? PAGE 374

• • • Chapter Outline

Leadership and Trait Theory

Leadership and Trust

Leaders versus Managers

An Overview of Four Major Classes of Leadership Theories

Leadership Trait Theory

Behavioral Leadership Theories

Basic Leadership Styles

Two-Dimensional Leadership Styles

The Leadership Grid®

Situational Approaches to Leadership

Contingency Leadership Model

Leadership Continuum Model

Path-Goal Model

Normative Leadership Model

Situational Leadership® Model

Comparing Leadership Models

Leadership Substitutes Theory

Contemporary Leadership Theories

Visionary Leaders

Charismatic Leaders

Transformational Leaders

Handling Complaints

Handling Employee Complaints

Handling Customer Complaints

You'll find answers to these questions throughout the chapter. To learn more about American Express, visit its website at www.americanexpress.com.

Sources: Information for this case was taken from the American Express website at http://www.americanexpress.com, accessed August 9, 2013.

LO 12-1

Compare the trait, behavioral, situational, and contemporary leadership theories.

LEADERSHIP AND TRAIT THEORY

Leadership is a key issue in management.[1] In this section, we discuss leadership and trust, the difference between leadership and management, and leadership trait theory.

Leadership and Trust

What Is Leadership and Why Is Trust Important? The manager's fundamental task is to influence others.[2] As defined in Chapter 1, *leadership* is the process of influencing employees to work toward achieving objectives. Leadership is typically understood as taking place in an organization where leaders and followers share a formal group membership.[3] So leadership includes a leader–follower relationship[4] (leader–member exchange—*LMX theory*), which needs to be based on trust,[5] because without trust you can't have a good management–employee relationship and truly influence employees.[6]

The late Steve Jobs is considered to be one of the most successful leaders of our time because he was skilled in motivating employees to achieve organizational objectives. Photo from Kimihiro Hoshino/ AFP/Getty Images.

The Importance of Leadership. Leadership matters a great deal,[7] because it has a direct affect on performance.[8] Enabling employees to achieve great things often comes down to the work of a single leader,[9] such as the late Steve Jobs at **Apple**. Unfortunately, an estimated one third of managers are either mediocre or just plain horrible, resulting in lower performance.[10] Recall your present and past managers. Where they effective at motivating you and really influencing you to achieve the organizational objectives?

Leadership Development. There are two age-old leadership questions: "Are leaders born or made?" and "Can leadership skills be developed?" The first question is actually kind of a trick question because the answer is both, and part of the answer to question 1 answers question 2. We are all born with different levels of natural leadership ability, but research shows that leadership skills can be developed.[11] Teaching leadership theories (as we do in this chapter) contributes to developing leaders' skills.[12] If leadership skills can't be developed, why would colleges offer management and leadership courses and companies (including **GE, IBM**, and **Apple**, just to name a few) spend millions on training and develop programs, especially leadership development?[13] So you can be trained to lead, and your team will follow.[14]

LO 12-2

Explain why the terms *manager* and *leader* are not interchangeable.

LEADERS VERSUS MANAGERS

People tend to use the terms *manager* and *leader* interchangeably. However, managers and leaders differ.[15] Leading is one of the four management functions (planning, organizing, leading, and controlling). Thus, management is broader in scope than leadership, but leadership is critical to management success.[16] A manager can have this position without being a true leader. There are managers—you may know of some—who are not leaders because they do not have the trust and ability to influence others. There are also good leaders who are not managers. An informal leader, an employee group member, is a case in point. You may have been in a situation in which one of your peers had more influence than the manager/coach. Effective managers/coaches also work with team leaders to influence teamwork and performance. Leadership is plural; there can be multiple leaders.[17] So you don't have to be a manager to be a leader.

An Overview of Four Major Classes of Leadership Theories

There are four major classifications of leadership theories. We present the theories in their historical development starting with leadership trait theory in this section, followed by behavior, situational, and contemporary leadership theories in the following three major sections. See Exhibit 12-1 for an overview of the leadership theories discussed in this chapter.

EXHIBIT 12-1   MAJOR LEADERSHIP THEORIES

Class of Leadership Theories	Specific Theory
Trait Theory attempts to determine a list of distinctive characteristics that account for leadership effectiveness.	**Trait theory leadership style** is based on the leader's personal traits and characteristics
Behavioral Leadership Theories attempt to determine distinctive styles used by effective leaders. *Leadership style* is the combination of traits, skills, and behaviors managers use in interacting with employees.	**Basic leadership** styles include autocratic, democratic, and laissez-faire. **Two-dimensional leadership styles** are four possible leadership styles that are based on the dimensions of job structure and employee consideration. **Leadership Grid®** identifies the ideal leadership style as incorporating a high concern for both production and people.
Situational Leadership Theories attempt to determine the appropriate leadership styles for particular situations using models.	**Contingency leadership model** is used to determine if leadership style is task or relationship oriented and if the situation matches the style. **Leadership continuum model** is used to determine which of seven styles of leadership, on a continuum from autocratic (boss centered) to participative (employee centered), is best for a given situation. **Path-goal model** is used to determine employee objectives and to clarify how to achieve them using one of four leadership styles. **Normative leadership model** is a time-driven or development-driven decision tree that assists a user in selecting one of five leadership styles (decide, consult individuals, consult group, facilitate, and delegate) to use in a given situation (based on seven questions/variables) to maximize a decision. **Situational Leadership® model** is used to select one of four leadership styles that match the employees' maturity level in a given situation. **Substitutes for leadership** are characteristics of the task, of subordinates, or of the organization that replace the need for a leader.
Contemporary Leadership Theories attempt to determine how effective leaders interact with, inspire, and support followers.	**Visionary leaders** create an image of the organization in the future that provides direction for setting goals and developing strategic plans. **Charismatic leaders** inspire loyalty, enthusiasm, and high levels of performance. **Transformational leaders** bring about continuous learning, innovation, and change.

Leadership Trait Theory

Early leadership studies were based on the assumption that leaders are born, not made. (Recall today, research supports the opposite.) Researchers wanted to identify a set of characteristics or traits that distinguished leaders from followers or effective leaders from ineffective ones. **Leadership trait theorists** *attempt to determine a list of distinctive characteristics that account for leadership effectiveness.* Researchers analyzed physical and psychological traits, such as appearance, aggressiveness, self-reliance, persuasiveness, and dominance in an effort to identify a set of traits that all successful leaders possessed.

Inconclusive Findings. In 70 years, more than 300 trait studies were conducted.[18] However, no one was able to compile a universal list of traits that all successful leaders possess. In all cases, there were exceptions. People also questioned whether traits such as assertiveness and self-confidence were developed before or after one became a leader. Even though it is generally agreed that no universal set of leadership traits or qualities exists, people continue to study and write about leadership traits.[19]

The Ghiselli Study. Edwin Ghiselli conducted probably the most widely publicized trait study. He studied more than 300 managers from 90 different businesses in the United States and published his results in 1971.[20] He concluded that certain traits are important to effective leadership, though not all of them are necessary for success. Ghiselli identified the following six traits, in order of importance, as being significant traits for effective leadership: (1) *supervisory ability*—getting the job done through others (basically, the ability to perform the four functions of management you are studying in this course), (2) *need for occupational achievement*, (3) *intelligence*, (4) *decisiveness*, (5) *self-assurance*, and (6) *initiative*.

At **American Express (Case Question 1)**, Ken Chenault uses supervisory ability to get subordinates to perform according to his expectations. This skill was evident early in his career when he was able to inspire managers in American Express's poorly performing merchandise unit to turn the unit into a profitable one. Chenault has also demonstrated a need for occupational achievement as one of only a few African Americans in top management in corporate America. His peers and former superiors also recognize him for his intelligence, decisiveness, and initiative. All of these traits no doubt played a large role in helping Chenault to reach the CEO position at American Express.

Personality Traits. Recall from Chapter 10 that your personality is made up of traits, and thus, personality is an important part of trait theory.[21] Organizations continue to select managers who have particular personality traits, as these affect leadership style and employee behavior and performance.[22] To be an effective leader, you must first be yourself (*authentic leadership*)[23] and be aware of who you are as a leader. You get to know yourself better through the self-assessment exercises throughout this book; however, you can change aspects of your personality and still be yourself.

Ethics and Spirituality in the Workplace. Personality and other traits do affect a leader's use of ethical or unethical behavior.[24] Managers that use unethical behavior and encouraging employees to be unethical do tend to influence employee behavior—bad apples.[25] But as discussed in Chapter 2, businesses are encouraging ethical behavior and social responsibility because it is the right thing to do and it pays.[26]

Related to ethics and values is spirituality. People are looking for meaning in life and at work. Organizations are offering programs to help employees and managers find this meaning. For example, many organizations are offering programs

WORK
APPLICATION 12-1

Of Ghiselli's six traits, which does your boss possess? Are there any that she or he does not possess?

leadership trait theorists Theorists who attempt to determine a list of distinctive characteristics that account for leadership effectiveness.

behavioral leadership theorists Theorists who attempt to determine distinctive styles used by effective leaders.

12-1 JOIN THE DISCUSSION ETHICS & SOCIAL RESPONSIBILITY

Dilbert

Through his cartoon character Dilbert, Scott Adams makes fun of managers. Adams distrusts top-level managers and has said that leadership is really about manipulating people to get them to do something they don't want to do when there may not be anything in it for them. Adams says that we may be hung up on leadership as part of our DNA. Apparently, we have always sought to put somebody above everybody else.

1. Do you agree with Scott Adams that leadership is basically manipulation?
2. Do we really need leaders?
3. Is it ethical and socially responsible to make fun of managers?

that focus on helping employees understand more about their values, spiritual principles, and sense of purpose. Some companies even have corporate chaplains.[27]

Evangelist Billy Graham identified four main character traits as personal qualities of leadership: (1) *integrity*, (2) *personal security*, (3) *sense of priority*, and (4) *vision*.[28] Zig Ziglar, best-selling author who trained people to be successful, and Peter Lowe, who conducts success seminars all over the world, both say that proper emphasis on the spiritual aspects of life is extremely important to success.[29] Research has shown that people who attend church regularly make more money, have better health, are happier with their jobs and family life, and have a much lower divorce rate. Ziglar states, "In short, they get more of the things that money can buy and all of the things that money can't buy."[30] Of course, not all successful leaders are spiritual.

BEHAVIORAL LEADERSHIP THEORIES

In the continuing quest to find the best leadership style for all situations, by the late 1940s, most leadership research focused on the behavior of leaders rather than on analyzing their traits. What behaviors are involved in effective leadership?[31] The success of teams often depends on helping behavior,[32] so it is important to understand leader behaviors[33] and how they affect employee behavior.[34] **Behavioral leadership theorists** *attempt to determine distinctive styles used by effective leaders.* Recall that Douglas McGregor, a behavioral theorist, developed Theory X and Theory Y (Chapter 1). Complete the Self-Assessment to determine your leadership behavior according to Theory X and Theory Y.

In this section, we discuss the basic leadership styles, two-dimensional leadership styles, the Leadership Grid®, and contemporary perspectives on behavioral leadership.

Basic Leadership Styles

Leadership style *is the combination of traits, skills, and behaviors managers use in interacting with employees.* Note that behavioral theorists focus on the leaders' behaviors. However, behaviors are based on traits and skills.

Leading teams requires leaders to interact with all team members. Behavioral leadership theory sheds insight on how a leader's actions influence outcomes. Photo from Photodisc/Thinkstock.

leadership style The combination of traits, skills, and behaviors managers use in interacting with employees.

12-1   SELF ASSESSMENT

Theory X and Theory Y Leadership Behavior

Beside each of the following 10 statements, place the letter (U, F, O, or S) that best describes what you would do as a manager. There are no right or wrong answers.

Usually (U)	Frequently (F)	Occasionally (O)	Seldom (S)

_____ 1. I would set the objectives for my department alone rather than include employees' input.

_____ 2. I would allow employees to develop their own plans rather than develop them myself.

_____ 3. I would delegate several tasks I enjoy doing to employees rather than do them myself.

_____ 4. I would allow employees to make decisions to solve problems rather than make them myself.

_____ 5. I would recruit and select new employees alone rather than use employees' input.

_____ 6. I would orient and train new employees myself rather than have employees do it.

_____ 7. I would tell employees only what they need to know rather than give them access to anything they want to know.

_____ 8. I would spend time praising and recognizing employees' work efforts rather than just giving criticism.

_____ 9. I would set several controls for employees to ensure that objectives are met rather than allow employees to set their own controls.

_____ 10. I would frequently observe my employees to ensure that they are working and meeting deadlines rather than leave them alone.

To better understand your own behavior toward employees, score your answers. For items 1, 5, 6, 7, 9, and 10, give yourself one point for each U, two points for each F, three points for each O, and four points for each S. For items 2, 3, 4, and 8, give yourself one point for each S, two points for each O, three points for each F, and four points for each U. Total all points. Your score should be between 10 and 40.

Theory X and Theory Y are on opposite ends of a continuum. Most people's behavior falls somewhere between the two extremes. Place a check on the continuum where your score falls.

Theory X Behavior   Theory Y Behavior

10_____   20_____   30_____   40_____

(More Autocratic)   (More Participative)

The lower your score, the stronger your Theory X behavior, and the higher your score, the stronger your Theory Y behavior. A score of 20 to 30 could be considered balanced between the two theories. Your score may not be an accurate measure of how you would behave in an actual managerial position. However, it should help you anticipate how you are likely to behave.

In the 1930s, before behavioral theory became popular, research was conducted by Kurt Lewin and associates at the **University of Iowa** on the managerial leadership style. The studies identified three basic leadership styles:[35] *autocratic* (similar to Theory X behavior), *democratic* (similar to Theory Y behavior), and *laissez-faire* (a leave-employees-alone approach).

LO 12-3

Discuss the major similarity and difference between two-dimensional leadership styles and the Leadership Grid®.

two-dimensional leadership styles Four possible leadership styles that are based on the dimensions of job structure and employee consideration.

Two-Dimensional Leadership Styles

Two-dimensional leadership styles *are four possible leadership styles that are based on the dimensions of job structure and employee consideration.*

Structuring and Consideration Styles. In 1945, the Personnel Research Board of **The Ohio State University** began a study to determine effective leadership styles.[36] In the process, researchers developed an instrument known as the Leader Behavior Description Questionnaire (LBDQ). Respondents to the questionnaire perceived leaders' behavior on two distinct dimensions:

1. *Structuring*—the extent to which the leader takes charge to plan, organize, lead, and control as the employee performs the task. This dimension focuses on getting the job done.

2. *Consideration*—the extent to which the leader communicates to develop trust, friendship, support, and respect. This dimension focuses on developing relationships with employees.

Job-Centered and Employee-Centered Styles. At approximately the same time as The Ohio State University studies began, the **University of Michigan**'s Survey Research Center initiated its own leadership studies.[37] This research identified the same two dimensions, or styles, of leadership behavior as the Ohio research. However, the Michigan researchers called the two styles *job centered* (analogous to structuring) and *employee centered* (analogous to consideration).

Using Two-Dimensional Leadership Styles. When interacting with employees, the manager can focus on getting the job done through directing (structuring, or job-centered behavior) and/or through developing supportive relationships (consideration, or employee-centered behavior). Combinations of the two dimensions of leadership result in the four leadership styles illustrated in Exhibit 12-2.

WORK APPLICATION 12-2

Recall a present or past boss. Which of the four leadership styles created by Ohio State's version of the two-dimensional leadership model did your boss use most often? Describe your boss's behavior.

EXHIBIT 12-2 THE OHIO STATE UNIVERSITY AND THE UNIVERSITY OF MICHIGAN TWO-DIMENSIONAL LEADERSHIP STYLES

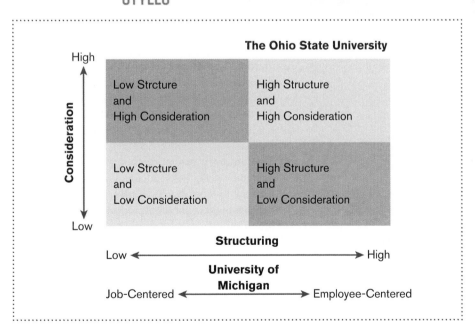

The Ohio State and University of Michigan leadership models are different in that the University of Michigan places the two leadership behaviors at opposite ends of the same continuum, making it one-dimensional with two styles. The Ohio State University model considers the two behaviors independent of one another, making it two-dimensional with four styles.

The Leadership Grid®

Robert Blake and Jane Mouton developed the Managerial Grid, which Blake and Anne Adams McCanse later transformed into the Leadership Grid.[38]

The Leadership Grid® builds on the Ohio State and Michigan studies. It is based on the same two leadership dimensions that they called "concern for production" and "concern for people." The Leadership Grid® *identifies the ideal leadership style as incorporating a high concern for both production and people.* A questionnaire is used to measure a manager's concern for people and production on a scale from 1 to 9, 1 being low concern and 9 being high concern. Five major leadership styles are highlighted on the grid:

- (1, 1) The leader with an *impoverished management style* has low concern for both production and people.
- (9, 1) The leader with an *authority-compliance management style* has a high concern for production and a low concern for people.
- (1, 9) The leader with a *country club management style* has a high concern for people and a low concern for production.
- (5, 5) The leader with a *middle-of-the-road management style* has balanced, medium concern for both production and people.
- (9, 9) The leader with a *team management style* has a high concern for both production and people. This leader strives for maximum performance and employee satisfaction.

WORK
APPLICATION 12-3

Recall a present or past boss. Which of the five major leadership styles did your boss use most often? Describe your boss's behavior.

12-1 APPLYING THE CONCEPT

The Leadership Grid®

Identify the leadership style described in each of the five situations.

A. impoverished
B. authority-compliance
C. country club
D. middle-of-the-road
E. team

____ 1. The department has adequate morale and an average productivity level. The leader is somewhat concerned about both people and production.

____ 2. The department has one of the lowest levels of morale in the company yet is one of the top performers. The leader is highly concerned about production but not about people.

____ 3. The department is one of the lowest producers in the company, with a low level of morale. The leader is not concerned about people or production.

____ 4. The department is one of the top performers. The members have high morale. The leader is highly concerned about both people and production.

____ 5. The department has very high morale; its members enjoy their work. The productivity level is one of the lowest in the company. The leader is highly concerned about people but not about production.

According to Blake, the team leadership style is the most appropriate style to use in all situations. However, most current researchers say there is no best style of leadership that should be used in all situations.[39] What do you think?

At **American Express (Case Question 2)**, Ken Chenault has used the team management style most frequently since assuming his post as CEO. However, in certain situations, he has adapted his style. For example, after the 2001 World Trade Center disaster, Chenault adopted a more country-club style as he expressed a greater concern for the immediate emotional and safety needs of employees while placing concerns about the company's production on the back burner.

Leadership Grid® A model that identifies the ideal leadership style as incorporating a high concern for both production and people.

SITUATIONAL LEADERSHIP THEORIES

Situational leadership theory is also called *contingency theory*.[40] Both trait and behavioral leadership theories were attempts to find the best leadership style in all situations. In the 1960s, it became apparent that no single leadership style is appropriate in all situations. Managers need to adopt different leadership styles,[41] as leadership success requires adapting leadership styles to meet the situation.[42] Thus, **situational approaches to leadership** *attempt to determine appropriate leadership styles for particular situations*. In this section, we discuss some of the most popular situational theories shown in Exhibit 12–1, which are called models.

Contingency Leadership Model

In 1951, Fred E. Fiedler began to develop the first situational approach to leadership—the contingency theory of leader effectiveness.[43] Fiedler believed that one's leadership style reflects one's personality and remains basically constant. That is, leaders do not change styles. The **contingency leadership model** *is used to determine if leadership style is task or relationship oriented and if the situation matches the style*.

Leadership Style. The first step is to determine whether your leadership style is task or relationship oriented. To do so, you fill in what Fiedler called the Least Preferred Coworker (LPC) scale. The LPC essentially answers this question: "Do you use a more task-oriented or relationship-oriented leadership style in working with others?"

Situational Favorableness Decision Tree. After determining leadership style, you determine situational favorableness. *Situational favorableness* refers to the degree to which a situation enables you to exert influence over followers. The more control you have over followers, the more favorable the situation. The three variables that determine situational favorableness are as follows:

1. *Leader–Follower Relations.* Is the relationship between you and followers good or poor? The better the relations, the more favorable the situation.
2. *Task Structure.* Is the task structured or unstructured? Do employees perform repetitive, routine, standard tasks that are easily understood? The more repetitive the jobs, the more favorable the situation.
3. *Position Power.* Do you have position power—the power to assign work, reward and punish, hire and fire, and give raises and promotions? The more position power, the more favorable the situation.

After determining your leadership style, you can answer the three questions pertaining to situational favorableness by following a decision tree to discover the best leadership style to a given situation. Exhibit 12-3 shows the decision tree.

Matching the Situation to the Leadership Style. If your preferred leadership style is the one indicated by the decision tree, you match and do nothing. If, however, your preferred leadership style is not ideal for the given situation, then the situation must be changed to match your leadership style. You can change your relationship, repetitiveness of the task, or your power.

One of the major criticisms of contingency theory is that it's often difficult to change a situation. Critics say that when a manager's leadership style does not match the situation, the style should be changed. All the other situational leadership theories disagree with changing the situation to match your leadership style; they advocate changing your leadership style to match the situation.

LO 12-4

State the primary difference between the contingency leadership model and other situational approaches to leadership.

WORK
APPLICATION 12-4

Classify your present or past boss's preferred style as task or relationship oriented. Think of a specific situation at work and use the contingency model to determine the appropriate style to use for this situation. Did the boss use the appropriate style?

situational approaches to leadership Theories that attempt to determine appropriate leadership styles for particular situations.

contingency leadership model A model used to determine if leadership style is task or relationship oriented and if the situation matches the style.

EXHIBIT 12-3   CONTINGENCY LEADERSHIP MODEL

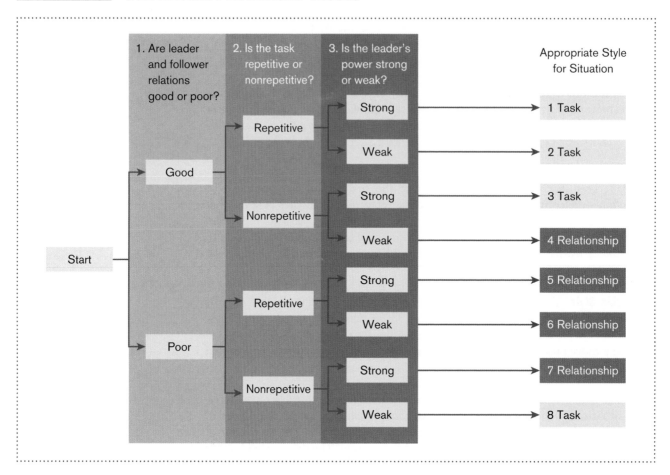

12-2   APPLYING THE CONCEPT

Contingency Leadership Theory

Using Exhibit 12–3, determine the appropriate leadership style under the given conditions.

  A   task-oriented
  B   relationship-oriented

____ 6. Nyota, the chair of a committee charged with recommending ways to increase organizational performance, is highly regarded by the volunteer members from a variety of departments

____ 7. Saul, a manager, oversees the assembly of mass-produced containers. He has the power to reward and punish. Saul is viewed as a hard-nosed boss.

____ 8. Aarti is a manager from the corporate planning staff; she helps departments plan. Aarti is viewed as being a dreamer who doesn't understand the company's various departments. Employees tend to be rude in their dealings with her.

____ 9. Juan, a manager, oversees the processing of canceled checks for a bank. He is well liked by the employees. Juan enjoys hiring and evaluating his employees' performance.

____ 10. Lakesha, the principal of a school, assigns teachers to classes and other various duties. She hires and decides on tenure appointments. The school atmosphere is tense.

Leadership Continuum Model

Robert Tannenbaum and Warren Schmidt developed a model of leadership that focuses on who makes the decisions. They viewed leadership behavior on a continuum from autocratic (boss centered) to participative (employee centered).

The continuum includes seven major styles from which a leader can choose. Exhibit 12-4 lists the seven styles.[44] The **leadership continuum model** *is used to determine which of seven styles of leadership, on a continuum from autocratic (boss centered) to participative (employee centered), is best for a given situation.* Before selecting one of the seven leadership styles, the leader must consider the following three variables: the *leader's preferred style*, the *followers' preferred style for the leader*, and *the situation.*

WORK
APPLICATION 12-5

Using the leadership continuum model, identify your boss's most commonly used leadership style. Now recall a specific situation in which this leadership style was used. Would you say this was the most appropriate leadership style in that situation? Explain.

EXHIBIT 12-4   THE LEADERSHIP CONTINUUM

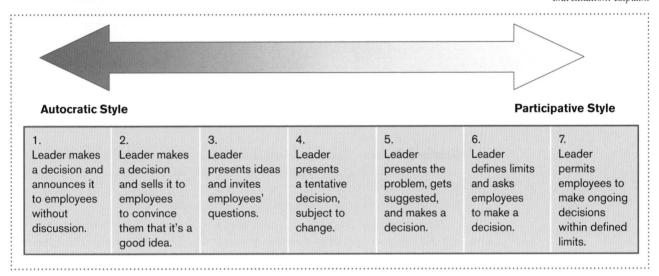

Autocratic Style — Participative Style

| 1. Leader makes a decision and announces it to employees without discussion. | 2. Leader makes a decision and sells it to employees to convince them that it's a good idea. | 3. Leader presents ideas and invites employees' questions. | 4. Leader presents a tentative decision, subject to change. | 5. Leader presents the problem, gets suggested, and makes a decision. | 6. Leader defines limits and asks employees to make a decision. | 7. Leader permits employees to make ongoing decisions within defined limits. |

Source: Adopted from Robert Tannenbaum and Warren Schmidt, "How to Choose a Leadership Pattern," *Harvard Business Review* (May/June, 1973).

12-3 APPLYING THE CONCEPT

Leadership Continuum

Refer to Exhibit 12–4 and indicate the leadership style exemplified in each statement.

A
B
C
D
E
F
G

____ 11. "From now on, this is the way it will be done. Does anyone have any questions about the procedure?"

____ 12. "These are the weeks when people can take their vacations. Let me know when you plan to take yours."

____ 13. "I'd like your ideas on how to stop the bottleneck on the production line. Then I'll choose a solution to implement."

____ 14. "Jose, I selected you to be transferred to the new department, but you don't have to go if you don't want to."

____ 15. "Sam, type up this memo for me right away."

Path-Goal Model

Robert House developed the path-goal leadership model. The **path-goal model** *is used to determine employee objectives and to clarify how to achieve them using one of four leadership styles.* The model focuses on how leaders influence employees' perceptions of their goals and the paths they follow toward goal attainment.[45] As shown in Exhibit 12-5, the path-goal model uses situational factors to determine the leadership style that affects goal achievement through performance and satisfaction.

leadership continuum model A model used to determine which of seven styles of leadership, on a continuum from autocratic (boss centered) to participative (employee centered), is best for a given situation.

path-goal model A model used to determine employee objectives and to clarify how to achieve them using one of four leadership styles.

EXHIBIT 12-5   A SUMMARY OF PATH-GOAL FACTORS AND STYLES

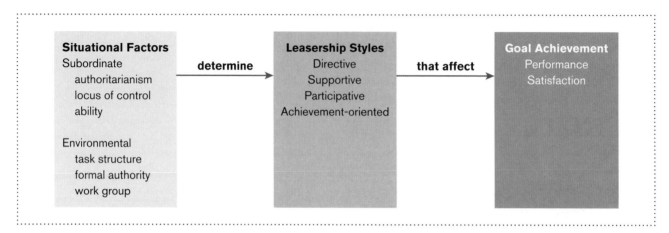

Situational Factors. *Subordinate* situational factors are (1) authoritarianism (the degree to which employees defer to leaders and want to be told what to do and how to do the job), (2) locus of control (Chapter 10), and (3) ability (the extent of employees' ability to perform tasks to achieve goals).

Environmental situational factors are (1) task structure (repetitiveness in the job), (2) formal authority (leader's power), and (3) work group (the extent to which coworkers contribute to job satisfaction).

Leadership Styles. Based on the situational factors, a leader can select the most appropriate of the following leadership styles:

1. *Directive.* The leader provides high structure. Directive leadership is appropriate when subordinates want authoritarian leadership, have an external locus of control, and have low ability. Directive leadership is also appropriate when the task is complex or ambiguous, formal authority is strong, and the work group provides job satisfaction.

2. *Supportive.* The leader provides high consideration. Supportive leadership is appropriate when subordinates do not want authoritarian leadership, have an internal locus of control, and have high ability. Supportive leadership is also appropriate when the task is simple, formal authority is weak, and the work group does not provide job satisfaction.

3. *Participative.* The leader considers employee input when making decisions. Participative leadership is appropriate when subordinates want to be involved, have an internal locus of control, and have high ability. Participative leadership is also appropriate when the task is complex, authority is either strong or weak, and job satisfaction from coworkers is either high or low.

4. *Achievement-oriented.* The leader sets difficult but achievable goals, expects subordinates to perform at their highest level, and rewards them for doing so. In essence, the leader provides both high structure and high consideration. Achievement-oriented leadership is appropriate when subordinates are open to authoritarian leadership, have an external locus of control, and have high ability. Achievement-oriented leadership is also appropriate when the environmental task is simple, authority is strong, and job satisfaction from coworkers is either high or low.

WORK
APPLICATION 12-6

Identify your boss's most commonly used leadership style. Now recall a specific situation in which this style was used. From the perspective of the path-goal model, was this the most appropriate leadership style based on the situational factors? Explain.

Normative Leadership Model

Recall that Chapter 4 presented Victor Vroom's normative participative decision-making model. The participative model is clearly a leadership model, although it focuses on making decisions. Return to Chapter 4 and review the text discussion and Exhibit 4–11. The trend today is toward higher levels of participation to improve decisions and performance.[46]

The normative leadership model is popular in the academic community because it is based on research. However, the model is not as popular with managers, who find it cumbersome to have to decide which version (time-driven or development-driven) of the model to use and follow a seven-question decision tree every time they have to make a decision.

Situational Leadership® Model

Paul Hersey and Ken Blanchard developed the Situational Leadership® model. The **Situational Leadership® model** *is used to select one of four leadership styles that match the employees' maturity level in a given situation.*[47] Their model identifies four leadership styles using the Ohio State University model in Exhibit 12–2.

To select a leadership style, you determine the followers' maturity level. "Maturity level" refers to the level of employee development (competence and commitment) or readiness to do the job (ability and willingness). If employee maturity is low, you use a *telling style*, giving employees explicit directions about how to accomplish a task. If employee maturity is moderate to low, you use a *selling style*, explaining decisions to gain understanding. If employee maturity is moderate to high, you use the *participating style* to facilitate decision making among subordinates. And if employee maturity is high, you use a *delegating style*, giving employees responsibility for decisions and their implementation.

Hersey has used a baseball metaphor to explain how this model helps managers: I can't give you the way to hit a home run every time at bat, but the model can help you increase your batting average.[48] Likewise, this book cannot teach you all the details of how to lead in every situation, but the theories and models presented here can help you increase your leadership skills and managerial success.

WORK
APPLICATION 12-7

Identify your boss's most commonly used normative leadership style. Now recall a specific situation in which this style was used. From the normative leadership perspective, was it the most appropriate leadership style? Explain.

WORK
APPLICATION 12-8

Identify your boss's most commonly used leadership style. Would you say this is the most appropriate leadership style based on the maturity level of the employees in your team or organization? Explain.

**Situational Leadership®
model** A model used to select one of four leadership styles that match the employees' maturity level in a given situation.

12-4 APPLYING THE CONCEPT

Situational Leadership Styles

For each of the following situations, identify the maturity level of the employee and the leadership style the manager should use so that the job gets done.

A. Low maturity of employee: The manager should use the telling style.

B. Low to moderate maturity of employee: The manager should use the selling style.

C. Moderate to high maturity of employee: The manager should use the participating style.

D. High maturity of employee: The manager should use the delegating style.

_____ 16. You told Shinji to fill the customer order in a specific way. However, he deliberately ignored your directions. The customer returned the order to you with a complaint.

_____ 17. Milani is an enthusiastic employee. You have decided to expand her job responsibilities to include a difficult task that she has never done before.

_____ 18. Part of Pete's job, which he has done properly many times, is to take out the trash when the bin is full. It is full now.

_____ 19. Nina usually does an excellent job and gets along well with her coworkers. For the past two days, you have noticed a drop in the quality of her work, and yesterday you saw her arguing with a coworker. You want Nina to return to her usual level of performance.

_____ 20. Mary Ann has never done a report before, but you know she can do it with a minimum amount of help from you.

In contrast to what Fiedler advocated with his contingency leadership model, **American Express's (Case Question 3)** Ken Chenault *does* change his leadership style as necessary to focus on tasks or relationships. For example, on 9/11, immediately after hearing that the World Trade Center had been attacked, Chenault used an autocratic style to make the decision to evacuate the American Express building across the street and to charter private planes and buses to transport stranded American Express customers. However, his most common leadership style is participative.

Comparing Leadership Models

The behavioral and situational leadership models we've discussed are all based on two dimensions of leadership, shown Exhibit 12–2. However, as you've seen, different authors use different terms for what are basically the same dimensions. Exhibit 12-6 provides a comparison of the behavioral and situational leadership models and uses *direction* and *support* to describe these two dimensions of leadership. The columns in the exhibit are headed "High direction/Low support," "High direction/High support," and so on. The terms that appear below these headings have basically the same meanings as the column headings.

EXHIBIT 12-6   A COMPARISON OF BEHAVIORAL AND SITUATIONAL LEADERSHIP MODELS

	High Direction/ Low support	High Direction/ High Support	Low Direction/ High Support	Low Direction/ Low Support
Behavioral Leadership Theories				
Basic Leadership Styles	Autocratic	Democratic		Laissez-faire
The Ohio State University Model (Exhibit 12-2)	High structure/ Low consideration	High structure/ High consideration	Low structure/High consideration	Low structure/Low consideration
University of Michigan Model (Exhibit 12-2)	Job centered			Employee centered
Leadership Grid	Authority-compliance (9, 1)	Team (9, 9)	Country club (1, 9)	Impoverished (1, 1)
	Middle of the road (5, 5)			
Situational Approaches to Leadership	Task		Relationship	
Contingency Leadership Model (Exhibit 12-3)	Style 1	Styles 2 and 3	Styles 4 and 5	Styles 6 and 7
Leadership Continuum Model (Exhibit 12-4)	Directive	Achievement oriented	Supportive	Participative
Path-goal Model (Exhibit 12-5)	Decide	Consult	Facilitate	Delegate
Normative Leadership Model (Exhibit 4-11)	Telling	Selling	Participating	Delegating

Leadership Substitutes Theory

The leadership theories and models that have been discussed so far assume that some leadership style will be effective in each situation. Steven Kerr and John Jermier argued that certain situational variables prevent leaders from affecting subordinates' attitudes and behaviors.[49] **Substitutes for leadership** *are characteristics of the task, of subordinates, or of the organization that replace the need for a leader.* These characteristics can also neutralize the effect of leadership behavior. That is, the following may substitute for or neutralize leadership by providing direction and/or support: *Characteristics of the task, subordinates, and the organization.* For routine *tasks* with highly skilled *subordinates* in mechanistic structured *organizations*, employees don't need supervisory instructions.

Contemporary Leadership Theories

As presented, leadership theories progressed from focusing on traits to behavior to the situation.[50] Today researchers try to put these theories together. **Contemporary leadership theories** *attempt to determine how effective leaders interact with, inspire, and support followers.* Three contemporary leadership theories (visionary, charismatic, and transformational) have a lot in common with a heavy focus on behavior.[51] These leaders articulate a compelling vision, emphasizing collective identities, expressing confidence and optimism, and referencing core values and ideas.[52] Contemporary leadership studies focus primarily on top level managers.

Visionary Leaders

Visionary leaders *create an image of the organization in the future that provides direction for setting goals and developing strategic plans.* They believe they are capable of creating a significant part of the future and controlling its effects on them. Visionary leaders try to prevent threats, not merely prepare for them, and to create opportunities, not merely exploit them. They envision a desirable future and invent ways of bringing it about.[53] Steve Jobs was a visionary leader as he developed **Apple** products and services before consumers knew they wanted them, including the PC/iPad and how we listen to and buy music (iPod/iPhone and iTunes). Visionary leadership also includes *strategic leadership*, as the vision is implemented through strategy.

Charismatic Leaders

Charismatic leaders *inspire loyalty, enthusiasm, and high levels of performance.* Their confident dynamic personal traits and behavior enable them to develop strong relationships with followers they may not even know personally, giving them strong influence over followers' behavior and performance. Charismatic leaders articulate a clear vision that is based on strongly held values, model those values, communicate high performance expectations, and display confidence in followers' ability to achieve the vision. Followers in turn trust charismatic leaders, are loyal to them, and are inspired to work hard to accomplish the leader's vision, goals, and strategy. The term *charismatic* has been applied to many leaders, from John F. Kennedy and Mother Teresa to Martin Luther King Jr. **Apple's** Steve Jobs was called a pied piper of charisma by Bill Gates of **Microsoft**.[54] Many studies have reported that charismatic leaders have a strong effect on performance, and at least one study found that charismatic leadership skills can be developed.[55]

Transformational Leaders

Transformational leaders *bring about continuous learning, innovation, and change.* They gain acceptance of the mission and group's purpose and motivate

WORK APPLICATION 12-9

Could the characteristics of the task, subordinates, or the organization substitute for your present or a past boss? In other words, is your boss necessary? Explain.

WORK APPLICATION 12-10

Identify the one leadership theory or model you prefer. State why.

WORK APPLICATION 12-11

Describe the type of leader you want to be.

substitutes for leadership Characteristics of the task, of subordinates, or of the organization that replace the need for a leader.

contemporary leadership theories Theories that attempt to determine how effective leaders interact with, inspire, and support followers.

visionary leaders Leaders who create an image of the organization in the future that provides direction for setting goals and developing strategic plans.

charismatic leadership A leadership style that inspires loyalty, enthusiasm, and high levels of performance.

transformational leaders Leaders who bring about continuous learning, innovation, and change.

Charismatic leaders like Mother Teresa have a strong influence on others. People are often willing to work hard to help a charismatic leader's vision become a reality. Photo from Tim Graham/Getty Images.

WORK
APPLICATION 12-12

Recall the top manager from an organization you work for or have worked for. Would you call this CEO a charismatic or transformational leader? Why or why not?

followers to go beyond their own self-interest (transcend) for the good of the organization and group.[56] Transformational leaders make their followers feel like a vital part of the firm and understand how their jobs fit with the vision or understand how to make the vision become a reality. Many charismatic leaders are also visionary and transformational leaders, but not all. Transformational leaders are good at overcoming resistance to change. They continue to bring about innovations in processes, products, and services by cultivating employee creativity.[57] They often increase performance beyond expectations, even more than their employees thought possible. Transformational leaders are especially need in firms with growth strategies competing in dynamic environments. CEO Alan Mulally transformed **Ford** from a company losing billions for nearly a decade to profitability while cutting its debt by more than a third, and his company was the only American automaker not to declare bankruptcy or take government bailout money.[58]

Transactional Leadership. Transformational leadership is often contrasted with transactional leadership. **Transactional leadership** *is a leadership style based on social exchange.* The exchange involves the principle that "you do this work for me and I'll give this reward to you, and I will punish you if you don't." Transactional leaders promote stability rather than change and are described as task and reward oriented, structured, and passive. Transactional leadership occurs mostly among middle and first-line managers, but some top-level managers are transactional. Employees generally prefer working for transformational leaders and perform at higher levels than for transactional leaders.

American Express CEO (Case Question 4) Ken Chenault is a visionary and charismatic leader, and it is his personal traits that make him charismatic. Tom Ryder, who competed with Chenault for the CEO position at American Express, said that when you work with Chenault, you feel you'll do anything for him. Chenault is also a transformational leader: before he was CEO, he had the courage to challenge the old culture and make changes. After the 9/11 attacks, Chenault assured employees that American Express would continue and that their lives and roles were valued. Two weeks after the 9/11 tragedy, he gathered employees together for a "town hall meeting," personally comforted grief-stricken employees, and vowed to donate $1 million of profits to the families of American Express victims. He told them, "You represent American Express. All the people of American Express are what this company is about. In fact, you are my strength and I love you."

HANDLING COMPLAINTS

No matter how hard you try to do a good job and to satisfy all employees' and customers' needs, complaints will arise. A *complaint* is an expression of dissatisfaction with a situation, often coupled with a request for change. Handling complaints requires strong leadership skills. The manner in which complaints are handled has a profound effect on the organization. In this section, we discuss how to handle employee and customer complaints; Skill Builder 12–2 will help you develop this skill.

transactional leadership A leadership style based on social exchange.

12-2 JOIN THE DISCUSSION ETHICS & SOCIAL RESPONSIBILITY

Leadership and Gender

Are there differences in the leadership styles of men and women? Some researchers say that women tend to be more participative, relationship-oriented leaders and men more task oriented. However, others say that men and women are more alike as leaders than different and are equally effective.

1. Is it ethical and socially responsible to say that people of a particular gender make better leaders?
2. Do you think men and women lead in the same way?
3. Are men or women more ethical and socially responsible as leaders?
4. Would you prefer to have a man or a woman as boss?

Handling Employee Complaints

Not handling employee complaints effectively can create resentment, low morale, low productivity, and increased turnover. So it is advisable to have an open-door policy that allows employees to feel free to come to you with a complaint. Try not to take complaints personally as a reflection on you or your leadership ability. Even the best managers have to deal with complaints. Do not become defensive, dismiss the complaint as being not valid, or try to talk the employee out of the complaint. There are five steps you should take when an employee comes to you with a complaint. These steps are summarized in Model 12–1.

Step 1. Listen to the complaint and paraphrase it. If you cannot accurately restate the complaint in your own words, you cannot resolve it. When listening to the complaint, distinguish facts from opinions. At times, employees think they know the facts when they do not. Sometimes, when facts are given, complaints are dropped immediately.

Step 2. Ask the complainer to recommend a solution. The complainer may have a good solution that you haven't thought of or one that is easier to implement than your solution. However, asking about a solution does not mean that you must implement it. In such cases, be sure to let the employee know why the suggestion will not be implemented.

Step 3. Schedule time to get all the facts and make a decision. Generally, the faster a complaint is resolved, the fewer the negative side effects. However, you may find it necessary to check records or talk to others about the complaint, including your own boss or colleagues, who may have handled a similar complaint. Simply saying "I'll get back to you" frustrates the employee and may make him or her think you have no intention of addressing the complaint. Tell the employee that you will take a specific amount of time to consider the complaint—set a deadline.

Step 4. Develop a plan for addressing the complaint. You may decide to accept the employee's recommendation for a solution, or you may be able to work with the employee in coming up with a different solution. If you decide to take no action to resolve the complaint, you should clearly explain to the employee why you are choosing not to act. Remind the employee of any mechanisms that are available for appealing your decision.

Step 5. Implement the plan and follow up. It is important to make sure that the plan for resolving the complaint is implemented; following up ensures that it is. Following up may involve meeting with the employee at some point after the solution is implemented. It is advisable to document the entire process in writing.

MODEL 12-1 **STEPS IN ADDRESSING EMPLOYEE COMPLAINTS**

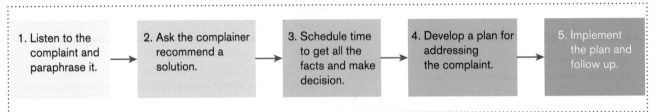

1. Listen to the complaint and paraphrase it. → 2. Ask the complainer recommend a solution. → 3. Schedule time to get all the facts and make decision. → 4. Develop a plan for addressing the complaint. → 5. Implement the plan and follow up.

WORK
APPLICATION 12-13

Identify a complaint you brought to a manager. State the complaint and identify which steps in the complaint-handling model the manager did or did not follow. If you have never complained, interview someone who has.

Handling Customer Complaints

Handling a customer complaint is somewhat different from handling an employee complaint, but it is critical, because customer satisfaction is the major goal of many organizations. Unfortunately, most customers are dissatisfied with the way firms handle their complaints.[59] Dissatisfied customers often complain to friends, with increasing use of the Internet, often result in lost customers and future sales.[60] The steps for handling customer complaints are listed in Model 12–2 and discussed below:

Step 1. **Admit the mistake and apologize.** As when handling employees' complaints, you should listen to the customer's complaint and paraphrase it. Then admit that a mistake was made and apologize by acknowledging the hurt or damage done.[61]

Step 2. **Agree on a solution.** You can tell the customer what you intend to do about the problem, but a better approach is to ask the customer to recommend a solution to the problem: "How would you like us to handle the situation?" Customers consistently recommend solutions that cost less than what managers might offer initially.

Step 3. **Implement the solution quickly.** Quick implementation has a direct effect on customer satisfaction.[62] Up to 95 percent of complainers will return to your business if the problem is resolved quickly.[63]

Step 4. **Prevent future complaints.** Taking quick corrective action will help prevent the mistake from happening again and decrease the possibility of future complaints. You can feature improvements in your marketing materials, such as blogs and your website.[64]

MODEL 12-2 **STEPS IN ADDRESSING CUSTOMER COMPLAINTS**

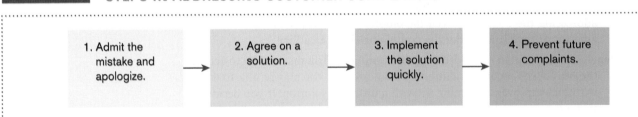

1. Admit the mistake and apologize. → 2. Agree on a solution. → 3. Implement the solution quickly. → 4. Prevent future complaints.

Handling complaints is very important to **American Express (Case Question 5)** because the company strives to attract and retain thousands of employees and millions of customers. Without employees and customers, it doesn't have a business. With 63,500 employees worldwide, American Express managers handle employee complaints every day. The company has grievance procedures to make sure that all employees are treated fairly. American Express also has a large full-time staff of customer service employees to handle customer complaints.

• • • CHAPTER SUMMARY

12-1. **Compare the trait, behavioral, situational, and contemporary leadership theories.**

All four theories have the same goal of determining what it takes to be an effective leader; however, their focus is different. Trait theorists try to find a list of distinctive characteristics that account for leadership effectiveness. Behavioral theorists try to determine distinctive styles used by effective leaders and the one leadership style that is best in all situations. Situational theorists try to find the appropriate leadership style for various situations and believe that the best leadership style varies from situation to situation. Contemporary theorists try to determine how effective leaders interact with, inspire, and support followers.

12-2. **Explain why the terms *manager* and *leader* are not interchangeable.**

Management is broader in scope than leadership. Leadership is the process of influencing employees to work toward achieving objectives. A person who is a manager can be a poor leader, and a person who is not a manager can be a good leader.

12-3. **Discuss the major similarity and difference between two-dimensional leadership styles and the Leadership Grid®.**

Both theories use basically the same two dimensions of leadership, although they give them different names. The major difference is that two-dimensional leadership theory has four major leadership styles (high structure/low consideration, high structure/high consideration, low structure/high consideration, and low structure/low consideration), whereas the Leadership Grid® identifies five major leadership styles (impoverished, authority-compliance, country club, middle-of-the-road, and team).

12-4. **State the primary difference between the contingency leadership model and other situational approaches to leadership.**

The contingency leadership model recommends changing the situation, not the leadership style. The other situational leadership approaches recommend changing the leadership style, not the situation.

• • • KEY TERMS

behavioral leadership theorists, 361
charismatic leadership, 371
contemporary leadership
    theories, 371
contingency leadership model, 365
leadership continuum model, 367
Leadership Grid®, 364

leadership style, 361
leadership trait theorists, 360
path-goal model, 367
situational approaches to
    leadership, 365
Situational Leadership® model, 369
substitutes for leadership, 371

transactional leadership, 372
transformational leaders, 371
two-dimensional leadership
    styles, 362
visionary leaders, 371

• • • KEY TERM REVIEW

Complete each of the following statements with one of this chapter's key terms.

1. _____ attempt to determine a list of distinctive characteristics that account for leadership effectiveness.

2. _____ attempt to determine distinctive styles used by effective leaders.

3. _____ is the combination of traits, skills, and behaviors managers use in interacting with employees.

4. _____ are four possible leadership styles that are based on the dimensions of job structure and employee consideration.

5. The _____ identifies the ideal leadership style as incorporating a high concern for both production and people.

6. _____ attempt to determine appropriate leadership styles for particular situations.

7. The _____ is used to determine if leadership style is task or relationship oriented and if the situation matches the style.

8. The _____ is used to determine which of seven styles of leadership, on a continuum from autocratic (boss centered) to participative (employee centered), is best for a given situation.

9. The _____ is used to determine employee objectives and to clarify how to achieve them using one of four leadership styles.

10. The _____ is used to select one of four leadership styles that matches the employees' maturity level in a given situation.

11. _____ are characteristics of the task, of subordinates, or of the organization that replace the need for a leader.

12. _____ attempt to determine how effective leaders interact with, inspire, and support followers.

13. _____ create an image of the organization in the future that provides direction for setting goal and developing strategic plans.

14. _____ inspire loyalty, enthusiasm, and high levels of performance.

15. _____ is a leadership style that brings about continuous learning, innovation, and change.

••• REVIEW QUESTIONS

1. What is leadership, and why is it important?

2. What are the three parts of leadership style?

3. What are the two determinants of leadership and the four possible leadership styles according to The Ohio State University and University of Michigan studies?

4. What are the five major leadership styles identified on the Leadership Grid®?

5. What are the two leadership styles identified by the contingency leadership model?

6. What are the two styles of leadership at either end of the leadership continuum model?

7. What are the four leadership styles identified by the path-goal leadership model?

8. What are the five leadership styles identified by the normative leadership model?

9. What are the four leadership styles identified by the Situational Leadership® model?

10. What are the three substitutes for leadership?

11. What is the difference between transformational and transactional leadership?

••• COMMUNICATION SKILLS

The following critical-thinking questions can be used for class discussion and/or as written assignments to develop communication skills. Be sure to give complete explanations for all questions.

1. Peter Drucker said it's not worth pointing out the differences between a leader and a manager. Do you agree? Why or why not?

2. What traits do you think are most important in a leader?

3. Should spirituality be allowed in the workplace? Should spirituality be encouraged in the workplace? Why or why not?

4. Based on the Self-Assessment, is your behavior more Theory X or Theory Y? How do you feel about your score? Will you make any changes?

5. The Ohio State University and University of Michigan two-dimensional leadership styles identified in the 1940s haven't changed much over the years, as they are still being taught and used today. However, the way we conduct business today is very different from the way it was conducted in the 1940s. Do you think it is time for a revolutionary approach to leadership styles? If so, please provide some suggestions/ideas.

6. Today, the Leadership Grid® is still being taught in colleges and by consultants to be used by managers. Do you agree that the team leadership style is the best leadership style for use in all situations? Why or why not?

7. What situational approach to leadership do you prefer? Why?

8. What percentage of top leaders would you say are really visionary, charismatic, and/or transformational? (Your answers can change for each of the three leadership theories.)

9. Do you believe that men and women lead differently?

10. What has been your experience with having your complaints handled as an employee and as a customer? How could management do a better job of handling complaints from both employees and customers?

••• CASE: APPLE'S LEADERSHIP TRANSITION FROM STEVE JOBS TO TIM COOK

Apple is the company and case of our lifetime. Its story is full of adventure, entrepreneurship, teamwork, legends, and leaderships. If you were alive in 1982, you would have most likely used the Apple Macintosh and felt like you were part of the future. The story has been told in books, most recently and successfully Steve Jobs by Walter Isaacson. The book was turned into a movie starring Ashton Kutcher as Steve Jobs.

But, if you look closer, you will see how Jobs used an unusual leadership style to invent, grow, leave, return, grow the company again, and eventually pass away at the height of his fame. This is his leadership journey.

Together with Apple cofounder Steve Wozniak, Steve Jobs helped popularize the personal computer in the late 1970s and is credited with bringing cheap, easy-to-use computers to the masses. When 21-year-old Jobs saw a computer that Wozniak had designed for his own use, he convinced Wozniak to assist him and started a company to market the computer. Apple Computer Co. was founded as a partnership on April 1, 1976. Though their initial plan was to sell just printed circuit boards, Jobs and Wozniak ended up creating a batch of completely assembled computers and thus entered the personal computer business. The first personal computer Jobs and Wozniak introduced, the Apple I, sold for $666.66, a number Wozniak came up with because he liked repeating digits. Its successor, the Apple II, was introduced the following year and became a huge success, turning Apple into an important player in the personal computer industry. In December 1980, Apple Computer became a publicly traded corporation, making Jobs a multimillionaire.[65]

In the early 1980s, the company struggled to compete against IBM and Microsoft in the lucrative business and corporate computing market, and IBM and Microsoft continued to gain market share at Apple's expense in the personal computer industry. Jobs decided that to compete, he needed to bring in professional management to grow the company. In 1983, Jobs lured John Sculley away from Pepsi-Cola to serve as Apple's CEO, challenging him, "Do you want to spend the rest of your life selling sugared water, or do you want a chance to change the world?" The following year, Apple set out to do just that, starting with a Super Bowl television commercial titled "1984." The Macintosh became the first commercially successful computer with a graphical user interface. An industrywide sales slump toward the end of 1984 caused a deterioration in Jobs's working relationship with Sculley, and at the end of May 1985—following an internal power struggle and an announcement of significant layoffs—Sculley relieved Jobs of his duties as head of the Macintosh division. In 1986, finding himself sidelined by the company he had founded, Jobs sold all but one of his shares in Apple. Around the same time, Jobs founded another computer company, NeXT Computer (a computer platform development company specializing in the higher education and business markets). NeXT technology would later play a large role in catalyzing two unrelated events: the World Wide Web and the return of Apple Computer. Also in 1986, Steve Jobs started what became Pixar Animated Studios,

of which he was CEO. Jobs contracted with Disney to produce a number of computer-animated feature films, which Disney would cofinance and distribute. The first film produced by the partnership, Toy Story, brought fame and critical acclaim to the studio when it was released in 1995. Over the next 10 years, the company would produce the box office hits *A Bug's Life* (1998), *Toy Story 2* (1999), *Monsters, Inc.* (2001), *Finding Nemo* (2003), *The Incredibles* (2004), and *Cars* (2006). In 2006, Jobs sold Pixar to Disney and remained on its board.

In 1996, Apple bought NeXT for $402 million, bringing Jobs back to the company he founded. With the purchase of NeXT, much of the company's technology found its way into Apple products. In 1997, Jobs became Apple's interim CEO. Under Jobs's guidance, the company increased sales significantly with the introduction of the iMac and other new products; since then, appealing designs and powerful branding have worked well for Apple. At the 2000 Macworld Expo, Jobs officially dropped the "interim" modifier from his title at Apple and once again became the CEO.

Since then, the company has branched out from personal computers, dropping the word "Computer" from its company name, to focus more on mobile electronic devices. With the introduction of the iPod portable music player and iTunes digital music software in 2001 and the iTunes Store in 2003, the company has made forays into consumer electronics and music distribution. In 2007, Apple entered the cellular phone business with the introduction of the iPhone, a multitouch-display cell phone, iPod, and Internet device. Also in 2007, the company released the Apple TV, a set-top video device that links up to a user's television and allows consumers to view photos, play music and podcasts, and watch movies and TV shows via the iTunes store, Netflix, and YouTube. Most recently, Apple introduced its much-anticipated media tablet, the iPad, which offers multitouch interaction with multimedia formats such as books, TV shows, and music. It also includes a mobile version of Safari, Apple's Internet browser, as well as access to Apple's App, iTunes, and iBooks stores.

Much has been made of Jobs's notorious micromanaging of his employees and his aggressive and demanding personality, and people who have worked for Jobs over the years have mixed reactions to his leadership style. Some call him temperamental, aggressive, tough, intimidating, and very demanding. He was known to verbally attack people who are not meeting goals and expectations. Many employees have admitted a fear of encountering Jobs while riding in the elevator, "afraid that they might not have a job when the doors opened"—a practice that became known as "getting Steved." Yet employees who performed to expectations were well rewarded. Many who feared him also had great respect for him, as he inspired loyalty, enthusiasm, and high levels of performance through continuous learning, innovation, and change. Many people believe that the reason Apple has had its continued, incredible turnaround since the late 1990s was due to the return of Steve Jobs's as leader of the company.

However, Jobs's health deteriorated, and everyone wondered what would happen when he passed away. Tim Cook was inserted as CEO while Jobs was still alive. Jobs did pass away October 5, 2011. Although expected, it was still a shock to Apple and the entire computer and technology industry.

Passing the torch from the entrepreneur that started a business to a person hired into the business can be very difficult. Under Tim Cook's watch, Apple introduced an iPad Mini. Although it was successful, it wasn't the breakout hit expected of Apple products. Jobs himself once said he didn't like the mini devices that other companies sold to try to beat the original larger-size iPad.[66]

Apple stock continued to languish almost two years after Jobs's death. Although the iPhone has been popular since being introduced, other smartphones from Samsung using Google's Android technology have often been more popular and more glamorous then the iPhones.

After two years as the CEO of Apple, Tim Cook's success is just starting to be measured. He is much quieter than Jobs was as leader. He is a more thoughtful and data-driven leader. He is known to be calm unless he becomes upset over an issue. At that point, he can reprimand an employee with one sentence that gets the point across quickly.

The most difficult moment in Cook's tenure was when the new Apple Maps app for the iPhone was released and did not work correctly. Cook took over for his lower-level executive. His first move was to fire the Apple executive. His second move was to issue a public apology to iPhone owners.

Cook has done a good job leading Apple during a time when Apple is a huge corporation. He has managed the maturing products such as the iPhone and iPad, which eventually had to experience a slower growth rate. Overall, most people are waiting for the next product from Apple that will change the world like the iPhone and iPad did a few years ago. [67] Is Tim Cook up to the challenge?

The answer might arrive sooner than we thought possible. In what appears to be a new start, Apple's most serious fans were out waiting in line at Apple stores around the globe days before the iPhone 5s and 5c went on sale in September of 2013.

The iPhone 5s features a new fingerprint scanner, an upgraded camera, and a much faster processor. The iPhone 5c is a cheaper model based upon the original iPhone 5.

Case Questions

1. Would you consider Steve Jobs a leader, a manager, or both?

2. Would you consider Tim Cook a leader, a manager, or both?

3. Would Ghiselli say that Steve Jobs or Tim Cook has the traits of a successful leader?

4. Which basic leadership style—autocratic, democratic, or laissez-faire—would Jobs's critics say he used? What is Cook's style?

5. Could you make a case for the Ohio State leadership style of high structure/low consideration or low structure/high consideration in analyzing Jobs versus Cook's leadership style?

6. Using the University of Michigan leadership style model, was Jobs or Cook job centered or employee centered?

7. Which Leadership Grid® style (1, 1) impoverished, (9, 1) authority-compliance, (1, 9) country club, (5, 5) middle-of-the-road, or (9, 9) team would Jobs's and Cook's critics say they used?

8. Was Steve Jobs a charismatic leader?

9. Was Jobs considered a transformational or transactional leader?

10. Is Tim Cook considered a transformational or transactional leader?

11. Which contingency leadership style, task oriented or relationship oriented, would Jobs's and Cook's critics say they use?

12. Did leadership play a role in the change in performance at Apple with and without Steve Jobs as CEO?

13. Would you have liked to have work for Steve Jobs? Why or why not?

14. Would you like to work for Tim Cook? Why or why not?

Cumulative Case Questions

15. Was Steve Jobs or Tim Cook an entrepreneur? Why or why not? (Chapter 1).

16. What external environment factor did Apple change for the business and general economy? (Chapter 2).

17. What decision-making model is used at Apple when selecting new products and transitions? (Chapter 3).

18. What is the strategic level of planning of this case, and what strategy is Apple using? (Chapter 4).

19. How did power change at Apple, and what role did conflict play? (Chapter 8)

• • • Skill Builder 12-1: The Situational Leadership® Model

Objective

To better understand situational leadership.

Skills

The primary skills developed through this exercise are:

1. *Management ski11*–interpersonal (leaders need good people skills to influence others)
2. *AACSB competency*—analytic skills
3. *Management function*—leading (through influencing others)

Think of a situation from a present or past job that required a boss to show leadership. Describe the situation in enough detail so that others can understand it and determine the maturity level of the employees.

For your situation, determine the maturity level of the follower(s) and select the situational leadership style appropriate for the situation (low, telling; moderate to low, selling; moderate to high, participating; high, delegating).

Apply It

What did I learn from this experience? How will I apply this knowledge in the future?

• • • Skill Builder 12-2: Handling Complaints

Objective

To develop experience and skills in resolving complaints.

Skills

The primary skills developed through this exercise are:

1. *Management skill*—interpersonal (handling complaints requires people skills)
2. *AACSB competency*—communication abilities
3. *Management function*—leading (through working with others)

In this activity, you will role play handling a complaint. To begin, think of a complaint—one you actually presented to a manager, one that was presented to you, one you heard about, or one you have made up. Write down details about the situation and the complaint, including any pertinent information that will help someone else play the role of the complainer (relationship to manager, knowledge level, years of employment, background, age, etc.).

The class will be divided into groups of three. One person in each group plays the role of the manager who must handle the complaint. This person gives his or her written complaint description to the person who is to present the complaint. The two ad lib the situation. A third person observes the role play and evaluates how the complaint is handled, writing comments on the observer form that follows. After each role play, group members should discuss how effectively the complaint was handled based on the observer's comments. After the discussion, group members switch roles and do another role play until each group member has had a chance to play each role.

Try to note something positive the person does at each step of the process as well as some ways the person might improve his or her handling of complaints. Be specific and descriptive in your comments, and be prepared to suggest alternative behaviors when discussing how the person might improve.

Step 1. How well did the manager listen? Was the manager open to the complaint? Did the manager try to talk the employee out of the complaint? Was the manager defensive? Did the manager get the full story without interruptions? Did the manager paraphrase the complaint?

Positive behavior:

Ways to improve:

Step 2. Did the manager ask the complainer to recommend a solution? How well did the manager react to the suggested solution? If the solution could not be used, did the manager explain why?

Positive behavior:

Ways to improve:

Step 3. Did the manager schedule time to get all the facts and/or make a decision? Was it a reasonable length of time? Did the manager set a specific time to get back to the person?

Positive behavior:

Ways to improve:

Step 4. Did the manager and the employee develop a plan?

Positive behavior:

Ways to improve:

Observer Form

Observe the role play to determine whether the person playing the role of manager followed the steps below.

Apply It

What did I learn from this experience? How will I use this knowledge in the future?

• • • SKILL BUILDER 12–3: MANAGEMENT STYLES

Refer to Chapter 1, Skill Builder 1–4, on pages 27–30 to complete this exercise.

• • • SKILL BUILDER 12–4: USING THE VROOM MODEL

Refer to Chapter 4, Skill Builder 4–2, on pages 121–122 to complete this exercise.

• • • STUDENT STUDY SITE

Visit the Student Study Site at **www.sagepub.com/lussier6e** to access to these additional study tools:

- Mobile-compatible self-assessment quizzes
- Mobile-compatible key term flashcards
- Video Links
- SAGE Journal Articles
- Web Links

13 Communication and Information Technology

• • • Learning Outcomes

After studying this chapter, you should be able to:

13-1. Describe the three ways communication flows through organizations. PAGE 384

13-2. List the four steps in the interpersonal communication process. PAGE 388

13-3. State the major advantages of oral communication and written communication. PAGE 392

13-4. State a general guide to channel selection. PAGE 395

13-5. List the five steps in the process of sending face-to-face messages. PAGE 396

13-6. Describe paraphrasing, and explain why it is useful. PAGE 397

13-7. List and explain the three parts of the process of receiving messages. PAGE 398

13-8. Define reflecting responses, and state when they should be used. PAGE 403

13-9. Discuss what should and should not be done to calm an emotional person. PAGE 403

13-10. Describe the three primary types of information systems and their relationship. PAGE 405

13-11. List the components of an information network. PAGE 406

IDEAS ON MANAGEMENT at Facebook

Facebook's mission is to give people the power to share and make the world more open and connected. Facebook is a social network service whose name stems from the colloquial name for the book given to students at the start of the academic year by some universities. It was founded in February 2004 by Mark Zuckerberg with his college roommates and fellow Harvard University computer science students Eduardo Saverin, Andrew McCollum, Dustin Moskovitz, and Chris Hughes.

Facebook went public with its initial public offering (IPO) in 2012, but the stock dropped in price. Investors were concerned about the corporation making enough profits to give the stockholders a good return on their money. However, Facebook made the *Fortune* 500 list, ranked at 482, based on its 2012 revenues of $5.1 billion and profits of $53 million. Facebook is also ranked in the top 50 of the *Fortune* World's Most Admired Companies, and Zuckerberg is ranked in the *Fortune* Top 10 Businesspersons of the Year ranking.

Zuckerberg's ultimate goal is to turn Facebook into the planet's standardized communication platform and main tool that people use to communicate for work and pleasure. With 1.1 billion members (this is around 15 percent of the world population of 7 billion and more than four times the population of America) already using Facebook, it seems he is well on his way.

1. What types of organizational communication are possible and which information technology does Facebook use? PAGE 386
2. When using a social networking site such as Facebook, which part of the message-sending process can be the most difficult to accomplish? PAGES 395, 398
3. How can you analyze information from messages received on Facebook? PAGE 399
4. Can social networking sites such as Facebook be a type of communication between individuals and companies? Why or why not? PAGE 407

• • • Chapter Outline

You'll find answers to these questions throughout the chapter. To learn more about Facebook, visit its website at www.facebook.com.

Sources: Information for this case and answers within the chapter were taken from Facebook's website at http://www.facebook.com, accessed August 20, 2013; "Largest U.S. corporations—Fortune 500," *Fortune* (May 20, 2013): 1–20; "The World's Most Admired Companies," *Fortune* (March 18, 2013): 137–139.

Organizational Communication and Information Technology

Communication *is the process of transmitting information and meaning.* From Chapter 1, communication is important to the management: skills, roles, and functions. So you need strong communications skills to manage effectively.[1] Given increasing worker interdependence, many organizations need employees to engage in greater communication and information exchange.[2] Strategy and structure are related.[3] Communicating information is so important that some firms design their organizational structures as a means to meet the information-processing requirements generated by individuals and groups.[4] The organizational strategy and goals must be communicated frequently.[5]

There are two major types, or levels, of communication: organizational and interpersonal. That is, communication takes place among organizations and among their units or departments, and communication takes place among individuals. Both companywide and individual communications are vital.[6] In this section, we discuss organizational communication and information technology. In subsequent sections, we focus on interpersonal communication, and in the last section, we discuss the use of information systems at both levels.

Organizational communication flows formally in vertical and horizontal directions and informally through the grapevine. Exhibit 13-1 illustrates these aspects of organizational communication.

Vertical Communication

Vertical communication *is the flow of information both downward and upward through the organizational chain of command.* It is also called *formal communication* because information that flows this way is recognized as the officially sanctioned information.

Downward Vertical Communication. When top-level management makes decisions or creates policies and procedures, these are often communicated down the chain of command to employees. Downward communication occurs when higher-level managers tell those below them what to do and how to do it. The delegation process occurs via downward communication.

Upward Vertical Communication. When employees send a message to their bosses, they are using upward communication. Upward communication is vital, as it gives employees participation in management decisions and improving performance.[7] To help facilitate upward communication, many organizations have adopted an open-door policy that allows employees to feel at ease in going to managers.

Horizontal Communication

Horizontal communication *is the flow of information between colleagues and peers.* It is formal communication, but it does not follow the chain of command; instead, it is multidirectional. Horizontal communication is needed to coordinate within a department, among team members, and among different departments.

LO 13-1

Describe the three ways communication flows through organizations.

---

communication The process of transmitting information and meaning.

vertical communication The flow of information both downward and upward through the organizational chain of command.

horizontal communication The flow of information between colleagues and peers.

EXHIBIT 13-1 ORGANIZATIONAL COMMUNICATION

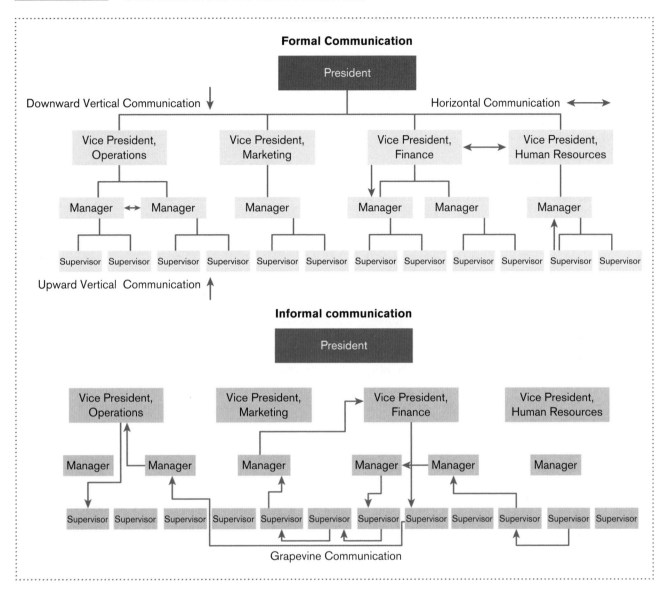

When the manager of the marketing department communicates with the manager of the production department or other departments, horizontal communication takes place. Most employees spend more time communicating with peers than with managers.

Grapevine Communication

The **grapevine** *is the informal flow of information in any direction throughout an organization.* It is informal communication because it is not official or sanctioned by management. The information is often called rumors and gossip. Grapevine information can begin with anyone in the organization and can flow in any direction. Employees complain, talk about sports and news events, discuss work-related matters such as layoffs and personnel changes, and whisper secrets about coworkers through the grapevine.

13-1 APPLYING THE CONCEPT

Communication Flow

Identify the form of communication flow occurring for each statement.

A. vertical downward
B. vertical upward
C. horizontal
D. grapevine

____ 1. "Arjun, please take this package to the mailroom for me right now."

____ 2. "Hey, Carl, have you heard that Paul and Helen were caught . . ."

____ 3. "Juanita, will you come here and hold this so I can get it straight?"

____ 4. "Tomas, here is the report you asked me to type. Check it and I'll make changes."

____ 5. "Kyra, I have two new customers who want to set up charge accounts. Please rush the credit check so we can increase business."

INFORMATION TECHNOLOGY

Today's technology has made communication faster and easier,[8] and technology will affect your career.[9] Many firms have computer information systems and an executive who oversees all aspects of information technology. Generally, this executive has the title of chief information officer (CIO).

Data are unorganized facts and figures, whereas *information* is data converted into a form that helps people do their jobs. Useful information has three qualities:

• Timely—current and available when you need it

• Relevant—suited to the situation, accurate, complete but concise

• Understandable—in a form that is easy to comprehend

Communication often takes place through the use of information technology. *Information technology (IT)* refers to the technology used to store, process, and distribute useful information. IT has enabled productivity gains that have reduced the cost of information and has created new opportunities. By effectively using IT in its warehousing, distribution, and inventory systems to keep its costs and prices low, **Walmart** is the leading retailer.

Let's discuss the Internet, e-commerce, wireless technology, and cloud computing briefly.

The Internet is a global collection of computer networks linked together to exchange data and information, and the *World Wide Web (WWW)* is a segment of the Internet in which information is presented in the form of Web pages. The Internet has opened up new avenues for communication, such as email, instant messaging, chat rooms, blogging, and VoIP, as well as e-commerce. More than 2 billion people, with a global population of 7 billion, use the Internet, and more than 80 percent of Americans have Internet access.[10]

Facebook (Case Question 1) can send information throughout an organization, as well as individually, horizontally, vertically, and through the grapevine, but its primary information technology channel used is the Internet, which can be wireless.

Electronic commerce (e-commerce) consists of the buying and selling of products and services over electronic systems, typically the Internet. Exhibit 13-2 illustrates the various types of e-commerce. **Amazon.com** is a leading retail e-commerce company, but you may not realize that **eBay** has a commerce platform

13-1 JOIN THE DISCUSSION ETHICS & SOCIAL RESPONSIBILITY

The Grapevine

The grapevine is commonly used to spread rumors and gossip. Most grapevine information is harmless and informs employees of what is going on in the firm. However, some, especially talk regarding work-related matters and coworkers, can destroy trust and sabotage productivity.

1. Have you or anyone you know been hurt by rumors or gossip? Explain the situation and how you or the other person was hurt.

2. Do rumors and gossip help or hurt individuals and the organization?
3. Is it ethical and socially responsible to spread rumors and gossip?
4. Should employees gossip and spread rumors when they are not sure of the accuracy of the information they are spreading?
5. How should managers handle rumors and gossip?

(including PayPal) that touches $175 billion of commerce, almost 20 percent of all e-commerce.[11] Companies are also using social media such as **Facebook** and **LinkedIn** to communicate and conduct business.[12]

The trend toward *wireless communication* continues, as people are becoming increasingly mobile. E-commerce is also being called *mobile commerce (m-commerce)* as wireless handheld devices such as cell phones and personal digital assistants (PDAs) are being used to conduct business. Have you bought anything using your cell phone?

The idea behind *cloud computing* is that companies store data and software on the Internet, then access it and run it all over the Web from their office computers, which thereby don't need as much storage space or as much expensive

EXHIBIT 13-2 E-COMMERCE

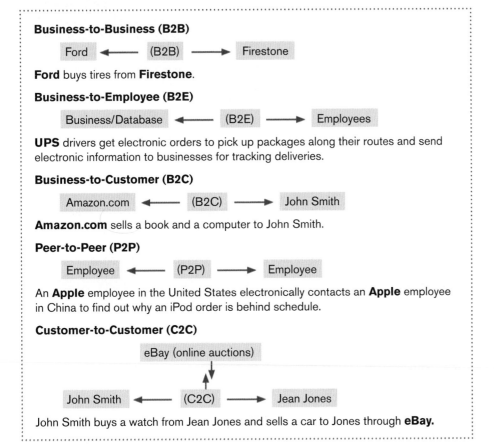

Business-to-Business (B2B)

Ford ◄——— (B2B) ———► Firestone

Ford buys tires from **Firestone**.

Business-to-Employee (B2E)

Business/Database ◄——— (B2E) ———► Employees

UPS drivers get electronic orders to pick up packages along their routes and send electronic information to businesses for tracking deliveries.

Business-to-Customer (B2C)

Amazon.com ◄——— (B2C) ———► John Smith

Amazon.com sells a book and a computer to John Smith.

Peer-to-Peer (P2P)

Employee ◄——— (P2P) ———► Employee

An **Apple** employee in the United States electronically contacts an **Apple** employee in China to find out why an iPod order is behind schedule.

Customer-to-Customer (C2C)

eBay (online auctions)

John Smith ◄——— (C2C) ———► Jean Jones

John Smith buys a watch from Jean Jones and sells a car to Jones through **eBay.**

software. Cloud-computing customers do not own the physical infrastructure where they store their data and software, instead avoiding capital expenditure by renting usage from a third-party provider. They consume resources as a service and pay only for resources that they use. Major cloud service providers include **Amazon.com, EMC2, Google, HP, IBM,** and **Salesforce**.

The Dark Side of the Internet and Cell phones. Let's discuss the negative side of IT.

In a survey, 81 percent of U.S. professionals say they *work harder* today than they did five years ago because of modern technology.[13] Cell phones and hand-held devices keep people connected to the office, *blurring work–life balance.* In a recent survey, 61 percent of respondents said that they take business-related calls and email after work hours and during weekends.[14] Do you?

As companies and consumers continue to use the Internet for business, computer *security* and *identity theft* have become problems. Scores of banks and e-commerce giants, from **JPMorgan** to **Walmart**, have been hit, sometimes repeatedly, by hackers and online fraud schemes. So organizations need to protect themselves against *cyber-theft.*[15]

Although technology is supposed to increase productivity, people *lose time* every day due to interruptions and distractions that deteriorate workers' ability to concentrate. As discussed in Chapter 5, Time Management, people multitasking by constantly checking their screens decrease the speed at which they can get their work done—as multitasking is a myth because you can't concentrate on two thinking tasks at the same time.

13-2 JOIN THE DISCUSSION ETHICS & SOCIAL RESPONSIBILITY

Should Personal Cell Phones Be Banned at Work?

As discussed, employees are wasting a lot of time at work either using their companies' computers or their own personal cell phones. To help prevent employees wasting time, organizations are monitoring the use of their company's technology and banning personal cell phones at work.

1. Is it ethical and socially responsible for employees to use company time and perhaps its technology for personal use? Should employees get paid for doing personal things at work?
2. Is it ethical and socially responsible for companies to monitor employee use of their technology? Should they monitor?
3. Is it ethical and socially responsible for companies to ban the use of employee personal technology on the job? Should they ban personal cell phones at work?

Every day many employees are *doing personal work on the job,* such as using the company computer to email and IM friends and family and to visit websites such as **Facebook** and to shop. Employees are wasting so much time that employers are blocking employee access to social media websites. Companies are also monitoring employee computer use and email to stop the abuse. But with monitoring comes the question of employee privacy and legal issues. Many employees are getting around the issue of using the company computer by using their personal cell phones, so some companies are banning the use of personal technology at work.[16] In a survey, 23 percent of recent graduates said they wouldn't take a job if they couldn't use their cell phones for personal calls/texts.[17] Would you?

LO 13-2

List the four steps in the interpersonal communication process.

THE INTERPERSONAL COMMUNICATION PROCESS AND COMMUNICATION BARRIERS

We now turn to interpersonal communications, or one-on-one and small-group communications.[18] You need to be able to talk to people.[19] We are expected to work well in groups and communicate with ease.[20] We need to be open to conversations, and asking questions and listening are crucial[21] as we all engage in the communication process. Exhibit 13-3 illustrates the communication process, which is discussed next, followed by barriers that interfere with interpersonal communications.

EXHIBIT 13-3   THE COMMUNICATION PROCESS

2. Message is transmitted through a channel.

1. Sender encodes the message and selects the transmission channel.

Sender

3. Receiver decodes the message and decides if feedback is needed.

Receiver

4. Feedback, response, or new message may be transmitted through a channel.

The sender and receiver continually change roles as they communicate.

The Interpersonal Communication Process

The **communication process** *takes place between a sender who encodes a message and transmits it through a channel to a receiver who decodes it and may give feedback.*

Stage 1. The sender encodes the Message and selects the transmission channel. The *sender* of the message is the person who initiates the communication. The *message* is the information and meaning communicated. **Encoding** *is the sender's process of putting the message into a form that the receiver will understand.* Your selection of words is important,[22] because your words and how you say them can help or hurt the flow of communications. The message is transmitted through a **communication channel**—*the means or medium by which a message is transmitted; the three primary channels are oral, nonverbal, and written.* You should determine the most appropriate channel to meet the needs of the situation. We will discuss message transmission channels in more detail in the next section of the chapter. Regardless of the channel, you need to use basic communication skills[23] that we discuss throughout this chapter.

Stage 2. The sender transmits the message. After the sender encodes the message and selects the channel, he or she transmits the message through the channel to the receiver(s).

Stage 3. The receiver decodes the message and decides if feedback is needed. The person receiving the message decodes it. **Decoding** *is the receiver's process of translating a message into a meaningful form.* The receiver interprets the meaning of the message and decides if feedback, a response, or a new message is needed. With oral communication, feedback is commonly given immediately. However, with written communication, feedback may be delayed.

communication process The process that takes place between a sender who encodes a message and transmits it through a channel to a receiver who decodes it and may give feedback.

encoding The sender's process of putting the message into a form that the receiver will understand.

communication channel The means or medium by which a message is transmitted; the three primary channels are oral, nonverbal, and written.

decoding The receiver's process of translating a message into a meaningful form.

WORK
APPLICATION 13-2

Give an example of a message that might be transmitted in a work setting. Be sure to illustrate the four steps in the communication process, state the channel, and note if feedback was given.

Stage 4. Feedback: A response or a new message may be transmitted. After the receiver decodes the message, he or she may give feedback to the sender. You should realize that the role of sender and receiver can be changed during a communication exchange. Remain open to messages being sent back from the receiver.

Communication Barriers

Exhibit 13-4 depicts a number of common barriers to communication.

EXHIBIT 13-4 MAJOR COMMUNICATION BARRIERS

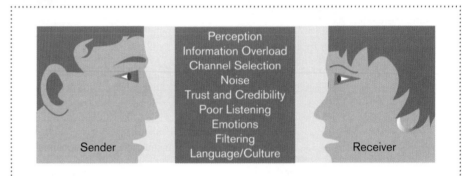

Perception. As messages are transmitted, receivers perceive them and translate them so that they make sense to them.[24] *Semantics* and *jargon* can be communication barriers, because the same word often means different things to different people.

To overcome perception problems, you need to consider how the other person will most likely perceive the message and try to encode and transmit it appropriately. Be careful not to use jargon with people who are not familiar with the terminology, especially people from countries with different cultures.

Information Overload. There is a limit to the amount of information people can understand at any given time. Information overload is a common problem because we are often presented with too much information to comprehend in a short time.

To minimize information overload, send messages in a quantity that the receiver can understand. When sending an oral message, do not talk for too long without checking to be sure the receiver understands the message as you intended.

Channel Selection. Use of an inappropriate channel can result in missed communication. For example, most young people like to text, but many older ones don't text.

Before sending a message, give careful thought to selecting the most effective channel. We discuss channel selection in the next section.

Noise. Noise during the transmission of a message can disturb or confuse the receiver. Noise is anything that interferes with message transmission. A machine or people may make noise that makes it difficult to hear, the sender may not speak loud enough for the receiver to hear well, or a radio/ TV or a phone call may distract the receiver, causing interpretation errors.

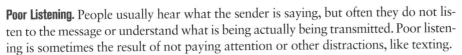

13-2 APPLYING THE CONCEPT

Communication Barriers

Identify the communication barrier indicated by each statement.

- A. perception
- B. information overload
- C. channel selection
- D. noise
- E. trust and credibility
- F. not listening
- G. emotions
- H. filtering

_____ 6. "Chill out. You shouldn't be upset."

_____ 7. "No questions" (meanwhile thinking, "I was lost back on step 1 and don't know what to ask").

_____ 8. "We are right on schedule" (meanwhile thinking, "We are actually behind, but we'll catch up").

_____ 9. "I said I'd do it in a little while. It's only been 15 minutes. Why do you expect it done by now?"

_____ 10. "You don't know what you are talking about. I'll do it my way."

To overcome noise, consider the physical surroundings before transmitting a message. Try to keep noise to a minimum. If possible, stop the noise or distraction or move to a quiet location.

Trust and Credibility. During communication, receivers take into account the trust they have in the senders, as well as the senders' credibility.[25] When receivers do not trust senders or do not believe senders know what they are talking about, they are reluctant to accept the message.[26]

To improve others' level of trust in you, be open and honest with people.[27] If people catch you in a lie, they may never trust you again. To gain and maintain credibility, get the facts straight before you communicate, and send clear, correct messages.

Poor Listening. People usually hear what the sender is saying, but often they do not listen to the message or understand what is being actually being transmitted. Poor listening is sometimes the result of not paying attention or other distractions, like texting.

One method to help ensure that people listen to your message involves getting their full attention and questioning them and having them paraphrase the message back to you. When listening, follow the listening tips presented later in this chapter.

Emotions. Everyone has emotions, and emotions can interfere with communication and make it difficult for people to be objective and to listen.[28]

When communicating, remain calm and be careful not to make others emotional through your behavior. Later in this chapter you will learn how to calm an emotional employee.

Filtering. _Filtering_ is the process of altering or distorting information to project a more favorable image. When people are asked to report progress toward objectives, they may stress the positive and deemphasize or even leave out the negative side.[29] Some people will even lie, but don't because the truth will catch up with you and you will lose trust and credibility.[30]

In today's global village, managers need to develop intercultural communication skills so they can work with people across cultures to achieve organizational goals. Photo from Blend Images/Superstock.

WORK
APPLICATION 13-3

Give two examples of different communication barriers you encountered at work. Explain how each barrier could have been overcome.

To help eliminate filtering, treat errors as a learning experience rather than as an opportunity to blame and criticize employees. You will learn about criticism later in this chapter. Using an open-door policy can create and support a two-way communication climate.

Language/Culture. In the global village, people that come from different cultures and speak different languages need to communicate. If you can't communicate in the same language, you will encounter a major barrier.

MESSAGE TRANSMISSION CHANNELS

When encoding a message, the sender should give careful consideration to selecting the channel. Channels (the ways in which messages are transmitted) include oral, nonverbal, and written forms. Exhibit 13-5 lists the major message transmission channels.

EXHIBIT 13-5   MESSAGE TRANSMISSION CHANNELS

Oral Communication	Nonverbal Communication	Written Communication
Face-to-face conversations	Setting	Memos
Meetings	Body language	Letters
Presentations	Facial expressions	Reports
Telephone conversations	Vocal quality	Email
Voice mail messages	Gestures	Faxes
	Posture	Bulletin boards
	Posters (pictures)	Posters (words)
		Newsletters

LO 13-3

State the major advantages and disadvantages of oral communication and written communication.

Oral Communication

Here we discuss the five most common channels for oral communication. The major advantages of oral communication are that it is usually easier and faster than written communication and it encourages feedback. The disadvantage is that there is usually no record of such communication. In the global village, video communications/Skype often replaces face-to-face meetings, and presentations.[31] Try not to say "um" or other annoying things when using oral communications.[32]

- *Face-to-face conversations* are important, even though we have phones and email/IM/texting,[33] especially between managers and employees.[34] It is the appropriate channel for delegating tasks, coaching, disciplining, sharing information, answering questions, checking progress toward objectives, and developing and maintaining good interpersonal relations.

- *Meetings are common today* (Chapter 8). The most common type of meeting is the brief, informal get-together of a manager with two or more employees. Meetings are appropriate for coordinating employee activities, delegating a task to a group, and resolving employee conflicts.

- *Presentations* are common in the workplace today, and few skills are more important to mangers.[35] The focus of your presentation should be on what you can do for the audience.[36] Be sure to (1) begin your presentation with a purpose statement and an overview of the main points to be covered, (2) discuss your main points in the detail necessary to get the message across, and (3) summarize the purpose, main points, and any action required of the audience. *The use of presentation software* such as PowerPoint (PP) is popular. However, there are some things to keep in mind.[37] The audience should be looking at you, not reading the PP slides. Flashy slides can actually distract from your message, so focus more on getting the point across clearly and concisely. Don't simply read your PP; the slides should just be an outline to help you talk to the audience about your topic points.

- The key to developing your presentation skills is preparation and practice. There are many websites and organizations, such as **Toastmasters International (www.toastmasters.org)**, that can help you develop your public speaking skills.

- *Telephone Conversations.* The amount of time employees spend on the telephone varies greatly with the job. The telephone is the appropriate channel for quick exchanges of information and for checking up on something; phone calls often save managers from having to travel. However, a telephone conversation is generally an inappropriate channel for discussing or dealing with personnel matters. Face-to-face and phone conversations are more effective and faster than email and responding back and forth multiple times.

- *Voice Mail.* Voice mail is most commonly used to leave messages for people who are unable to answer the phone and sometimes in place of written messages. Voice mail is appropriate for sending short messages containing information that need not be in written form.

Nonverbal Communication

Every time you talk to someone face to face, you also use nonverbal communication. **Nonverbal communication** *consists of messages sent without words.* It includes the *setting* of the communication (physical surroundings) and *body language.* The impact of any face-to-face communication is dependent on body language, which includes (1) facial expressions (eye contact and a wink or a smile, a frown, or a dirty look), (2) vocal quality (not the words used, but the way they are said—calmly or urgently, fast or slowly, softly or loudly), (3) gestures (such as moving the hands, pointing and signaling, and nodding the head),[38] and (4) posture (sitting up straight or slouching, leaning back or forward, crossing arms and/or legs). One of the weaknesses of writing (email/text) is you lose most of the nonverbal communications.[39]

To make communication effective, be aware of your nonverbal communication and make sure it is consistent with your oral communication.[40] When your oral communication conflicts with your nonverbal communication, people tend to give more weight to the nonverbal communication—actions speak louder than words. You also want to be aware of other people's nonverbal communication because it reveals their feelings and attitudes toward the communication. When talking to people, use nonverbal communication to convey openness to messages. Smile, face the person, and use appropriate eye contact for 3 to 5 seconds;[41] lean forward a bit and gesture frequently to convey that you are listening and are interested. Do not cross your arms or legs (signs of being closed to communication), and speak in a pleasant, calm tone of voice. A harsh tone of voice or a nasty look can be more humiliating than words.

nonverbal communication
Messages sent without words.

Advertising

Companies use oral, nonverbal, and written communication to advertise their products in order to increase sales. Selecting the best words to sell a product or service is important. However, some of the terms used in ads are misleading or deceptive, even though the words themselves are legal. For example, some food products are labeled with the word *natural* but are highly processed, such as products including a lot of white sugar. Also, ads for some processed snack foods use the word *natural,* which leads people to think the snacks are healthy, when in fact others

classify them as junk food, such as potato chips. The obesity task force of the Food and Drug Administration (FDA) is trying to crack down on misleading labels and ads and is calling for warnings and fines for violators.

1. Is it ethical and socially responsible for food companies to use terms (like *natural*) that can be misleading without a clear legal definition?
2. How should the FDA define *natural* so that the word is not used to mislead people?

Lovie Smith was the head coach of the **NFL Chicago Bears**. When Smith got mad, he stared straight ahead in silence. His players called it "the Lovie Look" and said it was more frightening—and more of a warning to play better—than his yelling angry words.[42]

Written Communication

With today's technology, we write all the time.[43] Nothing can reveal your communication weaknesses more clearly than poorly written letters, reports, emails, texts, and so on. Along with email, you are likely to encounter the following kinds of written communication in the workplace, many of which are used in conjunction with email:

WORK
APPLICATION 13-4

Give an example of an oral message and a written message you received at work, and specify the channel of each.

- *Memos* are commonly used to send intraorganizational messages.
- *Letters* are commonly used to communicate with people outside of the organization. Memos and letters are sent electronically (in the form of emails or faxes) more often than they are sent through the mail.
- *Reports* are used to convey information, evaluation, analysis, and/or recommendations to management or colleagues. Reports can also be sent by fax or as an attachment to email.
- *Bulletin board and blog notices* usually supplement other forms of communication. Many companies today have electronic bulletin boards and blogs for their employees to post on.
- *Posters (or signs)* are commonly used as reminders of important information, such as a mission statement or safety instructions. Posters can also be nonverbal, or graphic, communication. An example is the universal symbol that bans or forbids some activity: a picture of what you are not supposed to do, circled and with a line through it.
- *Newsletters* are used to convey general information to all employees. Many organizations send out company newsletters through email or post them on e-bulletin boards.

It is often recommended that you write like you talk.[44] Written communication is appropriate when detailed instructions are required, when something needs to be documented, for formal or official messages (especially those containing facts and figures), and when there is a need to give a number of people the exact same information. The major advantage of written communication is that it provides a record of what was communicated. The major disadvantages are that it usually takes longer and it hinders feedback.

13-3 APPLYING THE CONCEPT

Channel Selection

For each of the five communication situations, select the most appropriate channel for transmitting the message. If you would use a combination of channels, place the letter(s) of the additional channel you would use at the end of the situation.

Oral communication

A. face to face
B. meeting
C. presentation
D. telephone

Written communication

E. email
F. memo
G. letter
H. report

I. bulletin board
J. poster
K. newsletter

____ 11. You are waiting for FedEx to deliver an important letter, and you want to know if it is in the mail room yet. ____

____ 12. Employees have been leaving the lights on in the break room when no one is in it. You want them to shut the lights off. ____

____ 13. José, Jamal, and Sam will be working as a team on a new project. You need to explain the project to them. ____

____ 14. John has come in late for work again. You want this practice to stop. ____

____ 15. You have exceeded your departmental goals and want your boss to know about it, because this success should have a positive influence on your upcoming performance appraisal. ____

Combining Channels

Nonverbal communication and oral communication are almost always combined. You can also combine oral and written communication (as in a presentation) or even oral, nonverbal, and written communication. Using combined channels is appropriate when the message is important and you want to ensure that employees attend to and understand it. For example, managers sometimes send a memo, then follow up with a personal visit or telephone call to see if there are any questions. Managers often formally document a face-to-face meeting, particularly in a disciplinary situation.

Facebook (Case Question 2) involves using both nonverbal and written communication. Users can post pictures (nonverbal communication) and messages to their and others' Walls (written communication). Facebook includes other forms of written communication such as text messaging and instant messaging as well as traditional email. Facebook also wants to be your home page on your cell phone.

Selecting the Message Transmission Channel

Media richness refers to the amount of information and meaning conveyed through a channel. The more information and meaning, the "richer" the channel. Face-to-face communication is the richest channel because it allows the sender and receiver to take full advantage of both oral and nonverbal communication. The telephone is less rich than talking face to face because most nonverbal cues are lost when you cannot see facial expressions and gestures. All forms of oral communication are richer than written communication because oral communication allows transmission of at least some nonverbal cues, which are lost with written messages.

It's important to select the most appropriate channel of transmission for any message. As a general guide, use oral channels for sending difficult and unusual messages, written channels for transmitting simple and routine messages to several people or messages that contain facts and figures or detailed instructions, and combined channels for important messages that recipients need to attend to and understand.

LO 13-4

State a general guide to channel selection.

SENDING MESSAGES

We are constantly pitching our ideas.[45] An important part of a manager's job is to give instructions, which is sending a message. Have you ever heard a manager say, "This isn't what I asked for"? When this happens, it is usually the manager's fault. As a manager, you must take 100 percent of the responsibility for ensuring that your messages are transmitted clearly. This section discusses the processes of planning and sending messages and how to properly check the receiver's understanding of the message.

Planning the Message

The vast majority of messages you send and receive in the workplace are quite simple and straightforward: "Please copy this document." Many such messages are transmitted orally and face to face or in a brief memo email. Such straightforward messages need minimal planning, because they are routine. However, sometimes the message you need to transmit is difficult, unusual, or especially important. As noted earlier, for these kinds of messages, the richer the channel, the better. Before sending a message, answer these questions:

- *What?* What is the goal of the message? Set an objective.[46]
- *Who?* Determine who should receive the message.
- *How?* Plan how you will encode the message so that it will be understood. Select the appropriate channel(s) for the audience and situation.
- *When?* When will the message be transmitted? Timing is important.
- *Where?* Decide where the message will be transmitted (setting).

The Message-Sending Process

LO 13-5

List the five steps in the process of sending face-to-face messages.

As noted earlier, oral channels are richer than other channels, and face-to-face, oral communication is best when the message you must transmit is a difficult or complex one. When sending a face-to-face message, follow these steps in the message-sending process:

Step 1. **Develop rapport.** Put the receiver at ease. It is usually appropriate to begin communication with small talk related to the message to make a connection.[47]

Step 2. **State your communication objective.** It is helpful for the receiver to know the objective (result) of the communication before you explain the details.

Step 3. **Transmit your message.** Tell the receivers whatever you want them to know calmly and with respect.

Step 4. **Check the receiver's understanding.** When giving information, ask direct questions and/or paraphrase. Simply asking, "Do you have any questions?" does not check understanding.

Step 5. **Get a commitment and follow up.** If the message involves assigning a task, make sure that the message recipient can do the task and have it done by a certain time or date. Follow up to ensure that the necessary action has been taken.

message-sending process
A process that includes (1) developing rapport, (2) stating your communication objective, (3) transmitting your message, (4) checking the receiver's understanding, and (5) getting a commitment and following up.

Model 13–1 lists the five steps in the message-sending process.

MODEL 13-1 THE MESSAGE-SENDING PROCESS

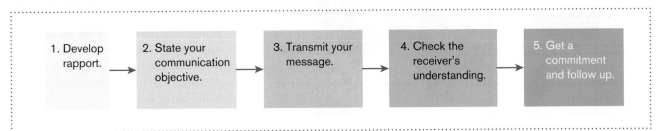

1. Develop rapport. → 2. State your communication objective. → 3. Transmit your message. → 4. Check the receiver's understanding. → 5. Get a commitment and follow up.

Checking Understanding: Feedback

Feedback *is information that verifies a message.* Questioning, paraphrasing, and inviting comments and suggestions are all means of obtaining feedback that check understanding. Ask for feedback,[48] because feedback increases performance.[49] The best way to make sure communication has taken place is to get feedback from the receiver of the message through questioning and paraphrasing.[50] **Paraphrasing** *is the process of restating a message in one's own words.* If the receiver of the message can answer the question or paraphrase the message, communication has taken place.

The Common Approach to Getting Feedback on Messages and Why It Doesn't Work. The most common approach to getting feedback is to send the entire message and then ask, "Do you have any questions?" Feedback usually does not follow because people tend not to ask questions. To ask a question, especially if no one else does, is often considered an admission of not paying attention or not being bright enough to understand the message.

After managers send a message and ask if there are questions, they often make another common error. They assume that if no one asks a question, the communication is complete. In reality, recipients may have misunderstood the message. When this occurs, the result is often wasted time, materials, and effort.

How to Get Feedback on Messages. Use the following four guidelines when seeking feedback on messages.

- *Be open to feedback.* There are no dumb questions, so invite questions.[51] When someone asks a question, be responsive and patiently answer and explain things clearly. If people sense that you get upset if they ask questions, they will not ask. Also, if managers get upset with employees who bring them bad news (negative feedback), employees will tend to avoid these managers and keep bad news to themselves.

- *Be aware of nonverbal communication.* Make sure that your nonverbal communication encourages feedback. For example, if you say, "I encourage questions," but you look at people as though they are stupid or you act impatient when they do ask, people will learn not to ask questions. You must also read nonverbal communication accurately. For example, if you are explaining a task to an employee and he or she has a puzzled expression, the employee is probably confused but may not be willing to say so. In such a case, you should stop and clarify things before going on.

- *Ask questions.* When you send messages, you should know whether recipients understand the messages before taking action. Direct questions

WORK APPLICATION 13-5

Recall a specific task that a boss assigned to you. Identify which steps in the face-to-face message-sending process he or she did and did not use.

LO 13-6

Describe paraphrasing, and explain why it is useful.

WORK APPLICATION 13-6

Recall a past or present boss. How effective was this person at getting feedback? Was the boss open to feedback and aware of nonverbal communication? Did the boss ask questions and ask you to paraphrase?

feedback Information that verifies a message.

paraphrasing The process of restating a message in one's own words.

Ending messages or presentations with "Do you have any questions?" is not the most effective way to get feedback. What are some more useful ways to obtain feedback? Photo from Vetta Stock Photo/iStockphoto.

about the specific information you have given will indicate if the receiver has been listening and whether he or she understands enough to give an appropriate reply. If the response is not accurate, you need to repeat the message, giving more examples or elaborating further.

- *Paraphrase.* The most accurate indicator of understanding is paraphrasing. How you ask the receiver to paraphrase will affect his or her attitude. For example, saying, "Tell me what I just said so that I can be sure you will not make a mistake as usual," would probably result in defensive behavior or an error by the employee. Consider these examples of proper requests for paraphrasing:

"Now tell me what you are going to do so that we will be sure we are in agreement."

"Would you tell me what you are going to do so that I can be sure that I explained myself clearly?"

Notice that the second statement takes the pressure off the employee. The sender is asking for a check on his or her own ability, not that of the employee. These types of requests for paraphrasing should result in a positive attitude toward the message and the sender. They show concern for the employee and for communicating effectively.

The most difficult part of the message-sending process to accomplish when using **Facebook (Case Question 2)** is checking the receiver's understanding. This is difficult because you do not know if the receiver has even read the message. Thus, it is impossible to give feedback if you do not know if all the receivers have read the message or not.

LO 13-7

List and explain the three parts of the process of receiving messages.

Receiving Messages

The third step in the communication process requires the receiver to decode the message and decide if feedback is needed. This section discusses the process of receiving messages.

The Message-Receiving Process

The **message-receiving process** *includes listening, analyzing, and checking understanding.* The parts of the message-receiving process are illustrated in Model 13–2.

message-receiving process A process that includes listening, analyzing, and checking understanding.

Listening. *Listening* is crucial,[52] and it is the process of giving a speaker your undivided attention. It is one of the most important business and personal skills you can develop. Complete Self-Assessment 13–1 to determine the level and the quality of your listening skills.

MODEL 13-2   THE MESSAGE-RECEIVING PROCESS

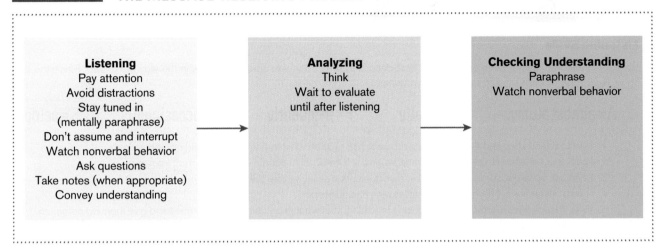

Analyzing. *Analyzing* is the process of thinking about, decoding, and evaluating the message. As the speaker sends the message, you should be doing two things:

- *Thinking.* To help overcome the discrepancy between your listening speed and people's rate of speaking, use the speed of your brain positively. Listen actively by mentally repeating or paraphrasing, organizing, summarizing, reviewing, and interpreting often. These activities will help you to do an effective job of decoding the message.

- *Waiting to Evaluate Until After Listening.* You should listen to the entire message first, then come to your conclusions. When you evaluate, base your conclusion on the facts presented rather than on stereotypes and politics.

When analyzing information on **Facebook (Case Question 3)**, you have to read the message carefully; think about the message, whether it be a written message or a nonverbal message such as a picture; evaluate the message; shape an opinion; and then formulate questions if you have any in order to get a better understanding.

Checking Understanding. *Checking understanding* is the process of giving feedback. After you have listened to the message (or while listening if it's a long message), check your understanding of the message by doing two things:

- *Paraphrasing.* Give feedback by paraphrasing the message back to the sender. When you can paraphrase the message correctly, you convey that you have listened and understood the other person.[54] Now you are ready to offer your ideas, advice, solution, decision, or whatever the sender of the message is talking to you about.

- *Watching nonverbal behavior.* As you speak, watch the other person's nonverbal communication. If the person does not seem to understand what you are talking about, clarify the message before finishing the conversation.

Do you talk more than you listen? Ask your boss, coworkers, or friends, who will give you an honest answer. Regardless of how much you listen, if you follow the guidelines discussed in this section, you will become a better listener. Review items 1, 4, 5, 6, 9, 12, 13, 14, and 15 in the Self-Assessment on page 400, which are the statements that describe good listening skills. Effective listening requires responding to the message to ensure mutual understanding.

13-1 SELF ASSESSMENT

Listening Skills

For each statement, select the response that best describes how often you actually behave in the way described. Place the letter A, U, F, O, or S on the line before each statement.

A = almost always   U = usually   F = frequently   O = occasionally   S = seldom

_____ 1. I like to listen to people talk. I encourage others to talk by showing interest, smiling, nodding, and so forth.

_____ 2. I pay closer attention to people who are more similar to me than to people who are different from me.

_____ 3. I evaluate people's words and nonverbal communication ability as they talk.

_____ 4. I avoid distractions; if it's noisy, I suggest moving to a quiet spot.

_____ 5. When people interrupt me when I'm doing something, I put what I was doing out of my mind and give them my complete attention.

_____ 6. When people are talking, I allow them time to finish. I do not interrupt, anticipate what they are going to say, or jump to conclusions.

_____ 7. I tune people out who do not agree with my views.

_____ 8. While another person is talking or a professor is lecturing, my mind wanders to personal topics.

_____ 9. While another person is talking, I pay close attention to the nonverbal communication so I can fully understand what he or she is trying to communicate.

_____ 10. I tune out and pretend I understand when the topic is difficult for me to understand.

_____ 11. When another person is talking, I think about and prepare what I am going to say in reply.

_____ 12. When I think there is something missing from or contradictory in what someone says, I ask direct questions to get the person to explain the idea more fully.

_____ 13. When I don't understand something, I let the other person know I don't understand.

_____ 14. When listening to other people, I try to put myself in their position and see things from their perspective.

_____ 15. During conversations, I repeat back to the other person what has been said in my own words to be sure I understand what has been said.

If people you talk to regularly answered these questions about you, would they have the same responses that you selected? To find out, have friends fill out the questions using "you" (or your name) rather than "I." Then compare answers.

To determine your score, give yourself 5 points for each A, 4 for each U, 3 for each F, 2 for each O, and 1 for each S for statements 1, 4, 5, 6, 9, 12, 13, 14, and 15. For items 2, 3, 7, 8, 10, and 11 the scores reverse: 5 points for each S, 4 for each

RESPONDING TO MESSAGES

The fourth and last step in the communication process is responding to the message. How we respond to messages is important.[55] However, not all messages require a response.

With oral communication, the sender often expects the receiver to respond to the message. When the receiver does respond, the roles are reversed, as the receiver now becomes the sender of a message. Roles can continue to change throughout the conversation. In this section, we discuss five response styles, how to deal with emotional people, and how to give and receive criticism.

Response Styles

As a sender transmits a message, how the receiver responds to the message directly affects the communication. The response should be appropriate for the situation. Five typical response styles are shown in Exhibit 13-6.

Suppose an employee voices the following complaint to her supervisor:

"You supervise me so closely that you disrupt my ability to do my job."

O, 3 for each F, 2 for each U, and 1 for each A. Write the number of points on the lines next to the response letters. Now add your total number of points. Your score should be between 15 and 75. Note where your score falls on the continuum below. Generally, the higher your score, the better your listening skills.

Poor listener   Good listener

15____20____25____30____35____40____45____50____55____60____65____70____75

With oral communication, the key to successfully understanding the message is listening.[53] As the speaker sends the message, you should be doing the following:

- *Paying attention.* When people begin to talk, stop what you are doing and give them your complete attention immediately. If you miss the first few words, you may miss the message.

- *Avoiding distractions.* Keep your eyes on the speaker. Do not fiddle with pens, papers, or other distractions like texting. If you are in a noisy or distracting place, suggest moving to a quiet spot or talking later.

- *Staying tuned in.* While the other person is talking, try not to let your mind wander. If the topic is difficult, ask questions. Do not think about what you are going to say in reply; just listen. As you listen, mentally repeat or paraphrase the message to stay tuned in so you don't drop information.

- *Not assuming and interrupting.* People make listening mistakes when they hear the first few words of a sentence, finish it in their own minds, and miss the second half. Listen to the entire message without interrupting the speaker.

- *Watching nonverbal behavior.* People sometimes say one thing and mean something else. So watch as you listen to be sure that the speaker's eyes, body, and face are sending the same message as the verbal message. If something seems out of sync, get it cleared up by asking questions.

- *Asking questions.* When you feel there is something missing or contradictory in what is being said, or when you just do not understand, ask direct questions to get the person to explain the idea more fully.

- *Taking notes (when appropriate).* In work settings, part of listening is writing down important things (such as instructions) so that you can remember them later and documenting them when necessary. Always be ready to take notes.

- *Conveying understanding.* The way to let the speaker know you are listening to the message is to use verbal cues, such as "uh-huh," "I see," and "I understand." You should also use nonverbal communication, such as eye contact, appropriate facial expressions, nodding of the head, or leaning slightly forward in your chair to indicate you are interested and listening.

We will consider how a manager might respond to this complaint using each response style.

Advising. *Advising responses* provide evaluation, personal opinion, direction, or instructions. Employees often come to a manager for advice on how to do something. Advising tends to close or limit discussion or direct the flow of communication away from the sender to the receiver.

Giving advice is appropriate when you are explicitly asked for it. However, automatically giving advice tends to build dependence. Develop employees' abilities to think things through and to make decisions. When asked for advice, ask, "What do you think is the best way to handle this situation?"

A manager's advising response to the employee's complaint might be "You need my directions to do a good job, since you lack experience" or "I disagree. You need my instructions, and I need to check your work." Note that in this situation the employee did not ask for advice, but it was given anyway.

Diverting. *Diverting responses* switch the focus of the communication to a new message—in other words, they change the subject. Like advising, diverting tends

WORK APPLICATION 13-7

Refer to the Self-Assessment. What is your weakest listening skill? Give an example of how your listening skills have had an impact on you at work.

EXHIBIT 13-6   FIVE TYPICAL RESPONSE STYLES

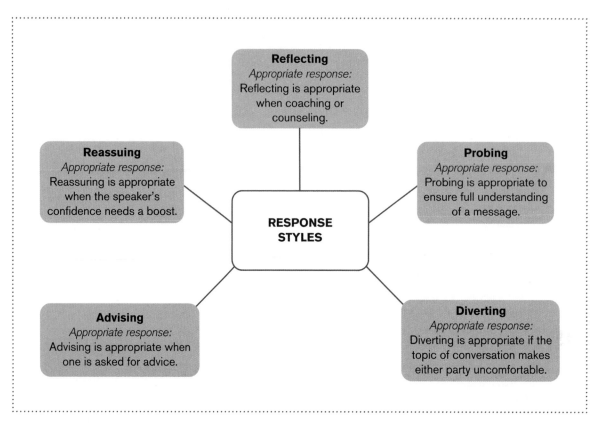

to redirect, close, or limit the flow of communication. Diverting responses used during the early stages of receiving the message may cause the sender to feel that the message is not worth discussing or that the other party's message is more important.

A diverting response can be appropriate when either party is uncomfortable with the topic, such as politics or religion.

A manager's diverting response to the employee's complaint might be, "You've reminded me of a manager I once had who . . ."

Probing. Probing responses ask the speaker to give more information about some aspect of the message. Probing can be useful when a listener needs to get a better understanding of the situation. When probing, "what" questions are preferable to "why" questions.

Probing is appropriate during the early stages of listening to a message to ensure that you fully understand the situation. After probing, responses in other styles are often needed.

A manager's probing response to the employee's complaint might be, "What do I do to cause you to say this?" Note that "Why do you feel this way?" is *not* an appropriate probing response.

Reassuring. Reassuring responses are given to reduce the intensity of the emotions associated with the message. Essentially you're saying, "Don't worry, everything will be OK" or "You can do it." You are trying to calm the sender.

Reassuring is appropriate when the other person lacks confidence. Encouraging responses that give praise can help employees develop confidence.

A manager's reassuring response to the employee's complaint might be, "Don't worry, I will not be supervising you so closely for much longer" or "Your work is improving, so I may be able to provide less direction soon."

Reflecting. **Reflecting responses** *paraphrase the message and communicate under-standing and acceptance to the sender.* When reflecting, be sure *not* to use the sender's exact words, or the person may feel you are mimicking him or her, not understanding, or not listening closely. Reflecting in your own words leads to the most effective communication and the best human relations.

Reflecting responses should be used when coaching and counseling. Such responses help make the sender feel listened to, understood, and free to explore the topic in more depth. As the communication progresses, it may be appropriate to change to other response styles. However, sometimes just reflective listening is all that is needed.[56]

A manager's reflecting response to the employee's complaint might be "My checking up on you annoys you?" or "You don't think I need to check up on you, is this what you mean?" Note that these responses allow the employee to express feelings and to direct the communication.

LO 13-8

Define reflecting responses, and state when they should be used.

WORK
APPLICATION 13-8

Recall two oral messages you received and your responses to them. Identify your response style, and give examples of responses you might have given using two other response styles.

13-4 APPLYING THE CONCEPT

Response Styles

Identify the response style exemplified in each statement.

A. advising
B. diverting
C. probing
D. reassuring
E. reflecting

Secretary: Boss, do you have a minute to talk?
Boss: Sure, what's up?
Secretary: Can you do something about all the swearing people do in the operations department? It carries

through these thin walls into my work area. It's disgusting. I'm surprised you haven't done anything.

Boss:

_____ 16. "I didn't know anyone was swearing. I'll look into it."

_____ 17. "You don't have to listen to it. Just ignore the swearing."

_____ 18. "Are you feeling well today?"

_____ 19. "So you find this swearing offensive?"

_____ 20. "What specific swear words are they saying that offend you?"

Dealing With Emotions

As a manager, you may receive a message from an employee or customer who is in an emotional state.[57] **Apple's** Steve Jobs was known to be emotional at times.[58] Emotions tend to complicate communication, but they can bring about new ideas and new ways of doing things. You should understand emotions and how to deal with them.

Emotions are important to an individual's behavior.[59] It doesn't really matter what people know or don't know; what counts is what they feel.[60] Understanding emotions to some extent depends on one's level of *emotional intelligence.* Emotional intelligence has five dimensions:[61] (1) self-awareness, or understanding your own emotions; (2) self-management, the ability to manage your own emotions; (3) self-motivation, the ability to persist through failure and setbacks; (4) empathy, the ability to understand others' emotions and to see things from their perspective; and (5) social skills that allow one to handle others' emotions. One's level of emotional intelligence is also called one's *emotional quotient,* or

LO 13-9

Discuss what should and should not be done to calm an emotional person.

reflecting responses Responses that paraphrase a message and communicate understanding and acceptance to the sender.

EQ (to parallel the notion of intelligence quotient, or IQ). Some companies have developed EQ tests that employees can take, as emotional intelligence is considered important to individual and organizational success. It has been said that you need an IQ, EQ, and "I got a clue" to succeed.

When dealing with emotional people, keep the following in mind:

- Feelings are subjective; they tell us people's attitudes and needs.
- Feelings are usually disguised as factual statements. For example, when people are hot, they tend to say "It's hot in here" rather than "I feel hot." When they are bored, they tend to say "This topic is boring" rather than "I'm feeling bored by this topic."
- Most important: feelings are neither right nor wrong.

Empathetic listening is one aspect of emotional intelligence. If you really want to understand where the other person is coming from, you need to see things from his or her perception. Photo from Digital Vision/Thinkstock.

People cannot choose their feelings or control them. However, they can control how they express feelings through behavior. For example, if Rachel, an employee, says "You *!!" (pick a word that would make you angry) to Louise, her manager, Louise will feel its impact. However, Louise has a choice about how she responds. She can express her feelings in a calm manner, or she can yell back, give Rachel a dirty look, write up a formal reprimand for Rachel's personnel file, and so on. Managers should encourage people to express their feelings in a positive way, but they can't allow employees to go around yelling at, swearing at, or intimidating others. Avoid getting caught up in others' emotions. Staying calm when dealing with an emotional person works much better than getting emotional, too.

Calming the Emotional Employee. When an employee comes to you in an emotional state, show some compassion,[62] as compassion is recognized as vital.[63] *Never* make condescending statements such as "You shouldn't be angry," "Don't be upset," "You're acting like a baby," or "Just sit down and be quiet." These types of statements only make the feelings stronger. You may get employees to shut up and show them who is boss, but effective communication will not take place. The problem will still exist, and your relations with the employee will suffer because of it, as will your relations with others who see or hear about what you said and did. So your responses should be empathetic.[64]

Reflective Empathic Responding. Empathic listening *is understanding and relating to another's feelings.* The empathic responder deals with feelings, content, and the underlying meaning being expressed in the message. Empathy is needed to develop human relationships based on trust.[65] Don't argue with emotional people. Instead, encourage them to express their feelings in a positive way. Empathically let them know that you understand how they feel. Do not agree or disagree with the feelings; simply identify them verbally. Paraphrase the feeling to the person. Use statements such as these: "You were *hurt* when you didn't get the assignment." "You *resent* Chani for not doing her share of the work; is that what you mean?" "You are *doubtful* that the job will be done on time; is that what you're saying?" After you make an empathic response, most employees will feel free to open up and tell you what's going on.

empathic listening Understanding and relating to another's feelings.

After you deal with emotions, you can proceed to work on content (solving problems). It may be wise to wait until a later time if emotions are very strong. You may find that just being willing to listen to others' feelings is often the solution.[66] Sometimes employees simply need to vent their emotions. A manager with strong listening skills may be just the solution employees need.

Criticism

While it's not something we look forward to, giving and getting criticism is a necessary part of life. Regardless of the role you are in, there are ways to give and receive criticism effectively.

Giving Criticism. An important part of the manager's job is to provide constructive criticism. Giving constructive criticism can lend much needed assistance to individuals by giving them feedback on things that can be improved and issues that can be avoided.[67] When providing criticism, do it quickly, concisely, and privately. Be honest, but don't be too negative, and give recommendations for improvement—improving should be the focus. Chapter 14 will provide more details on how to accomplish this task.

Criticism that moves upward is a different matter. Even when bosses ask, they usually don't want to hear personal criticism. If your boss asks you in a meeting for feedback on how good a manager he or she is or how he or she can improve, it may sound like the ideal opportunity to unload your complaints—but in such a situation, the first rule of thumb is to never publicly criticize your boss, even if specifically asked to do so. You are better off airing criticism in private. Don't criticize your boss behind his or her back, either; bosses often find out about it.

Getting Criticism. Criticism from your boss, peers, or employees is painful. People do not really enjoy being criticized, even when it is constructive, and many people handle it poorly. However, it is important to keep in mind that, more often than not, your boss and others want to help you succeed. Also, keep the phrase "no pain, no gain" in mind when it comes to criticism. If you want to improve your chances of having a successful career, seek honest feedback and use the feedback to improve your performance.[68] When you get criticism, whether you ask for it or not, view it as an opportunity to improve, stay calm (even when the other person is emotional), and don't get defensive. If you become defensive and emotional (and it is hard not to when you feel attacked), the person will stop giving feedback and you will not improve.[69]

INFORMATION SYSTEMS AND NETWORKS

Like any system, an information system has input, transformation, and output. Information systems (IS) have data as input, and they transform the data into information to help employees do their jobs and make decisions.[70] These systems are used to communicate with employees throughout organizations and on the interpersonal level.[71] In this section, we discuss types of information systems and information networks.

Types of Information Systems

Here are three primary types of information systems.

Transaction Processing Systems (TPS). *Transaction processing systems* are used to handle routine and recurring business matters. Organizations use transaction processing systems to record accounting transactions, such as accounts receivable

WORK
APPLICATION 13-9

Recall a situation in which a manager had to handle an emotional employee. Did the manager follow the guidelines for calming an emotional person? Did the manager use reflective, empathic responses?

WORK
APPLICATION 13-10

How would you rate yourself on your ability to accept criticism without getting emotional and defensive? How could you improve your ability to accept criticism?

LO 13-10

Describe the three primary types of information systems and their relationship.

and payable and payroll. Most large retail organizations use scanners to record sales transactions at the checkout counter. Banks process checks and deposits and record credit card transactions. Stockbrokers buy and sell stock for clients.

Management Information Systems (MIS). *Management information systems* transform data into the information employees need to do their work. Managers' work usually consists of running their units or departments, and the information provided by management information systems is commonly used for making routine decisions. Real-time tracking is done on MIS.

Executive information systems (EIS) are a form of MIS used by top-level managers. EISs place greater emphasis on integrating external data and information with internal information on critical success factors, which are often industry specific. In other words, EISs focus more on development and revision of nonroutine strategy, whereas MISs focus more on strategy implementation.

Decision Support Systems (DSS). Information processing is needed when making decisions,[72] and decision making has been professionalized with tools and procedures.[73] *Decision support systems* use managers' insights in an interactive computer-based process to assist in making nonroutine decisions. DSSs are more flexible than MISs. However, a decision support system can interact with a MIS. These data manipulations allow managers to evaluate the possible effects of alternative decisions. For example, capital budgeting decisions can be made with the help of a DSS. These systems can let managers know in days rather than months how a discounting promotion is affecting sales, for example. They can also spot a competitor's challenge before it does too much damage.

Expert systems are computer programs designed to imitate the thought processes of a human being. They build on a series of rules ("if–then" scenarios) to move from a set of data to a decision. **Boeing** uses an expert system called CASE (Connector Assembly Specification Expert). CASE produces assembly procedures for each of the 5,000 electrical connectors on Boeing airplanes.[74]

13-5   APPLYING THE CONCEPT

Types of Information Systems

Identify the type of information system that would be appropriate in each case.

A. transaction processing system
B. management information system
C. executive information system
D. decision support system
E. expert system

_____ 21. A manager wants to know if an important order has been shipped yet.

_____ 22. A manager wants to determine how many checkout counters to have in a new store.

_____ 23. A small business owner wants to use an accounting software program.

_____ 24. A manager intuitively knows how to schedule customers. A top manager wants to help others do a good job of scheduling, too.

_____ 25. The CEO is working on the company's strategic plan.

LO 13-11

List the components of an information network.

Information Networks

Information networks apply information technology to connect all employees of an organization to each other, to suppliers, to customers, and to databases. Information networks are used to integrate information systems, and at many organizations, networks are the primary means for employees to learn how to do their jobs, to find information, and to solve problems. Exhibit 13-7 illustrates the components of an information network. As you can see, much of the network is based on machine-to-machine (M2M) communications.

Facebook's (Case Question 4) social networking has proved to be a type of communication in that individuals can connect to one another via the Internet, and companies are also using social networking to recruit new people to hire and as promotional tools for their products.

EXHIBIT 13-7   INFORMATION NETWORK

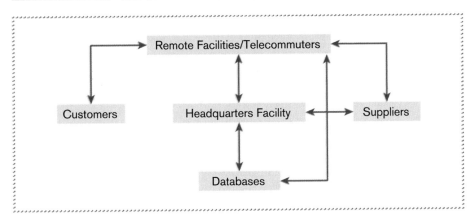

As we bring this chapter to a close, you should understand the flow of organizational communication, information technology (IT), the interpersonal communication process (sending receiving and responding to messages), and information systems (IS) and networks.

• • • CHAPTER SUMMARY

13-1. **Describe the three ways communication flows through organizations.**

Formal communication flows vertically downward and upward through the chain of command. Formal communication flows horizontally between colleagues and peers. Informal communication flows through the grapevine in any direction.

13-2. **List the four steps in the interpersonal communication process.**

The sender encodes the message and selects the transmission channel. (2) The sender transmits the message through a channel. (3) The receiver decodes the message and decides if feedback is needed. (4) The receiver may give feedback by making a response or sending a new message through a channel.

13-3. **State the major advantages and disadvantage of oral communication and written communication.**

The major advantages of oral communication are that it is usually easier and faster than written communication and it encourages feedback. The disadvantage is that there is usually no record of such communication.

The major advantage of written communication is that it provides a record of what was communicated. The major disadvantages are that it usually takes longer and it hinders feedback.

13-4. **State a general guide to channel selection.**

As a general guide, use rich oral channels for sending difficult and unusual messages, written channels for transmitting simple and routine messages to several people or messages that contain facts and figures or detailed information, and combined channels for important messages that recipients need to attend to and understand.

13-5. List the five steps in the process of sending face-to-face messages.

The face-to-face message-sending process involves five steps: (1) Develop rapport. (2) State your communication objective. (3) Transmit your message. (4) Check the receiver's understanding. (5) Get a commitment and follow up.

13-6. Describe paraphrasing, and explain why it is useful.

Paraphrasing is the process of restating a message in one's own words. The receiver uses paraphrasing to check understanding of the transmitted message. If the receiver can paraphrase the message accurately, communication has taken place. If not, communication is not complete.

13-7. List and explain the three parts of the process of receiving messages.

The three parts of the message-receiving process are listening, analyzing, and checking understanding. Listening is the process of giving a speaker your undivided attention. Analyzing is the process of thinking about, decoding, and evaluating the message. Checking understanding is the process of giving feedback.

13-8. Define reflecting responses, and state when they should be used.

Reflecting responses paraphrase the message and communicate understanding and acceptance to the sender. Reflecting responses are appropriate to use when coaching and counseling.

13-9. Discuss what should and should not be done to calm an emotional person.

To calm an emotional person, do not make statements that put the person down. Make reflective empathic responses that let the emotional person know that you understand how he or she feels. Paraphrase the feelings.

13-10. Describe the three primary types of information systems and their relationship.

Transaction processing systems (TPSs) are used to record routine, repetitive transactions. Management information systems (MISs) transform data into information and are used by managers to perform their work and to make routine decisions. Decision support systems (DSSs) are used by managers to make nonroutine decisions. A TPS is related to an MIS because its totals are included in the MIS. A DSS is related to an MIS, which includes TPS totals, because it uses MIS databases.

13-11. List the components of an information network.

The components of an information network include connections between employees from headquarters and remote locations, suppliers and customers, and databases.

• • • KEY TERMS

communication, 384
communication channel, 389
communication process, 389
decoding, 389
empathic listening, 404

encoding, 389
feedback, 397
grapevine, 385
horizontal communication, 384
message-receiving process, 398

message-sending process, 396
nonverbal communication, 393
paraphrasing, 397
reflecting responses, 403
vertical communication, 384

• • • KEY TERM REVIEW

Complete each of the following statements using one of this chapter's key terms.

1. _____ is the process of transmitting information and meaning.

2. _____ is the flow of information both downward and upward through the organizational chain of command.

3. _____ is the flow of information between colleagues and peers.

4. The _____ is the informal flow of information in any direction throughout an organization.

5. The _____ takes place between a sender who encodes a message and transmits it through a channel to a receiver who decodes it and may give feedback.

6. _____ is the sender's process of putting the message into a form that the receiver will understand.

7. A _____ is the means or medium by which a message is transmitted; the three primary ones are oral, nonverbal, and written.

8. _____ is the receiver's process of translating a message into a meaningful form.

9. _____ consists of messages sent without words.

10. The steps in the _____ are (1) developing rapport, (2) stating your communication objective, (3) transmitting your message, (4) checking the receiver's understanding, and (5) getting a commitment and following up.

11. _____ is information that verifies a message.

12. _____ is the process of restating a message in one's own words.

13. The _____ includes listening, analyzing, and checking understanding.

14. _____ paraphrase a message and communicate understanding and acceptance to the sender.

15. _____ is understanding and relating to another's feelings.

••• REVIEW QUESTIONS

1. What is the difference among vertical, horizontal, and grapevine communication?

2. What is the difference between encoding and decoding?

3. What is filtering?

4. What is the difference between nonverbal and oral and written communication?

5. What is the difference between setting and body language?

6. What is media richness?

7. What should be included in your plan to send a message?

8. What are the four ways to get feedback on messages?

9. Why should you listen, analyze, and then check understanding?

10. Why is criticism important to the individual and organization?

11. What takes place during the information systems process?

••• COMMUNICATION SKILLS

The following critical-thinking questions can be used for class discussion and/or as written assignments to develop communication skills. Be sure to give complete explanations for all questions.

1. Select an organization with which you are familiar. How can the flow of communication be improved?

2. Is the grapevine helpful or harmful to most organizations? Should managers try to stop grapevine communication? Why or why not?

3. Which e-commerce methods have you used? Which one do you use most often?

4. Wireless phones and handheld devices are blurring work and home life. Is this positive or negative? Should people stay connected and work while on vacation?

5. What does perception have to do with encoding and decoding?

6. Which communication barrier do you think is the most common, and which barrier do you believe has the most negative effects on communication?

7. Which message transmission channel do you use most often in your personal and professional life? What is your strongest and weakest channel? How can you improve on your weakness?

8. When sending messages, how effective are you at checking the receiver's understanding? Can you improve? If so, how?

9. When receiving messages, how effective are you at listening? Can you improve? If so, how?

10. Which response style do you use most often?

11. What is the relationship between information and the management functions?

12. What is the difference between a computer network and an information network?

••• CASE: WELLPOINT

WellPoint, Inc. is one of the largest health benefits companies in the United States. It is a for-profit independent licensee of the Blue Cross and Blue Shield Association serving members in several states. Through its networks nationwide, the company delivers a number of leading health benefit solutions through a broad portfolio of integrated health care plans and related services, along with a wide range of specialty products such as life and disability insurance benefits, dental, vision, and behavioral health benefit services, as well as long-term care insurance and flexible spending accounts. Health care is changing and WellPoint is leading the way to help improve the system, make health care easier for consumers to access and use, and improve the health of people by driving innovation to control costs and improve the quality of care everyone receives.

Joseph R. Swedish is the CEO, but day-to-day management of WellPoint is carried out by its executive leadership team. The team comprises top-tier business executives with a deep understanding of their respective operational areas, and it shapes the strategic actions that are undertaking to enhance the company's leadership position in an ever-changing industry. Team members work together to provide innovative health benefits solutions that address the health-care system's most pressing challenges: affordability and quality of care.

WellPoint and the health-care industry are facing two issues. First, communications among WellPoint and the government and health-care providers is critical, as is as patient records being electronic to help improve the quality of health care. Second, with the passage of the **Patient Protection and Affordable Care Act (PPACA)**, commonly called **Obamacare** or the **Affordable Care Act (ACA)**, it is not clear to everyone how they will be affected by it. Because it will be implemented over several years, there is a lot of uncertainty in the industry about how health-care providers will operate, especially regarding insurance, billing, and cost of health care and how businesses will provide health care benefits to their employees.

The ACA aims to increase the quality and affordability of health insurance, lower the uninsured rate by expanding public and private insurance coverage, and reduce the costs of health care for individuals and the government. It provides a number of mechanisms—including mandates, subsidies, and insurance exchanges—to increase coverage and affordability. The law also requires insurance companies to cover all applicants within new minimum standards and offer the same rates regardless of pre-existing conditions or sex. The ACA and its implementation continue to face challenges in Congress, in federal courts (including the Supreme Court), from some state governments, and business organizations and individual businesses. Only time will tell how the ACA will affect America.

Sources: Information for this case taken from WellPoint, Inc.'s website at http://www.wellpoint.com, accessed September 19, 2013; Wikipedia, "Patient Protection and Affordable Care Act." http://en.wikipedia.org/wiki/Affordable_Care_Act, accessed September 19, 2013.

Case Questions

1. Discuss WellPoint organizational communications and its use of information technology.

2. Describe some of the potential communication barriers created by the Affordable Care Act and how to overcome them.

3. Identify the types of information systems WellPoint needs to operate effectively.

4. Do some research and find out how WellPoint and other healthcare providers are dealing with changes brought about through the Affordable Care Act.

5. How has the Affordable Care Act affected you and your family and the organizations they work for?

Cumulative Case Questions

6. What types of external environment changes is WellPoint facing in the health-care industry? (Chapters 2 and 6)?

7. How do creative problems solving and decision making and innovation have to do with this case? (Chapters 4 and 6)

8. How does the Affordable Care Act affect human resources managers? (Chapter 9)

• • • SKILL BUILDER 13-1: GIVING INSTRUCTIONS

Objective

1. To develop your ability to send and receive messages (communication skills).

2. You will plan, give, and receive instructions for the completion of a drawing of three objects. No preparation is necessary except reading and understanding the chapter. The instructor will provide the original drawings.

Skills

The primary skills developed through this exercise are:

1. *Management skill*—interpersonal (giving directions is communicating)

2. *AACSB competency*—communication abilities

3. *Management function*—leading (influencing others through communicating instructions)

Procedure (15 minutes)

In this exercise, you will work with a partner. One person will play the role of manager, and the other person will play the role of employee. You will go through the exercise twice, switching roles before the second time so that each person has a chance to give instructions in the role of manager and receive them in the role of employee.

The task is for the person in the role of manager to describe for the person in the role of employee a drawing of three objects so that the employee can duplicate the drawing, based on what the manager describes. (Your instructor will provide the drawing to those playing the role of manager; a different drawing will be used in the second run-through, when people have switched roles and partners.) The objects must be drawn to scale, and the drawing must be a recognizable reproduction of the original. The exercise has four parts.

1. *Planning.* The manager plans how to instruct the employee in the task. The manager's plans may include written instructions to be shown to the employee but may not include any drawing.

2. *Instruction.* The manager gives the instructions he or she has developed. While giving instructions, the manager is not to show the original drawing to the employee. The instructions may be given orally or in writing, or both, but the manager should not use any hand gestures. The manager must give the instructions for all three objects before the employee begins drawing them.

3. *Drawing.* The employee makes a drawing. Once the employee begins drawing, the manager should watch but may no longer communicate in any way.

4. *Evaluation.* When the employee is finished drawing or when the time is up, the manager shows the employee the original drawing. Partners should discuss how each person did and should answer the questions in the Integration section.

Integration

Answer the following questions. You may select more than one answer. The manager and employee discuss each question, and the manager, not the employee, writes the answers.

1. The goal of communication was to _____.
   a. influence
   b. inform
   c. express feelings

2. The communication was _____.
   a. vertical downward
   b. vertical upward
   c. horizontal
   d. grapevine

3. The manager did an _____ job of encoding the message and the employee did an _____ job of decoding the message.
   a. effective
   b. ineffective

4. The manager transmitted the message through _____ communication channel(s).
   a. oral
   b. written
   c. combined

5. The manager spent _____ time planning.
   a. too much
   b. too little
   c. the right amount of

Questions 6 to 11 relate to the steps in the message-sending process.

6. The manager developed rapport (step 1).
   a. true
   b. false

7. The manager stated the objective of the communication (step 2).
   a. true
   b. false

8. The manager transmitted the message _____ (step 3).
   a. effectively
   b. ineffectively

9. The manager checked understanding by using _____ (step 4).
   a. direct questions
   b. paraphrasing
   c. both
   d. neither

10. The manager checked understanding _____.
    a. too frequently
    b. too infrequently
    c. about the right number of times

11. The manager got a commitment and followed up (step 5).
    a. true
    b. false

12. The employee did an _____ job of listening, an _____ job of analyzing, and an _____ job of checking understanding through the message-receiving process.
    a. effective
    b. ineffective

13. The manager and/or employee got emotional.
    a. true
    b. false

14. Were the objects drawn to scale? If not, why not?

15. Did manager and employee both follow the rules? If not, why not?

16. In answering these questions, the manager was ____ and the employee was ____ to criticism that could help improve communication skills.

    a. open

    b. closed

17. If you could do this exercise over again, what would you do differently to improve communication?

Apply It

What did I learn from this experience? How will I use this knowledge in the future?

••• SKILL BUILDER 13–2: ANALYZING COMMUNICATION STYLE

Objective

To develop skills for using the most appropriate communication style based on the situation.

Skills

The primary skills developed through this exercise are:

1. *Management skill*—interpersonal (understanding communication styles)

2. *AACSB competency*—communication abilities

3. *Management function*—leading (influencing others through communicating)

Preparing for Skill Builder 13–2

When you work with people outside your department, you have no authority to give them direct orders. You must use other means to achieve your goal. Through this Skill Builder, you will learn about communication styles and how to select the most appropriate communication style in a given situation. Begin by determining your preferred communication style by completing the Self-Assessment.

Self-Assessment: Determining Your Preferred Communication Style

To determine your preferred communication style, select the alternative that most closely describes what you would do in each of the following 12 situations. Do not be concerned with trying to pick the "correct" answer; simply circle the letter of the choice that best describes what you would actually do.

____ 1. Wendy, a knowledgeable person from another department, comes to you, the engineering supervisor, and requests that you design a product to her specifications. You would:

a. Control the conversation and tell Wendy what you will do for her.

b. Ask Wendy to describe the product. Once you understand it, you would present your ideas. Let her know that you are concerned and want to help with your ideas.

c. Respond to Wendy's request by conveying understanding and support. Help clarify what she wants you to do. Offer ideas, but do it her way.

d. Find out what you need to know. Let Wendy know you will do it her way.

____ 2. Your department has designed a product that is to be fabricated by Saul's department. Saul has been with the company longer than you have; he knows his department. Saul comes to you to change the product design. You decide to:

a. Listen to Saul explain the change and why it would be beneficial. If you believe Saul's way is better, change it; if not, explain why the original design is superior. If necessary, insist that it be done your way.

b. Tell Saul to fabricate it any way he wants.

c. Tell Saul to do it your way. You don't have time to listen and argue with him.

d. Be supportive; make changes together as a team.

____ 3. Upper managers call you to a meeting and tell you they need some information to solve a problem they describe to you. You:

a. Respond in a manner that conveys personal support and offer alternative ways to solve the problem.

b. Just answer their questions.

c. Explain how to solve the problem.

d. Show your concern by explaining how to solve the problem and why it is an effective solution.

____ 4. You have a routine work order that you typically place verbally, for work that is to be completed in three days. Su, the receiver, is very experienced and willing to be of service to you. You decide to:

a. Explain your needs, but let Su make the order decision.

b. Tell Su what you want and why you need it.

c. Decide together what to order.

d. Simply give Su the order.

____ 5. Work orders from the staff department normally take three days to fulfill; however, you have an emergency and need the job done today. Your colleague Javier, the department supervisor, is knowledgeable and somewhat cooperative. You decide to:

a. Tell Javier that you need the work done by three o'clock and will return at that time to pick it up.

b. Explain the situation and how the organization will benefit by expediting the order. Volunteer to help in any way you can.

c. Explain the situation and ask Javier when the order will be ready.

d. Explain the situation and together come to a solution to your problem.

_____ 6. Danielle, a peer with a record of high performance, has recently had a drop in productivity. You know Danielle has a family problem. Her problem is affecting your performance. You:

a. Discuss the problem; help Danielle realize that the problem is affecting her work and yours. Supportively discuss ways to improve the situation.

b. Tell the boss about it and let him decide what to do.

c. Tell Danielle to get back on the job.

d. Discuss the problem and tell Danielle how to improve the work situation; be supportive.

_____ 7. You buy supplies from Dev regularly. He is an excellent salesperson and very knowledgeable about your situation. You are placing your weekly order. You decide to:

a. Explain what you want and why. Develop a supportive relationship.

b. Explain what you want and ask Dev to recommend products.

c. Give Dev the order.

d. Explain your situation and allow Dev to make the order.

_____ 8. Jean, a knowledgeable person from another department, has asked you to perform a routine staff function in a different way. You decide to:

a. Perform the task to her specifications without questioning her.

b. Tell her that you will do it the usual way.

c. Explain what you will do and why.

d. Show your willingness to help; offer alternative ways to do it.

_____ 9. Tam, a salesperson, wants to place an order with your department but the order has a short delivery date. As usual, Tam claims it is a take-it-or-leave-it offer. He wants your decision now, or within a few minutes, because he is in the customer's office. Your action is to:

a. Convince Tam to work together to come up with a later date.

b. Give Tam a yes or no answer.

c. Explain your situation and let Tam decide if you should take the order.

d. Offer an alternative delivery date. Work on your relationship; show your support.

_____ 10. As a time-and-motion expert, you have been called by an operator who has a complaint about the standard time it takes to perform a job. As you analyze the entire job, you realize that one element of the job should take longer, but other elements should take less time, leading to a shorter total standard time for the job. You decide to:

a. Tell the operator and foreman that the total time must be decreased and why.

b. Agree with the operator and increase the standard time.

c. Explain your findings. Deal with the operator and/or foreman's concerns, but ensure compliance with your new standard.

d. Together with the operator, develop a standard time.

_____ 11. You approve budget allocations for projects. Maria, who is very competent in developing budgets, has come to you with a proposed budget. You:

a. Review the budget, make revisions, and explain them in a supportive way. Deal with concerns, but insist on your changes.

b. Review the proposal and suggest areas where changes may be needed. Make changes together, if needed.

c. Review the proposed budget, make revisions, and explain them.

d. Answer any questions or concerns Maria has and approve the budget as is.

_____ 12. You are a sales manager. A customer has offered you a contract for your product but needs to have it delivered soon. The offer is open for two days. The contract would be profitable for you and the organization. The cooperation of the production department is essential to meet the deadline. Tim, the production manager, has developed a grudge against you because of your repeated requests for quick delivery. Your action is to:

a. Contact Tim and try to work together to complete the contract.

b. Accept the contract and convince Tim in a supportive way to meet the obligation.

c. Contact Tim and explain the situation. Ask him if you and he should accept the contract, but let him decide.

d. Accept the contract. Contact Tim and tell him to meet the obligation. If he resists, tell him you will go to his boss.

To determine your preferred communication style, circle the letter you selected in each situation. The column headings indicate the style you selected.

	Autocratic	Consultative	Participative	Empowering
1.	a	b	c	d
2.	c	a	d	b
3.	c	d	a	b
4.	d	b	c	a
5.	a	b	d	c
6.	c	d	a	b
7.	c	a	b	d
8.	b	c	d	a
9.	b	d	a	c
10.	a	c	d	b
11.	c	a	b	d
12.	d	b	a	c
Total	_____	_____	_____	_____

Add up the number of circled items per column. The four totals should sum to 12. The column with the highest number represents your preferred communication style. The more evenly distributed the numbers are among the four styles, the more flexible your communications. A total of 0 or 1 in any column may indicate a reluctance to use that style. You could have problems in situations calling for the use of that style.

Selecting a Communication Style

As you saw from the Self-Assessment, communication styles can also be autocratic, consultative, participative, or empowering.

With the **autocratic communication style**, the communication is generally controlled by the sender of the message; little, if any, response is expected from the receiver, and his or her input is not considered. The communication is structured and either directive or informative. With the **consultative communication style**, the sender of the message makes it clear that he or she desires a response and tries to elicit a response by asking questions, showing concern for the other person's point of view, and being open to the person's feelings. The **participative communication style** involves trying to elicit the other person's ideas and being helpful and supportive. A manager using the **empowering communication style** conveys that the other person is in charge of the communication; the communication is very open.

There is no single communication style that is best for all situations. In determining the appropriate style for a given situation, managers must take into consideration four different variables: time, information, acceptance, and capability.

Time. In certain situations, there may not be enough time to engage in two-way communication. In an emergency, for example, the other three variables are not as important as the time factor; in such cases, the autocratic style is appropriate. Also, time is relative: In one situation, a few minutes may be sufficient for effective communication; in another situation, a month may be too little time.

Information. The amount of information the sender and the receiver each have helps determine which style of communication is appropriate in a given situation. For example, in a situation in which an employee has little information, the manager might use an autocratic communication style; if the employee has much information, the manager would be better off using a participative style.

Acceptance. The likelihood that the receiver of a message will accept it also influences communication style. If the receiver is likely to accept a message, the autocratic style may be appropriate. However, there are situations in which acceptance is critical to success, such as when a manager is trying to implement changes. If the receiver is reluctant to accept a message or is likely to reject it, the consultative, participative, or empowering styles may be appropriate.

Capability. An employee's capability refers to his or her ability and motivation to participate in two-way communication. If an employee has low capability, the autocratic style may be best; if an employee has outstanding capability, the empowering communication style may be ideal. In addition, capability levels can change as situations change: The employee with whom a manager used an autocratic style might be better addressed using a participative style in a different situation.

Successful managers rely on different communication styles, depending on the situation. In some situations, one of the variables discussed above may be more important than others. For example, a manager who is communicating with a highly capable employee might ordinarily use a consultative style. But if in a particular situation the manager already has the information she needs, the manager may use an autocratic style with that employee.

Reread the 12 situations in the Self-Assessment. For each one, consider the four variables discussed earlier. Refer to the Situational Communication Model in Model 13–3.

First, determine if there is sufficient time to engage in two-way communication. Second, assess the level of information you have and the other person's capability and likelihood of accepting a message. Then select the appropriate communication style for the situation based on your analysis. Did the analysis cause you to change your earlier responses?

MODEL 13-1 SITUATIONAL COMMUNICATION MODEL

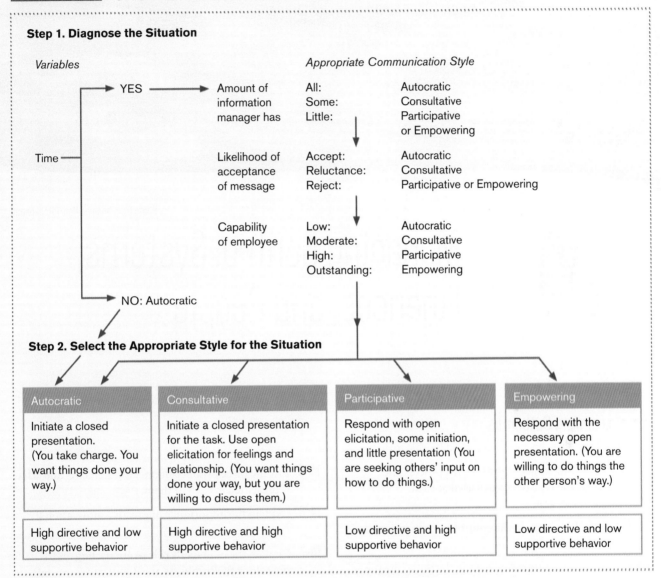

Step 1. Diagnose the Situation

Variables   *Appropriate Communication Style*

YES → Amount of information manager has
- All: Autocratic
- Some: Consultative
- Little: Participative or Empowering

Time

Likelihood of acceptance of message
- Accept: Autocratic
- Reluctance: Consultative
- Reject: Participative or Empowering

Capability of employee
- Low: Autocratic
- Moderate: Consultative
- High: Participative
- Outstanding: Empowering

NO: Autocratic

Step 2. Select the Appropriate Style for the Situation

Autocratic	Consultative	Participative	Empowering
Initiate a closed presentation. (You take charge. You want things done your way.)	Initiate a closed presentation for the task. Use open elicitation for feelings and relationship. (You want things done your way, but you are willing to discuss them.)	Respond with open elicitation, some initiation, and little presentation (You are seeking others' input on how to do things.)	Respond with the necessary open presentation. (You are willing to do things the other person's way.)
High directive and low supportive behavior	High directive and high supportive behavior	Low directive and high supportive behavior	Low directive and low supportive behavior

Apply It

What did I learn from this experience? How will I use this knowledge in the future?

••• STUDENT STUDY SITE

Visit the Student Study Site at **www.sagepub.com/lussier6e** to access to these additional study tools:

- Mobile-compatible self-assessment quizzes
- Mobile-compatible key term flashcards
- Video Links
- SAGE Journal Articles
- Web Links

14 Managing Control Systems, Finances, and People

• • • **Learning Outcomes**

After studying this chapter, you should be able to:

14-1. List the four stages of the systems process and describe the type of control used at each stage. PAGE 418

14-2. List the four steps in the control systems process. PAGE 421

14-3. Describe the differences among the three categories of control frequency. PAGE 424

14-4. Explain how the capital expenditures budget is different from the expense budget. PAGE 427

14-5. List the three primary financial statements and what is presented in each of them. PAGE 428

14-6. Explain the importance of positive motivational feedback in coaching. PAGE 431

14-7. Explain the manager's role in counseling and the role of the employee assistance program staff. PAGE 434

IDEAS ON MANAGEMENT at the Ranch Golf Club

Peter and Korby Clark were part owners of nearly 50 **Jiffy Lube** stores, most of which they sold to **Pennzoil**. The Clarks had many investment opportunities, but the Ranch grabbed their attention. The Clarks became one-third owners of the Ranch, and Pete is the managing partner overseeing day-to-day operations while Korby oversees an endless variety of things that need to get done.

The **Ranch Golf Club,** where every player is a special guest for the day, opened in 2001 in Southwick, Massachusetts. The Ranch's competitive advantage is that it is an upscale public course with links, woods, a variety of elevations, and "unsurpassed service." To communicate professionalism, all employees wear uniforms and are extensively trained to provide high-quality service.

From the start, the Ranch's goal was to be the best golf club in New England. In less than a year, the Ranch earned a four-star course rating, one of only four in New England. In the January 2003 issue of *Golf Digest,* the Ranch was rated number three in the country in the "new upscale public golf course" category, and it was ranked as the best public course in Massachusetts in 2007. The Ranch was voted in the top 50 of all Public Golf Courses in Golf World's 2010 Readers' Choice Awards; it was one of only two courses in all of New England that made the list.

1. How does the Ranch control the organizational system? **PAGE 419**
2. How does the Ranch use the control systems process, and how is it performing? **PAGE 424**
3. What control methods are used to achieve objectives and standards at the Ranch? **PAGE 426**
4. What are the major operating budget revenues and expenses at the Ranch? **PAGE 427**
5. How does the Ranch use capital expenditure budgets? How does the Ranch use financial statements and budgets? **PAGE 428**
6. Does Peter Clark coach his Jiffy Lube business, the Ranch, and sports teams the same way? **PAGE 432**
7. How does the Ranch get feedback to improve performance? **PAGE 434**

You'll find answers to these questions throughout the chapter. To learn more about the Ranch, visit its website at www.theranchgolfclub.com.

Source: Information for this case was taken from personal interviews with Peter and Korby Clark in August 2013.

••• Chapter Outline

LO 14-1

List the four stages of the systems process and describe the type of control used at each stage.

WORK
APPLICATION 14-1

Using Exhibit 14–1, identify the primary organizational inputs, transformation process, outputs, and customers of a firm you work for or have worked for. Also, identify the level of customer satisfaction.

ORGANIZATIONAL AND FUNCTIONAL AREA CONTROL SYSTEMS

Management control is about monitoring performance.[1] Controls describe the processes used to communicate, monitor, and reinforce objectives.[2] As defined in Chapter 1, *controlling* is the process of monitoring progress and taking corrective action when needed to ensure that objectives are achieved. In this section, we discuss controlling the organizational system and its functional areas.

Organizational Systems Control

With multiple types of organizations and stakeholders, there is no universally accepted external control system;[3] the control must fit the situation. So the focus here will be on the importance of integrating various controls through the systems approach. In Chapter 2, you learned about the systems process, which is now expanded to include types of control at each stage. Exhibit 14-1 illustrates the systems process, with appropriate types of control. The four different types of control needed at the different stages of the systems process are explained next.

EXHIBIT 14-1 THE SYSTEMS PROCESS WITH TYPES OF CONTROLS

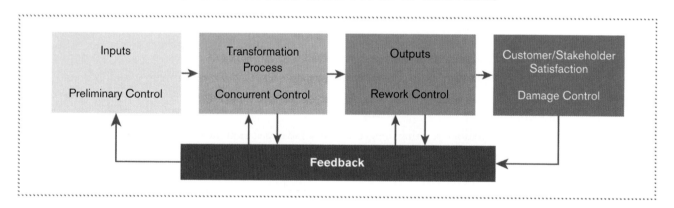

Preliminary Control (Inputs). **Preliminary control** *is designed to anticipate and prevent possible problems.* A major difference between successful and unsuccessful managers lies in their ability to anticipate and prevent problems rather than solving problems after they occur. Planning and organizing are the keys to preliminary control, which is also called *feedforward control.* A common preliminary control is preventive maintenance. Many companies routinely tune up their machines, engines, autos, planes, and so forth to prevent breakdowns that would cause problems.

preliminary control Action designed to anticipate and prevent possible problems.

concurrent control Action taken to ensure that standards are met as inputs are transformed into outputs.

rework control Action taken to fix an output.

damage control Action taken to minimize negative impacts on customers/stakeholders due to faulty outputs.

Concurrent Control (Transformation Process). **Concurrent control** *is action taken to ensure that standards are met as inputs are transformed into outputs.* It is more economical to reject faulty input parts than to wait and find out that the finished output does not work properly. Employees spend time checking quality during the transformation process.

Rework Control (Outputs). **Rework control** *is action taken to fix an output.* Rework is necessary when preliminary and concurrent controls have failed. Most organizations inspect the final output before it is sold. Sometimes rework is not cost effective or possible, and outputs have to be accepted as is, discarded, or sold for salvage, which can be costly.

Damage Control (Customer/Stakeholder Satisfaction). Damage control *is action taken to minimize negative impacts on customers/stakeholders due to faulty outputs.* When a faulty output gets to the customer, damage control is needed. Warranties, a form of damage control, require refunding the purchase price, fixing the product, reperforming the service (a form of rework), or replacing the product with a new one.

Feedback (Continuous Improvement). An important part of the systems process is the feedback loop, particularly from the customer and other stakeholders. The only way to continually increase customer satisfaction is to use feedback from the customer to continually improve the products and services. Restaurant and hotel/motel evaluation cards filled out by customers are examples of feedback.

Focus on Preliminary and Concurrent Types of Control. Remember that focusing on preliminary and concurrent controls cuts down on rework and damage. Relying on rework control is not effective because it is more costly to do things twice than to do them right the first time. This approach is particularly problematic with services, such as manicures and haircuts and auto repairs, which are delivered as they are produced. The best solution is to prevent poor quality from happening in the first place.

WORK
APPLICATION 14-2

Building on Work Application 14–1, give examples of preliminary, concurrent, rework, and damage controls for an organization you work for or have worked for.

14-1 APPLYING THE CONCEPT

Types of Control

Identify the type of control used or required as

A. preliminary
B. concurrent
C. rework
D. damage

____ 1. As Sayeed was scooping the ice cream, the cone split down the side.

____ 2. The manager, Amita, is using the time management system on Friday.

____ 3. The new shirt Carl bought today has a button missing.

____ 4. Ted just got his monthly budget report telling him how much he spent and his balance.

____ 5. Coach Lee is reviewing the plays to be used during the big game on Sunday.

The Ranch's (Case Question 1) major control systems inputs that require preliminary control include the practice facility, the golf course itself, the golf carts, and tee times. The transformation is the actual playing of golf, and the major concurrent control is the player assistance out on the course. If players are not satisfied, player assistance knows it early and can fix the problem quickly before the game is over. Rework and damage control (refunds or playing again at no cost) are not common.

Functional Area/Department Control Systems

Recall from Chapters 1 and 7 that firms are commonly organized into four major functional departments: operations, marketing, human resources, and finance. Information is a fifth major functional area that may be a stand-alone department or may fall under the finance functional area.

Although in most organizations the operations department is the only functional area that actually transforms the inputs into the outputs of goods and

WORK
APPLICATION 14-3

Building on Work Applications 14–1 and 14–2, illustrate the systems process for a department you work for or have worked for within an organization. Be sure to give examples of preliminary, concurrent, rework, and damage controls for your department.

WORK
APPLICATION 14-4

Building on Work Applications 14–1 through 14–3, illustrate the systems process you personally use within your department. Be sure to give examples of preliminary, concurrent, rework, and damage controls you personally use.

The making of products requires coordination and feedback among various departments to ensure customer satisfaction. Photo from F1 online digital Bildagentur GMBH/Alamy.

services (which are called *products*) that are sold to customers, all functional departments use the systems process. Note that damage control with the customer is primarily the function of the marketing department. The other department outputs stay within the organization and go to stakeholders, not to the customer; therefore, internal damage control is necessary when outputs are faulty. You will learn more about operations in Chapter 15.

The Feedback Process Within and Between Functional Areas/Departments. Within each department, employees also use the systems process to transform inputs into outputs. Other department members rather than other departments may receive their outputs. For example, on a production line making the **Ford** Taurus, each person works on one part of the car. When the work is completed, that person's output moves down the line to become the next person's input, and so on, until the Taurus is completed. Each employee should be using preliminary, concurrent, rework, and damage control.

Feedback is needed for improvements. Throughout the systems process, feedback should be circulated among all the functional areas/departments to improve organizational performance in the input, transformation, and output processes while continually increasing customer satisfaction. Exhibit 14-2 illustrates an effective feedback process between the functional departments. Note that operations, marketing, finance, and human resources provide feedback to one another and to the information department. To be effective, feedback should be given to all departments, not just to the information department for dissemination to the other departments.

EXHIBIT 14-2   THE FEEDBACK PROCESS BETWEEN FUNCTIONAL AREAS/DEPARTMENTS

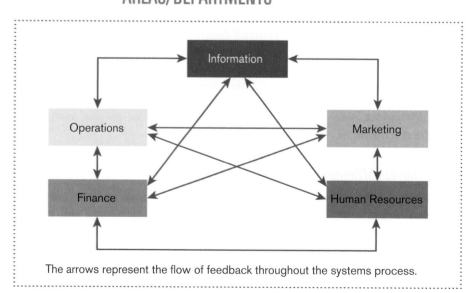

The arrows represent the flow of feedback throughout the systems process.

ESTABLISHING CONTROL SYSTEMS

In this section, we discuss the four steps in the control systems process and 10 specific control methods that can be used during the process.

The Control Systems Process

Controlling is about setting a level of performance and achieving it.[4] The steps in the **control systems process** *are (1) set objectives and standards, (2) measure performance, (3) compare performance to standards, and (4) correct or reinforce.* See Exhibit 14-3 for an illustration of the control systems process. The same control systems process steps should be followed on an organizational level and within each functional area.

Step 1. Set objectives and standards. Setting objectives (Chapter 5) is the starting point for both planning and controlling.[5] Recall (Chapter 11) that objectives increase commitment, motivation, and persistence toward goals[6] and that objectives should be challenging, not the minimum.[7] Setting objectives and standards is part of the input process, and the objectives and standards themselves are preliminary controls.

EXHIBIT 14-3   THE CONTROL SYSTEMS PROCESS

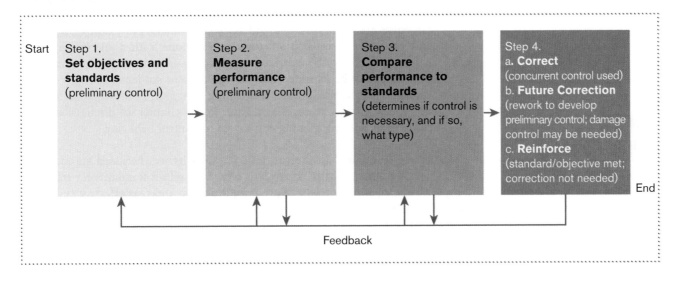

Start

Step 1. Set objectives and standards (preliminary control)

Step 2. Measure performance (preliminary control)

Step 3. Compare performance to standards (determines if control is necessary, and if so, what type)

Step 4.
a. **Correct** (concurrent control used)
b. **Future Correction** (rework to develop preliminary control; damage control may be needed)
c. **Reinforce** (standard/objective met; correction not needed)

End

Feedback

Controls convey performance standards.[8] Standards allow you to measure performance,[9] and measures (*metrics*) matter because if you can't measure performance, you can't control it.[10] For standards to be complete, they must cover five major areas. **Standards** *measure performance levels in the areas of quantity, quality, time, cost, and behavior.* Incomplete standards usually lead to negative results. For example, if employees are given only high quantity standards with a fast time limit, they will tend to focus only on how many products are produced and may ignore quality. Employees respond to what is measured and reinforced (Chapter 11), so the development of balanced standards is a key to business success.

- *Quantity.* How many units should employees produce to earn their pay? Some examples of quantity standards include the number of words a secretary must type, the number of loans a loan officer must make, and the number of classes a professor must teach.

control systems process
(1) Set objectives and standards, (2) measure performance, (3) compare performance to standards, and (4) correct or reinforce.

standards Measures of performance levels in the areas of quantity, quality, time, cost, and behavior.

- *Quality.* How well must a job be done? Some examples of quality standards include the number of typing errors an assistant may make, the number or percentage of delinquent loans a loan officer may make, and the acceptable number or percentage of poor student evaluations a professor may get. Quality standards are often difficult to establish and measure, but it must be done.

- *Time.* When should the task be completed? Or how fast?[11] When assigning a task, it is important to specify a time period. Deadlines are one form of time-based standard. And performance is generally measured with respect to a specific time period. Examples include how many words an assistant types per minute, how many loans a loan officer makes per month, and how many courses a professor teaches per semester or year.

- *Cost.* How much should it cost to do the job? How sophisticated a cost system should an organization have? An assistant's typing cost may be reflected in a salary limit. A loan officer's cost may include an expense account for entertaining customers, as well as the cost of an office, an assistant's help, and so on, although cost could be determined on the basis of delinquent loan losses only. The professor's cost may include a salary limit and an overhead cost. Organizations globally are focusing on cost controls.[12]

- *Behavior.* What should employees do and not do?[13] What behavior is ethical and unethical?[14] Standing plans of *policies, procedures,* and especially *rules* help control or limit behavior.[15] In addition, there may be specific directives about things to do and say to customers. For example, an assistant may be expected to answer the telephone with a specific greeting. A loan officer may be expected to process a loan in a certain manner. A professor may be expected not to date current students. In many earlier chapters you learned about controlling behavior, reinforcement motivation theory being one approach. Later in this chapter we discuss coaching, counseling, and disciplining employees to control behavior.

Complete Standards. In the previous paragraphs we discussed standards in terms of each of the five areas separately. Now we will set standards for the assistant, loan officer, and professor that combine all five areas, as effective standards should. The assistant's standard may be to type 50 words (quantity) per minute (time) with two errors or less (quality) at a maximum salary of $15.00 per hour (cost) and to answer the telephone with a specific greeting (behavior). The loan officer's standard may be to make $200,000 (quantity) in loans per quarter (time), with delinquency not to exceed $10,000 (quality and cost), while following procedures (behavior). The professor's standard may be to teach 24 semester hours (quantity) per year (time), with an acceptable department chair performance evaluation (quality), at a salary of less than $70,000 (cost), without dating current students (behavior). Each of these jobs would have additional standards as well.

Step 2. Measure performance. An important part of control monitoring is measuring performance.[16] If you don't measure performance, how do you know if your objectives are being met?[17]

After setting objectives, the next step—which may take place while setting standards—is to identify the critical success factors (CSFs). **Critical success factors** *are the limited number of areas in which satisfactory results will ensure successful performance, achieving the objective/standard.* You cannot control everything, so you should identify the few most important things to control—priorities.[18] For example, at the organizational level in supermarkets (including **Food Mart, Kroger, Safeway,** and **Stop & Shop**), maintaining the right product mix in each

WORK
APPLICATION 14-5

Give an example of a standard from an organization you work for or have worked for that has the five characteristics of a complete standard.

critical success factors The limited number of areas in which satisfactory results will ensure successful performance, achieving the objective/standard.

local store, having the products on the shelves, having them advertised effectively to pull shoppers into the store, and having them priced correctly (since profit margins are low in this industry) are the critical success factors. At the departmental and employee level, these CSFs must be implemented and monitored.

How often should you measure performance, and what methods of control should you use? It depends on the situation. Later in this section we will discuss 10 specific methods you can use to control CSFs.

Step 3. Compare performance to standards. After determining what, when, and how frequently to measure, you must follow up by comparing the actual results to the objective or standard in order to know if you are on schedule to achieve (or have achieved) the objective/standard.[19] This step is relatively easy if you have performed the first two steps correctly. This comparison determines the type of control, if any, needed in step 4. By comparing actual performance to standards, you are keeping score.[20]

A performance or variance report is commonly used to measure and evaluate performance. Performance reports usually show standards, actual performance, and deviations from standards. In Exhibit 14-4, the results, although under production and over cost, are acceptable because in both cases the deviation from standard (variance divided by standard) is less than 1 percent. When variances are significant, they should be explained.

WORK
APPLICATION 14-6

Give an example of the critical success factors for a job you have or had. Be sure to place them in priority order (most important first) and to explain why they are critical.

EXHIBIT 14-4   OPERATIONS PERFORMANCE REPORT

Outputs and Inputs	Standard/ Budget	Actual	Variance
Units produced (outputs)	10,000	9,992	−8
Production cost (inputs)	$ 70,000	$ 68,895	$ 1,105
Labor, including overtime	95,500	95,763	−263
Materials	4,750	4,700	+50
Supplies			
Totals	$170,250	$169,358	$892

Step 4. Correct or reinforce. If you are not meeting the objective, fix it quickly.[21] If you are, give positive reinforcement to continue meeting standards. During the transformation process, concurrent controls are used to correct performance to meet standards. When performance is complete and it is too late to take corrective action to meet the standard, the appropriate corrective action is to (1) analyze why the standard was not met, (2) use the information to develop preliminary control, and (3) feedback the preliminary control so as to take the corrective action necessary to meet the objective/standard next time. When performance has affected others, also use damage control.

Resistance to Control. Employees respond to incentives, and sometimes they resist controls.[22] When establishing control systems, especially standards, it is important to consider employee reactions to them and their possible resistance to change.[23] When employees perceive the controls as fair, they are less resistant to meeting them.[24] Methods of managing change (Chapter 6) should be used when establishing control systems. Allowing employees to be involved in establishing the control system is very helpful at gaining commitment to the objectives and standards.[25]

WORK
APPLICATION 14-7

Identify a situation in which corrective action was needed to meet an objective/standard. Describe the corrective action taken to meet the objective/standard.

14-1 JOIN THE DISCUSSION ETHICS & SOCIAL RESPONSIBILITY

Academic Grades

Recall the Join the Discussion about academic standards in Chapter 11. Successful managers establish and maintain high expectations for all their employees. As Lou Holtz said, we need to set a higher standard. While students are doing less work than in prior years, grades continue to go up, a trend called grade inflation. At one time, most colleges used a set grade point average (GPA) to determine honors. But today, because of grade inflation, most colleges use a system of ranking GPAs.

1. Why are professors giving higher grades today than were given 5, 10, or 20 years ago?
2. Are students who are putting in less time and getting higher grades being well prepared for a career with high standards after graduation?

3. Is it ethical and socially responsible for professors to drop standards and for colleges to award higher grades today than they did 5, 10, or 20 years ago?
4. Should colleges take action to raise standards? If so, what should they do?
5. An important part of a professor's job is to evaluate student learning through grading. Do you believe your learning is evaluated effectively? How could it improve?
6. Do you find consistency among your professors' standards in terms of the work required in their courses and the grades given, or do some professors require a lot more work and some give lots of As and others lots of lower grades? Should colleges take action to improve consistency among professors' standards? If so, what should they do?

Each year, **the Ranch (Case Question 2)** sets objectives, broken down by month, for each of its departments. The Ranch also has a sophisticated computer program that has set standards. Each month, a performance report is printed out that compares performance this month to objectives, standards, and past months. Corrective action is taken when needed, and performance is reinforced.

LO 14-3

Describe the differences among the three categories of control frequency.

Control Frequency and Methods

There are 10 specific methods you can use to measure and control performance. These 10 methods fall into three categories of **control frequency**: *constant, periodic, and occasional.*

Constant Controls. Constant controls are in continuous use:

- *Self-Control.* If managers are not watching or somehow monitoring performance, will employees do the job through self-monitoring?[26] The real issue is the degree of internal self-control employees are given versus external control imposed by managers.[27] Too much or too little imposed control can cause problems. Today's employees prefer to have control over when, where, and how much they work.[28]

- *Clan Control.* Clan or *group control* is a form of human resources control in which the organization relies heavily on its culture and norms to ensure specific behaviors through peer pressure.[29] Organizations that use teams tend to rely on clan control to enforce positive norms.[30]

- *Standing Plans.* Policies, procedures, and rules are developed to influence employees' behavior in recurring, predictable situations (Chapter 5).[31] Standards are similar to standing plans that are in constant use.

Periodic Controls. *Periodic controls* are used on a regular, fixed basis, such as once per hour or day, every week, or at the end of the month, quarter, or year.

- *Regular Meetings and Reports.* Regular reports can be oral or written. Regularly scheduled meetings with one or more employees to discuss progress and any problems are common in all organizations. These meetings may be scheduled daily, weekly, or monthly.

control frequency The rate of repetition—constant, periodic, or occasional—of measures taken to control performance.

14-2 APPLYING THE CONCEPT

Frequency and Methods of Control

Identify the one primary method of control.

Constant

A. self
B. clan
C. standing plans

Periodic

D. regular meetings and reports
E. budgets
F. audits

Occasional

G. observation
H. the exception principle
I. special reports
J. project

____ 6. The manager's desk is facing the employees.

____ 7. The assistant is working alone today since the boss is out of the office.

____ 8. The manager got the monthly operations performance report.

____ 9. The boss asked an employee to explain why the task is behind schedule.

____ 10. Signs are posted stating that helmets must be worn throughout the construction site.

- **Budgets.** Budgets are one of the most widely used control tools.[32] We discuss budgeting details in the next section of this chapter. The preparation of a new budget is a preliminary control. As the year progresses, the budget becomes a concurrent control. At year end, it is reworked for the next year. A budget may require damage control if significant changes, such as overspending, take place for some reason.

- **Audits.** There are two major types of audits: accounting and management. Part of the accounting function is to maintain records of the organization's transactions and assets. Most large organizations have an *internal auditing* person or department that checks periodically to make sure assets are reported accurately and to keep theft at a minimum. In addition to performing internal audits, many organizations hire a certified public accounting (CPA) firm to verify the organization's financial statements through an *external accounting audit.* The **management audit** *analyzes the organization's planning, organizing, leading, and controlling functions to look for improvements.* The analysis focuses on the past, present, and future.

Occasional Controls. Unlike periodic controls, which involve set time intervals, *occasional controls* are used on a sporadic basis when needed:

- **Observation.** Managers personally watch and talk to employees as they perform their jobs. Observation is also done by video camera and electronic devices.

- **The Exception Principle.** When the exception principle is used, control is left up to employees unless problems occur, in which case the employees go to the manager for help. Corrective action is then taken to get performance back on schedule.

- **Special Reports.** When problems or opportunities are identified, management often requests that a special report be compiled by one employee, a committee within the department/organization, or outside consultants who specialize in that area. Such reports vary in content and nature but are often designed to identify the cause of a problem as well as a solution—or an opportunity and a way to take advantage of it.

WORK
APPLICATION 14-8

Give an example of a constant, a periodic, and an occasional control method used by an organization you work for or have worked for. Identify each by name and explain why it is classified as such.

management audit Analysis of the organization's planning, organizing, leading, and controlling functions to look for improvements.

- **Project controls.** With nonrecurring or unique projects, the project manager needs to develop a control system to ensure the project is completed on time. Because planning and controlling are so closely linked, planning tools, such as Gantt charts and PERT networks (Chapter 15), are also project control methods.[33]

For a review of the systems process with its four types of controls and the methods of control categorized by frequency, see Exhibit 14-5. The types of control are listed separately because all four types may be used with any method and more than one method can be used at once. You need to be aware of the stage of the systems process you are in and the type of control used in that stage (Exhibit 14-1) and then select the most appropriate method(s) for the type of control.

EXHIBIT 14-5   TYPES, FREQUENCY, AND METHODS OF CONTROL

Types of Control	Frequency and Methods of Control		
Preliminary (input)	Constant Control	Periodic Control	Occasional Control
Concurrent (transformation process)	Self	Regular Meeting and Reports	Observation
Rework (output)	Clan	Budgets	Exception Principle
Damage (customer satisfaction)	Standing Plans	Audits	Special Reports Project

Employees at **the Ranch (Case Question 3)** can't be watched constantly, so managers also depend on self-control and clan control. One of the standing plans is the 10-foot rule: If you come within 10 feet of customers, you always greet them cheerfully and ask whether they need any assistance. Pete Clark has to communicate often with his staff, and nothing is more important to continually improving operations than their sitting down face to face during regular weekly meetings and listening to each other. The Ranch uses budgets and it also has audits. To offer unsurpassed service, all employees use observation. Player assistance uses the exception principle, as employees know to contact management if they can't handle any golfer's request. If any department is not meeting objectives, special reports are used to identify problems and solutions. Project control is used for golf tournaments and special events for corporate clients and other organizations, as well as for the dining facility.

FINANCIAL CONTROLS: THE MASTER BUDGETING PROCESS

Accounting is referred to as the language of business and profit is the primary measure of business success. If you want to advance and succeed in business, you must be able to work with budgets and financial statements to make important decisions.[34] In this section, we discuss budgeting and financial statements.

A **budget** *is a planned quantitative allocation of resources for specific activities.* Notice that the definition of *budget* does not include money. This is because all types of resources can be allocated. For example, in Exhibit 14-4, units of output were budgeted. Human resources, machines, time, and space can also be budgeted. However, for our purposes, when we use the term *budgeting* in this chapter, we are referring to the narrower, more common use of the term to mean financial budget.

The steps in the *master budgeting process* are to develop the (1) revenue and expenditure operating budgets, (2) capital expenditures budget, and (3) financial

budget A planned quantitative allocation of resources for specific activities.

budgeted cash flow, income statement, and balance sheet. The three steps, with their sub-steps, are illustrated in Exhibit 14-6. Notice the feedback loop that takes into account possible revisions in a prior budget due to other budget developments.

The budget usually covers a one-year period, broken down by month. The finance *controller* is responsible for the budgeting process that results in a *master budget* for the entire organization. Each department sub-mits its proposed budget to the controller/committee for approval. During the budget-ing process, the use of power and politics is common, and the negotiating conflict man-agement style (Chapter 10) is typically used to resolve the conflicts that arise when allocating scarce resources. The controller/committee may negotiate recommended revisions with department managers and/or use its position power to require revisions.

Accounting can be considered the language of business, and budgeting is the process to control financial performance. Photo from Dmitriy Shironosov/Alamy.

Operating Budgets

Many managers fear developing budgets because they have weak math or accounting skills. In reality, budgeting requires planning skills rather than math and accounting skills. You usually have the prior year's budget as a guide to use, which needs updating for the coming year. Using a computer spreadsheet makes the job even easier as it does the math for you.

The **operating budgets** *include the revenue and expense budgets*. You must first determine how much money you have or will have before you can plan how you are going to spend it. Therefore, the first step in the master budgeting process is to determine the revenue, and then the expenditure budgets can be determined. Good controls reduce budget overruns.[35] Success comes from increasing revenues and/or reducing expenses.[36]

Revenue Budgets. A *revenue budget* is a forecast of total income for the year. The revenue budget adds together projected income from all sources, such as sales for each product and/or location. The marketing/sales department commonly pro-vides the revenue figures for the entire firm based on the sales forecast.

Expense Budgets. An *expense budget* is a forecast of total operating spending for the year. It is common for each functional area/department manager to have an expenditure budget. Employee compensation is a major expense for many com-panies that have laid off employees to cut expenses during the last recession, and firms are controlling cost by being cautious in hiring new employees as the econ-omy expands slowly.[37]

The Ranch's (Case Question 4) revenues come from greens fees (which include use of the practice facility and a golf cart), the Tavern on the Green, function facil-ities, and the golf shop. Expenses include golf course and building maintenance, supplies and equipment (machines, fertilizers/chemicals, food and beverages), management and administration expenses, and employee compensation.

Capital Expenditures Budget

The second step in developing the master budget is to develop the capital expen-ditures budget. The **capital expenditures budget** *includes all planned major asset investments*. You may have heard that it takes money to make money—that's what

WORK
APPLICATION 14-9

Identify the major source(s) of revenue and expenses where you work or have worked.

LO 14-4

Explain how the capital expenditures budget is different from the expense budget.

operating budgets The revenue and expense budgets.

capital expenditures budget A projection of all planned major asset investments.

EXHIBIT 14-6   STEPS IN THE MASTER BUDGETING PROCESS

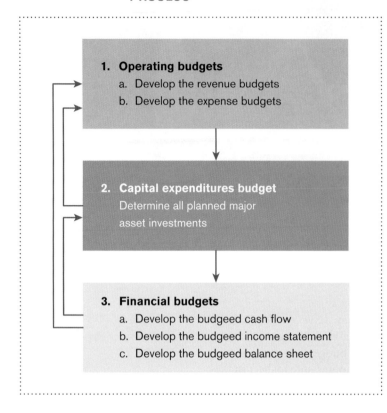

1. **Operating budgets**
   a. Develop the revenue budgets
   b. Develop the expense budgets

2. **Capital expenditures budget**
   Determine all planned major asset investments

3. **Financial budgets**
   a. Develop the budgeed cash flow
   b. Develop the budgeed income statement
   c. Develop the budgeed balance sheet

capital budgeting is all about. The major assets owned by an organization are those that last and are paid for over several years and enable the firm to make a profit. The major assets budgeted for usually include land, new buildings, and all types of equipment. Economic growth comes through capital investment, so governments and financial institutions provide funds to business to purchase capital assets to start and expand operations.[38] Businesses startups need capital for resources to launch a new venture.[39] Capital to start a new business is referred to as *risk capital* and *venture capital*.[40]

The business focus should be on increasing revenues, not simply cutting expenses. Although controlling expenses is important, you can only cut expenses so far, making the capital expenditures budget the most important budget because it is based on developing ways to bring in revenues through new and improved products and projects that will create customer value and profits. Companies must continually work to develop new products and plan to take advantage of opportunities.

It cost a lot of money to turn a farm into **the Ranch (Case Question 5a)**, to purchase equipment to maintain the course, and to renovate one of the old barns into a restaurant and the other into the functions facility, changing rooms, and a golf shop. It will take several years for the owners to get their investment back and start making a profit. That's what capital budgeting is all about. Prior to being a golf club, the property had been a dairy farm owned by the Hall family. The Hall family wanted to turn the farm into a golf club and provided the land, and investors were to supply the capital. The Ranch has a one-third ownership by the Halls, one-third by the investors and managing partners the Clarks, and one-third by investors Bernard Chiu and Ronald Izen.

Financial Budgets and Statements

The third step in the master budgeting process is to prepare financial budgets. In other words, before the year begins, the controller forecasts what each statement will be at year end. The financial budgets are prepared last because the operating and capital expenditures budget figures are needed to prepare them. If the budgeted financial statements do not meet expectations, the capital expenditures budget and/or operating budgets may need to be revised—hence the need for the feedback loop in the master budgeting process in Exhibit 14-6. Revisions are common when a net loss is projected.

Each statement commonly gives figures for the year, with each month and quarter presented. The difference between the budget, also called a *pro forma statement,* and actual statements is that actual statements report past results while the budget or pro forma statement projects future results.

Financial statements are used by the internal managers of the firm, as well as external suppliers, creditors, and investors, who make decisions about whether to conduct business with the firm by evaluating its performance. Although major corporations with public shareholders have to provide financial statements, only

LO 14-5

List the three primary financial statements and what is presented in each of them.

WORK
APPLICATION 4-10

Identify the major capital asset expenditures invested in by your present or a past organization.

14-2 JOIN THE DISCUSSION ETHICS & SOCIAL RESPONSIBILITY

Expenses

PricewaterhouseCoopers (PwC) is a large global accounting firm. When its employees traveled to and from clients' facilities and for clients, PwC paid the cost and then charged travel expenses to the client. PwC's practice was to charge the regular rate, when in fact it was getting discounts. Clients accused PwC of overcharging them for travel. PwC said there was nothing wrong with this practice, but it agreed to a several-million-dollar settlement to resolve an Arkansas lawsuit over travel rebates.

1. Is it ethical and socially responsible for PricewaterhouseCoopers to charge the full rate for travel expenses when it gets discounts?
2. If you worked for a company and knew it did this, would you say anything to anyone about it? If yes, to whom would you speak and what would you say?

---

around 7 percent of privately owned companies provide financial information to all their employees. However, advocates of doing so (called *open-book management*) report that it can improve the bottom line.[41]

The three primary **financial statements** are *the income statement, balance sheet, and cash flow statement*. (They are presented below in the order in which they appear in annual reports.)

Income Statement. The income statement presents revenue and expenses and the profit or loss for the stated time period. The income statement primarily covers one year. However, monthly and quarterly income statements are also developed to measure interim performance and to be used for concurrent control when necessary. Many people believe that college sports are profitable. However, only 22 of 337 (6.5 percent) of Division I colleges make a profit.[42] Some sports may make money, but the expenses of the other sport teams that lose money offset the overall profits. A workable balance sheet doesn't include too much debt.[43] Exhibit 14-7 shows an abbreviated income statement for **IBM** with $106,604,000 in profits for 2012.[44]

Balance Sheet. The *balance sheet* presents the assets and liabilities and owners' equity. Assets are owned by the organization; liabilities are debts owed to others; owners'/stockholders' equity is the assets minus the liabilities, or the share of assets owned. The balance sheet is called by that name because the total of the assets always equals the total of the liabilities plus owners' equity for a particular point in time. Exhibit 14-7 includes a balance sheet for **IBM** balancing at $119,213,000.[45]

Cash Flow Statement. The *cash flow statement* presents the cash receipts and payments for the stated period. (Checks are considered cash.) It commonly has two sections: operating and financial activities. Cash flow statements typically cover one year. However, monthly and quarterly statements are also developed to measure interim performance and to be used for concurrent control when necessary. The operating budgets and capital expenditures budget affect the cash flow statement as cash revenue is received and cash expenses and expenditures are paid.

Bonds versus Stocks. Companies that wish to expand need money to do so. Two commonly used options for large corporations are to sell bonds or stock. The sale of bonds and stocks doesn't affect the income statement, but it affects the balance sheet and cash flow statements. So what's the difference between bonds and stock? For this example, let's say the company wants to raise $1 million.

WORK
APPLICATION 14-11

Does the company you work for or have worked for make its financial statements available to the public? If it does, get copies and review them. Also, does the organization develop operating, capital expenditures, and financial budgets? If it does, try to get copies for review. If you are not sure, call or talk to your present or past boss to find out.

financial statements The income statement, balance sheet, and cash flow statement.

EXHIBIT 14-7 IBM FINANCIAL STATEMENTS (IN MILLIONS)

	Income Statement
Revenue	
[sales − cost = gross profit]	$44,364
Expenses [selling + administrative + R&D + taxes]	$27,760
Net Income (or Net Loss) [revenue − expenses]	$16,6045
	Balance Sheet
Assets	
[current − cash/accounts receivable + inventories + property and equipment] *Liabilities* and Stockholders' Equity	$119,213
Liabilities [current − accounts payable/accrued expenses/estimated product warranties + long-term − mortgages/notes/bonds]	$100,229
Stockholders' Equity	$18,984
Total Liabilities and Owners Equity	**$119,213**

Source: http://www.ibm.com, as of December 2012.

Bonds. If the company sells bonds, it must pay back the bond holders plus the rate of interest specified. The firm increases its assets of cash and its liabilities by $1 million. No ownership in the company has been given away. So if you buy bonds, you can expect to get your money back plus interest. Bonds are a low-risk investment, but the return is often less than with stocks.

Stock. If the company sells stock, it never has to pay back the stockholders because they become owners of the company. The firm increases its assets of cash and its owners' equity by $1 million. So if you buy stock, you hope the value of that stock goes up and that the company will pay dividends, earning you money back. You can lose money, however, if you sell the stock for less than you paid for it.

Note that the only time the company gets any money is when it first sells the stock—an initial public offering (IPO). When a stockholder sells the shares to another person, the company gets nothing, and it has to record the new owner of the stock. Stockbrokers make their money (commission) by buying and selling stock for their client investors.

The Ranch (Case Question 5b) prepares a financial budget (pro forma statement) for the year, and each month the budget is compared to actual financial statements as everyone tries to meet the budget. The regularly scheduled meetings devote time to financial statements.

Personal Finance

In your personal life, two key financial areas to focus on are managing credit wisely and saving for retirement. Using credit cards is a quick way to build a good credit history, which will result in better insurance and mortgage interest rates, as well as other benefits. One or two credit cards are enough for one individual. In selecting a credit card, mail offers are usually not good deals. Go to websites like www.rewardscards.com and www.creditcards.com to see side-by-side comparisons. Be sure to get no-fee cards plus cash back or other rewards plans, like free travel. Use a credit card for rent (if you can), food, and gas. But be sure to pay off the debt on time and in full to avoid carrying expensive balances. If you can't pay of the full balance monthly, use a credit card with a low interest rate—usually not one with any rewards.

On the retirement front, be sure to put the maximum amount possible into an employer's 401(k) program, or at least enough to get any company match— never decline free money. After maxing out the 401(k), or if you can't get one, put money into a good individual retirement account (IRA) with no-load funds, such as with **TIAA-CREF**. As stated in Chapter 9, if you start young (in your 20s) and put away $2,000 a year until retirement, you can become a millionaire.

MANAGING PEOPLE

As a manager, it's your job to have employees meet objectives and standards[46] and follow the rules.[47] You will have to impose practices and procedures to regulate, order, and control behavior.[48] You will have to confront problems.[49] So this section discusses how to coach, counsel, and discipline employees to maintain and increase their performance.

Coaching

Coaching includes a variety of behavioral techniques and methods to help improve performance.[50] **Coaching** *is the process of giving motivational feedback to maintain and improve performance.* Good coaching also improves communications and relationships.[51] Many people who hear the word coaching immediately think of athletes, but coaching is also an important management skill that is used to get the best results from each employee. Before reading about coaching, complete the Self-Assessment on Coaching to determine how well you do or can coach people to improve performance.

The Importance of Positive Feedback. As implied in the definition of coaching, feedback is the central part of coaching, and like the objective, it should be motivational.[52] You should give more positive than negative feedback. Have you ever noticed that when athletes make good plays, the coach and team members cheer them on? The same technique motivates people in the workplace; try it! Recall the importance of giving praise and how to give motivational praise from Chapter 11.

Determining Corrective Coaching Action. When an employee is not performing up to potential, even when acceptable standards are being met, the first step is to determine why,[53] using the performance formula: performance = ability × motivation × resources (Chapter 11).

When ability is holding back performance, training is needed. When motivation is lacking, motivational techniques, such as giving praise, may help. Talk to the employee to try to determine why motivation is lacking, and develop a plan together. If motivation does not work, you may have to use discipline, which will be discussed later. When resources are lacking, work to obtain them.

LO 14-6

Explain the importance of positive motivational feedback in coaching.

coaching The process of giving motivational feedback to maintain and improve performance.

14-1   SELF ASSESSMENT

Coaching

For each of the following 15 statements, select the response that best describes your actual behavior or what you would do when coaching others to improve performance. Place the number 5, 4, 3, 2, or 1 on the line before each statement.

Describes my behavior			Does NOT describe my behavior	
5	4	3	2	1

_____ 1. I know when to coach, counsel, and discipline people.

_____ 2. I don't try to be a psychological counselor or offer advice to solve personal problems, but I do refer people who need help to professionals.

_____ 3. I deal with mistakes as a learning opportunity rather than a reason to place blame and punish.

_____ 4. I make sure people are clear about my expectations rather than let them guess.

_____ 5. I take action to make sure people do at least the minimum rather than let them perform below standard.

_____ 6. I maintain a relationship with people when I coach them rather than let coaching hurt our relationship.

_____ 7. I coach soon after the incident rather than wait for a later time to talk about it.

_____ 8. I focus on showing concern for people and helping them improve performance for their own benefit rather than to get what I want done.

_____ 9. I show people how they can benefit by taking the action I suggest rather than just tell them what to do.

_____ 10. I offer very specific suggestions for improving rather than say general things like "You're not doing a good job" or "You need to do better."

_____ 11. I don't use words like "always" and "never" when talking about what the person does that needs to be improved. For example, I would say, "You were late twice this week" not "You're always late" or "You're never on time."

_____ 12. I focus on the behavior that needs to be improved rather than on the person. For example, I would say, "Why not set an earlier time to get to work—say, 7:45 instead of 8:00?" not "Why can't you be on time?"

_____ 13. I walk around and talk to people to help them improve rather than wait for them to come to me.

_____ 14. I feel comfortable giving people feedback rather than feeling uncomfortable or awkward.

_____ 15. I coach differently depending on the problem rather than always the same way.

_____ Total score

To determine your coaching score, add up the numbers for your 15 answers (between 15 and 75) and place the score on the total score line and on the following continuum.

Effective coaching							Not effective coaching
75_____70_____60_____50_____40_____30_____20_____15_____							

Pete Clark is unique, as he spent several years managing his own Jiffy Lube franchises and coaching high school baseball and football and college football teams before managing **the Ranch (Case Question 6)**. Pete says there are more similarities than differences among running a Jiffy Lube business, directing the Ranch Golf Club, and coaching sports. The focus is the same: high-quality service. You have to treat the customer or player right. Pete uses the same "3 I's" coaching philosophy at all three: You need *intensity* to be prepared to do the job right, *integrity* to do the right thing when no one is watching, and *intimacy* to be a team player. If one person does not do the job right, everyone is negatively affected. In business and sports, you need to strive to be the best. You need to set and meet challenging goals. Pete strongly believes in being positive and developing a supportive working relationship, which includes sitting down to talk and really listening to the other person.

The Coaching Model. Coaching should be viewed as a way to provide ongoing feedback to employees about their job performance. However, ask managers what they tend to put off doing and they'll likely say advising weak employees that they must improve their performance. Many managers are hesitant to confront employees, even to the point of jarred nerves and sleepless nights. Procrastinators hope that the employees will turn around on their own, only to find—often too late—that the situation gets worse. Part of the problem is that managers don't know how to coach or are not good at coaching.[54] Thus, Model 14–1 presents a four-step coaching model, and the steps are described after.

MODEL 14-1   COACHING

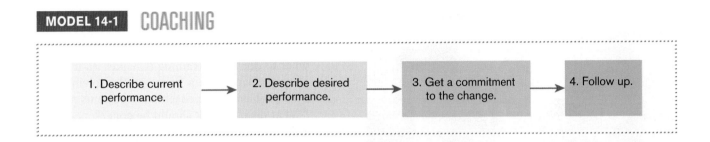

Step 1. Describe current performance. Using specific examples, describe the current behavior that needs to be changed, focusing on improving, not wrong behavior.

For example, don't say, "You are picking up the box wrong." Say, "Billie, there is a more effective way of picking the box up off the floor than bending at the waist."

Step 2. Describe desired performance. Tell the employees exactly what the desired performance is in detail. Show how they will benefit from following your advice.

For example: *Ability*—"If you squat down and pick up the box using your legs instead of your back, it is easier and there is less chance of injuring yourself. Let me demonstrate for you." *Motivation*—"Why should you squat and use your legs rather than your back to pick up boxes?"

Step 3. Get a commitment to the change. When dealing with an *ability* issue, it is not necessary to get employees to verbally commit to the change if they seem willing to make it. However, if employees defend their way and you're sure it's not as effective, explain why your proposed way is better. If you cannot get the employees to understand and agree, get a verbal commitment. This step is also important for *motivation* issues, because if the employees are not willing to commit to the change, they will most likely not make the change.

For example: *Ability* lacking—the employee will most likely be willing to pick up boxes correctly, so skip this step. *Motivation* lacking—"Will you squat rather than use your back from now on?"

Step 4. Follow up. Remember that some employees do what managers *inspect* (imposed control), not what they *expect*. You should follow up to ensure that employees are behaving as desired.

When dealing with an *ability* issue, if the person was receptive and you skipped step 3, say nothing. However, watch to be sure that the activity is done correctly in the future. Coach again, if necessary. For a *motivation* problem, make a statement that you will follow up and that there are possible consequences for repeat performance.

For example: *Ability*—say nothing, but observe. *Motivation*—"Billie, picking up boxes with your back is dangerous; if I catch you doing it again, I will take disciplinary action."

WORK
APPLICATION 14-12

How would you rate your present or past boss's coaching ability? Explain your answer using critical incidents.

Sam Walton, deceased founder and CEO of Walmart , was a great believer in Management By Walking Around (MBWA). Photo from Gilles Mingasson/Getty Images.

Management by Walking Around

As a leader, you help people,[55] and MBWA is one way to do so. **Management by walking around (MBWA)** *has three major activities: listening, teaching, and facilitating.*

- *Listening.* To find out what is going on, do a lot more listening than talking and be open to feedback.[56] Learn to talk last, not first. Open with a simple question like "How is it going?" Then use the communication skills from Chapter 13.

- *Teaching.* It does not mean telling employees what to do; this is training (Chapter 9). It means helping them to do a better job by solving their own problems. Use coaching statements such as "What do you think should be done?"

- *Facilitating.* It means taking action to help employees get their jobs done. The focus is primarily on improving the system to increase performance. By listening, find out what's getting in the way or slowing employees down. Your job is to run interference—to remove the stumbling blocks preventing employees from improving performance.

Sam Walton, deceased founder and CEO of **Walmart**, was a great believer in MBWA. Walton would visit every one of his stores every year. He would unexpectedly go into a store and walk up to customers and employees and talk to them about improving **Walmart**, writing notes on a little pad he carried around with him. Today, **Walmart** has too many stores (around 10,800 in 27 countries) for the CEO to visit every store annually. But, true to the philosophy, top executives are required to visit stores every year.[57]

Feedback is critical to success at **the Ranch (Case Question 7)**, as it tells the Clarks whether the players and diners are getting quality service and how to improve. The Clarks and employees are accepting of criticism because they realize that the only way to improve is to listen and make changes. In fact, Pete and Korby Clark spend much of their time at the Ranch managing by walking around, as they listen to employees, teach them how to improve through coaching, and help them satisfy golfers' requests. They also ask people about their experience, listening for suggestions for improvements and facilitating good ideas. The Clarks set clear objectives and have regular meetings with employees to get and give feedback on how the Ranch is progressing toward meeting its objectives.

LO 14-7

Explain the manager's role in counseling and the role of the employee assistance program staff.

management by walking around (MBWA) A type of supervision in which the three major activities are listening, teaching, and facilitating.

Counseling

When coaching, you are fine-tuning performance; with counseling and disciplining, you are dealing with a problem employee who is not performing to standards or is violating standing plans. Problem employees have a negative effect on performance.[58] Good human resource management (Chapter 9) skills can help you avoid hiring problem employees,[59] but you will most likely have to confront problem employees as a manager.[60]

Problem Employees. Problem employees display behavioral and performance-related issues. They do poor-quality work, they don't get along with coworkers, they display negative attitudes, and they frequently don't show up for work.[61] There are four types of problem employees: There are employees who do not have the *ability* to meet the job performance standards and should be transferred or terminated. There are employees who do not have the *motivation* to meet job performance standards or intentionally *violate standing plans* and often need discipline. There are also employees who have performed well in the past but have a job-related or personal *problem* negatively affecting their performance who many need counseling. It is not always easy to distinguish between the types of problem employees. Therefore, it is often advisable to start with coaching/counseling and change to discipline if the problem persists.

Management Counseling. When most people hear the term *counseling*, they think of psychological counseling or psychotherapy. That type of sophisticated help should not be attempted by a noncounseling professional such as a manager. Instead, **management counseling** *is the process of giving employees feedback so they realize that a problem is affecting their job performance and referring employees with problems to the employee assistance program.*

Most managers do not like to hear the details of personal problems. Doing so is not a requirement. Instead, your role as a manager is to help employees realize that they have problems and that those problems affect their work Your job is getting the employee back on track. You should not give advice on how to solve personal problems such as a relationship difficulty. When professional help is needed, you should refer the employee to the human resources department for professional help through the employee assistance program.

EAP. The **employee assistance program (EAP)** *has a staff of people who help employees get professional assistance in solving their problems.* Most large businesses have an EAP to help solve employees' personal problems.

To make the referral, you could say something like "Are you aware of our employee assistance program? Would you like me to set up an appointment with Jean in the HR department to help you get professional assistance?" However, if job performance does not return to standard, discipline is appropriate because it often makes the employee realize the seriousness of his or her problem and the importance of maintaining job performance. Some time off from work, with or without pay, depending on the situation, often helps the employee deal with the problem.

The Importance of Confronting Problem Employees. A manager's first obligation is to the organization's performance rather than to individual employees. Therefore, it is your job to confront problem employees.[62] Not taking action with problem employees because you feel uncomfortable confronting them, because you feel sorry for them, or because you like them does not help you or the employee. Not only do problem employees negatively affect their own productivity, but they also cause more work for you and other employees. Problem employees lower employee morale, as others resent them for not pulling their own weight. Team members will often use clan control to pressure problem employees to perform to norms and standards.[63] Thus, it is critical to take quick action with problem employees.

Disciplining

Coaching, which includes counseling, should generally be the first step in dealing with a problem employee. However, if an employee is unwilling or unable to change or a rule has been broken, discipline is necessary, especially for workplace deviance that causes problems.[64]

WORK
APPLICATION 14-13

Identify a problem employee you observed on the job. Describe how the person affected the department's performance.

management counseling The process of giving employees feedback so they realize that a problem is affecting their job performance and referring employees with problems to the employee assistance program.

employee assistance program (EAP) A benefit program staffed by people who help employees get professional assistance in solving their problems.

14-3 APPLYING THE CONCEPT

Guidelines for Effective Discipline

Identify which guideline is being followed—or not being followed—in the following statements. Use the guidelines in Exhibit 14-8 as the answers. Place the letter of the guideline (A–H) on the line before its statement.

_____ 11. "Come into my office so that we can discuss this matter now."

_____ 12. "The boss must have been upset to yell that loudly."

_____ 13. "It's not fair. The manager comes back from break late all the time; why can't I?"

_____ 14. "When I leave the place a mess, the manager reprimands me. When Helen does it, nothing is ever said."

_____ 15. "The boss gave me a verbal warning for being late for work and placed a note in my file."

The human resources department handles many of the disciplinary details and provides written disciplinary procedures. These procedures usually outline grounds for specific sanctions and dismissal, based on the violation.

EXHIBIT 14-8   GUIDELINES FOR EFFECTIVE DISCIPLINE

A.	Clearly communicate the standards and standing plans to all employees.
B.	Be sure that the punishment fits the crime.
C.	Follow the standing plans yourself.
D.	Take consistent, impartial action when the rules are broken.
E.	Discipline immediately, but stay calm and get all the necessary facts before you discipline.
F.	Discipline in private.
G.	Document discipline.
H.	When the discipline is over, resume normal relations with the employee.

Workplace Deviance and Discipline. Deviance is negative voluntary behavior of problem employees that violates significant organizational norms, threatens the well-being of the organization, and costs organizations as much as $200 billion annually. Deviant behavior includes rudeness, stealing, violence, vandalism, and frequently withholding effort, showing up late, leaving early, and absence from work.[65] Employees respond to incentives,[66] so it can be tempting to engage in deviant behavior for self-interest reasons.[67] It's your job as the manager to get employees to conform to standards and comply with standing plans,[68] and employees are easier to manage when they believe the standards and rules are fair.[69] **Discipline** *is corrective action to get employees to meet standards and standing plans.* The major objective of discipline is to change behavior. Secondary objectives may be to (1) let employees know that action will be taken when standing plans or performance requirements are not met and (2) maintain authority when challenged. Exhibit 14-9 lists eight guidelines for effective discipline. Generally, abusive supervisors[70] who yell[71] and hold grudges[72] have more discipline problems than do nonabusive supervisors.[73]

discipline Corrective action to get employees to meet standards and standing plans.

Progressive Discipline. Many organizations have a series of progressively more severe disciplinary actions. The progressive disciplinary steps are (1) oral warning, (2) written warning, (3) suspension, and (4) dismissal. All four steps are commonly followed for minor violations, such as being late for work or excessive absenteeism. For more important violations, such as stealing, steps may be skipped. Be sure to document each step.[74]

| 14-3 | **JOIN THE DISCUSSION** ETHICS & SOCIAL RESPONSIBILITY |

Disciplining Ethical Behavior

Unfortunately, some employees are rewarded for being unethical, while others are disciplined for being ethical. For example, some auto repair shops pay a commission for work done, so mechanics are paid more if they get customers to buy parts and services they don't need. Mechanics who have a below-average number of repairs may be considered underachievers and may be pressured, through discipline, to perform unneeded repair work.

Similarly, those in the medical field may push unnecessary tests or even treatments.

1. Have you ever been in or known of a situation in which people were rewarded for being unethical and disciplined for being ethical? If so, describe the situation.
2. Is it ethical and socially responsible for firms to establish controls that reward unethical behavior and discipline ethical behavior to make more money?

The Discipline Model. The steps in the discipline model should be followed when employees must be disciplined. The five steps are presented here and summarized in Model 14–2.

Step 1. Refer to past feedback. Begin the interview by refreshing the employee's memory. If the employee has been coached/counseled about the behavior or if he or she has clearly broken a known rule, state that.

For example: *Prior coaching*—"Billie, remember my telling you about the proper way to lift boxes with your legs?" *Rule violation*—"Billie, you know the safety rule about lifting boxes with your legs."

Step 2. Ask why the undesired behavior was used. Giving the employee a chance to explain the behavior is part of getting all the necessary facts before you discipline. If you used prior coaching and the employee committed to changing the behavior, ask why the behavior did not change.

For example: *Prior coaching*—"Two days ago you told me that you would use your legs rather than your back to lift boxes. Why are you still using your back?" *Rule violation*—"Why are you breaking the safety rule and using your back rather than your legs to lift the box?"

Step 3. Give the discipline. If there is no good reason for the undesirable behavior, give the discipline. The discipline will vary with the stage in the disciplinary progression.

For example: *Prior coaching*—"Because you have not changed your behavior, I'm giving you an oral warning." *Rule violation*—"Because you have violated a safety rule, I'm giving you an oral warning."

Step 4. Get a commitment to change and develop a plan. Try to get a commitment to change. If the employee will not commit, make note of the fact in the critical incidents file or use the procedures for a written warning. If a plan for change has been developed in the past, try to get the employee to commit to it again. Or develop a new plan if necessary.

For example: *Prior coaching or rule violation*—"Will you lift with your legs from now on?" "Is there a way to get you to remember to use your legs instead of your back when you lift?"

Step 5. Summarize and state the follow-up. Summarize the discipline and state the follow-up disciplinary action to be taken. Part of follow-up is to document the discipline. At the written warning and suspension all stages, get the employee's signature. If necessary, take the next step in the discipline model: dismissal.

For example: *Prior coaching or rule violation*—"So you agree to use your legs instead of your back when you lift. If I catch you again, you will be given a written warning, which is followed by a suspension and dismissal if necessary."

MODEL 14-2 DISCIPLINE

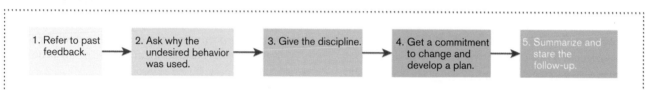

1. Refer to past feedback. → 2. Ask why the undesired behavior was used. → 3. Give the discipline. → 4. Get a commitment to change and develop a plan. → 5. Summarize and stare the follow-up.

WORK
APPLICATION 14-14

Review the discipline guidelines in Exhibit 14–9. Identify any guidelines your present or past boss did not follow.

As we bring this chapter to a close, you should be able to establish systems controls (preliminary, concurrent, rework, and damage controls), use the control systems process (set objectives and standards, measure performance, compare performance to standards, and reinforce or correct performance), and use control methods (constant, periodic, and occasional) to achieve organizational objectives. You should also understand the budgeting process (operating, capital expenditure, and financial budgets) and contents of financial statements (income statement, balance sheet, and cash flow statement). You should also be able to manage by walking around and coach, counsel, and discipline employees using behavioral models 14–1 and 14–2.

• • • CHAPTER SUMMARY

14-1. **List the four stages of the systems process and describe the type of control used at each stage.**

The first stage of the systems process is inputs. Preliminary control is designed to anticipate and prevent possible input problems. The second stage is the transformation process. Concurrent control is action taken to ensure that standards are met as inputs are transformed into outputs. The third stage is outputs. Rework control is action taken to fix an output. The fourth stage is customer/stakeholder satisfaction. Damage control is action taken to minimize negative impacts on customers/stakeholders due to faulty outputs. During the four stages, feedback is used to improve upon the process to continually increase customer satisfaction.

14-2. **List the four steps in the control systems process.**

The steps in the control systems process are (1) set objectives and standards, (2) measure performance,

(3) compare performance to standards, and (4) correct or reinforce, with a feedback loop for continuous improvement.

14-3. **Describe the differences among the three categories of control frequency.**

Constant controls are in continuous use. Periodic controls are used on a regular fixed basis, such as once a day or week. Occasional controls are used on a sporadic basis when needed.

14-4. **Explain how the capital expenditures budget is different from the expense budget.**

The capital expenditures budget includes all planned major asset investments. It shows funds allocated for investments in major assets that will last and be paid for over several years. The expense budget shows funds allocated to pay for operating costs during the budgeting year. With expense budgets, the focus is on cost control. With capital expenditures budgets, the focus is on the more important role of developing ways to bring in revenues through new and improved products and projects that will create customer value.

14-5. **List the three primary financial statements and what is presented in each of them.**

The *income statement* presents revenue and expenses and the profit or loss for the stated time period. The *balance sheet* presents assets, liabilities, and owners' equity. The *cash flow statement* presents the cash receipts and payments for the stated period.

14-6. **Explain the importance of positive motivational feedback in coaching.**

The objective of coaching is to improve performance. Positive feedback, such as praise, is used to motivate employees to maintain and improve their performance.

14-7. **Explain the manager's role in counseling and the role of the employee assistance program staff.**

The manager's role in counseling is to give employees feedback so they realize that a problem is affecting their job performance and to refer employees with problems to the employee assistance program. The role of the employee assistance program staff is to assist employees who need professional help to solve their problems.

••• Key Terms

budget, 426
capital expenditures budget, 427
coaching, 431
concurrent control, 418
control frequency, 424
control systems process, 421
critical success factors, 422

damage control, 418
discipline, 436
employee assistance program (EAP), 435
financial statements, 429
management audit, 425

management by walking around (MBWA), 434
management counseling, 435
operating budgets, 427
preliminary control, 418
rework control, 418
standards, 421

••• Key Term Review

Complete each of the following statements using one of this chapter's key terms.

1. _____ is designed to anticipate and prevent possible problems.

2. _____ is action taken to ensure standards are met as inputs are transformed into outputs.

3. _____ is action taken to fix an output.

4. _____ is action taken to minimize negative impacts on customers/stakeholders due to faulty outputs.

5. The steps are (1) set objectives and standards, (2) measure performance, (3) compare performance to standards, and (4) correct or reinforce.

6. _____ measure performance levels in the areas of quantity, quality, time, cost, and behavior.

7. _____ are the limited number of areas in which satisfactory results will ensure successful performance, achieving the objective/standard.

8. Categories of _____ include constant, periodic, and occasional.

9. The _____ analyzes the organization's planning, organizing, leading, and controlling functions to look for improvements.

10. A _____ is a planned quantitative allocation of resources for specific activities.

11. The _____ include the revenue and expense budgets.

12. The _____ includes all planned major asset investments.

13. The three primary _____ are the income statement, balance sheet, and cash flow statement.

14. _____ is the process of giving motivational feedback to maintain and improve performance.

15. _____ has three major activities: listening, teaching, and facilitating.

16. _____ is the process of giving employees feedback so they realize that a problem is affecting their job performance and referring employees with problems to the employee assistance program.

17. The _____ has a staff of people who help employees get professional assistance in solving their problems.

18. _____ is corrective action to get employees to meet standards and standing plans.

••• REVIEW QUESTIONS

1. Why is damage control important?

2. Why should you focus on preliminary and concurrent types of control rather than on rework and damage control?

3. Who are the primary customers/stakeholders for the outputs of the operations, marketing, human resources, finance, and information functional areas/departments?

4. What are the five areas of performance that standards measure?

5. Why is measuring performance important to an organization?

6. What is shown in a performance report?

7. What is the role of reinforcement in the control systems process?

8. What are the three constant control methods, the three periodic control methods, and the four occasional control methods?

9. What are the three steps in the master budgeting process?

10. Why is the capital expenditures budget the most important budget?

11. What is the difference between financial statements and financial budgets?

12. What is the objective of coaching?

13. How do managers commonly demotivate employees?

14. What is the performance formula, and how is it used with coaching?

15. What are the three activities of management by walking around, and what is the role of facilitating?

16. What are the differences among coaching, counseling, and disciplining?

••• COMMUNICATION SKILLS

The following critical-thinking questions can be used for class discussion and/or as written assignments to develop communication skills. Be sure to give complete explanations for all questions.

1. Recall a personal event that you had to help conduct, such as a party, shower, or wedding. Identify preliminary, concurrent, rework, and damage controls, as well as feedback. What did you learn from the experience and the textbook discussion that can help you to plan and control better in the future?

2. Apply the control systems process to your college education. What are your major objectives and standards? How do you measure and compare performance to your objectives and standards? What current and future corrective action have you taken? Do you reinforce your performance when meeting goals? If so, how?

3. Employees tend to resist control and sometimes break the rules. Give examples of things you or others have done to resist controls.

4. How does your professor in this course use controls to reduce and/or eliminate cheating on tests and other assignments?

5. How confident are you in your ability to develop budgets and read financial statements? What experience have you had in developing budgets and reading financial statements?

6. Do you feel that managers should spend more time on coaching and MBWA techniques? Explain.

7. Which of the eight discipline guidelines is most relevant to you personally? Explain.

8. Can the need for discipline be reduced? If so, how?

••• CASE: SUE LEE CLOTHES

About three years ago, Sue Lee started her small manufacturing company in the Garment District in New York City. Lee employs around 35 people. The five teams at Sue Lee work in one big room in which all clothes are made. One of the teams makes custom shirts for quality men's clothing stores.

Sue Lee works in a separate office and spends most of her time on marketing, finance, and human resources

management. She does not spend much time with the manufacturing employees. Team leaders are responsible for keeping team production records and hours worked, training team members, and helping them when there is a problem. Team leaders do not get involved with discipline.

Unlike some of her competitors, Sue Lee does not want to run a sweatshop, so she pays employees a salary rather than a low piece rate for actual work performed. However, if employees don't produce an average of 48 shirts, they lose their jobs. Sue Lee's employees have a higher rate of job satisfaction than competitors' employees do, and Lee has a quality reputation.

With all the competition, Sue Lee is not making much money. She wants to get employees to produce more shirts. Sue Lee thought about buying new machines as a capital expenditure, but she really did not have the money or the desire, because her current machines were working fine. Sue Lee also considered changing to piece-rate pay. However, she figured that paying employees more to produce more would have an offsetting effect and would not benefit her much. Sue Lee also feared that if she went to piece-rate pay, she might have quality problems, which she did not want to risk. Sue Lee prides herself on being ethical and socially responsible to all stakeholders.

Sue Lee came up with the idea of setting a new quota in addition to the 48-shirt standard. Employees could leave work early once they had met the new 53-shirt quota. Sue Lee figured that she was not pushing her employees too hard and that they could get out of work around a half-hour earlier each day if they want too.

Sue Lee met with the employees in the shirt team and told them, "I want to try a new idea, which I think is fair to everyone, for the next two weeks. If you produce 53 shirts, you can go home for the day and get your full pay. I figure you can get out around 4:30 instead of 5 o'clock without having to rush your work. The same level of quality is required, and quality will be checked as usual. If you want, you can continue to produce 48 shirts and work the full eight hours." They discussed the new system, and they all liked the idea of working less hours for the same pay. If it did not work, they would go back to the old system.

On the Monday following the first week, Sue Lee got her weekly production reports, which state the number of units made by each worker and the hours each employee worked, arranged by team. Sue Lee got around to reading them after closing time, as usual. She went right to the shirt team report to see how the new system was working. Sue Lee was happy to see that everyone was producing 53 shirts and getting out around 4:30. However, on Friday, Kay made 53 shirts and left at 2:30. Sue Lee did not understand how this was possible. She decided to talk to Kay to see what was going on.

On Tuesday morning, Sue Lee visited Kay at work and asked her how it was possible to get out at 2:30. Kay said, "All I did was adjust my machine and place this new gadget on it to speed it up. Plus I developed a new procedural sequence in which I make shirts. Watch how much faster I can sew now; especially placing buttons on is so much faster." Sue Lee watched her in amazement as she made a shirt. Sue Lee did not know what to say. She told her to keep up the good work and went back to her office.

As Sue Lee walked back to her office, she wondered to herself, "Should I continue to let her leave that early? Do the other workers think it's fair for Kay to get out so much earlier than they do? This is only a two-week trial, subject to changes that are fair to everyone. What is the fair thing to do?"

Case Questions

1. Which of the four types of organizational systems control did Sue Lee use in allowing employees to go home early when they finished their work?

2. Explain how Sue Lee used the control systems process in the case.

3. Did Sue Lee develop complete standards in all five areas and did employees resist the controls?

4. Which type of control frequency and method did Sue Lee personally use in letting employees leave when they had met the quota/standard of 53 shirts?

5. How was the new control method supposed to affect the financial performance of Sue Lee Clothes?

6. Are there any potential problems with Kay's adjusting of her machine?

7. Should Sue Lee keep the control system the way it is now and continue to let Kay leave two hours earlier than the other employees? If not, what should she do?

8. Does the increased production/productivity pose any potential threat to employees? Explain.

Cumulative Case Questions

9. Which internal environmental factor is the major issue in this case? (Chapter 2)

10. How does the global village affect Sue Lee Clothes? (Chapter 3)

11. (a) Was the change at Sue Lee a strategic or operational one? (b) What was the role of objectives in this case? (c) Which functional area was affected? (Chapter 5)

12. Which job design did Sue Lee use to increase productivity? (Chapter 7)

13. What type of change was made by Sue Lee to increase productivity? (Chapter 6)

14. What (a) content, (b) process, and (c) reinforcement motivation theories were used by Sue Lee when she changed the standard to allow employees to go home early? (Chapter 11)

••• SKILL BUILDER 14-1: BOLTON CONTROL SYSTEM

Objective

To improve your skill at developing a control system for an organization/department.

Skills

The primary skills developed through this exercise are:

1. *Management skill*—decision making (conceptual, diagnostic, analytical, critical-thinking, and quantitative-reasoning skills are needed to develop a control system for a business)
2. *AACSB competency*—analytic skills
3. *Management function*—controlling

Situation

Marie Bolton owns and operates the Bolton Clerical Employment Agency. As the name indicates, her agency focuses on providing clerical employees to its business clients. It has a file of clerical employees looking for jobs or better jobs. When employers place job orders with the agency, the agency recruiter tries to find a person who fits the job specifications. The agency sends possible candidates to the employer. The employment agency charges the employer a fee only when one of its referred candidates is hired by the company. The fee is based on the employee's first-year salary. The average fee paid by employers is $1,000.

Each agency recruiter gets 35 percent of the fee charged as a salary. Pay is 100 percent commission. Refunds are made if the person placed does not stay on the job for three months.

Marie has two employees called recruiters. With only two employees, Marie is also a full-time recruiter. She does the management functions in addition to recruiting.

Marie has no formal control methods because her two recruiters are very competent professionals who are paid only by commission; she places minimal restrictions on them. Marie is somewhat satisfied with the way her business is operating. However, through a professional association she found out that her business is not doing as well as the average employment agency. Being competitive by nature, Marie does not want to be below average.

Marie has asked you to set up a control system to help her improve her agency's performance. She has provided you with the following performance report, comparing her agency's figures to those of the average agency. The professional association forecasts that revenues for next year will not increase for the industry.

PERFORMANCE INFORMATION REPORT FOR LAST YEAR

	Bolton	Average
Placement revenue (refunds deducted, not taxes)	$230,000	$250,000
Recruiter commissions paid	$80,500	$87,500
Refunds	$8,000	$10,000
Number of placements	230	250
Number of company interviews	*	1,000
Number of full-time recruiters (including owners who recruit)	3	3

*Bolton does not keep records of the number of candidates it sends to companies for interviews.

Procedure

Identify the systems process for Bolton by identifying its primary inputs, transformation process, outputs, and customers/stakeholders:

Inputs	Transformation Process	Outputs	Customers/ Stakeholders

Identify major types of control for each stage of the systems process.

Preliminary	Concurrent	Rework	Damage

To set up a control system for Bolton, follow the steps in the control systems process.

Step 1. Setting Objectives and Standards

Marie's objective is to earn $250,000 in revenue for the next year, which is the industry average. Establish standards for the year that will enable Marie to reach her objective.

Quantity. Quantity of interviews per recruiter: ____

Quantity of placements per recruiter: ____

Calculate the number of additional interviews needed to meet the standard per recruiter: ____

Calculate the percentage increase: ____ %

Quality. State the dollar value of acceptable refunds per recruiter: $____

State the corresponding number of refunds: ____

Time. State the time period in which the quantity and quality standards should be met: ____

Cost. State the cost based on commissions per recruiter: $____

Behavior. Identify any behaviors employees should change to help them meet the standards.

Step 2. Measuring Performance

What are the critical success factors for employment agencies? Have you identified the critical success factors within your standards? If not, rework them. How often should Marie measure performance and what methods of control should she use?

Time frequency for measuring performance: ____

Quantity of interviews per recruiter for time period: ____

Quantity of placements per recruiter for time period: ____

List specific control methods to use:

Step 3. Comparing Performance to Standards

How should Marie compare her agency's performance to her new standards?

Step 4. Correcting or Reinforcing

What type of corrective action should Marie take if standards are not being met or what type of reinforcement if they are?

Assume that Bolton does exactly meet the standard. Calculate the rate of productivity for Bolton's past performance (average agency): ____

1. Calculate the rate of productivity for the new performance standard: ____

2. Is there a change in productivity? ____ yes ____ no

3. If yes, by what percentage did it increase or decrease? ____

4. Base the inputs on recruiter commissions only.

5. Calculate the past commission per employee (average agency): ____

6. Calculate the new commission per employee: ____

7. What percentage pay increase do recruiters get? ____

8. Do profits increase when the new standards are met? ____

9. How do you think the employees will react to your proposed control system? Do you think they will resist the control? Why or why not?

Apply It

What did I learn from this exercise? How will I use this knowledge in the future?

Your instructor may ask you to do this Skill Builder in class in a group. If so, the instructor will provide you with any necessary information or additional instructions.

• • • SKILL BUILDER 14-2: COACHING

Objective

To develop your skill at improving performance through coaching.

Skills

The primary skills developed through this exercise are:

1. *Management skill*—interpersonal (coaching takes communication skills to motivate employees)

2. *AACSB competency*—communication ability, (to resolve performance problems)

3. *Management function*—controlling

Procedure 1 (2–4 minutes)

Break into groups of three. Make some groups of two if necessary. Each member selects one of the following three situations in which to be the manager and a different one in which to be the employee. In each situation, the employee knows the standing plans; he or she is not motivated to follow them. You will take turns coaching and being coached.

Three Problem Employee Situations

1. Employee 1 is a clerical worker. The person uses files, as do the other 10 employees in the department.

The employees all know that they are supposed to return the files when they are finished so that others can find them when they need them. Employees should have only one file out at a time. The supervisor notices that Employee 1 has five files on the desk, and another employee is looking for one of them. The supervisor thinks that Employee 1 will complain about the heavy workload as an excuse for having more than one file out at a time.

2. Employee 2 is a server in an ice-cream shop. The employee knows that the tables should be cleaned up quickly after customers leave so that new customers do not have to sit at dirty tables. It's a busy night. The supervisor finds dirty dishes on two of this employee's occupied tables. Employee 2 is socializing with some friends at one of the tables. Employees are supposed to be friendly; Employee 2 will probably use this as an excuse for the dirty tables.

3. Employee 3 is an auto technician. All employees at the garage where this person works know that they are supposed to put a paper mat on the floor of each car so that the carpets don't get dirty. When the service supervisor got into a car Employee 3 repaired, the car did not have a mat and there was grease on the carpet. Employee 3 does excellent work and will probably make reference to this fact when coached.

Procedure 2 (3–7 minutes)

Prepare for coaching to improve performance. Below, each group member writes an outline of what he or she will say when coaching Employee 1, 2, or 3, following the steps below:

1. Describe current performance.

2. Describe desired performance. Get a commitment to the change.

3. Follow up.

Procedure 3 (5–8 minutes)

Role Playing. The manager of Employee 1, the clerical worker, coaches him or her as planned. (Use the actual name of the group member playing Employee 1.) Talk—do not read your written plan. Employee 1, put yourself in the worker's position. You work hard; there is a lot of pressure to work fast. It's easier when you have

more than one file. Refer to the workload while being coached. Both the manager and the employee will have to ad lib. The person not playing a role is the observer. He or she makes notes on the observer form that follows. Try to make positive comments and point out areas for improvement. Give the manager alternative suggestions about what he or she could have said to improve the coaching session.

Observer Form

1. How well did the manager describe current behavior?

2. How well did the manager describe desired behavior? Did the employee state why the behavior is important?

3. How successful was the manager at getting a commitment to the change? Do you think the employee will change?

4. How well did the manager describe how he or she was going to follow up to ensure that the employee performed the desired behavior?

Feedback. The observer leads a discussion of how well the manager coached the employee. (This should be a discussion, not a lecture.) Focus on what the manager did well and how the manager could improve. The employee should also give feedback on how he or she felt and what might have been more effective in getting him or her to change. Do not go on to the next interview until you are told to do so. If you finish early, wait for the others to finish.

Procedure 4 (5–8 minutes)

Same as procedure 3, but change roles so that Employee 2, the server, is coached. Employee 2 should make a comment about the importance of talking to customers to make them feel welcome. The job is not much fun if you can't talk to your friends.

Procedure 5 (5–8 minutes)

Same as procedure 3, but change roles so that Employee 3, the auto technician, is coached. Employee 3 should comment on the excellent work he or she does.

Apply It

What did I learn from this experience? How will I use this knowledge in the future?

• • • SKILL BUILDER 14-3: DISCIPLINING

Objective

To develop your ability to discipline an employee.

Skills

The primary skills developed through this exercise are:

1. *Management skill*—interpersonal (discipline requires communication skills to motivate employees to improve)
2. *AACSB competency*—communication ability (to resolve performance problems)
3. *Management function*—controlling

Procedure 1 (2–4 minutes)

Break into groups of three. Make some groups of two if necessary. Each member selects one of the three situations from Skill Builder 14–2. Decide who will discipline Employee 1, the clerical worker; Employee 2, the ice-cream shop server; and Employee 3, the auto technician. Also select a different group member to play the employee being disciplined.

Procedure 2 (3–7 minutes)

Prepare for the discipline session. Write a basic outline of what you will say to Employee 1, 2, or 3; follow the steps in the discipline model below.

1. Refer to past feedback. (Assume that you have discussed the situation before, using the coaching model.)
2. Ask why the undesired behavior was used. (The employee should make up an excuse for not changing.)
3. Give the discipline. (Assume that an oral warning is appropriate.)
4. Get a commitment to change and develop a plan.
5. Summarize and state the follow-up.

Procedure 3 (5–8 minutes)

Role Playing. The manager of Employee 1, the clerical worker, disciplines him or her as planned. (Use the actual name of the group member playing the employee.) Talk—do not read your written plan. Employee 1, put yourself in the worker's position. You work hard; there is a lot of pressure to work fast. It's easier when you have more than one file. Both the manager and the employee will need to ad lib.

The person not playing a role is the observer. He or she makes notes on the observer form that follows. For each of the following steps, try to make a statement about the positive aspects of the discipline and a statement about how the manager could have improved. Give alternative things the manager could have said to improve the discipline session. Remember, the objective is to change behavior.

Observer Form

1. How well did the manager refer to past feedback?
2. How well did the manager ask why the undesired behavior was used?
3. How well did the manager give the discipline?
4. Did the manager get a commitment to change? Do you think the employee will change his or her behavior?
5. How well did the manager summarize and state the follow-up? How effective will the follow-up be?

Feedback. The observer leads a discussion of how well the manager disciplined the employee. The employee should also give feedback on how he or she felt and what might have been more effective in getting him or her to change. Do not go on to the next interview until you are told to do so. If you finish early, wait until the others finish or the time is up.

Procedure 4 (5–8 minutes)

Same as procedure 3, but change roles so that Employee 2, the ice cream server, is disciplined. Employee 2, put yourself in the worker's position. You enjoy talking to your friends, and you're supposed to be friendly to the customers.

Procedure 5 (5–8 minutes)

Same as procedure 3, but change roles so that Employee 3, the auto technician, is disciplined. Employee 3, put yourself in the worker's position. You are an excellent technician. Sometimes you forget to put the mat on the floor.

Apply It

What did I learn from this experience? How will I use this knowledge in the future?

• • • STUDENT STUDY SITE

Visit the Student Study Site at **www.sagepub.com/lussier6e** to access to these additional study tools:

- Mobile-compatible self-assessment quizzes
- Mobile-compatible key term flashcards
- Video Links
- SAGE Journal Articles
- Web Links

Photo from Donald Heupel/Reuters/Landov.

15 Operations, Quality, and Productivity

• • • Learning Outcomes

After studying this chapter, you should be able to:

15-1. Describe time-based competition and why it is important. PAGE 447

15-2. Explain the differences among operations systems with respect to tangibility of products, levels of customer involvement, operations flexibility, and management of resources and technology. PAGE 448

15-3. Discuss what is meant by "quality is a virtue of design." PAGE 452

15-4. Explain product, process, cellular, and fixed-position facility layouts in terms of their level of customer involvement and flexibility. PAGE 453

15-5. Describe the similarities and differences among the planning sheet, Gantt chart, and PERT network. PAGE 455

15-6. Explain the relationship among inventory control, just-in-time (JIT) inventory, and materials requirement planning (MRP). PAGE 459

15-7. Explain how statistical process control (SPC) charts and the exception principle are used in quality control. PAGE 464

15-8. Describe how to measure productivity and list three ways to increase it. PAGE 466

IDEAS ON MANAGEMENT at Frito-Lay

In the 1930s, Elmer Doolin founded the Frito Company and Herman Lay founded H. W. Lay Company, each borrowing around $100 to start his business. In 1961, the Frito and Lay companies merged to form Frito-Lay, Inc. Today, Frito-Lay's 34 brands account for 59 percent of the U.S. snack chip industry. Since 1965, Frito-Lay is a wholly owned subsidiary of PepsiCo, Inc., whose CEO is Indra Nooyi, the only Indian woman to head a *Fortune* 500 company.

Frito-Lay is the world's leading snack food company that thinks globally and acts locally. To ensure that its products are developed to satisfy the taste preferences of people in various countries around the world, Frito-Lay has acquired foreign operations and brands through direct investment. The reasons Frito-Lay is so successful include aggressive marketing, an extensive distribution system, operating discipline to control consistent quality, and new product innovation.

1. How would Frito-Lay's operations systems be classified? PAGE 451
2. How would Frito-Lay's operations systems be described in terms of design? PAGE 455
3. How does Frito-Lay manage its operations systems and supply chain? PAGE 462
4. How does Frito-Lay control quality? PAGE 465

You'll find answers to these questions throughout the chapter. To learn more about Frito-Lay, visit its website at www.fritolay.com.

Source: Information for this case was taken from Frito-Lay North America, Inc., website at http://www.fritolay.com, accessed August 27, 2013.

TIME-BASED COMPETITION AND OPERATIONS

LO 15-1

Describe time-based competition and why it is important.

Time-based competition *refers to the use of strategies to increase the speed with which an organization goes from creativity to delivery.* The time required to complete this process is called throughput time. With globalization, the speed of competition has increased and the winners are the companies that adapt fastest.[1] By redesigning organizing processes to help consumers save time or more fully enjoy the time that they spend doing something, companies are more profitable.[2] Speed, efficiency, and cost control are the common goals of successful

● ● ● Chapter Outline

WORK
APPLICATION 15-1

Is your present or past organization concerned about time-based competition? If so, what functional areas are primarily responsible for speed?

LO 15-2

Explain the differences among operations systems with respect to tangibility of products, levels of customer involvement, operations flexibility, and management of resources and technology.

companies.[3] Through time-based competition, **3M** reduced its new product development time from two years to two months and **Motorola** cut its production lead time for cellular phones from several weeks to four hours. The **Apple** iPhone has a slower once-a-year upgrade cycle than its rivals, releasing several designs annually.[4]

Operations is the function concerned with transforming resource inputs into product outputs. A **product** is a good, a service, or a combination of the two. Because the mission of all organizations revolves around providing products, the operations department is a primary focus of efforts to improve speed.[5]

At its peak, manufacturing employees were 39 percent of the U.S. workforce, but today it is down to 9 percent, as America is more of a service economy.[6] However, around half of the large manufacturers plan to return some production to the United States, partly due to the efficiency of digital technology and *3-D printing* that is slowly transforming manufacturing.[7] **GE, Ford**, and **Mattel** are using 3-D printing to get products to their customers faster.[8] Your career will be affected by your ability to learn quickly and adapt to technology changes that come from operations.[9]

Operations is important because if you don't have a good product developed through effective operations that change quickly in a dynamic environment, you won't have a business.[10] Success at integrating the activities and resources leads to higher operational capabilities. Exhibit 15-1 lists the ways systems to manage operations are classified, designed, and managed.

EXHIBIT 15-1   HOW OPERATIONS SYSTEMS ARE CLASSIFIED, DESIGNED, AND MANAGED

Classifying Operations Systems	Designing Operations Systems	Managing Operations Systems
• Tangibility of products	• Product mix and design	• Planning schedules and project management
• Level of customer involvement	• Facility layout	• Inventory control
• Operations flexibility	• Facility location	• Materials requirement planning (MRP)
• Resources and technology management	• Capacity planning	• Supply chain management
		• Quality control

time-based competition The use of strategies to increase the speed with which an organization goes from creativity to delivery.

operations The function concerned with transforming resource inputs into product outputs.

product A good, a service, or a combination of the two.

CLASSIFYING OPERATIONS SYSTEMS

Operations systems can be classified by the tangibility of products, level of customer involvement, operations flexibility, and management of resources and technology.

Tangibility of Products

The *tangibility of products* refers to whether the products are tangible, intangible, or mixed.

Tangible Products. *Goods,* such as **Toyota** automobiles, **Dell** computers, and this textbook, are *tangible products.*

Intangible Products. *Services,* such as haircuts, dry cleaning, and legal advice, are *intangible products.*

Mixed Products. *Mixed products* are made up of both tangible and intangible products. Major appliance retail stores, like **Sears**, not only sell appliances but also offer extended warranties and service what they sell.

Level of Customer Involvement

It is important to view operations from the customer's perspective. The level of customer involvement *refers to the amount of input from customers, which determines whether operations are make to stock, assemble to order, or make to order.*

Make-to-Stock (MTS) Operations. *Make-to-stock operations* produce products with a common design and price in anticipation of demand. Therefore, there is a low level of customer involvement. Most goods that you see in retail stores are from make-to-stock operations. While most services, such as haircuts, cannot be made to stock, some, such as scheduled transportation on airline flights, can.

Assemble-to-Order (ATO) Operations. *Assemble-to-order operations* produce a standard product with some customized features. Some services and goods, such as those built with optional features, can be produced only after the receipt of an order. Therefore, there is a moderate level of customer involvement. Relatively expensive goods, such as automobiles, mainframe computer systems, and furniture, are commonly assembled to order. Services can also be assembled to order. Standard training consulting packages and accounting and legal services can be customized to fit the needs of an organization.

15-1 APPLYING THE CONCEPT

Level of Customer Involvement

Identify each product by its level of customer involvement.

A. make-to-stock
B. assemble-to-order
C. make-to-order

_____ 1. A UPS Store customer wants copies made and sent
_____ 2. An Apple iPad
_____ 3. A haircut by Pierre
_____ 4. A soft drink by 7-Up in a can
_____ 5. Coffee ice cream in a sugar cone from Sundae School

Make-to-Order (MTO) Operations. *Make-to-order operations* are carried out only after an order has been received from a specific customer. Here, there is a high level of customer involvement. Many services, such as auto repair, tailoring, development of a business's accounting system, criminal legal defense, and medical services, have to be made to order. Some goods, such as custom clothing and **Dell** computers, are also made to order.

Operations Flexibility

Operations flexibility refers to the amount of variety in the products an operation produces, which determines whether the products are produced continuously, repetitively, in batches, or individually. Flexibility is based on product volume (how many units of one product are produced) and variety (how many different products the operation produces). The trend is toward more flexible manufacturing, such as printing custom sayings on **M&Ms**.

customer involvement The amount of input from customers, which determines whether operations are make to stock, assemble to order, or make to order.

operations flexibility The amount of variety in the products an operation produces, which determines whether products are produced continuously, repetitively, in batches, or individually.

Continuous Process Operations (CPO). Continuous process operations produce outputs that are not in discrete units, such as **Bay State** gas and **Shell** oil. They tend to produce goods rather than services. With little to no variety and high volume, continuous process operations are the least flexible of the operations systems. Therefore, they are used for made-to-stock goods.

Repetitive Process Operations (RPO). Repetitive process operations produce outputs in an assembly-line structure having each unit follow the same path, such as **GM** automobiles. All kinds of consumer and industrial goods are repetitive-process-operations outputs. Some services can also be assembly line oriented, such as an automatic car wash or dog-grooming service. ROPs are primarily used for made-to-stock or assembled-to-order goods.

Batch Process Operations (BPO). Batch process operations produce different outputs with the same resources, such as a stove being used to cook and bake all kinds of different products. **Fine** wood furniture maker uses the same people and machines to make dining room tables and chairs, desks, and bedroom dressers. A few services, such as **United Cleaning** services with business accounts, can also use batch process operations. Batch process operations are primarily used for made-to-stock or assembled-to-order goods. They also require more controls over the systems process than do continuous process and repetitive process.

15-2 APPLYING THE CONCEPT

Flexibility of Operations

Identify the operations system that would be used to produce each product.

A. CPO
B. RPO
C. BPO
D. IPO
E. PPO

____ 6. The new student union built at Springfield College
____ 7. A BMW M3 car
____ 8. A swimming pool sold and installed by Teddy Bear Pools
____ 9. The asphalt for a driveway delivered by Juan's Asphalt Company
____ 10. Packages of Trident gum

Individual Process Operations (IPO). *Individual process operations* produce outputs to customer specifications. They have high variety and low volume and so are used for made-to-order goods and services. In manufacturing, individual process operations are known as *job shops*. Used by the large majority of retailers and service organizations, individual process operations have the most flexibility. Like batch process operations, individual process operations require more controls to maintain an even flow of business.

Project Process Operations (PPO). *Project process operations* have low volume and high variety. Commonly completed by sending the resources to the customer's site rather than working on the project at the seller's facilities, project process operations are used, for example, in general contracting and the construction industry. Consulting services often blend individual process with project process operations: a client gives the consultant a project to complete, and the work may be divided between the two sites.

Resources and Technology Management

Operations is the function through which inputs are transformed into product outputs, but **technology** *is the process used to transform inputs into outputs.* Rapid changes in technology require flexibility.[11] Important operations decisions concerning the management of resources and technology include how labor and capital intensive the operations to make the product will be and how the customer will be served.

Intensity. In *capital-intensive operations,* machines do most of the work. Manufacturing companies that use continuous and repetitive operations processes (such as oil, automobile, and steel companies) are generally capital intensive. These companies tend to use high levels of technology, much of which has been developed by other companies, such as **Modern Controls.**

In *labor-intensive operations,* human resources do most of the work. Organizations that use individual process operations tend to be labor intensive. Education and consulting, as well as personal services such as haircutting, auto repair, accounting, and legal services, tend to be very labor intensive.

Manufacturing firms use a *balance of capital and labor* in batch and individual process operations, because it takes skilled workers to use flexible machines. So a balance is in the middle of the continuum between capital and labor intensity. With the increasing costs of labor, companies are replacing workers with technology. The new **Nike** Flyknit running shoe is spun, not sewn, reducing not only labor cost but also time, materials, and weight. The most labor-intensive part of the footwear manufacturing process is gone, requiring fewer workers.[12]

Ways of Serving Customers. Customers can be served by people, machines, or both. **Bank of America** provides service via tellers, automated teller machines, the Internet, and the telephone. Another consideration is where customers will be served. Today, some banks will send a loan officer to your home or office to take a mortgage loan application; others will do it over the phone and Internet. **Honda**, like many businesses, relies on intermediaries—a network of dealers—to serve and sell to customers.

Multiple Classifications

Exhibit 15-2 shows the four criteria for classifying operations systems. Notice that the focus on the left side of the exhibit is on manufacturing goods, while the focus on the right side is on providing services. However, it is not always easy to classify an organization's operations system, either because it falls at some intermediate point on the continuum or because it encompasses more than one type of operation.

Frito-Lay (Case Question 1) offers tangible goods produced through make-to-stock operations. It uses a repetitive process for its high-volume products and a batch process for its lower-volume products. A batch process is also used for different-sized portions of the same product. Frito-Lay's resources are balanced in intensity, as its manufacturing plants and trucks are expensive, but it also has thousands of well-paid employees. Customer service is important, and that is why Frito-Lay makes frequent deliveries and stocks shelves for customers.

DESIGNING OPERATIONS SYSTEMS

In a changing environment, operations systems must be continually redesigned.[13] **Toyota** built a new assembly-line factory in Mississippi, but it looks nothing like the traditional car plant.[14] The interrelated areas of product mix and design, facility layout, facility location, and capacity planning must all be considered. **GE** has a reputation for managing costs and complicated production operations.[15]

WORK APPLICATION 15-2

Using Exhibit 15-2, identify the operations system where you work or have worked based on product tangibility, customer involvement, flexibility, and resources.

WORK APPLICATION 15-3

List the product mix for an organization for which you work or have worked. Be sure to identify the number of major product lines, the number of products within one of the major lines offered, and the mixture of goods and services within that one major line.

technology The process used to transform inputs into outputs.

EXHIBIT 15-2 CLASSIFYING OPERATIONS SYSTEMS

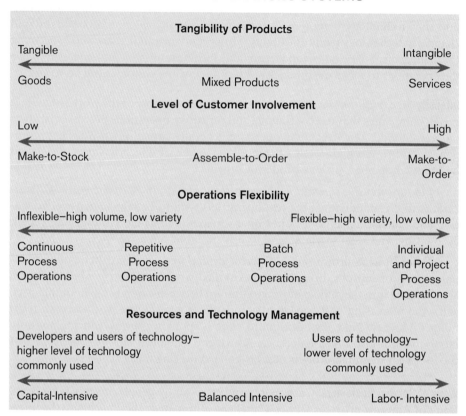

Product Mix and Design

Based on the organization's mission and objectives, top-level managers select the product mix. The *product mix* includes the number of product lines, the number of products offered within each line, and the mixture of goods and services within each line. **Apple** expanded its product mix from PCs to diversify into mobile devices to include the iPod, iPhone, and iPad.

Product design refers to new or improved product development. Successful companies integrate design and manufacturing rather than treating them as separate steps in product development. Many successful companies include suppliers and customers in the design process to help ensure the success of new products.

Quality is a virtue of design. The throughput stages, Exhibit 15-3, must be well coordinated and controlled. As you can see, the first stage is to design the product. "*Quality is a virtue of design*" means that if products are well designed, with cross-functional team input to ensure customer value, there will be fewer operations problems, the product will be easier to sell, and servicing the product will be less costly.

Toyota had multiple design problems, leading to more than 8 million cars being recalled, which cost millions of dollars to repair. **Snapple's** original bottle design was poor because it wouldn't fit into a car cup holder. **Apple** is known for its great designs, but the iPhone 4 was dogged by reports of reception problems. All of these problems hurt sales. Companies use design consulting help to ensure great designs. **IDEO** fashioned the first **Apple** mouse.[16]

Balancing time-based competition and design. While companies need to increase innovation and speed products to market, they also need to have quality products to succeed. Rushing through the design process can lead to operations problems that can't be easily fixed, in turn leading to sales problems and high repair costs. Thus, it can result in companies' losing money rather than making profits.

LO 15-3

Discuss what is meant by "quality is a virtue of design."

EXHIBIT 15-3 THROUGHPUT STAGES

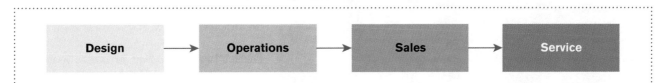

FACILITY LAYOUT

Facilities are the physical resources used in the operations process. The building, machines, furniture, and so on are part of the facility. **Facility layout** *refers to the spatial arrangement of physical resources relative to each other*. The type of facility layout selected is based on the classification of the operations system and the product design. Exhibit 15-4 compares the four types of layouts with

LO 15-4

Explain product, process, cellular, and fixed-position facility layouts in terms of their level of customer involvement and flexibility.

EXHIBIT 15-4 FACILITY LAYOUT

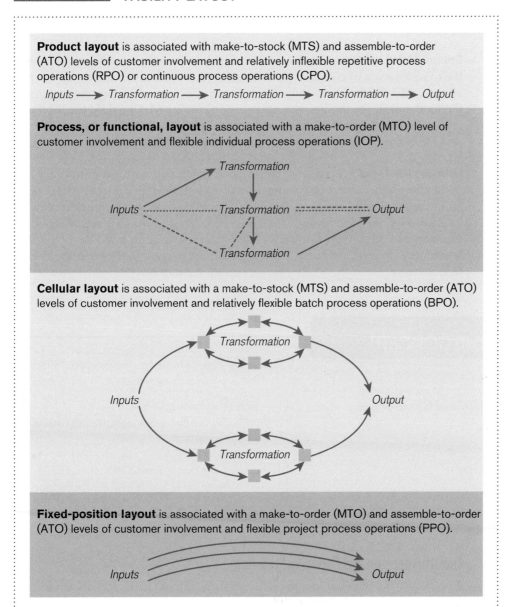

facility layout The spatial arrangement of physical resources relative to each other—operations use product, process, cellular, or fixed-position layouts.

Many fast-food companies, such as Burger King, use a cellular layout to more efficiently serve customers. Photo from Gavin Rodgers/Alamy.

respect to their level of customer involvement and flexibility of operations and provides an illustration of each systems process, which are discussed below.

Product Layout. *Product layout* is associated with make-to-stock and assemble-to-order levels of customer involvement, relatively inflexible repetitive process or continuous process operations, and capital intensity with high volume and low variety. Product layout is common in assembly-line manufacturing, like **Chrysler** cars, as the product must go through each step of the process in sequence.

Process Layout. *Process* or *functional layout* is associated with a make-to-order level of customer involvement, flexible individual process operations, and labor intensity or a balanced intensity. **Macy's** retail stores and **Mercy Hospital** providers use process layouts so that customers/patients can go to particular departments to find what they need. They don't need to go through a set sequence through every aisle in the store or department in the hospital, as in a product layout.

Cellular Layout. *Cellular layout* is associated with make-to-stock and assemble-to-order levels of customer involvement, relatively flexible batch process operations, and a balanced intensity. In restaurants, operations are in the making of the food, not in the dining area, and most, including **McDonald's**, use a cellular layout. Even your home kitchen is set up cellularly. Grouping technology into cells provides some of the efficiencies of both product and process layouts.

Fixed-Position Layout. *Fixed-position layout* is associated with make-to-order and assemble-to-order levels of customer involvement, flexible project process operations, and balanced intensity. **Boeing** makes planes using fixed-position layout. In many fixed-position layouts, the business must go to the customer. **Chatelaine Contractors** and construction crews have to go to the lot to build the house, and **United Rug Cleaners** and **Cieco Lawn Services** have to come to the house to perform their services.

WORK APPLICATION 15-4

Identify the facility layout used where you work or have worked. Draw the physical arrangement of the facilities.

15-3 APPLYING THE CONCEPT

Facility Layout

Identify the facility layout that would be used to produce each product.

A. product
B. process
C. cellular
D. fixed-position

___ 11. A pizza being made at Domino's
___ 12. The Mazda plant that makes eight different cars using the same equipment
___ 13. A DVD player by RCA
___ 14. A house being built by Jones Contractors, Inc.
___ 15. A set of fingernails at Juanita's full-service salon

Facility Location and Capacity Planning

Location is the physical geographic site of facilities. The facility location must be determined based on the classification of the operations system and the

JOIN THE DISCUSSION ETHICS & SOCIAL RESPONSIBILITY
15-1

Factory Conditions

Many companies in the past, including Gap, have been criticized for not monitoring factory conditions. To address the criticism, the firm set standards for its manufacturers and developed a thorough factory inspecting system. Gap's vendor compliance officers (VCOs) inspect factories around the world and check compliance with Gap factory standards. These standards include suppliers not employing anyone under the age of 14 and factories not permitting physical or nonphysical abuse. Gap will terminate its business relationship or require the factory to implement a corrective action plan if this code is violated. In fact, since 2003, Gap has closed some 200 factories due to persistent or severe violations of standards.

1. Is it ethical and socially responsible for Gap to revoke contracts, causing poor workers to lose their jobs?
2. Is it ethical and socially responsible to Gap's stockholders to pay higher labor costs than necessary, thus possibly reducing profits and their dividends?

Source: Information taken from the Gap, Inc. website at http://www.gap.com, accessed August 26, 2013.

---

organization's product mix, layout requirements, and capacity planning. Major factors that are considered when making the location decision include cost; proximity to inputs, customers, and/or competitors; availability of transportation; access to human resources; and number of facilities. **General Mills** and **Pillsbury** are both located in Minneapolis, Minnesota, where they can get easy access to grains for processing into their products.

Another part of the facility decision is capacity planning. **Capacity** *is the amount of products an organization can produce.* Should a facility be built to produce 200 or 500 **BMWs** per day? How many checkout/teller stations should **Big Y** supermarket and **Citibank** have? Should a **Red Lobster** restaurant have 50 or 100 tables? How many rooms should a **Hilton Hotel** build? How many beds should an intensive care unit of **Westfield Hospital** have? **Apple** doesn't make most of its products; manufacturing is outsourced, mostly to China. To ensure its contractors meet its capacity needs for products, Apple invested in outfitting its contractor factories in Asia.[17]

Frito-Lay (Case Question 2) has expanded its convenience-food product mix in recent years. It is also focusing on health and wellness by making snacks with less fat, sugar, sodium, and calories. It has removed trans fats from its products and is offering Baked! versions of multiple products. Product packaging and design are important to make the product stay fresh longer and look good to potential buyers. Frito-Lay uses product and cellular layouts to make the snacks, and it has 33 facility locations in the United States, with flexible capacity to meet fluctuating demand and optimize production and distribution.

MANAGING OPERATIONS SYSTEMS AND THE SUPPLY CHAIN

After operations systems have been designed, they must be managed. The principles of organization (Chapter 7) must be used. In this section, we discuss planning schedules and project management, inventory control, materials requirement planning, supply chain management, and quality control.

Planning Schedules and Project Management

Scheduling is important.[18] In fact, scheduling has been called the most critical task a business does day in and day out.[19] Using project management scheduling tools is important.[20] So here we discuss three techniques—the planning sheet, the Gantt chart, and the PERT network—which are often designed for specific projects.

LO 15-5

Describe the similarities and differences among the planning sheet, Gantt chart, and PERT network.

WORK
APPLICATION 15-5

Identify which priority scheduling method(s) the organization for which you work or have worked uses.

capacity The amount of products an organization can produce.

Scheduling is the process of listing activities that must be performed to accomplish an objective; the activities are listed in sequence, along with the time needed to complete each one. Scheduling answers the planning questions: "Which employees will make which products?" "When, how, and where will they be produced?" "How many of each will be produced?"

An important part of scheduling is routing. **Routing** *is the path and sequence of the transformation of a product into an output.* Routing for each of the four facility layouts is illustrated with arrows in Exhibit 15-4. Notice that with process and cellular layouts, routing is complex.

Priority scheduling *is the continuing evaluation and reordering of the sequence in which products will be produced.* The method of priority scheduling depends on the layout used. Three simple methods are used to schedule operations:

- *First come–first served.* Jobs are scheduled in the order in which they are received. This method is common in service organizations.
- *Earliest due date.* The job with the earliest promised delivery date is scheduled first.
- *Shortest operating time.* Jobs that take the least amount of time are scheduled first.

Many organizations use a combination of the three methods.

The Planning Sheet. Planning sheets *state an objective and list the sequence of activities required to meet the objective, when each activity will begin and end, and who will complete each activity.* The planning sheet in Exhibit 15-5 shows the transformation process for a monthly marketing letter, which is mailed to 300 potential customers. It is commonly used with simple, singular tasks to be accomplished.

Gantt Chart. Gantt charts *use bars to graphically illustrate a schedule and progress toward the objective over a period.* The different activities to be performed are usually listed vertically, with time shown horizontally. The resources to be allocated, such as people or machines, are also commonly shown on the vertical axis. Gantt charts, like planning sheets, are appropriate when independent sequential steps are needed to accomplish the objective. The Gantt chart has an advantage over the planning sheet in that it places progress toward the objective on the chart as a control technique.

Another important advantage of the Gantt chart over the planning sheet and PERT is that it can show multiple projects on one chart. This helps in prioritizing and scheduling project activities that use the same resources.

Exhibit 15-6 illustrates a Gantt chart for multiple orders in an operations department. Each bar extends from the start time to the end time, with the shaded portion indicating the part completed to date. Using the chart, you can see at a glance how orders are progressing. If you become aware that a project is behind schedule, you can take corrective action to get it back on schedule. If today is day 1 of week 3 in May, the end of the shaded portion of the bar will be directly under the second 3 if the project is exactly on schedule. What is the status of each of the four projects on the chart in Exhibit 15-6? The answer is at the bottom of the exhibit.

Performance Evaluation and Review Technique (PERT). Multiple activities are considered to be independent when they can be performed simultaneously; they are considered to be dependent when one must be completed before the next activity can begin. Planning sheets and Gantt charts are useful tools when the activities

WORK
APPLICATION 15-6

Give an example of a project in an organization for which you work or have worked that is suitable for scheduling using the planning sheet.

routing The path and sequence of the transformation of a product into an output.

priority scheduling The continuing evaluation and reordering of the sequence in which products will be produced.

planning sheet A scheduling tool that states an objective and lists the sequence of activities required to meet the objective, when each activity will begin and end, and who will complete each activity.

Gantt chart A scheduling tool that uses bars to graphically illustrate a schedule and progress toward the objective over a period.

EXHIBIT 15-5   PLANNING SHEET

Objective: To mail a personalized form letter to all target clients by the 15th of each month.

Responsible: Latoya/Joel

Due date: 15th of each month

Control checkpoints: 7th and 12th of each month

Starting date: 1st of each month

Priority: High

	Activities	When Start		End	Who
1.	Type letter on computer.	1st		2nd	Latoya
2.	Deliver letter to printer.	3rd	or	4th	Joel
3.	Print letters on company stationery.	5th		6th	printer
4.	Pick up letters at printer.	6th	or	7th	Joel
5.	Use mail merge to type names and addresses on letters and envelopes.	7th		9th	Joel
6.	Sign each letter.	9th	or	10th	Latoya
7.	Fold each letter and put in an envelope.	10th		11th	Joel
8.	Bundle letters to meet bulk mailing specifications.	12th		13th	Joel
9.	Deliver to U.S. Postal Bulk Mail Center.	13th			Joel
10.	Mail letters.	14th	or	15th	U.S. Mail

EXHIBIT 15-6   GANTT CHART (ORDERS BY WEEK)

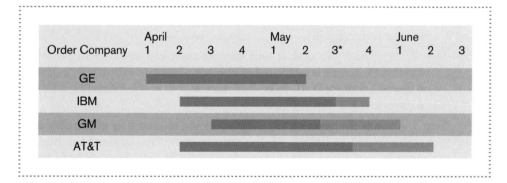

follow each other in a dependent series. However, when some activities are dependent and some are independent, PERT (critical path) is more appropriate. **PERT** *is a network scheduling technique that illustrates the dependence of activities.* Exhibit 15-7 shows a PERT network.

The key components of PERT are activities, events, times, and the critical path. With complex projects, it is common to have multiple activities represented as one event. For example, in automobile production, building the engine would be an event that requires multiple activities to complete. Time can be measured in a variety of ways (seconds, minutes, hours, days, weeks, months, years, etc.) to determine the critical path. The **critical path** *is the most time-consuming series*

PERT A network scheduling technique that illustrates the dependence of activities.

WORK
APPLICATION 15-7

Give an example of a project in an organization for which you work or have worked that would be appropriate to schedule using a Gantt chart.

of activities in a PERT network. The critical path is important to know because it determines the length of time needed to complete a project. It is shown by the double lines in Exhibit 15-7. Any delay in the steps in the critical path will delay the entire project. The cost of each activity is sometimes shown with the time.

EXHIBIT 15-7   PERT NETWORK

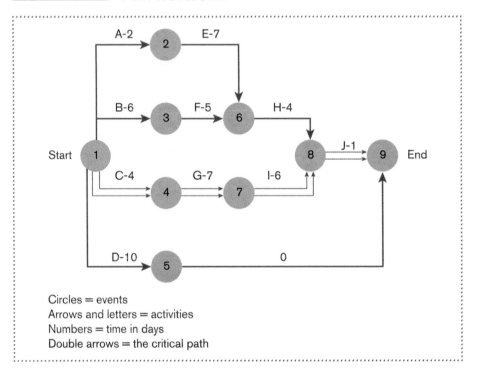

Circles = events
Arrows and letters = activities
Numbers = time in days
Double arrows = the critical path

The following steps explain how the PERT network in Exhibit 15-7 was completed:

Step 1. List all the activities/events that must be completed to reach the specific objective. Assign a letter to each one. Exhibit 15-7 shows 10 activities, labeled A through J.

Step 2. Determine the time it will take to complete each activity/event. In Exhibit 15-7, time is measured in number of days as follows: A, 2 days; B, 6 days; C, 4 days; D, 10 days; E, 7 days; F, 5 days; G, 7 days; H, 4 days; I, 6 days; and J, 1 day.

Step 3. Arrange the tasks on the diagram in the sequence in which they must be completed. In Exhibit 15-7, A must be completed before E can begin; E must be completed before H can begin; and H must be completed before J can begin.

For example, before you can place a box of cereal on a shelf for sale (J), it must be ordered (A), received (E), and priced (H). Notice that activity D is independent. An arrow as well as a letter represents each activity. The numbered circles signify the completion of an event leading to the desired outcome. All activities originate and terminate at a circle. The 1 represents the start of the project, and 9 its end or completion.

Step 4. Determine the critical path. To do this, you must total the time required for each path from start (1) to end (9). Path 1–2–6–8–9 takes 2 + 7 + 4 + 1 days, for a total of 14 days. Path 1–3–6–8–9 takes 6 + 5 + 4 + 1 days, for a total of 16 days. Path 1–4–7–8–9 takes 4 + 7 + 6 + 1 days, for a total of

critical path The most time-consuming series of activities in a PERT network.

18 days. Path 1–5–9 takes 10 + 0 days, for a total of 10 days. The critical path, indicated by the double arrow, is 1–4–7–8–9. The program or project should take 18 days to complete. If the job was supposed to be done in two weeks, you would know before you even started that it could not be done on time. You would have to change the completion date or maybe abandon the project.

To summarize, planning sheets and Gantt charts are commonly used to develop procedures for routine standing plans, whereas PERT is commonly used for single-use program plans for a complex project with dependent activities. However, all three types of schedules can be used for either standing or single-use plans.

WORK
APPLICATION 15-8

Give an example of a project in an organization for which you work or have worked that would be appropriate to schedule using a PERT network.

15-4 APPLYING THE CONCEPT

Scheduling Tools

Select the most appropriate scheduling tool for each situation.

  A. planning sheet
  B. Gantt chart
  C. PERT network

_____ 16. A plan will be created for building a new submarine.

_____ 17. The registrar's office is working on the schedule of its rooms and courses.

_____ 18. A production department is scheduling the making of eight products on six different types of machines.

_____ 19. Plans are being developed for building a new house.

_____ 20. Procedures for a new method of reporting absenteeism is being created.

Inventory Control

Inventory *is the stock of materials held for future use.* Thus, inventory is an idle resource needed to transform inputs into outputs. Inventory control, also called *materials control,* is an important responsibility of the operations manager.

Inventory control *is the process of managing raw materials, work in process, finished goods, and in-transit goods.* Exhibit 15-8 illustrates how inventory control fits into the systems process.

- *Raw Materials.* Raw materials are input materials that have been received but have not yet been transformed in any way by the operations department, such as eggs at a restaurant or steel at an automaker. Important preliminary controls include purchasing raw materials and scheduling their delivery to your facility so that they will be there when needed.

- *Work in Process.* Work in process is material that has had some transformation but is not yet an output, such as an egg that is being cooked or a car on the assembly line. Concurrent controls are used to ensure that products meet standards before they become finished goods.

- *Finished Goods.* Finished goods are transformed outputs that have not yet been delivered to customers, such as cooked eggs sitting on a plate waiting to be served to a customer or a car sitting at the factory waiting to be shipped to a dealer. Rework control may be needed, such as reheating the eggs if they get cold while waiting for the server or fixing the car if it cannot be driven off the assembly line.

LO 15-6

Explain the relationship among inventory control, just-in-time (JIT) inventory, and materials requirement planning (MRP).

inventory The stock of materials held for future use.

inventory control The process of managing raw materials, work in process, finished goods, and in-transit goods.

- *In-Transit (pipeline) Goods.* In-transit goods are finished goods being delivered to the customer, such as eggs being carried to the table by a server or cars being delivered by truck to the dealer. Damage control may be needed. For example, if the server drops the eggs on the way to the table, the order must be redone; or if the car is damaged in delivery, it will need to be returned or fixed by the dealer at the manufacturer's expense. Deliverers of products commonly have insurance to cover the cost of damaged and lost goods.

Retailing and Services Inventory. Retail inventory control, including *purchasing,* is concerned almost exclusively with finished goods for resale as is. However, many retailers, such as the **Home Shopping Network,** catalog seller **L.L. Bean,** and major furniture and appliance stores, do have in-transit inventory.

EXHIBIT 15-8   INVENTORY CONTROL WITHIN THE SYSTEMS PROCESS

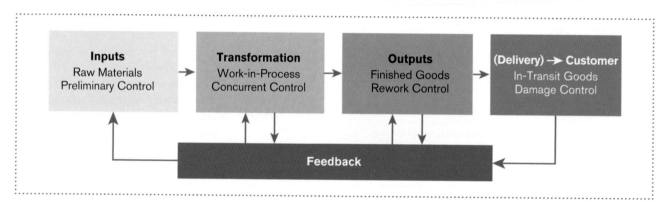

Most service organizations deal only with the finished-goods inventory they create by providing the service. However, some services have in-transit inventory—for example, accounting statements and legal documents are commonly delivered to clients.

Just-in-Time (JIT) Inventory. The objective of inventory control is to have the correct amount of all four types of inventory available when and where they are needed while minimizing waste and the total cost of managing and storing inventory. To accomplish this objective, many organizations now use JIT. **Just-in-time (JIT) inventory** *is a method by which necessary parts and raw materials are delivered shortly before they are needed.*

Toyota was a pioneer in lean manufacturing, including JIT inventory management. Very few parts are stored at the plant waiting to be installed as cars move through the assembly line. Instead, the factories rely on suppliers to get the needed raw materials and parts to the factory floor when they are required during the production process.

Materials Requirement Planning (MRP)

Materials requirement planning (MRP) *is a system that integrates operations and inventory control with complex ordering and scheduling.* MRP involves developing a process for ordering raw materials and components at the right time and in the right quantity so that they arrive shortly before their scheduled transformation into outputs and appropriate work in process is ready as needed. JIT is part of inventory control, which is part of MRP. MRP is becoming more important as retailers are placing smaller orders with less lead time.

just-in-time (JIT) inventory A method by which necessary parts and raw materials are delivered shortly before they are needed.

materials requirement planning (MRP) A system that integrates operations and inventory control with complex ordering and scheduling.

MRP is commonly used by firms that have different delivery systems and lead times. **Lockheed Martin, Texas Instruments**, and **Westinghouse** all use MRP because they need hundreds of parts in vastly different quantities, with arrival times that vary from hours to months. Coordinating and controlling such a complex system is virtually impossible for any manager. However, MRP software can manage such a system fairly easily.

Enterprise Resource Planning (ERP). ERP takes MRP a step further, as it collects, processes, and provides information about a firm's entire enterprise. Ordering, product design, production, purchasing, inventory, distribution, human resources, receipt of payments, and forecasting of future demand are incorporated into one network system. For example, anyone with access can check the current inventory, a sales rep can enter an order and see what the actual delivery date will be, and an engineer can see how a decision about product design will affect production schedules and resource needs. **SAP** ERP software, as well as other software by companies, makes ERP possible.

Economic Order Quantity (EOQ). The *EOQ* is the optimal quantity of a product to order, determined on the basis of a mathematical model. The more often you order, the higher the ordering cost—but if you order less often, your holding cost goes up. By using the EOQ, you can minimize ordering and holding costs without running out of stock.

Calculating EOQs is a part of MRP. However, many small businesses that want to calculate EOQs don't need MRP. Such businesses can determine EOQ using a calculator, as follows:

$$EOQ = \sqrt{\frac{2RS}{H}} = \sqrt{\frac{2(5,000)(25)}{2}} = \sqrt{5,000(25)} = \sqrt{125,000} = 353.55$$

where

EOQ = optimal quantity to reorder

R = total required over planning horizon (usually one year); here, 5,000

S = cost of preparing one order (or setup); here, $25

H = cost of holding one unit for the planning horizon; here, $2

supply chain management The process of coordinating all the activities involved in producing a product and delivering it to the customer.

Supply Chain Management

Supply chain management *is the process of coordinating all the activities involved in producing a product and delivering it to the customer.* Managing the supply chain is challenging work,[21] and it is a growing field.[22] To provide high-quality products at the lowest cost, supply chain management starts with forecasting demand for a product and then moves on to planning and managing supply and demand, acquiring materials, scheduling and producing the product, warehousing, controlling inventory, distributing the product, and delivering it. The final stage involves customer service. Supply chain management focuses heavily on purchasing and inventory control. Raw materials, including component parts, are expensive for many manufacturers. Thus, keeping inventory costs down while ensuring that good-quality materials are available when needed is important in the supply chain. Just-in-time inventory is used to control costs and to avoid stocking inventories that may not be sold.

FedEx doesn't just deliver packages; it provides services to help businesses manage their entire supply chain. Photo from Victor J. Blue/Bloomberg via Getty Images.

With the growth in online sales, deliveries are on the increase, and managing the delivery portion of the supply chain is becoming an increasingly important part of doing business. When you think of **UPS** and **FedEx**, you probably think of shipping packages. But they provide help throughout the entire supply chain to businesses of all sizes focusing on logistics.

Dell is a global leader at supply chain management. It does not make monitors or keep them in inventory, and it buys its computer components on a just-in-time basis. Dell specializes in customizing computers, putting suppliers' components together to customer specifications. By selling directly to the customer, it has eliminated entire steps in the supply chain, thus keeping inventory to a bare minimum. Tim Cook is an operations expert who was hired as the master of **Apple's** supply chain and was promoted to CEO.[23]

Radio-Frequency Identification (RFID) Technology. *Radio-frequency identification (RFID)* is an automatic identification method, relying on storing and remotely retrieving data using devices called RFID tags.[24] An RFID tag is an object that can be stuck on or incorporated into a product, animal, or person for the purpose of identification using radio waves. These tags are so small they can be placed anywhere, even in paper. RFID is used in supply chain management to improve the efficiency of inventory tracking and management. To learn more about RFID, visit www.rfidt.com.

Frito-Lay (Case Question 3) plans and schedules the production and delivery of its products. Its raw materials include tons of potatoes, corn, cheese, and many other ingredients, which it buys on a just-in-time basis from suppliers to make the products (work in process and finished goods inventory) that are shipped to customers. It offers just-in-time inventory to most of its customers, as it restocks shelves frequently so that many customers carry no stored inventory at all—it's all on the shelves. Within its supply chain management program, Frito-Lay uses ERP to integrate all its B2B and EDI activities with those of suppliers and customers. When products are delivered and sold, data are sent in real time so that supply, production, and inventory information can be adjusted quickly for effective inventory control.

QUALITY CONTROL

The cost of poor quality is typically 20 to 30 percent of revenues. Because quality is such an important issue, it has been covered throughout the text; however, we discuss it in more detail here.

Quality control *is the process of ensuring that all types of inventory meet standards.* As you can tell by the definition, quality control and inventory control overlap. The top row in Exhibit 15-8 shows the systems process steps, the second row shows the four inventory stages, and the third row shows the four types of quality control. Quality control is just as important for goods as it is for services; it applies to the scrambled eggs in a restaurant as well as to the car produced by an automaker.

Quality assurance requires that you "build in" quality; you cannot "inspect it in." Recall from Chapter 14 that the quality focus should be on preliminary and concurrent control, not rework and damage control, and that quality is a virtue of design.

Customer Quality Control. Exhibit 15-9 lists five rules that will help ensure quality customer service. If you follow these rules, you will increase your chances of developing effective human relations skills and ensuring a high-quality product for your customers. And remember that everyone you deal with is a customer.

quality control The process of ensuring that all types of inventory meet standards.

EXHIBIT 15-9 FIVE RULES OF CUSTOMER HUMAN RELATIONS

1. Put people before things.
2. Always be nice—no matter how busy you are.
3. Take your time with people.
4. Be polite; say "please," "thank you," and "you're welcome."
5. Don't discriminate with your service (treat everyone well).

Unfortunately, quality problems are rather common. The United States healthcare system is plagued with quality problems including rising costs. Several drug manufacturing companies have had quality problems, including **Johnson & Johnson, Merck,** and **GlaxoSmithKline. Toyota** has had several quality problems and recalls and dropped in ranking in the **J.D. Power & Associates** Initial Quality Survey in 2009, trailing some U.S. car makers.

Total Quality Management (TQM). The four major TQM principles are (1) focus on delivering customer value, (2) continually improve systems and processes, (3) focus on managing processes rather than people, and (4) use teams to continually improve. A few of the differences between TQM (discussed in Chapter 2) and quality control follow:

The money saved by skimping on quality control can be very costly and can damage a company's reputation in both the short and long term. Pictured here is Tony Hayward, former chief executive of oil and energy company BP. Photo from Edstock/ iStockphoto.

- TQM is much broader in scope than quality control because part of its core value is to make it the job of everyone in the organization to improve quality. Under quality control, the operations department is solely responsible for product quality.

- With TQM, quality is determined by customers, who compare actual use with requirements to determine value, or purchasing benefits. With quality control, quality is determined by the standards set for acceptability.

- The focus in TQM is not on acceptance or rejection of the product but on continuous improvement. With quality control, if products don't meet quality requirements, corrective action is taken to make them acceptable or they are rejected.

The board and top management at **BP** knew something was wrong with safety quality for years but ignored TQM. BP deferred repairs that were a critical factor in the Gulf of Mexico explosion. BP may have saved money by skimping on quality repairs, but the explosion cost billions of dollars.[25] It wasn't worth it.

The International Standards Organization. The International Standards Organization (ISO) *certifies firms that meet set quality standards.* Both manufacturing and services sectors are applying for ISO certification to improve their management systems and operational control. JIT and TQM are part of ISO 9000 certification, as organizations must document policies that address quality management, continuous improvement, and customer satisfaction. Most multinational corporations have

International Standards Organization (ISO) An organization that certifies firms that meet set quality standards.

15-2 JOIN THE DISCUSSION ETHICS & SOCIAL RESPONSIBILITY

Social Accountability International

Social Accountability International, or SAI (http://www.sa-intl .org), is a U.S.-based nonprofit organization dedicated to the development, implementation, and oversight of voluntary verifiable social accountability standards. SAI works to improve workplaces and combat sweatshops through the expansion and further development of the current international workplace standards. SAI gets key stakeholders to develop consensus-based voluntary standards and promotes understanding and implementation

of standards worldwide. Like ISO 9000 certification, SA8000 certification verifies compliance of qualified organizations with international workplace standards.

1. Should global multinationals eliminate sweatshops by having SA8000-certified facilities?
2. Should global multinationals require all their suppliers to get SA8000 certification?
3. How might working toward SA8000 certification affect cost, revenues, and profits?

WORK
APPLICATION 15-10

Explain quality control in an organization where you work or have worked.

ISO 9000 certification, and they require the suppliers they do business with to be certified in order to ensure the quality of materials used. For more information on ISO 9000 and other certifications, visit the ISO website at http://www.iso.org.

Six Sigma. Six Sigma's goal is only 3.4 defects or mistakes per million operations. *Sigma* is a letter from the Greek alphabet used to represent a statistical measure of deviations from a standard. Most companies operate at the Three-Sigma level of 66,000 defects per million. Six Sigma can reduce costs, rejects, lead times, and capital spending while raising employee skill levels and strengthening overall financial results. Six Sigma is grounded in math, statistics, data analysis, finance, and computer skills. There is a heavy emphasis on measurement and achieving measurable bottom-line results.

Motorola invented Six Sigma in 1987, but **GE** popularized it. Since then, Motorola has reported more than $17 billion in savings. But Six Sigma is not just for manufacturing. **Capital One** says it has launched a Six Sigma initiative to drive continuous improvement, and **Dunkin' Brands** uses it to lift its bottom line.

LO 15-7

Explain how statistical process control (SPC) charts and the exception principle are used in quality control.

Statistical Quality Control. *Statistical quality control* is a management science technique that uses a variety of statistical tests based on probability to improve the quality of decision making. Statistics are employed to improve the probability of identifying and eliminating quality problems. The most common test is statistical process control, a standard TQM technique that is part of Six Sigma.

Statistical process control (SPC) *aids in determining whether quality is within an acceptable standard range.* It is called a process control because it is concurrent; quality is measured and corrected during the transformation process. SPC is used to monitor operations and to minimize variances in the quality of products. **McDonald's**, for example, goes to great lengths to ensure that the quality of its Big Mac is the same all over the country. Service organizations can also benefit from statistical process control. Implementing SPC requires four steps.

First you set the upper and lower levels of acceptable quality. Second, you select the sampling technique and the frequency of measuring quality. Third, you (or the machine) measure actual performance and compare it to the standard on the SPC chart. Last, you use the exception principle—accept or reject the level of quality.

statistical process control (SPC) A statistical test that aids in determining whether quality is within an acceptable standard range.

An example of an SPC chart for 16-ounce bags of Lay's Potato Chips is shown in Exhibit 15-10. As long as the bags of chips weigh between 15.80 and 16.20 ounces, the machine continues to produce them. However, if the measured weight

EXHIBIT 15-10 STATISTICAL PROCESS CONTROL CHART FOR 16-OUNCE BAGS OF LAY'S POTATO CHIPS

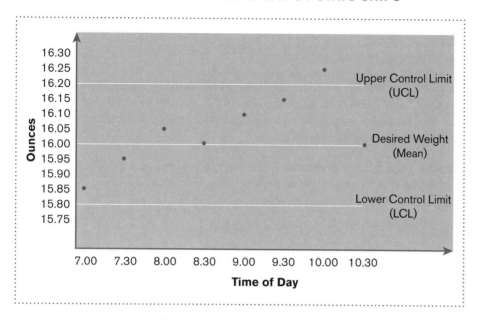

goes out of this range, as it did at 10:00, the machine stops and is adjusted so as to produce the desired mean weight of 16 ounces, as shown at 10:30.

Frito-Lay (Case Question 4) is very concerned about the quality of its products. It uses TQM to make sure that all of its ingredients (potatoes, corn, cheese, etc.) are of consistent quality and uniformly combined in its manufacturing plants so that each product always tastes the same. Packing supplies are also important so that products remain fresh until the expiration date on the package. Frito-Lay is ISO 9000 certified and requires its manufacturing suppliers to be certified, too. As illustrated in Exhibit 15-10, Frito-Lay uses SPC to ensure quality.

Contributions by Quality Gurus. The beginning of the quality revolution dates back to May 16, 1924, when Walter Shewhart wrote a memo to his boss at **Bell Labs** stating that he wanted to use statistics to improve the quality of Bell telephones. Shewhart started the focus on concurrent control by delegating the role of inspector to employees.

W. Edwards Deming. In the 1950s, he went to Japan to teach quality and is credited with being instrumental in turning Japanese industry into an economic world power. In fact, the highest Japanese award for quality is the Deming Prize. Deming said that improving quality would automatically improve productivity and called for a focus on customer value and continuous improvement. He directed managers' attention to the fact that most quality problems—up to 90 percent—are not the fault of employees; rather, the system is to blame. Deming developed the world-famous 14 points to improve quality.

Joseph M. Juran. He developed the Juran Trilogy: planning, control, and improvement. Juran stated that 20 percent of the reasons for out-of-control performance cause 80 percent of the quality problems. He called this the Pareto principle, more commonly known as the 80–20 rule. When performance is out of control, first look at the usual "vital few" reasons (20 percent), and most of the time (80 percent) they will have a standing-plan solution. Have you ever noticed how manufacturers commonly have a place in the product manual for troubleshooting that says, "If you have a problem, try 1, 2, 3, 4"?

Armand V. Feigenbaum. He made his mark in the 1950s by publishing material on "total quality control," now more commonly called TQM. Feigenbaum worked to fight the myth that maintaining quality is expensive and focused on improving quality as an important way to lower costs.

Philip B. Crosby. He popularized the concepts "quality is free," "do it right the first time," and "zero defects" in the late 1970s. Crosby believed that it was possible and necessary to measure the costs of poor quality in order to combat the notion that quality was expensive.

Genichi Taguchi. He advocated designing quality into each product. Hence, he emphasized quality as a virtue of design.

Productivity and the Balanced Scorecard

Employees would like to get paid more. However, if they are paid more without producing more, a company must cut costs and/or raise product prices to offset the additional wage cost in order to maintain profits. This causes inflation. The only real way to increase our standard of living is to increase productivity.[26] As a manager, you need to understand how to measure and increase productivity. In this section, we discuss measuring and increasing productivity and the balanced scorecard that is a method of increasing productivity.

Measuring and Increasing Productivity

As discussed in Chapter 14, metrics matter.[27] A study found that employees are only productive 5 hours a day.[28] Measuring productivity can be complex, but it doesn't have to be. Here is a simple yet realistic approach for you to use on the job.

Calculating Productivity. Productivity *is a performance measure relating outputs to inputs.* In other words, productivity is measured by dividing the outputs by the inputs. Suppose a trucking company wants to measure productivity of a delivery. The truck traveled 1,000 miles and used 100 gallons of gas. Its productivity was 10 miles to the gallon:

$$\frac{\text{Output}}{\text{Input}} = \text{Productivity}$$

$$\frac{1,000 \text{ miles}}{100 \text{ gallons}} = 10 \text{ mpg}$$

The inputs can be in a variety of forms. In the preceding example, the inputs were gallons of gas. Inputs could also be labor hours, machine hours, number of workers, the cost of labor, and so on.

Following is another fairly simple example, involving measuring the productivity of an accounts payable department:

Step 1. Select a base period, such as an hour, day, week, month, quarter, or year. In this example we will use a week.

Step 2. Determine how many bills were sent out during that period (outputs). The records show that 800 bills were sent out.

WORK APPLICATION 15-11

Are any of the gurus' quality contributions used where you work or have worked? Explain how.

LO 15-8

Describe how to measure productivity and list three ways to increase it.

productivity A performance measure relating outputs to inputs.

Step 3. Determine the cost of sending out the bills (inputs). Determining cost can become complicated if you include overhead, depreciation, and so forth. In this instance, calculate cost based on direct labor charges for three employees who are each paid $10 per hour. They each worked 40 hours during the week, or a total of 120 hours. The total cost is $10 per hour times 120 hours, or $1,200.

Step 4. Divide the number of outputs (bills) by the inputs (labor costs) to determine the productivity rate of .67 (800 ÷ $1,200 = .67). Performance is usually stated as a ratio (in this case, .67:1) or as a percentage (67 percent). It can also be stated as a labor cost per unit. To determine the labor cost per unit, reverse the process and divide the input by the output. In this case, it cost $1.50 to send out each bill ($1,200 ÷ 800).

Calculating Productivity Percentage Changes. The .67 productivity rate is set as the base standard. The next week, the accounting department again sent out 800 bills, but because of machine problems, concurrent corrective action of having employees work overtime was needed to meet the standard output, at an additional cost of $100. The productivity rate went down to .62 (800 ÷ $1,300). The labor cost per unit went up to $1.63 ($1,300 ÷ 800). To determine the percentage change, use this formula:

Current productivity rate	62
−Base standard productivity rate	−67
Change	5

Change ÷ Base productivity rate = 5 ÷ 67 = .0746

There was a 7.46 percent decrease in productivity. Note that it is not necessary to use the decimals on .67 and .62 in this calculation. Also, when the current productivity rate is less than the standard, there is a decrease in productivity, but it is not necessary to use a negative number.

Production versus Productivity. It is important to calculate productivity rather than just production output, because it is possible to increase production but decrease productivity. If the accounts payable department sends out 850 bills (production) but uses 10 hours of overtime to do so (time-and-a-half at $15.00 per hour × 10 hours = $150), productivity has decreased from .67 to .63 (850 ÷ 1,350). In other words, if you measure only output production and it increases, you can be fooled into thinking you are doing a better job when in reality you are doing a worse job. Do you believe smartphones have increased productivity? Although people are busier, in general, smartphones have done nothing to improve productivity.[29]

Productivity Comparisons. Productivity measures are more meaningful when they are compared to other productivity rates. You can compare your department's productivity to that of other organizations and/or departments. This was done in Skill Builder 14–1.

Most important, you should compare your department's productivity during one period to its productivity in other periods. This comparison will enable you to identify increases or decreases in productivity over time. Unfortunately, as your level of productivity increases, it often becomes increasingly difficult to continuously improve it. A productivity rate can also be set as the standard, and you can compare your department's productivity to the standard on an ongoing basis. This is done in Applying the Concept 15–5.

15-5 APPLYING THE CONCEPT

Measuring Productivity

The standard monthly productivity rate in your department is

$$\frac{\text{Outputs of 6,000 units}}{\text{Inputs of \$9,000 cost}} = .67$$

For the first five months of the year, calculate the current productivity rate and show it as a ratio and a percentage. Also, calculate the percentage productivity change, compared to the standard, stating whether it is an increase or a decrease. January: outputs of 5,900, inputs of $9,000

_____ ratio, _____ percent, increase/decrease of _____ percent
February: outputs of 6,200, inputs of $9,000
_____ ratio, _____ percent, increase/decrease of _____ percent
March: outputs of 6,000, inputs of $9,300
_____ ratio, _____ percent, increase/decrease of _____ percent
April: outputs of 6,300, inputs of $9,000
_____ ratio, _____ percent, increase/decrease of _____ percent
May: outputs of 6,300, inputs of $8,800
_____ ratio, _____ percent, increase/decrease of _____ percent

Increasing Productivity. Increasing productivity is about working smarter (using our brains), not simply working harder, and doing more with less. We continue to produce more stuff with fewer workers.[30] Recall that motivating employees has been shown to increase productivity.[31] As a manager, you should work with your employees to measure productivity and continually increase it to provide better customer value.

There are three ways to increase productivity:

1. Increase the value of the outputs but maintain the value of the inputs ($\uparrow$ O $\leftrightarrow$ I).

2. Maintain the value of the outputs but decrease the value of the inputs ($\leftrightarrow$ O $\downarrow$ I).

3. Increase the value of the outputs but decrease the value of the inputs ($\uparrow$ O $\downarrow$ I).

In simple terms, you can reduce labor costs, improve outputs, or both.[32] **Volkswagen** and other auto makers cut labor costs,[33] and **Nike's** spun running shoe also reduced labor cost to increase productivity.[34] The more technologically advanced farms and manufacturing become, the fewer people they employ as they continue to increase productivity.[35]

The Balanced Scorecard

Is your organization achieving its mission? If you don't have a quick and accurate answer, then, besides financial measures, you need a balanced scorecard (BSC).[36] Researchers Robert Kaplan and David Norton concluded that financial measures alone were not sufficient to measure performance; other factors in the new economy were missing from traditional financial reporting.[37]

The **balanced scorecard (BSC)** *measures financial, customer service, and internal business performance, as well as learning and growth performance.* All four dimensions of the scorecard are equally important, and results relate to one another through the systems effect. Let's face it, you have to make a profit (financial performance), but without customers (customer service performance), you don't have a business,[38] and without employee development (learning and growth performance) and continuously improving operations (internal business performance), you will not be successful. So you need a multimeasure scorecard.[39] See Exhibit 15-11 for an overview of the BSC.

balanced scorecard (BSC) A management tool that measures financial, customer service, and internal business performance, as well as learning and growth performance.

EXHIBIT 15-11 THE BALANCED SCORECARD

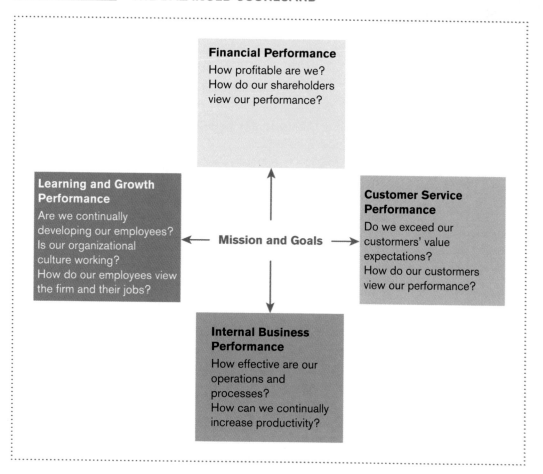

Employees develop a control system with targets, measures, outcomes, and initiatives to guide improvement in all four dimensions of the BSC. *Targets* are objectives (or metrics) that employees set to improve in the areas critical to success. *Measures* are compared to *outcomes* to determine whether targets are being achieved. *Initiatives* are the strategies and tactics (plans) designed to achieve targets. Rather than simply measuring the past, the targets and measures create focus for the future, as the BSC is both a planning and a control method.

As you can see, the BSC plays to the well-known management adage "if you want to manage it, you've got to measure it, and you get what you measure and reinforce." If you are not measuring your financial, customer service, internal business, and learning and growth performance, you and other stakeholders really don't know how well you are doing. If your team is without a scorecard, it isn't playing the game; it's only practicing.[40]

As we bring this chapter to a close, you should understand the importance of time-based competition, to be able to classify operations systems, to know how operations systems are designed, to realize how operations and the supply chain are managed, and how to measure and increase productivity and understand the parts of the balanced scorecard.

15-1 SELF ASSESSMENT

Putting It All Together

For this self-assessment, refer to prior self-assessments and skill builders; write down a few things you have learned about yourself, focusing on strengths and areas for improvement.

Chapter 1, Management Traits, p. 5

_____

_____

Chapter 2, How Ethical Is Your Behavior?, pp. 46–47

_____

Chapter 3, Country of Origin of Products, p. 64

_____

Chapter 3, Attitude about Women and Minorities Advancing, p. 80

_____

_____

Chapter 4, Decision-Making Styles, p. 95

_____

_____

Chapter 5, Effective Planning, p. 126

_____

_____

Chapter 5, Time Management Techniques, p. 148

_____

_____

Chapter 6, Entrepreneurial Qualities, p. 176

_____

_____

Chapter 7, Organizational Preference, p. 198

_____

_____

Chapter 7, Personal Priorities, p. 203

_____

_____

Chapter 8, Are You a Team Player?, p. 217

_____

_____

Chapter 8, Management Styles in Group Situations, p. 242

_____

_____

Chapter 9, Career Development, p. 260

_____

_____

Chapter 10, Personality Profile, pp. 295–296

_____

Chapter 10, Job Satisfaction, p. 300

_____

Chapter 10, Use of Political Behavior, p. 305

_____

Chapter 10, Personality Type and Stress, p. 320

_____

Chapter 11, What Motivates You?, p. 338

_____

Chapter 11, Acquired Needs, p. 339

_____

Chapter 12, Theory X and Theory Y Leadership Behavior, p. 362

_____

Chapter 13, Listening Skills, pp. 400–401

_____

_____

Chapter 13, Analyzing Communication Style, p. 412

_____

_____

Chapter 14, Coaching, p. 432

_____

_____

Based on your review, how can you use this knowledge to help you in your career development?

Develop a plan to apply your self-assessments in both your personal and your professional life. What specific areas will you work on improving? How will you improve? How will you know if you have improved?

• • • CHAPTER SUMMARY

15-1. **Describe time-based competition and why it is important.**

Time-based competition refers to the use of strategies to increase the speed with which an organization goes from creativity to delivery. It is important because speed gives an organization a first-mover competitive advantage.

15-2. **Explain the differences among operations systems with respect to tangibility of products, levels of customer involvement, operations flexibility, and management of resources and technology.**

A product can be a tangible good, an intangible service, or a combination of the two. The three levels of customer involvement refer to whether a standard product is made to stock, customer-specific products are made to order, or a standard product with some customized features is assembled to order. Operations flexibility refers to whether the products are produced continuously in nondiscrete units, repetitively on an assembly line for one product, in batches with the same resources used for multiple products, individually to customer specifications at the seller's facilities, or individually over a long time at sites including the customer's facilities. Resources may be capital intensive (if machines do most of the work), labor intensive (if human resources do most of the work), or a balance of the two.

15-3. **Discuss what is meant by "quality is a virtue of design."**

"Quality is a virtue of design" means that if products are well designed, with cross-functional team input to ensure customer value, there will be fewer operations problems, the product will be easier to sell, and servicing the product will be less costly. Therefore, it is important for cross-functional teams to work together on the design of new products.

15-4. **Explain product, process, cellular, and fixed-position facility layouts in terms of their level of customer involvement and flexibility.**

Product layout is associated with make-to-stock and assemble-to-order levels of customer involvement and relatively inflexible repetitive or continuous process operations. Process layout is associated with a make-to-order level of customer involvement and flexible individual process operations. Cellular layout is associated with make-to-stock and assemble-to-order levels of customer involvement and relatively flexible batch process operations. Fixed-position layout is associated with make-to-order and assemble-to-order levels of customer involvement and flexible project process operations.

15-5. **Describe the similarities and differences among the planning sheet, Gantt chart, and PERT network.**

Similarities include the fact that all three are scheduling techniques and list activities that must be performed to accomplish an objective. Activities are listed in sequence, with the time needed to complete each. The primary differences concern their format and use. Planning sheets state an objective and list the sequence of activities required to meet the objective, when each activity will begin and end, and who will complete each activity. Gantt charts use bars to graphically illustrate a schedule and progress toward the objective over a period. Gantt charts, like planning sheets, are appropriate when independent sequential steps are needed to accomplish the objective. The Gantt chart has an advantage over the planning sheet in that it places progress toward the objective on the chart as a control technique. PERT is a network scheduling technique that illustrates the dependence of activities. When some activities are dependent and some independent, PERT is more appropriate.

15-6. **Explain the relationship among inventory control, just-in-time (JIT) inventory, and materials requirement planning (MRP).**

Inventory control is the process of managing raw materials, work in process, finished goods, and in-transit goods. JIT is an inventory method in which necessary parts and raw materials are delivered shortly before they are needed. MRP is a system that integrates operations and inventory control. JIT is part of inventory control, and both are part of MRP.

15-7. **Explain how statistical process control (SPC) charts and the exception principle are used in quality control.**

The statistical process control chart is used to graph actual performance to see whether it is within an acceptable standard range. According to the exception principle, if performance is within the acceptable range, do nothing; if it is out of the control limits, take corrective action.

15-8. **Describe how to measure productivity and list three ways to increase it.**

Productivity is measured by dividing outputs by inputs. Productivity can be increased by

(1) increasing the value of the outputs while maintaining the value of the inputs, (2) maintaining the value of the outputs while decreasing the value of the inputs, or (3) increasing the value of the outputs while decreasing the value of the inputs.

• • • KEY TERMS

balanced scorecard (BSC), 468
capacity, 455
critical path, 458
customer involvement, 449
facility layout, 453
Gantt chart, 456
International Standards
   Organization (ISO), 463
inventory, 459

inventory control, 459
just-in-time (JIT) inventory, 460
materials requirement planning
   (MRP), 460
operations, 448
operations flexibility, 449
PERT, 457
planning sheet, 456
priority scheduling, 456

product, 448
productivity, 466
quality control, 462
routing, 456
statistical process control (SPC), 464
supply chain management, 462
technology, 451
time-based competition, 448

• • • KEY TERM REVIEW

Complete each of the following statements using one of this chapter's key terms.

1. _____ refers to the use of strategies to increase the speed with which an organization goes from creativity to delivery.

2. _____ is the function concerned with transforming resource inputs into product outputs.

3. A _____ is a good, a service, or a combination of the two.

4. _____ refers to the amount of input from customers, which determines whether operations are make to stock, assemble to order, or make to order.

5. _____ refers to the amount of variety in the products an operation produces, which determines whether the products are produced continuously, repetitively, in batches, or individually.

6. _____ is the process used to transform inputs into outputs.

7. _____ refers to the spatial arrangement of physical resources relative to each other.

8. _____ is the amount of products an organization can produce.

9. _____ is the path and sequence of the transformations of a product into an output.

10. _____ is the continuing evaluation and reordering of the sequence in which products will be produced.

11. A _____ states an objective and lists the sequence of activities required to meet the objective, when each activity will begin and end, and who will complete each activity.

12. A _____ uses bars to graphically illustrate a schedule and progress toward the objective over a period.

13. _____ is a network scheduling technique that illustrates the dependence of activities.

14. The _____ is the most time-consuming series of activities in a PERT network.

15. _____ is the stock of materials held for future use.

16. _____ is the process of managing raw materials, work in process, finished goods, and in-transit goods.

17. _____ is an inventory method in which necessary parts and raw materials are delivered shortly before they are needed.

18. _____ is a system that integrates operations and inventory control with complex ordering and scheduling.

19. _____ is the process of coordinating all the activities involved in producing a product and delivering it to the customer.

20. _____ is the process of ensuring that all types of inventory meet standards.

21. The _____ certifies firms that meet set quality standards.

22. _____ aids in determining whether quality is within an acceptable standard range.

23. _____ is a performance measure relating outputs to inputs.

24. A _____ measures financial, customer service, and internal business performance, as well as learning and growth performance.

REVIEW QUESTIONS

1. What does the operations department do?
2. Is the level of customer involvement highest with make-to-stock, assemble-to-order, or make-to-order operations? Why?
3. Which type of process operation is the most flexible? Least flexible?
4. Which type of process operation is most commonly used by retailers and service organizations?
5. Are services generally more capital or labor intensive than manufacturing? Why?
6. Why is it important to balance time-based competition and design?
7. Which two facility layouts are the most flexible? Which two layouts are the least flexible?
8. Why is capacity planning so important?
9. Why is scheduling important?
10. What does a Gantt chart show that a planning sheet and a PERT network don't show?
11. When would you use a PERT network rather than a Gantt chart?
12. What are the four types of inventory?
13. What does materials requirement planning integrate?
14. What is the relationship between inventory and quality control?
15. What are the five rules of customer relations?
16. Why should you measure productivity rather than just production?

COMMUNICATION SKILLS

The following critical-thinking questions can be used for class discussion and/or as written assignments to develop communication skills. Be sure to give complete explanations for all questions.

1. Why are some companies (such as Apple) innovative when it comes to changing products and processes, while others (such as Eastman Kodak) are slow to innovate and change?
2. Can a standard make-to-stock product (such as soda) also be made to order? If so, how?
3. Is the trend toward broader product mix with unrelated diversification? Why or why not?
4. Think about your career and the ideal job you are planning to obtain. Use Exhibit 15-2 to classify the operations systems and Exhibit 15-4 to identify the facility layout where you will work.
5. Assume you are planning a major event or project, such as a big wedding. (If you have an actual future event or project, use it rather than selecting an assumed event.) Would you use the planning sheet, Gantt chart, or PERT to plan and control the event?

Why? Identify the major things that you need to plan for and make, and put them on the actual form using either Exhibit 15-5, 15-6, or 15-7 as a guide.

6. Many companies are now using radio-frequency identification (RFID) technology. RFID is revolutionary and is helping businesses improve supply chain management. However, critics are concerned about protecting people's privacy. For example, with RFID, businesses will better know consumers' shopping habits and purchases. Do you want businesses to know where you live and the products you have in your house? Explain.
7. What is your view of the quality of products you have purchased over the past year compared to previous years? Did you have to return and exchange products or have them repaired? Do you think that quality is getting better with time?
8. The balanced scorecard (BSC) calls for measuring performance in four areas. If a business is making good profits, should it bother with the other three nonfinancing measures? Why or why not?

CASE: TOYOTA

Toyota Motor Corporation, commonly known simply as Toyota, is a Japanese multinational corporation. It also manufactures the Lexus and Scion brands. Toyota has long been recognized as an industry leader in manufacturing, and its production system, more than any other aspect of the company, is responsible for having made Toyota the company it is today.

Over the years, Toyota was aggressive in cutting costs, and no detail was too small. For instance, Toyota designers took a close look at the grip handles mounted above the door inside most cars. They managed to cut the number of parts in the handles from 34 to 5, which helped cut procurement costs by 40 percent. The change slashed the time needed for installation by 75 percent—to 3 seconds. Toyota is often given credit for popularizing the now-famous just-in-time (JIT) inventory system. Toyota managed to slash the time it took to bring models into production once a design was final to about 12 months, compared with an industry average of between 24 and 36 months. Toyota also began to design parts for many of its cars that were cheaper and lighter, further cutting costs for the company. With the heavy focus on cutting costs, the company's top U.S. executive, Jim Press, warned his bosses in Japan that vehicle quality was slipping. But his warning had no apparent effect.

Toyota's fortunes began to change, and its focus on cost cutting rather than quality caught up with it. Three separate but related recalls of automobiles occurred at the end of 2009 and start of 2010 after reports that several vehicles experienced unintended acceleration. Toyota also issued a separate recall for hybrid antilock brake software. When all was said and done, Toyota had announced recalls of more than 11 million vehicles for the problems. Sales of multiple recalled models were suspended for several weeks as a result of the recalls, with the vehicles awaiting replacement parts. Some owners that had their recalled vehicles repaired still reported accelerator pedal issues, leading to investigations and the finding of improper repairs. The recalls further led to additional investigations, along with multiple lawsuits against Toyota. As a result of the recalls, Toyota had to pay a record $48.8 million in fines, and there are still pending lawsuits against the company. But quality problems didn't stop. In October 2012, Toyota announced a recall of 7.43 million vehicles worldwide to fix malfunctioning power window switches.

Toyota got carried away chasing high-speed growth, market share, and productivity gains year in and year out. All that slowly dulled the commitment to quality embedded in Toyota's corporate culture. Toyota needs to absorb a painful lesson about what happens to a great company when ambition gets too far ahead of tradition.

Sources: A. Ohnsman, J. Green, and K. Inoue, "The Humbling of Toyota," BusinessWeek (March 11, 2010), http://www.businessweek.com/magazine/content/10_12/b4171032583967.htm, accessed December 21, 2010; K. Thomas and T. A. Husaka, "Toyota to Pay $32.4 Million in Extra Fines," Yahoo! News (December 21, 2010), http://news.yahoo.com/s/ap/20101221/ap_on_bi_ge/as_toyota_recall, accessed December 21, 2010; and Wikipedia's entry on Toyota at http://en.wikipedia.org/wiki/Toyota, accessed September 19, 2013.

Case Questions

1. How is Toyota's operations system and facility layout classified?

2. Which types of inventory does Toyota have?

3. Which area of the balanced scorecard is causing problems at Toyota?

4. Can Toyota get quality back on track and stop the recalls? As the chief operations officer, what would you do to improve quality?

Cumulative Case Questions

5. Discuss the ethical issues surrounding this case. (Chapter 2)

6. Where in the decision-making process might Toyota have erred when it decided to cut vehicle production costs? (Chapter 4)

7. Discuss whether Toyota's cost-cutting tactics fit its competitive strategy. (Chapter 5)

8. How would you rate Toyota's ability to change through innovation, and what type of changes has it been making? (Chapter 6)

9. Discuss why negotiation skills are so important at Toyota. (Chapter 10)

10. Discuss the importance of motivation (Chapter 11) and leadership (Chapter 12) at Toyota.

11. Discuss the need for a team approach at Toyota. (Chapter 8)

• • •   SKILL BUILDER 15–1: DEVELOPING A PLAN TO OPEN A MOVIES AND MUSIC SHOP

Objective

To develop your skills in planning using a Gantt chart and PERT network.

Skills

The primary skills developed through this exercise are:

1. *Management skill*—decision making (conceptual, diagnostic, analytical, critical-thinking, and quantitative reasoning skills are needed to develop a schedule to open a business)

2. *AACSB competency*—analytic skills

3. *Management function*—controlling

You have decided to open and manage Smith (your last name) Movies & Music Shop on April 1. It is now late December. You plan to move in one month before the store opens in order to set up. During March, your assistant will help you set up while you train him or her. Assume that you have decided to use (1) a Gantt chart and (2) a PERT network. Develop both, in whichever order you prefer, following the text guides for their development. Assume that you have identified the activities and completion times listed below (the activities may not be given in sequence) and that you will start to implement the plan on January 2.

a. Lease the fixtures necessary to display your DVDs and CDs; it will take 2 weeks to get them.

b. Order and receive DVDs and CDs. This will take 1 week.

c. Recruit and select an assistant (3 weeks or less).

d. Install the fixtures, paint, decorate, and so on (2 weeks).

e. Form a corporation (4 weeks).

f. Make arrangements to buy DVDs and CDs on credit (2 weeks).

g. Find a store location (6 weeks or less).

h. Unpack and display the DVDs and CDs (1 week).

i. Train the assistant (1 week).

j. Select the DVDs and CDs you plan to stock (1 week).

k. Determine start-up costs and cash outflows per month through April 30; your rich uncle will lend you this amount (1 week).

Gantt Chart

When developing the Gantt chart, use the following format, based on weeks. You may want to change the letter sequence to match the starting dates.

Gantt Chart

PERT

When developing the PERT chart, draw arrows from the start to your circles for the independent activities. Place the letter of the activity inside the circle. On the arrow to the activity, place the number of weeks needed to complete it. Then draw an arrow to the end. Also from the start, draw the first dependent activity, followed by the next dependent activity, and so on, until you get to the last one; then draw an arrow to the end.

Gantt Chart				
Activity Letter	January 1 2 3 4	February 1 2 3 4	March 1 2 3 4	April 1
_____				
_____				
_____				
_____				
_____				
_____				
_____				
_____				
_____				
_____				
_____				

Be sure to put the number of weeks and activity/event letters on your network. After all activities have been listed, determine the critical path and draw the second arrow to indicate it. *Hint:* You should have five arrows to activities coming from the start; you can begin the process with either selecting movies/music or finding a store location.

PERT
(with critical path)

Start   End

Conclusion

Is Gantt or PERT more appropriate for this type of plan?

Apply It

What did I learn from this experience? How can I use this knowledge in the future?

• • • SKILL BUILDER 15–2: ECONOMIC ORDER QUANTITY

Objective

To develop your skill at calculating EOQ.

Skills

The primary skills developed through this exercise are:

1. *Management skill*—decision making (quantitative reasoning skills are needed to determine EOQ)

2. *AACSB competency*—analytic skills

3. *Management function*—controlling

Calculate the EOQ for each of the following four situations:

1. $R = 2,000$, $S = \$15.00$, $H = \$5.00$

2. $H = \$10.00$, $R = 7,500$, $S = \$40.00$

3. $R = 500$, $H = \$15.00$, $S = \$35.00$

4. $S = \$50.00$, $H = \$25.00$, $R = 19,000$

Apply It

What did I learn from this experience? How will I use this knowledge in the future?

• • • SKILL BUILDER 15-3: INCREASING PRODUCTIVITY

Objective

To gain experience in determining ways to increase productivity.

Skills

The primary skills developed through this exercise are:

1. *Management skill*—decision making (conceptual, diagnostic, analytical, critical-thinking, and quantitative reasoning skills are needed to develop cost-cutting ideas)
2. *AACSB competency*—analytic skills
3. *Management function*—controlling

1. Select a place where you work or have worked. Identify the few critical success factors (Chapter 14)

that were/are important for your job/department success.
2. Determine ways to cut input costs but maintain outputs in order to increase productivity. Identify ways to save time and money. How can things be done more cheaply?
3. Determine ways to increase outputs but maintain inputs in order to increase productivity. What can be done to produce more? How can things be done quicker and better?

Apply It

What did I learn from this experience? How will I use this knowledge in the future?

• • • SKILL BUILDER 15-4: YOUR COURSE SELF-ASSESSMENT

Objective

To review your course Self-Assessments.

Skills

The primary skills developed through this exercise are:

1. *Management skill*—decision making
2. *AACSB competency*—reflective thinking skills

3. *Management function*—controlling

Break into groups and discuss your answers to the Self-Assessment, Putting It All Together. Focus on helping each other improve career development plans.

Apply It

What did I learn from this experience? How will I use this knowledge in the future?

• • • SKILL BUILDER 15-5: THE MOST IMPORTANT THINGS I GOT FROM THIS COURSE

Objective

To review your course learning, critical thinking, and skill development.

Skills

The primary skills developed through this exercise are:

1. *Management skill*—decision making
2. *AACSB competency*—reflective thinking skills
3. *Management function*—controlling

Think about and write/type the three or four most important things you learned or skills you developed through this course and how they are or will help you in your personal and/or professional lives.

Apply It

What did I learn from this experience? How will I use this knowledge in the future?

• • • STUDENT STUDY SITE 📱

Visit the Student Study Site at **www.sagepub.com/lussier6e** to access to these additional study tools:

- Mobile-compatible self-assessment quizzes
- Mobile-compatible key term flashcards
- Video Links
- SAGE Journal Articles
- Web Links

··· Glossary

acquisition Occurs when one business buys all or part of another business.

adaptive strategies Overall strategies for a line of business, including prospecting, defending, and analyzing.

arbitrator A neutral third party who resolves a conflict by making a binding decision.

assessment centers Places job applicants undergo a series of tests, interviews, and simulated experiences to determine their potential.

attitudes Positive or negative evaluations of people, things, and situations.

attribution The process of determining the reason for someone's behavior and whether that behavior is situational or intentional.

authority The right to make decisions, issue orders, and use resources.

balanced scorecard (BSC) A management tool that measures financial, customer service, and internal business performance, as well as learning and growth performance.

BCF statement A statement that describes a conflict in terms of behaviors, consequences, and feelings, in a way that maintains ownership of the problem.

behavioral leadership theorists Theorists who attempt to determine distinctive styles used by effective leaders.

behavioral theorists Researchers who focus on people to determine the best way to manage in all organizations.

benchmarking The process of comparing an organization's products and services and processes with those of other companies.

bona fide occupational qualification (BFOQ) An occupational qualification that may be discriminatory but that is reasonably necessary to normal operation of a particular organization.

brainstorming The process of suggesting many possible alternatives without evaluation.

budget A planned quantitative allocation of resources for specific activities.

business portfolio analysis The corporate process of determining which lines of business the corporation will be in and how it will allocate resources among them.

capacity The amount of products an organization can produce.

capital expenditures budget A projection of all planned major asset investments.

career development The process of gaining skill, experience, and education to achieve career objectives.

career planning The process of setting career objectives and determining how to accomplish them.

centralized authority Important decisions are made by top managers.

change agent The person responsible for implementing an organizational change effort.

charismatic leadership A leadership style that inspires loyalty, enthusiasm, and high levels of performance. **transformational leaders** Leaders that *bring about continuous learning, innovation, and change.*

citizenship behavior Employee efforts that go above and beyond the call of duty.

classical theorists Researchers who focus on the job and management functions to determine the best way to manage in all organizations.

coaching The process of giving motivational feedback to maintain and improve performance.

coalition A network of alliances that help achieve an objective. **conflict** A situation in which people are in disagreement and opposition.

collaborative conflict resolution model A conflict resolution model that calls for (1) stating the problem in a BCF statement, (2) getting the other party to acknowledge the problem or conflict, (3) asking for and/or presenting alternative resolutions to the conflict, and (4) coming to an agreement.

collective bargaining The negotiation process resulting in a contract between employees and management that covers employment conditions.

command groups Groups that consist of managers and the employees they supervise.

communication channel The means or medium by which a message is transmitted; the three primary channels are oral, nonverbal, and written.

communication process The process that takes place between a sender who encodes a message and transmits it through a channel to a receiver who decodes it and may give feedback.

communication The process of transmitting information and meaning.

compensation The total of an employee's pay and benefits.

competitive advantage Specifies how an organization offers unique customer value.

competitive advantage specifies how an organization offers unique customer value

concurrent control Action taken to ensure that standards are met as inputs are transformed into outputs.

consensus mapping The process of developing group agreement on a solution to a problem.

contemporary leadership theories Theories that attempt to determine how effective leaders interact with, inspire, and support followers.

content motivation theories Theories that focus on identifying and understanding employees' needs.

contingency leadership model A model used to determine if leadership style is task or relationship oriented and if the situation matches the style.

contingency plans Alternative plans to be implemented if uncontrollable events occur.

contingency theorists Researchers who focus on determining the best management approach for a given situation.

contract manufacturing Contracting a foreign firm to manufacture products a company will sell as its own.

control frequency The rate of repetition—constant, periodic, or occasional—of measures taken to control performance.

control systems process (1) Set objectives and standards, (2) measure performance, (3) compare performance to standards, and (4) correct or reinforce.

Controlling The process of monitoring progress and taking corrective action when needed to ensure that objectives are achieved.

creative process The approach to generating new ideas that involves three stages (1) preparation, (2) incubation and illumination, and (3) evaluation.

creativity A way of thinking that generates new ideas.

criteria The standards that an alternative must meet to be selected as the decision that will accomplish the objective.

critical path The most time-consuming series of activities in a PERT network.

critical success factors The limited number of areas in which satisfactory results will ensure successful performance, achieving the objective/standard.

customer involvement The amount of input from customers, which determines whether operations are make to stock, assemble to order, or make to order.

customer value The perceived benefit of a product, used by customers to determine whether or not to buy the product.

damage control Action taken to minimize negative impacts on customers/stakeholders due to faulty outputs.

decentralized authority Important decisions are made by middle and first-line managers.

decision making The process of selecting a course of action that will solve a problem.

decision-making conditions Certainty, risk, and uncertainty.

decision-making model model A six-step process for arriving at a decision and involves (1) classifying and defining the problem or opportunity, (2) setting objectives and criteria, (3) generating creative and innovative alternatives, (4) analyzing alternatives and selecting the most feasible, (5) planning and implementing the decision, and (6) controlling the decision.

decision-making skills The ability to conceptualize situations and select alternatives to solve problems and take advantage of opportunities.

decoding The receiver's process of translating a message into a meaningful form. nonverbal communication Messages sent without words.

delegation The process of assigning responsibility and authority for accomplishing objectives.

departmentalization The grouping of related activities into units.

development Ongoing education to improve skills for present and future jobs.

devil's advocate approach Group members focus on defending a solution while others try to come up with reasons the solution will not work.

direct feedback An OD intervention in which the change agent make sa direct recommendation for change.

direct investment The building or buying of operating facilities in a foreign country.

Disability a mental or physical impairment that substantially limits an individual's ability.

discipline Corrective action to get employees to meet standards and standing plans.

discontinuous change A significant breakthrough in technology that leads to design competition and a new technology cycle.

discrimination An illegal practice that gives unfair treatment to diversity groups in employment decisions.

divisional structure Departmentalization based on semiautonomous strategic business units.

embargo A total ban on the importing of a product from one or more countries.

empathic listening Understanding and relating to another's feelings.

employee assistance program (EAP) A benefit program staffed by people who help employees get professional assistance in solving their problems.

encoding The sender's process of putting the message into a form that the receiver will understand.

entrepreneur Someone who starts a small-business venture

equity theory Theory that proposes that employees are motivated when their perceived inputs equal outputs.

ERG theory Theory that proposes that employees are motivated by three needs: existence, relatedness, and growth.

ethics Standards of right and wrong that influence behavior.

ethnocentrism Regarding one's own ethnic group or culture as superior to others.

expatriates Individuals who live and work outside their native country.

expectancy theory Theory that proposes that employees are motivated when they believe they can accomplish a task and the rewards for doing so are worth the effort.

external environment The factors outside of an organization's boundaries that affect its performance.

facility layout The spatial arrangement of physical resources relative to each other—operations use product, process, cellular, or fixed-position layouts.

feedback Information that verifies a message.

financial statements The income statement, balance sheet, and cash flow statement.

first-mover advantage Offering a unique customer value before competitors do sobusiness plan Written description of a new venture, describing its objectives and the steps for achieving them

forcefield analysis An OD intervention that diagrams the current level of performance, the forces hindering change, and the forces driving toward change.

Franchising An entrepreneurial venture in which a franchisor licenses a business to the franchisee for a fee and royalties.

functional conflict A situation in which disagreement and opposition support the achievement of organizational objectives.

functional strategies Strategies developed and implemented by managers in marketing, operations, human resources, finance, and other departments.

Gantt chart A scheduling tool that uses bars to graphically illustrate a schedule and progress toward the objective over a period.

giving praise model A four-step technique for providing feedback to an employee (1) Tell the employee exactly what was done correctly; (2) tell the employee why the behavior is important; (3) stop for a moment of silence; (4) encourage repeat performance.

glass ceiling The invisible barrier that prevents women and minorities from advancing to the top jobs in organizations.

global sourcing Hiring others outside the organization to perform work worldwide.

global village Refers to companies conducting business worldwide without boundaries.

global virtual teams Teams whose members are physically located in different places but work together as a team.

goal-setting theory Theory that proposes that achievable but difficult goals motivate employees.

grand strategy An overall corporate strategy for growth, stability, or turnaround and retrenchment, or for some combination of these.

grapevine The informal flow of information in any direction throughout an organization.

group cohesiveness The extent to which members stick together.

group composition The mix of members' skills and abilities.

group performance model Group performance is a function of organizational context, group structure, group process, and group development stage.

group process dimensions Roles, norms, cohesiveness, status, decision making, and conflict resolution.

group process The patterns of interactions that emerge as members perform their jobs.

group roles Group task roles, group maintenance roles, and self-interest roles.

group structure dimensions Group type, size, composition, leadership, and objectives.

group types Formal or informal, functional or cross-functional, and command or task.

group Two or more members with a clear leader who perform independent jobs with individual accountability, evaluation, and rewards.

growth strategies Strategies a company can adopt in order to grow concentration, backward and forward integration, and related and unrelated diversification.

hierarchy of needs theory Theory that proposes that employees are motivated by five levels of needs: physiological, safety, social, esteem, and self-actualization.

horizontal communication The flow of information between colleagues and peers.

human resources management process Planning for, attracting, developing, and retaining employees.

incremental change Continual improvement that takes place within the existing technology cycle.

innovation The implementation of a new idea.

internal environment Factors that affect an organization's performance from within its boundaries.

international company An organization based primarily in one country but transacts business in other countries.

International Standards Organization (ISO) An organization that certifies firms that meet set quality standards.

interpersonal skills The ability to understand, communicate, and work well with individuals and groups through developing effective relationships.

intrapreneur Someone who starts a new line of business within a larger organizationsmall business A business that is independently owned and operated with a small number of employees and relatively low volume of sales

inventory control The process of managing raw materials, work in process, finished goods, and in-transit goods.

inventory The stock of materials held for future use.

job characteristics model A conceptual framework for designing or enriching jobs that focuses on core job dimensions, psychological states of employees, and the strength of employees' need for growth.

job description Identifies the tasks and responsibilities of a position.

job design The process of identifying tasks that each employee is responsible for completing.

job enrichment The process of building motivators into a job to make it more interesting and challenging.

job evaluation The process of determining the worth of each job relative to the other jobs within the organization.

job specifications Identify the qualifications needed by the person who is to fill a position.

joint venture Two or more firms sharing ownership of a new company.

just-in-time (JIT) inventory A method by which necessary parts and raw

materials are delivered shortly before they are needed.

knowledge management Involving everyone in an organization in sharing knowledge and applying it continuously to improve products and processes.

labor relations The interactions between management and unionized employees.

large-group intervention An OD technique that brings together participants from all parts of the organization, and often key outside stakeholders, to solve problems or take advantage of opportunities.

leadership continuum model A model used to determine which of seven styles of leadership, on a continuum from autocratic (boss centered) to participative (employee centered), is best for a given situation.

Leadership Grid® A model that identifies the ideal leadership style as incorporating a high concern for both production and people.

leadership style The combination of traits, skills, and behaviors managers use in interacting with employees.

leadership trait theorists Theorists who attempt to determine a list of distinctive characteristics that account for leadership effectiveness.

Leading The process of influencing employees to work toward achieving objectives.

learning organization An organization with a culture that values sharing knowledge so as to adapt to the changing environment and continuously improve.

levels of authority The authority to inform, the authority to recommend, the authority to report, and full authority.

levels of culture Behavior, values and beliefs, and assumptions.

levels of management Top managers, middle managers, and first-line managers.

licensing The process of a licensor agreeing to licensee the right to make its products or services or use its intellectual property in exchange for a royalty.

line authority The responsibility to make decisions and issue orders down the chain of command.

management audit Analysis of the organization's planning, organizing, leading, and controlling functions to look for improvements.

management by objectives (MBO) The process in which managers and their employees jointly set objectives for the employees, periodically evaluate performance, and reward according to the results.

management by walking around (MBWA) A type of supervision in which the three major activities are listening, teaching, and facilitating.

management counseling The process of giving employees feedback so they realize that a problem is affecting their job performance and referring employees with problems to the employee assistance program.

management functions Planning, organizing, leading, and controlling.

management role categories The categories of roles—interpersonal, informational, and decisional—managers play as they accomplish management functions.

management science theorists Researchers who focus on the use of mathematics to aid in problem solving and decision making.

management skills The skills needed to be an effective manager, including technical, interpersonal, and decision-making skills.

manager The individual responsible for achieving organizational objectives through efficient and effective utilization of resources.

manager's resources Human, financial, physical, and informational resources.

materials requirement planning (MRP) A system that integrates operations and inventory control with complex ordering and scheduling.

mediator A neutral third party who helps resolve a conflict.

merger Occurs when two companies form one corporation.

message-sending process A process that includes (1) developing rapport, (2) stating your communication objective, (3) transmitting your message, (4) checking the receiver's understanding, and (5) getting a commitment and following up.

micromanagement A management style generally used as a negative term for when a manager closely observes or controls the work of his or her employees.

mission An organization's purpose or reason for being.

motivation process The process of moving from need to motive to behavior to consequence to satisfaction or dissatisfaction.

motivation The willingness to achieve organizational objectives or to go above and beyond the call of duty (organizational citizenship behavior).

multinational corporation (MNC) An organization that has ownership in operations in two or more countries.

networking The process of developing relationships for the purpose of career building and socializing. networking The process of developing relationships for the purpose of career building and socializing.

new venture A small business or a new line of business

nominal grouping The process of generating and evaluating alternatives using a structured voting method.

nonprogrammed decisions Significant decisions that arise in nonrecurring and nonroutine situations, for which the decision maker should use the decision-making model.

normative leadership model A time-driven or development-driven decision tree that assists a user in selecting one of five leadership styles (decide, consult individuals, consult group, facilitate, and delegate) to use in a given situation (based on seven questions/variables) to maximize a decision.

norms Expectations about appropriate behavior that are shared by members of a group.

objectives Statements of what is to be accomplished that is expressed in singular, specific, and measurable terms with a target date.

OD interventions Specific actions taken to implement specific changes.

one-minute self-sell An opening statement used in networking that quickly summarizes your history and career plan and asks a question.

operating budgets The revenue and expense budgets.

operational planning The process of setting short-range objectives and determining in advance how they will be accomplished.

operations flexibility The amount of variety in the products an operation produces, which determines whether products are produced continuously, repetitively, in batches, or individually.

operations The function concerned with transforming resource inputs into product outputs.

organization chart A graphic illustration of an organization's management hierarchy and departments and their working relationships.

organizational behavior The study of actions that affect performance in the workplace.

organizational change Alterations of existing work routines and strategies that affect the whole organization.

organizational culture The values, beliefs, and assumptions about appropriate behavior that members of an organization share.

organizational development (OD) The ongoing planned process of change used as a means of improving performance through interventions.

Organizing The process of delegating and coordinating tasks and allocating resources to achieve objectives.

orientation The process of introducing new employees to the organization and their jobs.

paraphrasing The process of restating a message in one's own words. message-receiving process A process that includes listening, analyzing, and checking understanding.

participative decision-making model A time-driven or development-driven decision tree that assists a user in selecting one of five leadership styles to use in a given situation to maximize a decision.

path-goal model A model used to determine employee objectives and to clarify how to achieve them using one of four leadership styles. Situational Leadership® model A model used to select one of four leadership styles that match the employees' maturity level in a given situation.

performance appraisal The ongoing process of evaluating employee performance.

performance formula Performance = ability × motivation × resources.

Performance Means of evaluating how effectively and efficiently managers utilize resources to achieve objectives.

personality A combination of behavioral, mental, and emotional traits that define an individual. perception The process of selecting, organizing, and interpreting environmental information.

PERT A network scheduling technique that illustrates the dependence of activities.

planning sheet A scheduling tool that states an objective and lists the sequence of activities required to meet the objective, when each activity will begin and end, and who will complete each activity.

planning The process of setting objectives and determining in advance exactly how the objectives will be met.

Planning The process of setting objectives and determining in advance exactly how the objectives will be met.

policies General guidelines to be followed when making decisions.

politics The process of gaining and using power.

power The ability to influence others' behavior.

preliminary control Action designed to anticipate and prevent possible problems.

priority scheduling The continuing evaluation and reordering of the sequence in which products will be produced.

priority-determination questions Questions that help determine the priority of tasks to be completed.

problem solving The process of taking corrective action to meet objectives.

problem The situation that exists whenever objectives are not being met.

procedure A sequence of actions to be followed in order to achieve an objective.

process consultation An OD intervention designed to improve team dynamics.

process motivation theories Theories that focus on understanding how employees choose behaviors to fulfill their needs.

product A good, a service, or a combination of the two.

productivity A performance measure relating outputs to inputs.

programmed decisions Decisions that arise in recurring or routine situations, for which the decision maker should use decision rules or organizational policies and procedures.

Pygmalion effect The theory that managers' attitudes toward and expectations and treatment of employees largely determine their performance.

quality control The process of ensuring that all types of inventory meet standards.

quality A measure of value determined by comparing a product's actual functioning to requirements.

quota Sets a limit on the number or volume of a product that can be imported or exported during a set time.

reciprocity The mutual exchange of favors and privileges to accomplish objectives.

recruiting The process of attracting qualified candidates to apply for job openings.

reflecting responses Responses that paraphrase a message and communicate understanding and acceptance to the sender.

reinforcement theory Theory that proposes that the consequences of their behavior will motivate employees to behave in predetermined ways.

responsibility The obligation to achieve objectives by performing required activities.

rework control Action taken to fix an output.

routing The path and sequence of the transformation of a product into an output.

rules Statements of exactly what should or should not be done.

selection The process of choosing the most qualified applicant recruited for a job.

single-use plans Programs and budgets developed for handling nonrepetitive situations.

situation analysis An analysis of those features in a company's environment that most directly affect its options and opportunities.

situational approaches to leadership Theories that attempt to determine appropriate leadership styles for particular situations.

social responsibility The conscious effort to operate in a manner that creates a win-win situation for all stakeholders.

sociotechnical theorists Researchers who focus on integrating people and technology.

span of management The number of employees reporting to a manager.

staff authority The responsibility to advise and assist other personnel.

stages of group development Forming, storming, norming, performing, and termination.

stages of the change process Denial, resistance, exploration, and commitment.

stakeholders' approach to ethics Creating a win-win situation for all relevant stakeholders so that everyone benefits from the decision.

standards Measures of performance levels in the areas of quantity, quality, time, cost, and behavior.

standing plans Policies, procedures, and rules developed for handling repetitive situations.

statistical process control (SPC) A statistical test that aids in determining whether quality is within an acceptable standard range.

status The perceived ranking of one member relative to other members in a group.

strategic alliance An agreement to share resources that does not necessarily involve creating a new company.

strategic human resources planning The process of staffing the organization to meet its objectives.

strategic planning The process of developing a mission and long-range objectives and determining in advance how they will be accomplished.

strategy A plan for pursuing a mission and achieving objectives.

stress The body's reaction to environmental demands.

subsidies Form of financial support, including government grants, loans, and tax breaks given to domestic companies.

substitutes for leadership Characteristics of the task, of subordinates, or of the organization that replace the need for a leader.

supply chain management The process of coordinating all the activities involved in producing a product and delivering it to the customer.

survey feedback An OD intervention that uses a questionnaire to gather data to use as the basis for change.

sustainability Meeting the needs of the present world without compromising the ability of future generations to meet their own needs.

SWOT analysis A determination of an organization's internal environmental strengths and weaknesses and external environmental opportunities and threats.

symbolic leaders Leaders who articulate a vision for an organization and reinforce the culture through slogans, symbols, and ceremonies.

synectics The process of generating novel alternatives through role playing and fantasizing.

systems process The method used to transform inputs into outputs.

systems theorists Researchers who focus on viewing the organization as a whole and as the interrelationship of its parts.

tariff A direct tax on imports to make them more expensive.

task groups Employees selected to work on a specific objective.

team building An OD intervention designed to help work groups increase structural and team dynamics and performance.

team leaders Empower members to take responsibility for performing the management functions and focus on developing effective group structure and group process and on furthering group development.

team A small number of members with shared leadership who perform interdependent jobs with both individual and group accountability, evaluation, and rewards.

technical skills The ability to use methods and techniques to perform a task.

technology The process used to transform inputs into outputs.

time-based competition The use of strategies to increase the speed with which an organization goes from creativity to delivery.

total quality management (TQM) The process that involves everyone in an organization focusing on the customer to continually improve product value.

training The process of teaching employees the skills necessary to perform a job.

transactional leadership A leadership style based on social exchange.

transformational leaders Leaders who bring about continuous learning, innovation, and change.

two-dimensional leadership styles Four possible leadership styles that are based on the dimensions of job structure and employee consideration.

two-factor theory Theory that proposes that employees are motivated by motivators rather than by maintenance factors.

types of change Changes in strategy, in structure, in technology, and in people.

types of managers General managers, functional managers, and project managers.

vertical communication The flow of information both downward and upward through the organizational chain of command.

vestibule training Training that develops skills in a simulated setting.

visionary leaders Leaders who create an image of the organization in the future that provides direction for setting goals and developing strategic plans.

···Endnotes

Chapter 1

1. B. Benjamin and C. O'Reilly, "Becoming a Leader: Early Career Challenges Faced by MBA Graduates," *Academy of Management Learning & Education* 10, no. 3 (2011): 452–472.

2. N. Breugst, H. Patzelt, D. A. Shepherd, and H. Aguinis, "Relationship Conflict Improves Team Performance Assessment Accuracy: Evidence From a Multilevel Study," *Academy of Management Learning & Education* 11, no. 2 (2012): 187–206.

3. G. Yukl, "Effective Leadership Behavior: What We Know and What Questions Need More Attention," *Academy of Management Perspectives* 26, no. 4 (2012): 66–85.

4. W. J. Henisz, "Leveraging the Financial Crisis to Fulfill the Promise of Progressive Management," *Academy of Management Learning & Education* 10, no. 2 (2011): 298–321.

5. R. E. Silverman, "Who's the Boss? There Isn't One," *The Wall Street Journal* (June 20, 2012), B1.

6. G. Hirst, D. Van Knippenberg, Ch. H. Chen, and D. A. Sacramento, "How Does Bureaucracy Impact Individual Creativity? A Cross-Level Investigation of Team Orientation-Creativity Relationships," *Academy of Management Journal* 54, no. 3 (2011): 624–641.

7. P. C. Patel and B. Conklin, "Perceived Labor Productivity in Small Firms—The Effects of High-Performance Work Systems and Group Culture Through Employee Retention," *Entrepreneurship Theory and Practice* 36, no. 2 (2012): 205–231.

8. J. B. Oldroyd and S. S. Morris, "Catching Falling Stars: A Human Resource Response to Social Capital's Detrimental Effect of Information Overload on Star Employees," *Academy of Management Review* 37, no. 3 (2012): 396–418.

9. B. A. Campbell, R. Coff, and D. Kryscynski, "Rethinking Sustained Competitive Advantage from Human Capital," *Academy of Management Review* 37, no. 3 (2012): 378–395.

10. S. Nifadkar, A. S. Tsui, and B. E. Ashforth, "The Way You Make Me Feel and Behave: Supervisor-Triggered Newcomer Affect and Approach-Avoidance Behavior," *Academy of Management Journal* 55, no. 2 (2012): 1146–1168.

11. B. L. Hallen and K. M. Eisenhardt, "Catalyzing Strategies and Efficient Tie Formation: How Entrepreneurial Firms Obtain Investment Ties," *Academy of Management Journal* 55, no. 1 (2012): 35–70.

12. S. Garg, "Venture Boards: Distinctive Monitoring and Implications for Firm Performance," *Academy of Management Review* 38, no. 1 (2013): 90–108.

13. E. R. Crawford and J. A. Lepine, "A Configural Theory of Team Process: Accounting for the Structure of Taskwork and Teamwork," *Academy of Management Review* 38, no. 1 (2012): 32–48.

14. H. K. Gardner, F. Gino, and D. R. Staats, "Dynamically Integrating Knowledge in Teams: Transforming Resources into Performance. How You Manage the Organization's Resources Affects Its Performance," *Academy of Management Journal* 55, no. 4 (2012): 998–1022.

15. R. Nag and D. A. Gioia, "From Common to Uncommon Knowledge: Foundations of Firm-Specific Use of Knowledge as a Resource," *Academy of Management Journal* 55, no. 2 (2 2012): 421–457.

16. C. B. Bingham and J. P. Davis, "Learning Sequences: Their Existence, Effect, and Evolution," *Academy of Management Journal* 55, no. 3 (2012): 611–641.

17. A. M. Carton and J. N. Cummings, "A Theory of Subgroups in Work Teams," *Academy of Management Review* 37, no. 3 (2012): 441–470.

18. R. Fisman and T. Sullivan, "In Defense of the CEO," *Wall Street Journal* (January 12–13, 2013): C1–C2.

19. J. Nickerson, C. J. Yen, and J. T. Mahoney, "Exploring the Problem-Finding and Problem-Solving Approach for Designing Organizations," *Academy of Management Perspectives* 26, no. 1 (2012): 52–72.

20. C. Rose, "Charlie Rose Talks to Donald Gogel," *BusinessWeek* (May 28–June 3, 2012): 52.

21. Patel and Conklin, "Perceived Labor Productivity in Small Firms."

22. *The Wall Street Journal* (November 14, 1980): 33.

23. G. Petriglieri, J. D. Wood, and J. L. Petriglieri, "Up Close and Personal: Building Foundations for Leaders' Development through the Personalization of Management Learning," *Academy of Management Learning & Education* 10, no. 3 (2011): 430–450.

24. M. Mayo, M. Kakarika, J. C. Pastor, and S. Brutus, "Aligning or Inflating Your Leadership Self-Image? A Longitudinal Study of Responses to Peer Feedback in MBA Teams," *Academy of Management Learning & Education* 11, no. 4 (2012): 631–652.

25. Yukl, "Effective Leadership Behavior."

26. M. Feys, F. Anseel, and B. Wille, "Improving Feedback Reports: The Role of Procedural Information and Information Specificity," *Academy of Management Learning & Education* 10, no. 4 (2011): 661–681.

27. R. B. Kaiser and R. B. Kaplan, "Outgrowing Sensitivities: The Deeper Work of Executive Development," *Academy of Management Learning & Education* 5, no. 4 (2006): 463–483.

28. T. Semrau and A. Werner, "The Two Sides of the Story: Network Investments and New Venture Creation," *Journal of Small Business Management* 50, no. 1 (2012): 159–180.

29. Breugst et al., "Relationship Conflict Improves Team Performance Assessment Accuracy."

30. J. Ankeny, "The Good Sir Richard," *Entrepreneur* (June 2012): 31–38.

31. M. Wang, H. Liao, Y. Zhan, and J. Shi, "Daily Customer Mistreatment and Employee Sabotage against Customers: Examining Emotion and Resource Perspectives," *Academy of Management Journal* 54, no. 2 (2011): 312–334.

32. Benjamin and O'Reilly, "Becoming a Leader."

33. Fisman and Sullivan, "In Defense of the CEO."

34. R. Klimoski and B. Amos, "Practicing Evidence-Based Education in Leadership Development," *Academy of Management Learning & Education* 11, no. 4 (2012): 685–702.

35. Yukl, "Effective Leadership Behavior."

36. AACSB International, *Eligibility Procedures and Accreditation Standards for Business Accreditation* (Tampa, FL: Author, 2012). www.aacsb.edu/accreditation/standards-busn-jan2012.pdf. Retrieved April 12, 2013.

37. E. Ghiselli, *Exploration in Management Talent* (Santa Monica, CA: Goodyear Publishing, 1971).

38. Crawford and Lepine, "A Configural Theory of Team Process."

39. N. Bloom, C. Genakos, R. Sadu, and J. Van Reenen, "Management Practices across Firms and Countries," *Academy of Management Perspectives* 26, no. 1 (2012): 12–33.

40. H. G. Halvorson, "How to Be a Better Boss in 2013," *The Wall Street Journal* (January 2, 2012), B1, B6.

41. E. Fauchart and M. Gruber, "Darwinians, Communitarians, and Missionaries: The Role of Founder Identity in Entrepreneurship," *Academy of Management Journal* 54, no. 5 (2011): 935–957.

42. Q. M. Roberson and I. O. Williamson, "Justice in Self-Managing Teams: The

Role of Social Networks in the Emergence of Procedural Justice Climates," *Academy of Management Journal* 55, no. 3 (2012): 685–701.

43. R. Kark, "Games Managers Play: Play as a Form of Leadership Development," *Academy of Management Learning & Education* 10, no. 3 (2012): 507–527.

44. J. Collins, "Collins on Chaos," *Fortune* (October 17, 2011): 157–170.

45. Garg, "Venture Boards."

46. Collins, "Collins on Chaos."

47. L. A. Hill, *Becoming a Manager: Mastery of a New Identity* (Boston: Harvard Business School Press, 1992).

48. Kark, "Games Managers Play."

49. H. Mintzberg, *The Nature of Managerial Work* (New York: Harper & Row, 1973).

50. Yukl, "Effective Leadership Behavior."

51. Fisman and Sullivan, "In Defense of the CEO."

52. D. A. Shepherd, H. Patzelt, and M. Wolfe, "Moving Forward from Project Failure: Negative Emotions, Affective Commitment, and Learning from the Experience," *Academy of Management Journal* 54, no. 6 (2011): 1229–1259.

53. L. Schhoedt, E. Monsen, A. Person, T. Barnett, and J. J. Chrisman, "New Venture and Family Business Teams: Understanding Team Formation, Composition, Behaviors, and Performance," *Entrepreneurship Theory and Practice* 37, no. 1 (2013): 1–15.

54. Ankeny, "The Good Sir Richard."

55. F. W. Taylor, *Principles of Scientific Management* (New York: Harper & Brothers, 1911).

56. H. Fayol, *General and Industrial Management,* trans. by J. A. Conbrough (Geneva: International Management Institute, 1929).

57. F. Roethlisberger and W. Dickson, *Management and the Worker* (Boston: Harvard University Press, 1939).

58. A. Maslow, *Motivation and Personality,* 2nd ed. (New York: Harper & Row, 1970).

59. D. McGregor, *The Human Side of Enterprise* (New York: McGraw-Hill, 1960).

60. R. Ackoff, *Creating the Corporate Future* (New York: Wiley, 1981).

61. H. Koontz, "The Management Theory Jungle Revisited," *Academy of Management Review* 5 (April 1980). 175; D. Katz and R. Khan, *The Social Psychology of Organizations,* 2nd ed. (New York: Wiley, 1978).

62. E. L. Trist and K. W. Bamforth, "Some Social and Psychological Consequences of the Longwall Method of Coalgetting," *Human Relations* 4 (1951): 3–38; F. E. Emery and E. L. Trist, *Socio-Technical Systems,* Vol. 2 of *Management Science: Methods and Techniques* (London: Pergamon, 1960).

63. T. Burns and G. Stalker, *The Management of Innovation* (London: Tavistock, 1961).

64. M. W. McCarter, J. T. Mahoney, and G. B. Northcraft, "Testing the Waters: Using Collective Real Options to Manage the Social Dilemma of Strategic Alliances," *Academy of Management Review* 36, no. 4 (2011): 621–640.

65. S. A. Mohrman and E. E. Lawler, "Generating Knowledge That Drives Change," *Academy of Management Perspectives* 26, no. 1 (2012): 41–51.

66. M. R. Barrick, M. K. Mount, and N. Li, "The Theory of Purposeful Work Behavior: The Role of Personality, Higher-Order Goals, and Job Characteristics," *Academy of Management Review* 38, no. 1 (2013): 132–153.

67. Gardner et al., "Dynamically Integrating Knowledge in Teams."

68. J. D. Hoover, R. C. Giambatista, and L. Y. Belkin, "Eyes On, Hands On: Vicarious Observational Learning as an Enhancement of Direct Experience," *Academy of Management Education & Learning* 11, no. 4 (2012): 591–608.

69. M. Reinholt, T. Pedersen, and N. J. Foss, "Why a Central Network Position Isn't Enough: The Role of Motivation and Ability for Knowledge Sharing in Employee Networks," *Academy of Management Journal* 54, no. 6 (2011): 1277–1297.

70. Carton and Cummings, "A Theory of Subgroups in Work Teams."

71. S. D. Charlier, K. G. Brown, and S. L. Rynes, "Teaching Evidence-Based Management in MBA Programs: What Evidence Is There?" *Academy of Management Education & Learning* 10, no. 2 (2012): 222–236.

72. S. D. Parks, *Leadership Can Be Taught: A Bold Approach for a Complex World* (Boston: Harvard Business School Press, 2005).

73. T. T. Baldwin, J. R. Pierce, R. C. Joines, and S. Farouk, "The Elusiveness of Applied Management Knowledge: A Critical Challenge for Management Education," *Academy of Management Education & Learning* 10, no. 4 (2011): 583–605.

74. D. F. Baker and S. J. Baker, "To Catch the Sparkling Glow: A Canvas for Creativity in the Management Classroom," *Academy of Management Education & Learning* 11, no. 4 (2012): 704–721.

75. P. Bansal, S. Bertels, T. Ewart, P. MacConnachie, and J. O'Brian, "Bridging the Research-Practice Gap," *Academy of Management Perspectives* 26, no. 1 (2012): 73–92.

76. Feys et al., "Improving Feedback Reports."

77. Klimoski and Amos, "Practicing Evidence-Based Education."

78. G. Dokko and V. Gaba, "Venturing into New Territory: Career Experiences of Corporate Venture Capital Managers and Practice Variation," *Academy of Management Journal* 55, no. 3 (2012): 563–583.

79. C. Newport, "Practice the Hard Stuff," *The Wall Street Journal* (January 2, 2013): B6.

80. Klimoski and Amos, "Practicing Evidence-Based Education."

81. B. E. Kaufman, "Strategic Human Resource Management Research in the United States," *Academy of Management Perspectives* 26, no. 2 (2012): 12–36.

Chapter 2

1. C. Rose, "Charlie Rose Talks to eBay's John Donahoe," *BusinessWeek* (February 4–10, 2013): 38.

2. Information taken from Toyota's website, http://www.toyota.com, accessed May 6, 2013.

3. Information taken from Walmart's corporate website, http://www.walmartstores.com, accessed May 6, 2013.

4. Information taken from the Springfield College website, http://www.spfldcol.edu, accessed May 6, 2013.

5. K. Leavitt, S. J. Reynolds, C. M. Barnes, P. Schilpzan, and S. T. Hannah, "Different Hats, Different Obligations: Plural Occupational Identities and Situated Moral Judgments," *Academy of Management Journal* 55, no. 6 (2012): 1316–1333.

6. J. Welch and S. Welch, "Dealing with the Morning-After Syndrome at Facebook," *Fortune* (March 19, 2012): 92.

7. D. Brady and John Chambers *BusinessWeek* (August 27–September 2, 2012): 76.

8. Welch and Welch, "Dealing."

9. B. A. Campbell, R. Coff, and D. Kryscynski, "Rethinking Sustained Competitive Advantage from Human Capital," *Academy of Management Review* 37, no. 3 (2012): 378–395.

10. R. Nag and D. A. Gioia, "From Common to Uncommon Knowledge: Foundations of Firm-Specific Use of Knowledge as a Resources," *Academy of Management Journal* 55, no. 2 (2012): 421–457.

11. J. K. Summers, S. E. Humphrey, and G. R. Ferris, "Team Member Change, Flux in Coordination, and Performance: Effects of Strategic Core Roles, Information Transfer, and Cognitive Ability," *Academy of Management Journal* 55, no. 2 (2012): 314–338.

12. A. H. Jordan and P. G. Audia, "Self-Enhancement and Learning from Performance Feedback," *Academy of Management Review* 27, no. 2 (2012): 221–231.

13. Summers et al., "Team Member Change."

14. J. Gehman, L. K. Trevino, and R. Garud, "Values Work: A Process Study of the Emergence and Performance of Organizational Values Practices," *Academy of Management Journal* 56, no. 1 (2013): 84–112.

15. Welch and Welch, "Dealing."

16. Gehman et al., "Values Work."
17. J. M. W. N. Lepoutre and M. Valente, "Fols Break Out: The Role of Symbolic and Material Immunity in Explaining Institutional Nonconformity," *Academy of Management Journal* 55, no. 2 (2012): 285–313.
18. Lepoutre and Valente, "Fols Break Out."
19. Welch and Welch, "Dealing."
20. A. Lashinsky, "Larry Page Interview," *Fortune* (February 6, 2012): 98–99.
21. Welch and Welch, "Dealing."
22. Lepoutre and Valente, "Fols Break Out."
23. J. D. Hoover, R. C. Giambatista, and L. Y. Belkin, "Eyes On, Hands On: Vicarious Observational Learning as an Enhancement of Direct Experience," *Academy of Management Education & Learning* 11, no. 4 (2012): 591–608.
24. H. K. Gardner, F. Gino, and D. R. Staats, "Dynamically Integrating Knowledge in Teams: Transforming Resources into Performance. How You Manage the Organization's Resources Affects Its Performance," *Academy of Management Journal* 55, no. 4 (2012): 998–1022.
25. S. A. Mohrman and E. E. Lawler, "Generating Knowledge That Drives Change," *Academy of Management Perspectives* 26, no. 1 (2012): 41–51.
26. Mohrman and Lawler, "Generating Knowledge That Drives Change."
27. Gardner et al., "Dynamically Integrating Knowledge in Teams."
28. Campbell et al., "Rethinking Sustained Competitive Advantage."
29. Staff, "It's Not His Mess, Just His to Clean Up," *BusinessWeek* (January 28–February 2, 2013): 14.
30. Summers et al., "Team Member Change."
31. J. L. Ray, L. T. Baker, and D. A. Plowman, "Organizational Mindfulness in Business Schools," *Academy of Management Learning & Education* 10, no. 2 (2011): 188–203.
32. T. R. Crook, J. G. Combs, D. J. Jetchen, and H. Aguinis, "Organizing around Transaction Costs: What Have We Learned and Where Do We Go From Here?" *Academy of Management Perspectives* 27, no. 1 (2013): 63–79.
33. P. Klarner and S. Raisch, "Move to the Beat: Rhythms of Change and Firm Performance," *Academy of Management Journal* 56, no. 1 (2013): 160–184.
34. Leavitt et al., "Different Hats, Different Obligations."
35. R. Ackoff, *Creating the Corporate Future* (New York: Wiley, 1981).
36. M. Ji, W. H. Mobley, and A. Kelly, "When Do Global Leaders Learn Best to Develop Cultural Intelligence? An Investigation of the Moderating Role of Experiential Learning Styles," *Academy of Management Education & Learning* 12, no. 1 (2013): 32–50.
37. Exhibit 2–5 is based on systems theory and was designed by Dr. Abbas Nadim of the University of New Haven. The author added the word *culture* in the segment whose label now reads "Management and Culture."
38. N. M. Pless, T. Maak, and D. A. Waldman, "Different Approaches towards Doing the Right Thing: Mapping the Responsibility Orientations of Leaders," *Academy of Management Perspectives* 26, no. 4 (2012): 51–65.
39. A. Rasche, K. U. Gilbert, and I. Schedel, "Cross-Disciplinary Ethics Education in MBA Programs: Rhetoric or Reality?" *Academy of Management Learning & Education* 12, no. 1 (2013): 71–85.
40. B. C. Gunia, L. Wang, L. Huang, J. Wang, and J. K. Murnighan, "Contemplation and Conversation: Subtle Influences on Moral Decision Making," *Academy of Management Journal* 55, no. 1 (2012): 13–33.
41. P. Zak, *The Moral Molecule* (New York: Penguin, 2012).
42. R. L. Hughes, R. C. Ginnett, and G. J. Curphy, *Leadership: Enhancing the Lessons of Experience,* 7th ed. (Burr Ridge, IL: McGraw-Hill, 2011).
43. R. Murphree, "Visionary Leader: Gospel is Key to Unlimited Success," *AFA Journal* (March 2013): 11.
44. C. Bonanos, "The Lies We Tell at Work," *BusinessWeek* (February 4–10, 2013): 71–73.
45. Zak, *The Moral Molecule.*
46. C. Downs, "Liar, Liar–Back's on Fire," *AARP Magazine* (October/November 2012): 22.
47. Leavitt et al., "Different Hats, Different Obligations."
48. Gunia et al., "Contemplation and Conversation."
49. D. Lange and N. T. Washburn, "Understanding Attributions of Corporate Social Irresponsibility." *Academy of Management Journal* 37, no. 2 (2012): 300–326.
50. J. R. Detert and M. C. Edmondson, "Implicit Voice Theories: Taken-for-Granted Rules of Self-Censorship at Work," *Academy of Management Journal* 54, no. 3 (2011): 461–488.
51. D. Ariely, "Why We Lie," *Wall Street Journal* (May 2–6–27, 2012): C1–C2.
52. Bonanos, "The Lies We Tell at Work."
53. C. A. Rusnak, "Are You Confusing People with Your Leadership Style?" *Costco Connection* (March 2012): 11.
54. J. Geisler, "Forgive? Forget? Not Likely," *Costco Connection* (December 2012): 10.
55. Bonanos, "The Lies We Tell at Work."
56. Ariely, "Why We Lie."
57. M. K. Duffy, K. L. Scott, J. D. Shaw, B. J. Tepper, and K. Aquino, "A Social Context Model of Envy and Social Undermining," *Academy of Management Journal* 55, no. 3 (2012): 643–666.
58. D. M. Mayer, K. Aquino, R. L. Greenbaum, and M. Kuenzi, "Who Displays Ethical Leadership, and Why Does It Matter? An Examination of Antecedents and Consequences of Ethical Leadership," *Academy of Management Journal* 55, no. 1 (2011): 151–171.
59. Ariely, "Why We Lie."
60. Gunia et al., "Contemplation and Conversation."
61. Gunia et al., "Contemplation and Conversation."
62. Bonanos, "The Lies We Tell at Work."
63. Ariely, "Why We Lie."
64. Ariely, "Why We Lie."
65. S. D. Levitt and S. J. Dubner, "SuperFreakonomics: Global Cooling, Patriotic Prostitutes, and Why Suicide Bombers Should Buy Life Insurance," *Academy of Management Perspectives* 25, no. 2 (2011): 86–87.
66. Ariely, "Why We Lie."
67. Leavitt et al., "Different Hats, Different Obligations."
68. Ariely, "Why We Lie."
69. Ariely, "Why We Lie."
70. Bonanos, "The Lies We Tell at Work."
71. Bonanos, "The Lies We Tell at Work."
72. Ariely, "Why We Lie."
73. Bonanos, "The Lies We Tell at Work."
74. Ariely, "Why We Lie."
75. Bonanos, "The Lies We Tell at Work."
76. Bonanos, "The Lies We Tell at Work."
77. R. L. Dufrensne and E. H. Offstein, "Holistic and Interntional Student Character Development Process: Learning from West Point," *Academy of Management Learning & Education* 11, no. 4 (2012): 570–590.
78. Zak, *The Moral Molecule.*
79. Zak, *The Moral Molecule.*
80. Gunia et al., "Contemplation and Conversation."
81. Ariely, "Why We Lie."
82. A. Simha and J. B. Cullen, "Ethical Climates and Their Effects on Organizational Outcomes: Implications from the Past and Prophecies for the Future," *Academy of Management Perspectives* 26, no. 4 (2012): 20–34.
83. J. M. Schauboeck, "Embedding Ethical Leadership Within and Across Organizational Levels," *Academy of Management Journal* 55, no. 5 (2012): 1053–1078.
84. Mayer et al., "Who Displays Ethical Leadership?"
85. Ariely, "Why We Lie."
86. J. Welch and S. Welch, "Whisteblowers: Why You Should Heed Their Warning," *Fortune* (June 11, 2012): 86.
87. J. Palazzolo, "Is It a Bribe . . . or Not?" *Wall Street Journal* (July 22, 2013): R3.
88. Rasche et al., "Cross-disciplinary Ethics Education."
89. Lange and Washburn, "Understanding Attributions."
90. M. Driver, "An Interview with Michael Porter: Social Entrepreneurship and the Transformation of Capitalism," *Academy of Management Learning & Education* 11, no. 3 (2012): 421–431.

91. A. M. Grant, "Giving Time, Time after Time: Work Design and Sustained Employee Participation in Corporate Volunteering," *Academy of Management Review* 37, no. 4 (2012): 589–615.

92. A. Edmans, "The Link between Job Satisfaction and Firm Value, with Implications for Corporate Social Responsibility," *Academy of Management Perspectives* 26, no. 4 (2012): 1–19.

93. Staff, "Master Class," *BusinessWeek* (May 6–12, 2013): 83.

94. Lange and Washburn, "Understanding Attributions."

95. R. Cohen, "Five Lessons from the Banana Man," *Wall Street Journal* (June 2–3, 2012): C2.

96. E. L. Worsham, "Reflections and Insights on Teaching Social Entrepreneurship: An Interview with Greg Dees," *Academy of Management Learning & Education* 11, no. 3 (2012): 442–452.

97. B. Mycoskie, *Start Something That Matters* (New York: Spiegel & Grau, 2012), 193.

98. Definition developed by the Brundtland Commission.

99. A. Nadim and R. N. Lussier, "Sustainability as a Small Business Competitive Strategy," *Journal of Small Strategy* 21, no. 2 (2012): 79–95.

100. S. B. Banerjee, "Embedding Sustainability across the Organization: A Critical Perspective," *Academy of Management Learning & Education* 10, no. 4 (2011): 719–731.

101. H. Paulson, "Fortune Global Forum," *Fortune* (April 29, 2013): 20.

102. A. A. Marcus and A. R. Fremeth, "Green Management Matters Regardless," *Academy of Management Perspectives* 23, no. 3 (2009): 17–26.

103. K. K. Dhanda and P. J. Murphy. "The New Wild West Is Green: Carbon Offset Markets, Transactions, and Providers." *Academy of Management Perspectives* 25, no. 4 (2011): 37–49.

104. Nadim and Lussier, "Sustainability."

105. N. M. Scarborough, *Essentials of Entrepreneurship and Small Business* (Upper Saddle River, NJ: Prentice Hall, 2011).

106. Information taken from Wikipedia's entry on chief sustainability officer at http://en.wikipedia.org/wiki/Chief_sustainability_officer, accessed May 22, 2013.

107. Staff, "Who's the Greenest of Them All?" *BusinessWeek* (November 28–December 2, 2011): 59.

108. Walmart website, www.walmart.com, accessed May 22, 2013.

109. Staff, "Briefs: Wal-Mart," *BusinessWeek* (February 13–19, 2012): 28.

110. K. Weise, "Sustainability: I'm with Wal-Mart," *BusinessWeek* (November 28–December 2, 2011) 60.

111. B. Dumaine, "Google's Zero-Carbon Quest," *Fortune* (July 23, 2012): 75–78.

112. Information taken from the World Business Council for Sustainable Development's website, http://www.wbcsd.org, accessed May 22, 2013.

113. IISD website, http://www.iisd.org, accessed May 22, 2013.

114. Inventors, http://inventors.about.com/library/inventors/bllego.htm.

115. R. Matthews, "Lego and Mattel Bow to Greenpeace Pressure and Eliminate Unsustainable Packaging," September 23, 2011, *Green Conduct,* http://www.greenconduct.com/news/2011/09/23/lego-and-mattel-bow-to-greenpeace-pressure-and-eliminate-unsustainable-packaging/#sthash.dlTVVBiM.dpuf.

116. Lego Progress Report 2012, cache.lego.com/r/aboutus/-/media/ . . . /Progress_Report2012.pdf

117. Green.tv, *Lego and Sustainability,* accessed October 4, 2013, http://green.tv/videos/lego-and-sustainability/

Chapter 3

1. M. Li, W. H. Mobley, and A. Kelly, "When Do Global Leaders Learn Best to Develop Cultural Intelligence? An Investigation of the Moderating Role of Experiential Learning Styles," *Academy of Management Education & Learning* 12, no. 1 (2013): 32–50.

2. S. T. Hannah, B. J. Avolio, and D. R. May, "Moral Maturation and Moral Conations: A Capacity Approach to Explaining Moral Thought and Action," *Academy of Management Review* 36, no. 4 (2011): 663–685.

3. Information taken from the FedEx website, http://www.fedex.com, accessed May 16, 2013.

4. Ji et al., "When do global leaders learn best?"

5. J. H. Marler, "Strategic Human Resource Management in Context," *Academy of Management Perspectives* 26, no. 2 (2012): 6–11.

6. C. Rose, "Charlie Rose Talks to EBay's John Donahue," *BusinessWeek* (February 4–10, 2013): 38.

7. Amazon.com website, www.amazon.com, accessed May 25, 2013.

8. C. Rogers and S. Terlep, "Fiat Chief Pulls Out the Deal Wrench," *Wall Street Journal* (May 25–26, 2013), B1, B2.

9. D. Mattoli, D. Cimilluca, and D. Kesmodel, "China Makes Biggest U.S. Play," *Wall Street Journal* (May 30, 2013), A1.

10. PepsiCo website, www.pepsico.com, accessed May 25, 2013.

11. Ad, "Investing in America and American Jobs," *Fortune* (May 20, 2013), S1.

12. Staff, "Where Clothes Come From," *Fortune* (June 10, 2013), 17.

13. J. R. Hagerty, "'Made in America' Has Its Limits," *Wall Street Journal* (November 23, 2012), B1.

14. Hannah et al., "Moral Maturation."

15. Ad, *BusinessWeek* (November 5–11, 2012): S3.

16. R. Karlgaard, "Energy in 2050," *Forbes* (April 23, 2012): 34.

17. C. Kenny, "The Case for Second Place," *BusinessWeek* (October 17–23, 2011): 14–15.

18. Staff, "US Seeks Talks with India over Poultry Imports Ban," *Yahoo!* (March 6, 2012). News link.

19. K. Bradsher, "WTO Rules against China's Limits on Imports," *New York Times* (August 12, 2009): 13.

20. G. Williams, "News on the Road Column," *San Antonio Express–New* (March 2, 2006), p. 3.

21. W. Ma and M. Dalton, "China Solar Firms Seek Truce," *Wall Street Journal* (May 24, 2013): B3.

22. P. Coy, "Mapping the Way to a Global Free-Trade Deal," *BusinessWeek* (June 4–10, 2012): 24–26.

23. Information taken from the World Trade Organization's website, http://www.wto.org, accessed May 27, 2013.

24. Coy, "Mapping."

25. M. Murphy, "Putting Down Roots in Mexico," *Wall Street Journal* (May 28, 2013), B9.

26. Information taken from the CAFTA-DR website, http: http://www.caftadr.net, accessed May 16, 2013.

27. Information taken from the European Union website, http://europa.eu, accessed May 16, 2013.

28. Information taken from the Association of Southeast Asian Nation website, http://www.aseansec.org, accessed May 22, 2013.

29. J. Clenfield, "What's Good for Toyota Isn't Always Good for Japan," *BusinessWeek* (April 29–May 5, 2013), 11–12.

30. Staff, "The Big Mac Index," *Economist* (January 14, 2012), accessed May 27, 2013, http://www.economist.com/node/21542808.

31. N. Gulati and R. Ahmed, "India Has 1.2 Billion People but Not Enough Drink Coke," *Wall Street Journal* (June 27, 2012): B1, B5.

32. H. Binswanger, "Outsourcing is the U.S. at Its Best," *Forbes* (August 20, 2012): 28.

33. B. Einhorn and C. Winter, "Want Some Milk with Your Green Tea Oreos?" *BusinessWeek* (May 7–13, 2012): 25–26.

34. J. Jargon and L. Burkitt, "KFC's China Flap Holds Lessons for Investors," *Wall Street Journal* (January 12–13, 2013): B1, B3.

35. S. Jakab, "GM Moves On Past Government Motors," *Wall Street Journal* (May 2, 2013): C1.

36. Bloomberg News, "Card Issuers Battle for a Slot in China's Wallets," *BusinessWeek* (May 6–12, 2013): 44–45.

37. Gulati and Ahmed, "India."

38. Binswanger, "Outsourcing."

39. Staff, "It's Not His Mess, Just His to Clean Up," *BusinessWeek* (January 28–February 2, 2013): 14.

40. C. Murphy and L. Burkett, "Hershey Launches New Brand in China," *Wall Street Journal* (May 21, 2013): B1.

41. Fanatics website, accessed June 1, 2013, www.Fanatics.com.

42. Nike website, accessed May 27, 2013, www.nike.com.

43. Subway website, accessed May 27, 2013, www.subway.com.

44. McDonald's website, accessed May 27, 2013, www.mcdonalds.com.

45. Foxconn website, www.foxconn.com, accessed May 27, 2013.

46. A. Satariano and D. MacMillan, "Usain Bolt: The App," *BusinessWeek* (May 13–19, 2013): 41–42.

47. Garmin Press Release, Garmin website, www.garmin.com, accessed May 28, 2013.

48. D. Person and S. T. Stub, "E-car Venture's Fall Is Blow to Renault," *Wall Street Journal* (May 28, 2013): B3.

49. T. Ying and A. Ho, "In Some Chinese Cities, the Tags Cost More Than the Car," *BusinessWeek* (April 29–May 5, 2012): 19–20.

50. C. Rauwald, "Daimler, Beiqi Foton Link Deal on China Truck Joint Venture," *Wall Street Journal* (July 16, 2010): B1.

51. V. Bajaj, "After a Year of Delays, the First Starbucks Is to Open in Team Loving India," *New York Times* (January 30, 2012): accessed online.

52. Einhorn and Winter, "Want Some Milk?"

53. J. Corman, R. N. Lussier, and R. Baeder, "Global Strategies for the Future: Large vs. Small Business," *Journal of Business Strategies* 8, no. 2 (1991): 86–93.

54. Einhorn and Winter, "Want Some Milk?"

55. Export-Import Bank website, www.exim.gov, accessed May 17, 2013.

56. Einhorn and Winter, "Want Some Milk?"

57. P. Sonne and M. Colchester, "France, the U.K. Take Aim at Digital Pirates," *Wall Street Journal* (April 15, 2012): B1.

58. K. L. Ashcraft, "The Glass Slipper: Incorporating Occupational Identity in Management Studies," *Academy of Management Review* 38, no. 1 (2013): 6–31.

59. J. Gehman, L. K. Trevino, and R. Garud, "Values Work: A Process Study of the Emergence and Performance of Organizational Values Practices," *Academy of Management Journal* 56, no. 1 (2013): 84–112.

60. Census, "The U.S. Population," *Wall Street Journal* (December 21, 2012): A1.

61. National Public Radio, "News Broadcast," on WFCR (March 30, 2011).

62. M. Jordan, "Births Fuel Hispanic Gains," based on Census Data, *Wall Street Journal* (July 15, 2011). A3.

63. M. Jordan, "Asians Top Immigration Class," *Wall Street Journal* (June 19, 2012): A3.

64. C. Dougherty and M. Jordan, "Minority Births Are New Majority," *Wall Street Journal* (May 17, 2012): A6.

65. C. Dougherty, "New Faces of Childhood," based on Census Data, *Wall Street Journal* (April 6, 2011): A3.

66. M. Jordan, "Illegals Estimated to Account for 1 in 12 U.S. Births," *Wall Street Journal* (August 12, 2010): A1–A2.

67. Staff, "More White Americans Died," *Wall Street Journal* (June 13, 2013): A1, A8.

68. C. Dougherty, "U.S. Nears Racial Milestone," *Wall Street Journal* (June 11, 2010): A3.

69. S. Reddy, "Latinos Fuel Growth in Decade," based on Census Data, *Wall Street Journal* (March 25, 2011): A2.

70. U.S. Census Bureau, reported in the *Wall Street Journal* (December 13, 2012): A3.

71. Li et al., "When Do Global Leaders Learn?"

72. E. B. King, J. F. Dawson, M. A. West, V. L. Gilrane, and L. Bustin, "Why Organizational and Community Diversity Matters: Representativeness and the Emergence of Incivility and Organizational Performance," *Academy of Management Journal* 54, no. 6 (2011): 1103–1116.

73. J. L. Turnock, "ELC Diversity Ad," *Forbes* (June 25, 2012): 83–86.

74. S. J. Shin, T. Y. Kim, J. Y. Lee, and L. Bian, "Cognitive Team Diversity and Individual Team Member Creativity: A Cross-Level Interaction," *Academy of Management Journal* 55, no. 1 (2012): 195–212.

75. King et al., "Why Organizational and Community Diversity Matters."

76. Travelers ad, *Forbes* (July 16, 2012): 56.

77. J. L. Petriglieri, "Under Threat: Responses to and the Consequences of Threats to Individuals' Identities," *Academy of Management Review* 36, no. 4 (2011): 641–662.

78. S. R. Rhodes, "Age-Related Differences in Work Attitudes and Behavior," *Psychological Bulletin* 92 (1983): 328–367.

79. A. Fisher, "Wanted: Aging Baby-Boomers," *Fortune* (September 30, 1996): 204.

80. G. M. McEvoy and W. F. Cascio, "Cumulative Evidence of the Relationship between Employee Age and Job Performance," *Journal of Applied Psychology* 74 (1989): 11–17.

81. Staff, "Statistics & Data: Quick Stats on Women Workers, 2009," www.dol.gov, accessed May 30, 2013.

82. Staff, "Women's Earning as a Percentage of Men's 2010," Labor Statistics, www.bls.gov, accessed May 30, 2013.

83. K. A. Brower and E. Dwoskin, *BusinessWeek* (May 21–27, 2012): 33–34.

84. D. Bevelander and M. J. Page, "Ms. Trust: Gender, Networks and Trust—Implications for Management Education," *Academy of Management Learning & Education* 10, no. 4 (2011): 623–642.

85. J. Bussey, "How Women Can Get Ahead: Advice from Female CEOs," *Wall Street Journal* (May 18, 2012): B1, B2.

86. G. Zampano, "Italy to Push Pink Quotas," *Wall Street Journal* (June 6, 2012): B1, B2.

87. Staff, "Charge Statistics: FY 1997 through FY 2010," EEOC, www.eeoc.gov, accessed May 30, 2013.

88. E. O. Wright and J. Baxter, "The Glass Ceiling Hypothesis: A Reply to Critics," *Gender & Society* 14 (2000): 814–821.

89. Ashcraft, "The Glass Slipper."

90. W. Mosseberg, "After Leaning In," *Wall Street Journal* (June 3, 2013): D1.

91. Warren Buffett, "Warrant Buffett Is Bullish . . . on Women," *Fortune* (May 20, 2013): 121–124.

92. Travelers ad, *Forbes* (July 16, 2012): 56.

93. A. M. Carton and A. S. Rosette, "Explaining Bias against Black Leaders: Integrating Theory on Information Processing and Goal-Based Stereotyping," *Academy of Management Journal* 54, no. 6 (2011): 1141–1158.

94. Black Entrepreneur Profile website, accessed May 31, 2013, www.blackentrepreneurprofile.com.

95. Staff, "Charge Statistics FY 1997 through FY 2008," www.eeoc.gov, accessed May 30, 2013.

96. Staff, "Fortune 500 Black, Latino, Asian CEOs," *Diversity Inc.* (n.d.).

97. E. Fry, "Serving Up the American Dream," *Fortune* (May 20, 2013): 34.

98. Ad, "Power through Partnership," *Fortune* (May 20, 2013): S1, S2.

99. Ad, "Investing in America and American Jobs," *Fortune* (May 20, 2013): S2.

100. ADA website, www.ada.gov, accessed May 31, 2013.

101. Staff, "2007 Disability Status Report," www.ilr.cornell.edu, accessed May 31, 2013.

102. R. Greenwood and V. A. Johnson, "Employer Perspectives on Workers with Disabilities," *Journal of Rehabilitation* 53 (1987): 37–45.

103. T. E. Narashimban and G. Babu, "The Chosen Ones," *Business Standard* (March 11, 2012).

104. Shin et al., "Cognitive Team Diversity."

105. A. Simha and J. B. Cullen, "Ethical Climates and Their Effects on Organizational Outcomes: Implications from the Past and Prophecies for the Future," *Academy of Management Perspectives* 26, no. 4 (2012): 20–34.

106. Xerox website, www.xerox.com, access June 1, 2013.

107. Travelers ad, *Forbes* (July 16, 2012): 56.

108. J. Bussey, "How Women Can Get Ahead."

109. Frito-Lay website, www.fritolay.com, accessed June 1, 2013.

110. N. D. Cakar and A. Erturk, "Comparing Innovation Capability of SME: Examining the Effects of Organizational

Culture and Empowerment," *Journal of Small Business Management* 48, no. 3 (2010): 325–359.

111. Li et al., "When Do Global Leaders Learn?"

112. Li et al., "When Do Global Leaders Learn?"

113. King et al., "Why Organizational and Community Diversity Matters."

114. G. Hofstede, "Motivation, Leadership, and Organizations: Do American Theories Apply Abroad?" *Organizational Dynamics* (Summer 1980): 42–63.

115. Adapted from M. Javidan and R. J. House, "Cultural Acumen for the Global Manager: Lessons from Project GLOBE," *Organizational Dynamics* 29, no. 4 (2001): 289–305.

116. C. Joinson, "No Return," *HR Magazine* (November 1, 2002): 70.

117. J. and S. Welch, "Why Joe Biden Is Wrong about Private Equity Execs," *Fortune* (July 2, 2012): 42.

118. W. Arthur and W. Bennett, "The International Assignee: The Relative Importance of Factors Perceived to Contribute to Success," *Personnel Psychology* 48 (1995): 99–114.

119. C. Suddath, "Sheryl-Sandberg's 'Lean In' Brand Goes Global," *Business-week.com*, March 22, 2013.

120. S. Sandberg, *Lean In* (New York: Alfred A. Knopf, 2013), 171.

121. Sandberg, *Lean In*, 7.

122. Sandberg, *Lean In*, 8.

Chapter 4

1. J. R. Detert and A. C. Edmondson, "Implicit Voice Theories: Taken-for-Grated Rules of Self-Censorship at Work," *Academy of Management Journal* 54, no. 3 (2011): 461–488.

2. T. R. Crook, J. G. Combs, D. J. Jetchen, and H. Aguinis, "Organizing around Transaction Costs: What Have We Learned and Where Do We Go from Here?" *Academy of Management Perspectives* 27, no. 1 (2013): 63–79.

3. M. Pennington, "The 99% Movement Scorns American Creativity," *Forbes* (June 4, 2012): 30.

4. S. Power, "BP Cites Crucial Mistake," *Wall Street Journal* (May 25, 2010): A1.

5. D. J. Sleesman, D. E. Conlon, G. McNamara, and J. E. Miles, "Cleaning Up the Big Muddy: A Meta-Analytic Review of the Determinants of Escalation of Commitment," *Academy of Management Journal* 55, no. 3 (2012): 541–562.

6. D. Kestenbaum, "Why We Fall for This," *AARP Magazine* (April 28, 2011): 48–51.

7. Pennington, "The 99% Movement."

8. A. Lashinsky, "Larry Page Interview," *Fortune* (February 6, 2012): 98–99.

9. Detert and Edmondson, "Implicit Voice Theories."

10. B. P. Owens and D. R. Hekman, "Modeling How to Grow: An Inductive Examination of Humble Leader Behaviors, Contingencies, and Outcomes," *Academy of Management Journal* 55, no. 4 (2012): 787–818.

11. W. Allen, "The Woody Allen School of Productivity," *BusinessWeek* (June 25–July 1, 2012): 86.

12. T. Evans, "Be a Temp Forever," *Business-Week* (December 17–23, 2012): 83.

13. S. D. Levitt and S. J. Dubner, "SuperFreakonomics," *Academy of Management Perspectives* 25, no. 2 (2011): 86–87.

14. Sleesman et al., "Cleaning Up the Big Muddy."

15. W. Amos, "Patience Pays," *Costco Connection* (October 2012): 13.

16. K. Cashman, "The Cure for Knee-Jerking," *Costco Connection* (April 2013): 13.

17. J. McGregor, "Smart Management for Tough Times," *BusinessWeek* (March 12, 2009): 30–34.

18. M. Javidan and R. J. House, "Cultural Acumen for the Global Manager: Lessons from Project GLOBE," *Organizational Dynamics* 29, no. 4 (2001): 289–305.

19. K. E. Van Oorschot, H. Akkermans, K. Sengupta, and L. N. Van Wassenhove, "Anatomy of a Decision Trap in Complex New Product Development Projects," *Academy of Management Journal* 56, no. 1 (2013): 285–307.

20. S. Mantere and M. Ketokivi, "Reasoning in Organization Science," *Academy of Management Review* 38, no. 1 (2013): 70–89.

21. M. Voronov and R. Vince, "Integrating Emotions into the Analysis of Institutional Work," *Academy of Management Review* 37, no. 1 (2012): 58–81.

22. P. C. Nutt, "Expanding the Search for Alternatives During Strategic Decision-Making," *Academy of Management Executive* 18, no. 4 (2004): 13–28.

23. W. J. Henisz, "Leveraging the Financial Crisis to Fulfill the Promise of Progressive Management," *Academy of Management Learning & Education* 10, no. 2 (2011): 298–321.

24. Owens and Hekman, "Modeling How to Grow."

25. B. Casselman, "Risk-Averse Cultures Infects U.S. Workers, Entrepreneurs," *Wall Street Journal* (June 3, 2013): A1, A14.

26. Sleesman et al., "Cleaning Up the Big Muddy."

27. P. Puranam, M. Raveendran, and T. Knudsen, "Organization Design: The Epistemic Interdependence Perspective," *Academy of Management Review* 37, no. 3 (2012): 419–440.

28. Mantere and Ketokivi, "Reasoning in Organization Science."

29. Puranam et al., "Organization Design."

30. Mantere and Ketokivi, "Reasoning in Organization Science."

31. A. H. Jordan and P. G. Audia, "Self-Enhancement and Learning from Performance Feedback," *Academy of Management Review* 37, no. 2 (2012): 221–231.

32. S. B. Sitkin and J. R. Hackman, "Developing Team Leadership: An Interview with Coach Mike Krzyzewski," *Academy of Management Learning & Education* 10, no. 3 (2011): 494–501.

33. E. R. Burris, "The Risk and Rewards of Speaking Up: Managerial Responses to Employee Voice," *Academy of Management Journal* 55, no. 4 (2012): 851–875.

34. H. A. Richardson and S. G. Taylor, "Understanding Input Events: A Model of Employees' Responses to Requests for Their Input," *Academy of Management Review* 37, no. 3 (2012): 471–491.

35. Owens and Hekman, "Modeling How to Grow."

36. J. K. Summers, S. E. Humphrey, and G. R. Ferris, "Team Member Change, Flux in Coordination, and Performance: Effects of Strategic Core Roles, Information Transfer, and Cognitive Ability," *Academy of Management Journal* 55, no. 2 (2012): 314–338.

37. B. J. McHenry, "When Do Chief Marketing Officers Have Influence on Top Management Teams?" *Academy of Management Perspectives* 25, no. 2 (2011): 79–80.

38. S. J. Shin, T. Y. Kim, J. Y. Lee, and L. Bian, "Cognitive Team Diversity and Individual Team Member Creativity: A Cross-Level Interaction," *Academy of Management Journal* 55, no. 1 (2012): 195–212.

39. H. J. Klein, J. C. Molloy, and C. T. Brinsfield, "Reconceptualzing Workplace Commitment to Redress a Stretched Construct: Revisiting Assumptions and Removing Confounds," *Academy of Management Review* 37, no. 1 (2012): 130–151.

40. N. Breugst, A. Domurath, H. Patzelt, and A. Klaukien, "Perceptions of Entrepreneurial Passion and Employees' Commitment to Entrepreneurial Ventures," *Entrepreneurship Theory and Practice* 36, no. 1 (2012): 171–201.

41. Sitkin and Hackman, "Developing Team Leadership."

42. Jordan and Audia, "Self-Enhancement and Learning."

43. Staff, "Don't Blame Apple for Keeping Its Money," *BusinessWeek* (May 27–June 2, 2013): 12.

44. Puranam et al., "Organization Design."

45. A. Van Anz, "5 lessons from Adrian Van Anz," *Forbes* (June 25, 2012): 142.

46. Jordan and Audia, "Self-Enhancement and Learning."

47. L. Kwoh, "You Call That Innovation?" *Wall Street Journal* (May 23, 2012): B1, B8.

48. Shin et al., "Cognitive Team Diversity."

49. M. Baer, "Putting Creativity to Work: The Implementation of Creative Ideas in Organizations," *Academy of Management Journal* 55, no. 5 (2012): 1102–1119.

50. Kwoh, "You Call That Innovation?"

51. Pennington, "The 99% Movement."

52. D. Eng, "Bringing Design to Corporate America," *Fortune* (April 29, 2013): 25–28.

53. S. Shellenbarger, "What Makes a Risk-Taker," *Wall Street Journal* (May 22, 2013): D1, D3.

54. Sitkin and Hackman, "Developing Team Leadership."

55. S. Berfield and L. Patton, "What's So Hard about a 24/7 McMuffin?" *BusinessWeek* (May 6–12, 2013): 22–24.

56. Baer, "Putting Creativity to Work."

57. J. Lehrer, "How to Be Creative," *Wall Street Journal* (May 10–11, 2012): C1, C2.

58. Lehrer, "How to Be Creative."

59. Puranam et al., "Organization Design."

60. Richardson and Taylor, "Understanding Input Events."

61. Summers et al., "Team Member Change."

62. Van Anz, "5 Lessons."

63. Shin et al., "Cognitive Team Diversity."

64. Burris, "The Risk and Rewards."

65. B. Helm, "The Dubbing of 'Bing,'" *BusinessWeek* (June 15, 2009): 23.

66. Klein et al., "Reconceptualzing Workplace Commitment."

67. Information taken from http://www .professionalartistmag.com, accessed June 6, 2013.

68. Van Oorschot et al.," Anatomy of a Decision Trap."

69. Staff, "Crunch Two Data Sets, Call Me in the Morning," *BusinessWeek* (May 2–27, 2012): 40–41.

70. Kestenbaum, "Why We Fall for This."

71. W. Isaacson, "Steve Jobs: The Biography . . . His Rivalry with Bill Gates," *Fortune* (November 7, 2011): 97–112.

72. Breugst et al., "Perceptions of Entrepreneurial Passion."

73. Nutt, "Expanding the Search."

74. Evans, "Be a Temp Forever."

75. Van Oorschot et al.," Anatomy of a Decision Trap."

76. Sleesman et al., "Cleaning Up the Big Muddy."

77. Kestenbaum, "Why We Fall for This."

78. Allen, "The Woody Allen School of Productivity."

79. V. H. Vroom, "Leadership and the Decision-Making Process," *Organizational Dynamics* 28, no. 4 (2000): 82–94.

Chapter 5

1. R. N. Lussier and C. E. Halabi, "A Three-Country Comparison of the Business Success Versus Failure Prediction Model," *Journal of Small Business Management* 48, no. 3: 360–377.

2. P. Klarner and S. Raisch, "Move to the Beat: Rhythms of Change and Firm Performance," *Academy of Management Journal* 56, no. 1 (2013): 160–184.

3. N. Breugst, A. Domurath, H. Patzelt, and A. Klaukien, "Perceptions of Entrepreneurial Passion and Employees' Commitment to Entrepreneurial Ventures," *Entrepreneurship Theory and Practice* 36, no. 1 (2012): 171–201.

4. P. C. Fiss, "Building Better Causal Theories: A Fuzzy Set Approach to Typologies in Organizational Research," *Academy of Management Journal* 54, no. 2 (2011): 393–420.

5. H. Yang, Z. Lin, and M. W. Peng, "Behind Acquisitions of Alliance Partners: Exploratory Learning and Network Embeddedness," *Academy of Management Journal* 54, no. 5 (2011): 1169–1080.

6. M. Nippa, U. Pidun, and H. Rubner, "Corporate Portfolio Management: Appraising Four Decades of Academic Research," *Academy of Management Perspectives* 25, no. 4 (2011): 50–66.

7. Klarner and Raisch, "Move to the Beat."

8. J. Welch and S. Welch, "Dealing with the Morning-After Syndrome at Facebook," *Fortune* (March 19, 2012): 92.

9. C. Rose, "Charlie Rose talks to eBay's John Donahoe," *BusinessWeek* (February 4–10, 2013): 38.

10. Welch and Welch, "Dealing with the Morning-After Syndrome at Facebook."

11. A. Lashinsky, "Larry Page Interview," *Fortune* (February 6, 2012): 98–99.

12. R. Murphree, "Visionary Leader: Gospel Is Key to Unlimited Success," *AFA Journal* (March 2013): 11.

13. A. M. Grant, "Leading with Meaning: Beneficiary Contact, Prosocial Impact, and the Performance Effects of Transformational Leaders," *Academy of Management Journal* 55, no. 2 (2012): 458–476.

14. Welch and Welch, "Dealing with the Morning-After Syndrome at Facebook."

15. J. L. Ray, L. T. Baker, and D. A. Plowman, "Organizational Mindfulness in Business Schools," *Academy of Management Learning & Education* 10, no. 2 (2011): 188–203.

16. Fiss, "Building Better Causal Theories."

17. M. Porter, "How Competitive Forces Shape Strategy," *Harvard Business Review* 57, no. 2 (1979): 137–145.

18. Welch and Welch, "Dealing with the Morning-After Syndrome at Facebook."

19. B. A. Campbell, R. Coff, and D. Kryscynski, "Rethinking Sustained Competitive Advantage from Human Capital," *Academy of Management Review* 37, no. 3 (2012): 378–395.

20. G. Hirst, D. Van Knippenberg, C. H. Chen, and D. A. Sacramento, "How Does Bureaucracy Impact Individual Creativity? A Cross-Level Investigation of Team Orientation-Creativity Relationships," *Academy of Management Journal* 54, no. 3 (2011): 624–641.

21. R. Karlgaard, "Energy in 2050: Shell's Peter Voser," *Forbes* (April 23, 2012): 34.

22. B. Dumaine, "Google's Zero-Carbon Quest," *Fortune* (July 23, 2012): 75–78.

23. Murphree, "Visionary Leader."

24. C. R. Wanberg, J. Zhu, R. Kanfer, and Z. Zhang, "After the Pink Slip: Applying Dynamic Motivation Frameworks to the Job Search Experience," *Academy of Management Journal* 55, no. 2 (2012): 261–284.

25. M. E. Douglas, Indiana State University.

26. A. H. Jordan and P. G. Audia, "Self-Enhancement and Learning from Performance Feedback," *Academy of Management Review* 37, no. 2 (2012): 211–231.

27. S. Kapner, "Citi's CEO is Keeping Score," *Wall Street Journal* (March 5, 2013): C1.

28. S. K. Johnson, L. O. Garrison, G. H. Broome, J. W. Fleenor, and J. L. Steed, "Go for the Goals: Relationships between Goal Setting and Transfer of Training Following Leadership Development," *Academy of Management Learning & Education* 11, no. 4 (2012): 555–569.

29. F. Bridoux, R. Coeurderoy, and R. Durand, "Heterogeneous Motives and the Collective Creation of Value," *Academy of Management Review* 36, no. 4 (2011): 711–730.

30. J. Shin, M. S. Taylor, and M. G. Seo, "Resources for Change: The Relationships of Organizational Inducements and Psychological Resilience To Employees' Attitudes and Behaviors toward Organizational Change," *Academy of Management Journal* 55, no. 3 (2012): 727–748.

31. Breugst et al., "Perceptions of Entrepreneurial Passion."

32. Kapner, "Citi's CEO is Keeping Score."

33. Kapner, "Citi's CEO is Keeping Score."

34. Nippa et al., "Corporate Portfolio Management."

35. Nippa et al., "Corporate Portfolio Management."

36. P. Burrows, "Google's Bid to be Everything to Everyone," *BusinessWeek* (February 20–26, 2012): 37–38.

37. WD-40 website, www.wd40.com, accessed June 11, 2013.

38. E. Glazer, E. Byron, D. K. Berman, and J. S. Lublin, "P&G's Stumbles Put CEO on Hot Seat for Turnaround," *Wall Street Journal* (September 27, 2012): A1, A16.

39. D. Cimilluca, "UBS to Cut 10,000 Staff in Overhaul," *Wall Street Journal* (October 29, 2012): C1, C3.

40. V. Fuhrmans and F. Geiger, "Siemens to Slice Its Costs Sharply," *Wall Street Journal* (November 9, 2012): B3.

41. www.kraft.com, accessed June 11, 2013.

42. Dr Pepper Snapple Group website, www.drpeppersnapplegroup.com, accessed June 11, 2013.

43. S. Terlep and M. Ramsey, "Ford Bets $5 Billion on Made in China," *Wall Street Journal* (April 20, 12): B1, B2.

44. E. Curran, "Ford Shift Shows New Power of Care Center," *Wall Street Journal* (May 24, 2013): B1, B2.

45. Staff, "Google: Mulling Brick and Mortar," *BusinessWeek* (February 25–March 3, 2012): 19.

46. ArcelorMittal website, www.arcelormittal.com, accessed June 11, 2013.

47. S. Carey and A. Gonzalez, "Delta to Buy Refinery in Effort to Lower Jet-Fuel Costs," *Wall Street Journal* (May 1, 2012): B3.

48. Information taken from the Virgin Group's website, http://www.virgin.com, accessed June 11, 2013.

49. M. A. L. Navarro, L. C. Fiol, and M. A. M. Tena, "Long-Term Orientation and Commitment in Export Joint Ventures among SMEs," *Journal of Small Business Management* 51, no. 1 (2013): 100–113.

50. Yang et al., "Behind Acquisitions of Alliance Partners."

51. P. Monin, N. Noorderhaven, E. Vaara, and D. Kroon, "Giving Sense to and Making Sense of Justice in Postmerger Integration," *Academy of Management Journal* 56, no. 1 (2013): 256–284.

52. X. Yin and M. Shanley, "Industry Determinants of the 'Merger Versus Alliance' Decision," *Academy of Management Review* 33, no. 2 (2008): 473–491.

53. C. Guglielmo, "Google's New Shopping List," *Forbes* (April 23, 2012): 40–41.

54. A. Efrati, "Google's Mobile Balancing Act," *Wall Street Journal* (May 23, 2012): B3.

55. S. Raice, "New Tech Spenders in Feeding Frenzy," *Wall Street Journal* (May 14, 2012): B1, B2.

56. Nippa et al., "Corporate Portfolio Management."

57. K. Linebaugh, "GE Weighs Cuts to Lending Units," *Wall Street Journal* (June 12, 2012): B1.

58. Google website, www.google.com, accessed June 12, 2013.

59. Coca-Cola website, www.coca-cola.com, accessed June 12, 2013.

60. R. Dezember, S. Banjo, and S. Terlep, "After Umbro Sale, Nike Turns to Cole Haan," *Wall Street Journal* (October 25, 2012): B4.

61. Fiss, "Building Better Causal Theories."

62. Fiss, "Building Better Causal Theories."

63. Groupon website, www.groupon.com, accessed June 12, 2013.

64. "Largest U.S. Corporations–Fortune 500," *Fortune* (May 20, 2013): 1–20.

65. Fiss, "Building Better Causal Theories."

66. Wilson website, www.wilson.com, accessed June 12, 2013.

67. Fiss, "Building Better Causal Theories."

68. S. E. Brunk, "From Theory to Practice: Applying Miles and Snow's Ideas to Understand and Improve Firm Performance," *Academy of Management Executive* 4, no. 1 (2003): 105–108.

69. Efrati, "Google's Mobile Balancing Act."

70. Microsoft website, www.microsoft.com, accessed June 12, 2013.

71. M. Porter, *Competitive Strategy: Techniques for Analyzing Industries and Competitors* (New York: The Free Press, 1980), 15.

72. Campbell et al., "Rethinking Sustained Competitive Advantage from Human Capital."

73. Coca-Cola website, www.coca-cola.com, accessed June 12, 2013.

74. C. Dawson, "For Datsun Revival, Nissan Gambles on $3,000 Model," *Wall Street Journal* (October 2, 2012): A1, A16.

75. Z. Tang and C. Hull, "An Investigation of Entrepreneurial Orientation, Perceived Environmental Hostility, and Strategy Application among Chinese SMEs," *Journal of Small Business Management* 50, no. 1 (2012): 132–158.

76. A. Preuschat, "Asics Races to Build Its Brand," *Wall Street Journal* (February 14, 2012): B8.

77. Fiss, "Building Better Causal Theories."

78. Amazon.com website, www.amazon.com, accessed June 12, 2013.

79. L. P. Tost, "An Integrative Model of Legitimacy Judgments," *Academy of Management Review* 36, no. 4 (2011): 686–710.

80. A. Simha and J. B. Cullen, "Ethical Climates and Their Effects on Organizational Outcomes: Implications from the Past and Prophecies for the Future," *Academy of Management Perspectives* 26, no. 4 (2012): 20–34.

81. M. Voronov and R. Vince, "Integrating Emotions into the Analysis of Institutional Work," *Academy of Management Review* 37, no. 1 (2012): 58–81.

82. B. A. Scott, C. M. Barnes, and D. T. Wagner, "Chameleonic or Consistent? A Multilevel Investigation of Emotional Labor Variability and Self-Monitoring," *Academy of Management Journal* 55, no. 4 (2012): 905–926.

83. Ray et al., "Organizational Mindfulness."

84. J. E. Mathieu and W. Schulze, "The INFLUENCE of Team Knowledge and Formal Plans on Episodic Team Process–Performance Relationships," *Academy of Management Journal* 49, no. 3 (2006): 605–619.

85. A. Dizik, "Services to Help Us Stop Dawdling Online," *Wall Street Journal* (January 28, 2010): D2.

86. S. Shellenberger, "No Time to Read This? Read This," *Wall Street Journal* (November 18, 2009): D1, D5.

87. Staff, "Make Time This Week," *Costco Connection* (September 2012): 23.

88. R. E. Silverman, "Here's Why You Won't Finish This Article," *Wall Street Journal* (December 12, 2012): B1, B6.

89. S. Shellenberger, "How Productivity Tools Can Waste Your Time," *Wall Street Journal* (January 30, 2013): D1, D5.

90. S. Shellenberger, "Conquering the To-Do List," *Wall Street Journal* (December 28, 2011): D1, D2.

91. C. Suddath, "My Life as an Efficiency Squirrel," *BusinessWeek* (October 29–November 4, 2012): 88–89.

92. Shellenberger, "Conquering the To-Do List."

93. J. Ankeny, "Appointments with Success," *Entrepreneur* (March 2012): 49.

94. J. Perry, "How to Be a Better Procrastinator," *Wall Street Journal* (August 11–12, 2012): C3.

95. M. Beck, "Inside the Minds of the Projectionists," *Wall Street Journal* (October 30, 2012): D1, D4.

96. Suddath, "My Life as an Efficiency Squirrel."

97. J. Robinson, "E-Mail Is Making You Stupid," *Entrepreneur* (March 2010): 61–63.

98. C. Wallis, "The Multitasking Generation," *TIME* (March 19, 2006): online.

99. Robinson, "E-Mail Is Making You Stupid."

100. Robinson, "E-Mail Is Making You Stupid."

101. K. Kanter, "Effective Multitasking," *Orange County Business Journal* (May 7, 2007).

102. Kanter, "Effective Multitasking."

103. "Multitasking the Right Way," *Spherion Staffing Services* (June 2007): online.

104. Robinson, "E-Mail Is Making You Stupid."

105. Silverman, "Here's Why You Won't Finish This Article."

106. S. Shellenberger, "How Productivity Tools Can Waste Your Time," *Wall Street Journal* (January 30, 2013): D1, D5.

107. S. Shellenberger, "At Work, Do Headphones Really Help?" *Wall Street Journal* (Mat 29, 2012): D1, D4.

108. Klarner and Raisch, "Move to the Beat."

109. R. B. MacKay and R. Chia, "Choice, Chance, and Unintended Consequences in Strategic Change: A Process Understanding of the Rise and Fall of Northco Automotive," *Academy of Management Journal* 56, no. 1 (2013): 201–230.

110. Jordan and Audia, "Self-Enhancement and Learning from Performance Feedback."

111. BlackBerry, "A Short History of the Blackberry," http://www.bbscnw.com/a-short-history-of-the-blackberry.php.

112. FoxNews.com, "BlackBerry Unveils New Smartphones, Drops RIM Name," http://www.foxnews.com/tech/2013/01/30/rims-last-shot-new-blackberry-smartphones-unveiled/.

113. L. Latiff, "Samsung Reports a 50 Percent Jump in Profits Thanks to Galaxy S4 Success," *The Inquirer,* July 26, 2013.

114. VentureBeat, "BlackBerry's Next Potential Turnaround Strategy: Going Private," http://venturebeat.com/2013/08/09/

blackberrys-next-potential-turn around-strategy-going-private/#Kxe bOxWAGR7vvBJm.99.

115. http://techcrunch.com/2013/09/20/blackberry-confirms-massive-layoffs-reveals-1-billion-loss-in-q2-2014/

116. W. Collins, "BlackBerry Strikes Preliminary Go-Private Deal for $4.7 Billion," *WSJ Online* (September 23, 2013).

Chapter 6

1. S. J. Shin, T. Y. Kim, J. Y. Lee, and L. Bian, "Cognitive Team Diversity and Individual Team Member Creativity: A Cross-Level Interaction," *Academy of Management Journal* 55, no. 1 (2012): 195–212.

2. W. M. Murphy, "From E-Mentoring to Blended Mentoring: Increasing Students' Developmental Initiation and Mentors' Satisfaction," *Academy of Management Education & Learning* 10, no. 4 (2011): 606–622.

3. G. Hirst, D. Van Knippenberg, C. H. Chen, and D. A. Sacramento, "How Does Bureaucracy Impact Individual Creativity? A Cross-Level Investigation of Team Orientation-Creativity Relationships," *Academy of Management Journal* 54, no. 3 (2011): 624–641.

4. M. Baer, "Putting Creativity to Work: The Implementation of Creative Ideas in Organizations," *Academy of Management Journal* 55, no. 5 (2012): 1102–1119.

5. J. K. Summers, S. E. Humphrey, and G. R. Ferris, "Team Member Change, Flux in Coordination, and Performance: Effects of Strategic Core Roles, Information Transfer, and Cognitive Ability," *Academy of Management Journal* 55, no. 2 (2012): 314–338.

6. J. Shin, M. S. Taylor, and M. G. Seo, "Resources for Change: The Relationships of Organizational Inducements and Psychological Resilience to Employees' Attitudes and Behaviors toward Organizational Change," *Academy of Management Journal* 55, no. 3 (2012): 727–748.

7. D. Brady, "John Chambers," *BusinessWeek* (August 27–September 2, 2012): 76.

8. S. Shellenbarger, "What Makes a Risk-Taker," *Wall Street Journal* (May 22, 2013): D1, D3.

9. C. Guglielmo, "Apple's Secret Plan for Its Cash Stash," *Forbes* (May 7, 2012): 116–120.

10. Z. Tang and C. Hull, "An Investigation of Entrepreneurial Orientation, Perceived Environmental Hostility, and Strategy Application Among Chinese SMEs," *Journal of Small Business Management* 50, no. 1 (2012): 132–158.

11. P. Klarner and S. Raisch, "Move to the Beat: Rhythms of Change and Firm Performance," *Academy of Management Journal* 56, no. 1 (2013): 160–184.

12. B. Casselman, "Risk-Averse Cultures Infects U.S. Workers, Entrepreneurs," *Wall Street Journal* (June 3, 2013): A1, A14.

13. L. Kwoh, "Memo to Staff: Take More Risks," *Wall Street Journal* (March 20, 2013): B8.

14. Klarner and Raisch, "Move to the Beat."

15. M. Cuban, "Motivate Yourself," *BusinessWeek* (April 11, 2013).

16. A. Langley, C. Smallman, H. Tsoukas, and A. H. Van De Venn, "Process Studies of Change in Organization and Management: Unveiling Temporality, Activity, and Flow," *Academy of Management Journal* 56, no. 1 (2013): 1–13.

17. T. R. Crook, J. G. Combs, D. J. Jetchen, and H. Aguinis, "Organizing around Transaction Costs: What Have We Learned and Where Do We Go from Here?" *Academy of Management Perspectives* 27, no. 1 (2013): 63–79.

18. Shin et al., "Resources for Change."

19. Shin et al., "Cognitive Team Diversity."

20. B. Stone, "Here Comes Amazon's Kindle TV-Set-Top Box," *BusinessWeek* (April 29–May 5, 2012): 34–35.

21. Brady, "John Chambers."

22. R. B. MacKay and R. Chia, "Choice, Chance, and Unintended Consequences in Strategic Change: A Process Understanding of the Rise and Fall of Northco Automotive," *Academy of Management Journal* 56, no. 1 (2013): 201–230.

23. Brady, "John Chambers."

24. P. C. Fiss, "Building Better Causal Theories: A Fuzzy Set Approach to Typologies in Organizational Research," *Academy of Management Journal* 54, no 2 (2011): 393–420.

25. Microsoft website, www.microsoft.com, accessed June 17, 2013.

26. H. Bresman, "Changing Routines: A Process Model of Vicarious Group Learning in Pharmaceutical R&D," *Academy of Management Journal* 56, no. 1 (2013): 35–61.

27. Bresman, "Changing Routines."

28. Summers et al., "Team Member Change."

29. Murphy, "From E-Mentoring to Blended Mentoring."

30. K. Hill, "Unified Command," *Forbes* (June 4, 2012): 48.

31. Summers et al., "Team Member Change."

32. D. Eng, "Bringing Design to Corporate America," *Fortune* (April 29, 2013): 25–28.

33. Klarner and Raisch, "Move to the Beat."

34. S. E. Ante, "IBM's Chief to Employees: Think Fast, Move Fast," *Wall Street Journal* (April 25, 2013): B1, B2.

35. I. Sherr and D. FitzGerald, "New Xbox One Moves Beyond Games," *Wall Street Journal* (May 22, 3013): B8.

36. J. E. Lessin and G. Bensinger, "Apple Plays Up Its Core," *Wall Street Journal* (June 11, 2013): B1, B5.

37. C. Edwards, "Fighting for 3D Survival," *BusinessWeek* (April 25–May 1, 2011): 38–40.

38. M. Ramsay, "Real 4G Standards Ratified by ITU," *Wireless Week* (January 19, 2012): online.

39. NCR website, www.ncr.com, accessed June 18, 2013.

40. L. Kwoh, "You Call That Innovation?" *Wall Street Journal* (May 23, 2012): B1, B8.

41. Bresman, "Changing Routines."

42. A. Simha and J. B. Cullen, "Ethical Climates and Their Effects on Organizational Outcomes: Implications from the Past and Prophecies for the Future," *Academy of Management Perspectives* 26, no. 4 (2012): 20–34.

43. B. Stone, "Inside the Moonshot Factory," *BusinessWeek* (May 27–June 2, 2013): 56–77.

44. Staff, "Don't Blame Apple for Keeping Its Money," *BusinessWeek* (May 27–June 2, 2013): 12.

45. E. R. Burris, "The Risk and Rewards of Speaking Up: Managerial Responses to Employee Voice," *Academy of Management Journal* 55, no. 4 (2012): 851–875.

46. J. Liang, C. I. C. Farh, and J. L. Farh, "Psychological Antecedents of Promotive and Prohibitive Voice: A Two-Wave Examination," *Academy of Management Journal* 55, no. 1 (2012): 71–92.

47. K. Cashman, "The Cure for Knee-Jerking," *Costco Connection* (April 2013): 13.

48. Staff, "The World's Most Innovative Companies," *BusinessWeek* (April 24, 2006).

49. Staff, "Fail Often, Fail Well," *Economist* (April 16, 2011): 74.

50. W. J. Henisz, "Leveraging the Financial Crisis to Fulfill the Promise of Progressive Management," *Academy of Management Learning & Education* 10, no. 2 (2011): 298–321.

51. N. D. Cakar and A. Erturk, "Comparing Innovation Capability of SME: Examining the Effects of Organizational Culture and Empowerment," *Journal of Small Business Management* 48, no. 3 (2010): 325–359.

52. Stone, "Inside the Moonshot Factory."

53. E. Almirall and R. Casdesus-Masanell, "Open versus Closed Innovation: A Model of Discovery and Divergence," *Academy of Management Review* 35, no. 1 (2010): 27–47.

54. T. Daniels, "Starbucks Sponsors the Betacup Challenge to Spur Challenge Problem-Solving," thebetacup.com, http://www.thebetacup.com/2010/03/15/starbucks-sponsors-the-betacup-challenge-to-spur-creative-problem-solving, accessed June 18, 2013.

55. Shin et al., "Resources for Change."

56. P. Monin, N. Noorderhaven, E. Vaara, and D. Kroon, "Giving Sense to and Making Sense of Justice in Postmerger Integration," *Academy of Management Journal* 56, no. 1 (2013): 256–284.

57. Shin et al., "Resources for Change."
58. J. L. Petriglieri, "Under Threat: Responses to and the Consequences of Threats to Individuals' Identities," *Academy of Management Review* 36, no. 4 (2011): 641–662.
59. Shin et al., "Resources for Change."
60. M. Pennington, "The 99% Movement Scorns American Creativity," *Forbes* (June 4, 2012): 30.
61. Henisz, "Leveraging the Financial Crisis."
62. Kwoh, "Memo to Staff."
63. A. H. Jordan and P. G. Audia, "Self-Enhancement and Learning from Performance Feedback," *Academy of Management Review* 37, no. 2 (2012): 211–231.
64. N. Wingfield, "Microsoft Faces the Post-PC World," *Wall Street Journal* (August 15, 2011): B1, B2.
65. J. Battilana and T. Casciaro, "Change Agents, Networks, and Institutions: A Contingency Theory of Organizational Change," *Academy of Management Journal* 55, no. 2 (2012): 381–398.
66. S. K. Johnson, L. O. Garrison, G. H. Broome, J. W. Fleenor, and J. L. Steed, "Go for the Goals: Relationships between Goal Setting and Transfer of Training Following Leadership Development," *Academy of Management Learning & Education* 11, no. 4 (2012): 555–569.
67. Monin et al., "Giving Sense."
68. R. Karlgaard, "Energy in 2050: Shell's Peter Voser," *Forbes* (April 23, 2012): 34.
69. L. P. Tost, "An Integrative Model of Legitimacy Judgments," *Academy of Management Review* 36, no. 4 (2011): 686–710.
70. Henisz, "Leveraging the Financial Crisis."
71. Cuban, "Motivate Yourself."
72. Shin et al., "Resources for Change."
73. M. Selman, "Manipulate Creative People," *BusinessWeek* (April 11, 2013): 92.
74. Karlgaard, "Energy in 2050."
75. K. Hultman, *The Path of Least Resistance* (Austin, TX: Learning Concepts, 1979).
76. J. Gehman, L. K. Trevino, and R. Garud, "Values Work: A Process Study of the Emergence and Performance of Organizational Values Practices," *Academy of Management Journal* 56, no. 1 (2013): 84–112.
77. M. Smets, T. Morris, and R. Greenwood, "From Practice to Field: A Multilevel Model of Practice-Driven Institutional Change," *Academy of Management Journal* 55, no. 4 (2012): 887–904.
78. B. P. Owens and D. R. Hekman, "Modeling How to Grow: An Inductive Examination of Humble Leader Behaviors, Contingencies, and Outcomes," *Academy of Management Journal* 55, no. 4 (2012): 787–818.

79. Battilana and Casciaro, "Change Agents, Networks, and Institutions."
80. Smets et al., "From Practice to Field."
81. Karlgaard, "Energy in 2050."
82. Summers et al., "Team Member Change."
83. Klarner and Raisch, "Move to the Beat."
84. Battilana and Casciaro, "Change Agents, Networks, and Institutions."
85. M. Voronov and R. Vince, "Integrating Emotions into the Analysis of Institutional Work," *Academy of Management Review* 37, no. 1 (2012): 58–81.
86. Owens and Hekman, "Modeling How to Grow."
87. Battilana and Casciaro, "Change Agents, Networks, and Institutions."
88. Johnson et al., "Go for the Goals."
89. S. B. Sitkin and J. R. Hackman, "Developing Team Leadership: An Interview with Coach Mike Krzyzewski," *Academy of Management Learning & Education* 10, no. 3 (2011): 494–501.
90. Summers et al., "Team Member Change."
91. GE website, www.ge.com, accessed June 20, 2013.
92. Y. Lee, "Grand Ambitions," *BusinessWeek* (July 2013): 31–44.
93. D. A. Gregoire and D. A. Shepherd, "Technology-Market Combinations and the Identification of Entrepreneurial Opportunities: An Investigation of the Opportunity-Individual Nexus," *Academy of Management Journal* 55, no. 4 (2012): 753–785.
94. J. D. Hansen, G. D. Deitz, M. Tokman, L. D. Marino, and K. M. Weaver, "Cross-National Invariance of the Entrepreneurial Orientation Scale," *Journal of Business Venturing* 26, no. 1 (2011): 61–78.
95. V. C. Hahn, M. Frese, C. Binnewies, and A. Schmitt, "Happy and Proactive? The Role of Hedonic and Eudemonic Well-Being in Business Owners' Personal Initiative," *Entrepreneurship Theory and Practice* 36, no. 1 (2012): 97–113.
96. J. C. Hayton and M. Cholakova, "The Role of Affect in the Creation and Intentional Pursuit of Entrepreneurial Ideas," *Entrepreneurship Theory and Practice* 36, no. 1 (2012): 41–59.
97. C. Shane, "Reflections of the 2010 AMR Decade Award: Delivering on the Promise of Entrepreneurship as a Field of Research," *Academy of Management Review* 37, no. 1 (2012): 10–20.
98. K. L. Johnson, "The Role of Structural and Planning Autonomy in the Performance of Internal Corporate Ventures," *Journal of Small Business Management* 50 (2012): 469–497.
99. K. W. Seawright, I. H. Smith, R. K. Mitchell, and R. McClendon, "Exploring Entrepreneurial Cognition in Franchisees: A Knowledge-Structure Approach," *Entrepreneurship Theory and Practice* 37, no. 2 (2013): 201–227.

100. Small Business Association website, www.sba.gov website, accessed April 17, 2013.
101. U.S. Department of Labor website, www.bls.gov, accessed October 3, 2012.
102. A. D. Cruz, C. Howorth, and E. Hamilton, "Intrafamily Entrepreneurship: The Formation and Membership of Family Entrepreneurial Teams," *Entrepreneurship Theory and Practice* 37, no. 1 (2013): 17–46.
103. J. Y. K. Lim, L. W. Busentz, and L. Chidambaram, "New Venture Teams and the Quality of Business Opportunities Identified: Faultlines Between Subgroups of Founders and Investors," *Entrepreneurship Theory and Practice* 37, no. 1 (2013): 47–67.
104. N. Classen, A. Van Gils, Y. Bammens, and M. Carree, "Accessing Resources from Innovation Partners: The Search Breadth of Family SMEs," *Journal of Small Business Management* 50 (2012): 191–215.
105. K. Pajo, A. Coetzer, and N. Guenole, "Formal Development Opportunities and Withdrawal Behaviors by Employees in Small and Medium-Sized Enterprises," *Journal of Small Business Management* 48 (2010): 281–301.
106. "Largest U.S. corporations—Fortune 500," *Fortune* (May 20, 2013): 1–20.
107. Shane, "Reflections."
108. Tang and Hull, "An Investigation."
109. Johnson, "The Role of Structural and Planning Autonomy."
110. E. Fauchart and M. Gruber, "Darwinians, Communitarians, and Missionaries: The Role of Founder Identity in Entrepreneurship," *Academy of Management Journal* 54, no. 5 (2011): 935–957.
111. C. Powell, "Battle Ready," *Forbes* (June 4, 2012): 50.
112. S. Blank, "Business as Art," *Entrepreneur* (March 2012): 51–52.
113. B. K. Brockman, M. A. Jones, and R. C. Becherer, "Customer Orientation and Performance in Small Firms: Examining the Moderating Influence of Risk-Taking, Innovativeness, and Opportunity Focus," *Journal of Small Business Management* 50, no. 3 (2012): 429–446.
114. S. L. Newbert and E. T. Tornikoski, "Resource Acquisition in the Emergence Phase: Considering the Effects of Embeddedness and Resource Dependence," *Entrepreneurship Theory and Practice* 37, no. 2 (2013): 249–280.
115. R. N. Lussier and C. E. Halabi, "A Three-Country Comparison of the Business Success versus Failure Prediction Model," *Journal of Small Business Management* 48, no. 3 (2010): 360–377.

116. D. H. B. Welsh, A. E. Davis, D. E. Desplaces, and C. M. Falbe, "A Resource-Based View of Three Forms of Business in the Startup Phase: Implications for Franchising," *Journal of Small Business Strategy* 22, no. 1 (2012): 47–65.

117. B. R. Barringer and R. D. Ireland, *Entrepreneurship* (Upper Saddle River, NJ: Prentice Hall, 2012).

118. B. A. Campbell, R. Coff, and D. Kryscynski, "Rethinking Sustained Competitive Advantage from Human Capital," *Academy of Management Review* 37, no. 3 (2012): 378–395.

119. J. Ankeny, "The Good Sir Richard," *Entrepreneur* (June 2012): 31–38.

120. P. C. Patel and B. Conklin, "Perceived Labor Productivity in Small Firms—The Effects of High-Performance Work Systems and Group Culture Through Employee Retention," *Entrepreneurship Theory and Practice* 36, no. 2 (2012): 205–231.

121. M. Uasu, G. Huang, and O. Kharif, "Sony's First-Mover Disadvantage," *BusinessWeek* (May 6–12, 2013): 35–36.

122. B. Honig and M. Samuelsson, "Planning and the Entrepreneur: A Longitudinal Examination of Nascent Entrepreneurs in Sweden," *Journal of Small Business Management* 50, no. 3 (2012): 365–388.

123. Richard Branson, "Richard Branson on the Secret to Virgin's Sustained Success," *Entrepreneur*, http://www.entrepreneur.com/article/228382#ixzz2fXCblflp.

124. Richard Branson, "Richard Branson on the Secret to Virgin's Sustained Success," *Entrepreneur*, http://www.entrepreneur.com/article/228382#ixzz2fXCblflp.

Chapter 7

1. P. C. Patel and B. Conklin, "Perceived Labor Productivity in Small Firms—the Effects of High-Performance Work Systems and Group Culture through Employee Retention," *Entrepreneurship Theory and Practice* 36, no. 2 (2012): 205–231.

2. T. R. Crook, J. G. Combs, D. J. Jetchen, and H. Aguinis, "Organizing around Transaction Costs: What Have we Learned and Where Do We Go from Here?" *Academy of Management Perspectives* 27, no. 1 (2013): 63–79.

3. P. C. Fiss, "Building Better Causal Theories: A Fuzzy Set Approach to Typologies in Organizational Research," *Academy of Management Journal* 54, no. 2 (2011): 393–420.

4. Crook et al., "Organizing around Transaction Costs."

5. R. Karlgaard, "Energy in 2050: Shell's Peter Voser," *Forbes* (April 23, 2012): 34.

6. A. P. Cowen, "An Expanded Model of Status Dynamics: The Effects of Status Transfer and Interfirm Coordination," *Academy of Management Journal* 55, no. 5 (2012): 1169–1186.

7. P. Lawrence and J. Lorsch, *Organization and Environment* (Burr Ridge, IL: Irwin, 1967).

8. Karlgaard, "Energy in 2050."

9. M. A. Hogg, D. Van Knippenberg, and D. E. Rast, "Intergroup Leadership in Organizations: Leading across Group and Organizational Boundaries," *Academy of Management Review* 37, no. 2 (2012): 232–255.

10. Cowen, "An Expanded Model."

11. Karlgaard, "Energy in 2050."

12. E. M. Wong, M. E. Ormiston, and P. E. Tetlock, "The Effects of Top Management Team Integrative Complexity and Decentralized Decision Making on Corporate Social Performance," *Academy of Management Journal* 54, no. 6 (2011): 1207–1228.

13. Information taken from Wikipedia's entry on micromanagement at http://en.wikipedia.org/wiki/Micromanagement, accessed June 24, 2013.

14. P. Puranam, M. Raveendran, and T. Knudsen, "Organization Design: The Epistemic Interdependence Perspective," *Academy of Management Review* 37, no. 3 (2012): 419–440.

15. Staff, "Step Away This Year," *Costco Connection* (September 2012): 23.

16. General Motors, www.gm.com, accessed June 24, 2013.

17. Cowen, "An Expanded Model."

18. G. Colvin, "The Next Management Icon: Would You Believe He's from China?" *Fortune* (July 25, 2011): 77.

19. Crook et al., "Organizing around Transaction Costs."

20. Puranam et al., "Organization Design."

21. Pepsico, www.pepsico.com, accessed June 24, 2013.

22. M. Carney, E. R. Gedajlovic, P. P. M. A. R. Heugens, M. Van Essen, and J. Van Oosterhout, "Business Group Affiliation, Performance Context, and Strategy: A Meta-Analysis," *Academy of Management Journal* 54, no. 3 (2013): 437–460.

23. M. Hammer and J. Champy, *Reengineering the Corporation: A Manifesto for Business Revolution* (New York: Harper & Row, 1993).

24. C. Rose, "Despite the Rhetoric I Hear, Thank God Employers Are Still in the Health-Care System," *BusinessWeek* (March 4–10, 2013): 32.

25. J. R. Hollenbeck, B. Beersma, and M. E. Schouten, "Beyond Team Types and Taxonomies: A Dimensional Scaling Conceptualization for Team Descriptions," *Academy of Management Review* 37, no. 1 (2013): 82–106.

26. H. Bresman, "Changing Routines: A Process Model of Vicarious Group Learning in Pharmaceutical R&D," *Academy of Management Journal* 56, no. 1 (2013): 35–61.

27. H. Yang, Z. Lin, and M. W. Peng, "Behind Acquisitions of Alliance Partners: Exploratory Learning and Network Embeddedness," *Academy of Management Journal* 54, no. 5 (2011): 1169–1080.

28. W. Li, R. Veliyath, and J. Tan, "Network Characteristics and Firm Performance: An Examination of the Relationships in the Context of a Cluster," *Journal of Small Business Management* 51, no. 1 (2013): 1–22.

29. J. D. Hoover, R. C. Giambatista, and L. Y. Belkin, "Eyes On, Hands On: Vicarious Observational Learning as an Enhancement of Direct Experience," *Academy of Management Education & Learning* 11, no. 4 (2012): 591–608.

30. H. K. Gardner, F. Gino, and D. R. Staats, "Dynamically Integrating Knowledge in Teams: Transforming Resources into Performance," *Academy of Management Journal* 55, no. 4 (2012): 998–1022.

31. Crook et al., "Organizing around Transaction Costs."

32. A. M. Grant, "Leading with Meaning: Beneficiary Contact, Prosocial Impact, and the Performance Effects of Transformational Leaders," *Academy of Management Journal* 55, no. 2 (2012): 458–476.

33. J. L. Ray, L. T. Baker, and D. A. Plowman, "Organizational Mindfulness in Business Schools," *Academy of Management Learning & Education* 10, no. 2 (2011): 188–203.

34. Hammer and Champy, *Reengineering the Corporation*.

35. A. M. Grant, "Giving Time, Time after Time: Work Design and Sustained Employee Participation in Corporate Volunteering," *Academy of Management Review* 37, no. 4 (2012): 589–615.

36. Hollenbeck et al., "Beyond Team Types and Taxonomies."

37. Bresman, "Changing Routines."

38. R. Hackman and G. Oldham, *Work Redesign* (Reading, MA: Addison-Wesley, 1980).

39. D. Liu, T. R. Mitchell, T. W. Lee, B. C. Holtom, and T. R. Hinkin, "How Employees Are Out of Step with Coworkers: How Job Satisfaction Trajectory and Dispersion Influence Individual- and Unit-Level Voluntary Turnover," *Academy of Management Journal* 55, no. 6 (2012): 1360–1380.

40. Grant, "Giving Time."

41. S. Shellenberger, "Conquering the To-Do List," *Wall Street Journal* (December 28, 2011): D1, D2.

42. V. Harnish, "Five Ways to Get Your Strategy Right," *Fortune* (April 11, 2011): 42.

43. Staff, "Make Time This Week," *Costco Connection* (September 2012): 23.

44. Harnish, "Five Ways."

45. C. Rose, "Charlie Rose Talks to eBay's John Donahoe," *BusinessWeek* (February 4–10, 2013): 38.

46. M. Beck, "Inside the Minds of the Perfectionists," *Wall Street Journal* (October 30, 2012): D1, D4.

47. C. Suddath, "My Life as an Efficiency Squirrel," *BusinessWeek* (October 29–November 4, 2012): 88–89.

48. Shellenberger, "Conquering the To-Do List."

49. This section and Skill Builder 7–1 are adapted from Harbridge House training materials (Boston).

50. C. Suddath, "My Life as an Efficiency Squirrel."

51. Staff, "Make Time This Week."

52. http://www.businessweek.com/articles/2013-06-06/costco-ceo-craig-jelinek-leads-the-cheapest-happiest-company-in-the-world

53. Costco, "History," http://www.costco.com.au/About/History.html.

54. http://www.businessweek.com/articles/2013-06-06/costco-ceo-craig-jelinek-leads-the-cheapest-happiest-company-in-the-world

Chapter 8

1. J. R. Hollenbeck, B. Beersma, and M. E. Schouten, "Beyond Team Types and Taxonomies: A Dimensional Scaling Conceptualization for Team Descriptions," *Academy of Management Review* 37, no. 1 (2013): 82–106.

2. H. Bresman, "Changing Routines: A Process Model of Vicarious Group Learning in Pharmaceutical R&D," *Academy of Management Journal* 56, no. 1 (2013): 35–61.

3. M. Korn, "Business Schools Know How You Think, But How Do You Feel?" *Wall Street Journal* (May 2, 2013): B1.

4. J. Welch and S. Welch, "Why Joe Biden Is Wrong about Private Equity Execs," *Fortune* (July 2, 2012): 42.

5. AACSB website, Aacsb.edu, accessed June 28, 2013.

6. S. B. Sitkin and J. R. Hackman, "Developing Team Leadership: An Interview with Coach Mike Krzyzewski," *Academy of Management Learning & Education* 10, no. 3 (2011): 494–501.

7. Hollenbeck et al., "Beyond Team Types and Taxonomies."

8. Sitkin and Hackman, "Developing Team Leadership."

9. R. E. Silverman, "Who's the Boss? There Isn't One," *Wall Street Journal* (June 20, 2012): B1, B8.

10. G. Colvin, "The Next Management Icon: Would You Believe He's from China?" *Fortune* (July 25, 2011): 77.

11. Hollenbeck et al., "Beyond Team Types and Taxonomies."

12. Sitkin and Hackman, "Developing Team Leadership."

13. B. J. McHenry, "When Do Chief Marketing Officers Have Influence on Top Management Teams?" *Academy of Management Perspectives* 25, no. 2 (2011): 79–80.

14. Colvin, "The Next Management Icon."

15. M. A. Hogg, D. Van Knippenberg, and D. E. Rast, "Intergroup Leadership in Organizations: Leading across Group and Organizational Boundaries," *Academy of Management Review* 37, no. 2 (2013): 232–255.

16. J. Liang, C. I. C. Farh, and J. L. Farh, "Psychological Antecedents of Promotive and Prohibitive Voice: A Two-Wave Examination," *Academy of Management Journal* 55, no. 1 (2012): 71–92.

17. Sitkin and Hackman, "Developing Team Leadership."

18. S. J. Shin, T. Y. Kim, J. Y. Lee, and L. Bian, "Cognitive Team Diversity and Individual Team Member Creativity: A Cross-Level Interaction," *Academy of Management Journal* 55, no. 1 (2012): 195–212.

19. E. B. King, J. F. Dawson, M. A. West, V. L. Gilrane, and L. Bustin, "Why Organizational and Community Diversity Matters: Representativeness and the Emergence of Incivility and Organizational Performance," *Academy of Management Journal* 54, no. 6 (2011): 1103–1116.

20. Sitkin and Hackman, "Developing Team Leadership."

21. Hollenbeck et al., "Beyond Team Types and Taxonomies."

22. B. Gates, "My Advice to Students: Get a Sound Broad Education," *Costco Connection* (February 1999): 13.

23. Hollenbeck et al., "Beyond Team Types and Taxonomies."

24. J. K. Summers, S. E. Humphrey, and G. R. Ferris, "Team Member Change, Flux in Coordination, and Performance: Effects of Strategic Core Roles, Information Transfer, and Cognitive Ability," *Academy of Management Journal* 55, no. 2 (2012): 314–338.

25. B. C. Gunia, L. Wang, L. Huang, J. Wang, and J. K. Murnighan, "Contemplation and Conversation: Subtle Influences on Moral Decision Making," *Academy of Management Journal* 55, no. 1 (1 2012): 13–33.

26. A. M. Grant, "Leading with Meaning: Beneficiary Contact, Prosocial Impact, and the Performance Effects of Transformational Leaders," *Academy of Management Journal* 55, no. 2 (2012): 458–476.

27. Gunia et al., "Contemplation and Conversation."

28. Grant, "Leading with Meaning."

29. J. M. W. N. Lepoutre and M. Valente, "Fols Break Out: The Role of Symbolic and Material Immunity in Explaining Institutional Nonconformity," *Academy of Management Journal* 55, no. 2 (2012): 285–313.

30. S. S. Wang, "Under the Influence: How the Group Changes What We Think," *Wall Street Journal* (May 3, 2011): D1, D3.

31. M. K. Duffy, K. L. Scott, J. D. Shaw, B. J. Tepper, and K. Aquino, "A Social Context Model of Envy and Social Undermining," *Academy of Management Journal* 55, no. 3 (2012): 643–666.

32. Duffy et al., "A Social Context Model."

33. J. Battilana and T. Casciaro, "Change Agents, Networks, and Institutions: A Contingency Theory of Organizational Change," *Academy of Management Journal* 55, no. 2 (2012): 381–398.

34. M. Voronov and R. Vince, "Integrating Emotions into the Analysis of Institutional Work," *Academy of Management Review* 37, no. 1 (2012): 58–81.

35. Wang, "Under the Influence."

36. Wang, "Under the Influence."

37. Wang, "Under the Influence."

38. K. Leavitt, S. J. Reynolds, C. M. Barnes, P. Schilpzan, and S. T. Hannah, "Different Hats, Different Obligations: Plural Occupational Identities and Situated Moral Judgments," *Academy of Management Journal* 55, no. 6 (2012): 1316–1333.

39. M. Krzyzewski, "Hard Choices," *BusinessWeek* (July 16–22, 2012): 72.

40. King et al., "Why Organizational and Community Diversity Matters."

41. Sitkin and Hackman, "Developing Team Leadership."

42. Krzyzewski, "Hard Choices."

43. A. P. Cowen, "An Expanded Model of Status Dynamics: The Effects of Status Transfer and Interfirm Coordination," *Academy of Management Journal* 55, no. 5 (2012): 1169–1186.

44. Wang, "Under the Influence."

45. Cowen, "An Expanded Model of Status Dynamics."

46. Hogg et al., "Intergroup Leadership in Organizations."

47. Wang, "Under the Influence."

48. McHenry, "When Do Chief Marketing Officers Have Influence?"

49. Gunia et al., "Contemplation and Conversation."

50. Sitkin and Hackman, "Developing Team Leadership."

51. King et al., "Why Organizational and Community Diversity Matters."

52. Hogg et al., "Intergroup Leadership in Organizations."

53. J. R. Detert and A. C. Edmondson, "Implicit Voce Theories: Taken-for-Grated Rules of Self-Censorship at Work," *Academy of Management Journal* 54, no. 3 (2011): 461–488.

54. Bresman, "Changing Routines."

55. A. Langley, C. Smallman, H. Tsoukas, and A. H. Van De Venn, "Process Studies of Change in Organization and Management: Unveiling Temporality, Activity, and Flow," *Academy of Management Journal* 56, no. 1 (2013): 1–13.

56. Sitkin and Hackman, "Developing Team Leadership."

57. Summers et al., "Team Member Change."

58. Summers et al., "Team Member Change."

59. McHenry, "When Do Chief Marketing Officers Have Influence?"

60. Hollenbeck et al., "Beyond Team Types and Taxonomies."

61. J. and S. Welch, "Why Joe Biden Is Wrong."

62. A. Fox, "Help Managers Shine," *HR Magazine* (February 2013): 43–46.

63. AACSB website, www.aacsb.edu, accessed July 3, 2013.

64. E. Krell, "Get Sold on Training Incentives," *HR Magazine* (February 2013): 57–60.

65. Battilana and Casciaro, "Change Agents, Networks, and Institutions."

66. Sabre Holdings website, www.Sabre-Holdings.com, accessed July 3, 2013.

67. Hogg et al., "Intergroup Leadership in Organizations."

68. Sitkin and Hackman, "Developing Team Leadership."

69. J. Shin, M. S. Taylor, and M. G. Seo, "Resources for Change: The Relationships of Organizational Inducements and Psychological Resilience to Employees' Attitudes and Behaviors toward Organizational Change," *Academy of Management Journal* 55, no. 3 (2012): 727–748.

70. Sitkin and Hackman, "Developing Team Leadership."

71. Krell, "Get Sold."

72. Patience and Nicholson website, http://www.pandn.co.nz, accessed July 3, 2013.

73. R. E. Silverman, "Where's the Boss? Trapped in a Meeting," *Wall Street Journal* (February 14, 2012): B1.

74. S. Shellenbarger, "Meet the Meeting Killers," *Wall Street Journal* (May 16, 2012): D1, D3.

75. M. Milian, "It's Not You, It's Meetings," *BusinessWeek* (June 11–17, 2012): 51–52.

76. Sitkin and Hackman, "Developing Team Leadership."

77. Shellenbarger, "Meet the Meeting Killers."

78. Milian, "It's Not You, It's Meetings."

79. Shellenbarger, "Meet the Meeting Killers."

80. Milian, "It's Not You, It's Meetings."

81. Milian, "It's Not You, It's Meetings."

82. Shellenbarger, "Meet the Meeting Killers."

83. Milian, "It's Not You, It's Meetings."

84. Asana website, www.asana.com, accessed July 3, 2013.

85. Milian, "It's Not You, It's Meetings."

86. Shellenbarger, "Meet the Meeting Killers."

87. Staff, "Master Class," *BusinessWeek* (May 13–19, 2013): 83.

88. Shellenbarger, "Meet the Meeting Killers."

89. Liang et al., "Psychological Antecedents."

90. Liang et al., "Psychological Antecedents."

91. Shellenbarger, "Meet the Meeting Killers."

92. E. Bernstein, "Speaking Up Is Hard to Do: Researchers Explain Why," *Wall Street Journal* (February 7, 2012): D1, D4.

93. Shellenbarger, "Meet the Meeting Killers."

94. Shellenbarger, "Meet the Meeting Killers."

95. Shellenbarger, "Meet the Meeting Killers."

96. Shellenbarger, "Meet the Meeting Killers."

97. Target website, https://corporate.target.com/about/mission-values.

98. Lydia Dishman, "How Target's CEO Inspires Teamwork at a Massive Scale," Fast Company, http://www.fastcompany.com/3001988/how-targets-ceo-inspires-teamwork-massive-scale.

99. Matt Golosinski, "With Teamwork, Gregg Steinhafel '79 Hits the Bull's-Eye at Target," Kellogg World, http://www.kellogg.northwestern.edu/kwo/sum07/features/steinhafel.htm, retrieved October 3, 2013.

100. Target website, https://corporate.target.com/india/life-at-target.html.

101. Target website, https://corporate.target.com/corporate-responsibility/team-members.

Chapter 9

1. X. Liang, J. H. Marler, and Z. Cui, "Strategic Human Resource Management in China: East Meets West," *Academy of Management Perspectives* 26, no. 2 (2012): 55–70.

2. J. H. Marler, "Strategic Human Resource Management in Context: A Historical and Global Perspective," *Academy of Management Perspectives* 26, no. 2 (2012): 6–11.

3. M. Festing, "Strategic Human Resource Management in Germany," *Academy of Management Perspectives* 26, no. 2 (2012): 37–54.

4. A. J. Nyberg and R. E. Ployhart, "Context-Emergent Turnover (CET) Theory: A Theory of Collective Turnover," *Academy of Management Review* 38, no. 1 (2013): 109–131.

5. A. Lenung, M. Der Foo, and S. Chaturvedi, "Imprinting Effects of Founding Core Teams on HR Values in New Ventures," *Entrepreneurship Theory and Practice* 37, no. 1 (2013): 87–106.

6. K. Jiang, D. P. Lepak, J. Hu, and J. C. Baer, "How Does Human Resource Management Influence Organizational Outcomes? A Meta-Analytic Investigation of Mediating Mechanisms," *Academy of Management Journal* 55, no. 6 (2012): 1264–1294.

7. A. Konrad, "Virtual-Workforce Manager," *Fortune* (July 23, 2012): 32.

8. Staff, "Compliance Conundrum," *HR Magazine* (February 2013): 22.

9. R. J. Grossman, "No Federal Regulatory Relief in Sight," *HR Magazine* (February 2013): 22–27.

10. EEOC website, www.eeoc.gov, accessed July 8, 2013.

11. A. Smith, EEOC to focus on hiring, pay, and harassment. *HR Magazine* (February 2013): 11.

12. R. J. Ely, H. Ibarra, and D. M. Kolb, "Taking Gender into Account: Theory and Design for Women's Leadership Development Programs," *Academy of Management Journal* 55, no. 6 (2012): 1264–129.

13. J. L. Petriglieri, "Under Threat: Responses to and the Consequences of Threats to Individuals' Identities," *Academy of Management Review* 36, no. 4 (2011): 641–662.

14. Smith, "EEOC to Focus on Hiring, Pay, and Harassment."

15. EEOC website, www.eeoc.gov, accessed July 8, 2013.

16. Staff, "Sex and the Workplace," *BusinessWeek* (May 14–20, 2012): 92.

17. EEOC website, www.eeoc.gov, accessed July 8, 2013.

18. Marler, "Strategic Human Resource Management in Context."

19. Jiang et al., "How Does Human Resource Management Influence Organizational Outcomes?"

20. Festing, "Strategic Human Resource Management in Germany."

21. Liang et al., "Strategic Human Resource Management in China."

22. Land's End website, www.landsend.com, accessed July 8, 2013.

23. T. Lytle, "Streamline Hiring," *HR Magazine* (April 2013): 63–65.

24. A. Fox, "Put Plans into Action," *HR Magazine* (April 2013): 27–31.

25. J. Sandberg, "Short Hours, Big Pay and Other Little Lies from Your Future Boss," *Wall Street Journal* (October 22, 2003): B1.

26. C. R. Wanberg, J. Zhu, R. Kanfer, and Z. Zhang, "After the Pink Slip: Applying Dynamic Motivation Frameworks to the Job Search Experience," *Academy of Management Journal* 55, no. 2 (2012): 261–284.

27. V. Harnish, "Five Steps to Find (and Keep) Stars," *Fortune* (July 1, 2013): 22.

28. Lytle, "Streamline Hiring."

29. K. L. Ashcraft, "The Glass Slipper: Incorporating Occupational Identity in Management Studies," *Academy of Management Review* 38, no. 1 (2013): 6–31.

30. A. Edmans, "The Link between Job Satisfaction and Firm Value, with Implications for Corporate Social Responsibility," *Academy of Management Perspectives* 26, no. 4 (2012): 1–19.

31. E. Silverman and L. Weber, "An Inside Job: More Firms Opt to Recruit from Within," *Wall Street Journal* (May 30, 2012): B1, B8.

32. Procter & Gamble website, www .pg.com, accessed July 8, 2013.

33. CareerBuilder, "Bad Hires Can Be Costly," *HR Magazine* (February 2013): 18.

34. A. Lashinsky, "Larry Page Interview," *Fortune* (February 6, 2012): 98–99.

35. EEOC website, www.eeoc.gov, accessed July 9, 2013.

36. Lytle, "Streamline Hiring."

37. J. Alsever, "How to Get a Job: Show, Don't Tell," *Fortune* (March 19, 2012): 29–31.

38. CareerBuilder, "Bad Hires Can Be Costly."

39. C. Suddath, "Imaginary Friends," *BusinessWeek* (January 21 -27, 2013): 68.

40. D. M. Cable and V. S. Kay, "Striving for Self-Verification during Organizational Entry," *Academy of Management Journal* 55, no. 2 (2012): 360–380.

41. D. Meinert, "Cultural Similarities Influence Hiring Decisions," *HR Magazine* (February 2013): 18.

42. S. Lau, "Rejecting Candidates, Paid Meal Breaks, Global Talent," *HR Magazine* (February 2013): 23.

43. Alsever, "How to Get a Job."

44. Lytle, "Streamline Hiring."

45. Meinert, "Cultural Similarities Influence Hiring Decisions."

46. Jiang et al., "How Does Human Resource Management Influence Organizational Outcomes?"

47. Cable and Kay, "Striving for Self-Verification."

48. D. M. Sluss, R. E. Ployhart, M. G. Cobb, and B. E. Ashforth, "Generalizing Newcomers' Relational and Organizational Identifications: Process and Prototypicality," *Academy of Management Journal* 55, no. 4 (2012): 949–975.

49. R. E. Silverman, "First Day on Job: Not Just Paperwork," *Wall Street Journal* (May 28, 2013), D1.

50. Silverman, "First Day on Job."

51. S. K. Johnson, L. O. Garrison, G. H. Broome, J. W. Fleenor, and J. L. Steed, "Go for the Goals: Relationships between Goal Setting and Transfer of Training Following Leadership Development," *Academy of Management Learning & Education* 11, no. 4 (2012): 555–569.

52. Festing, "Strategic Human Resource Management in Germany."

53. E. Krell, "Get Sold on Training Incentives," *HR Magazine* (February 2013): 57–60.

54. A. Fox, "Help Managers Shine," *HR Magazine* (February 2013): 43–46.

55. B. Schyns, T. Kiefer, R. Kerschreiter, and A. Tymon, "Teaching Implicit Leadership Theories to Develop Leaders and Leadership: How and Why It Can Make a Difference," *Academy of Management Learning & Education* 10, no. 3 (2011): 397–408.

56. Johnson et al., "Go for the Goals."

57. Harnish, "Five Steps."

58. M. Magni, C. Paolino, R. Cappetta, and L. Proserpio, "Diving Too Deep: How Cognitive Absorption and Group Learning Behavior Affect Individual Learning," *Academy of Management Learning & Education* 12, no. 1 (2013): 51–69.

59. M. Li, W. H. Mobley, and A. Kelly, "When Do Global Leaders Learn Best to Develop Cultural Intelligence? An Investigation of the Moderating Role of Experiential Learning Styles," *Academy of Management Education & Learning* 12, no. 1 (2013): 32–50.

60. J. Welch and S. Welch, Dealing with the morning-after syndrome at Facebook, *Fortune* (March 19, 2012): 92.

61. M. W. Ohland, "The Comprehensive Assessment of Team Member Effectiveness: Development of BARS for Self- and Peer Evaluation," *Academy of Management Education & Learning* 11, no. 4 (2012): 609–630.

62. S. Brutus, M. B. L. Donia, and S. Ronen, "Can Business Students Learn to Evaluate Better? Evidence from Repeated Exposure to a Peer-Evaluation System," *Academy of Management Education & Learning* 12, no. 1 (2012): 18–31.

63. Ely et al., "Taking Gender into Account."

64. Festing, "Strategic Human Resource Management in Germany."

65. Johnson et al., "Go for the Goals."

66. Staff, "Master Class," *BusinessWeek* (May 6–12, 2013): 83.

67. Ad, "Need Coaching?" *HR Magazine* (February 2013): 66.

68. K. Gurchiek, "New HR Standard on Performance Management," *HR Magazine* (April 2013): 74.

69. ANSI website, www.ansi.org, accessed July 10, 2013.

70. M. K. Duffy, K. L. Scott, J. D. Shaw, B. J. Tepper, and K. Aquino, "A Social Context Model of Envy and Social Undermining," *Academy of Management Journal* 55, no. 3 (2012): 643–666.

71. Nyberg and Ployhart, "Context-Emergent Turnover (CET) Theory."

72. D. Liu, T. R. Mitchell, T. W. Lee, B. C. Holtom, and T. R. Hinkin, "How Employees Are Out of Step with Coworkers: How Job Satisfaction Trajectory and Dispersion Influence Individual- and Unit-Level Voluntary Turnover," *Academy of Management Journal* 55, no. 6 (2012): 1360–1380.

73. Edmans, "The Link between Job Satisfaction and Firm Value."

74. D. C. Wyld, "Do Employees View Stock Options the Same Way as Their Bosses Do?" *Academy of Management Perspectives* 25, no. 4 (2011): 91–92.

75. Staff, "Master Class."

76. G. O. Trevor, G. Reilly, B. Gerhart, "Reconsidering Pay Dispersion's Effect on the Performance of Interdependent Work: Reconciling Sorting and Pay Inequality," *Academy of Management Journal* 55, no. 3 (2012): 585–610.

77. Wyld, "Do Employees View Stock Options?"

78. D. Zielinski, "Tech Support," *HR Magazine* (February 2013): 34–38.

79. Trevor et al., "Reconsidering Pay Dispersion's Effect."

80. MetLife ad, "A Win-Win Solution," *Fortune* (July 1, 2013): 22.

81. D. Tobenkin, "Stay Well Together," *HR Magazine* (February 2013): 63–66.

82. Grossman, "No Federal Regulatory Relief in Sight."

83. B. Leonard, "A Holistic Approach to an Onsite Health Clinic," *HR Magazine* (April 2013): 14.

84. G. Jasen, "Your First Job? Think about Retirement," *Wall Street Journal* (December 3, 2012): R9.

85. M. Tytel, "Work–Life Balance," *BusinessWeek* (February 1, 2007): http://www .businessweek.com/innovate/next/blog/ smallbiz/tips/archives/2007/02/work-life_balan.html, accessed September 7, 2010.

86. The Staff of the Corporate Executive Board, "The Increasing Call for Work–Life Balance," *BusinessWeek* (March 27, 2009): http://www.businessweek. com/managing/content/mar2009/ ca20090327_734197.htm, accessed September 7, 2010.

87. L. M. Leslie, C. F. Manchester, T. Y. Park, and S. A. Mehng, "Flexible Work Practices: A Source of Career Premiums or Penalties?" *Academy of Management Journal* 55, no. 6 (2012): 1407–1428.

88. N. Shah, "More Americans Working Remotely," *Wall Street Journal* (March 6, 2013): A3.

89. Jiang et al., "How Does Human Resource Management Influence Organizational Outcomes?"

90. R. Maurer, "Corporations Urged to Push Suppliers on Worker Safety," *HR Magazine* (February 2013): 15.

91. OSHA website, www.osha.gov, accessed July 10, 2013.

92. S. Greenhouse, "BP to Pay Record Fine for Refinery," *New York Times* (August 12, 2010): B1.

93. R. N. Lussier, "Maintaining Civility in the Laboratory," *Clinical Leadership and Management Review* 19, no. 6 (2005): 1–4; and R. N. Lussier, "Dealing with Anger and Preventing Workplace Violence," *Clinical Leadership and Management Review* 18, no. 2 (2004): 117–119.

94. BLS website, www.bls.gov, accessed July 11, 2013.

95. K. Naughton, T. Higgins, and D. Welch, with C. Trudell, "At Ford, Staying Solvent Has Its Costs," *BusinessWeek* (August 1–7 2011): 24–25.

96. A. Simha and J. B. Cullen, "Ethical Climates and Their Effects on Organizational Outcomes: Implications from the Past and Prophecies for the Future," *Academy of Management Perspectives* 26, no. 4 (2012): 20–34.

97. Liu et al., "How Employees Are Out of Step With Coworkers."

98. S. Ovide, "Groupon Staff Feel the Heat," *Wall Street Journal* (August 13, 2012): B1, B2.

99. Lytle, "Streamline Hiring."

100. A. R. Gardner, "No Finding of Race Discrimination in Failure-to-Promote Case," *HR Magazine* (April 2013): 74.

101. Wanberg et al., "After the Pink Slip."

102. Google website, http://www.google.com/about/jobs/teams/people-operations/ retrieved October 2, 2013.

103. F. Manjoo, "The Happiness Machine: How Google Became Such a Great Place to Work," Slate.com, accessed January 21, 2013.

104. F. Manjoo, "The Happiness Machine: How Google Became Such a Great Place to Work." *Slate*. January 21, 2013, pp. 1–2. Retrieved from www.slate.com/articles/technology/technology/2013/01/google_people_operations_the_secrets_of_the_world_s_most_scientific_human.2.html

105. ibid

106. Leslie et al., "Flexible Work Practices."

107. Leslie et al., "Flexible Work Practices."

108. A. Gumbus and R. N. Lussier, "Career Development: Enhancing Your Networking Skill," *Clinical Leadership & Management Review* 17 (2003): 16–20.

109. J. Hempel, "LinkedIn: How It's Changing Business," *Fortune* (July 1, 2013): 69–74

110. B. Haislip, "It Pays to Be Polite," *Wall Street Journal* (November 12, 2012): R6.

111. Riley Guide website, www.rileyguide.com, accessed July 12, 2013.

112. M. Baer, "Putting Creativity to Work: The Implementation of Creative Ideas in Organizations," *Academy of Management Journal* 55, no. 5 (2012): 1102–1119.

113. C. Galunic, G. Ertug, M. Gargiulo, "The Positive Externalities of Social Capital: Benefiting from Senior Brokers," *Academy of Management Journal* 55, no. 5 (2012): 1213–1231.

114. C. Farrell, "It's Not What Grads Know, It's Who They Know," *BusinessWeek* (June 16–24, 2012): 9–10.

115. This section is adapted with permission from A. Gumbus and R. N. Lussier, "Career Development."

116. J. Jantsch, "Referral Offers Your Customers Can't Refuse," *Entrepreneur* (May 2009): 96.

117. J. Hempel, "Three Degrees of Reid Hoffman," *Fortune* (February 6, 2012): 32.

Chapter 10

1. B. Schyns, T. Kiefer, R. Kerschreiter, and A. Tymon, "Teaching Implicit Leadership Theories to Develop Leaders and Leadership: How and Why It Can Make a Difference," *Academy of Management Learning & Education* 10, no. 3 (2011): 397–408.

2. M. B. Eberly, E. C. Holley, M. D. Johnson, and T. R. Mitchell, "Beyond Internal and External: A Dyadic Theory of Relational Attributions," *Academy of Management Journal* 36, no. 4 (2011): 731–753.

3. J. Battilana and T. Casciaro, "Change Agents, Networks, and Institutions: A Contingency Theory of Organizational Change," *Academy of Management Journal* 55, no. 2 (2012): 381–398.

4. T. Evans, "Be a Temp Forever," *BusinessWeek* (December 17–23, 2012): 83.

5. S. Cacciola, "Motivating Athletes the German Way," *Wall Street Journal* (August 7, 2012): D9.

6. P. J. Zak, "The Trust Molecule," *Wall Street Journal* (April 28–29, 2012): C1, C2.

7. M. Korn, "Business Schools Know How You Think, But How Do You Feel?" *Wall Street Journal* (May 2, 2013): B1.

8. Cacciola, "Motivating Athletes the German Way."

9. E. Bernstein, "Speaking Up Is Hard To Do: Researchers Explain Why," *Wall Street Journal* (February 7, 2012): D1, D4.

10. H. St. Lifer, "Weight Loss Mood & Food," *AARP Magazine* online, accessed July 18, 2013.

11. K. M. Hmieleski and R. A. Baron, "Entrepreneurs' Optimism and New Venture Performance: A Social Cognitive Perspective," *Academy of Management Journal* 52, no. 3 (2009): 473–488.

12. Cacciola, "Motivating Athletes the German Way."

13. Korn, "Business Schools."

14. J. Paskin, "Finding the I in Team," *BusinessWeek* (February 18–24, 2013): 78.

15. A. M. Grant, "Leading with Meaning: Beneficiary Contact, Prosocial Impact, and the Performance Effects of Transformational Leaders," *Academy of Management Journal* 55, no. 2 (2012): 458–476.

16. S. S. Wang, "Why Placebos Work Wonders," *Wall Street Journal* (January 3, 2012): D1, D2.

17. E. Fauchart and M. Gruber, "Darwinians, Communitarians, and Missionaries: The Role of Founder Identity in Entrepreneurship," *Academy of Management Journal* 54, no. 5 (2011): 935–957.

18. D. Sánchez-Teruel and M. A. Robles-Bello, "Model 'Big Five' Personality and Criminal Behavior," *International Journal of Psychological Research* 6, no. 1 (2013): 102–109.

19. Staff, "Master Class," *BusinessWeek* (May 13–19, 2013): 83.

20. Korn, "Business Schools."

21. J. B. D. Garcia, A. I. R. Escudero, and N. N. Cruz, "Influence of Affective Traits on Entrepreneurs' Goals and Satisfaction," *Journal of Small Business Management* 50, no. 3 (2012): 408–428.

22. P. Monin, N. Noorderhaven, E. Vaara, and D. Kroon, "Giving Sense to and Making Sense of Justice in Postmerger Integration," *Academy of Management Journal* 56, no. 1 (2013): 256–284.

23. G. Colvin, "What Really Has the 99% up in Arms," *Fortune* (November 7): 87.

24. Eberly et al., "Beyond Internal and External."

25. Colvin, "What Really Has the 99% up in Arms."

26. Battilana and Casciaro, "Change Agents, Networks, and Institutions."

27. J. Shin, M. S. Taylor and M. G. Seo, "Resources for Change: The Relationships of Organizational Inducements and Psychological Resilience to Employees' Attitudes and Behaviors toward Organizational Change," *Academy of Management Journal* 55, no. 3 (2012): 727–748.

28. Evans, "Be a Temp Forever."

29. J. R, Detert and A. C. Edmondson, "Implicit Voice Theories: Taken-for-Grated Rules of Self-Censorship at Work," *Academy of Management Journal* 54, no. 3 (3 2011): 461–488.

30. J. C. Santora and M. Esposito, "Do Happy Leaders Make for Better Team Performance?" *Academy of Management Perspectives* 25, no. 4 (2011): 88–90.

31. A. Edmans, "The Link between Job Satisfaction and Firm Value, with Implications for Corporate Social Responsibility," *Academy of Management Perspectives* 26, no. 4 (2012): 1–19.

32. D. R. Soriano, "Can Goal Setting and Performance Feedback Enhance Organizational Citizenship Behavior?" *Academy of Management Perspectives* 22, no. 1 (2008): 65–66.

33. B. A. Scott, C. M. Barnes, and D. T. Wagner, "Chameleonic or Consistent? A Multilevel Investigation of Emotional Labor Variability and Self-Monitoring," *Academy of Management Journal* 55, no. 4 (2012): 905–926.

34. A. Lashinsky, "Larry Page Interview," *Fortune* (February 6, 2012): 98–99.

35. K. Hannon, "It's Never Too Late to Love Your Job," *AARP Magazine* (May 2013): 44–45.

36. E. Bernstein, "Train Your Brain to Be Positive, and Feel Happier Every Day: It Only Sounds Corny," *Wall Street Journal* (August 28, 2012): D1, D2.

37. B. J. McHenry, "When Do Chief Marketing Officers Have Influence on Top Management Teams?" *Academy of Management Perspectives* 25, no. 2 (2011): 79–80.

38. N. D. Cakar and A. Erturk, "Comparing Innovation Capability of SME: Examining the Effects of Organizational Culture and Empowerment," *Journal of Small Business Management* 48, no. 3 (2010): 325–359.

39. Bernstein, "Speaking Up is Hard to Do."

40. J. Antonakis, M. Fenley, and S. Liechti, "Can Charisma Be Taught? Tests of Two Interventions," *Academy of Management*

Learning & Education 10, no. 3 (2011): 374–396.

41. V. Harnish, "Five Ways to Close Big Deals Now," *Fortune* (February 4, 2013): 32.

42. L. P. Tost, "An Integrative Model of Legitimacy Judgments," *Academy of Management Review* 36, no. 4 (2011): 686–710.

43. R. Cohen, "Five Lessons from the Banana Man," *Wall Street Journal* (June 2–3, 2012): C2.

44. Cohen, "Five Lessons."

45. N. W. Biggart and R. Delbridge, "Systems of Exchange," *Academy of Management Review* 29, no. 1 (2004): 28–49.

46. B. Haislip, "It Pays to Be Polite," *Wall Street Journal* (November 12, 2012): R6.

47. D. R. Soriano, "Political Skills in Organizations: Do Personality and Reputation Play a Role?" *Academy of Management Perspectives* 22, no. 1 (2008): 66–68.

48. C. Farrell, "It's Not What Grads Know, It's Who They Know," *BusinessWeek* (June 16–24, 2012): 9–10.

49. C. H. Chang, C. C. Rosen, and P. E. Levy, "The Relationship between Perceptions of Organizational Politics and Employee Attitudes, Strain and Behavior: A Meta-Analytic Examination," *Academy of Management Journal* 52, no. 4 (2009): 779–801.

50. Monin et al., "Giving Sense."

51. J. Liang, C. I. C. Farh, and J. L. Farh, "Psychological Antecedents of Promotive and Prohibitive Voice: A Two-Wave Examination," *Academy of Management Journal* 55, no. 1 (2012): 71–92.

52. D. M. Sluss, R. E. Ployhart, M. G. Cobb, and B. E. Ashforth, "Generalizing Newcomers' Relational and Organizational Identifications: Process and Prototypicality," *Academy of Management Journal* 55, no. 4 (2012): 949–975.

53. B. P. Owens and D. R. Hekman, "Modeling How to Grow: An Inductive Examination of Humble Leader Behaviors, Contingencies, and Outcomes," *Academy of Management Journal* 55, no. 4 (2012): 787–818.

54. Harnish, "Five Ways."

55. L. M. Leslie, C. F. Manchester, T. Y. Park, and S. A. Mehng, "Flexible Work Practices: A Source of Career Premiums or Penalties?" *Academy of Management Journal* 55, no. 6 (2012): 1407–1428.

56. S. B. Sitkin and J. R. Hackman, "Developing Team Leadership: An Interview with Coach Mike Krzyzewski," *Academy of Management Learning & Education* 10, no. 3 (2011): 494–501.

57. Sitkin and Hackman, "Developing Team Leadership."

58. B. Weissenberger, "Gossip in the Workplace," *BusinessWeek.com* (November 3, 2009): http://www.businessweek.com/

managing/content/nov2009/ca2009113_999372.htm, accessed July 22, 2013.

59. Staff, "Forgive? Forget? Not Likely," *Costco Connection* (December 2012): 10.

60. E. R. Burris, "The Risk and Rewards of Speaking Up: Managerial Responses to Employee Voice," *Academy of Management Journal* 55, no. 4 (2012): 851–875.

61. C. Hann, "The Masters," *Entrepreneur* (March 2012): 55–58.

62. E. Hochuli, "Admit a Mistake," *BusinessWeek* (May 12, 2012): 78.

63. E. Bernstein, "I'm Very, Very, Very Sorry . . . Really?" *Wall Street Journal* (October 19, 2010): D1, D2.

64. W. M. Murphy, "From E-Mentoring to Blended Mentoring: Increasing Students' Developmental Initiation and Mentors' Satisfaction," *Academy of Management Education & Learning* 10, no. 4 (2011): 606–622.

65. T. R. Crook, J. G. Combs, D. J. Jetchen, and H. Aguinis, "Organizing around Transaction Costs: What Have We Learned and Where Do We Go from Here?" *Academy of Management Perspectives* 27, no. 1 (2013): 63–79.

66. W. S. Helms, C. Oliver, and K. Webb, "Antecedents of Settlement on a New Institutional Practice: Negotiation of the ISO 26000 Standard of Social Responsibility," *Academy of Management Journal* 55 (5, 2012): 1120–1145.

67. C. Suddath, "The Art of Haggling," *BusinessWeek* (November 26–December 2, 2012): 98.

68. J. Welch and S. Welch, "Why Joe Biden Is Wrong about Private Equity Execs," *Fortune* (July 2, 2012): 42.

69. S. Raice, S. E. Ante, and E. Glazer, "In Facebook Deal, Board Was All But out of Picture," *Wall Street Journal* (April 18, 2012): A1, A2.

70. Harnish, "Five Ways."

71. R. Lussier, "The Negotiation Process," *Clinical Leadership & Management Review* 14, no. 2 (2000): 55–59.

72. Suddath, "The Art of Haggling."

73. Harnish, "Five Ways."

74. Suddath, "The Art of Haggling."

75. D. Kestenbaum, "Why We Fall for This," *AARP Magazine* (April 28, 2011): 48–51.

76. V. Barret, "Silicon Valley Cinderella," *Forbes* (April 9, 2012): 98–102.

77. Harnish, "Five Ways."

78. Suddath, "The Art of Haggling."

79. Kestenbaum, "Why We Fall for This."

80. Barret, "Silicon Valley Cinderella."

81. Suddath, "The Art of Haggling."

82. B. Urstadt, "The Business Case for Being Nice," *BusinessWeek* (April 8–14, 2013): 74.

83. Harnish, "Five Ways."

84. T. Lenski, "Talk It Out," *BusinessWeek* (December 10–16, 2012): 85.

85. R. Fehr and M. J. Gelfand, "The Forgiving Organization: A Multilevel Model of Forgiveness at Work," *Academy of Management Review* 37, no. 4 (2012): 664–688.

86. A. M. Grant and S. V. Patil, "Challenging the Norm of Self-Interest: Minority Influence and Transitions to Helping Norms in Work Units," *Academy of Management Review* 37, no. 4 (2012): 547–568.

87. Lenski, "Talk It Out."

88. E. B. King, J. F. Dawson, M. A. West, V. L. Gilrane, and L. Bustin, "Why Organizational and Community Diversity Matters: Representativeness and the Emergence of Incivility and Organizational Performance," *Academy of Management Journal* 54, no. 6 (2011): 1103–1116.

89. Fehr and Gelfand, "The Forgiving Organization."

90. E. Berstein, "Friendly Fight: A Smarter Way to Say I'm Angry," *Wall Street Journal* (April 19, 2011): D1, D4.

91. Detert and Edmondson, "Implicit Voice Theories."

92. Lenski, "Talk It Out."

93. Urstadt, "The Business Case for Being Nice," *BusinessWeek* (April 8–14, 2013): 74.

94. Berstein, "Friendly Fight."

95. Lenski, "Talk It Out."

96. Berstein, "Friendly Fight."

97. M. A. Hogg, D. Van Knippenberg, and D. E. Rast, "Intergroup Leadership in Organizations: Leading across Group and Organizational Boundaries," *Academy of Management Review* 37, no. 2 (2013): 232–255.

98. S. Shellenbarger, "When Stress Is Good For You," *Wall Street Journal* (January 24, 2012): D1, D5.

99. C. R. Wanberg, J. Zhu, R. Kanfer, and Z. Zhang, "After the Pink Slip: Applying Dynamic Motivation Frameworks to the Job Search Experience," *Academy of Management Journal* 55, no. 2 (2012): 261–284.

100. S. Shellenbarger, "Are You Hard-Wired to Boil over from Stress?" *Wall Street Journal* (February 13, 2013): D3.

101. J. Schramm, "Manage Stress, Improve the Bottom Line," *HR Magazine* (February 2013): 80.

102. J. Schramm, "Manage Stress, Improve the Bottom Line."

103. Shellenbarger, "When Stress Is Good for You," *Wall Street Journal* (January 24, 2012): D1, D5.

104. The Car Dealer Negotiation confidential information is from A. G. Woodside, Tulane University. The Car Dealer Game is part of a paper, "Bargaining Behavior in Personal Selling and Buying Exchanges," presented by Dr. Woodside at the Eighth Annual Conference of the Association for Business Simulation and Experiential Learning (ABSEL): Orlando, Florida, 1980. It is used with Dr. Woodside's permission.

Chapter 11

1. D. C. Wyld, "Do Employees View Stock Options the Same Way as Their Bosses Do?" *Academy of Management Perspectives* 25, no. 4 (2011): 91–92.

2. M. A. Hogg, D. Van Knippenberg, and D. E. Rast, "Intergroup Leadership in Organizations: Leading across Group and Organizational Boundaries," *Academy of Management Review* 37, no. 2 (2013): 232–255.

3. A. M. Grant, "Leading with Meaning: Beneficiary Contact, Prosocial Impact, and the Performance Effects of Transformational Leaders," *Academy of Management Journal* 55, no. 2 (2012): 458–476.

4. F. Bridoux, R. Coeurderoy, and R. Durand, "Heterogeneous Motives and the Collective Creation of Value," *Academy of Management Review* 36, no. 4 (2011): 711–730.

5. Grant, "Leading with Meaning."

6. M. Cuban, "Motivate Yourself," *BusinessWeek* (April 11, 2013).

7. V. Barret, "Silicon Valley Cinderella," *Forbes* (April 9, 2012): 98–102.

8. V. Harnish, "Five Ways to Close Big Deals Now," *Fortune* (February 4, 2013): 32.

9. D. Liu, H. Liao, and R. Loi, "The Dark Side of Leadership: A Three Level Investigation of the Cascading Effect of Abusive Supervision on Employee Creativity," *Academy of Management Journal* 55, no. 5 (2011): 1187–1212.

10. Staff, "Master Class," *BusinessWeek* (March 4–10, 2013): 79.

11. K. Hannon, "It's Never Too Late to Love Your Job," *AARP Magazine* (May 2013): 44–45.

12. Staff, "Master Class."

13. Harnish, "Five Ways to Close Big Deals Now."

14. A. Maslow, "A Theory of Human Motivation," *Psychological Review* 50 (1943): 370–396; Motivation and Personality (New York: Harper & Row, 1954).

15. H. A. Richardson and S. G. Taylor, "Understanding Input Events: A Model of Employees' Responses to Requests for Their Input," *Academy of Management Review* 37, no. 3 (2012): 471–491.

16. C. Adlerfer, "An Empirical Test of a New Theory of Human Needs," *Organizational Behavior and Human Performance* (April 1969): 142–175; Existence, Relatedness, and Growth (New York: Free Press, 1972).

17. F. Herzberg, "One More Time: How Do You Motivate Employees?" *Harvard Business Review* (January/February 1968): 53–62.

18. S. Boivie, S. D. Graffin, and T. G. Pollock, "Time for Me to Fly: Predicting Director Exit at Large Firms," *Academy of Management Journal* 55, no. 6 (2012): 1334–1359.

19. Grant, "Leading with Meaning."

20. A. Edmans, "The Link between Job Satisfaction and Firm Value, with Implications for Corporate Social Responsibility," *Academy of Management Perspectives* 26, no. 4 (2012): 1–19.

21. Hannon, "It's Never Too Late."

22. H. Murray, *Explorations in Personality* (New York: Oxford Press, 1938).

23. J. Atkinson, *An Introduction to Motivation* (New York: Van Nostrand Reinhold, 1964); D. McClelland, *The Achieving Society* (New York: Van Nostrand Reinhold, 1961); D. McClelland and D. H. Burnham, "Power Is the Great Motivator," *Harvard Business Review* (March/April 1978): 103.

24. Staff, "Master Class."

25. S. Cacciola, "Motivating Athletes the German Way," *Wall Street Journal* (August 7, 2012): D9.

26. J. S. Adams, "Toward an Understanding of Inequity," *Journal of Abnormal and Social Psychology* 67 (1963): 422–436.

27. P. Monin, N. Noorderhaven, E. Vaara, and D. Kroon, "Giving Sense to and Making Sense of Justice in Post Merger Integration," *Academy of Management Journal* 56, no. 1 (2013): 256–284.

28. M. K. Duffy, K. L. Scott, J. D. Shaw, B. J. Tepper, and K. Aquino, "A Social Context Model of Envy and Social Undermining," *Academy of Management Journal* 55, no. 3 (2012): 643–666.

29. C. P. Long, C. Bendersky, and C. Morrill, "Fairness Monitoring: Linking Managerial Controls and Fairness Judgments in Organizations," *Academy of Management Journal* 54, no. 5 (2011): 1045–1068.

30. Edmans, "The Link."

31. G. Colvin, "What Really Has the 99% up in Arms," *Fortune* (November 7): 87.

32. G. O. Trevor, G. Reilly, and B. Gerhart, "Reconsidering Pay Dispersion's Effect on the Performance of Interdependent Work: Reconciling Sorting and Pay Inequality," *Academy of Management Journal* 55, no. 3 (2012): 585–610.

33. K. Leavitt, S. J. Reynolds, C. M. Barnes, P. Schilpzan, and S. T. Hannah, "Different Hats, Different Obligations: Plural Occupational Identities and Situated Moral Judgments," *Academy of Management Journal* 55, no. 6 (2012): 1316–1333.

34. Long et al., "Fairness Monitoring."

35. E. Locke, "Guest Editor's Introduction: Goal-Setting Theory and Its Applications to the World of Business," *Academy of Management Executive* 18, no. 4 (2004): 124–125.

36. J. Raelin, "Does Action Learning Promote Collaborative Leadership?" *Academy of Management Learning & Education* 5, no. 2 (2006): 152–168.

37. H. J. Klein, J. C. Molloy, and C. T. Brinsfield, "Reconceptualzing Workplace Commitment to Redress a Stretched Construct: Revisiting Assumptions and Removing Confounds," *Academy of Management Review* 37, no. 1 (2012): 130–151.

38. C. Ricketts, "Hit List: Lou Holtz," *Wall Street Journal* (December 23, 2006): P2; L. Holtz, "Setting a Higher Standard," *Success Yearbook* (Tampa, FL: Peter Lowe International, 1998): 74.

39. Staff, "Master Class."

40. N. Breugst, A. Domurath, H. Patzelt, and A. Klaukien, "Perceptions of Entrepreneurial Passion and Employees' Commitment to Entrepreneurial Ventures," *Entrepreneurship Theory and Practice* 36, no. 1 (2012): 171–201.

41. V. Vroom, Work and Motivation (New York: John Wiley & Sons, 1964).

42. B. F. Skinner, *Beyond Freedom and Dignity* (New York: Alfred A. Knopf, 1971).

43. S. D. Levitt and S. J. Dubner, "SuperFreakonomics," *Academy of Management Perspectives* 25, no. 2 (2011): 86–87.

44. Staff, "Master Class."

45. R. McCammon, "Approval Ratings," *Entrepreneur* (February 2012): 16–17.

46. Staff, "Master Class."

47. Cacciola, "Motivating Athletes the German Way."

48. McCammon, "Approval Ratings."

49. Boivie et al., "Time for Me to Fly."

50. Bridoux et al., "Heterogeneous Motives and the Collective Creation of Value."

51. Edmans, "The Link."

52. McCammon, "Approval Ratings."

53. M. Baer, "Putting Creativity to Work: The Implementation of Creative Ideas in Organizations," *Academy of Management Journal* 55, no. 5 (2012): 1102–1119.

54. G. Colvin, "Great Job!" *Fortune* (August 12, 2013): 62–66.

55. K. Jiang, D. P. Lepak, J. Hu, and J. C. Baer, "How Does Human Resource Management Influence Organizational Outcomes? A Meta-Analytic Investigation of Mediating Mechanisms," *Academy of Management Journal* 55, no. 6 (2012): 1264–1294.

56. Levitt and Dubner, "SuperFreakonomics."

57. M. Pennington, "The 99% Movement Scorns American Creativity," *Forbes* (June 4, 2012): 30.

58. L. M. Leslie, C. F. Manchester, T. Y. Park, and S. A. Mehng, "Flexible Work Practices: A Source of Career Premiums or Penalties?" *Academy of Management Journal* 55, no. 6 (2012): 1407–1428.

59. A. Lashinsky, "Larry Page Interview," *Fortune* (February 6, 2012): 98–99.

60. Wyld, "Do Employees View Stock Options the Same Way as Their Bosses Do?"

61. T. Demos, "Motivate Without Spending Millions," *Fortune* (April 12, 2010): 37–38.

62. P. Amos, "We're Having a Bad Year. How Can I Keep Employees Motivated without Giving Bonuses?" *Fortune* (November 24, 2008): 28.

63. Demos, "Motivate Without Spending Millions."

64. Demos, "Motivate Without Spending Millions."

65. McCammon, "Approval Ratings."

66. Barret, "Silicon Valley Cinderella."

67. National Public Radio, aired April 30, 2013.

68. M. Selman, "Manipulate Creative People," *BusinessWeek* (April 11, 2013): 92.

69. McCammon, "Approval Ratings."

70. K. Blanchard and S. Johnson, *The One-Minute Manager* (New York: William Morrow & Co., 1982).

71. McCammon, "Approval Ratings."

72. Staff, "Master Class."

73. McCammon, "Approval Ratings."

74. S. Cendrowski, "Applied Materials CEO's Best Advice: The Buck Stops Here," *Fortune* (September 16, 2010): 58.

75. G. Hofstede, "Motivation, Leadership, and Organizations: Do American Theories Apply Abroad?" *Organizational Dynamics* (Summer 1980): 55.

76. M. Javidan, P. W. Dorfman, M. S. de Luque, and R. J. House, "In the Eye of the Beholder: Cross Cultural Lessons in Leadership from Project GLOBE," *Academy of Management Perspectives* 20, no. 1 (2006): 67–90.

Chapter 12

1. M. A. Hogg, D. Van Knippenberg, and D. E. Rast, "Intergroup Leadership in Organizations: Leading across Group and Organizational Boundaries," *Academy of Management Review* 37, no. 2 (2013): 232–255.

2. A. Fox, "Help Managers Shine," *HR Magazine* (February 2013): 43–46.

3. Hogg et al., "Intergroup Leadership in Organizations."

4. B. P. Owens and D. R. Hekman, "Modeling How to Grow: An Inductive Examination of Humble Leader Behaviors, Contingencies, and Outcomes," *Academy of Management Journal* 55, no. 4 (2012): 787–818.

5. C. Leahey, "Building Trust Inside Your Company," *Fortune* (March 19, 2012): 35.

6. Fox, "Help Managers Shine."

7. J. Antonakis, M. Fenley, and S. Liechti, "Can Charisma Be Taught? Tests of Two Interventions," *Academy of Management Learning & Education* 10, no. 3 (2011): 374–396.

8. S. B. Sitkin and J. R. Hackman, "Developing Team Leadership: An Interview with Coach Mike Krzyzewski," *Academy of Management Learning & Education* 10, no. 3 (2011): 494–501.

9. C. Hann, "The Masters," *Entrepreneur* (March 2012): 55–58.

10. Fox, "Help Managers Shine."

11. Antonakis et al., "Can Charisma Be Taught?"

12. B. Schyns, T. Kiefer, R. Kerschreiter, and A. Tymon, "Teaching Implicit Leadership Theories to Develop Leaders and Leadership: How and Why It Can Make a Difference," *Academy of Management Learning & Education* 10, no. 3 (2011): 397–408.

13. S. K. Johnson, L. O. Garrison, G. H. Broome, J. W. Fleenor, and J. L. Steed, "Go for the Goals: Relationships between Goal Setting and Transfer of Training Following Leadership Development," *Academy of Management Learning & Education* 11, no. 4 (2012): 555–569.

14. Fox, "Help Managers Shine."

15. Fox, "Help Managers Shine."

16. Staff, "Master Class," *BusinessWeek* (April 29–May 5, 2013): 71.

17. Sitkin and Hackman, "Developing Team Leadership."

18. B. M. and R. Bass, *The Bass Handbook of Leadership,* 3rd ed. (New York: Free Press, 2008).

19. Antonakis et al., "Can Charisma Be Taught?"

20. E. Ghiselli, *Explorations in Management Talent* (Santa Monica, CA: Goodyear, 1971).

21. Owens and Hekman, "Modeling How to Grow."

22. J. C. Santora and M. Esposito, "Do Happy Leaders Make for Better Team Performance?" *Academy of Management Perspectives* 25, no. 4 (2011): 88–90.

23. Hann, "The Masters."

24. D. M. Mayer, K. Aquino, R. L. Greenbaum, and M. Kuenzi, "Who Displays Ethical Leadership, and Why Does It Matter? An Examination of Antecedents and Consequences of Ethical Leadership," *Academy of Management Journal* 55, no. 1 (2011): 151–171.

25. J. M. Schauboeck, "Embedding Ethical Leadership within and across Organizational Levels," *Academy of Management Journal* 55, no. 5 (2012): 1053–1078.

26. N. M. Pless, T. Maak, and D. A. Waldman, "Different Approaches towards Doing the Right Thing: Mapping the Responsibility Orientations of Leaders," *Academy of Management Perspectives* 26, no. 4 (2012): 51–65.

27. M. Oppenheimer, "The Rise of the Corporate Chaplain," *BusinessWeek* (August 23, 2012): 58–61.

28. B. Graham, "Leadership and Spirituality," *Success Yearbook* (Tampa, FL: Peter Lowe International, 1998), 54.

29. Z. Ziglar, "Formula for Complete Success," *Success Yearbook* (Tampa, FL: Peter Lowe International, 1998), 30, 105; P. Lowe, "The Fifth Level of Life," *Success Yearbook* (Tampa, FL: Peter Lowe International, 1998), 91–93.

30. Ziglar, "Formula for Complete Success."

31. Owens and Hekman, "Modeling How to Grow."

32. A. M. Grant and S. V. Patil, "Challenging the Norm of Self-Interest: Minority Influence and Transitions to Helping Norms in Work Units," *Academy of Management Review* 37, no. 4 (2012): 547–568.

33. J. R. Detert and A. C. Edmondson, "Implicit Voice Theories: Taken-for-Grated Rules of Self-Censorship at Work," *Academy of Management Journal* 54, no. 3 (2011): 461–488.

34. Mayer et al., "Who Displays Ethical Leadership?"

35. K. Lewin, R. Lippert, and R. K. White, "Patterns of Aggressive Behavior in Experimentally Created Social Climates," *Journal of Social Psychology* 10 (1939): 271–301.

36. R. Likert, *New Patterns of Management* (New York: McGraw-Hill, 1961).

37. R. M. Stogdill and A. E. Coons, eds., *Leader Behavior: Its Description and Measurement* (Columbus: Ohio State University Bureau of Business Research, 1957).

38. R. Blake and J. Mouton, *The Leadership Grid III: Key to Leadership Excellence* (Houston: Gulf Publishing, 1985); R. Blake and A. A. McCanse, *Leadership Dilemmas–Grid Solutions* (Houston: Gulf Publishing, 1991).

39. Grant and Patil, "Challenging the Norm of Self-Interest."

40. Z. Tang and C. Hull, "An Investigation of Entrepreneurial Orientation, Perceived Environmental Hostility, and Strategy Application among Chinese SMEs," *Journal of Small Business Management* 50, no. 1 (2012): 132–158.

41. Owens and Hekman, "Modeling How to Grow."

42. Sitkin and Hackman, "Developing Team Leadership."

43. F. Fiedler, *A Theory of Leadership Effectiveness* (New York: McGraw-Hill, 1967).

44. R. Tannenbaum and W. Schmidt, "How to Choose a Leadership Pattern," *Harvard Business Review* (May/June 1973): 166.

45. R. House, "A Path-Goal Theory of Leadership Effectiveness," *Administrative Science Quarterly* 16, no. 2 (1971): 321–329.

46. H. A. Richardson and S. G. Taylor, "Understanding Input Events: A Model of Employees' Responses to Requests for Their Input," *Academy of Management Review* 37, no. 3 (2012): 471–491.

47. P. Hersey and K. Blanchard, "Life-Cycle Theory of Leadership," *Training and Development Journal* (June 1979): 94–100.

48. J. R. Schermerhorn, "Situational Leadership: Conversations with Paul Hersey," *Mid-American Journal of Business* 12, no. 2 (1998): 5–11.

49. S. Kerr and J. Jermier, "Substitutes for Leadership: The Meaning and Measurement," *Organizational Behavior and Human Performance* 22 (1978): 375–403.

50. Owens and Hekman, "Modeling How to Grow."

51. Schyns et al., "Teaching Implicit Leadership Theories."

52. A. M. Grant, "Leading with Meaning: Beneficiary Contact, Prosocial Impact, and the Performance Effects of Transformational Leaders," *Academy of Management Journal* 55, no. 2 (2012): 458–476.

53. R. Ackoff, *Creating the Corporate Future* (New York: Wiley, 1981).

54. W. Isaacson, "Steve Jobs: The Biography . . . His Rivalry with Bill Gates," *Fortune* (November 7, 2011): 97–112.

55. Antonakis et al., "Can Charisma Be Taught?"

56. Grant, "Leading with Meaning."

57. S. J. Shin, T. Y. Kim, J. Y. Lee, and L. Bian, "Cognitive Team Diversity and Individual Team Member Creativity: A Cross-Level Interaction," *Academy of Management Journal* 55, no. 1 (2012): 195–212.

58. Staff, "Epiphany at Ford," *Economist* (December 11–17, 2010): 83–85.

59. D. MacMillan, "Why It Pays to Apologize," *BusinessWeek* (October 12, 2009): 22.

60. P. Edwards and S. Edwards, "Sales Smart, Customer Foolish," *Costco Connection* (August 2013): 13.

61. Information taken from Perfect Apology's page on corporate apologies at http://www.perfectapology.com/corporate-apologies.html, accessed August 8, 2013.

62. Edwards and Edwards, "Sales Smart, Customer Foolish."

63. S. Rand, "Customer Complaints: How to Handle Them and Keep Customers Happy," Associated Content, Inc. (July 15, 2005), http://www.associatedcontent.com/article/5111/customer_complaints_how_to_handle_them.html, accessed August 8, 2013.

64. Edwards and Edwards, "Sales Smart, Customer Foolish."

65. Apple website, http://apple-history.com/h1.

66. http://www.businessinsider.com/uh-oh-apple-may-be-making-a-smaller-ipad-the-one-steve-jobs-hated-2012-4.

67. Poormina Gupta and Peter Henderson, "INSIGHT—At Apple, Time Cooks Leads a Quiet Cultural Revolution," *Reuters*, http://www.reuters.com/article/2013/08/22/usa-apple-cook-idINDEE97L05320130822, accessed October 4, 2013.

68. Chris O'Brien and Andrea Chang, "Apple Fans Line Up to Buy iPhone 5s, 5c; Gold in Short Supply," *Los Angeles Times*, http://www.latimes.com/business/technology/la-fi-tn-apple-faithful-lineup-to-buy-iphone-5s-and-5c-20130919,0,2043189.story.

Chapter 13

1. A. Konrad, "Virtual-Workforce Manager," *Fortune* (July 23, 2012): 32.

2. H. A. Richardson and S. G. Taylor, "Understanding Input Events: A Model of Employees' Responses to Requests for their Input," *Academy of Management Review* 37, no. 3 (2012): 471–491.

3. P. C. Fiss, "Building Better Causal Theories: A Fuzzy Set Approach to Typologies in Organizational Research," *Academy of Management Journal* 54, no. 2 (2011): 393–420.

4. P. Puranam, M. Raveendran, and T. Knudsen, "Organization Design: The Epistemic Interdependence Perspective," *Academy of Management Review* 37, no. 3 (2012): 419–440.

5. A. Fox, "Put Plans into Action," *HR Magazine* (April 2013): 27–31.

6. Fox, "Put Plans into Action."

7. J. R. Detert and A. C. Edmondson, "Implicit Voice Theories: Taken-for-Grated Rules of Self-Censorship at Work," *Academy of Management Journal* 54, no. 3 (2011): 461–488.

8. Fox, "Put Plans into Action."

9. W. M. Murphy, "From E-Mentoring to Blended Mentoring: Increasing Students' Developmental Initiation and Mentors' Satisfaction," *Academy of Management Education & Learning* 10, no. 4 (2011): 606–622.

10. K. Mehrotra, "A Glimmer of Hope for India's Web Darling," *BusinessWeek* (April 22–28, 2013): 33–34.

11. C. Rose, "Charlie Rose Talks to eBay's John Donahoe," *BusinessWeek* (February 4–10, 2013): 38.

12. Konrad, "Virtual-Workforce Manager."

13. Margin note, *Entrepreneur* (December 2008): 40.

14. R. Estuar and G. Hechanova, "Mobile Phones Affect Work/Life Balance," http://business.inquirer.net/money/topstories/view/20091108-235051/Mobile-phones-affect-worklife-balance, accessed August 15, 2013.

15. H. Paulson, "*Fortune* Global Forum," *Fortune* (April 29, 2013): 20.

16. C. Matsuda, "Hello, You've Got a Job to Do," *Entrepreneur* (March 2010): 73.

17. L. Weber, "No Personal Calls on the Job? No Thanks," *Wall Street Journal* (May 9, 2012): B10.

18. Fox, "Put Plans into Action."

19. V. Harnish, "Five Steps to Find (and Keep) Stars," *Fortune* (July 1, 2013): 22.

20. J. Paskin, "Finding the I in Team," *BusinessWeek* (February 18–24, 2013): 78.

21. E. Bernstein, "The Hidden Benefits of Chitchat," *Wall Street Journal* (August 13, 2013): D1, D2.

22. R. McCammon, "Cool Rules," *Entrepreneur* (May 2012): 22–23.

23. R. McCammon, "Voice Lessons," *Entrepreneur* (March 2012): 20–21.

24. K. E. Van Oorschot, H. Akkermans, K. Sengupta, and L. N. Van Wassenhove, "Anatomy of a Decision Trap in Complex New Product Development Projects," *Academy of Management Journal* 56, no. 1 (2013): 285–307.

25. S. B. Sitkin and J. R. Hackman, "Developing Team Leadership: An Interview with Coach Mike Krzyzewski," *Academy of Management Learning & Education* 10, no. 3 (2011): 494–501.

26. J. A. Colquitt, J. A. Lepine, C. P. Zapata, and R. E. Wild, "Trust in Typical and High-Reliability Contexts: Building and Reacting to Trust among Firefighters," *Academy of Management Journal* 54, no. 5 (2011): 999–1015.

27. C. A. Rusnak, "Are You Confusing People with Your Leadership Style?" *Costco Connection* (March 2012): 11.

28. E. Bernstein, "Big Explosions, Small Reasons," *Wall Street Journal* (October 16, 2012): D1, D2.

29. Van Oorschot et al., "Anatomy of a Decision Trap."

30. Rusnak, "Are You Confusing People?"

31. Fox, "Put Plans into Action."

32. McCammon, "Cool Rules."

33. J. Fluhr, "My Advice," *Fortune* (July 23, 2012): 60.

34. Fox, "Put Plans into Action."

35. Rusnak, "Are You Confusing People?"

36. R. McCammon, "Talking Points," *Entrepreneur* (April 2012): 18–19.

37. M. Michalowicz, "Not Just for Laughs," *Costco Connection* (October 2012): 13.

38. McCammon, "Talking Points."

39. S. Parker, "Time for Airtime," *Forbes* (June 25, 2012): 34.

40. Rusnak, "Are You Confusing People?"

41. Michalowicz, "Not Just for Laughs," *Costco Connection* (October 2012): 13.

42. C. Hymowitz, "Two Football Coaches Have a Lot to Teach Screaming Managers," *Wall Street Journal* (January 29, 2007): B1.

43. McCammon, "Voice Lessons."

44. McCammon, "Voice Lessons."

45. McCammon, "Cool Rules."

46. Fox, "Put Plans into Action."

47. R. McCammon, "Accentuate the Negative," *Entrepreneur* (October 2012): 18–19.

48. Rusnak, "Are You Confusing People?"

49. A. H. Jordan and P. G. Audia, "Self-Enhancement and Learning from Performance Feedback," *Academy of Management Review* 37, no. 2 (2012): 211–231.

50. Bernstein, "The Hidden Benefits of Chitchat."

51. Staff, "Master Class," *BusinessWeek* (April 29–May 5, 2013): 71.

52. Bernstein, "The Hidden Benefits of Chitchat."

53. Sitkin and Hackman, "Developing Team Leadership."

54. E. Bernstein, "Putting the Honey Back in Honey, I'm Home," *Wall Street Journal* (October 4, 2011): D4.

55. Richardson and Taylor, "Understanding Input Events."
56. Bernstein, "Putting the Honey Back."
57. Bernstein, "Big Explosions, Small Reasons."
58. W. Isaacson, "Steve Jobs: The Biography . . . His Rivalry with Bill Gates," *Fortune* (November 7, 2011): 97–112.
59. J. B. D. Garcia, A. I. R. Escudero, and N. N. Cruz, "Influence of Affective Traits on Entrepreneurs' Goals and Satisfaction," *Journal of Small Business Management* 50, no. 3 (2012): 408–428.
60. G. Colvin, "What Really Has the 99% Up in Arms," *Fortune* (November 7): 87.
61. D. Goleman, *Emotional Intelligence* (New York: Bantam, 1995) and *Working with Emotional Intelligence* (New York: Bantam, 1999).
62. L. T. Madden, D. Duchon, T. M. Madden, and D. A. Plowman, "Emergent Organizational Capacity for Compassion," *Academy of Management Review* 37, no. 4 (2012): 689–708.
63. P. W. B. Atkins and S. K. Parker, "Understand Individual Compassion in Organizations: The Role of Appraisals and Psychological Flexibility," *Academy of Management Review* 37, no. 4 (2012): 524–546.
64. McCammon, "Accentuate the Negative."
65. B. Schyns, T. Kiefer, R. Kerschreiter, and A. Tymon, "Teaching Implicit Leadership Theories to Develop Leaders and Leadership: How and Why It Can Make a Difference," *Academy of Management Learning & Education* 10, no. 3 (2011): 397–408.
66. Bernstein, "Putting the Honey Back."
67. Jordan and Audia, "Self-Enhancement and Learning from Performance Feedback."
68. Rusnak, "Are You Confusing People?"
69. S. E. Moss and J. I. Sanchez, "Are Your Employees Avoiding You? Managerial Strategies for Closing the Feedback Gap," *Academy of Management Executive* 18, no. 1 (2004): 32–44.
70. M. Milian, "It's Not You, It's Meetings," *BusinessWeek* (June 11–17, 2012): 51–52.
71. Fox, "Put Plans into Action."
72. Puranam et al., "Organization Design."
73. Van Oorschot et al., "Anatomy of a Decision Trap."
74. A. Kupfer, "Now, Live Experts on a Floppy Disk," *Fortune* (October 12, 1987): http://money.cnn.com/magazines/fortune/fortune_archive/1987/10/12/69664/index.htm, accessed August 19, 2013.

Chapter 14

1. T. R. Crook, J. G. Combs, D. J. Jetchen, and H. Aguinis, "Organizing around Transaction Costs: What Have We Learned and Where Do We Go from Here?" *Academy of Management Perspectives* 27, no. 1 (2013): 63–79.
2. C. P. Long, C. Bendersky, and C. Morrill, "Fairness Monitoring: Linking Managerial Controls and Fairness Judgments in Organizations," *Academy of Management Journal* 54, no. 5 (2011): 1045–1068.
3. A. M. Grant and S. V. Patil, "Challenging the Norm of Self-Interest: Minority Influence and Transitions to Helping Norms in Work Units," *Academy of Management Review* 37, no. 4 (2012): 547–568.
4. A. H. Jordan and P. G. Audia, "Self-Enhancement and Learning from Performance Feedback," *Academy of Management Review* 37, no. 2 (2012): 211–231.
5. A. Fox, "Put Plans into Action," *HR Magazine* (April 2013): 27–31.
6. S. K. Johnson, L. O. Garrison, G. H. Broome, J. W. Fleenor, and J. L. Steed, "Go for the Goals: Relationships between Goal Setting and Transfer of Training Following Leadership Development," *Academy of Management Learning & Education* 11, no. 4 (2012): 555–569.
7. Staff, Master Class," *BusinessWeek* (March 4–10, 2013): 79.
8. Long et al., "Fairness Monitoring."
9. Fox, "Put Plans into Action."
10. T. Lytle, "Streamline Hiring," *HR Magazine* (April 2013): 63–65.
11. Lytle, "Streamline Hiring."
12. S. Chandra and S. Matthews, "Afraid to Hire," *BusinessWeek* (October 8–14, 2012): 13–14.
13. J. M. W. N. Lepoutre and M. Valente, "Fols Break Out: The Role of Symbolic and Material Immunity in Explaining Institutional Nonconformity," *Academy of Management Journal* 55, no. 2 (2012): 285–313.
14. K. Leavitt, S. J. Reynolds, C. M. Barnes, P. Schilpzan, and S. T. Hannah, "Different Hats, Different Obligations: Plural Occupational Identities and Situated Moral Judgments," *Academy of Management Journal* 55, no. 6 (2012): 1316–1333.
15. B. A. Scott, C. M. Barnes, and D. T. Wagner, "Chameleonic or Consistent? A Multilevel Investigation of Emotional Labor Variability and Self-Monitoring," *Academy of Management Journal* 55, no. 4 (2012): 905–926.
16. M. Wright, "Private Equity: Managerial and Policy Implications," *Academy of Management Perspectives* 27, no. 1 (2013): 1–6.
17. Fox, "Put Plans into Action."
18. Fox, "Put Plans into Action."
19. Fox, "Put Plans into Action."
20. D. Meinert, "An Open Book," *HR Magazine* (April 2013): 43–46.
21. J. Lopez, "The Woody Allen School of Productivity," *BusinessWeek* (June 25–July 1, 2012): 86.
22. S. D. Levitt and S. J. Dubner, "SuperFreakonomics," *Academy of Management Perspectives* 25, no. 2 (2011): 86–87.
23. Jordan and Audia, "Self-Enhancement and Learning from Performance Feedback."
24. Long et al., "Fairness Monitoring."
25. S. B. Sitkin and J. R. Hackman, "Developing Team Leadership: An Interview with Coach Mike Krzyzewski," *Academy of Management Learning & Education* 10, no. 3 (2011): 494–501.
26. Scott et al., "Chameleonic or Consistent?"
27. M. B. Eberly, E. C. Holley, M. D. Johnson, and T. R. Mitchell, "Beyond Internal and External: A Dyadic Theory of Relational Attributions," *Academy of Management Journal* 36, no. 4 (2011): 731–753.
28. L. M. Leslie, C. F. Manchester, T. Y. Park, and S. A. Mehng, "Flexible Work Practices: A Source of Career Premiums or Penalties?" *Academy of Management Journal* 55, no. 6 (2012): 1407–1428.
29. Long et al., "Fairness Monitoring."
30. J. Battilana and T. Casciaro, "Change Agents, Networks, and Institutions: A Contingency Theory of Organizational Change," *Academy of Management Journal* 55, no. 2 (2012): 381–398.
31. Scott et al., "Chameleonic or Consistent?"
32. K. E. Van Oorschot, H. Akkermans, K. Sengupta, and L. N. Van Wassenhove, "Anatomy of a Decision Trap in Complex New Product Development Projects," *Academy of Management Journal* 56, no. 1 (2013): 285–307.
33. Van Oorschot et al., "Anatomy of a Decision Trap."
34. Meinert, "An Open Book."
35. Van Oorschot et al., "Anatomy of a Decision Trap."
36. C. Rose, "Charlie Rose Talks to Michael Porter," *BusinessWeek* (March 4–10, 2013): 32.
37. Chandra and Matthews, "Afraid to Hire."
38. H. Paulson, "*Fortune* Global Forum," *Fortune* (April 29, 2013): 20.
39. D. De Clercq, D. S. K. Lim, and C. H. Oh, "Individual-Level Resources and New Business Activity: The Contingent Role of Institutional Context," *Entrepreneurship Theory and Practice* 37, no. 2 (2013): 303–330.
40. Wright, "Private Equity."
41. Meinert, "An Open Book."
42. Associated Press, "News Release," Charter.net posted on homepage news August 10, 2011.
43. J. and S. Welch, "Why Joe Biden Is Wrong about Private Equity Execs," *Fortune* (July 2, 2012): 42.
44. IBM website, www.ibm.com, accessed August 21, 2013.
45. IBM website, www.ibm.com, accessed August 21, 2013.
46. Long et al., "Fairness Monitoring."
47. Scott et al., "Chameleonic or Consistent?"
48. G. Hirst, D. Van Knippenberg, C. H. Chen, and D. A. Sacramento, "How

Does Bureaucracy Impact Individual Creativity? A Cross-Level Investigation of Team Orientation-Creativity Relationships," *Academy of Management Journal* 54, no. 3 (2011): 624–641.

49. J. R. Detert and A. C. Edmondson, "Implicit Voice Theories: Taken-for-Grated Rules of Self-Censorship at Work," *Academy of Management Journal* 54, no. 3 (2011): 461–488.

50. J. Segers, D. Vloeberghs, E. Henderickx, and I. Inceoglu, "Structuring and Understanding the Coaching Industry: The Coaching Cube," *Academy of Management Learning & Education* 2, no. 2 (2011): 204–221.

51. Ad, "Need Coaching?" *HR Magazine* (February 2013): 66.

52. Johnson et al., "Go for the Goals."

53. Jordan and Audia, "Self-Enhancement and Learning from Performance Feedback."

54. Segers et al., "Structuring and Understanding the Coaching Industry."

55. Staff, "Master Class."

56. Johnson et al., "Go for the Goals."

57. Walmart website, www.walmart.com, accessed August 22, 2013.

58. S. Shellenbarger, "Meet the Meeting Killers," *Wall Street Journal* (May 16, 2012): D1, D3.

59. CareerBuilder, "Bad Hires Can Be Costly," *HR Magazine* (February 2013): 18.

60. Detert and Edmondson, "Implicit Voice Theories."

61. CareerBuilder, "Bad Hires Can Be Costly."

62. Detert and Edmondson, "Implicit Voice Theories."

63. Grant and Patil, "Challenging the Norm of Self-Interest."

64. R. E. Kidwell, "A Strategic Deviance Perspective on Franchise Form or Organizing," *Entrepreneurship Theory and Practice* 35, no. 3 (2011): 467–482.

65. M. S. Christian and A. P. J. Ellis, "Examining the Effects of Sleep Deprivation on Workplace Deviance: A Self-Regulatory Perspective," *Academy of Management Journal* 54, no. 5 (2011): 913–934.

66. Levitt and Dubner, "SuperFreakonomics."

67. B. C. Gunia, L. Wang, L. Huang, J. Wang, and J. K. Murnighan, "Contemplation and Conversation: Subtle Influences on Moral Decision Making," *Academy of Management Journal* 55, no. 1 (2012): 13–33.

68. M. Voronov and R. Vince, "Integrating Emotions into the Analysis of Institutional Work," *Academy of Management Review* 37, no. 1 (2012): 58–81.

69. Long et al., "Fairness Monitoring."

70. D. Liu, H. Liao, and R. Loi, "The Dark Side of Leadership: A Three Level Investigation of the Cascading Effect of Abusive Supervision on Employee Creativity," *Academy of Management Journal* 55, no. 5 (2011): 1187–1212.

71. S. Shellenbarger, "When the Boss Is a Screamer," *Wall Street Journal* (August 15, 2012): D1, D2.

72. T. Lenski, "Talk It Out," *BusinessWeek* (December 10–16, 2012): 85.

73. E. R. Burris, "The Risk and Rewards of Speaking Up: Managerial Responses to Employee Voice," *Academy of Management Journal* 55, no. 4 (2012): 851–875.

74. A. R. Gardner, "No Finding of Race Discrimination in Failure-to-Promote Case," *HR Magazine* (April 2013): 74.

Chapter 15

1. Staff, "Meeting of the Minds," *Fortune* (July 22, 2013): 21.

2. J. L. Ray, L. T. Baker, and D. A. Plowman, "Organizational Mindfulness in Business Schools," *Academy of Management Learning & Education* 10, no. 2 (2011): 188–203.

3. S. Chandra and S. Matthews, "Afraid to Hire," *BusinessWeek* (October 8–14, 2012): 13–14.

4. Staff, "Briefs–Apple," *BusinessWeek* (July 30–August 5, 2012): 23

5. C. Boulton, "Barbies, Auto Parts Hot off the Press," *Wall Street Journal* (June 6, 2013): B1, B5.

6. G. Colvin, "Why Obama Is Wrong on Where to Find More American Jobs," *Fortune* (September 26, 2011): 92.

7. J. Koten, "A Revolution in the Making," *Wall Street Journal* (June 11, 2012): R1, R2.

8. Boulton, "Barbies, Auto Parts Hot off the Press."

9. W. M. Murphy, "From E-Mentoring to Blended Mentoring: Increasing Students' Developmental Initiation and Mentors' Satisfaction," *Academy of Management Education & Learning* 10, no. 4 (2011): 606–622.

10. Staff, "Meeting of the Minds."

11. Murphy, From E-Mentoring to Blended Mentoring."

12. M. Townsend, "Is Nike's Flyknit the Swoosh of the Future?" *BusinessWeek* (March 19–25, 2012): 31–32.

13. Ray et al., "Organizational Mindfulness in Business Schools," *Academy of Management Learning & Education* 10, no. 2 (2011): 188–203.

14. M. Maynard, "Toyota, Mississippi," *Forbes* (July 16, 2012): 44–46.

15. S. Gorkoluk, "It's Not His Mess, Just His to Clean Up," *BusinessWeek* (January 28–February 3, 2013): 12–13.

16. D. Eng, "Bringing Design to Corporate America," *Fortune* (April 29, 2013): 25–28.

17. C. Guglielmo, "Apple's Secret Plan for Its Cash Stash," *Forbes* (May 7, 2012): 116–120.

18. K. E. Van Oorschot, H. Akkermans, K. Sengupta, and L. N. Van Wassenhove, "Anatomy of a Decision Trap in Complex New Product Development Projects," *Academy of Management Journal* 56, no. 1 (2013): 285–307.

19. J. Ankeny, "Appointments with Success," *Entrepreneur* (March 2012): 49.

20. Van Oorschot et al., "Anatomy of a Decision Trap."

21. Ad, "Risky Business," *Fortune* (July 22, 2013): 84–87.

22. M. Korn, "Hot New MBA: Supply-Chain Management," *Wall Street Journal* (June 6, 2013): B6.

23. Guglielmo, "Apple's Secret Plan."

24. R. E. Silverman, "Tracking Sensors Invade the Workplace," *Wall Street Journal* (March 7, 2013): B1, B2.

25. P. Coy and S. Reed, "Lessons of the Spill," *Business Week* (May 10–May 16, 2010): 48–54.

26. D. K. Berman, "Why Aren't Smartphones Making Us More Productive?" *Wall Street Journal* (May 1, 2013): B1, B2.

27. T. Lytle, "Streamline Hiring," *HR Magazine* (April 2013): 63–65.

28. News, "Productivity," *NPR Radio,* aired April 30, 2013.

29. Berman, "Why Aren't Smartphones Making Us More Productive?"

30. Colvin, "Why Obama Is Wrong."

31. S. Cacciola, "Motivating Athletes the German Way," *Wall Street Journal* (August 7, 2012): D9.

32. Berman, "Why Aren't Smartphones Making Us More Productive?"

33. M. Ramsey, "VW Chops Labor Costs in U.S.," *Wall Street Journal* (May 23, 2011): B1, B2.

34. Townsend, "Is Nike's Flysknit the Swoosh of the Future?"

35. Colvin, "Why Obama Is Wrong."

36. A. Gumbus and R. N. Lussier, "Entrepreneurs Use a Balanced Scorecard to Translate Strategy into Performance Measures," *Journal of Small Business Management* 44, no. 3 (2006): 407–425.

37. R. Kaplan and D. P. Norton, "Using the Balanced Scorecard as a Strategic Management System," *Harvard Business Review* (January–February 1996): 75–85.

38. P. and S. Edwards, "Sales Smart, Customer Foolish," *Costco Connection* (August 2013): 13.

39. G. Elders, "Tracking Company Sustainability," *Bloomberg Markets* (July 2013): 121.

40. Gumbus and Lussier, "Entrepreneurs Use a Balanced Scorecard."

···Author Index

··· Subject Index

···Company Index

researchmethods

The essential online tool for researchers from the world's leading methods publisher

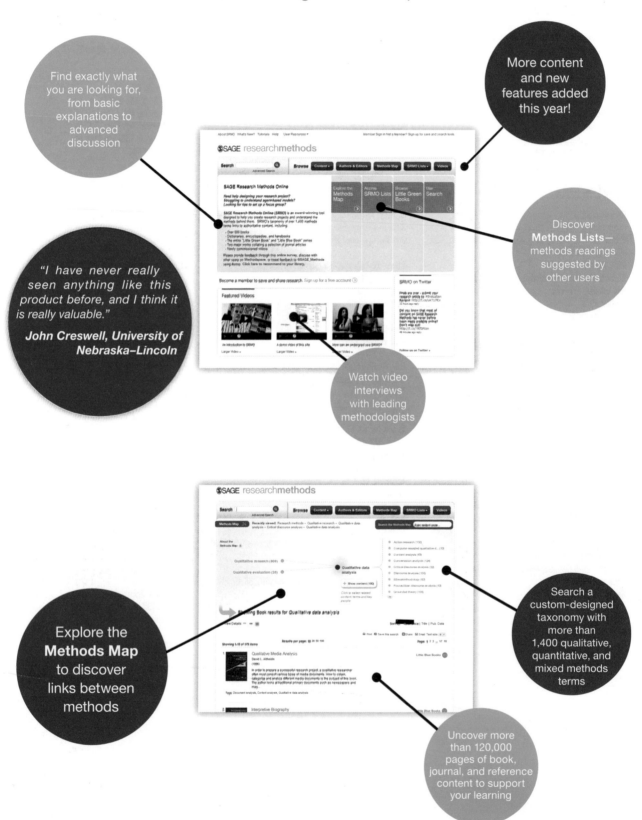

Find exactly what you are looking for, from basic explanations to advanced discussion

More content and new features added this year!

"I have never really seen anything like this product before, and I think it is really valuable."

John Creswell, University of Nebraska–Lincoln

Discover **Methods Lists**— methods readings suggested by other users

Watch video interviews with leading methodologists

Explore the **Methods Map** to discover links between methods

Search a custom-designed taxonomy with more than 1,400 qualitative, quantitative, and mixed methods terms

Uncover more than 120,000 pages of book, journal, and reference content to support your learning

Find out more at
www.sageresearchmethods.com